EXCAVATIONS AT JALAME

EXCAVATIONS CONDUCTED BY A JOINT EXPEDITION
OF THE UNIVERSITY OF MISSOURI
AND
THE CORNING MUSEUM OF GLASS

EXCAVATIONS AT JALAME

Site of a Glass Factory in Late Roman Palestine

Edited by Gladys Davidson Weinberg

University of Missouri Press
Columbia, 1988

Library of Congress Cataloging-in-Publication Data

Excavations at Jalame.
    "Excavations conducted by a joint expedition of the University
of Missouri and the Corning Museum of Glass"—P.
    Bibliography: p.
    Includes index.
    1. Jalamet el-Asafna Site (Israel). 2. Glass manufacture—Israel.
3. Romans—Israel. 4. Excavations (Archaeology)—Israel. 5. Israel—
Antiquities, Roman.
I. Weinberg, Gladys Davidson. II. University of Missouri–Columbia.
III. Corning Museum of Glass.
DS110.J34E93   1987   933   86–16121
ISBN 0–8262–0409–0 (alk. paper)

This volume was published with the assistance of the J. Paul Getty Trust, the
Corning Museum of Glass, the Smithsonian Institution, and private donors.

This volume is gratefully dedicated to the memory of Eliyahu Dobkin and Sheikh Abdullah Khayr. These two men shared a common love for the land. They were both passionate explorers of its history and gave of their knowledge with unfailing generosity and good will. They assisted this expedition in vital ways and were close and sympathetic observers of its progress and results. Their contributions were symbolic of the kindness, cooperation, and hospitality that we met with on every hand.

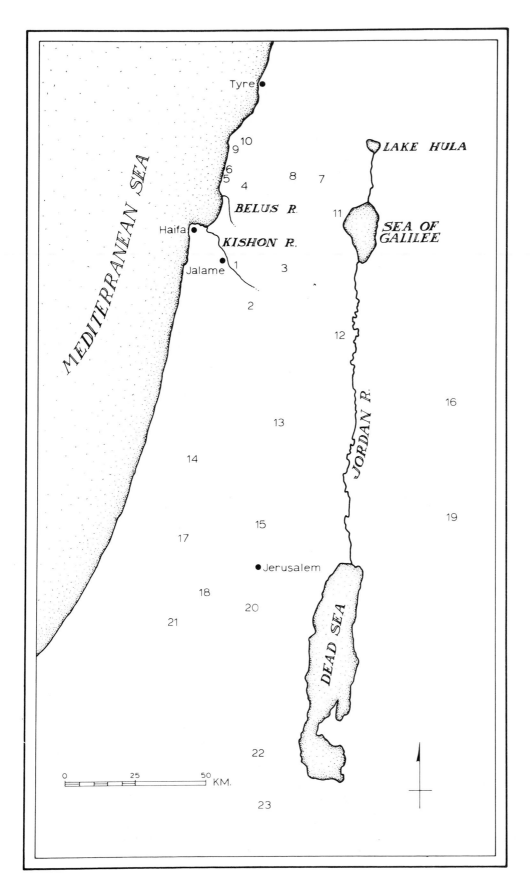

Map showing some of the ancient Palestinian sites where glass comparable to that from Jalame has been found.

1 Beth Shearim

2 Megiddo

3 Nazareth

4 Kafr Yasif

5 Shavei Zion

6 Nahariya

7 Meiron

8 Peqiin

9 El Bassa

10 Hanita

11 Huqoq

12 Beth Shan

13 Samaria

14 Rosh Ha'ayin

15 Tell en-Nasbeh

16 Gerasa

17 Gezer

18 Beit Nattif

19 Amman

20 Beit Fajjar

21 Beit Govrin

22 Horvat Usa

23 Mezad Tamar

Preface

Since the purpose and conduct of the excavation at Jalame are explained in the Introduction, it is unnecessary to discuss these here. It should be remembered that the area explored was of limited extent and isolated from important centers. Consisting mainly of a small residential and industrial compound, it was little affected by larger events in the late Roman empire. Only the years when glassmaking was carried on as a commercial enterprise differentiate it from other such establishments, and it is this aspect that has been our main focus. Contemporaneous historical events are described in Chapter 2 (p. 16).

During four excavation seasons, as well as before and after regular field work, many individuals, in addition to members of the staff, encouraged and aided us in our task. Most of them have, happily, survived the long wait for this publication; we are most grateful for their help and cooperation.

The excavation staff consisted of the following:

In 1964 (5 1/2 weeks) Paul N. Perrot was Administrative Director, Gladys D. Weinberg Field Director. The other members were Robert H. Brill, Gloria S. Merker, Irwin Merker, Saul S. Weinberg. Nina Travlou (now Einhorn) served as architect and draftsman.

In 1965 (7 weeks) Perrot and G. D. Weinberg directed the dig as before. Sidney M. Goldstein and Eleanor Tomb (undergraduate and graduate students respectively) were new additions, and for shorter periods Prof. Frederick R. Matson, ceramic technologist, of Pennsylvania State University and John F. Wosinski, Project Manager Refractories, Corporate Engineer at Corning Glass Works, took part in the work. Nina Travlou again served as architect, assisted during the last three weeks by the artist Jörg Schmeisser.

In 1966 (7 1/2 weeks) the staff consisted of Perrot, G. D. Weinberg, Goldstein, G. Merker, R. Luebbers (photographer), Schmeisser, Travlou, and S. Weinberg.

In 1967 (3 weeks) the staff included G. D. Weinberg, Barbara L. Johnson, Dean Moe, Schmeisser, S. Weinberg, and others for shorter periods.

Brief supplementary probes were conducted in 1968 and 1971.

During the first season ten to fifteen workmen were employed; these were chiefly newly arrived immigrants whose lack of experience and variety of languages occasionally taxed the ability of the staff. One experienced digger, Ezra Asher, was lent us by the French Archaeological Mission in Israel. In 1965, twenty to twenty-five workmen were supplemented by a number of volunteers (students and others). In 1966, ten to twelve volunteers, for varying lengths of time, and twenty-five to thirty workmen were employed. In 1967 we depended only on a few volunteers, as the dig was confined to a small area.

In preparing for the publication, artists, draftsmen, and photographers contributed their services, both in Israel and in the United States. Besides those on the staff, the following artist-draftsmen may be mentioned: the late Iro Athanassiadou, Dona Barton, John Huffstot, Carolyn Long, Anna Spanou.

(We apologize to those inadvertently omitted.) Most of the black-and-white photographs of objects for the final publication were prepared by Cathy Callaway.

Since none of the staff had excavated previously in Israel, we depended to a great extent on those who were familiar with the country, the language, and the customs. It will be obvious to readers that our approach was necessarily based on our Greek experience, and therefore this volume does not correspond exactly with typical archaeological publications produced in Israel.

During all our excavation seasons, we received complete cooperation from the Department of Antiquities and Museums of the Government of Israel: from the Director, Dr. Avraham Biran; from the Administrative Assistant, Miss Hannah Katzenstein, to whom we owe more than we can ever express; and from the local inspectors. Essential to the success of our work was the help of Mr. Yehudah Naor, who had discovered the site, his wife Brachah, and the members of Kibbutz Shaar Ha-amakim, which provided housing for us during part of our first season. Material assistance and hospitality were generously offered by Mr. Eliyahu Dobkin, the noted glass collector; valuable excavation equipment was lent us during several seasons by Dr. Jean Perrot, Director of the French Archaeological Mission; two houses at the site were lent us for our work by the Haifa Police Department.

We warmly thank Prof. Dan Barag, who gave us the benefit of his expertise not only in the field but also in Columbia, Missouri, during the early stages of our post-excavation research. Mrs. Gusta Lehrer (now Lehrer-Jacobson), Curator of the Glass Pavilion of the Haaretz Museum, participated in the dig for short periods and offered the resources of the museum for comparative study. At our request, Dr. Donald B. Harden made a trip to Israel in 1968 for the purpose of examining the site and giving us the benefit of his knowledge and experience. The problems involved in glass technology were first discussed with Dr. Frederic Schuler, formerly on the staff of Corning Glass Works and subsequently The Corning Museum of Glass. His knowledge and support have been indispensable throughout the years.

During the years before the final scientific report (Chap. 9) was available, a number of glass analyses were provided by Dr. Edward V. Sayre, Director of Brookhaven National Laboratory; other analyses were carried out by Dr. Constance Barsky, then on the staff of the Department of Geology, University of Missouri–Columbia; information concerning clays and related materials was furnished by Prof. Walter D. Keller of the Geology Department, and members of his staff. The late Dr. Henry E. Bent, Prof. of Chemistry, was helpful in many ways. To these and to other specialists and scholars who offered advice during the excavations and afterward, we are most grateful.

A debt impossible to repay dates from 1972, when we first became acquainted with Mr. Dominick Labino and his wife, Elizabeth. Well known for his pioneer work in art glass, Labino had by then experimented with the reproduction of ancient techniques, and he agreed to extend this work to the Jalame products, to clarify ancient methods that hitherto had not been studied or fully understood. During the years since then, he conducted many experiments; these are described in the text. His death in January of 1987 was a great loss, and to us an additional disappointment in that we shall not be able to present him the completed work.

Financial support for the excavations and subsequent studies came from a variety of sources. The collaborating institutions—The Corning Museum of Glass and the University of Missouri–Columbia—furnished the services of their respective staffs and provided funds for equipment and labor. They could not, however, finance the entire project, as expenses for a large undertaking mount very quickly.

It was Dr. Robert Caldwell of the U.S. Department of State (now retired) who first called our attention to the existence of PL480 funds available in the currency of certain countries for archaeological work. This offered our first chance to obtain a sizable grant that paid for the initial survey in the fall of 1963 and for our campaign the following year. In 1965 such funds were temporarily withdrawn, but we were fortunate to obtain a grant from the National Science Foundation that enabled us to continue the excavations and also to purchase major equipment. In 1966 administration of the counterpart (PL480) funds was transferred to the Smithsonian Institution under its For-

eign Currency Program. From the Smithsonian's Office of International Activities we obtained two grants, which sufficed for the remainder of the field work and most of the drafting, drawing, and so forth, required for the publication. In this connection we wish to thank Mr. Kennedy B. Schmertz, then Program Director, and Mrs. Betty Wingfield, his assistant, for their help and their patience. Mr. A. W. Lampe, formerly Supervisor of Research Grants at the University of Missouri, was invariably cooperative and understanding.

The expense involved in producing this publication was shared, in varying degree, by the University of Missouri Press, the Corning Museum of Glass, the Smithsonian Institution, the J. Paul Getty Trust, and private donors.

It should be noted that, in view of the many years required to bring this project to its final state, not all the chapters were written at the same time, and it has not been possible to revise and update every one. In addition, we have not attempted to impose the views of one author upon another's, unless absolutely essential to the whole work. The reader may, therefore, find some contradictory statements among the chapters; these we have allowed to remain out of respect for personal views.

Errors of omission or commission are of course the responsibility of the editor.

Gladys Davidson Weinberg
February 1988

Contents

PAUL N. PERROT

Introduction

Twenty-five years have passed since Gladys Weinberg and I first discussed the possibility that the Corning Museum of Glass, which I then directed, and the University of Missouri might join forces to carry out the first planned excavation of an ancient glass factory site. At the onset of our discussions, we made it clear to each other that we were not concerned with finding objects that would delight the eye or expand the already large vocabulary of glass forms uncovered from antiquity but, rather, that we would seek out a site or sites that showed promise of providing data on the technology of glassmaking in antiquity. We were concerned with finding out what types of furnaces were used, the nature and form of the melting pots, the kinds of tools used, in what form the raw materials needed for the batch were obtained, and what sorts of fuels were employed. In short, we were concerned with questions that were unglamorous yet essential to a further understanding of glassmaking technology.

The period of most concern to us included the first centuries of our era, when glass vessels became household objects, so it was natural that we turned to the eastern Mediterranean as the most promising region for our search. It is there, undoubtedly, that the first blown glass vessels were produced, and, historically, this area had been a center for glass trade in the centuries preceding the development of blown glass. Traditionally, as is well demonstrated by archaeological evidence, the trade in glass was particularly well known in and around Tyre and Sidon. However, glass making had also been carried out at numerous sites to the south and east of Lebanon, over a protracted period.

Thus, in the fall of 1963, we undertook a survey of possible glass manufacturing sites in Israel. The reception we were accorded by the director and staff of the Department of Antiquities, as well as by the historians and archaeologists of the Hebrew University, was overwhelmingly open and enthusiastic in support of our quest. We were warmly welcomed and virtually inundated with offers of assistance and suggestions concerning promising sites. Equipped with lists that had been prepared for us, introductions to local museum directors and archaeologists, and a few admonitions, we took off to visit various sites that had been suggested as well as to seek out new ones.

Our trip took us from Jerusalem to Tel Aviv, up the coast to Ramat Gan, Rishpon, Caesarea, Athlit, Dor, Haifa, farther north to Akko, Nahariya, inland to Shamir and Hagoshrim, southward to Abu Sinan, Kafr Yasif, Beth Shearim, Jalame, Elyakim, Khirbet Ksas (Ruin of Glass), Tiberias, and Beth Shan. In all, we must have seen a dozen sites that in one way or another suggested glass manufacturing activity, ranging from Hellenistic times through the first five or six centuries of our era. None of these sites had been systematically excavated and, indeed, on most only the surface had been examined.

Wherever we went, we were guided by members of the staff of the Department of Antiquities or by enthusiastic and knowledgeable members of kibbutzim, whose usual pastime was to explore the countryside and, as it were, seek their roots, bridging the gap of the Diaspora and finding in this newly acquired land of theirs not only physical sustenance but intellectual and spiritual renewal. Their eagerness, keen sense of inquiry, and generosity in sharing their findings, as well as their hospitality, made this trip an immensely enriching personal experience.

In seeking a site for excavation, we had a few prerequisites: that the surface evidence be sufficiently rich and varied to demonstrate that glass activities had taken place for more than a short period of time; that the site be located close enough to a settlement that suitable labor could be obtained without undue expense or hardship; that the locality be free of complex logistical problems involving access, water supply, or nature of terrain.

One site above all met the prerequisites. On a rocky hill known as Jalamet el Asafna, a few hundred meters from a police post (a military structure of the Mandate period guarding the road from Haifa where it branches toward Megiddo and Nazareth), we saw the remains of rock-hewn olive presses and an abundance of glass fragments, chunks of raw glass, cullet, and vessels. These were associated with potsherds that appeared to date to about the 4th century, in an area that seemed to have remained undisturbed. The site was shown us by its discoverer, Yehudah Naor of nearby Kibbutz Shaar Ha-amakim, and the eager welcome and hospitality offered us by Yehudah and his wife, Brachah, and the kibbutz in general, were as attractive as the archaeological evidence. Jalame had still another advantage: it was located near Kiryat Tivon, a bustling community that provided logistical support; even more important, it was near the necropolis of Beth Shearim, thus enabling the team, at little extra expense, to explore the nature of the strange huge block located in the center of the cemetery's main cistern. This later proved to be one of the most exciting discoveries in the field of ancient glass: the first incontrovertible evidence of the use of a glassmaking tank in antiquity.

During the course of our survey another promising site was located at Kafr Yasif. There, in the olive groves, Sheikh Abdullah Khayr, the prominent Druse leader residing close by at Abu Sinan, showed us a large amount of glass fragments scattered on the surface. Sheikh Abdullah exemplified the warm hospitality of the Near East and had a profound interest in exploring the history of his ancestral lands. While he had not searched particularly for glass, he was an avid antiquarian and had collected through more than forty years a large and fascinating assemblage of antiquities of the region, local costumes, and antique utensils. He espoused with alacrity the prospect of having his sites explored, even though it was recognized that they did not hold as much promise as did Jalame. Thus, two weeks of exhausting and exhilarating touring, visits, exploration, and interchange ended.

The following months were consumed with the complicated process of laying the groundwork for excavation. This was started in June 1964 and continued for three seasons. It is the result of this work, plus years of study, that is presented in this volume.

Many of the questions we sought to answer still remain. In spite of expert advice from specialists on three continents, we cannot determine precisely the form of the furnace used at Jalame. What we have learned about it is summarized in the following pages. We do, however, know far more than we did about manufacturing processes and the range of vessel forms that would have been produced in a factory of the 4th century. In some cases our finds establish a chronology and in others they corroborate previous conclusions. We have confirmed what the Talmud suggests, that the glassmaking process in antiquity was a two-stage one; the raw materials were melted into ingots or cullet in one place and then shipped to be remelted and shaped into objects in another. The evidence of this seems clear at Jalame, where the second part of the process was carried out.

The glass factory did not function in limbo: we received an added bonus from the investigation of the country estate into which the factory was introduced about the middle of the 4th century. The "villa" that crowned the top of the hill, with olive presses and other installations, its wine press serving both for water supply and as status symbol, was functioning before the glass factory was introduced. The period during which it worked could be established by the significantly large number of coins dating ca. 351–383. Before and after this span of commercial activity, the coins were few, as one would expect in a private residential establishment. The enormous amount of pottery found at the site was unexpected, and its publication here serves to focus attention on ceramics of a period that has been much neglected in this region. The hundreds of lamps and lamp fragments are also of great interest, and the "minor finds," despite the removal of valuables by the 4th-century inhabitants, offer useful information on the daily life of the time. It is no exaggeration to say that all the hard work and protracted study and discussions among the excavators and other archaeologists and scientists have proved, in the end, worthwhile. This volume hopes to show that.

Preliminary Excavation Reports

"Glass Factories in Western Galilee" (communicated by the excavators), *IEJ* 14 (1964) 286–88.

"Search for Glass Factories" (news item), *Archaeology* 10 (1964) 283–84.

"Jalamet el Asafna" (communication de Mrs. G. Weinberg et de Mr. Paul N. Perrot), *RBibl* 72 (1965) 577–79.

Notes (Joint expedition of the Corning Museum of Glass and the University of Missouri . . ."), *Journal of Glass Studies* 7 (1965) 134–35.

Saul S. and Gladys D. Weinberg, "Roman Glass Factories," paper read at 66th General Meeting of the Archaeological Institute of America, Seattle, Dec. 1964; *AJA* 69 (1965) 177–78 (summary).

Gladys D. Weinberg, "Roman Glass Factories in Western Galilee," paper read at meeting of Classical Association of Middle West and South, Toledo, April 1965; *Classical Journal* 61 (1965) 8–10 (summary).

Paul N. Perrot, "The Excavation of Two Glass Factory Sites in Western Israel," International Congress on Glass, *Comptes Rendus* II (Brussels, 1965) paper 258, 1–4.

Saul and Gladys Weinberg, "Further Investigation of Glass Factories in Western Galilee," paper read at 67th General Meeting of the AIA, Providence, Dec. 1965; *AJA* 70 (1966) 196–97 (summary).

Notes ("The second season of excavations in Israel . . ."), *JGS* 8 (1966) 141–42.

"Jelemiye, Beth Shearim, Kafr Yasif" (communicated by the excavators), *IEJ* 16 (1966) 283–84.

Saul and Gladys Weinberg, "Glass Factories in Western Galilee: Third Campaign," paper read at 68th General Meeting of the AIA, Toledo, Dec. 1966; *AJA* 71 (1967) 195–96 (summary).

"Jalamet el Asafna" (communication de Mrs. Gladys D. Weinberg), *RBibl* 74 (1967) 88–90.

Gladys D. Weinberg, "Roman Glass Factories in Galilee," Museum Haaretz *Bulletin* 10 (1968) 49–50.

"Excavations at Jalame 1964–1967" (unsigned), *MUSE* 2 (1968) 13.

Notes ("The third season of excavations . . ."), *JGS* 9 (1967) 144.

"Specialized Production in a Late Roman Glass Factory," *Eretz-Israel* 19, Jerusalem (1987) 62–70 (Michael Avi-Jonah Memorial Volume).

Terminology

All measurements are given in meters.

All dates are after Christ (A.C.) unless otherwise noted.

All depths mentioned are from the surface, except a few which are stated as being below the *datum*.

G is omitted before inventory numbers in Chapter 4 and for window glass in Chapter 8. Similarly, P is omitted in Chapter 7.

Abbreviations Used in the Catalogues

Av	Average
B	Bone
D	Diameter
Est H	Estimated Height
Est W	Estimated Width
G	Glass
H	Height
L	Length
M	Metal
Max dim	Maximum dimension
P	Pottery
PH	Preserved Height
PL	Preserved Length
PW	Preserved Width
S	Stone
T	Terracotta
Th	Thickness
W	Width

Glassmaking

The definitions for the glass terminology have been adapted from several sources. There is considerable variation in terminology among glassmakers as well as among writers about glassmaking.

Annealing: gradual cooling of finished glass objects in order to prevent internal strain

Batch: the mixture of raw materials prepared for heating in order to make glass

Block: a hollowed block of hard wood used to shape a gather of glass in the initial blowing stage (the block is always kept wet, to prevent burning and to keep hot glass from adhering to the surface)

Blowpipe (or blowing iron): a metal tube used for blowing glass

Bubbles: air pockets trapped in the glass during manufacture; very small bubbles are called "seed"

Coil: see *Trail*

Cracking-off: removing a vessel from the blowpipe (*see* Moil)

Crown: the part of a furnace forming the top or roof

Crucible (or pot): container placed in the furnace for melting glass

Cullet: chunks of glass or broken vessel that can be remelted to form vessels

Folding in: making a roll or fold on the interior of a vessel wall

Folding out: making a roll or fold on the exterior of a vessel wall

Free-blowing (or offhand-blowing): forming glassware without the aid of molds

Gather (or gob): a mass of molten glass taken from the furnace on the blowpipe or pontil; also, to take glass from the furnace on a blowpipe or pontil

Kick: depression made in the bottom of a vessel while it is hot

Knocking-off: removing a vessel from the pontil

Marver: a flat surface of stone or metal on which the gather is rolled to smooth and shape it

Moil (also called overblow): the glass originally in contact with the lower end of the blowpipe, which becomes cullet after the vessel is removed from it

Mold: a form of one or more parts in which glass is shaped; few have survived from ancient times

Mold-blowing: blowing the parison into a mold (see Chaps. 3 and 4 for special kinds of mold-blowing)

Paddle (or pallet): a wooden tool usually kept wet, sometimes used for shaping vessels, flattening rims or bottoms, etc.

Parison (or paraison): a preliminary shape from which a vessel or other object is to be formed

Pig (or yoke): support in front of a furnace opening, on which to rest the blowpipe or pontil

Polishing: (1) fire-polishing: smoothing and rounding glass by reheating; (2) wheel-polishing: grinding and smoothing by the use of a wheel and a polishing agent

Pontil (or punty): a solid metal rod to which vessels may be transferred from the blowpipe for further working; also used for applying handles and trails.

Pontil mark: a scar left on the bottom of a vessel after it has been knocked off the pontil

Siege (or bench): surface on which pots (crucibles) are placed in the furnace

Slag: waste from glassmaking—partially fused or overflowed glass and other waste

Striations (or blowing spirals): streaks in glass caused by the rotary motion of the blowpipe and marks from the tools (see Chap. 9)

Trail: a strip of glass applied hot to a vessel, either to form a handle or for decoration; a very thin trail is often called a *thread*; thick ones may be *coils*

Weathering: changes on the surface of glass produced by interaction with its environment; various kinds are: iridescence, white film, enamel-like weathering varying from white to brown, pitting (the most severe form)

Glass

Base (or foot): an addition or extension to the vessel, as opposed to "bottom," which is the underside of the body

Coil base: a thread or coil of glass trailed on to form a ring on which the vessel stands

Pad base: formed by applying another parison beneath the body and splaying out the edges; the pad may also be solid

Pushed-in base: base ring formed by pushing in the bottom of the parison and folding it (see Fig. 3–9)

Tubular base ring: hollow ring added to the bottom

Body: globular, ovoid, oval, piriform (greatest diameter at bottom); bulbous (not regular enough to be called globular)

Bottom: flat, sometimes concave—used where there is not a definite base

Mouth: used only when it is a distinct feature, as on jugs and bottles

Neck: found on bottles and jugs; they may be: cylindrical, tapering upward or downward, funnel-shaped, inverted cone.

Rim: the upper part of a vessel, above the sides, down to a point where the wall turns in or out, or some kind of decoration (e.g., trails) forms a boundary; "lip" or "edge" is used when required

Folded rim: solid or hollow with air space in the fold

Polished rim: ground and polished with a wheel

Rounded rim: smoothed by reheating

Unworked rim: sharp, unfinished edge

Wall: the portion between rim (and neck, if present) and bottom or base

Pottery

Base: the resting surface of a vessel that is clearly set off by a groove or ridge. It may also take the form of a solid disc

Bottom: the resting surface of a vessel without a foot. It may be flat, convex, or concave and is not distinctly set off from the body wall

Burnishing: a shiny surface often showing vertical or horizontal strokes resulting from the polishing of a vessel with a pebble, seashell, and so forth

Clay: the material of which a pottery vessel is made may show several colors through the fabric as a result of firing. The following terms are used:

Banded: two or more definite bands of color through a section

Core: a band through the center of the section that is different in color from the clay at either side

Variegated: several colors through the section of a vessel that do not appear in distinct bands

Combing: decorative grooves made with a single- or multiple-toothed tool

Floor: the interior bottom of a vessel

Foot: the lowest part of a vessel, that on which it stands

Ring foot: a projecting resting surface clearly set off from the body wall at both the inner and outer edges

False ring foot: a partially projecting resting surface in which the outer edge of the foot forms the termination of the body wall and the inner edge is clearly set off from the underside of the vessel

Glaze: applied only to the few examples of Arab pottery that have a true glaze. In all other instances the more proper term *slip* is used

Gouging: decorative lines cut into the exterior surface of a vessel

Ribbing: ridges (flat, rounded, or sharp) around the exterior and/or interior of a vessel resulting from the process of manufacture. Sometimes these ridges are enhanced to serve a decorative purpose

Rim: termination of the wall at the upper part of a vessel. For pottery the term *lip* is not used

Knob rim: a thickened rim, in section a roughly rounded triangle

Rouletting: decoration made by rolling a decorated spool along the surface of a vessel

Radial feather rouletting: overlapping chattered rouletted decoration around the floor and/or interior wall of African Red Slip Ware

Slip: a liquid coating of clay applied to part or all of the surfaces of a vessel before firing. It may be the same color as the vessel or different. A slip may serve simply to provide a smooth surface or as decoration. It may be of a single color or variegated (mottled)

Turning or trimming marks: lines resulting from smoothing the surface of a vessel or cutting away excess clay

Maps and Plans

A. View of the site from north. Slope of Mt. Carmel at right. See Chapter 1, p. 1.

B. Masses of glass cullet and waste, mostly from factory dump. See Chapter 3, pp. 24, 28.

Color Plate 1.

A. Section of fill in firing chamber of glass furnace (north side, near east wall). See Chapter 3, p. 31.

D. Partly baked brick, from wall of glass furnace. See Chapter 3, p. 33.

B. Siege fragment, showing depressions for glass crucibles. See Chapter 3, p. 31.

E. Section of fill in Trench C-68, showing layers of burned earth. See Chapter 3, p. 33.

C. Glass parallelepiped, from crucible. See Chapter 3, p. 31.

Color Plate 2.

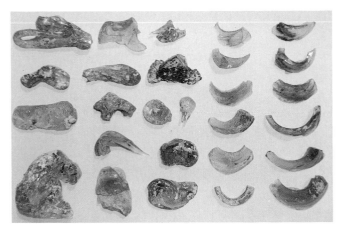

A. Knock-offs from blowpipes and pontils; various waste pieces. See Chapter 3, p. 35.

B. Drops, trails, and other glass waste. See Chapter 3, p. 35.

D. Small glass jar, intact (Chap. 4, No. 357). H .05.

C. Glass vessel fragments with applied dark blue-green trails. Top row: Chap. 4, Nos. 205, 330, 130, 124. Bottom row: Nos. 367, 364, 204, 368, 214.

Color Plate 3.

xx

A. Bases of cups, bowls, and jugs. Top row: Chap. 4, Nos. 237, 145, 170. Bottom row: with No. 174, Nos. 234, 235, 161.

B. Fragments of vessels with cobalt blue blobs. Top row: Chap. 4, Nos. 405, 406, 407, 423. Middle row: Nos. 414, 429, 433, 435, 416, 424. Bottom row: Nos. 413, 419, 422, 420, 428, 432.

C. Menorah with conical glass lamps—mosaic in synagogue at Hammath Tiberias. See Chapter 4, p. 90.

Color Plate 4.

Abbreviations

Note: Books and articles cited more than once are included in this listing; single citations are found in the text.

AASOR: *Annual of the American Schools of Oriental Research*
ActaA: *Acta Archaeologica*
ADAJ: *Annual of the Department of Antiquities in Jordan*
Adan, "Fountain of Siloam"
  D. Adan-Bayewitz, "The Fountain of Siloam and 'Solomon's Pool' in the First Century C.E. Jerusalem," *IEJ* 29 (1979) 92–100
Adan, "Horvat Ammudim"
  D. Adan-Bayewitz, "The Ceramics from the Synagogue of Horvat 'Ammudin and Their Chronological Implications," *IEJ* 32 (1982) 13–31
Aharoni, "Cave of Horror"
  Y. Aharoni, "The Expedition to the Judean Desert, 1961, Expedition B: The Cave of Horror," *IEJ* 12 (1962) 186–99
Aharoni, *Ramat Rahel, 1959–1960*
  Y. Aharoni et al. *Excavations at Ramat Rahel, Seasons 1959 and 1960* (Rome, 1962)
Aharoni, *Ramat Rahel, 1961–1962*
  Y. Aharoni, *Excavations at Ramat Rahel, Seasons 1961 and 1962* (Rome, 1964)
AIHV: Association Internationale pour l'Histoire de Verre
AJA: *American Journal of Archaeology*
Alarcão, *Conimbriga* 1965
  J. and A. Alarcão, *Vidros Romanos de Conimbriga* (Coimbra, 1965)
Alarcão, *Conimbriga* 6
  J. Alarcão et al., *Fouilles de Conimbriga 6, Ceramiques diverses et verres* (Paris, 1976)
Alcock, *Dinas Powys*
  L. Alcock, *Dinas Powys, an Iron Age, Dark Age and Early Medieval Settlement in Glamorgan* (Cardiff, 1963)
Amiran, "Citadel"
  R. Amiran and A. Eitan, "Excavations in the Courtyard of the Citadel, Jerusalem, 1968–69 (Preliminary Report)," *IEJ* 20 (1970) 9–17
Antioch 3: See Waagé, *Antioch 3*
AntJ: *Antiquaries Journal*
ArchDelt: *Archaiologikon Deltion*
ArchJ: *Archaeological Journal*
Atiqot: *'Atiqot, Journal of the Israel Department of Antiquities*: Hebrew Series—Arabic numerals; English Series—Roman numerals
Auth, *Newark Glass*
  S. H. Auth, *Ancient Glass at the Newark Museum from the Eugene Schaefer Collection of Antiquities* (Newark, 1976)
Avigad, "Beth Shearim 1953"
  N. Avigad, "Excavations at Beth She'arim, 1953," *IEJ* 4 (1954) 88–107
Avigad, "Beth Shearim 1954"
  N. Avigad, "Excavations at Beth She'arim, 1954: Preliminary Report," *IEJ* 5 (1955) 205–39
Avigad, *Beth Shearim* 3
  N. Avigad, *Beth She'arim, Report on the Excavations during 1953–1958* 3, *Catacombs 12–23* (Jerusalem, 1976)
Avigad, "Jewish Quarter 1970"
  N. Avigad, "Excavations in the Jewish Quarter of the Old City of Jerusalem, 1970 (Second Preliminary Report)," *IEJ* 20 (1970) 129–40
Avigad, "Jewish Quarter 1972"
  N. Avigad, "Excavations in the Jewish Quarter of the Old City of Jerusalem, 1971," *IEJ* 22 (1972) 193–200

Avigad, "Rock-Cut Tombs"
  N. Avigad, "Jewish Rock-Cut Tombs in Jerusalem and in the Judean Hill-Country," *Eretz Israel* 8 (1967) 119–42
BA: *The Biblical Archaeologist*
Bagatti, *Ain Karim*
  B. Bagatti, *Il Santuario della Visitazione ad 'Ain Karim (Montana Judaeae)*, SBF 5 (Jerusalem, 1948)
Bagatti, *Emmaus*
  B. Bagatti, *I Monumenti di Emmaus el-Qubeibeh e dei dintorni. Resultato degli scavi e sopralluoghi negli anni 1873, 1887–1890 e 1940–1944*, SBF 4 (Jerusalem, 1947)
Bagatti, "Museo Francescano"
  B. Bagatti, "I Vetri del Museo Francescano di Nazaret," *LA* 17 (1967) 222–40
Bagatti, *Nazareth*
  B. Bagatti, *Excavations in Nazareth* 1, *From the Beginning till the XII Century*, SBF 17 (Jerusalem, 1969)
Bagatti, "Nuovi Apporti"
  B. Bagatti, "Nuovi apporti archaeologici sul Pozzo di Giacobbe in Samaria," *LA* 16 (1966) 127–64
Bagatti, "S. Giuseppe"
  B. Bagatti, "Scavo presso la Chiesa di S. Giuseppe a Nazaret (Agosto 1970)," *LA* 21 (1971) 5–32
Bagatti, "Terre sigillate"
  B. Bagatti, "'Terre sigillate' in Palestina nei secoli V e VI," *Faenza* 39 (1953) 70–75
Bagatti-Milik
  B. Bagatti and J. T. Milik, *Gli Scavi del "Dominus Flevit"* 1, *La Necropoli del Periodo Romano*, SBF 13 (Jerusalem, 1958)
Baly, *Nessana* 1: See Colt, *Nessana*
Bar-Adon, "En el-Ghuweir"
  P. Bar-Adon, "Another Settlement of the Judean Desert Sect at 'En el-Ghuweir on the Shores on the Dead Sea," *BASOR* 227 (1977) 1–25
Bar-Adon, "Expedition C"
  P. Bar-Adon, "Expedition C," *IEJ* 11 (1961) 25–35
Barag, "Cave of Horror"
  D. Barag, "Glass Vessels from the Cave of Horror," *IEJ* 12 (1962) 208–14
Barag, "Glass Vessels"
  D. Barag, "Glass Vessels of the Roman and Byzantine Periods in Palestine," diss. (in Hebrew), Hebrew University, Jerusalem, 1970
Barag, *Hanita*
  D. Barag, "Hanita, Tomb XV, A Tomb of the Third and Early Fourth Century CE," *Atiqot* XIII (1978)
Barag, "Nahariya"
  D. Barag, "A Tomb Cave at Givath Katznelson-Nahariya," *Bulletin Museum Haaretz* 7 (1965) 29
Barag, "Nahariya Congress"
  D. Barag, "Glass Vessels from a Roman Tomb at Nahariya," *Proceedings of the 7th International Congress on Glass* (Brussels, 1965) 1–4, paper no. 243
Barag, "Netiv"
  D. Barag, "A Tomb Cave of the Byzantine Period near Netiv Ha-Lamed He," *Atiqot* 7 (1974) 81–87
Barag, "Survey of Pottery"
  D. Barag, "A Survey of Pottery Recovered from the Sea off the Coast of Israel," *IEJ* 13 (1963) 13–19
Baramki, "Beit Nattif"
  D. C. Baramki, "Two Roman Cisterns at Beit Nattīf," *QDAP* 5 (1936) 3–10
Baramki, "Karm al-Shaikh"

D. C. Baramki, "Note on a Cemetery at Karm al-Shaikh, Jerusalem," *QDAP* 1 (1932) 3–10
Baramki, "Kh. El Mefjer"
    D. C. Baramki, "The Pottery from Kh. El Mefjer," *QDAP* 10 (1942) 65–103
Baramki, "Tomb Chamber"
    D. C. Baramki, "An Ancient Tomb Chamber at Wa'r Abu eṣ Ṣafa Near Jerusalem," *QDAP* 4 (1935) 168–69
BASOR: Bulletin of the American Schools of Oriental Research
Baur, "Dura Glass"
    P. V. C. Baur, "Glass," *Excavations at Dura-Europos—Preliminary Report of Fourth Season of Work, October 1930–March 1931* (New Haven, 1933) 252–54
Baur, *Dura Lamps*
    P. V. C. Baur, *The Excavations at Dura-Europos Conducted by Yale University and the French Academy of Inscriptions and Letters. Final Report* 4, part 3, *The Lamps* (New Haven, 1947)
Baur, "Gerasa Glass"
    P. V. C. Baur, "Glassware," in *Gerasa: City of the Decapolis*, C. H. Kraeling, ed. (New Haven, 1938) 513–46
Beck, "Beads"
    H. Beck, "Classification and Nomenclature of Beads and Pendants," *Archaeologia* 77 (1928) 1–76
Bennett, "Citadel"
    C. M. Bennett, "Excavations at the Citadel (El Qal'ah), Amman, Jordan," *Levant* 10 (1978) 1–9
Ben-Tor, "Horvat Usa"
    A. Ben-Tor, "Excavations at Ḥorvat 'Uṣa," *Atiqot* 3 (1966) 1–24
Ben-Tor, "Tel Yoqneam"
    A. Ben-Tor and R. Rosenthal, "The First Season of Excavations at Tel Yoqne'am, 1977," *IEJ* 28 (1978) 57–82
Berger, *Vindonissa*
    L. Berger, *Römische Gläser aus Vindonissa* (Basel, 1960; rev. ed., 1980)
BJ: Bonner Jahrbücher
BMBeyrouth: Bulletin du Musée de Beyrouth
Bomford Coll.
    Ancient Glass, The Bomford Collection of Pre-Roman and Roman Glass on loan to the City of Bristol Museum and Art Gallery (Bristol, 1976)
Bovon, *Lampes*
    A. Bovon, *Lampes d'Argos*, École Française d'Athènes, *Études Péloponnésiennes* 5 (Paris, 1966)
Brodribb, *Shakenoak*
    A. C. C. Brodribb, A. R. Hands, D. R. Walker, *Excavations at Shakenoak Farm, Near Wilcote, Oxfordshire*, parts 1–4 (Oxford, 1968–1973)
Broneer, *Corinth Lamps*
    O. Broneer, *Corinth, Results of Excavations Conducted by the American School of Classical Studies at Athens* 4, part 2, *Terracotta Lamps* (Cambridge, Mass., 1930)
Broshi, "Zion Gate"
    M. Broshi and Y. Tsafrir, "Excavations at the Zion Gate, Jerusalem," *IEJ* 27 (1977) 28–37
BSA: British School at Athens, *Annual*
Bucovală, *Sticlă*
    M. Bucovală, *Vase Antice de Sticlă la Tomis* (Constantsa, 1968)
Charlesworth, "Glass"
    D. Charlesworth, "Glass," in I. Stead, *Excavations at Winterton Roman Villa and Other Roman Sites in North Lincolnshire 1958–1967*; Department of the Environment Archaeological Report 9 (London, 1976) 244–50
Chavane, *Salamine*
    M. Chavane, *Salamine de Chypre* 6, *Les petits objets* (Paris, 1975)
Christensen, *Hama*
    A. P. Christensen and C. F. Johansen, *Hama, Fouilles et Recherches 1931–1938* 3, 2 *Les poteries hellenistiques et les terres sigillées orientales* (Copenhagen, 1971)

Clairmont, *Dura Glass*
    C. W. Clairmont, *The Excavations at Dura-Europos. Final Report* 4, 5, *The Glass Vessels* (New Haven, 1963)
Cohen, "Horvat Haluqim"
    R. Cohen, "Excavations at Ḥorvat Ḥaluqim," *Atiqot* XI (1976) 34–50
Colt, *Nessana*
    H. D. Colt, ed., *Excavations at Nessana (Auja Hafir, Palestine)* 1 (London, 1962)
Corbo, *Kh. Siyar el-Ghanam*
    V. Corbo, *Gli Scavi di Kh. Siyar el-Ghanam (Campo dei Pastori) e i Monasteri dei dintorni, SBF* 11 (Jerusalem, 1955)
Corbo, *Monte degli Ulivi*
    V. Corbo, *Ricerche Archeologiche al Monte degli Ulivi, SBF* 16 (Jerusalem, 1965)
Corbo, *Sinagoga*
    V. Corbo et al., *La Sinagoga di Cafarnao, SBF* Minor Collections 9 (Jerusalem, 1970)
Crowfoot, *Samaria* 3
    J. W. Crowfoot, G. M. Crowfoot, K. M. Kenyon et al., *Samaria-Sebaste, Reports of the Work of the Joint Expedition in 1931–1933 and of the British Expedition in 1935*, No. 3, *The Objects from Samaria* (London, 1957)
Crowfoot-FitzGerald, "Tyropoeon"
    J. W. Crowfoot and G. M. FitzGerald, "Excavations in the Tyropoeon Valley, Jerusalem, 1927," *PEFA* 5 (1929) 98–99
Cunliffe, *Fishbourne*
    B. Cunliffe, *Excavations at Fishbourne* 2, *The Finds, Reports of the Society of Antiquaries of London* 27 (London, 1971)
Cunliffe, *Portchester*
    B. Cunliffe, *Excavations at Portchester Castle* 1, *Roman, Reports of the Research Committee of the Society of Antiquaries of London* 32 (London, 1975)
DarSag
    Daremberg and Saglio, *Dictionnaire des antiquités grecques et romaines d' après les textes et les monuments* (Paris, 1877–1919)
Delougaz-Haines
    P. Delougaz and R. C. Haines, *A Byzantine Church at Khirbat al-Karak*, University of Chicago Oriental Institute Publication 85 (Chicago, 1960)
Dothan, *Ashdod* 2–3
    M. Dothan, *Ashdod 2–3: The Second and Third Seasons of Excavations, 1963, 1965, Soundings in 1967, Atiqot* IX–X (1971)
Dothan, *Hammath Tiberias*
    M. Dothan, *Hammath Tiberias: Early Synagogues and the Hellenistic and Roman Remains* (Jerusalem, 1983)
Dothan-Freedman, *Ashdod* 1
    M. Dothan and D. N. Freedman, "Ashdod 1: The First Season of Excavations," *Atiqot* VII (1967)
Dunand-Duru, *Oumn el Amed*
    M. Dunand and R. Duru, *Oumn el-'Amed, une ville de l'époque héllénistique aux échelles de Tyr* (Paris, 1962)
Edgar, *Glass*
    C. C. Edgar, *Graeco-Egyptian Glass (Catalogue général des antiquités égyptiennes du Musée du Caire)* (Cairo, 1905)
Eitan, "Rosh Ha'ayin"
    A. Eitan, "Excavations at the Foot of Tel Rosh Ha'ayin," *Atiqot* 5 (1969) 49–68
Erdmann, "Mezad Tamar"
    E. Erdmann, "Die Glasfunde von Mezad Tamar (Kasr Gehainije) in Israel," *Saalburg Jahrbuch* 34 (1977) 98–146
Fisher-McCown, "Jerash"
    C. S. Fisher and C. C. McCown, "Jerash-Gerasa 1930," *AASOR* 11 (1929–1930) 1–50
FitzGerald, "Beth-Shan"
    G. M. FitzGerald, "Excavations at Beth-Shan in 1931," *PEFQ* (1932) 138–48
FitzGerald, *Beth-Shan* 3

G. M. FitzGerald, *Beth-Shan Excavations, 1921–1923: The Arab and Byzantine Levels* 3 (Philadelphia, 1931)

Forbes, *Studies*
R. J. Forbes, *Studies in Ancient Technology* (Leiden, 1964–1972)

Fremersdorf, *Denkmäler*
F. Fremersdorf, *Die Denkmäler des Römischen Köln*, 8 vols. (Cologne, 1928–1967)

Fremersdorf, "Köln-Müngersdorf"
F. Fremersdorf, "Der römische Gutshof Köln-Müngersdorf," *Rom. Germ. Forschungen* 6 (Berlin, Leipzig, 1933)

Frere, *Verulamium*
S. S. Frere, *Verulamium Excavations* 1 (London, 1972)

Gichon, "Byzantine Wares"
M. Gichon, "Fine Byzantine Wares from the South of Israel," *PEQ* 106 (1974) 119–39

Gichon, "En Boqeq"
M. Gichon, "Das Kastell En Boqeq," *BJ* 171 (1971) 386–406

Goldman, *Tarsus* 1
H. Goldman, ed., *Excavations at Gözlü Kule Tarsus* 1, *The Hellenistic and Roman Periods* (Princeton, 1950)

Goodenough, *Symbols*
E. R. Goodenough, *Jewish Symbols in the Greco-Roman Period*, 13 vols., Bollingen Series 37 (New York, 1953–1968)

Hamilton, "North Wall"
R. W. Hamilton, "Excavations Against the North Wall of Jerusalem, 1937–8," *QDAP* 10 (1940) 1–54

Harden, *Karanis*
D. B. Harden, *Roman Glass from Karanis Found by the University of Michigan Archaeological Expedition in Egypt, 1924 1929*, University of Michigan Studies, Humanistic Series, 41 (Ann Arbor, 1936)

Harden, "Nessana Glass": See Colt, *Nessana*

Harden, "Tomb-groups"
D. B. Harden, "Tomb-groups of Glass of Roman Date from Syria and Palestine," *Iraq* 11 (1949) 151–59

Harden, "Vasa"
D. B. Harden, "Roman Tombs at Vasa: The Glass," *RDAC* 1940–1948 (1955) 46 60

Harding, "Jebel Jofeh"
G. L. Harding, "A Roman Family Vault on Jebel Jofeh, 'Amman," *QDAP* 14 (1950) 81–94

Hayes, *LRP*
J. W. Hayes, *Late Roman Pottery* (London, 1972)

Hayes, *LRP Suppl.*
J. W. Hayes, *Supplement to Late Roman Pottery* (London, 1980)

Hayes, *Toronto Glass*
J. W. Hayes, *Roman and Pre-Roman Glass in the Royal Ontario Museum* (Toronto, 1975)

Hayes, *Toronto Pottery*
J. W. Hayes, *Roman Pottery in the Royal Ontario Museum* (Toronto, 1976)

Hesperia: Hesperia, Journal of the American School of Classical Studies at Athens

Husseini, "Ain Yabrud"
S. A. S. Husseini, "A Rock-Cut Tomb-Chamber at 'Ain Yabrūd," *QDAP* 6 (1937) 54–55

Husseini, "Beit Fajjar"
S. A. S. Husseini, "A Fourth-Century A.D. Tomb at Beit Fajjār," *QDAP* 4 (1935) 175–77

Ibrahim, "Survey"
M. Ibrahim et al., "The East Jordan Valley Survey, 1975," *BASOR* 222 (1976) 41–66

IEJ: Israel Exploration Journal

Iliffe, "El Bassa"
J. H. Iliffe, "A Tomb at el Bassa of c. A.D. 396," *QDAP* 3 (1934) 81–91

Iliffe, "Sigillata Wares"
J. H. Iliffe, "Sigillata Wares in the Near East," *QDAP* 6 (1938)

4–53

Iliffe, "Tarshiha"
J. H. Iliffe, "Rock-Cut Tomb at Tarshīhā," *QDAP* 3 (1934) 9–16

Isings, *Roman Glass*
C. Isings, *Roman Glass from Dated Finds* (Groningen, 1957)

Ivanyi, *Pannonische Lampen*
D. Ivanyi, *Die pannonische Lampen*, Dissertationes Pannonicae, Series 2, No. 2 (Budapest, 1935)

JEA: Journal of Egyptian Archaeology

JGS: Journal of Glass Studies

JIV: Journeés Internationales du Verre (now *AIHV*)

Kahane, "Huqoq"
P. P. Kahane, "Rock-Cut Tombs at Huqoq. Notes on the Finds," *Atiqot* III (1961) 126–47

Kahane, "Pottery Types 1"
P. P. Kahane, "Pottery Types from the Jewish Ossuary-Tombs Round Jerusalem 1," *IEJ* 2 (1952) 125–39

Kahane, "Pottery Types 2"
P. P. Kahane, "Pottery Types from the Jewish-Ossuary Tombs Round Jerusalem 2," *IEJ* 2 (1952) 176–82

Kahane, "Pottery Types 3"
P. P. Kahane, "Pottery Types from the Jewish Ossuary-Tombs Round Jerusalem 3," *IEJ* 3 (1953) 48–54

Kelso, *Bethel*
J. L. Kelso et al., "The Excavations of Bethel (1934–1960)," *AASOR* 39 (1968)

Kelso-Baramki, *Jericho and en-Nitla*
J. L. Kelso and D. C. Baramki, "Excavations at New Testament Jericho and Khirbet en-Nitla," *AASOR* 29 30 (1949–1951)

Kennedy, *Berytus* 14
C. A. Kennedy, "The Development of the Lamp in Palestine," *Berytus* 14 (1963) 67–115

Kisa, *Glas*
A. Kisa, *Das Glas im Altertume*, 3 vols. (Leipzig, 1908)

LA: Liber Annuus

Lamon-Shipton, *Megiddo* 1
R. S. Lamon and G. M. Shipton, *Megiddo 1: Seasons of 1925–34, Strata 1–5* (Chicago, 1939)

Lancel, *Tipasa*
S. Lancel, *Verrerie antique de Tipasa* (Paris, 1967)

Landgraf, *Tell Keisan*
J. Landgraf, "Byzantine Pottery," 51–99, in J. Briend and J. B. Humbert, *Tell Keisan (1971–1976)* (Göttingen, 1980)

Lehner, "Novaesium"
H. Lehner, "Die Einzelfunde von Novaesium," *BJ* 111/112 (1904) 313–19, 416–17, and pl. 35

Libyca: Libyca, Bulletin du Service des Antiquités (Algeria)

Loeschcke, *Vindonissa*
S. Loeschcke, *Lampen aus Vindonissa* (Zurich, 1919)

Loffreda, *Cafarnao* 2
S. Loffreda, *Cafarnao 2. La Ceramica*, *SBF* 19 (Jerusalem, 1974)

Loffreda, "Capernaum"
S. Loffreda, "The Late Chronology of the Synagogue of Capernaum," *IEJ* 23 (1973) 37–42

Loffreda, "Capharnaum"
S. Loffreda, "The Synagogue of Capharnaum: Archaeological Evidence for Its Late Chronology," *LA* 22 (1972) 5–29

Loffreda, "La ceramica"
S. Loffreda, "La ceramica della Sinagoga di Cafarnao," *LA* 20 (1970) 53–105

Loffreda, *et-Tabgha*
S. Loffreda, *Scavi di et-Tabgha*, *SBF* Minor Collections 7 (Jerusalem, 1970)

Loffreda, "Evoluzione"
S. Loffreda, "Evoluzione di un piatto-tegame secondo gli scavi di Cafarnao," *LA* 19 (1969) 237–63

Loffreda, "Kafr Kanna"
S. Loffreda, "Scavi a Kafr Kanna," *LA* 19 (1969) 328–48

Loffreda, *Sinagoga*
 S. Loffreda, "La Ceramica della Sinagoga di Cafarnao," in V. Corbo et al., *La Sinagoga di Cafarnao, SBF* Minor Collections 9 (Jerusalem, 1970)
Loffreda, "Stampi"
 S. Loffreda, "Stampi su terre sigillate di Cafarnao," *LA* 21 (1971) 286–315
Macalister, *Gezer*
 R. A. S. Macalister, *The Excavations at Gezer*, 3 vols. (London, 1912)
McCown, *Nasbeh 1*
 C. C. McCown et al., *Tell en-Nasbeh 1, Archaeological and Historical Results* (Berkeley and New Haven, 1947)
Mader, *Mambre*
 A. E. Mader, *Mambre, Die Ergebnisse der Ausgrabungen im heiligen Bezirk Râmet El-Ḫalîl in Südpalästina, 1926–1928* (Freiburg, Germany, 1957)
Maisler, "Tell Qasile"
 B. Maisler, "The Excavations at Tell Qasîle," *IEJ* 1 (1950–1951) 61–76, 125–40, 194–218
Makhouly, "el Jish"
 N. Makhouly, "Rock-Cut Tombs at el Jîsh," *QDAP* 8 (1939) 45–50
Masri, "Hama Glass"
 A. Masri, "Collection de verres du Musée de Hama," *Bulletin JIV* 3 (1964) 72–74
Materialy: Materialy i Issledovania po Arkheologii SSSR
Menzel, *Antike Lampen*
 H. Menzel, *Antike Lampen in Römisch-Germanischen Zentralmuseum zu Mainz*, Catalogue No. 15 (Mainz, 1969)
Meyers, "Gush Halav"
 E. M. Meyers et al., "Preliminary Report on the 1977 and 1978 Seasons at Gush Halav (el-Jish)," *BASOR* 233 (1979) 33–58
Meyers, *Khirbet Shema*
 E. M. Meyers et al., *Ancient Synagogue Excavations at Khirbet Shema', Upper Galilee, Israel, AASOR* 42 (1976)
Meyers, "Meiron, 1971–1972"
 C. L. Meyers et al., "Excavations at Meiron in Upper Galilee, 1971–1972: A Preliminary Report," *BASOR* 214 (1974) 2–25
Meyers, "Meiron 1974, 1975"
 C. L. Meyers et al., "Excavations at Meiron in Upper Galilee, 1974, 1975: Second Preliminary Report," *AASOR* 43 (1978) 73–98
Meyers, "Meiron 1976"
 E. M. Meyers et al., "The Meiron Excavation Project: Archaeological Survey in Galilee and Golan, 1976," *BASOR* 230 (1978) 1–24
Milne, *Instruments*
 J. Milne, *Surgical Instruments in Greek and Roman Times* (Oxford, 1907)
MSCC
 Munsell Soil Color Charts (Baltimore: Munsell Color Company, 1971)
Negev, "Mampsis"
 A. Negev and R. Sivan, "The Pottery of the Nabataean Necropolis at Mampsis," *RCRF Acta* 17/18 (1977) 109–31
Negev, "Nabataean Sigillata"
 A. Negev, "Nabataean Sigillata," *RBibl* 79 (1972) 381–98
Negev, *Oboda*
 A. Negev, *The Nabataean Potter's Workshop at Oboda* (Bonn, 1974)
Netzer-Meyers, "Jericho"
 E. Netzer and E. M. Meyers, "Preliminary Report on the Joint Jericho Excavation Project," *BASOR* 228 (1977) 15–27
ÖJh: Jahreshefte des Österreichischen Archäologischen Instituts
Oppenländer Coll.
 A. von Saldern, B. Nolte, P. La Baume, T. E. Haevernick, *Gläser der Antike, Sammlung Erwin Oppenländer* (Mainz, 1974)
OpusArch: *Opuscula Archaeologica*

OpusAth: *Opuscula Atheniensia*
PEFA: *Palestine Exploration Fund Annual*
PEFQ: *Palestine Exploration Fund Quarterly Statement*
PEQ : *Palestine Exploration Quarterly*
Perlzweig, *Agora Lamps*
 J. Perlzweig, *The Athenian Agora. Results of Excavations Conducted by the American School of Classical Studies at Athens 7, Lamps of the Roman Period, 1st to 7th Century After Christ* (Princeton, 1961)
Petrie, *Daily Use*
 W. M. F. Petrie, *Objects of Daily Use, BSAE* 42 (London, 1927)
Petrie, *Ehnasya*
 W. M. F. Petrie, *Roman Ehnasya (Herakleopolis Magna)* (London, 1904)
Petrie, *Gerar*
 W. M. F. Petrie, *Gerar, BSAE* 43 (London, 1928)
Petrie, *Tools and Weapons*
 W. M. F. Petrie, *Tools and Weapons, BSAE* 30 (London, 1917).
Prausnitz, *Shavei Zion*
 M. Prausnitz, *Excavations at Shavei Zion*, Monografie di Archeologia e d'Arte 2 (Rome, 1967)
QDAP: *The Quarterly of the Department of Antiquities in Palestine*
Rahmani, "Maon Synagogue"
 L. Y. Rahmani, "The Maon Synagogue (The Small Finds and Coins)" in Louis M. Rabinowitz Fund for the Exploration of Ancient Synagogues, *Bulletin* 3 (1960) 14–18
Rahmani, "Mirror-Plaques"
 L. Y. Rahmani, "Mirror-Plaques from a Fifth-Century A.D. Tomb," *IEJ* 14 (1964) 50–60
Rahmani, "Raqafot"
 L. Y. Rahmani, "Roman Tombs in Nahal Raqafot," *Atiqot* XI (1976) 77–88
Rahmani, "Romema"
 L. Y. Rahmani, "Jewish Tombs in the Romema Quarter of Jerusalem," *Eretz Israel* 8 (1967) 186–92
Rahmani, "Shmuel ha-Navi"
 L. Y. Rahmani, "Roman Tombs in Shmuel ha-Navi Street, Jerusalem," *IEJ* 10 (1960) 140–48
Rau, "Facettschliffgläser"
 H. G. Rau, "Facettschliffgläser und die Chronologie der Spätkaiserzeit," *Archäologisches Korrespondenzblatt, 4, Sonderdruck* (1973) 441–45
Rau, "Körpergräber"
 H. G. Rau, "Körpergräber mit Glasbeigaben des 4th A.C. in Oder-Weichelsraum," *Acta Praehistorica et Archaeologica* 3 (1972) 109–214
RBibl: *Revue Biblique*
RCRF Acta: *Rei Cretariae Romanae Fautorum, Acta*
RDAC: *Report of the Department of Antiquities, Cyprus*
Reed, *Dibon*
 W. L. Reed, *The Excavations at Dibon (Dhîbân) in Moab, Second Campaign, AASOR* 36–37 (1964) 37–79
Reisner, *Samaria 1*
 G. A. Reisner, C. S. Fisher, and D. G. Lyon, *Harvard Excavations at Samaria (1908–1910)* (Cambridge, Mass., 1924)
Riley, "Caesarea Hippodrome"
 J. A. Riley, "The Pottery from the First Season of Excavation in the Caesarea Hippodrome," *BASOR* 218 (1975) 25–63
Riley, "Coarse Pottery"
 J. A. Riley, "Coarse Pottery," in J. A. Lloyd, ed., *Excavations at Sidi Khrebish, Benghazi (Berenice)* 2, Supplement to *Libya Antiqua* 5
Ritterspach, "Meiron Cistern"
 A. D. Ritterspach, "The Meiron Cistern Pottery," *BASOR* 215 (1974) 19–29
Robertson, *Bar Hill*
 A. Robertson, M. Scott, and L. Keppie, *Bar Hill: A Roman Fort and Its Finds*, British Archaeological Report 16 (London, 1975)

Robinson, *Agora Pottery*
Henry S. Robinson, *The Athenian Agora. Results of the Excavations Conducted by the American School of Classical Studies at Athens 5, Pottery of the Roman Period, Chronology* (Princeton, 1959)

Robinson, *Olynthus 10*
D. M. Robinson, *Excavations at Olynthus 10* (Baltimore, 1941)

Robinson-Graham, *Olynthus 8*
D. M. Robinson and J. W. Graham, *Excavations at Olynthus 8, The Hellenic House* (Baltimore, 1938)

Saldern, *Sardis Glass*
A. von Saldern, *Ancient and Byzantine Glass from Sardis*, Sardis Monograph 6 (jointly as Corning Monograph) (Cambridge, Mass., 1980)

Saller, *Bethany*
S. J. Saller, *Excavations at Bethany* 1949–1953, *SBF* 12 (Jerusalem, 1957)

Samaria 1: See Reisner, *Samaria 1*

Samaria 3: See Crowfoot, *Samaria 3*

SBF: Publications of the *Studium Biblicum Franciscanum*

SCE: *The Swedish Cyprus Expedition: Finds and Results of the Excavations in Cyprus 1927–1931* (Stockholm, 1934–1956)

Schneider, *Mount Nebo*
H. Schneider, *The Memorial of Moses on Mount Nebo 3, The Pottery, SBF* 1 (Jerusalem, 1950)

Schuler, "Blowing"
F. Schuler, "Ancient Glassmaking Techniques, the Blowing Process," *Archaeology* 12 (1959) 116–22

Sellers-Baramki
O. R. Sellers and D. Baramki, "A Roman-Byzantine Burial Cave in Northern Palestine," *BASOR, Supplementary Studies* 15–16, 1953

Smith, "Herodian Lamp"
R. H. Smith, "The 'Herodian' Lamp of Palestine: Types and Dates," *Berytus* 14 (1961–1963) 53–65

Smith, "Household Lamps"
R. H. Smith, "The Household Lamps of Palestine in New Testament Times," *BA* 29 (1966) 2–36

Smith, *Pella*
R. H. Smith et al., *Pella of the Decapolis 1, The 1967 Season of the College of Wooster Expedition to Pella* (Wooster, Ohio, 1973)

Smith *Coll.*
R. W. Smith, *Glass from the Ancient World: The Ray Winfield Smith Collection* (Corning, 1957)

Sorokina, "Facettenschliffgläser"
N. Sorokina, "Facettenschliffgläser des 2en–3en Jhd. u.Z. aus dem Schwarzmeergebiet, *Annales* AIHV 7 (Berlin, 1977) 111–22

Sorokina, "Nuppengläser"
N. Sorokina, "Nuppengläser von der Nordküste des Schwarzen Meeres," *Annales* AIHV 5 (1970) 71–79

Sorokina, "Panticapaeum"
N. Sorokina, "Glass from the Excavations of Panticapaeum, 1945–1959" (Russian), *Materialy* 103 (1962) 210–40

SovArch: Sovietskaya Archaeologia

Stern, *Custodia*
E. M. Stern, *Ancient Glass at the Fondation Custodia*, Collection Frits Lugt (Utrecht, 1977)

Strange, "French Hill"
J. F. Strange, "Late Hellenistic and Herodian Ossuary Tombs at French Hill, Jerusalem," *BASOR* 219 (1975) 39–67

Sussman, *Jewish Art*
V. Sussman, *Jewish Art on Lamps in the Time of the Mishna*. The Israel Museum, Jerusalem, Cat. No. 74, Summer 1970

Sussman, *Jewish Lamps*

V. Sussman, *Ornamented Jewish Oil-Lamps from the Destruction of the Second Temple Through the Revolt of Bar Kokhba* (Jerusalem, 1972)

Sussman, "Kefar Ara"
V. Sussman, "A Burial Cave at Kefar 'Ara," *Atiqot* XI (1976) 92–101

Sussman, "Rehovot"
V. Sussman, "Ancient Burial Cave at Rehovot," *Atiqot* 5 (1969) 69–71

Szentleléky, *Lamps*
T. Szentleléky, *Ancient Lamps* (Amsterdam, 1969)

Talmud
The Babylonian Talmud, ed. I. Epstein (English translation) (London, 1952)

Tsori, "Kyrios Leontis"
N. Tsori, "The House of Kyrios Leontis at Beth-Shean," *Eretz Israel* 11 (1973) 229–47

Tufnell, *Lachish*
O. Tufnell, *Lachish 3, The Iron Age* (London, 1953)

Turkowski, "Agriculture"
L. Turkowski, "Peasant Agriculture in the Judaean Hills," *PEFQ* 101 (1969) 21–33

Tushingham, *Dibon*
A. D. Tushingham, *The Excavations at Dibon (Dhîbân) in Moab: The Third Campaign, 1952–53*, *AASOR* 40 (1972)

Tzori, "House of Kyrios Leontis"
N. Tzori, "The House of Kyrios Leontis at Beth Shean," *IEJ* 16 (1966) 123–34

de Vaux, "Khirbet Qumran"
R. de Vaux, "Fouilles au Khirbet Qumrân," *RBibl* 60 (1953) 83–106

Vessberg, "Cyprus Glass"
O. Vessberg, "Roman Glass in Cyprus," *OpusArch* 7 (1952) 109–65

Vessberg, "Cyprus Lamps"
O. Vessberg, "Terracotta Lamps," *SCE* 4, part 3, 184–93

Waagé, *Antioch 3*
F. O. Waagé, "Lamps," in *Antioch on-the-Orontes 3, The Excavations, 1937–1939*, ed. R. Stillwell (Princeton, 1941) 55–82

Walters, *Lamps*
H. B. Walters, *Catalogue of the Greek and Roman Lamps in the British Museum* (London, 1914)

Wampler, *Nasbeh 2*
J. C. Wampler, *Tell en-Nasbeh 2, The Pottery* (Berkeley and New Haven, 1947)

White, *Equipment*
K. D. White, *Farm Equipment of the Roman World* (Cambridge, England, 1975)

White, *Implements*
K. D. White, *Agricultural Implements of the Roman World*, (Cambridge, England, 1967)

Yadin, *Cave of Letters*
Y. Yadin, *The Finds from the Bar Kokhba Period in the Cave of Letters* (Jerusalem, 1963)

Yeivin, "Khorazin"
Z. Yeivin, "Excavations at Khorazin," *Eretz Israel* 11 (1973) 144–57

Zemer, *Storage Jars*
A. Zemer, *Storage Jars in Ancient Trade* (Haifa, 1977)

Zevulun-Olenik, *Talmudic Period*
U. Zevulun and Y. Olenik, *Function and Design in the Talmudic Period*, Haaretz Museum Publications (Tel Aviv, 1978)

Zori, "Beth-Shean"
N. Zori, "The Ancient Synagogue at Beth-Shean," *Eretz Israel* 8 (1967) 14–67

G.D. AND S.S. WEINBERG

The Site

The ancient site designated here as Jalame[1] is located on a small, sloping ridge that juts off a foothill on the northeast side of Mount Carmel and runs in a north-south direction (Color Pl. 1A and Pl. 1–1). It lies about ten kilometers southeast of Haifa, at the junction of the road running east from Haifa to Nazareth and that branching off to the south-southeast toward Megiddo. The ridge slopes steeply on its east and west sides but falls off more gently to the north and south (Fig. 1–1). Just north of the highest part of the ridge is point 592'z on the National grid, which is 41.9 m above sea level; the top of the ridge is enclosed by the 45 m contour line, while its base is the 20 m contour line, where the land flattens out rather abruptly.

On the southern part of the top of this ridge a police post was built in 1940–1941 and still remains there (Fig. 1–1); more recently two houses for guards were constructed farther to the north, just along the east side of the 45 m level. Otherwise, the west, north, and east slopes of the ridge are now without structures. After the survey, described in the Introduction, in which major signs of ancient occupation, particularly concentrations of glass fragments, were found on the west slope of the ridge slightly below its top, several seasons of excavation opened an area with a maximum extent of about 65 m east-west and 45 m north-south. The total excavated area was about 1,800 sq m.

The top of the ridge is almost entirely denuded, with earth fill remaining only in crevices in bedrock. In this exposed rock were two circular cuttings that proved to belong to an olive press; the northern one of the two, taken as the datum point for the excavations, is about 44

m above sea level. The highest point in the excavated area is at +0.83 m, very close to the top of the ridge, while the lowest point reached was –8.42 m, at the bottom of the western slope. Thus the total drop in the 65 m east-west extent of the excavation was 9.25 m, from bedrock on the east to virgin soil on the west. This 14 percent grade explains the shifting of the fill from the upper parts of the ridge to the lower slopes, to the extent that fills over 2 m in depth were recorded along the western edges of the excavated area.

Following the survey in 1963, the first season of excavation began on 8 June 1964. In a little more than six weeks we uncovered, in a series of trenches chosen by surface appearance, enough of the important features of the site so that a second campaign appeared desirable. Eventually there were three full-length seasons of digging, in the summers of 1964, 1965, and 1966, a shorter one in the autumn of 1967, and a number of probes in 1968 and 1971.

We first dug a series of test trenches in various parts of the site. Find spots were recorded by using a grid (see Fig. 1–2). During our second season we attempted to fill in gaps between the trenches of the first season, and during the third season, which concentrated on the glass factory dump, we resorted to the square system, with 1 m balks between the squares.

To summarize the excavating done in each season, we show a plan with the trenches indicated (Fig. 1–2). Those excavated in 1964 were: A, A–1, A–2, A–3, B, C, D, E, F, G, H, I, J, K, and L. In 1965 we excavated trenches A–4, A–5, A–6, F–1 to F–6, J–1 to J–3, L, L–1 to L–3, M, M–1, M–2, P, Q, S, and Y. In 1966 we excavated X–1 to X–4, D, F, Y–1 to Y–3 and Y–3S, J–6 to J–13, S–1, OP, OP–1 to OP–3. In 1967 we excavated X–1 to X–3. In 1968 various test trenches were made and in 1971 some further probes. With this the excavation was terminated.

Chronology and Stratigraphy

The most precise indications of the periods of use or occupation of the site come from the coins and lamps. A

---

1. *Jalame* has been chosen as a compromise among the many variations in the names the site has been called. The complete name is now generally written as *Jalamet el-Asafna*; however, the *British Survey of Western Palestine* (1878) identified the site on its map, sheet V, as *Khirbet el Asafnh*, marked as a little to the north of a small village named *Jelmeh*. E. H. Palmer, *The Survey of Western Palestine* (London, 1881) lists the site as *Khûrbet el 'Asâfneh*. On the survey of the Mandatory Government (1929–1930) the place is identified as *Kh. el Jalama*. The 1:100,000 map of 1936 and later editions mark the area simply as Jalama.

There is considerable uncertainty as to the meaning of the name. Since this is irrelevant to the purpose of our excavations, the several opinions that have been offered are not mentioned here. (All the above information was kindly provided by Prof. D. Barag.)

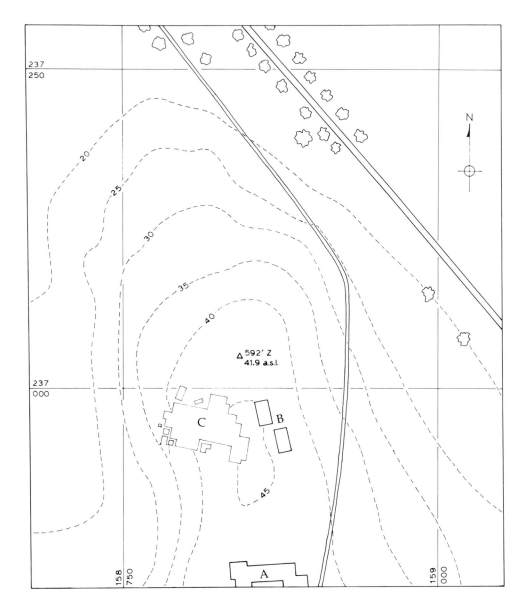

Fig. 1–1. Contour plan of Jalame ridge (adapted from Israel Government survey map). A, police post; B, guards' houses; C, excavated area.

single coin has a beginning date of 18/17 B.C. and remained current until A.C. 114/115. The next coins have beginning dates of A.C. 211/217. On the other hand, there are lamps and lamp fragments that indicate use of the site during at least part of the time for which there are no coins. A single Hellenistic lamp fragment (Chap. 6, No. 1) can have little significance, for it is not until the mid- or late 1st century A.C. that a continuous sequence of lamps appears. Most of the earlier lamps belong to the last quarter of the 1st century and the first quarter of the 2nd. A few of these are complete and, together with early pottery and fragments of sarcophagi, suggest that the top of the ridge was used for a half-century or more as a cemetery. We know of graves farther south on the ridge that were discovered during the construction of the police post (see Chap. 2, Appendix). At the same time, a con-

centration of lamp fragments on the western slope, in and below the area later occupied by the glass factory, suggests some occupation here in this relatively early period. One of these lamps (Chap. 6, No. 6), of the early 2nd century, was found in the southeast corner of the space later occupied by the glass furnace. It lay in fragments under a large ashlar block situated below the furnace floor (see Chap. 3). This may be the only ashlar block on the site still in its original position.

The sequence of early lamps seems to go no farther than the mid–2nd century; after this there is a blank until the lamp series starts again in the last quarter of the 3rd century. The coins, on the other hand, begin again early in the 3rd century, two having beginning dates of 211 and two more beginning dates of 218; the next coins belong to the third quarter of the century, six having

Fig. 1–2. Excavated area with numbered trenches and coordinates. (Grid divisions were placed every half-meter. On the plan above, those at 5-meter intervals are indicated.)

beginning dates between 251 and 255. After another gap of twenty years, an unbroken series of coins starts in the last quarter of the 3rd century and continues to the mid-4th. Thirty-two coins have beginning dates in these seventy-five years; but only thirteen lamp fragments can be assigned to the late 3rd and early 4th centuries.

It seems clear that there was a gap in the occupation of the site from about 125 to 275; both lamps and coins indicate renewed occupation by the latter date, again on the west slope, where the glass factory was later built. During the next seventy-five years, from 275 to 350, occupation seems to have spread to the top of the ridge. It was probably with the coming of Christianity, during the rule of Constantine (314–337) and his followers, that respect for the cemetery along the top of the ridge ceased and it was possible to build on this advantageous site. After some tentative extensions upward of the building that had existed on the slope, a large country house, or

"villa," was constructed on top of the ridge. Before mid-century, a wine press and a large olive press complex were added.

Everywhere on the site are signs of greatly increased activity after the year 350. Issues of Constantius II (351–361) and of the House of Constantine (351–363) account for 55 of the 207 identified coins from the site; this compares with 43 coins dating before 350. These were reinforced by 10 coins of Julian (355–363), 6 of Valentinian I (364–375), 12 of Valens (364–375), 2 of Gratian (378–383), 4 of Theodosius I (379–383), 38 of the Houses of Valentinian and Theodosius (364–383), and 3 of Valentinian II (375–392). Thus, 130 of the 207 identifiable coins have issuing dates between 351 and 378. This clearly was the period of operation of the glass factory, for these coins are everywhere associated especially with the dumped debris of the factory that occupies most of the southwest corner of the excavated area. Besides the building of the glass furnace in unit V (See Fig. 2–1), there were only minor alterations in the building on the west slope; no evidence remains for any changes in the villa.

Architecturally and numismatically there is a break at 383. This is the beginning date of the latest lots of coins: those of Theodosius I (383–395), Flacilla (383–386), Arcadius (383–392), Honorius (393–408), and the Houses of Valentinian and Theodosius (383–408). These account for 36 coins that represent the quarter-century from 383 to 408. They were found above the debris of the glass factory and are associated with the final architectural phase, which involved major rebuilding of the villa, rebuilding of the structure on the west slope, and possibly the tying together of the two complexes. The much smaller number of coins is probably due to the cessation of commercial activities, though the country house seems still to have been in use.

Architecturally, the very latest sign of activity is the addition of a large drain diagonally across the south end of the villa. At its northwest end it turns toward a stone-lined pit (Trench G, see Fig. 2–1) that existed in the Period 4 complex, but a connection between drain and pit is uncertain. Such crude constructions may have been added in the early 5th century. There are five coins with beginning dates of 425 and two with a beginning date of 457. Thus, occupation seems to have extended into the early 5th century, but how long it continued is uncertain.

Later remains were scant: pottery and glass fragments dropped by passers-by and more than forty Muslim burials (see Chap. 2).

2

SAUL S. WEINBERG

The Buildings and Installations

Period 1 (ca. 75–125)

Everywhere along the top of the ridge and down the west slope, the building remains incorporate re-used ashlar blocks. Only one block adjacent to the east side of the glass furnace of Period 3, just south of its center (Pl. 2–1A), seems to be in its original position. The lamp (Chap. 6, No. 6) found beneath the west side of this block is a strong indication that this original use dated in the early 2nd century. Possibly more digging elsewhere, beneath later buildings, would have revealed other ashlar blocks in situ. We may postulate that the re-used ashlars derived from early structures on the west slope of the ridge, in the general area of the later glass factory. The extent of the earliest occupation is indicated by the find spots of the earliest coin (Chap. 5, No. 1), current to 114/115, and of eight lamp fragments of the late 1st and early 2nd century. All these were found on the west slope in the area of the building that we consider to be of Period 2 (see below). Many other objects datable to the 1st and 2nd centuries also come from here. Following this early phase a long time must have passed before the next building phase began, for there are no signs of occupation for a century and a half (ca. 125–275).

Period 2 (275–350)

The renewed occupation of the site apparently began with construction in the same area on the west slope, in part re-using material from the earlier building. This new construction can be seen best in units I, II, and III (Fig. 2–2), where it was not buried or obliterated by later overbuilding. The complex extended to the north, east, and south but not to the west. The best evidence for dating these walls is the fact that debris from the glass factory, which ultimately filled the slope south of unit II and west of the long west wall of the latest building complex (Period 4), had covered the south wall of unit II and some of the area of III. In fact, two walls, each a single line of stones, which run westward from the west side of unit II (Pl. 2–1B), were probably retaining walls built in the following period (Period 3) to restrict the northward extension of the factory debris.

Since the walls of the later phases have been, to a large degree, left in place, and since they generally followed the lines of earlier walls, it is difficult to say much about the extent of building activity in Period 2. In many instances earlier walls can be seen underlying those of Period 4. Considering again the find spots of coins and other objects dating before 350, it is clear that the whole area, including units I to XV, was already occupied in Period 2. Further, unit XVI seems also to have had its main use in Period 2; then it appears to have been a courtyard with three clay ovens and a large stone basin (Pl. 2–1C). From this area came most of the fragments of basins cut from soft stone (see Chap. 8, Nos. 126–31), which are among the early features on the site. The doorways at the west end of unit XVI and in the four walls of unit XVIII and, in fact, in the whole block formed by XVII, XVIII, and XIX probably belong to this phase (Pl. 2–1D), for here too the latest walls are built upon earlier ones.

In attempting to reconstruct the buildings of Period 2 (Phase A), the well-constructed doorways, most with carefully cut jambs and some with good thresholds, are the best guide.[1] In addition, there are clearly early walls in some places beneath the walls of Period 4. These give evidence for two structural phases, probably the result of an earthquake that caused at least partial destruction of this complex. That is most obvious in the south wall of units XII and XV, which shows two contiguous foundations, the earlier one on the south, ca. .75 wide and preserved for one or two courses to a height of .35 (see Pl. 2–1C). The collapse of this wall is indicated graphically by the debris found south of it, which covered the entire

---

1. A number of cut blocks from L-shaped jambs were found scattered about the site. Measured drawings of them are shown in Fig. 2–2.

Period 1
75–125

Periods 2 & 3
275–383
Phase A
Beginning 275

Periods 2 & 3
275–383
Phase B
Beginning ca. 325

Periods 2 & 3
275–383
Phase C
Beginning ca. 350

Period 4
383–425

Fig. 2–1. Plan of Site

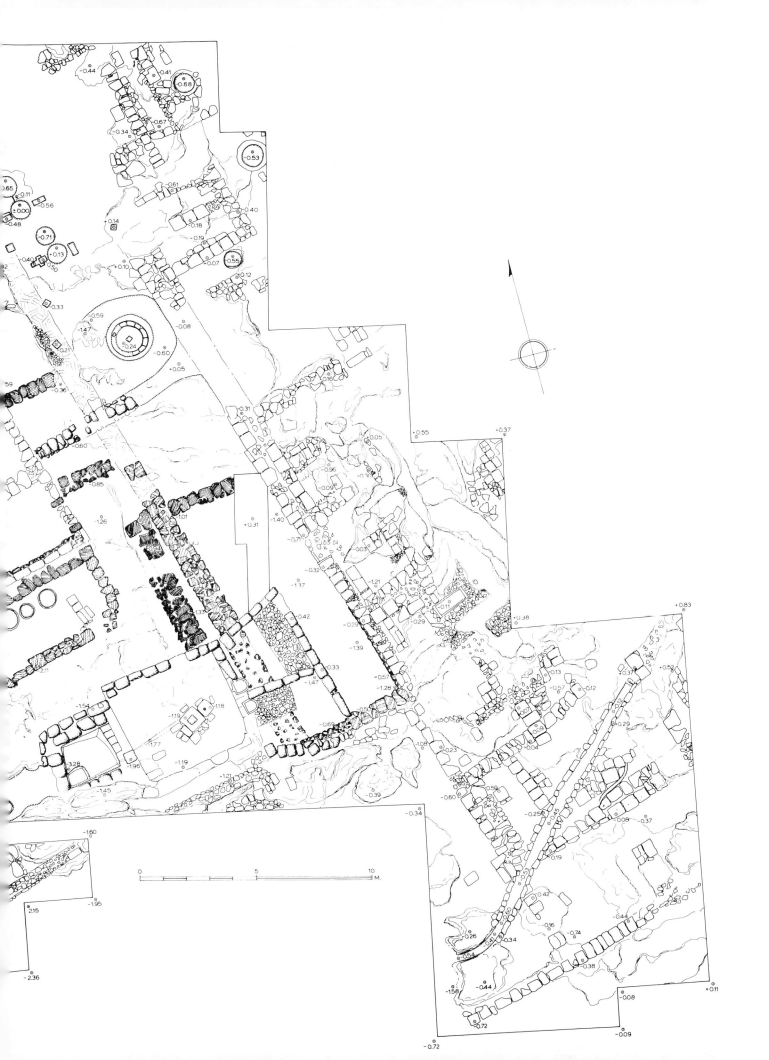

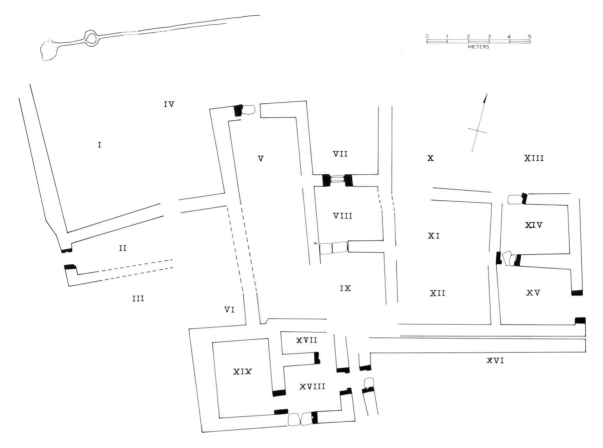

Fig. 2–2. Plan of buildings of Period 2.

long narrow unit (XVI) and destroyed the three ovens. Here were found numerous fragments of wall stucco, many of them painted (see Chap. 8, Nos. 165–66); similar fragments were found to the north and northwest, as far as units I and IV. Other evidence of earthquake damage was found in the southeast corner of unit VIII (Pl. 2–1E). The destroyed wall of unit XVI was replaced by another built immediately north of it (Phase B); at the eastern end of this was placed a typical L-shaped door post, used here to form a good corner (Pl. 2–1F). Together with this reconstruction, there was a general raising of floor levels that also involved raising the levels of the thresholds.

To this reconstruction we can probably attribute the unusual juxtaposition of the west wall of unit XVI and the east wall of XVIII, each with a doorway in the same position, and each door opening to the west (Pl. 2–2A); the two walls are only .50 apart, and the doors could not have functioned at the same time. The door of XVI would seem to be the earlier one, forming a good corner with the earlier (southern) foundation of this unit. Here, too, it is clear that the floors were raised ca. .50 and new thresholds laid.

Our picture of the large architectural complex of

Period 2 (Phase A) is incomplete, since none of the later walls was removed by our excavation except around unit V, where the glass furnace was later built. Using the doorways as a guide, the building (apparently a single structure) is judged to have been ca. 26 m long, measuring from the wide doorway in the east wall of unit XV to the smaller one in the west end of unit II. However, the lighter constructions west of unit VI were probably parts of courtyards and sheds, with the main building only about 20 m long. Its width, from the south wall of unit XVIII to the north wall of unit V, was about 16 m.

The widest doorway, possibly the main entrance to the building, is in the south wall of unit XVIII (Pl. 2–2B). It is 1.20 m wide: unit XVIII is exceptional in having doors in all four walls. That in the east wall, already mentioned, is .75 wide; it may have communicated with a courtyard replacing one that seems to have existed here (unit XVI) in the building's earlier phase. There is no east doorpost for the doorway between units XVII and XVIII, but the door opened into the former. Both doorposts in the wall between units XVIII and XIX have simple rectangular sections, indicating that there was only an opening.

Another wide entranceway from the exterior is in the

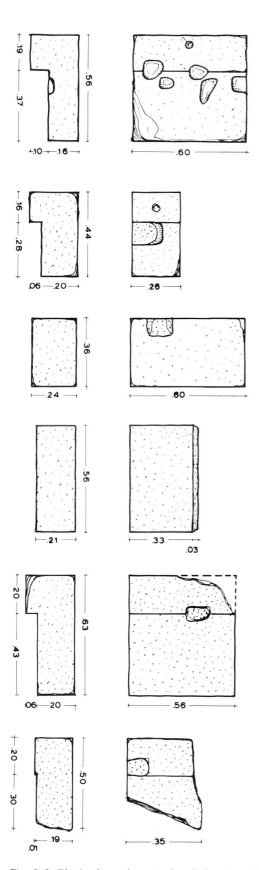

Fig. 2–3. Blocks from door jambs. Side view, left; front view, right.

east wall of unit XV; it may have had double doors or a large gate, for the jambs have no stops. This large room may have served as a courtyard or stable; it communicated with unit XIV, which in turn led into XIII (if this existed at the time). There is no apparent communication between this row of rooms on the east side of the complex and those to the west; possibly they were storage or work rooms, separate from the rest of the building.

We can say almost nothing of units XI and XII, immediately west of the series just described; we are not even sure what divisions there may have been in Period 2. The next row to the west, however, is clearer. Unit VII was evidently a kitchen in the last period and may have served a similar purpose in earlier phases. The opening between it and unit VIII, about .70 wide, may not have had a door, since the jambs have no stops, but it has one of the best threshold blocks in the complex (Pl. 2–2C). Between units VIII and IX was an opening, ca. 1.25 wide (Pl. 2–2D), but no jambs and, most likely, no doors. The form of unit IX in Period 2 is unclear, for earthquake damage and subsequent reconstruction have left little of its original plan. This is also true of unit V, west of VII and VIII. Here considerable change occurred in Period 3, when the glass furnace was installed. That there was already a substantial doorway in the north wall in Period 2 seems sure; the western L-shaped jamb is still in situ, as are two large, rough blocks that formed the threshold (Pl. 2–2E). The west wall of unit V in Period 2 has been taken to be the line of ashlar blocks extending north at a low level from unit XIX; the line is continued by other groups of blocks, finally joining the north wall. Again, the furnace built in the next period obliterated much of this construction.

Unit XIX probably had the same form from Period 2 onward, for on all four sides are indications of walls beneath those of Period 4. Whether or not the west wall continued to the north as the west wall of unit VI is problematical. What we do know is that a large area with a floor of beaten brown earth covered much of unit II and extended south into III and east into VI. The north wall of unit II, of lighter construction than most of the walls and probably belonging to a shed, rested partly on this floor and thus must have been built later in Period 2 than the main building. There was a large deposit of pottery on this floor in both unit III and VI; it was cut by the west wall of Period 4, which rested partly on the floor and partly on bedrock. Consequently, evidence of an earlier wall is lacking.

It is likely that the entire area north of unit XIX and west of unit V comprised courtyard and work areas. We have noted the long, shed-like structure extending west of unit V; its north and west walls (the latter with a doorway) are well preserved, as is a short return of the south wall from the west wall. However, constructions on the north and west sides of unit III, which were added to the long west wall in Period 4, did considerable damage in this area. The west wall of unit II is in line with what may have been the courtyard's west wall: at its south end the foundations abut against a rock outcrop. How far to the north this unit extended is unknown, but a few blocks in the northwest corner of the excavated area are parallel and very close to the north wall of Period 4; these may mark the northern extremity of the compound. Through this area runs an east-west drain, partly cut in rock and partly lined with blocks. It extends under the late west wall, into a small, rock-cut pit, and then into a larger one, where it ends. This drain is earlier than Period 4, but how much earlier is unknown.

The presence in the courtyard of a large stone weight (Pl. 2–2F), of the kind used in an early type of olive press, may indicate that such a press existed here before an olive press with screw mechanism was built up the slope to the east (see below). In addition to the work areas northwest of the main building in Period 2 (very likely in Period 3 as well) we have mentioned unit XVI, along the south side of the eastern half of this building. That there was also a work area here, probably a kitchen, is indicated by three storage bins or ovens adjacent to the earlier south wall (Pl. 2–3A) and a large stone mortar somewhat to the west in the same line. The bins or ovens are made of a thin shell of clay built up in rings (Pl. 2–3B), smoothed over when in place and fired from within. They rest on foundations of small stones (Pl. 2–3C) and had packings of such stones around the outside at the base. Their diameters east to west are .60, .40, and .60 m. All were found badly crushed under the stones of the collapsed wall; the bottom of each was found filled with a white powder, possibly ash, either from the original firing in situ or from use as ovens.[2]

There is evidence that the work areas west of the building extended southward as well, to the edge of the excavated area. When uncovering a series of working floors associated with the glass factory (see below), located in the area southwest of unit XIX, it was found that beneath the upper four floors, which were full of glass fragments, were two more floors of a fine white clay. These, in contrast to the floors above, have no glass associated with them. The lowest floor is founded on rock and virgin soil, separated from the one above by about .12 m of dark brown fill. The lowest floor (Pl. 2–3D) is by far the most carefully laid, but the one above it also is well made of about .10 of light clay. These two must have been laid down in Period 2 and been part of the working areas.

While the picture of the building of Period 2 is incomplete, it indicates a country house of some size, surrounded by work areas, some incorporated into the building itself. The well-built doorways, the numerous ashlar blocks, and some very good floors indicate a structure made with care.

It is also likely that during the latter part of Period 2 (Phase B) construction was pushed farther up the ridge, possibly even to its top. We have already suggested that with the coming of Christianity in the reign of Constantine (314–337), the cemetery along the top of the ridge was no longer sacrosanct and was built over. The great building on top of the ridge (see Fig. 2–1) was probably a large Roman villa. Its length has been uncovered for a stretch of 45 m; we seem to have found the south end, but the building may have extended farther north. Unfortunately, the top of the ridge has been eroded to bedrock, but wall foundations appear on the western slope. Many foundations show two construction phases: the later one is typical of Period 4, but the underlying foundations resemble those of the buildings farther down the west slope. The outstanding feature of the building on the ridge is its long west foundation, or the rock-cut bedding for it. This can be traced for about 35 m, with an average width of 1.15. From this long wall, spur wall foundations extend to the east. There are also some north-south interior walls. These are all so scrappy and the fill so shallow that we can say only that they are the remains of a series of small basement rooms, with two phases of construction.

Some features may belong to the first phase of the villa. At its southern end, possibly forming an entranceway through the south wall, is an area paved with large limestone slabs (Pl. 2–3E). At its northern end this paved area was disturbed by a long drain built late in Period 4; another smaller drain runs through the pavement in an S-curve. The large slabs shown in Pl. 2–3E may have formed a threshold about 2 m wide through the south wall, and the pavement seems to have continued northward, probably into a court. At about 10 m north of the "threshold" is a small rectangular tank (1.55 x .60), with walls ca. .10 thick, preserved not more than a centimeter or two above its fine plastered floor (Pl. 2–3F). In the area just south of this tank fragments of terracotta flues and circular bricks were found (see Chap. 8, Nos. 149–53). These indicate either that a bathing establishment existed in the southern part of the villa or, more likely, that some of the rooms were heated (See Pl. 8–10). In the northern part are three ovens like those in unit XVI; the northernmost and best preserved (Pl. 2–4A) had a diameter of .90 m. The next one to the south is even larger (exterior diameter ca. 1.20 m), the largest oven found at Jalame. The third oven is much smaller, only .60–.70 m in diameter. These ovens or bins indicate that the domestic portion of the villa was at the north.

Roughly parallel to the long wall, and 2.20–2.50 west

2. Similar bins were found outside a shop and along the paved Herodian street in Area C at Tel Aphek (M. Kochavi, *Aphek-Antipatris, Five Seasons of Excavation at Tel Aphek-Antipatris* 1972–1976 [Tel-Aviv, 1977] 12).

of it, another foundation about 1 m wide has been traced, through either actual masonry remains (Pl. 2–4B left) or the rock-cut bedding for them, for a length of ca. 29 m. These two walls must be part of the same plan and can be assumed to be contemporary. The western one ends on the south at living rock well to the north of the other, but between the two must have been a long corridor or road-way, for a clear path leads from the rock on the south to the most northerly extent of the excavations, a stretch of about 36 m. This path was later interrupted by two con-structions (see olive presses, below).

It must be noted that there are foundations east of the large building down the slope that were cut by the west-ern long wall just mentioned. One of these is built of heavy blocks, resembling those of the north wall of unit XVI and (with a gap) continuing its line to the east; it therefore seems part of the same construction program. Tied into this foundation is another one extending south-ward, a little west of the western long wall; it was uncovered to the point where it disappears beneath the wine press (Pl. 2–4B center), as did the long wall. Thus, there are at this point three building phases. The earliest is the foundation west of the western long wall, and its connected east-west foundation, which crosses the cor-ridor; a narrow section of unexcavated fill remains here. To this phase probably also belong two more east-west foundations of similar construction, both cut by the western long wall; one is ca. 2.40 m north of the angle formed by the two early walls just described, the other ca. 4.30 m farther north. From these walls one gets the impression that the first construction up the slope was an extension of the existing building of Period 2. How much time elapsed before the second phase, which included the two long walls and the villa, is difficult, per-haps impossible, to tell. Although the two long walls were originally part of the same architectural scheme, the western one was put out of use at its southern end by the construction of the wine press vats (see below). In the fill over its foundation and .50 m below the floor of the northern vat was found a coin of Constantine dated to 336–337 (Chap. 5, No. 24), which gives a *terminus post quem* for the filling. Confirming the date is the fact that in this fill there were almost no traces of glass, indicating that it was laid down before the glass factory began oper-ation (Period 3). It follows that the western long wall went out of use at its southern end some time before 350 and that the vats were then probably constructed. Thus the villa and the wine press must have been built about 335, for the western long wall was part of the villa com-plex and the vats were the latest part of the wine press construction. The whole architectural development at the top of the ridge can be placed within Period 2, proba-bly between 325 and 350, though possibly beginning a little earlier.

The Wine Press (Phase C)

One of the more complete and interesting installations is the wine press.[3] This comprises two vats at a level higher than an adjacent room with a plain white mosaic floor bordered by niches, a settling basin, and a large tank lower down, with an interior settling basin (Fig. 2–4, Pl. 2–4C). The whole has an extent of more than 60 sq m. Apparently this was not part of the original plan for the villa, since its construction involved dismantling part of the western long wall, built only a short time before. The dismantling did not occur, it seems, until after the western two-thirds of the whole installation were built, for the east wall of the mosaic room does not impinge on the western long wall. The construction of the niches necessitated removing only a portion of this wall (Fig. 2–4, section). The walls for the vats were built last.

The processing of the grapes began in the two upper vats. Here the grapes were deposited. The vat walls, only one course of which is preserved, were a single line of ashlar blocks laid as stretchers averaging .35 m; their foundation is rubble laid on the fill (Pl. 2–4D). They do not bond with the east wall of the mosaic room but only abut on it. The south wall of the southern vat is different in character, and it continues eastward to the front wall of the villa. This wall is probably part of a later alteration. When the vats were built the northern one was tra-pezoidal, ca. 3 m east-west and decreasing from 3.40 north-south on the east side to 2.50 on the west side; the southern one was roughly rectangular, 3 m east-west and ca. 2.30 north-south. These areas were then filled to the level of the tops of the niches and a cobblestone floor was laid. The floor of the north vat was found almost completely preserved (Pl. 2–4E), despite the fact that it lay only .10–.15 m below the surface. Its level is about that of the preserved tops of the walls. The floor is made of a single layer of cobblestones of various sizes, averag-ing fist-size; these are laid on the fill and are closely packed with smaller stones. Fragments of plaster were seen scattered among the cobbles. Plaster was found in all this area, mainly fallen from the walls. Certainly juice

3. This installation is typical of one of the more common types of wine presses, designated Type 8.0.1 by Rafael Frankel in his thorough study, "The History of the Processing of Wine and Oil in Galilee in the Period of the Bible, the Mishna and the Talmud" (Diss., Tel Aviv University, April 1984; Hebrew with English summary), 2 vols. The schematic plan is shown in Pl. 32, top left, while the occurrence and distribution appear on the map for type 8.0. The Jalame assemblage, which is not included in this work, extends the distribution of the type to the northwest of the desig-nated area, almost into western Galilee.

The Jalame wine press is, however, the only one for which there is reli-able internal dating evidence. Both the coin of Constantine just men-tioned and the lack of glass debris beneath the vats strongly suggest a date ca. 350 for the construction of our wine press. This is thus the earliest known; all the others are dated not earlier than the 6th c. Most of them, however, are isolated installations cut into rock, offering little evidence for dating.

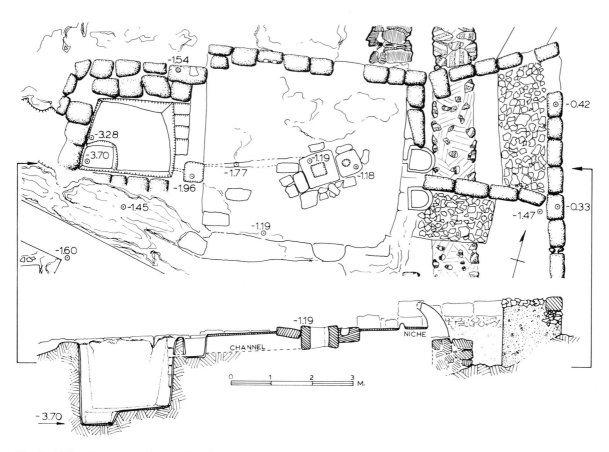

Fig. 2–4. The wine press, plan and section.

from the grapes would have seeped through the cobblestone floor, but once the earth beneath became satu-
rated, the vats would have held their contents. Only the
northern part of the southern vat floor is preserved (see
Pl. 2–4E), probably owing to later rebuilding in Period 4.
The narrow vat walls cannot have been higher than a few
courses; they were probably plastered both inside and
out.

The largest unit of the wine press is the central room,
used for treading the grapes. It is 4.75–5 m in length east-
west and ca. 4.20 wide north-south (see Pl. 2–4E right).
The north side is formed by a wall of ashlar blocks, two
courses of which are preserved, with a single block of a
third course at the east end. The exterior of this wall is
plastered, with the plaster continuing around the corner
onto the east wall (Pl. 2–4F). From the east end another
wall, also of two courses, extends south at right angles
(Pl. 2–4G). The southern half of the central room, like the
south wall of the tank, rests on living rock, but at least
one wall course seems to have been bedded on the rock,
as is shown by a cutting for a corner block at the east end
of its south wall and another at its west end (Pl. 2–5A-B).
The east wall of the large tank probably served as the
west wall of the central room (see Pl. 2–4C). All the walls

of this room were coated with plaster, now preserved to
a maximum of .18 above the floor.

The pavement of the central room consists of plain
white stone tesserae (see Pl. 2–4G), one row along the
edges of the room and the rest obliquely across it. The
tesserae are laid on a fine plaster surface, .08–.10 thick,
preserved over a larger area than the mosaic itself; thousands of tesserae were found loose in the fill. The plaster
surface rests on a basis of large rough stones (Pl. 2–5C);
six found in a test trench occupied a 1 m square.

In the east wall of the room are two niches, flanking
the east-west cross-wall that separates the upper vats (Pl.
2–5D), not quite centered on the east-west axis of the
room but ca. .40 south of it. Each niche is more than
semicircular in plan; the northern one is .52 wide and .58
long; the southern .48 wide and .52 long. Each has a
mosaic floor (Pl. 2–5E), its level about .10 above the floor
of the central room. A single row of tesserae follows the
curve of the niche; the rest are laid in straight rows. The
niches rose in semi-domical form; they were built of cobblestones laid in plaster, the interior lined with potsherds and then plastered; this plaster is now preserved
to a maximum of .10 above the niche floor. The dome of
the northern niche rises to .245 above its floor, that of the

southern to .32; in each case the top of the dome is level with the pavement of the vat. There probably was a small channel through each dome to allow liquid from the vat to flow into the niche; these are not preserved (Fig. 2-4, section). The western side of each niche was closed with a low barricade formed by an ashlar block. In the northern niche is an outlet (Pl. 2-5F) through which liquid flowed onto the mosaic floor; in the southern niche this is not preserved. The area of the upper vats was apparently filled with earth up to the level of the foundation for the wall separating the vats from the mosaic room. The niches were then built, based on this fill. The backs of the niches were waterproofed with a rough plaster coating (Pl. 2-6A); then each was carefully reinforced by a row of large fieldstones following the contour of the niche (Pl. 2-6B). Finally, the vats were filled with earth to the level of the tops of the niches, and cobblestone floors were laid down. (Pl. 2-4E shows the floors as found; later, parts were removed to disclose earlier construction.)

While no other niches are preserved, it seems certain there was at least one each on the north and south sides of the room. On the south side, an almost semicircular cutting in the rock, .85 wide and .50 deep, appears to indicate a niche; just opposite on the north side is a gap in the wall .80 wide and .48 deep, probably the position of a niche (see Fig. 2-4, plan). There is no evidence for additional niches.

Liquid from the vats flowed through the niches on the east side, then across the floor of the large central room (Fig. 2-4, section): the floor slopes .15-.20 from east to west. The middle of the central room was disturbed by a group of ashlar blocks, their tops roughly level with the mosaic (Pl. 2-6C). At the center of this group is a large block, .80 x .85, in which is cut a hole .30 square; the block is set obliquely, with its corners almost at the cardinal points. On its northeast side is a smaller dressed block, ca. .55 square, with rounded corners, through which a round hole (D .15) is cut a little off to one side. Cut blocks lie to the north, west, and south of the blocks with holes. From beneath the large block a well-made channel (Pl. 2-6D), partly constructed and partly cut in the rock, with plastered interior, leads westward to the northeast corner of the settling basin above the large tank (Pl. 2-6E). The channel is ca. .20 wide at the northwest corner of the large block; it narrows toward the settling basin and has a maximum depth of .35. No connection between channel and basin is visible; however, the basin has three coats of plaster, and it is possible that a former connection was closed by a later coat of plaster. It is certainly logical that the channel would connect with the settling basin.

It would seem that in the original scheme the block with the square hole lay over the channel, and juices from a screw press flowed into the channel, to be carried to the settling basin and the tank below. Whether or not the mosaic floor was graded to channel liquids to this central point is not now ascertainable. Most likely, at least some of the liquid flowed over the mosaic floor and then into the settling basin.[4]

In their present positions the blocks in the center of the floor must represent a secondary use, also with a screw press, in which the channel no longer connected with the settling basin and the square hole in the large block no longer led into the channel. This later use, probably in Period 4, would also have been as a wine press. It is likely that a large deposit of jars found immediately southwest of the tank (see Chap. 7, n. 109) was associated with the wine press. In this period the mosaic was partially destroyed, as shown by tesserae found in the channel fill.

Most of the area the wine press occupies seems not to have been used earlier, for here living rock comes close to the surface (see Fig. 2-4, section), or was actually exposed. The large lower tank of the wine press fills a natural depression in the rock; this may have been enlarged on the north (Pl. 2-6F). Almost no construction was required for the south side of the tank, but the other three sides have built walls; the north wall is ca. 1 m wide, the east ca. .75, and the west .50-1.00. The present depth of the tank is ca. 1.70; it is trapezoidal, the north and south sides being roughly parallel, about 2 m apart; the south side is ca. 2.30 long, the north ca. 1.90. Along the east side, five steps, recessed into the wall, lead from the north down into the tank. Because of the curve of the east wall, the steps become narrower as they descend, varying from .45 at the top to .30 at the bottom; they are .20-.36 high. The bottom step is about .40 from the tank floor, which lies 3.25-3.28 below datum (Pl. 2-6G). In the southwest corner of the tank is a roughly rectangular settling basin about .40 m deep; its south side is ca. .80 long, its east side ca. .55.

The interior of the tank, including the settling basin as well as the steps, is coated with plaster. The original plaster had a base of coarse potsherds; over it are two more coats of plaster. While the plaster is preserved in some places to the present top of the walls, it is not finished off and one must assume at least one more course of blocks. This is also indicated on the east side, where a barrier was required to control the flow of liquid and channel it into the upper settling basin. In addition, the exterior of the tank's north wall was plastered down to the level of the rock (see Pl. 2-4F). The floors of both the tank and its settling basin, on the other hand, are

4. Two additional wine presses, very close in scheme to the Jalame press, are being published by L. Y. Rahmani: "Two Byzantine Wine Presses of Jerusalem," in press. They offer the closest parallels to many of the features of our press; we are grateful to the author for supplying us with the text of his article well before it was submitted for publication.

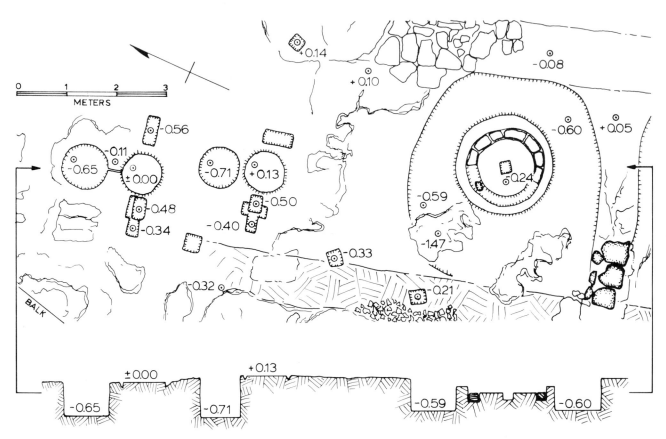

Fig. 2–5. Olive presses, plan and section.

paved with tesserae like those of the central room. They
are laid obliquely, except for two rows bordering the settling basin.

The liquid flowed into the tank through the basin
above its southeast corner (Fig. 2–4, section). The basin's
dimensions are .45 x .50, its depth .40. From the bottom
of its west side a channel ca. .07 in diameter led into the
large tank. This channel was partially blocked by a small
rough stone, evidently intended as a filter. No outlet
from the large tank could be determined from the preserved remains.

On the interior tank walls are two distinct water lines,
one .63 from the bottom, the other .93. These indicate
that water stood in the tank except during the wine-making season. Lime accretions on the mosaic floor also indicate that water stood on it during the rainy season.

Installations like that at Jalame are well known at other
sites, and the wine-making process has been thoroughly
discussed recently and in older accounts as far back as
the Mishnah and the Talmud.[5] Since our wine press
offers no features basically different from others, there is

no need to describe the process in detail. With the
author's permission, the following account of this process is adapted from Rahmani's article cited above (n. 4).

After the grapes were deposited on the floors of the
upper vats, they might be left for several days to exude their
juice. This, flowing into the small vats (those with niches),
produced the highly prized sweet wine known as *protropum*
or *mustum lixivum*. Alternatively, the grapes might have
been left to dry in the sun for several days; these, when
trodden, produced the no less prized *passum* (raisin wine).

Fermentation of the must could have taken place within
the niches, where it would have been shielded, under their
half-domes, from direct sunlight, and could have collected
heat while also being protected from the night's dew. In case
such high-priced wine was not in demand at some time, the
channels leading from the niches could be unstopped and
the must added to the juice produced by treading the grapes
on the large central mosaic floor, or that obtained from the
final squeezing of the vines and the grape skins by means of
the screw press. The juice then flowed into the large tank
below, where it continued to ferment, and finally was ladled
out into casks or jars.

Finally, in Period 4, the large tank was filled with
earth. That this was done at one time, with material
brought from elsewhere, is indicated by the lack of strati-

fication, confirmed by the fact that joins have been made of glass vessel fragments from various depths in the fill (see Chap. 4, No. 273).

The Olive Presses (Phase C)

The cultivation of olives and the use of olive oil are known from early times; the installation at Jalame is one of many that existed in the region during the Roman period. It comprised the usual crushing mill for the first pressing of the olives and, what is less common, two adjacent presses instead of a single one. Most unusual is the fact that the bases for the mill and the two presses were cut in the living rock;[6] as a result they are completely preserved in situ (Fig. 2–5 and Pl. 2–7A).

Like the wine press, the olive presses must postdate the building of the villa's west wall and the wall parallel to it, for the form of the walkway around the crushing mill is dictated by the presence of these walls on east and west. Rather than having the usual circular form, it is quasi-rectangular with rounded corners; only the north side is curved, suggesting that the wall that crossed the corridor south of the mill was also in place when the mill was cut from bedrock. On the other hand, small square rock cuttings in the line of the western long wall, as well as one in the villa's west wall, must be for wooden posts to support the roof over the installation. These suggest that the western wall and perhaps also the villa's west wall were already partially out of use, as we have seen to be true for the section beneath the vats of the wine press. Thus the olive press, like the wine press, cannot have been constructed much before 350 and probably was in use through the second half of the 4th century.

The press complex is a fairly standard type of installation for the period, except that there were two presses instead of one. They were surely of the screw type.[7] The crushing mill base is a cylinder 2 m in diameter, about .10 larger than that at Khorazin (see n. 7), and is roughly .52 high (Pl. 2–7B); the exterior of the drum is rough-picked but quite regular. The top of the mill has a horizontal lip ca. .20 wide, within which the upper surface seems to have been cut down for about .16. At the center is a square hole, ca. .20 on a side, for a vertical post. This would have been attached at its top to a horizontal beam and have served as the pivot for the stone

wheel that revolved in a channel (.25–.30 wide) worn into the top of the drum just inside the lip. Such a channel is not a usual feature of crushing mills. Since it was later filled with small stones cut to fit it and bring its surface up to the level of the central part of the drum, it is clear that the bedrock was softer than stone usually used for this purpose; it thus wore away under the pressure of the revolving wheel and was repaired by the addition of harder stones. A similar row of filling stones can be seen in a crushing mill of an olive press found on the Upper Citadel at Amman, dated to the 5th or 6th century. The base of this mill is almost identical in size with ours—2 m across, .60 high.[8]

The oddly shaped corridor around the mill varies in width from .80 at the east to 1.50 at the west; probably a person rather than an animal was required to push the wheel around, for there was little space. At two points, northwest and southwest of the circular base, declivities in the rock extend below the surface of the corridor. That to the northwest, with a maximum depth of .87 below the corridor level, seems to have served as a natural reservoir into which oil ran through a narrow channel cut from just inside the rim of the base down to its bottom (Pl. 2–7C). We can assume that these interruptions in the corridor floor were bridged in some manner; a few boards would have served.

After being crushed in the mill, the olive pulp, contained in wicker baskets, was brought to the presses, which lie in a line directly north (see Pl. 2–7A). As far as we know, it is exceptional to have two presses in close proximity. All that remains of them, as in the case of the mill, are cuttings in the rock, but they are informative in relation to what we know of other installations. The two presses at Jalame are almost identical. What remains of each is a circular floor cut in the rock with a smoothed upper surface, and an adjacent collecting pit.

The southern press (Pl. 2–7D) lies some 2.50 north of the corridor around the mill, and along the western edge of the corridor that had existed between the villa and the parallel wall to the west. Its circular surface, quite smooth and lying at +.13, has a diameter of ca. .82; it is surrounded by a narrow rock-cut channel. There was undoubtedly a channel (ca. .12 long) leading to the collecting pit north of it, but the rock is now chipped away at this point. The diameter of the pit is the same as that of the press, and it is .80–.84 deep. The pressing floor is flanked by deep cuttings in the rock intended for upright posts (see Pl. 2–7D). That to the east (ca. .55 long, .25 wide) runs north-south; it lies .18 east of the pressing floor. The corresponding cutting on the west was recut at

---

6. Dr. Frankel informs us that there is one other example (unpublished) of an olive press cut entirely from rock, at Hurvat Kalil, east of Amka in western Galilee. For Frankel's publication of the oil presses of Galilee, see his dissertation, cited in n. 3 above.

7. A. G. Drachmann, *The Mechanical Technology of Greek and Roman Antiquity* (Copenhagen, 1963) 129, fig. 50a, shows a reconstruction of such a press based on Hero's text. For the reconstruction of a similar single screw press at Khorazin, dated 3rd c., see Zeev Yeivin, "Two Ancient Oil Presses," *Atiqot* 3 (1966) 62, fig. 10 (English summary pp. 6–8). In addition, see also Drachmann, "Ancient Oil Mills and Presses," *Archaeologisk-Kunsthistoriske Meddelelser udgivne af det Kgl. Danske Videnskabernes Selskab*, vol. 1 (Copenhagen, 1932).

8. F. Zayadine, "Excavations on the Upper Citadel of Amman, Area A (1975 and 1977)," *ADAJ* 22 (1977–1978) 20 and 22, fig. 2. Zayadine remarks (p. 20): "As the wheel was of harder stone, it wore away the bottom of the basin, which was repaired with small slabs."

least once. The first cutting may have been almost the same as the eastern one; it is ca. .50 deep. However, it is now T-shaped, with an east-west section .20 wide and .30 long: this may have been cut at the same time as the north-south cutting. Clearly later is the rectangular east-west cutting (.25 wide, .35 long), its eastern edge very close to the pressing floor; it is .10 deeper than the earlier one. Some remodeling of the support for the screw press is indicated here.

The northern press (Pl. 2–7E) is quite similar. Its circle is slightly larger (D .85); the channel around it is wider, and its inner face shows clear chisel marks. Here the channel connecting with the collecting pit is clearly marked, ca. .11 deep and .30 long, almost three times the length of the now missing channel in the southern press. The pit is larger (ca. .95, depth .65). Both pits were lined with smooth plaster, damaged near the top in the northern pit, intact in the southern. The cuttings for the supports in the northern press are both east-west, but that on the west shows some remodeling. The eastern cutting (.25 wide, .60 long, .56 deep) lies .20 east of the circular pressing floor. The western cutting seems originally to have been .25 wide, probably as long as that on the east and at the same distance from the circle; it was .34 deep. However, a rectangular recutting .40 wide and .45 long was made .14 deeper; it reaches almost to the western edge of the circle, as in the southern press. The original cutting west of the northern press must have impinged on the western wall, for it is in line with one of the cuttings for the roof supports. Again, some alteration of the supports was called for. While the plan surely indicates that these were for screw presses, we cannot be sure whether these were single or twin screw. The presence of two presses, clearly contemporaneous, seems to indicate a commercial enterprise rather than just an establishment serving a household.

Period 3 (351–383)

By the middle of the 4th century, this country establishment had become a large architectural complex that, to judge by the size of the villa and the presses, reflected prosperity and tranquillity. Only earthquake damage disrupted some seventy-five years of occupation.

A marked change occurred in the year 351, reflected most vividly in the sudden increase in the number of coins found, many with a beginning date of 351. Whereas for the seventy-five years of Period 2 there are only 32 decipherable coins, the number of coins with a beginning date of 351 totals 55! Coins with beginning dates between 351 and 383 total 130, almost two-thirds of the identifiable coins from the site. This can be explained only by assuming a great increase of commercial activity that, in turn, must be associated with a glass factory that operated here during these three decades.

The drastic change must, however, be associated as well with the cataclysmic events of the year 351 that affected this region in particular. The Jewish revolt against Gallus Caesar broke out at Sepphoris in Galilee in June 351[9] and spread rapidly from Tiberias to Lydda. The Roman army reacted quickly, and the main encounter with the rebels took place in the Akko plain; after this the Roman forces moved southeastward in Galilee, destroying as they went. Beth Shearim, very close to Jalame, was completely demolished. Avi-Yonah remarks: "It appears, however, that the open country suffered much more than the cities."[10] Several thousand dead are mentioned, and "after the revolt of Gallus no more Jews are mentioned in three cities and fifteen villages, most of them in Galilee or the western part of the Jezreel Valley, the rest in the coastal plain."[11] The occupation by the Roman army began with great severity but gradually became milder.

The country house at Jalame was in the path of the worst destruction by the Roman army following the revolt, yet there is no structural evidence that the site suffered at this time. It may well have changed hands. We have no idea whether the previous occupants were Jews; if they were, they may have left or have been removed. All we do know is that a glass factory was set up during or very shortly after the year 351, its furnace occupying part of one of the rooms farthest down the slope (unit V), and that it flourished for the next three decades.

The evidence for the glass factory comprises three separate, related parts: the furnace and a series of working floors around it (see Chap. 3), sorting floors found between 8 and 16 m south of the furnace and west of the long outer wall of the last period of construction (west of units IV, VI and XIX, see Fig. 2–2), and, finally, a huge area of dumped debris from the factory. This debris occupied the entire southwest corner of the excavated area, including everything south of the two parallel retaining walls that extend westward from unit II, and west of the sorting floors. The dump area extends about 20 m east-west, to the very lowest limit of the slope that has been tested, where it drops rather precipitously between the 33 and 30 m contour lines (see Fig. 1–1). From the retaining walls along the north to the southernmost point excavated is about 12 m, but the dump continues beyond the excavated area toward the south for an unknown distance.

The Glass-Sorting Floors

While the heart of the glass factory was the furnace

9. The account of the revolt used here is that given by M. Avi-Yonah in *The Jews of Palestine: A Political History from the Bar Kokhba War to the Arab Conquest* (New York, 1976) 176–81.
10. Ibid., 180.
11. Ibid.

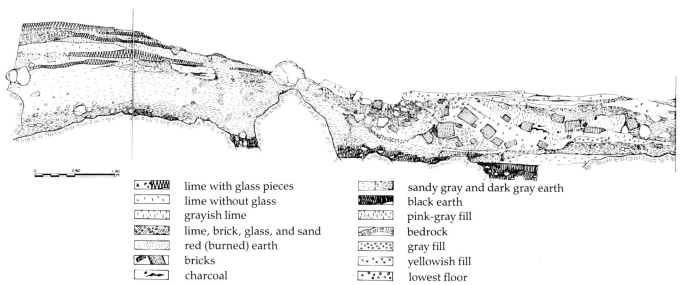

lime with glass pieces
lime without glass
grayish lime
lime, brick, glass, and sand
red (burned) earth
bricks
charcoal

sandy gray and dark gray earth
black earth
pink-gray fill
bedrock
gray fill
yellowish fill
lowest floor

Fig. 2–6. Section of sorting floors.

and the work areas surrounding it, activities connected with glass production spread well beyond to the south and west.

Along the southern two-thirds of unit XIX, the southwest corner room of the building complex in Period 2 and apparently in Period 3 as well, a series of six floors presumed to be for sorting glass extended southward to the edge of the excavated area (Fig. 2–6; Pls. 2 7F, 2 8A-D). The width of the area used for these floors reached at least 6 or 7 m westward from the long west wall of the Period 4 complex. The northernmost point to which they could be traced was within 8 m of the furnace; here they are only 2 m wide at most, and beyond this begins the factory dump. (Possibly the width was originally greater in the northern section and only toward the end of the furnace's period of use did the dumped debris back up onto the sorting floors.) The area that has been investigated is thus a large triangle. The possibility that originally the sorting floors spread along the south side of unit XIX has been mentioned. The northeast edge of the floors is cut by the trench for the foundations of the long west wall of the Period 4 building (Pl. 2-7F); thus, they clearly antedate the final building period. No traces of such floors were found east of the long wall.

The two lowest floors (designated 1 and 2), which were uncovered from the south edge of the excavated area northward for ca. 4 m, certainly belong to the period before the factory, as the fill associated with them is totally devoid of glass. North of this point the area is rocky and irregular (see Fig. 2–6). The only dating evidence for Floors 1 and 2 is a coin of Diocletian, of the year 293 (Chap. 5, No. 15); it came from the dark fill beneath the lowest floor, just above bedrock.

Above this the situation is entirely different. Appar-

ently this area was preempted for glass sorting as soon as the factory began operating. Over Floor 2 a considerable amount of fill (including bricks and stone) was laid down to raise the level above the protruding bedrock and to extend the working area farther to the north (see Fig. 2–6; Pl. 2-8A). In some places the top of this fill is a thin, dark crumbly layer, full of glass chunks and vessel fragments. Immediately over this was laid Floor 3, of hard white clay .01–.06 thick, covering the entire working area (Pl. 2-8B). Under the floor, in the extreme northern part of this area, was found a coin of Constantius II, 351–361 (Chap. 5, No. 53), giving a *terminus post quem* of 351 for the laying of the earliest glass sorting floor. In debris over this floor were found two more coins of Constantius II (Chap. 5, Nos. 47, 63); the latter has a beginning date of 355, showing that Floor 3 could not have been laid before this date. There are patches of black earth with bits of carbon on Floor 3, some hard-burned brick and much debris that seem to be from the glass furnace (see Chap. 3). The soft brown fill between Floor 3 and Floor 4 (some .10–.20) contains much glass, some of it large lumps of cullet and small chips resulting from smashing the cullet. In the northeast corner of the area, on top of the fill, was a hard layer, Floor 3a, about .06 thick, entirely filled with small splinters of glass (see Pl. 2-8B), like those found in the topmost floor (see below).

Another white clay floor (Floor 4), as much as .10 thick in some places, was laid over the entire area (Pl. 2-8C) some time after 355. The clay is fairly sterile, with only a few lumps of glass here and there. This floor, like the others, sloped somewhat to south and west, following the contours of the hill. At about its center, it was broken by a dump of brick and small stone fragments; with these was a coin of Theodosius I, an issue of 383–395

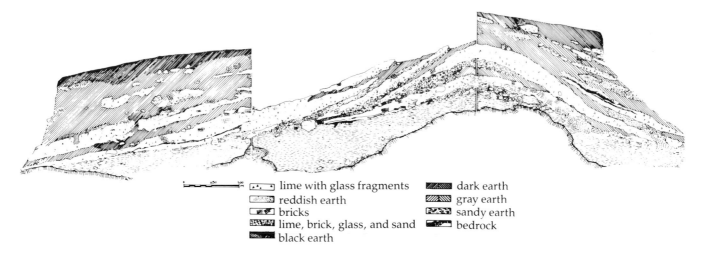

lime with glass fragments dark earth
reddish earth gray earth
bricks sandy earth
lime, brick, glass, and sand bedrock
black earth

Fig. 2–7. Glass factory dump, section through Trench Y–3S, from west.

(Chap. 5, No. 136), indicating a pit dug through the floors after 383. The floors above are not nearly so well preserved as those already described, since they were close to the surface and subject to disturbances. But it is clear that after about .10 of debris accumulated or was deposited over Floor 4, another white clay floor (Floor 5) was laid down (Pl. 2–8D); it is full of tiny bits of glass. Some .07 of red earth separates Floor 5 from Floor 6, the topmost. This earth contains a considerable amount of glass, but not nearly so much as the floor above it. In the red earth was found a coin of Theodosius I (Chap. 5, No. 135), an issue of 379–383; this indicates that Floor 6 was laid not before 379. Also of clay some .10–.20 thick (see Pl. 2–7F), it must originally have been white like the others, but it had become dark gray, almost black, in color. It was full of an infinite number of glass splinters as well as larger glass fragments, while on its surface lay pieces of cullet, glass chips, knock-offs, and waste pieces that might be from containers used to melt glass (see Chap. 3).

The four superimposed sorting floors (3–6) and the debris that accumulated between them give a vivid picture of one of the working areas of the glass factory. Here would have been brought the glass chunks, to be broken up and then melted down for making vessels. To these would be added carefully sorted vessel fragments, to be remelted. Some of these were certainly brought from elsewhere, but there were also vessels from the Jalame factory that had been poorly formed, or cracked during annealing, etc. The glass found to be unsuitable for remelting was discarded, most of it to the dump, but some was left and was trodden into the floors or accumulated on them. Much evidence for the manufacturing process comes from the debris in, on, and between these sorting floors.

The Glass Factory Dump

The dump was investigated over an area of approximately 150 sq m in the southwest corner of the excavations. Much of this was dug in large areas horizontally and to varying depths, not always down to the pre-factory fill. But in the southwest corner, where the dump showed the greatest depth, several stratigraphic cuts were made through it. The area used for the dump, like that of the glass-sorting floors, was occupied in part by large outcroppings of bedrock. There seems to have been no use of the dump area before the glass factory began operation; the debris in it was hauled here for disposal. Where the rock did not jut above ground, there was dark, rather soft fill over hardpan, varying in depth from a few centimeters to as much as a meter. In the fill were many small bits of pottery but no glass. We do not know where dumping began when the glass factory started operation; it would have been logical to start close to the factory by filling in and leveling the ground. Eventually the entire area was brought above the level of the rocky outcrops, but debris was dumped over as well as around the jutting rocks, as the section cut through the dump in Trench Y–3S shows clearly (Fig. 2–7). Here the layers conform to the shape of the rock dome over which they lie (Pl. 2–8E). On the other hand, the section taken through the length of Trench L (Fig. 2–8), down the slope at the very bottom for a length of about 9 m, indicates that some of the greatest irregularities were already evened out before much dumping was done.

The most recognizable features of the dump are the lenses of whitish limey conglomerate that occur throughout it, one above the other, with softer fills separating them (Pl. 2–9A). The conglomerate is full of glass of all sorts—vessel fragments, cullet, waste fragments of

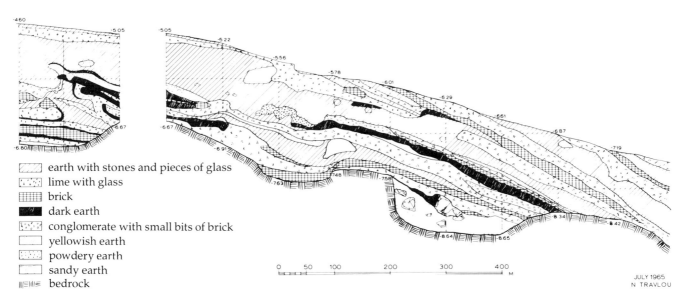

earth with stones and pieces of glass
lime with glass
brick
dark earth
conglomerate with small bits of brick
yellowish earth
powdery earth
sandy earth
bedrock

JULY 1965
N TRAVLOU

Fig. 2–8. Glass factory dump, section through Trench L, south and east sides.

all shapes and sizes; but this conglomerate also contains brick fragments (Pl. 2–9B), much broken pottery, lamps, coins, and other debris. It is evident, from the manner in which the lenses of conglomerate conform to the contours of the area, that the material was discarded in powdery form, and through the action of air and water turned into hard conglomerate layers (see Chap. 9). The fill between these layers was full of much the same kind of debris, though there were also piles of partially baked bricks, large stone pieces, and fragments of stone blocks with a curved surface, partially burnt; all this seems to be debris from glass furnaces, which must have been rebuilt frequently or repaired (see Chap. 3). Besides furnace debris, there are all sorts of glass fragments resulting from the manufacturing process: drops, threads, knock-offs, etc. One small intact glass vessel (Chap. 4, No. 357, somewhat deformed) was embedded in the conglomerate (Pl. 2–9C). All this waste material gives us a picture of the products of the factory.

Coins found both in the conglomerate masses and in the fill between them offer a fairly close dating for the accumulation of debris in the dump. It is clear that dumping began immediately after the factory started, during or only shortly after 351. There is no set number of conglomerate layers. Some are large and thick, others of lesser extent and quite thin, with variations in between (see Fig. 2–7). But we know from coins that in the section in Trench Y–3S, for instance, the lower of the two thick conglomerate masses over the large dome of rock (see Pl. 2–8E) was not laid down until after 355; the thicker mass above it was deposited after 364, and we can see that two or more layers follow the same contour, at least on one side. Thus the debris from the dump complements that from the sorting floors in recording the three decades of

the glass factory's existence; the site of the factory itself cannot offer such evidence since the furnace must have been repaired and renewed from time to time and the area cleaned out, sending that part of the record down to the dump.

Period 4 (383–early 5th century)

After three decades, the glass factory ceased operating as abruptly as it had begun, probably because fuel within an economical radius had been used up. Then followed the last major structural phase at the site, involving a complete reconstruction of the buildings in a new and different masonry style. The building on the slope was fitted into an enclosed rectangular form. To do this required the addition of rooms to form the southwest corner, perhaps some also in the northeast corner, and the cutting off from the complex of the whole western area, which had been used for glass-sorting floors, work areas, and the dump: the courts on the north remained within the enclosure. While the scant remains of the villa show the same reconstruction in the same new masonry style, too little is preserved to indicate more than that the reconstruction involved the entire architectural complex.

The date of this reconstruction can be fixed with considerable accuracy by coins found in the upper levels. In the fill over the last debris on the dump, over the top sorting floor, and on the few floors that have escaped erosion in top levels, were found coins with a beginning date of 383: there are 23 such coins, whereas there are only 11 that begin later than 383. These 34 coins indicate a great drop in commercial activity when the glass factory ceased to function, for we have seen that there were 130 decipherable coins from the factory's three decades. While the beginning date of period 4 is well fixed, its

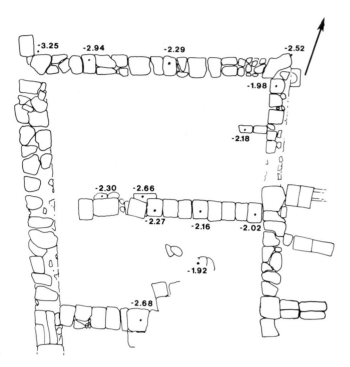

Fig. 2–9. Plan of Unit V, Period 4. Depths below datum.

final date is more difficult to determine. The coins offer some clues. Of the 34 late issues mentioned, all but 7 fall in the years 383–408, and the latest beginning date for any of these is 393. There is then a gap to 425; there are 5 coins with that year as their beginning date. The two latest have beginning dates of 457. The lamps tell much the same story: 16 items in the catalogue date from the late 4th and early 5th centuries, about half the number from the three decades of Period 3. Five lamp fragments postdate this period.

It is of interest that all the 7 late coins and all but one of the late lamp fragments were found in a strip about 5 m wide along the northern edge of the excavated area (Trench A–1—Trench A–6). The western part of this strip was largely courtyard, and the eastern part contained a couple of rooms, now much denuded. They would seem to have had little or nothing to do with the building complex; from this it may be concluded that the building of Period 4 was no longer in use by 425. Most of the site may have been deserted a decade or more before that.

The most striking architectural feature is the long west wall of Period 4, which was cleared for a length of 32.50. For the length of unit XIX only (see Fig. 2–2) it is superimposed on walls of Periods 2 and 3; this fact may have determined its position. It is also likely that the steep, rocky character of the areas farther downhill (to the west) made it undesirable to build beyond the main part of the earlier building. To the north of unit XIX this great wall, which bends slightly westward at the northwest corner of XIX (Pl. 2–9D), gave a new western limit for units VI

and V, the latter where the glass furnace had been. Unit V took on an entirely different character, with a new west wall and with a new east-west wall that divided it into two rooms, the northern one ca. 3.80 wide, the southern ca. 2.60 wide (Fig. 2–9). Beyond this, the western wall traversed the large northern court, going over the E-W drain. It seems to have come to an end and turned east in the northwest corner of the excavated area; a small section of the north wall is preserved.

To the south of unit XIX the long west wall of Period 4 continued in an almost straight line, bounding a group of three new rooms, forming a southwest corner of the complex that extends slightly beyond the excavated area (a small area was opened to define the corner). The east-west wall that forms the southern limit of the Period 4 complex is much slighter than the west wall, but it has been traced throughout most of its length of ca. 20 m to the point where it reached the south wall of the southern wine press vat. This long and narrow room seems also to have been a work area, perhaps a courtyard. In its southwest corner is a circular structure, possibly a storage pit, that antedates Period 4. In the southeast corner of the long room is a light structure, apparently a storage room for large water jars, a great heap of which was found beneath the collapsed walls (Pl. 2–10A; see also Chap 7, Nos. 798–808 and n. 109).

Except for the west and south exterior walls, the building of Period 4 retained much the same rooms as in Periods 2 and 3, plus the three rooms added in the southwest corner and possibly a few in the northeast. The walls of units X and XIII seem to be entirely of this last period, with no earlier foundations below. All the old interior walls were re-used and new floors were laid at a considerably higher level. Few floors of Period 4 could be traced, as they were not much below the surface. Almost all the extant walls must be foundations, with little or no construction above floor levels; thus there are no doorways. The doorways of Period 2 had already been filled to a considerable height and new thresholds and floors laid at ca. .50 above them, probably following an earthquake in Period 2 or 3. Since the floor levels were now raised still farther, we cannot tell whether the positions of doorways remained the same, though it is likely they did.

There is a marked contrast between the masonry of the old walls used as foundations and the new foundations of Period 4. The former are largely of ashlar masonry, usually a single row laid as headers, with some chinking. The new walls, by contrast, are built of large, roughly worked stones, most of them fieldstones, chinked with smaller stones. An occasional ashlar block remains from earlier construction, worked in with the fieldstones. This contrast is shown in a view from the east across units VII and V (Pl. 2–10B), showing the east and north walls of unit V in the new rough masonry, while the south wall of unit VII (left foreground), with its fine doorway, remains from an earlier period. However, to complicate matters, the new wall laid east-west across unit V (upper left) is also made of ashlar blocks laid as headers, but it rests on a poor fieldstone foundation (Pl. 2–10C), unlike those of the earlier ashlar walls. Details of the new masonry style are shown in Pl. 2–10D, from the east-west wall of unit V, and Pl. 2–9D, a view along the west outer wall, where it bounds unit XIX in the foreground and unit VI behind it. In the long west wall of the villa, just east of the wine press vats, is a section of wall with the new coarse masonry on top of the earlier ashlar wall (Pl. 2–10E).

One of the most extensive floors of Period 4 lies along the northern edge of the excavated area (Trench A–3—Trench A–6). It was found at .50–.60 below the surface, just where the tops of the walls begin to appear (Pl. 2–11A); this is 2.17–2.27 below datum. The floor is largely of white clay or plaster, with patches of brown earth. A white lime floor of considerable extent was found only .30–.40 below the surface in the area south of the earlier shed (unit II) that stood outside the long west wall. Only the west end of the south wall of the shed (Period 2) was preserved, while a new wall was built in the same line at a higher level (Period 4), its east end abutting the long west wall. From its west end a wall runs southward. Thus a small room (unit III) was formed outside the main complex, and in its northeast corner, partially recessed into the north wall, was built a stone cist formed of upright slabs (Pl. 2–11B). The cist had two compartments, a narrow one at the east (if indeed this is part of the cist) and a larger, almost square one at the west, about .50 on a side. In the latter was found a spherical pounding stone (Chap. 8, No. 80). Similar cists of this period occur in other rooms: a stone cist abuts the east side of the long wall (Pl. 2–11C); in unit XIII are two cists formed of bricks standing on end, one against the west wall of the room, the other close by to the northeast.

Besides the small room with the stone cist (unit III) another small structure was appended to the exterior of the long west wall near its northern end, just where it ran over the earlier east-west drain. A wall built parallel to and just south of the drain is preserved for about 1 m. The corner thus formed has a coating of coarse plaster on both the long wall and the new wall (see Pl. 2–2F), which is preserved for a maximum of .38 above the natural rock floor. The plaster is extant for 1.55 from the corner along the long wall. Fragments of fine stucco with painted decoration were found in the fill (see Chap. 8, No. 166). The south side of the room lies just along the drain, suggesting that this room was a latrine. The drain was later used for a Muslim burial (Pl. 2–11D).

Because of the shallow fill over the remains of Period 4,

it is difficult to say how and when the occupation ended. That it may have come about piecemeal is suggested by a late drain built diagonally northeast to southwest across the southernmost part of the villa (Pl. 2–11E). The channel is partly cut in rock, the sides are formed of stone slabs standing on end; no cover slabs were found. At its southwest end the channel turns westward and runs through a rock outcrop. The circular pit mentioned was dug in the corner formed by the west and south outer walls of the late building complex (see Pl. 2–11C). In fact, both these walls run over this circular pit, indicating that the latter predates Period 4. However, during excavation, this area was found to be full of debris from the collapsed walls, except in the circle of the pit. This would indicate that debris was cleared from this circular area to allow its continued use after the outer walls had collapsed; such use may have been contemporary with the late drain, and the two may possibly have been connected.

Everywhere within the building complexes, fallen wall blocks lay close beneath the surface. There was no pattern to suggest earthquake destruction; rather, the fall seems to have been due to abandonment and gradual collapse of the structures, which apparently occurred not later than 425. Little use was made of the area even during the early Arab occupation of the land in the 7th century. Some time later the entire slope became a Muslim cemetery, but in more than forty burials excavated nothing gave any indication of their date. Typically, those interred lay on their right side, facing Mecca; there were no grave offerings. Some burials were found directly beneath the surface; others lay at a depth of as much as 2 m. The gradual shifting of soil from the top of the ridge to the lower slopes accounts for the difference in depth.

Appendix: Outlying Structures

1. South of the excavations, in area of Jalame Police Post

In the 1941 excavations for the Jalame Police Post and the terrace before it, three rock-cut tombs were disclosed; another tomb was reported to have been opened much earlier. Two of the tombs cleared in 1941 were described in reports by N. Makhouly, the local Inspector for Antiquities. (We are indebted for these, and for the plan of one tomb, to the Department of Antiquities and Museums.) A summary of Makhouly's reports follows:

a. Report of 12 March 1941. In excavating the rock on the northwest side of the new Police Post building for leveling a wide terrace in front of it, a rock-cut tomb was discovered. The tomb (Fig. 2–10) consisted of a central vestibule, three burial niches arranged as *kokhim*, one burial recess, two small niches probably for offerings, and a door in the east wall. Originally there had been two more burial *kokhim* in the southern wall. The ves-

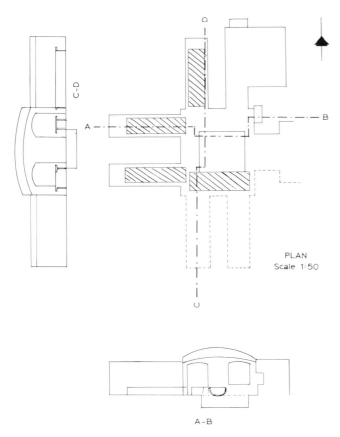

Fig. 2–10. Rock-cut tomb under Police Post terrace,
plan and section.

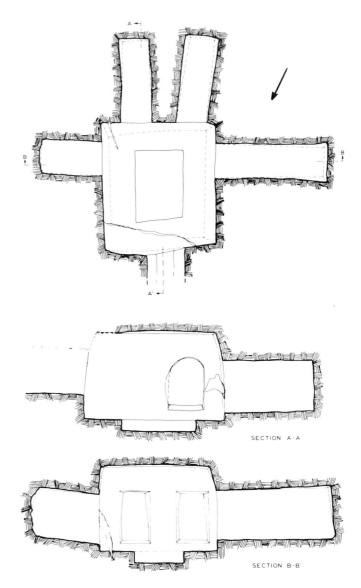

Fig. 2–11. Rock-cut tomb at north end of ridge, plan and sections.

tibule has in the middle a nearly square depression .35
deep. A large clay coffin lay on the platform south of this
depression, a small stone ossuary for a child lay on the
northern platform. To the west of the vestibule were two
kokhim, in each of which was a full-sized clay coffin. Off
the north side was a single *kokh* with a similar clay coffin,
while to the west of this was a large recess for more burials. In the northern wall of this recess, opposite its
entrance, was a small niche for offerings cut at a higher
level. A similar niche was cut to the north of the door in
the east wall. No finds other than the clay coffins and the
stone ossuary were reported.

b. Report of 22 March 1941. In the course of continuing
excavations of the rock for the terrace before the building, a tomb containing clay coffins was found. The tomb
consisted of a central vestibule and five *kokhim*. Three
rough steps, different in size and form and arranged
along the western wall, indicated the position of the
doorway, of which no traces were found. One niche was
cut in each of the northern, southern, and western walls,
while two niches were cut in the eastern wall. The niche
in the western wall was found empty and closed at the
mouth with a rubble wall .20 thick. The *kokh* in the south
wall contained a life-size clay coffin, which yielded a few

pieces of broken glass vessels and fragments of an iron
blade. The northern niche in the east wall contained fragments of a stone ossuary, which yielded a bronze coin,
two terracotta lamps, two glass vessels, and a group of
glass fragments. The niche in the north wall also contained a life-size clay coffin, which yielded no artifacts.
[The finds from these tombs cannot now be located.]

2. North of the excavations, along the northern slopes of
the ridge

A surface survey of the northern, lower slopes of the
ridge revealed traces of numerous man-made cuttings in
the rock, varying greatly in size and nature. Several of
these were tested, and two that proved of interest were
more fully cleaned out or excavated.

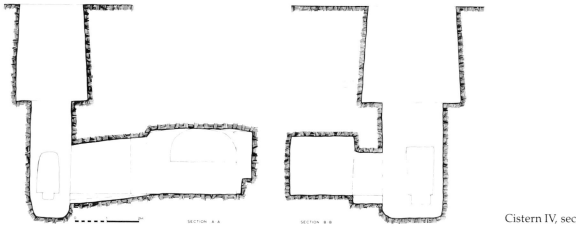

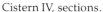
Cistern IV, sections.

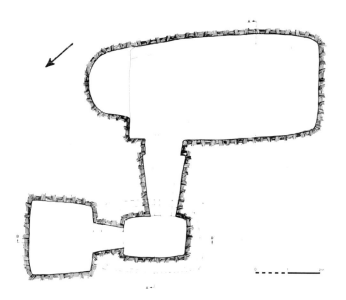

Fig. 2 12. Cistern IV, plan.

a. Rock-cut Tomb I. A hole in the roof of the tomb, approximately over its original entrance, gave access to the central chamber, which was found almost empty and had apparently been entered often in recent times. The roughly rectangular central vestibule measured ca. 2.80 x 2.40; the depressed inner rectangle, ca. .20 deep, measured 1.43 x 1 m (Fig. 2–11). There were four *kokhim* (*cubicula*), one each off the northeast and southwest sides and two off the southeast side; the single ones were ca. .70 wide, the pair ca. .60 wide. Their lengths are 1.20 for the northwest one, 1.84 for the pair, 2.40 for that on the southwest. The height of the central chamber is ca. 1.76. The single niches have arched entrances and vaulted ceilings; the pair have flat ceilings and entrances. The cutting of floors, walls, and ceilings was noted to have been done with considerable accuracy, resulting in right-angle joins. A few fragments of clay sarcophagi and some scattered bones were the only finds.

b. Cistern IV. This was found some 15 m north of Tomb I, approximately at the 25 m contour line. The cistern consists of a large rectangular shaft, with two side chambers extending from the lower part, a large one to the east and a smaller one to the north. The plan and sections show clearly the form and size of these features (Fig. 2–12). The shaft was loosely filled with stones of various sizes mixed with earth; the uppermost part was filled only with brush. This fill had not penetrated beyond the tops of the entrance passages to the chambers; these were found empty. All the rock-cut surfaces had originally been coated with plaster; in the east chamber three layers of plaster remained in some places, only two layers in others. There was much fallen plaster and it is possible that all the walls originally had three layers. The ceiling and floor were likewise plastered. In the shaft, on the other hand, plaster remained only on the north wall, where it was ca. .017 thick; probably the entire shaft was once plastered.

The east chamber presented several interesting features, beginning with its well-cut doorway. A large semicircular niche occupied the upper half of the north wall. Just below the east end of this niche a ramp began to rise along the east wall, extending the entire length of the wall to a platform about twice as wide as the ramp, along the south wall. Niche, ramp, and platform were all plastered. A narrow channel had been cut into the floor, beginning just inside the east chamber and extending the length of its entrance passageway, emptying into the shaft.

The only evidence for the date of the cistern complex was a cooking pot (Chap. 7, No. 604) and a few sherds found on a ledge where the shaft narrows. On this ledge remained a wedge of fine, dark soil that continued around the shaft; here the cooking pot was found, broken but almost complete. It has been dated to the late 1st or early 2nd century, indicating that the cistern complex was dug during Period 1.

3

GLADYS D. WEINBERG

The Glass Factory and Manufacturing Processes

The existence of a glass factory at Jalame has been established beyond any doubt by masses of raw glass and cullet, heaps of waste accumulated during manufacture, and thousands of vessel fragments (Color Pl. 1B). The amount of material excavated exceeds by far that found in connection with any other factory of any ancient period. In reports concerning other glass factories, the paucity of glass remains—vessel fragments, pontil knock-offs, drops, etc.—is often mentioned by the excavators. The contrary is true at Jalame: here glass was obviously cheap, and relatively little of it seems to have been collected for remelting.

The area excavated was chosen because of the quantities of glass visible on the surface as well as architectural features that protruded above ground. Further excavation, deeper in certain places and extending the area, would certainly have produced many more glass fragments. Decisions as to where to stop and where to continue had to be made constantly during the course of the excavation.

The Jalame factory produced mainly household vessels. There were probably many glasshouses in the area manufacturing similar utilitarian vessels, but since Jalame is the only center in the region that has been systematically excavated, it offers a unique opportunity to study manufacturing methods as well as the vessels themselves. Complete glass vessels come mainly from tombs, less often from habitations, where they are usually fragmentary. Neither tombs nor dwellings can shed light on manufacturing methods, except insofar as the vessels themselves offer clues. Consequently, much stress is placed here on manufacturing methods. Hundreds of vessels like those produced at Jalame exist, but many are in collections, without any indication of provenience except "possibly Syria," "probably Palestine," etc. There are also many more that have not been published at all.

Explanations have been offered elsewhere concerning manufacturing techniques, but little effort has been made to reconstruct shapes. Our approach has been, wherever possible, to reproduce the vessels, to determine which implements were used in the glassmaking process and which were *not* used, to discover which parts of the process were difficult and which easy for the ancient glassmaker—in general, to understand the processes of manufacturing glass vessels in the 4th century rather than only to present a typology. Thus, the composition of the glass used at the factory is important, and even more important are actual experiments. Such experiments do not *prove* what methods were used by the Jalame glassblowers, but they do indicate possible methods.

Study of the Jalame material provides information regarding chronology. We can state whether or not a particular vessel type was made at Jalame; we can also state what kinds of vessels may not have been made there. But the vessel types found at Jalame can be dated only to a certain extent: that is, they could have been made during, before, or after the time in which the factory operated, for this was less than thirty-five years, and types usually persisted for much longer. The Jalame factory was in no sense a pioneer establishment; the glassblowers had certainly worked elsewhere before, and they and their successors probably continued to work at other places after leaving Jalame. Where they came from and where they moved to, before and after the Jalame operation, is not known. One may guess that they did not wander very far from this area.

The Belus River, famous in antiquity for the excellent quality of its sand, flowed to the sea not far north of Jalame (see map on p. vi).[1] From the finds in the Syro-

1. Pliny (*Natural History* 5.75), Strabo (*Geography* 7.16.25), and Josephus (*De Bello Iudaico* 2.10.2) are among the sources mentioning the fame of the Belus River for glass sand. The texts of these and other Classical writers are discussed by M. L. Trowbridge, *Philological Studies in Ancient Glass*, University of Illinois Studies in Language and Literature, 13 (Urbana, 1928) 95 ff. Evidence for the use of Belus River sand as late as the 17th c. is offered by a French traveler who visited the Holy Land in 1652: "Quelque fois, quoy que fort rarement, quelques vaisseaux d'Italie en ont chargé pour cet effect" (M. I. Doubdan, *Voyage de la Terre Sainte* [Paris, 1657] 599,

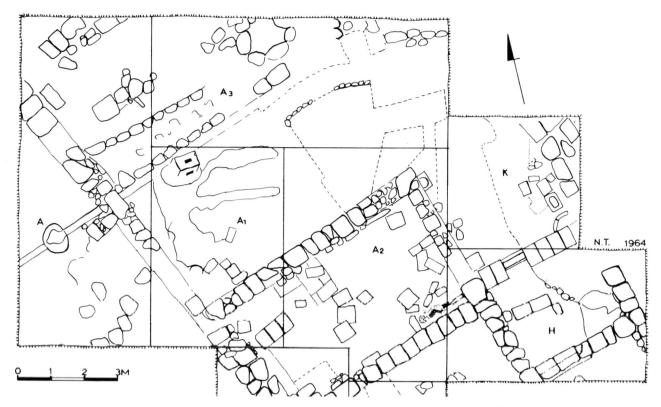

Fig. 3–1. Plan of Trenches A, A–1, A–2, with buildings of upper level.

Palestinian region as well as from the literature it is known that here, in Roman times, glass was worked in two stages. The raw materials were first melted together, resulting in the production of large blocks. These were then broken into smaller chunks and shipped to factories where vessels were produced.[2] Jalame was clearly one of these secondary establishments. The great glass slab found at Beth Shearim, not far from Jalame,[3] is an example of an unsuccessful first melting; other, smaller blocks, doubtless produced in the vicinity, would have supplied factories in the area. It appears that the whole

region was once wooded and that glassblowers moved their operations once they had exhausted the economically available fuel.

The first trench excavated (Trench A) proved to be near the center of the factory's activity. The second (Trench A–1) was still closer, and in the third (Trench A–2) we came upon the remains of the furnace itself (see Pls. 3–1A- E and 3–2). The furnace was not immediately recognized, for large stone blocks of the post-factory period (see Chap. 2, Period 4) lay fallen everywhere. These had to be removed, with considerable labor, before work could proceed (Fig. 3–1).

The distribution of the glass fragments helped to delineate the area of the factory's operation. As mentioned in Chap. 2, the fill was very shallow in some areas; this prevented certainty regarding the construction of the furnace and structures associated with it.

At the northern edge of the main excavated area glass was relatively scarce, and a trench farther north (Trench C) was soon abandoned when almost no glass appeared. Similarly, Trench B provided no finds of any consequence. The eastern edge of the excavated area, where bedrock is nearly or actually on the surface, was also comparatively unproductive of glass. The central portion, around the furnace, produced much more, especially vessel fragments, and in pockets a good deal of glass waste was found. Hard floors of packed clay and

as quoted by E. D. Clarke, *Travels in Various Countries of Europe, Asia and Africa*, pt. II, sec. 1 [London, 1812] 379). Clarke remarks about the Belus: "It seemed to us to be muddy, and mixed with various impurities; we afterwards regretted that we did not collect a portion, in order to examine whether it naturally contains an alkali."

2. Information concerning raw glass transported to factories in the form of lumps broken from a large slab is derived from the Babylonian Talmud (Shabbath 154b), where Rabbi Huna (3rd c.) explains a passage of the Mishnah relating to rules for observing the Sabbath. If a man's animal is loaded with glass and the Sabbath has commenced without his realizing it, he is instructed as follows (free translation): "If his animal is loaded with glass vessels, he may bring pillows and blankets and lay them underneath, then loosen the cords and the sack will fall down. But if his animal is loaded with [glass] lumps, he must just loosen the cords and let the sacks fall down, even if the glass breaks." The word for "lump" is the Greek βῶλος, written in Hebrew letters.

3. See Chap. 9. Another slab almost as large was found at Rishpon (Arsuf), on the coast north of Tel-Aviv. This has not been fully published; large chunks of it are stored in the Glass Pavilion, Museum Haaretz, Tel-Aviv.

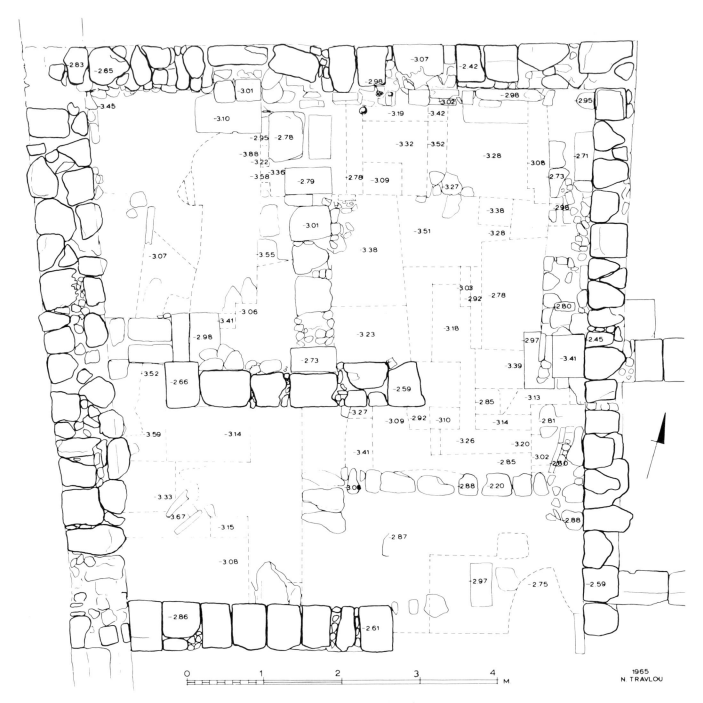

Fig. 3–2. Plan of trial trenches dug in enclosure (Trench A–2). Depths below datum.

lime appear to have been associated with glassmaking. In some places the floors were so hard that a pickax could not penetrate them, while in others it was possible to uncover a series of floors that had evidently been renewed from time to time.

Glass vessel fragments were also found in earth between the stones of walls built after the factory ceased work. Removing one of these walls, we found, in the earth packing between two large boulders, an almost intact glass pin (Chap. 8, No. 24), as well as fairly large fragments of vessel (see Pl. 2–10D).

South of the room eventually identified as the furnace a series of late walls tended to obscure all construction related to glassmaking, but just to the southwest of the long north-south wall, where the slope drops off sharply, a series of floors, each containing untold quan-

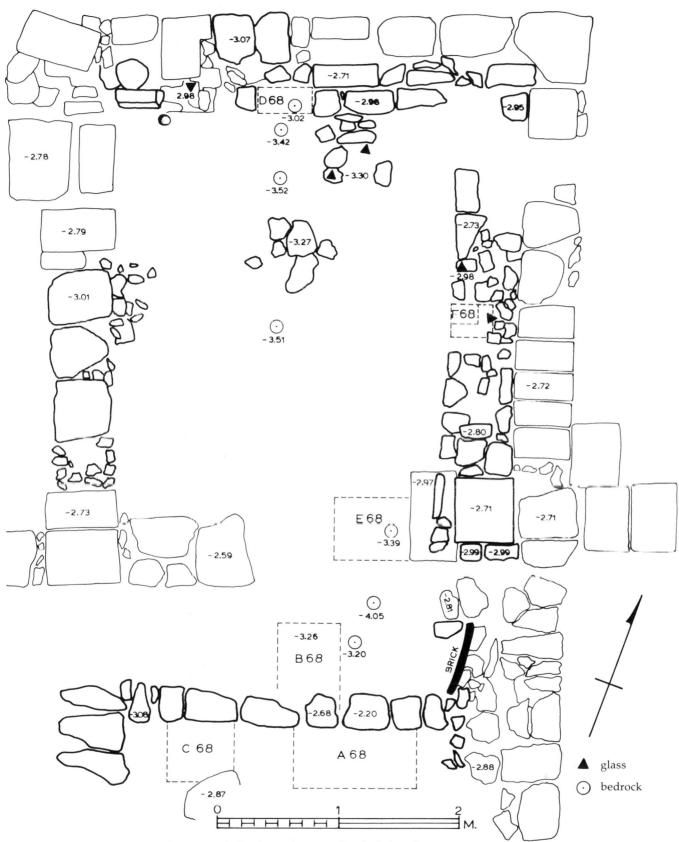

Fig. 3–3. Plan of furnace room after removal of unburned stones. Depths below datum.

tities of minute glass fragments, are thought to have been used for sorting broken glass, to be remelted (see Chap. 2, Period 3, Fig. 2–5, Pl. 2–7F).

The most abundant source of glass in all stages of manufacture was the dump where factory waste was discarded (see Pls. 2–8E, 2–9A–C). The excavated portion of the dump comprises about 150 sq m; it was seen to extend beyond to the south and west. From this area came not only glass (Color Pl. 1B) but many bricks (see below) and other material apparently used in constructing the furnace, as well as quantities of household pottery. The sections showing the stratification of the dump (Figs. 2–6 and 2–7) indicate its great extent, both horizontally and vertically. (For a detailed description see Chap. 2, where the chronological correlation of coins found there is also noted.) Lack of time and money prevented us from excavating the whole dump down to bedrock, but this would probably not have changed the picture.

The Furnace

As mentioned, our third trench (Trench A–2, see Fig. 3–1) proved to include what remained of the furnace in situ. Directly beneath the surface many large fieldstones and a few dressed stone blocks lay tumbled about, fallen from walls (Pl. 3–1A). These extended to a depth of ca. .50. Among them, in the topsoil, were numerous potsherds and a small chunk of cullet. Beneath the fallen stones was a mixture of brown topsoil and reddish brown earth that was characteristic of the whole site. The walls of an enclosure (north and east sides) now became identifiable (see Fig. 3–1); these were constructed of reused ashlar blocks and fieldstones. Beneath them were smaller stones, the surfaces of which had been severely calcined (Pl. 3–1B). Below this point the fill was brighter red and very gritty, mixed with grayish, somewhat clayey material. The area was therefore nicknamed the "Red Room." Thinking this might indicate the presence of a furnace, we proceeded to explore the interior of the enclosure by digging many small trial trenches (Fig. 3–2).

Eventually this enclosure was cleared sufficiently to ascertain that a furnace might have been located here, and this proved to be the only place on the site that showed evidence of having been heated sufficiently to melt glass. Reconstruction of the appearance of the furnace and its method of functioning was extremely difficult because of the proximity of the remains to the surface, as well as later overbuilding in Period 4. The reconstruction must, therefore, be considered tentative.

In order to establish which blocks could have belonged to a furnace and which to later construction, all the blocks and fieldstones that showed no traces of heating were removed, after being drawn and pho-

tographed. A low stone foundation was thus revealed, several courses high in some places, composed of partly calcined stones (Pl. 3–1C through 3–2B). The superstructure evidently had collapsed when the furnace was abandoned; much of it was removed and a substantial structure built there in Period 4 (see Chap. 2).

The presumed furnace foundations occupied a rectangular space measuring ca. 2.40 east-west and probably ca. 3.60 north-south (not including the walls).[4] The north-south measurement is uncertain, as few of the original stones remained at the south end under the heavy walls of Period 4.

A level basis for the floor of the firing chamber was made by filling depressions in the bedrock with earth and tamping it down. The foundations are mostly of stone, occasionally interspersed with baked bricks. On the west side three large, flat stones (total length ca. 1.40) suggest an entrance to the fire chamber.[5] Above them were stones of Period 4.

The plan of the furnace, as far as it could be determined, is shown in Fig. 3–3. The stones and bricks believed to belong to the furnace walls (all those partially calcined) are drawn in heavy outline; later ones are outlined lightly. Photographs of these walls (from the interior looking outward) are shown in Pls. 3–1D and 3–2A–B, and drawings of the same walls (Fig. 3–4) furnish more detail than a photograph can supply. Fig. 3–4A shows the entrance on the west; Fig. 3–4B (Pl. 3–1D) is the northwest corner of the furnace, with the door jamb and threshold of Period 4 in the center and an unexcavated area at the left. The nearer block of the two on the right, its south side calcined, must have formed part of the furnace wall. Fig. 3–4C (Pl. 3–1 D, E) shows the west end of the north side, again with door jamb and threshold. In front of that is a row of partly calcined stones and one baked brick. In Fig. 3–4D (Pl. 3–2A) the northeast corner is seen, showing the lower, partly calcined stones, the later ashlar additions, and some fill (in front) not excavated at the time. Fig. 3–4E (Pl. 3–2B) shows the east wall. The lower stones are part of the furnace wall; the upper rows (in outline) are of Period 4. The lowest ashlar block (extreme right) was covered by the earth of the fire chamber floor and was not burned. Beneath the level of this block (see Pl.2–1A) was found a lamp (Chap.

---

4. These measurements happen to approximate those specified by Theophilus (12th c.): 15 x 10 feet (4.44 x 2.96 m). See J. G. Hawthorne and C. S. Smith, *On Divers Arts: The Treatise of Theophilus* (Chicago, 1963) 49–50.

5. While the form of the Jalame furnace is far from certain in details, it is unlike many other wood-burning glass furnaces in that the fire chamber did not have a flue extending the length of the structure but apparently had only one entrance on the long western side. The cracks between the bricks of the structure would have provided exits for the fumes. The situation of the furnace furnished a natural draft: the almost constant wind funneling up the valley from the coast may have made a proper flue unnecessary. Such an arrangement would necessitate the removal of ash and debris from the one entrance. The form of other contemporary furnaces in the area is yet to be discovered.

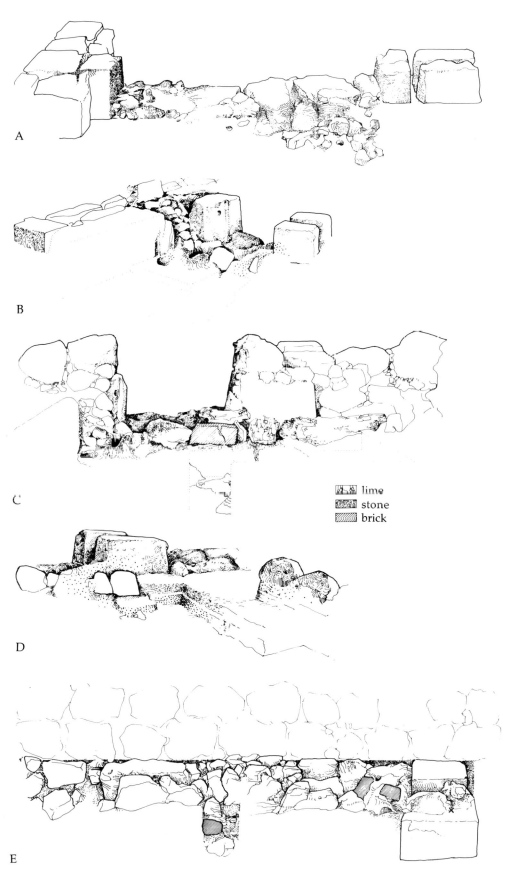

lime
stone
brick

Fig. 3–4. Furnace foundation walls,
seen from interior. A: west side;
B: northwest corner; C: north side;
D: northeast corner; E: east side.
Drawings by J. Schmeisser.

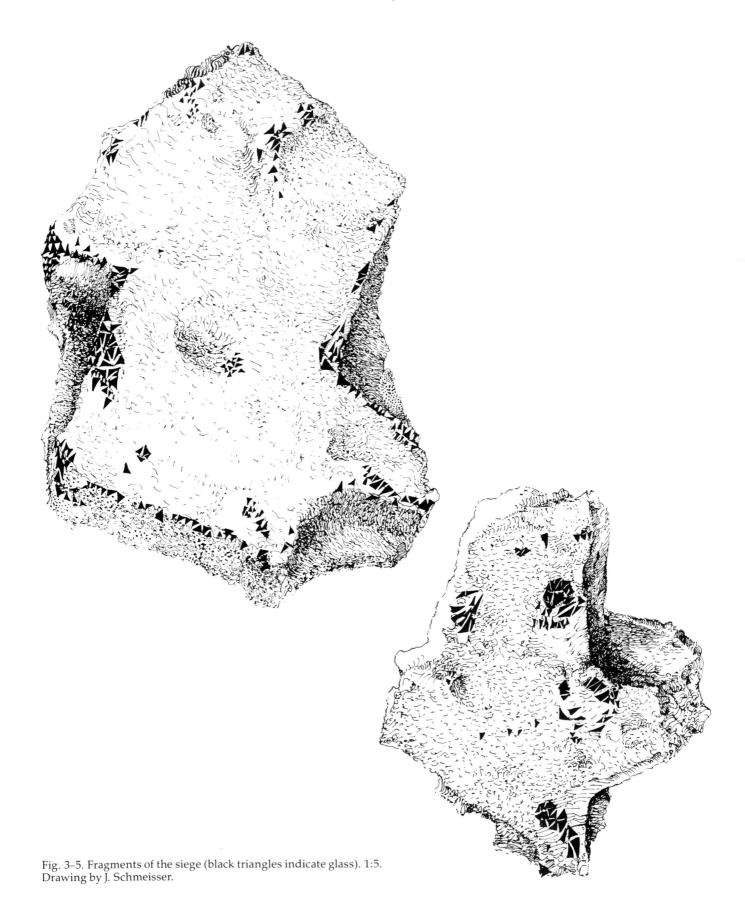

Fig. 3–5. Fragments of the siege (black triangles indicate glass). 1:5.
Drawing by J. Schmeisser.

6, No. 6) of the early 2nd century.

Pl. 3-2C is a view from the east and somewhat above, with dashed lines drawn in to indicate the approximate extent of the furnace. The unevenness of the area within the furnace walls is the result of the exploratory trenches dug in an effort to comprehend the complex.

The character of the fill in the fire chamber, from its basis on leveled bedrock to a height of ca. .60, is unique on the site (Color Pl. 2A). Its totally different aspect was at once apparent. The strata in the many test trenches made, which varied in depth, included red, granular, burned material, soft ashy layers, and buff-colored clayey earth on bedrock. This lowest stratum is not the black earth found on bedrock everywhere else on the site but a deliberately laid base for the fire chamber. Finds from the fill were minimal—a few coarse potsherds of common types and some small chunks of glass. (For a detailed description of the fill in the fire chamber and analysis of the contents, see Chap. 9.)

From the burned foundation walls and the fill, not much of the original appearance of the furnace could be reconstructed, but with the aid of discarded stones, bricks, portions of the siege, or bench, and other debris found mostly in the factory dump (see Chap. 2), partial understanding of the furnace structure became possible. We assume that the gritty red fill represents the accumulation of ash from the fire and bits of debris from parts of the superstructure, which must have collapsed from time to time.

Fragments of slabs found in the factory dump appear to have formed part of the siege, on which rested crucibles or containers for melting glass to form vessels. The largest of these siege fragments (Fig. 3-5 left; Pl. 3-3A-B) has a maximum length of .56, maximum width of .54, and is ca. .04 thick. One face of the slab is roughly flat, the other, thought to be the upper surface, is presumed also to have been flat, but in it are preserved parts of three rectangular depressions. These seem to indicate that where the crucibles stood, the siege gradually built up to a thickness of .08–.11 as a result of the spilling of molten glass and the eventual disintegration of the containers. A smaller slab fragment (Fig. 3-5 right, Color Pl. 4B) displays a similar formation. Rectangular parallelepipeds of glass, with traces of the container still clinging to the sides, were found; the best preserved (Pl. 3-3C) measured ca. .15 x .05 x .12 (see also Color Pl. 2C). The presumed siege appears to have been of a composite material—limestone containing gritty nodules and irregular areas of glass that melted and then hardened.[6] The heat would have risen through openings in the siege and reverberated onto the glass in the containers.

It has generally been assumed that in Roman times glass was melted in ceramic crucibles.[7] At Jalame, however, this was not the case. Among the thousands of potsherds found on the site not one bears a trace of melted glass, nor do any glass fragments show signs of contact with ceramic containers. The evidence strongly indicates that the crucibles were rectangular containers, made of limestone, which could have served only for a single melting of a relatively small quantity of glass. The thickness of their walls, which is not known, would have been a factor in their durability.[8]

It was impossible to discover how much of the furnace area was occupied by the siege or to determine exactly where the containers were placed and how many there were, but several must have been in use at the same time. Obviously, they had to be accessible from the exterior of the furnace. The largest fragment identified as part of the siege (see Fig. 3-5 left) may have been a corner slab. Outside the furnace, hard clay floors with masses of glass drippings and other glass waste embedded in them indicate where the molten glass was extracted and worked. Such floors are well preserved on the north and south; on the east a kitchen of Period 4 almost obliterated their traces, and on the west the entrance to the fire chamber took up most of the length of the wall.

How the siege was supported is uncertain. A number of blocks of peculiar shape may be relevant (Fig. 3-6, Pl. 3-4A). These are made of *nari*.[9] Most were found in the

SiO_2	Silicon dioxide	30.76
R_2O_3	Total R_2O_3	8.99
CaO	Calcium oxide	34.38
MgO	Magnesium oxide	1.26
Na_2O	Sodium oxide	2.35
K_2O	Potassium oxide	0.47
	Loss on ignition	21.33
		99.54

A test of a piece of the largest fragment of siege, together with a small chunk of raw glass found on the site, was conducted by heating the two objects in a laboratory kiln to a temperature of 1080° C. At this temperature the glass attained a consistency apparently compatible with blowing, while the siege fragment remained unchanged in appearance. How long the latter could resist such a high temperature was not tested. The siege fragment, however, did not disintegrate immediately.

7. For examples see G. Thill, "Une Verrerie Gallo-romaine au Titelberg," *Hemecht* 4 (1968) 521-28 (3rd–4th c.); E. M. Alekseeva and T. M. Arseneva, "Evidence of a Glass Industry in Tanais" (in Russian), *SovArch* 1966, no. 2, 176-83 (3rd c.).

8. The corner of a rectangular container is described in Chap. 8 (No. 140). The limestone is of the chalky kind that forms parts of the hill and could easily be cut with a sharp instrument. This fragment bears no trace of contact with molten glass.

9. Nari—"A variety of *caliche* that forms by surface or near-surface alteration of permeable calcareous rocks (dissolution and redeposition of calcium carbonate) and that occurs in the drier parts of the Mediterranean region. It is characterized by a fine network of veins surrounding unreplaced remnants of the original rock, and it often contains clastic particles (rocks and shells)." R. L. Bates and J. A. Jackson, eds., *Glossary of Geology*, 2nd ed. (Falls Church, Va., 1980). Mr. Y. Mimron and other members of the Geological Survey of Israel provided this identification.

6. Chemical analysis of a section of the largest slab fragment produced these results:

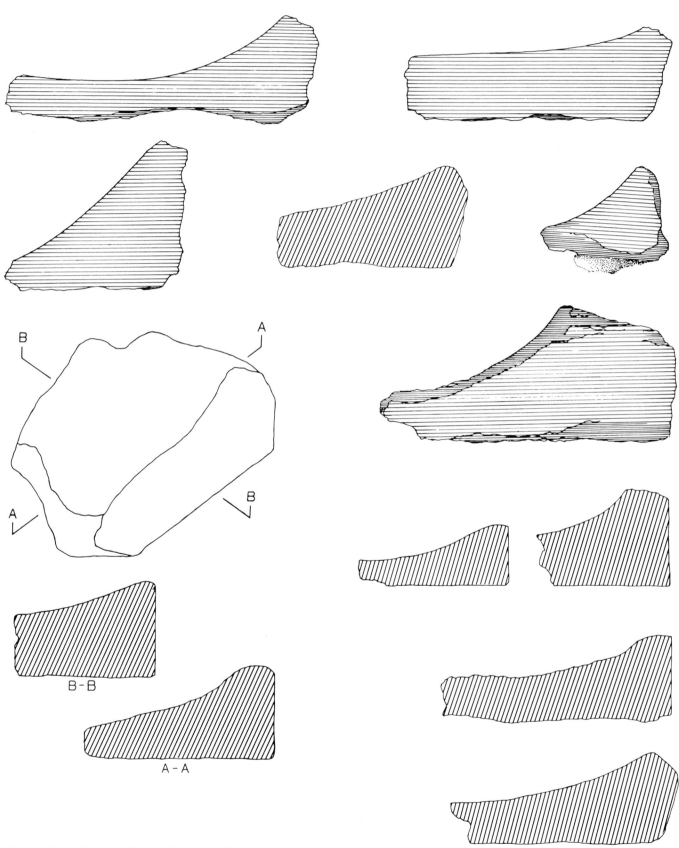

Fig. 3–6. Stone blocks with curved surfaces. 1:4.

Fig. 3-7. Tentative reconstruction of Jalame glass furnace (section E-W). Cross-hatched members exist.

factory dump; one fragment was in the furnace fill. Since all show signs of having been heated, chiefly on the concave face, they must have been discarded from the furnace area. Each has two large surfaces, one flat, the other concave, joined by a smaller face. The most complete block found is .32 in preserved length, .118 in height, and .31 in width. There is no evidence as to how these blocks might have been used in the furnace structure, but a tentative reconstruction is presented in Fig. 3-7. A small group of irregular stones on bedrock near the center of the fire chamber may indicate a support for the siege (see Fig. 3-3).

The form of the crown (roof) is easier to determine. Many mud bricks and fragments of bricks, fired on one face only, were found, chiefly in the factory dump (Fig. 3-8, Pl. 3-4B, Color Pl. 2D). Some are flat, others curved; on the latter the concave face is invariably baked, the convex face unbaked. The crown must, therefore, have been a barrel vault, built of unbaked bricks, the cracks between them plastered with clay or mud. When the furnace was first fired, the roof would have become a sturdy vault providing a reverberatory effect. Some apertures must have been left in the vault to produce a draft and to allow smoke to escape. This method—building a furnace from unbaked bricks and then firing it—is still found today in primitive glass factories.[10]

An annealing oven would normally have been contiguous to the working furnace. Although all the area around the latter was excavated, no separate structure could be definitely identified as intended for annealing. The southern third of the furnace could, however, have served this purpose. A long narrow fieldstone foundation extending three courses above bedrock was found at the south end of the furnace (it is abutted by trial trenches A68, B68, and C68; see Fig. 3-3). These test

trenches, dug in 1968 after the regular campaigns had ended, revealed this foundation. Its east end is bounded by a baked brick, slightly curved, .60 long, but the north wall (presuming there was one) had mostly disappeared. Trench C68 (Color Pl. 2F) showed clearly the bright red earth that also appeared in the fill of the main glass furnace, farther north (see Color Pl. 2A). Details concerning access to the annealing oven and the method of introducing and removing the vessels were all lost when the walls of Period 4 were constructed. Annealing in the modern sense was hardly possible, and the need for it was greatly reduced because of the thinness of most glass vessels produced at Jalame. But most of the failures in production occurred during annealing, because of strains in the glass. Zigzag and curved breaks are the result of this problem (Pl. 3-7). There must also have been a good deal of breakage after annealing, as is indicated by the thousands of fragments recovered from the factory dump.

Protection of the furnace from inclement weather must have been furnished—at least a shed. But of this no trace was found.

Manufacturing Methods

Glassblowing in ancient times was in most respects similar to the process used today. By the 4th century, when the Jalame factory was in operation, most of the basic "secrets" of glassmaking were known.[11]

Hardly any implements that could be associated with glassmaking were found at Jalame. When the workers departed, they took with them everything they consid-

10. A wood-burning furnace observed in Cairo has no definite openings to allow smoke to escape; it seeps out through cracks between the bricks. For such furnaces see D. Charlesworth, "A Primitive Glass Furnace in Cairo," *JGS* 9 (1967) 129-32; N. H. Henein, *Le Verre soufflé en Égypte* (Cairo, 1974); C. Imam et al., "L'Artisanat du verre à Damas," *Bulletin des Études Orientales* 27 (1974) 141-81.

11. For descriptions of glassblowing processes see *Tools of the Glassmaker* (Corning Museum of Glass, 1980); *How Glass is Made*, Museum News 15, no. 1 (Toledo Museum of Art, n.d.); Schuler, "Blowing"; Jennifer Price, "Glass," in D. Strong and D. Brown, *Roman Crafts* (New York, 1976) 111-25; Dominick Labino, *Visual Art in Glass*, Studies in Art Series, (Dubuque, Iowa, 1968). See also G. H. Kenyon, *The Glass Industry of the Weald* (Leicester, 1967). This volume offers much information useful for the study of ancient glassmaking, even though the factories discussed are far removed from Jalame both in place and time.

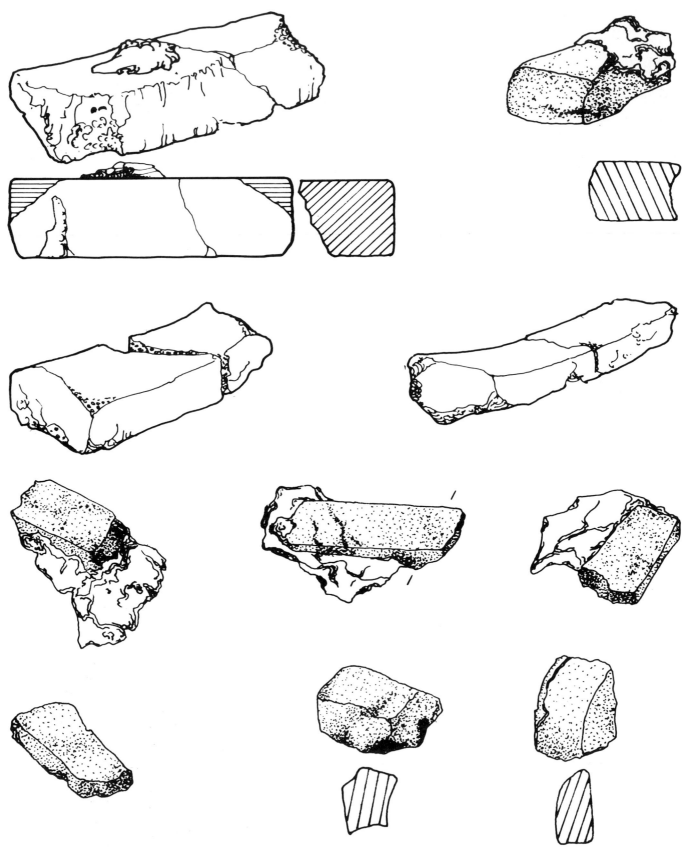

Fig. 3–8. Mud bricks fired on one face, from furnace walls and crown. Ca. 1:8.

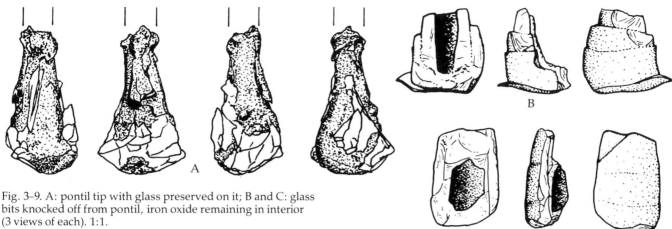

Fig. 3–9. A: pontil tip with glass preserved on it; B and C: glass bits knocked off from pontil, iron oxide remaining in interior (3 views of each). 1:1.

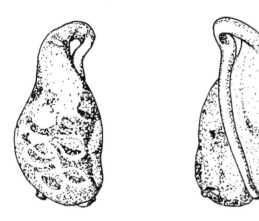

Fig. 3–10. Blob pulled out and tooled. 1:1.

ered of value, forgetting little. That they used blowpipes is obvious from the waste glass found (Pl. 3–5). Small lengths of pontils with glass still attached were discovered (see Fig. 3–9, Pl. 3–5A-C); we know from these, as well as from waste knocked off from pontils and scars on vessel bottoms (Pl 3–5D-F, Color Pl. 3A), that the pontil was in use.[12] Some of the blowpipe and pontil knockoffs and the moils include flakes of iron oxide.[13]

From the manner in which some of the vessels were formed it is clear that metal jacks were used (see Fig. 3–11),[14] but not a trace of any was found. Of wooden

tools there were no remains, but their forms can be conjectured with some assurance. A conscientious search through all the glass fragments found disclosed none showing marks of shears, so we conclude that these were not used in glassmaking at Jalame, although shears were certainly employed at that time for other purposes. The use of other metal implements is shown by blobs of glass with random tool marks (Fig. 3–10, Pl. 3 6C) as well as by many vessels that show signs of tooling.

Drops and threads, numbering in the hundreds of thousands, are similar to those found on the floor of every glass factory where blowing is practiced (Pl. 3–8A, Color Pl. 3B).

Vessels deformed during blowing (almost all found in the factory dump) are relatively few. Examples are shown in Fig. 3–12A-D and Pl. 3–6E. Accidents were common, however, during the necessarily inefficient annealing process. A curious object (Fig. 3–12F, Pl. 3–7B) was perhaps intended to be the base of a vessel; it is broken in many places. The breaks are sharp and clean; the disk was found as a unit but fell in pieces when picked up. Other fragments (Fig. 3–12E, Pl. 3–7A) give evidence of annealing failure, and still others included in the catalogue in Chap. 4 indicate that annealing presented a serious problem.

In addition to decorative trails on vessels, a few trails that had been discarded before being attached to vessels were found (Pl. 3–6D and E). And some curious objects we have called *wound trails* turned up in the factory dump (Pl. 3–6A-B). These were hot gobs of glass from which a trail was pulled out and wound a great many

12. Discarded bits of glass (moils, knock-offs) from both blowpipes and pontils were found in all colors. Bluish green (both light and dark), green, and brown are the most common, but there were also examples in olive green, colorless, and purple.

13. This was determined not only visually but also by microscopic examination. Dr. Constance Barsky, formerly of the Geology Department, University of Missouri-Columbia, examined surface rinds and inclusions on knock-offs and moils by electron microprobe techniques. To summarize the report, "The variations in iron and silicon content observed for the rinds, inclusions, and glass confirmed that the glass, while in the molten state, was in contact with a pure iron or iron-oxide containing material."

14. The experiment shown in Fig. 3–11 was carried out by the glass artist Grant Randolph in Santa Barbara, Calif., at the request of Frederic Schuler. Randolph described the method as follows: After the bulb is

formed, a groove is cut near the base with the jacks (Fig. 3–11A). Next, a paddle is pressed against the bottom in order to collapse and flatten the glass below the groove (B). The jacks are then inserted and forced into the now indented base (C). Pressure is applied with the jacks while alternating their placement from the recess in the foot to the original groove until the walls come into contact with one another (D). When the desired contact point is achieved, the vessel can then be finished as a bottle, bowl, etc.

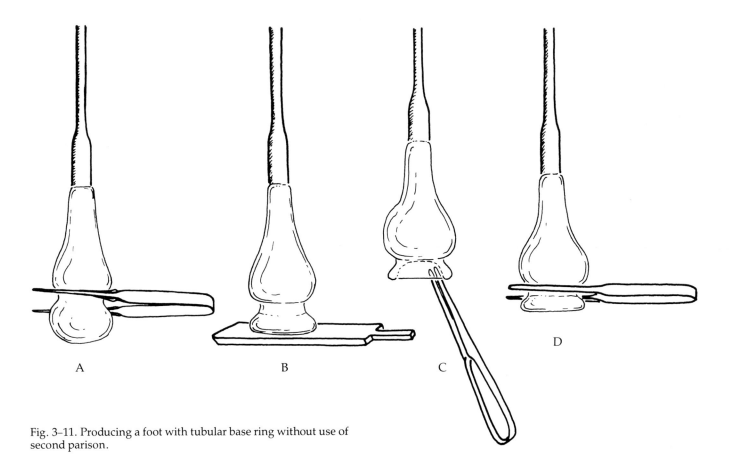

Fig. 3–11. Producing a foot with tubular base ring without use of second parison.

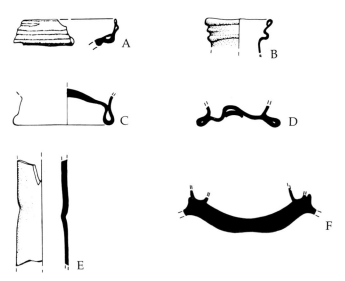

Fig. 3–12. A-D: vessels deformed during blowing; E-F: vessels damaged during annealing. 1:2.

times in haphazard fashion. Their purpose may have been to test the viscosity of glass to be blown, or perhaps they were simply demonstrations of the glassmakers' ability to handle the material.

A most interesting group of objects, found in some quantity, was the "test drops" (Pl. 3–8B). These came to light chiefly in the factory dump (find-spot mentioned in the Catalogue only when not the dump). While such objects seem not to have been noted at ancient or medieval glasshouse sites, they are easily explained by reference to modern glassmaking procedures. When a new batch is prepared, a small amount of glass is taken from the furnace on the end of a pontil and allowed to hang down, thus forming an elongated drop. By examining the quality and viscosity of this drop, the glassmaker determines whether the batch is sufficiently melted and the quality of the glass satisfactory.

The drops are greenish blue or green; one is olive green. They end in a globular form, and their stems are rather flat. All are broken off at the top. The flattening of the upper part clearly indicates that they were not intended as implements for cosmetic or other purposes; in any case, most of them are too large for such use. In almost all of them vertically elongated bubbles can be observed, and in many there are also swirls in the glass. Weathering is generally slight and of the usual white sort; only one is heavily weathered and pitted.

Dependable evidence concerning the marketing of the factory's products is lacking. It seems likely that the finished vessels were packed in containers, loaded on animals or carried by individuals, and sent to nearby towns to be sold in shops, for Jalame is an isolated place on a steep hill, to which few customers would have cared to come in order to buy common household vessels.

There is, nevertheless, a possible indication of where the money received was kept. Near the south wall of the furnace (at U-V:26, Fig. 1–2) a curious small structure was uncovered in a trial trench, at a depth of .40, in crumbly red earth like that associated with the furnace (Pl. 3–8). Here were found tumbled pieces of tile (like the sarcophagus fragments shown in Chap. 8, No. 182, Fig. 8–21), and at the west end of the trench there was a sort of box, two sides formed by roughly rectangular stones, one end closed by tile fragments (each .13 x .19). Just outside these tiles lay pieces of a large coarse pot, the bottom of a Gaza amphora (P19–65). Further excavation revealed only a few more tile fragments, bits of glass vessel, and part of a stone basin (Chap. 8, No. 137b).

I propose that this may have been the repository for cash received at the factory. The shattered condition of the pot would show that when the glassmakers departed, they removed it from the box, dumped out coins that had been in it, and scattered the pieces. This theory is obviously impossible to prove, but it seems worth consideration.

Pontils and Pontil Knock-offs

1 (M 62–66). PL .04; D shaft .009, head ca. .016

Iron pontil, lower end preserved, badly corroded. Ovoid (?) head tapering to shaft. End covered with bluish green glass. **Fig. 3–9A; Pl. 3–5A.**

2 (454–66). PL .021; D knock-off .019, pontil ca. .008

Pontil knock-off with part of vessel. Light green glass, white weathering. Interior retains traces of iron pontil; on the bottom is a small fragment of the vessel from which it was detached. **Fig. 3–9B; Pl. 3–5B.**

3 (502–64). PH .025; D knockoff ca. .02, pontil ca. .011

Pontil knock-off. Light green glass, white weathering. Traces of iron pontil inside. **Fig. 3–9C; Pl. 3–5C.**

4 (265–66). PH .013–.006; D .022–.013

Nine pontil knock-offs. Approximately disk-shaped with concave tops on which remain traces of iron oxide.

Rounded or flat bottoms, one with remains of vessel. Bluish green, light green, and one colorless. One shows traces of copper (red and blue). **Pl. 3–5D.**

Tooled Lumps

5 (199–66). Max dim .06; Max Th .02

Blob, smooth on all sides, except for one break. Greenish blue, white weathering. The piece was twisted and tooled when hot. It shows numerous short jabs of a flat tool. Apparently a trail (now broken off) extended from the blob. **Fig. 3–10, Pl. 3–6C.**

Vessels Deformed during Blowing

6 (256–64). PH .014; D rim uncertain

Bowl (?). Greenish blue, white weathering. Shape like No. 72, Chap. 4, but with irregular air spaces below the rim. **Fig. 3–12A.**

7 (142–66). PH .02; D rim .036

Bottle (?). Pale greenish blue, white weathering. Infolded rim, with additional (unintentional) folds below. The neck appears cylindrical. **Fig. 3 12B.**

8 (226–65). PH .018; D base .054

Bowl (?). Olive green. High folded base with irregular tubular ring. Thick concave bottom, traces of nearly vertical wall. (Also Chap. 4, No. 245.) **Fig. 3–12C.**

9 (310 66). PH .013; D .046

Bowl (?). Yellowish green, white weathering. Pushed-in base with tubular ring, deformed. Slightly concave bottom with pontil lump remaining. **Fig. 3–12D.**

Vessels Damaged during Annealing

10 (112–66). PH .053; D .028; Th wall .003–.004

Bottle, greenish blue, bubbles and blowing spirals, slight weathering. Neck broken off at both ends. Tooled constriction at about the middle. **Fig. 3–12E; Pl. 3–7A.**

11 (152–66). Max dim .066

Greenish blue, tiny bubbles, surface dulled. Circular object, raised concentric rings around edge and one raised ring below. Possibly intended as a vessel base. The breaks are sharp and clean. **Fig. 3–12F; Pl. 3–7B.**

4

GLADYS D. WEINBERG AND SIDNEY M. GOLDSTEIN

The Glass Vessels

The factory's production was limited to certain types of vessels. If hundreds of fragments of similar vessels are found, we assume them to have been made at Jalame. If there are only a few fragments of a vessel type, they are considered to have been imported, possibly already in a damaged condition and intended for remelting.

Most of the vessel fragments are contemporary with the factory; among these are many from vessels probably not made at the site. In the filling of the wine press tank, which was deposited all at one time (see Chap. 2), were found vessels of the factory's period of operation as well as some that probably are later. Although not a single coin or lamp fragment was found in the earth cleared from the tank, it is likely that the filling was done near the end of Period 4, that is, early 5th century.[1]

From the time after the abandonment of the site, there are very few glass vessel fragments (Nos. 386–97), a few potsherds of the 9th century (Chap. 7, Nos. 880–82), and two of Crusader times (Chap. 7, 883–84). The only finds later than these are modern—a few bits of bottles and some remnants of the "plastic age," the present time.

Classification is difficult when fragments constitute the chief evidence. It is obvious that the glassmakers were accustomed to producing many kinds of rims and bases and that they assembled these in various ways. Therefore it is not always certain whether a particular base fragment belongs to a shallow bowl or a deep one, or even if it is to be assigned to a bowl, cup, or dish.

Measurements are often helpful. A vessel with a large rim diameter must be a dish or a shallow bowl. A cup must have a reasonably convenient circumference for handling. But some bottles are very large, and the rim and neck that would theoretically serve for a cup might instead belong to a large bottle. Profiles are often more useful than photographs. The photographic illustrations are intended to show the appearance, texture, and condition of the glass, as well as the quantity, rather than the shapes of vessels.

The description of colors is difficult, for standard color charts do not correspond to transparent glass colors.[2] The kind of light used for the examination and assessment of color also produces marked variations. But fine distinctions are not particularly important here. The so-called natural colors all contain the same ingredients in varying amounts (see Chap. 9); the only real difference is caused when manganese is added to the batch. This makes the glass colorless or, when added in large amounts, purple. The colors most prevalent are bluish green in various shades, green, yellowish green, and, less common, brown, olive green, colorless, and purple.[3] Raw glass (cullet) of all these colors has been found in quantities comparable to the numbers of vessel fragments of each color. While no colorless chunks were found, there is some purple cullet. Colorless vessels are often streaked with purple, showing that the manganese was not thoroughly mixed into the batch. Handles, especially, tend to be streaked with various colors, yellow and greenish blue together, and other combinations.

A more intense greenish blue was used almost entirely for decorative trailing and blobs, occasionally for small handles. Such decoration is found on vessels from many Syro-Palestinian sites. The shapes of these vessels are not always easy to determine, since most of the fragments are small, but some can be definitely assigned:

Bowls: Nos. 27, 100, 122–26, 129–32
Jugs and Bottles: Nos. 214, 221, 222, 252, 257, 330, 334
Lamps or Beakers: Nos. 203–5, 403, 408, 438
Jars: Nos. 362, 364–68, 375
Amphoriskos: No. 383

---

1. Catalogued items found in the wine press tank are the following: Nos. 19, 30, 34, 79, 107, 122, 187, 191, 192, 207, 229, 230, 235, 261, 262 (only mentioned), 273, 276, 311, 327, 336, 343, 346, 518.

2. The terms for colors used here are based on visual observation alone and are different from the descriptions in Chap. 9, where the chemical composition of each color is explained.

3. In the color called "bluish green," the green appears dominant, in "greenish blue" the blue is dominant, etc.

A selection of the numerous fragments with applied greenish blue trails is shown on Color Pl. 3C. Most of these were found in the factory dump, the tiniest from sifting the excavated earth. The glass to which these trails were applied is usually pale bluish green or colorless with a bluish green tinge. In general, trailing is found on thin-walled, delicate vessels. Besides those catalogued or mentioned, 40 fragments with deep greenish blue decoration are inventoried. Most are from the factory dump. Cobalt blue was also used for decoration, but usually as blobs on vessels with cracked-off rims—lamps and bowls (see Nos. 404–11). Small chunks of cobalt blue cullet were found.

The surface condition of Jalame vessels is extremely varied. While some fragments are clear and almost unweathered, most exhibit at least some degree of weathering. This is usually a milky white film covering part or, more rarely, all of the surface, and underneath it appears iridescence. Other manifestations are a dulling of the surface unaccompanied by iridescence, a scratched surface that perhaps came from tumbling the fragments as they were discarded, a network of cracks indicating devitrification, or pitting, which is the most advanced stage of surface deterioration. A few fragments have a hard, dark weathering film, found chiefly on colorless and intense greenish blue glass (see Chap. 9 for detailed discussion of weathering).

Grinding and wheel-polishing, a finishing method often used, makes the glass weather more severely than fire-polishing. A curious feature, noted on many fragments, is weathering on one face, while the other is almost unweathered. Examination by various methods has failed to indicate any difference in composition between glasses with weathered and unweathered surfaces.

In general, the material seems to be of good quality. Bubbles are few; impurities are found mainly in handles, in moils, and in knock-offs, points immediately adjacent to the blowpipe or pontil.

Glassblowers of Roman times generally produced thin-walled vessels, which contrast with the cast vessels made before blowing was introduced. At Jalame the only types of vessels that are consistently thick-walled are the conical lamps and the bowls that were made by the same method (see Nos. 404–92). A few bottle rims and some body and base fragments are quite thick; these are exceptional.

A fundamental distinction between types of vessels produced at Jalame is the result of two different methods of manufacture. These are: (1) using the blowpipe to form the parison and finishing the vessel with the aid of the pontil, which makes it possible to reheat the rim and shape it in various ways, as well as to add handles and decorative elements; (2) using the blowpipe and other implements but not the pontil (thus producing cracked-off rims). The first method is most commonly used at Jalame; vessels made in this way will be discussed first.

The shapes include bowls, cups, jugs, bottles, and jars. Using the number of fragments of each kind of vessel as a guide to determining whether or not it was produced on the site, we have found that there was a considerable amount of specialization in factories, and that at Jalame probably only a limited number of shapes were produced.[4]

In describing each category of vessels, the arrangement follows this scheme: (1) number of fragments found at the site; (2) exact provenience, when known; (3) description of features of the type, including average sizes, proportions, etc.; (4) quality of the material, including bubbles, swirls, etc.; weathering, discussed above and in Chap. 9, is described only when it is unusual; (5) colors, common and rare, and decoration when present; (6) method of producing the shape; (7) similar vessels from other sites, geographic distribution; (8) catalogue (almost all pieces are illustrated).

Bowls with Rounded Rims

This general category includes several thousand rim fragments; these are more numerous than any other rim types found. The rim was rounded by reheating while the vessel was held on the pontil. Most of the rims are also thickened by reheating and then pressing the edge against a flat surface, probably a wooden paddle.

The bowl shapes, which are quite varied, must be determined on the evidence of rim and base fragments (very few joining) as well as by resemblances to better preserved examples found elsewhere. The wall fragments, calculated to be about 50,000 in number, seldom can be assigned to any particular shape of bowl. There is also the problem of distinguishing between bowls and cups. While the rim diameter is a clue, some of the bowls are very small, so this distinction may not be valid. When there is doubt, a vessel has been called a bowl rather than a cup.

The bases show less variation, the pushed-in base (several varieties) outnumbering other types. There are also tubular ring bases, a few coil bases, and solid folded bases. These have been associated with the rims whenever possible.

The rims are arranged according to the height of the vessels, proceeding from shallow to deep. The bases are in the same order, as far as possible, in a following group. Exceptions are a few restorable vessels. The rim diameter and the inclination of the wall often indicate whether a vessel is shallow or deep, and the base may offer even

---

4. See G. D. Weinberg, "Specialized Production in a Late Roman Glass Factory," *Eretz-Israel* 19, Jerusalem (1987) 62–70.

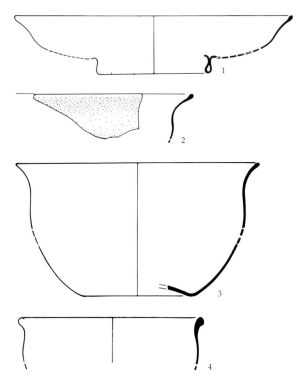

Fig. 4–1. Bowls with flaring rim. No. 1, 1:3; others, 1:2.

better clues to a vessel's shape, but hundreds of fragments cannot be classified in this manner.

Flaring Rim (Nos. 1–5)

These occur in relatively small numbers: 30–40 examples have been identified, and many small fragments probably have not been recognized. Most were found in the factory dump; about one-fifth elsewhere on the site. Those catalogued have been selected for variety of shape.

The rims, measuring more than .20 in diameter, are thickened to varying extents. They contain a considerable amount of small impurities (iron oxide from the blowpipe). Shallow bowls such as No. 1 had pushed-in bases. Rim diameters of the presumably deep bowls range from .10 to ca. .18. In some cases, as No. 3, there is no definite base but only a concave, thickened bottom. It is probable, however, that most of these bowls did have a base. The commonest colors are bluish green and yellowish green; there are a few olive green, colorless, and at least two purple specimens. No decoration is found on any of them. The weathering is the usual kind; a few exceptions are mentioned in the catalogue.

Such bowls are fairly common in many places. At Samaria remains of more than 40 small bowls with slightly flaring rims were found in 3rd–4th c. contexts.[5]

From tombs at Hanita, to the north, came a number of shallow and deep bowls with slightly flaring rims and various kinds of bases.[6] Cyprus is a prolific source of such bowls—generally, it seems, with high folded bases; definite contexts are lacking.[7] The shape is said to be rare in western Europe; those cited by Isings are dated to the 2nd c.[8]

1 (206–65). Est H .04; D base .09; D rim .22
    Pale green, impurities in rim. Fragments preserving nearly complete profile. **Fig. 4–1; Pl. 4–1.**

2 (115–64). Est D rim .21
    Light yellowish green. Body deeper than preceding. **Fig. 4–1.**

3 (342–66). Est H .07; D rim ca. .13
    Pale greenish blue. Fragments preserving nearly complete profile. **Fig. 4–1.**

4 (389–66). D rim .10
    Pale green. Slight patchy weathering. **Fig. 4–1.**

5 (128–65). PH .012; D rim .10
    Purple, dark weathering. Fragment of rim and body. Shape like preceding.

Thickened Rim, Straight Wall (Nos. 6–11)

There are about 100 fragments in this category, two-thirds found in the factory dump, one-third elsewhere on the site. Probably others have not been identified; these simple bowls were obviously for everyday use. Their common characteristics are thickened, rounded rims and walls that contract downward, some slightly concave, others slightly bulging. The angles of the walls differ; in no case could a base be assigned to a rim. Shallow bowls seem fewer than deep ones, the relation of rim diameter to height cannot be accurately estimated. The bases were probably the pinched-in kind.

The material is, in general, rather poor. Many fragments have impurities (iron oxide) near the rim, and most have long horizontal bubbles (depending on the size of the fragment preserved). Two exceptional fragments (Nos. 7 and 10) show traces of wheel-polishing outside.

The colors are the usual greenish blue and greens, the latter predominating; there are a few yellowish brown and colorless rims. This would suggest (as do the wheel-polished examples) that different qualities of bowls of one shape were made, to be sold at different prices.

The variety is rather common at both Hanita and

5. Crowfoot, *Samaria* 3, 410 and fig. 94.15. It is stated that most of these are pale blue (greenish blue?).

6. Barag, *Hanita*, 13–15, nos. 16–21 (shallow); nos. 37–38 (deep). References are given to unpublished bowls from Nahariya, as well as to vessels from other sites in Israel and Cyprus.
7. Vessberg, "Cyprus Glass," 114–15 and pl. 2, nos. 13–15.
8. Isings, *Roman Glass,* Form 87.

Nahariya,[9] though the outfolded rim seems more favored.

6 (287-65). D rim .12

Greenish blue, small bubbles. **Fig. 4-2; Pl. 4-1.**

7 (392-66). D rim .125

Light greenish blue, few tiny bubbles, impurities in the rim. Traces of wheel-polishing. **Fig. 4-2.**

8 (370-66). D rim .12

Light blue, tiny bubbles, almost no weathering. Two purple rim fragments (280-65, 512-64) are similar. **Fig. 4-2.**

9 (287-64). D rim .13

Light yellowish green, horizontal bubbles. **Fig. 4-2.**

10 (53-65). D rim ca. .13

Colorless, grayish tone, long bubbles, surface dulled. Shape like preceding. Traces of wheel-polishing outside.

11 (352-64, 364-64). D rim .08

Light green, long horizontal bubbles, black impurities, dark weathering. This might be a cup but it lacks the characteristic horizontal thread (see Nos. 162-66). A tiny light purple rim fragment (Th .002) with dark weathering (351-66) is similar. A yellowish brown rim fragment (314b-66, D .12) was also found. **Fig. 4-2.**

Outfolded Rim (single fold) (Nos. 12-44)

Rim fragments of this kind were found in the thousands. Most came from the factory dump, many were scattered around the site, and a few were found in the wine press tank, including the only nearly complete example of the shape (No. 19).

The common characteristic is the rounded rim (often thickened) folded out, down, and inward, usually but not always with an air space in the fold. The rim may flare out or follow the line of the vertical or slanting wall, or even incline inward. The walls, usually thin, curve gently toward the bottom when the bowl is shallow, or slant downward in a straighter line to form a deep bowl. The convex floor of the bowl is thick, with a conspicuous pontil mark on the bottom. All the bases (Nos. 37-44 and fragments [Pl. 4-2]) seem to be of the pushed-in base-ring variety, some with tubular rings, others with elongated air space, still others with a "high pushed-in base-ring" (see No. 41). The sizes of the bowls vary greatly. Some rim diameters are as large as .40 or .45. The deeper bowls may have diameters as small as .104.

The quality of the glass is, in general, not very good. The great quantity of discarded fragments indicates not

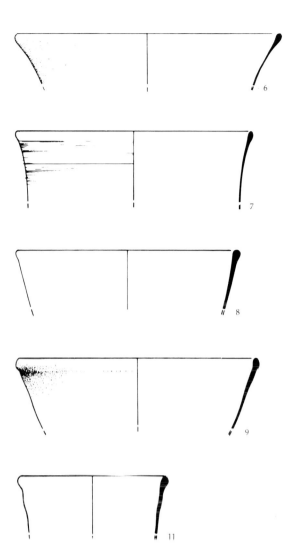

Fig. 4-2. Bowls with thickened rim and straight walls. 1:2.

only extensive production but also a lack of care in manufacture. The colors are mostly greenish blue, followed in quantity by various shades of green (light to pale), olive green, yellowish green, and brown. A few are colorless. The weathering varies but is present to some extent on all the fragments.

A complete bowl of this shape is shown on Pl. 4-1[10] and also representative fragments from Jalame on Pls. 4-2 (rims) and 4-3 (bases). The method of manufacture probably was as follows: The parison was blown into a sphere, then lengthened; the bottom was pushed in to form the base-ring. The vessel was then removed to a pontil and the rim rounded by heating, folding, and, finally, opening out. Long horizontal bubbles result from

9. Barag, *Hanita*, 13, no. 10 shallow, 21, no. 38 deeper, both with pushed-in base-ring; others rather similar have the tubular base-ring or a pad base; for Nahariya see Barag, "Glass Vessels," Type 3.16, with tooled base.

10. Museum of Art and Archaeology, University of Missouri-Columbia, No. 70.299. Light green, deep greenish blue trail wound around below rim. H .062; D rim .173. Photo courtesy of the museum.

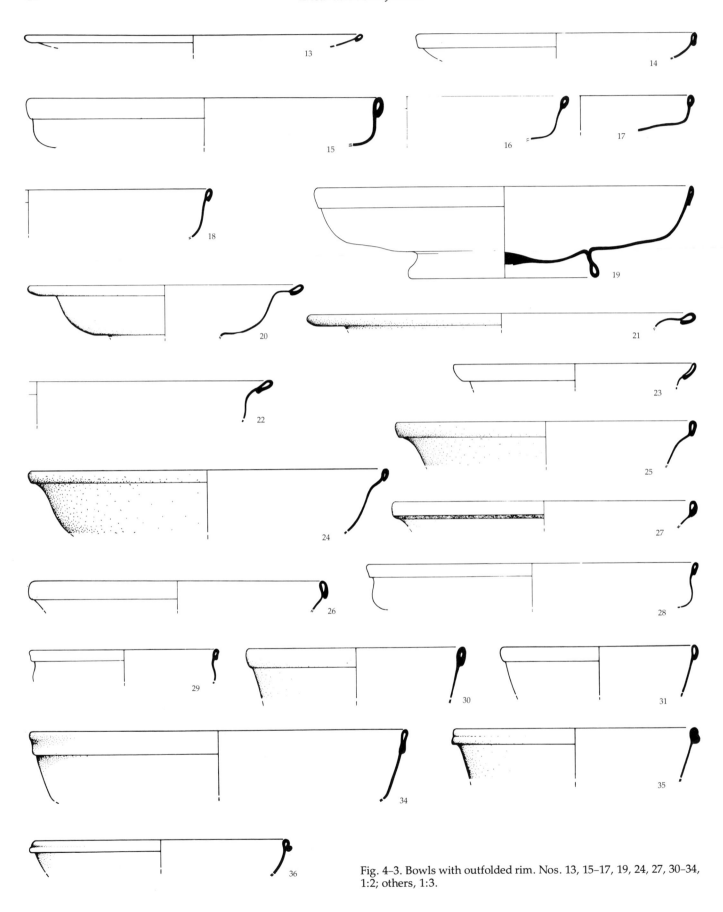

Fig. 4–3. Bowls with outfolded rim. Nos. 13, 15–17, 19, 24, 27, 30–34, 1:2; others, 1:3.

this final step. In the base fragments hardly any bubbles are visible, and none is lengthened.

Such dishes and bowls are common in the Syro-Palestinian area as well as in Cyprus. Close parallels are offered by sites in western Galilee: Nahariya, Hanita, Peqi'in, Yehiam. The fullest discussion may be found in the publication of the Hanita tombs,[11] which date to the 3rd and early 4th c. The type of rim is discussed by Erdmann,[12] who mentions only Eastern parallels except for a vessel from a grave in Cologne[13] which is thought to contain Eastern vessels. For such a simple shape one would expect Western parallels, but the type is not found in Isings except for the Cologne piece just mentioned.[14] The shape is found in Egypt, notably at Karanis, but the bases are almost invariably pads, often with tooling, seldom pushed-in base-rings such as those most common at Jalame.[15] The relatively few tooled bases at Jalame seem to be of the same material as the other fragments. There was certainly Egyptian influence, probably the result of imitation rather than importation.

One form of rim, the "wide obtuse-angled contour," as it is called by Harden,[16] was found at Jalame in some numbers (see No. 26) but does not seem to have existed at nearby sites. The Karanis example, with a tooled pad base, has a rim diameter of .152.

The Cypriote bowls have tubular base-rings or pad bases and some pushed-in base-rings as well. This variety is to be expected from the island's central position, where it received influences from both east and south.[17]

Decoration on these bowls is rare. The only example at Jalame is No. 27, with a deep greenish blue trail beneath the rim. The Missouri bowl (see n. 10 above) has similar decoration.

Rim Fragments

12 (5–67). D rim ca. .50

Olive green. Unusually good material, little weathering. A thick fragment of vessel floor with large pontil mark may belong to this vessel, presumed to be a flat dish. **Pl. 4–1.**

13 (222–65). D rim .18

Greenish blue. Very shallow dish. **Fig. 4–3.**

14 (36–64). D rim ca. .22

Pale green, slightly deeper than preceding. **Fig. 4–3.**

11. Barag, *Hanita*, 11 ff (Nos. 3–9, shallow; Nos. 31–34, deep).
12. Erdmann, "Mezad Tamar," 105 and n. 64 for bibliography. The author remarks that in the East such bowls generally start in the 3rd c. and continue through the 4th and 5th.
13. Fremersdorf, "Köln-Müngersdorf," 95, pl. 51, no. 16.
14. Isings, *Roman Glass*, Form 115.
15. Harden, *Karanis*, 76–77, nos. 117–21, the only examples at Karanis with pushed-in base-ring.
16. Ibid., no. 107.
17. Vessberg, "Cyprus Glass," 112–14 (shallow bowls), 114–17 (deep bowls).

15 (388–66). D rim .19

Yellowish green, no weathering. Wall vertical, then bending sharply inward. **Fig. 4–3.**

16 (91–64). D rim ca. .17

Pale green. Shape like preceding. **Fig. 4–3.**

17 (11–66). D rim .12

Light bluish green. Shape somewhat like preceding. **Fig. 4–3.**

18 (213–65). D rim ca. .29

Olive green. Wall curves gently into bottom. **Fig. 4–3; Pl. 4–1.**

19 (388–64). H .048; D rim .20; D base .10

Pale greenish blue. Entire profile preserved. No air space in rim fold. Gentle curve to high pushed-in base-ring. Thickened floor, pontil mark. From wine press tank. **Fig. 4–3; Pl. 4–1 (2 views).**

20 (21–66). D rim .22

Light olive green. Wall forms a ledge, then curves down and inward. **Fig. 4–3.**

21 (124–66). D rim ca. .31

Light green. Streaks, long bubbles, unusually heavy white weathering and pitting. Shape like preceding. **Fig. 4–3; Pl. 4–1.**

22 (387–66). D rim ca. .37

Light green. Interior pitted, slight weathering outside. Like preceding but deeper. **Fig. 4–3.**

23 (45–64). D rim .195

Pale greenish blue. Shape like preceding. **Fig. 4–3.**

24 (18–65). D rim .18

Pale greenish blue. Rim more vertical than in preceding. **Fig. 4–3.**

25 (139–66). D rim .24

Pale green. Shape like preceding. **Fig. 4–3.**

26 (315–64). D rim .24

Light olive green. Wall contracts sharply below rim—presumably a fairly deep bowl. **Fig. 4–3.**

27 (167–65). D rim .165

Pale green, deep greenish blue trail around wall at base of fold. Shape like preceding. **Fig. 4–3.**

28 (356–66). D rim ca. .25

Pale greenish blue. Wall spreads to form a squat bulbous body. **Fig. 4–3.**

29 (342–64). D rim .15

Light green. Shape like preceding. **Fig. 4–3.**

30 (367–64, 386–64). D rim .11

Light green. Wall tapers in a straight line. A fairly deep bowl. From wine press tank. **Fig. 4–3.**

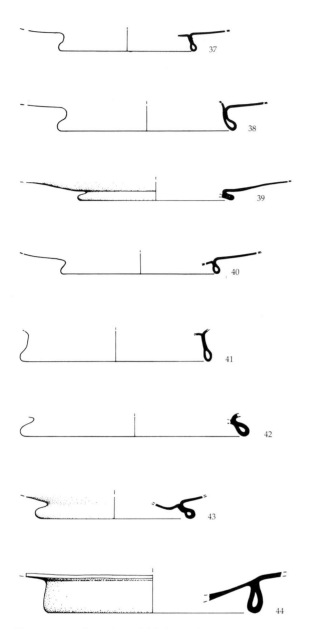

Fig. 4–4. Bowls with outfolded rim (bases). Nos. 43–44, 1:2; others, 1:3.

31 (291–66). D rim .104

Greenish blue, heavy white weathering. Shape like preceding. **Fig. 4–3.**

32 (508–64). D rim .18

Light yellowish green. Shape like preceding. **Pl. 4–3.**

33 (463–64). D rim .12

Light green, many black impurities and long bubbles in rim. Shape like preceding but material much poorer. **Pl. 4–3.**

34 (423–64). D rim .20

Greenish blue. Somewhat like preceding, with longer air space and thickened lip. Found in wine press tank. **Fig. 4–3.**

35 (456–66). D rim ca. .13

Pale green. Thickened rim folded into a double rib by tooling. Tiny air space. Wall tapers in a straight line. **Fig. 4–3.**

36 (169–64). D rim ca. .136

Pale greenish blue. Rim folded as on preceding. Wall curves gently inward. **Fig. 4–3.**

Base Fragments

37 (340–64). D base .109

Greenish blue. Pushed-in base-ring. Floor and wall almost horizontal. **Fig. 4–4; Pl. 4–3.**

38 (217–65). D base .14

Light yellowish green. Pushed-in base-ring, bending outward. Wall almost horizontal; floor rises sharply. **Fig. 4–4.**

39 (300–65). D base .13

Light greenish blue. Pushed-in base-ring. Wall slopes upward. **Fig. 4–4; Pl. 4–3.**

40 (61–66). D base .12

Light greenish blue. Pushed-in base-ring. Wall slopes upward, floor slopes downward toward center. **Fig. 4–4.**

41 (163–64). D base ca. .16

Light greenish blue. High pushed-in base-ring. Wall slopes upward; floor seems horizontal. **Fig. 4–4.**

42 (309–64). D base ca. .20

Light greenish blue, good material, almost no weathering. Pushed-in base-ring, unusually thick. Wall turns sharply out. **Fig. 4–4.**

43 (332–64). D base .08

Pale yellowish green. Pushed-in base-ring. Wall flares outward; floor dips and rises toward center. **Fig. 4–4.**

44 (97–66). D base .13

Light greenish blue. Pushed-in base-ring. Thick wall slopes down sharply to center of floor; wall rises obliquely upward. **Fig. 4–4.**

Thickened, Incurving Rim (Nos. 45–48)

Only about 25 of these have been identified, about two-thirds from the factory dump, the others scattered.

The distinguishing feature is the thickened rim, with a curve inward—more pronounced on some fragments than on others. Rim diameters range from .11 to .20; some are impossible to calculate. The angle of wall inclination varies, suggesting both shallow and deep bowls. No complete shape could be restored. The quality of the material varies; weathering is of the usual type; exceptions are noted in the catalogue. The colors are mostly shades of green; one is dark greenish blue, others of the same color are lighter (Pl. 4–4).

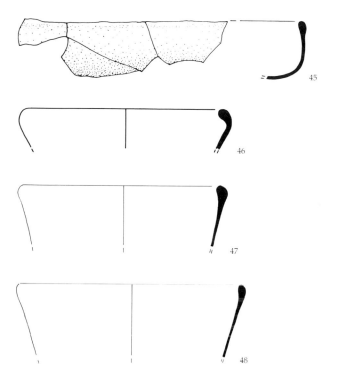

Fig. 4–5. Bowls with incurving rim. 1:2.

Similar bowls were found at Nahariya[18] and Hanita.[19] The shape also appears in Cyprus, where it seems to be earlier.[20] In the West, such bowls are dated from 1st through 4th c.[21]

45 (173–65). D rim .20

Light green, with bubbles, streaks, and impurities, dark weathering. Rim unevenly finished (perhaps from contact with a rough surface while hot). **Fig. 4–5; Pl. 4–4.**

46 (348–64). D rim .11

Yellowish green, white weathering. **Fig. 4–5.**

47 (490–66). D rim .12

Light yellowish green, brownish weathering. **Fig. 4–5.**

48 (518–64). D rim .11

Greenish blue, exterior pitted. Long horizontal bubbles in edge of rim. **Fig. 4–5.**

Horizontal Rib (Nos. 49–70)

This bowl is recognizable at Jalame from rim and wall fragments alone (Pls. 4–4, 4–5). The entire shape is, how-

ever, known (see Pl. 4–4),[22] and it is safe to assume that the bases were folded or there was a tubular base-ring. More than 200 rim fragments indicate local manufacture. Most of the pieces were found in the factory dump, a few around the buildings on the site, only one in the wine press tank.

The vessel has a rounded, not thickened, lip. Below it, around the outside, is the horizontal rib that is its distinguishing feature. Rim diameters that can be determined vary from .15 to .35—a wide span. The smaller diameters probably indicate deep bowls, while the larger (more numerous) represent shallow vessels.

Great variation exists in the proportions of rim to rib. Rarely is the rib directly below the lip; there are high rims and prominent ribs, low rims and prominent ribs, high rims and shallow ribs. It is almost impossible to find two identical examples. Some bowls are rather thick-walled, others extremely thin (the latter all greenish blue). Despite the thinness of some walls—a few less than .001 but usually ca. .0015—the rim diameter seems never less than .15. Thicker pieces have somewhat larger diameters; most are .20–.30. The profiles in Fig. 4–7 (Nos. 49–68) show the main variations.

The method by which the horizontal rib was formed has been in doubt. From observation of fragments under magnification, it appears that the rib is not an added trail but part of the vessel wall. Most of the rims have a concavity inside corresponding to the rib outside, but some have a smooth interior face.

Experimentation carried out by Dominick Labino resulted in finding a plausible method of making such bowls. The steps are as follow: (1) A gather of glass is taken from the furnace with the blowpipe. (2) The gather is blown slightly, forming a small parison. (3) The rib is pinched out all around the vessel at the point desired. At this stage the rib is quite thick. (4) The base, a separate parison, is attached and pushed in to form a tubular ring. (5) The pontil is attached to the bottom and the blowpipe removed. (6) The rim is opened out with the aid of a tool. This process produces the long bubbles visible in every rim fragment of this type at Jalame. (7) The lip is rounded by reheating and the floor is then flattened, if desired. (8) After the vessel is annealed, wheel-polishing is possible. Such polishing is seen on almost every rim and wall fragment; it is especially conspicuous on weathered surfaces. While we cannot be sure that this was the method actually followed, it has been shown to produce the desired effect, while other methods that have been suggested are less likely to have been successful.

The material of the bowls is generally good; a few impurities are occasionally seen near the lip. More than

18. Barag, "Glass Vessels," Type 3.23, with rounded bottom, no base.

19. Barag, *Hanita*, 23, no. 42. This has an almost vertical wall and a tubular base-ring.

20. Vessberg, "Cyprus Glass," 115 and pl. I, 27.

21. Isings, *Roman Glass*, Form 85, which includes bowls with pushed-in base as well as others with coil base. The sites mentioned range from Britain to Italy.

22. Green bowl, H .06, D rim .285, in Rockefeller Museum, Jerusalem (G 269).

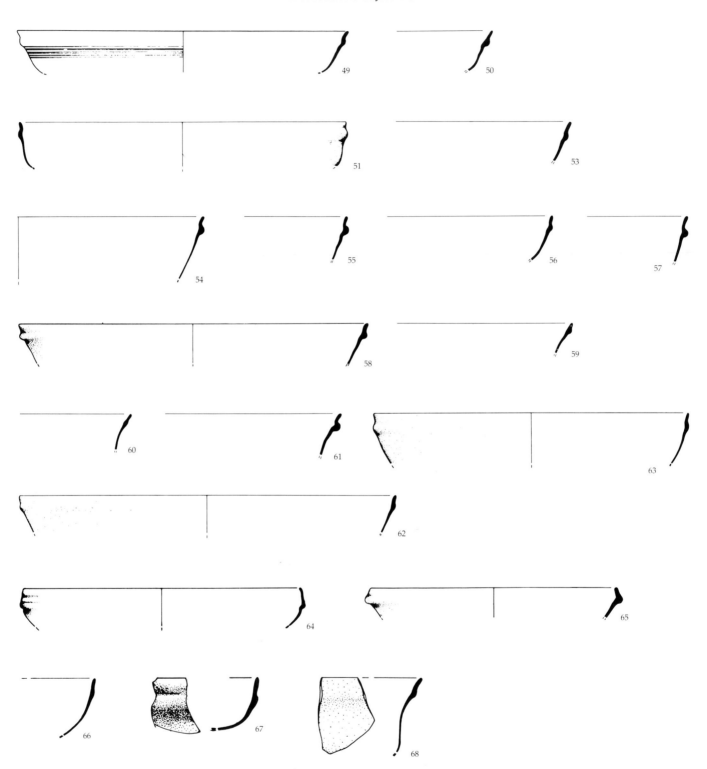

Fig. 4–6. Bowls with horizontal rib. Nos. 49–65, 1:3; others, 1:2.

half the fragments are various shades of greenish blue. About one-third are green or light green, a few are olive green and yellowish brown, and one (No. 62) is colorless with purple streaks. The weathering varies considerably. In general, greenish blue fragments are weathered more than others. Some of each color are entirely unweathered; others have white weathering; still others are pitted and dulled. Some are weathered only outside. On some the weathering crust flakes off and iridescence is seen underneath; on others the crust clings to the surface. A few pieces (dark greenish blue) have dark weathering.

The shape is not common elsewhere, or at least not published. There are examples from Hanita[23] and Nahariya (unpublished), but they are not recorded at other Palestinian sites, at Karanis, or in Cyprus. Some are in museum collections, without provenience.[24]

Rim Fragments

49 (344–64). D rim .26

Greenish blue. Wheel-polishing on exterior of this and following fragments unless otherwise stated. **Fig. 4–6; Pl. 4–4.**

50 (487–66). Est D rim .32

Pale green. **Fig. 4–6; Pl. 4–4.**

51 (170–65). D rim .28

Greenish blue. **Fig. 4–6; Pl. 4–4.**

52 (282–65). Est D rim .26

Light green, no weathering. **Pl. 4–4.**

53 (489–66). Est D rim .35

Light greenish blue. Almost no weathering. **Fig. 4–6.**

54 (415–66). Est D rim ca. .28

Greenish blue. **Fig. 4–6; Pl. 4–4.**

55 (507–65). Est D rim .33

Pale green. **Fig. 4–6.**

56 (32–66). Est D rim ca. .27

Pale green. **Fig. 4–6; Pl. 4–4.**

57 (514–64). Est D rim .33

Light green. **Fig. 4–6.**

58 (359–64). D rim ca. .275

Greenish blue, tiny black impurities. Unweathered outside, slight weathering inside. No polishing visible. **Fig. 4–6; Pl. 4–4.**

59 (515–64). Est D rim .35

Pale green. **Fig. 4–6.**

60 (508–65). Est D rim .25

Light greenish blue. **Fig. 4–6.**

61 (488–66). Est D rim .35

Pale green. **Fig. 4–6.**

62 (189–65). D rim ca. .30

Colorless, greenish tinge, horizontal purple streaks. Pitting and dark clinging weathering outside, interior unweathered. **Fig. 4–6; Pl. 4–4.**

63 (229–65). D rim ca. .25

Greenish blue. **Fig. 4–6.**

64 (337–66). D rim ca. .22

Pale greenish blue, faint purple streak, small black impurities in rim. Wall unusually curved. **Fig. 4–6.**

65 (20–64). D rim ca. .19

Light green, surface pitted, with clinging white weathering (typical of surface finds). Wall unusually thick, turning sharply inward below rib. **Fig. 4–6.**

66 (283–65). D rim unknown

Pale green. **Fig. 4–6.**

67 (203–66). D rim unknown

Greenish yellow. **Fig. 4–6.**

68 (62–66). D rim unknown

Light green. Interior slightly indented. Possibly the shape was distorted by fire. **Fig. 4–6.**

69 (249–64). D rim ca. .24

Pale greenish blue. Very shallow rib. Apparently damaged during manufacture. **Pl. 4–4.**

70 (121–64). D rim .28 or larger

Light green. A brown rim fragment (314–66a), D rim .23, was also found. **Pl. 4–4.**

Folded Collar (Nos. 71–76)

Of this shape[25] about 100 fragments could be identified (Pl. 4–5). The distinguishing characteristic is the broad collar made by folding the rim. The bases may have been of various kinds. The great majority came from the factory dump; some (mostly greenish blue) turned up in the central area. The three profiles shown (Fig. 4–7, Nos. 71–73) are the most typical of the Jalame examples, but other specimens (too fragmentary to illustrate) have a more swelling wall curve. The large diameters of some rims indicate shallow bowls, while others were deeper. The height of the folded collar seems to be proportionate to the rim diameter. Statistics are not reliable since most of the fragments do not preserve the entire height of the collar. The range in size is considerable, from tiny specimens (rim diameter as small as .09) to several of .34 and .35.

23. Barag, *Hanita*, 15, no. 26.
24. Hayes, *Toronto Glass*, 103, nos. 370–71 (the parallels given to excavated examples at Samaria and Jalame are inaccurate).
25. Isings, *Roman Glass*, Form 118.

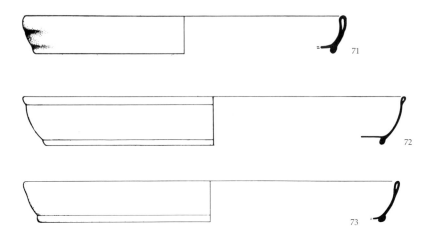

Fig. 4–7. Bowls with folded collar. 1:3.

The colors are, in order of frequency, greenish blue, green (light or pale), colorless (with yellow or purple tinge), olive green, brown, purple.[26] The last three are rare. The material and weathering are like other Jalame vessels. There is no decoration on any example.

The method used to produce the rim was probably as follows: Before the vessel was blown to its full size, the base was pushed in and the vessel removed from the blowpipe to a pontil. The edge of the rim (reheated) was folded either in or out (this differs on various examples) and downward to form a flange that was then pressed against the side of the vessel. After this, the rim was opened out to the desired diameter; the long horizontal bubbles that can be clearly seen in most of the collar fragments are evidence of this procedure.

These bowls are particularly interesting because they were certainly produced at Jalame and yet few have been published from the Near East. The only site where they appeared in any quantity is Meiron (eight published); they can be dated to the mid-4th century. These, and two fragments from Mesad Tamar, are the only ones in the Syro-Palestinian area with certain proveniences.[27] A vessel said to be from Beth Shan is in Toronto, another in a group of glasses reportedly from Tyre,[28] and a fragment was found at Karanis.[29]

In Europe the examples known cover an unusually wide area. They are as follows: a fragment at Corinth;[30] a complete bowl from a grave at Cologne;[31] and two fragments from Conimbriga.[32] A bowl formerly in Wheaton College[33] may have an Eastern provenience; others (unpublished) are reported from Istanbul, Beirut, and Gerasa. It is obvious that more bowls of this kind must have existed; undoubtedly the Jalame factory produced them for export. The dates assigned vary considerably; most are not based on sound evidence. Jalame clearly indicates a 4th c. date; none of the evidence presented elsewhere contradicts this.

71   (229–64). D rim ca. .265

Light olive green. Long air space in upper fold, none in lower, which turns inward. **Fig. 4–7; Pl. 4–5.**

72   (1–64). D rim .30

Light greenish blue. Small air space in upper fold, lower fold turns inward. Floor horizontal as far as preserved. **Fig. 4–7.**

73   (357–64). D rim ca. .30

Light green. Lower fold turns outward. **Fig. 4–7; Pl. 4–5.**

74   (484–66). Est D rim .34

Light green. Outer surface dulled, interior unweath-

seem exactly like ours, but the description conforms to the other examples, and it has been considered similar by those who have cited it, including Barag, "Glass Vessels," Type 2.16.

29. Harden, *Karanis*, 71, no. 88, pl. 12 (olive green, D rim ca. .22).

30. Davidson, *Corinth* 12, 99, no. 632, fig. 8 (light green, D rim ca. .28), found out of context and wrongly dated to the 2nd c.

31. Fremersdorf, "Köln-Müngersdorf," 94, pl. 51, no. 10 (pale green, D rim .35, D pad base .165). The grave contained three conical beakers, an oval plate with pad base, three dishes with out-turned rims and pushed-in bases, and a shallow bowl with ground rim, on which a hunting scene is represented in abrasion technique. The grave was dated by a coin of Valens to ca. 370. Fremersdorf believed all the vessels originated in Cologne, but Harden (and Isings, following Harden) remarked that the oval plate, the bowl, and the beakers are all probably Egyptian. It seems, however, that some are Syro-Palestinian.

32. Alarcão, *Conimbriga* 1965, 116, no. 192, pl. 7 (moss-green, D rim .352); *Conimbriga* 6, 193, no. 197, pl. 41 (green, no diameter given).

33. E. Dusenbery, "Ancient Glass in the Collections of Wheaton College," *JGS* 13 (1971) 21, no. 27, fig. 26 (light green, D rim .22).

26. Since relatively few purple glass fragments were found, most of them too small to categorize, it may be well to note that purple glass is not as rare as it might seem. Thirteen vessel fragments have been catalogued:
Bowls: 5, 8, 11 (last two only mentioned), 92, 93, 159, 490
Jugs and bottles: 223, 250–51, 288, 381 (mentioned)
Cup with purple trail: 166.
There are many tiny vessel fragments, a good many small cullet chunks, some purple trails. The amount is not great, but perhaps enough to suggest manufacture on the spot. Most of the material is from the factory dump.

27. E. M. Meyers et al., *Excavations at Ancient Meiron, Upper Galilee, Israel, 1971–72, 1974–75, 1977.* American Schools of Oriental Research (Cambridge, Mass. 1981) 70–71, fig. 3.28; pl. 9.10, nos. 15, 16; pl. 9.11, nos. 1–4; Erdmann, "Mezad Tamar," 105, no. 274 (green, D rim .256), no. 275 (colorless, D rim .242).

28. Hayes, *Toronto Glass*, 120, no. 468, fig. 13, pl. 30 (light green, D rim ca. .281). The bowl has a tubular ring-base. Harden, "Tomb-groups," 152, fig. 1,7 (light green, D rim .23). Judging from the profile, the bowl does not

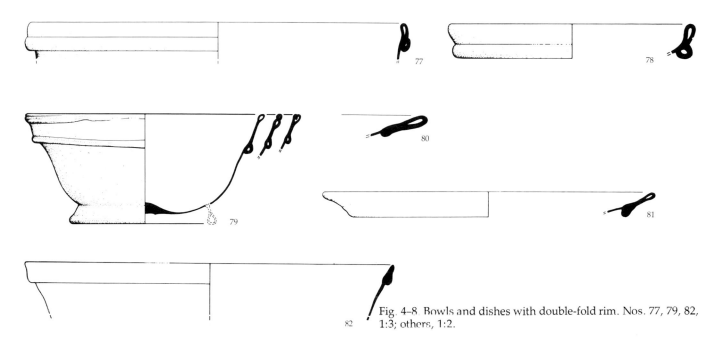

Fig. 4–8. Bowls and dishes with double-fold rim. Nos. 77, 79, 82, 1:3; others, 1:2.

ered. Long narrow air space in upper fold, none in lower fold, turned inward. **Pl. 4–5.**

75 (302–64). Est D .32

Light green. Similar, but lower fold turned outward. **Pl. 4–5.**

76 (47–65). D rim ca. .24

Light greenish blue, severe pitting and weathering. Very thin folded rim with long narrow air space. Lower fold not preserved. **Pl. 4–5.**

Rim with Double Fold (Nos. 77–82)

Closely related to the folded-collar rim (Nos. 71–76) is the rim with double fold. This is found, with variations, on deep bowls and shallow dishes, but it is uncommon at Jalame, and it is unlikely that such vessels were produced there. Of the few fragments, two are from the dump, one from the wine press tank, no others from a significant context. The rim is rounded, thickened, folded outward and then sharply back to the sloping wall, thus producing either two air spaces or a very thick ridge at the lower edge.

The material is of the ordinary kind, and the colors are the usual green and greenish blue. Yellowish brown (314c–66) is rare.

Nos. 77–78 are apparently from deep bowls; the latter bears some resemblance to a bowl found at Hanita, which has a pad base.[34] No. 79, with the profile nearly complete, was found in the wine press tank. The base was probably added on. No exact parallel has been noted.

34. Barag, *Hanita*, 21, no. 40 (rim D .26). This deep bowl is light bluish green.

No. 80, the rim of a large plate (Est rim D .45) has parallels at nearby sites. The most interesting is one found in a Beth Shearim catacomb (Fig. 4–9): its rim diameter is .52.[35] The importance of this plate lies in the remarkable representation incised on the exterior, which has been discussed in detail by Avigad.[36] Some of the figured objects have significance for vessels made at Jalame (see n. 212, below). No other decorated plate of this shape has been found, nor any other so large. Those from other sites, in descending order of rim diameters, are: El Bassa .44 and .34,[37] Shavei Zion .31,[38] Nazareth ca. .31.[39] The smallest shallow bowl with double fold rim is No. 81 (D .17). A bowl with similar rim was found at Hanita.[40] All these plates and the bowl have been assigned to the second half of the 4th c. Where the bottom is preserved, the center of the floor is thick, with a pontil mark.

77 (437–66). D rim ca. .30

Light greenish blue, heavy white weathering. Deep, with rather straight wall. **Fig. 4–8.**

78 (31–66). D rim ca. .13

Pale green, long horizontal bubbles. Like preceding but shallower. **Fig. 4–8.**

79 (405–64). Est H ca. .088; D rim .19

Numerous fragments forming nearly complete profile

35. Avigad, *Beth Shearim* 3, 207, no. 49; 209–13, fig. 100, pl. 69. Profile reproduced courtesy of the author.
36. Ibid., 209–13.
37. Iliffe, "El Bassa," 88, figs. 19, 20.
38. Barag in Prausnitz, *Shavei Zion*, 67, no. 13, fig. 16.
39. Bagatti, *Nazareth*, 312, no. 12, fig. 237.
40. Barag, *Hanita*, 11–12, no. 9 (D rim .26). He suggests (n. 14) this is a misshapen example of Hayes, *Toronto Glass*, 120, no. 468, and Isings, *Roman Glass*, Form 118, but it seems a distinct variation.

Fig. 4–9. Bowl with double-fold rim. After *Beth Shearim 3*, 210, fig. 100.

(base missing). Greenish blue, a few large bubbles, slight white weathering. Rim folded, hollow at top and bottom. The shape of the fold varies, as the profile shows. Thin wall, floor thickened in the center. Large pontil mark (D ca. .02). A pushed-in base is assumed. Found in wine press tank. **Fig. 4–8.**

80   (305–64). Est D rim ca. .45

Light greenish blue, small elongated bubbles around the rim, no weathering. **Fig. 4–8; Pl. 4–6.**

81   (35–66). D rim .17

Light green. From factory dump. **Fig. 4–8; Pl. 4–6.**

82   (414–64). PH .04; D rim ca. .29; Th wall .002

Two fragments of rim and body, not joining. Bluish green, a few long bubbles. Thickened, rounded rim folded out and downward, forming heavy flange .014 below edge. Corresponding convexity inside. From factory dump. **Fig. 4–8; Pl. 4–6.**

Triangular Lip (Nos. 83–87)

About 40 examples of this type have been identified, and probably there are more (Pl. 4–6). At least three-quarters of them come from the factory dump. The shapes appear to be deep bowls, none very large. The rim diameters range from .10 to .16, most of them .15–.16. The material and weathering are like other factory products. A few bubbles are seen in most fragments.

The colors are generally green and greenish blue, with a few yellow, one light brown, a few colorless.

The form of the lip is a variation on the plain, thickened rim. It was made by reheating the rim and then tooling it to a flattened triangular shape, often with rounded corners. On those vessels where the lip is truly triangular in section, traces of horizontal wheel-polishing appear on the exterior, extending a short distance down the wall.

This kind of lip seems to appear seldom, but illustrations are not always sufficiently clear to show such small details. One rim fragment from Karanis seems to be similar.[41] A small cup found at Mesad Tamar approaches this shape.[42] At Samaria there are none, nor at Hanita. A shallow bowl with this kind of lip, flat-bottomed without a definite base, is in Toronto.[43] There may be some in Cyprus; Vessberg's illustrations[44] are insufficiently detailed to make identification certain.

83   (104–64). D rim .125

Light green. Probably a deep bowl. Wheel-polished. **Fig. 4–10; Pl. 4–6.**

84   (157–64). D rim .15

Light green. Shape like preceding. Wheel-polished. **Pl. 4–6.**

85   (124–65). D rim .11

Light bluish green, a few black impurities. Deep bowl, wall irregular. Wheel-polished. **Fig. 4–10; Pl. 4–6.**

86   (266–65). D rim .11

Light green. Lip rounded. Wheel-polished. A similar example is light brown, with a rim D .10 (314c–66). **Fig. 4–10.**

87   (463–66). D rim unknown

Yellowish green. Bubbly material, wall almost vertical. **Fig. 4–10.**

Infolded Rim (Nos. 88–93)

The few fragments with this kind of rim, almost all found in the factory dump, are from bowls of various sizes and heights. The only one that might indicate defective manufacture, and hence local production, is No. 90, which was found near the furnace. Bowls with rims of this sort appear to have been uncommon; the infolded rim is more often found on flasks and jugs. No. 93, probably to be dated earlier than the factory, may be compared with a bottle rim (No. 288).

88   (160–66). D rim ca. .16

Olive green. Probably a shallow bowl. Rim and wall unusually thick. A small rim fragment of the same color (325–66) has a similar fold, but the wall appears to be nearly vertical. **Fig. 4–11; Pl. 4–6.**

89   (174–66). D rim ca. .15

Olive green. A smaller vessel, like the preceding. **Pl. 4–6.**

41. Harden, *Karanis,* no. 348, classified with "Bowls of uncertain shape."
42. Erdmann, "Mezad Tamar," 106, 127, no. 415, pl. 4.

43. Hayes, *Toronto Glass,* 120, no. 469, fig. 13, pl. 30. D of rim .22. It is "from Syria, 4th c. (?)."
44. Vessberg, "Cyprus Glass."

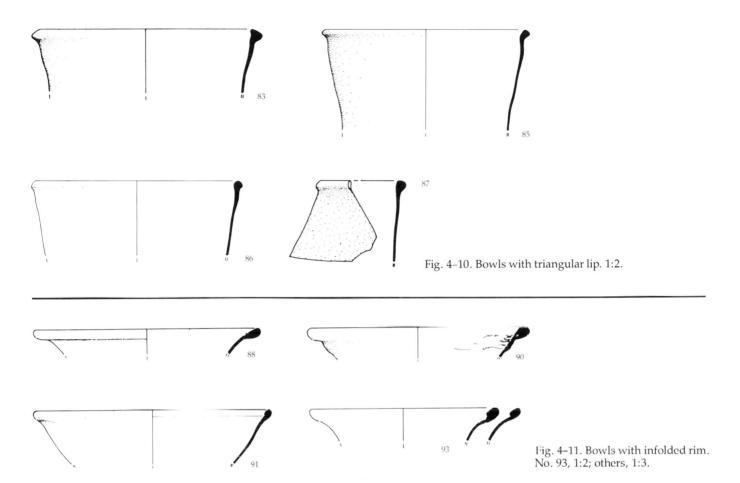

Fig. 4-10. Bowls with triangular lip. 1:2.

Fig. 4-11. Bowls with infolded rim. No. 93, 1:2; others, 1:3.

90 (276–64). D rim .18

Pale bluish green. Small air space in rim. Probably a shallow bowl. Unusually large bubbles just below lip seem to indicate defective blowing. **Fig. 4–11; Pl. 4–6.**

91 (65–65). D rim .19

Yellowish green. Fairly deep bowl. **Fig. 4 11; Pl. 4–6.**

92 (271–66). D rim ca. .065

Purple. Wall tapers slightly. Possibly a cup.

93 (302–66). D rim .102

Purple. Found in pre-351 context. **Fig. 4–11.**

Overhanging Rim (Nos. 94–97)

Few vessels of this kind were found; they seem to have been small, deep bowls. Three distinct kinds of rims are represented by the four fragments catalogued; and there are a few more of each kind. More than half were found in the factory dump, the remainder around the site.

The first variety (No. 94) has a slightly thickened rim flaring out and downward, while the wall tapers gradually. The second variety (No. 95) has a much thicker rim, folded out and downward close to the bulging wall. The body may have been globular. The third variety (Nos.

96–97) has a slightly thickened rim resembling the first variety but, in addition, a thin trail of the same color was applied just beneath the rim. On some specimens the wall contracts; on others it splays out. The rim diameters of bowls with applied trails range from .11 to .14.

The material is like that of other vessels; the colors are the usual greenish blue, yellowish brown, and various shades of green. No. 95 has marks of wheel-polishing on the exterior; Nos. 96 and 97 have long bubbles in the edge of the rim, indicating that it was opened out.

Such rims seem to be rare. The closest parallel is a bowl from Hanita, which has wheel-abraded bands on the rim and near the base.[45] Others, in the Nazareth Museum, may be similar.[46] Two rim fragments found farther east, at Dura, resemble our Nos. 96–97 in form; they are colorless, dated 2nd or 3rd c.[47] Colorless rims of the same sort found in Portugal are datable to the second half of the 2nd c. or the 3rd c.[48]

94 (182–65). D rim .085

Pale green. **Fig. 4-12.**

45. Barag, *Hanita*, 20–21, no. 35, with a low tubular base-ring.
46. Bagatti, "Museo Francescano," 234, figs. 6 and 7, no. 143.
47. Clairmont, *Dura Glass*, 54, nos. 226–27 (D rims .104, .098).
48. Alarcão, *Conimbriga* 6, 186, no. 166 (D rim .11).

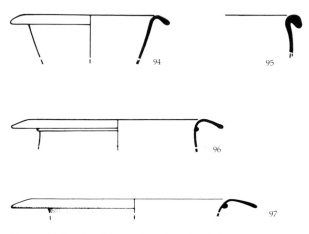

Fig. 4–12. Bowls with overhanging rim. 1:2.

95   (227–64). D rim ca. .20

Light yellowish green. Wheel-polished outside.
Fig. 4–12.

96   (66–65). D rim .11

Light greenish blue, long bubbles around edge of rim.
Trail of same color below rim. **Fig. 4–12.**

97   (408–64). D rim ca. .13

Light olive green. Like preceding but unweathered. A
similar fragment, yellowish brown (316–64, D rim .14),
was found in the factory dump. **Fig. 4–12.**

Collar Rim (Nos. 98–101)

About a dozen fragmentary rims, all from the factory
dump, seem to be from small bowls somewhat like Nos.
102 and 104. The rim diameters are .10–.145. Each has a
thickened rim, approximately vertical collar, and a sharp
bend inward and downward. All but No. 101 have a trail
around the base of the collar; on two (No. 100 and 47–66,
uncatalogued) it is dark greenish blue. The bowls were
probably rather deep, either with flat bottom or added
base. They are various shades of green and have the
usual type of weathering.

98   (411–64). D rim ca .135

Yellowish green, trail of same color around base of collar.
Fig. 4–13.

99   (374–66). D rim .115

Light yellowish green, tiny bubbles, horizontal striations below rim. Trail of same color around base of collar.
Fig. 4–13.

100   (237–66). D rim .14

Yellowish green, long horizontal bubbles. Thickened
rim, slight polishing traces outside. Deep greenish blue
trail around base of collar (also on 47–66). **Fig. 4–13.**

101   (41–66). D rim .145

Greenish blue, long horizontal bubbles, slight weathering inside, almost none outside. Slightly thickened rim.
Fig. 4–13.

Tooled-out Fold (Nos. 102–7)

Few rims with this feature were found, and none
could be associated with a base. As far as can be determined, all those catalogued, except No. 107, are from
fairly deep, small bowls. A few were found in the factory
dump, the rest scattered around the site. Most are greenish blue or green; the weathering is unremarkable. The
profiles vary: In No. 102 the rim and body form an S-
curve, interrupted by the fold; Nos. 103–4 have vertical
rims; in Nos. 105–6 the rims flare above the fold. No. 107
is quite different from the others (see discussion below).

Small bowls with tooled-out fold do not appear often
on Syro-Palestinian sites; they seem more common in
Cyprus, where they have either flat or concave bottoms,
or pad bases.[49] In addition to bowls without provenience,[50] there is a goblet (or lamp) from Beth Shearim,
with a tooled-out fold beneath the rim (D ca. .08); the
beaded stem is commonly found on late vessels.[51]

It seems that the tooled-out fold alone is not adequate
for determining either date or origin of these vessels. The
feature appears on bowls, cups, and possibly jars in both
East and West, from the 1st through 4th c.[52] Examples
from Italy and farther west date to the 1st and 2nd c. and
possibly later.

No. 107, apparently a flat dish (there is no clue to the
form of the base), is unique at the site, found in the wine
press tank. Parallels are elusive. A dish from Tyre (see n.
28 above) seems somewhat similar.

102   (165–64). D rim .11

Pale greenish blue. Rim forms S-curve with wall.
Fig. 4–14.

103   (153–64). D rim .08

Pale green. Rim tapers slightly toward tooled-out fold.
Fig. 4–14; Pl. 4–6.

104   (147a–64). D rim .11

Light greenish blue. Like preceding. Wall turns inward.
Fig. 4–14.

49. Vessberg, "Cyprus Glass," 147, pl. 9, nos. 37, 38 (no base); nos. 40,
41 (pad base). These were dated by comparison with pottery forms to
1st–2nd c. Isings remarks, however (*Roman Glass*, 90), that these Cyprus
vessels are undatable. See also Harden, "Vasa," 49, no. 11, fig. 20i (dated
before 250); no. 13, fig. 20k (unstratified).

50. Hayes, *Toronto Glass*, 80, no. 295, has a rim profile rather like our No.
102 and is dated 2nd or 3rd c.; no. 369 with a folded base and trail decoration is assigned to the second half of the 4th c.

51. Barag in Avigad, *Beth Shearim* 3, 205, no. 42, fig. 98. Parallels for the
beaded stem are given to vessels from Gerasa and elsewhere, but for the
upper part no parallel could be offered.

52. Isings, *Roman Glass*, Form 69a, citing numerous parallels, including
one from a 4th c. cemetery at Nijmegen, thought to be an heirloom.

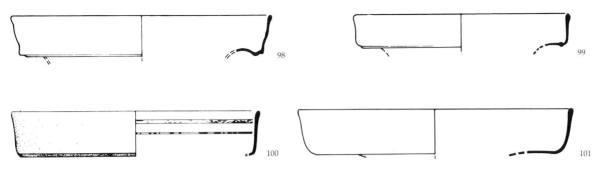

Fig. 4–13. Bowls with collar rim. 1:2.

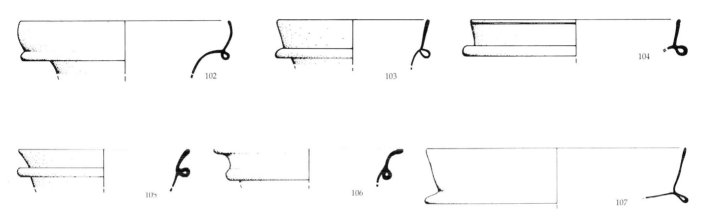

Fig. 4–14. Bowls with tooled-out fold. No. 107, 1:3; others, 1:2.

105 (172–65). D rim .09

Light greenish blue. Slightly flaring rim. **Fig. 4–14;**
Pl. 4–6.

106 (204–65). D rim .10

Light greenish blue. Rim flares above tooled out fold.
Fig. 4–14.

107 (336–64). PH .045; D rim ca. .208

Greenish blue, short horizontal bubbles in rim and a
few in the floor; almost no weathering. Slightly thickened
rim, tapering wall with elongated tooled-out fold at junction with floor. From wine press tank. **Fig. 4–14.**

Double Fold in Wall (Nos. 108–17)

These fragments were found in relatively small numbers, but enough to indicate that this was a local variety
even if not produced at Jalame. About half the fragments
were found in the factory dump, the rest around the site.

The feature common to all the examples is the double
fold formed as shown in Fig. 4–15—the rim folded
inward, then upward and again down. The vessel forms
vary considerably, and in most cases only a small part of
the body is preserved; no entire shape could be restored.
Rim diameters vary from .09 to .18, with a concentration
at .14–.15. Most of the fragments are green or greenish

blue; the material and the weathering are like most of the
Jalame glass.

No. 108 is the horizontal rim of a rather shallow bowl,
probably with tubular base-ring like some found in the
Judean Desert caves;[53] other forms with the double fold
dating 1st or 2nd c. have been found in Europe.[54] Nos.
109–17, from deeper bowls, seem later in date.

An extensive discussion of vessels with the double
fold is found in connection with fragments from Mesad
Tamar; these are thought to be not later than 3rd c.[55] Both
eastern and western parallels are noted, as well as the
long chronological spread of the double fold. Some fragments from Portugal indicate that this feature probably
was used all across Europe.[56] A deep bowl from a

53. Barag, "Cave of Horror," 208–10, nos. 1, 5; Barag in Yadin, *Cave of
Letters*, 104–5, no. 7 (a deep bowl that seems to be unique in having
crimped trails [see Nos. 118–21] as well as the double fold); Barag-Weinberg in P. and N. Lapp, *Discoveries in the Wâdī ed-Dâliyeh*, AASOR 41 (1974)
105, pl. 39, nos. 9, 10; Barag in Dothan, *Ashdod* 2–3, 204, no. 16, fig.
105:12.

54. Berger, *Vindonissa*, 82, no. 210, pl. 22, no. 94; E. Ritterling, *Das
frührömische Lager bei Hofheim in Taunus*, Annalen des Vereins für
Nassauische Altertumskunde und Geschichtsforschung, vol. 40, 1912
(Wiesbaden, 1913) 369, Form 6, pl. 38, 6.

55. Erdmann, "Mezad Tamar," 108, 141, nos. 872–75, pl. 7. The rim
diameters resemble the measurements of our examples, and the shapes
(only the rims preserved) appear similar.

56. Alarcão, *Conimbriga* 1965, 151, nos. 297–98, pl. 12; *Conimbriga* 6,
nos. 282, 284, pl. 45. They have no datable context.

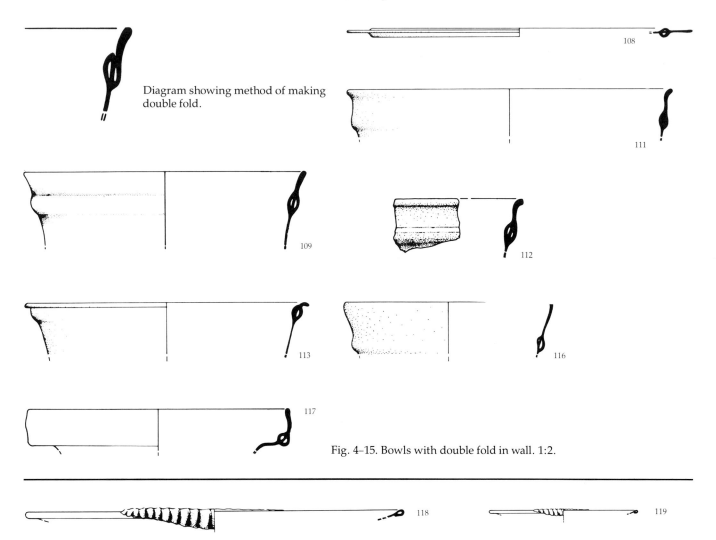

Diagram showing method of making double fold.

Fig. 4–15. Bowls with double fold in wall. 1:2.

Fig. 4–16. Bowls with crimped trails on rim. 1:3.

Nahariya tomb[57] suggests relationship with our Nos. 109–11. Judging from the quantity of the fragments at Jalame alone, one would think them contemporary with the factory.

108 (130–65). D rim ca. .18
  Light greenish blue, horizontal bubbles in rim. **Fig. 4–15; Pl. 4–7.**

109 (34–66). D rim .15
  Light green. **Fig. 4–15; Pl. 4–7.**

110 (435–66). D rim .14
  Light greenish blue, horizontal bubbles. Shape like preceding. **Pl. 4–7.**

111 (286–65). D rim .17
  Greenish blue. **Fig. 4–15.**

57. Barag, "Glass Vessels," Type 3.18.

112 (175–64). Est D rim .18
  Greenish blue, a few bubbles. **Fig. 4–15.**

113 (149–65). D rim ca. .15
  Greenish blue, dark weathering. **Fig. 4–15; Pl. 4–7.**

114 (143–65). D rim .09
  Pale greenish blue. Shape like preceding. **Pl. 4–7.**

115 (149a–65). D rim ca. .15
  Greenish blue, dark weathering. Shape like preceding. **Pl. 4–7.**

116 (221–64). D rim .11
  Pale greenish blue. **Fig. 4–15; Pl. 4–7.**

117 (197–65). D rim .14
  Yellowish green. A light yellowish brown fragment (422–66) has the same profile but lacks the rim. **Fig. 4–15; Pl. 4–7.**

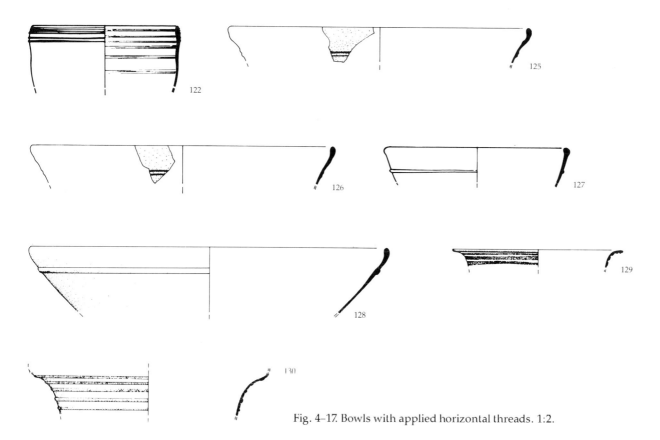

Fig. 4–17. Bowls with applied horizontal threads. 1:2.

Crimped Trails on Rim (Nos. 118–21)

The shape, which varies little, is shown on Pl. 4–7.[58] Characteristic are two heavy trails of the same color as the vessel, applied to opposite sides of the rim and tooled into a series of ribs. The rim is folded outward; the base may be pushed-in or be an added ring. Only four fragments of such rims have been found at Jalame, two in the factory dump. All are greenish blue; none preserves much of the vessel itself. No. 118 is unusually large.

This type has been dated from the 1st to early 3rd c. The most reliable dating (first third of 2nd c.) is based on pieces found in Judean Desert caves[59] and at Wadi ed-Daliyeh.[60] Similar bowls have been found at Palestinian sites,[61] but there are also examples from Sardis, Cyprus, Corinth, South Russia, Rumania, and western Europe.[62]

58. Museum of Art and Archaeology, University of Missouri-Columbia, No. 68.154. Purchased in Jerusalem. Light green. H .05, D rim .138. Photo courtesy of the museum.
59. See n. 53 above.
60. Barag-Weinberg as in n. 53, 104, pl. 39:4. The rim diameter is estimated to be .30.
61. Crowfoot, *Samaria* 3, 415 and fig. 96.5 with references to many other Eastern examples.
62. Saldern, *Sardis Glass*, 21–22, nos. 94–101; Vessberg, "Cyprus Glass," 114, pl. 1, 16; Davidson, *Corinth* 12, 98, nos. 612–13 in 2nd c. context; Sorokina, "Panticapaeum," 221, fig. 3:2; Bucovală, *Sticlă*, 40, no. 35; Isings, *Roman Glass*, Form 43, dated 1st–2nd c. (examples from Switzerland, Austria, etc.)

A find in a cemetery not far from Jalame (unpublished) offers a rare insight into poverty and human tragedy. The grave of a small girl was found to contain, besides the skeleton, only one object: a "frilled band" broken from a bowl of this kind, placed upon the child's head like a diadem.[63]

118 (17–66). D rim ca. .30

Greenish blue, dark weathering. Outfolded rim. Heavy tooled trail tapering at both ends, applied to rim. Wall slopes sharply inward. **Fig. 4–16; Pl. 4–7.**

119 (298–66). D rim ca. .162

Light greenish blue. **Fig. 4–16; Pl. 4–7.**

120 (136–65). D rim ca. .16

Light bluish green. **Pl. 4–7.**

121 (309–66). Max dim .034

Greenish blue. Small fragment of rim and body. **Pl. 4–7.**

Applied Horizontal Trails (Nos. 122–32)

Few bowl rims with trail decoration were found, some in the factory dump, others randomly on the site. Six or more have deep greenish blue trails (not marvered in) wound around the rim and upper part of the body; a few

63. The grave and contents were seen in the museum of Kibbutz Hazorea.

Fig. 4–18. Bowl with horizontal ribbing. 1:2.

others have trails of the same color as the vessel. The sizes vary greatly; some examples may be cups rather than bowls. The glass is of the usual kind, the colors green and greenish blue.

This type of decoration seems more common on jars and flasks. In view of the scarcity of Jalame examples, we have not attempted to offer parallels except for many fragments found at Mesad Tamar.[64] This kind of decoration continues in the 5th c.[65]

122   (296–64). D rim .076

Pale greenish blue. Thickened rim, slightly tapering wall. Thin deep greenish blue trails outside, scratched horizontal lines inside. From wine press tank. **Fig. 4–17; Pl. 4–7.**

123   (422–64). D rim .08

Pale greenish blue. Shape like preceding. Four thin trails, deep greenish blue. **Pl. 4–7.**

124   (250–64). D rim .06

Pale greenish blue. Shape like preceding. Six thin trails, deep greenish blue. **Pl. 4–7 and Color Pl. 3C.**

125   (205–65). D rim .016

Pale green. Thickened rim curving inward, tapering wall. Two deep greenish blue trails. **Fig. 4–17; Pl. 4–7.**

126   (214–66). D rim ca. .164

Pale green. Shape like preceding. Two deep greenish blue trails. **Fig. 4–17; Pl. 4–7.**

127   (145–64). D rim .10

Light greenish blue. Thickened rounded rim, trail of same color. **Fig. 4–17.**

128   (199–65). D rim ca. .19

Light green, impurities near rim, cream-colored weathering. Rounded rim, slightly thickened, curving inward. Single trail of same color. A small fragment of a similar bowl (247–66) is greenish blue, D rim .18. **Fig. 4–17.**

129   (39–66). D rim .09

Pale greenish blue. Deep greenish blue trail wound around rim and neck six times. **Fig. 4–17.**

130   (306–64). Max dim .126

Pale greenish blue. Body flaring upward toward the rim, which is not preserved. Five deep greenish blue trails wound around upper body. **Fig. 4–17; Color Pl. 3C.**

64. Erdmann, "Mezad Tamar," 107, nos. 569, 578 ff.
65. Barag in Prausnitz, *Shavei Zion*, 66, no. 8, fig. 16.

131   (193–65). Max dim .031

Very pale green. Shape like preceding. Two deep greenish blue trails preserved.

132   (140–65). D rim .08

Pale greenish blue. Thickened rim flaring slightly from cylindrical body. Deep greenish blue trail.

Horizontal Ribbing (Nos. 133–38)

A few fragments of vessels with this peculiar feature are all from the factory dump. The rims are rounded and thickened. Below the rim is a series of horizontal ribs that protrude both inside and out. This effect was apparently produced by pattern molding.

The surfaces are almost unweathered; the glass is of good quality but contains some bubbles and an occasional impurity. Two fragments (Nos. 136–37) have pitted exterior surfaces, which may indicate wheel-polishing. Fine abraded lines are faintly visible on No. 136. All seem to be shallow bowls, though this is not certain. Parallels are thus far lacking.

133   (171–66). D rim .142; Th rim .003

Pale bluish green, long bubble near rim, slight weathering. Thickened rim, horizontal ribbing down to point where wall curves inward. **Fig. 4–18; Pl. 4–8.**

134   (437–64). D rim ca. .10 (uncertain); Th rim .0035

Pale yellowish green, a few small bubbles and impurities. Shape like preceding. **Pl. 4–8.**

135   (494a–66). D rim .12; Th rim .002

Pale greenish blue, small bubbles, almost no weathering. Wall curves inward at bottom of fragment. **Pl. 4–8.**

136   (494b–66). D rim .17; Th rim .002

Bluish green, long bubbles in rim, exterior pitted, traces of wheel-polishing. Shape like preceding; ribbing is fainter. **Pl. 4–8.**

137   (494c–66). D rim .16; Th rim .002

Bluish green, long bubbles and impurities, exterior pitted. Shape like preceding, ribbing hardly noticeable. **Pl. 4–8.**

138   (494d–66). D rim .18; Th rim .003

Greenish blue, tiny bubbles, almost no weathering. Rim thicker than preceding. Wall curves inward. **Pl. 4–8.**

Miscellaneous Bowl Rims (Nos. 139–44)

139   (78–66). D rim ca. .20

Colorless with green tinge, dark weathering, pitting inside; outside mostly unweathered. Thickened, out-splayed rim, with shallow groove cut around upper surface. Interior wheel-polished, exterior fire-polished. Owing to weathering, it is uncertain whether the vessel was cast or blown. Found in factory dump. **Fig. 4–19.**

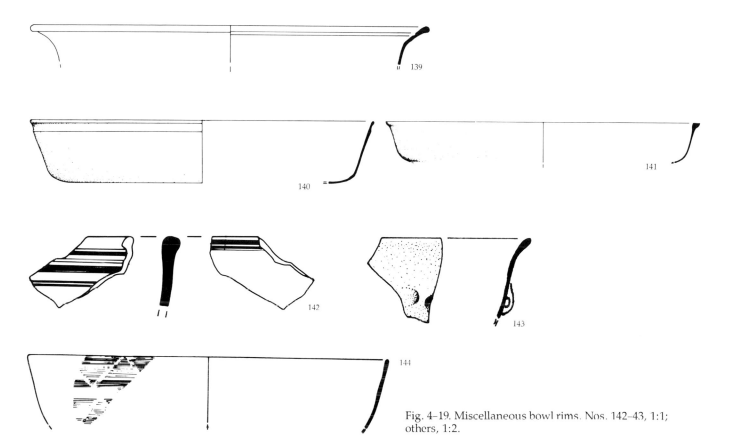

Fig. 4–19. Miscellaneous bowl rims. Nos. 142–43, 1:1; others, 1:2.

This seems somewhat like the so-called Alexandrian bowls of the 2nd c. Found in the Near and Middle East as well as in various parts of Europe, they are generally considered to have been cast, but this is not always certain. Most of the bowls comparable to our fragment are more angular in outline.[66]

140   (96–65). PH .031; D rim .18

Greenish blue, white weathering and pitting outside; iridescence inside. Slightly thickened rim. Wall tapers inward, then bends sharply to a nearly horizontal line. Wide, shallow groove outside just below the rim edge; wheel-polishing below this for .02 from the top. **Fig. 4–19.**

This resembles the bowl with collar rim (see No. 101), but it alone has a groove and polished exterior.

141   (251–66). PH .034; D rim .24

Light yellowish green, patchy white weathering. Four fragments of rim and body, two joining. Thickened rim, rounded but cracked off sharply, probably during annealing. Two of the fragments show wheel-polishing outside. From factory dump. **Fig. 4–19; Pl. 4–8.**

142   (304–65). PH .02; D rim unknown; Th .005–.003

Greenish blue, very fine glass, almost no weathering. Thickened, rounded rim, wheel-polished. Bands of fine abraded lines outside, one band inside. This tiny fragment

66. E.g., Barag, "Cave of Horror," 210–11, no. 6, D rim ca. .148; Clairmont, *Dura Glass*, 24, no. 90. References to similar vessels from Europe and North Africa are listed in Alarcão, *Conimbriga* 6, no. 96 (172, n. 50).

is unique at the site. Its exact provenience has been lost. A 4th c. date is probable. **Fig. 4–19.**

143   (208–65). D rim uncertain

Pale green, iridescence and patches of dark weathering. Shallow bowl, fragment of rim and body. Rounded, flaring rim. Horizontal pinch .015 below rim. From factory dump. (For discussion of this type see Nos. 370ff.). **Fig. 4–19.**

Miscellaneous Bowl Rims (Islamic) (No. 144)

Only seven recognizable fragments of Islamic glass were found, all on the surface. Pottery of the Islamic period is equally rare (see Chap. 7, Nos. 880–81). The decoration on the glass fragments is of two kinds: a design impressed with tongs on both sides of the vessel while hot (also called pinched or pincered decoration) and incision (one fragment).

These fragments seem to have no connection with the Muslim graves found on the hill (see Chap. 2); they were probably dropped by passersby. Glasses with tong-impressed designs are usually dated 8th or 9th c.;[67] the incised decoration is later, probably 10th c.[68]

67. C. Clairmont, *Catalogue of Ancient and Islamic Glass*, Benaki Museum (Athens, 1977) 69–70; C. J. Lamm, *Mittelalterliche Gläser und Steinschnittarbeiten* (Berlin, 1929–1930) 66–67, pl. 17. See also Harden," Glass," in Colt, *Nessana* 1, 80–81.

68. Clairmont, as in n. 67, 75–76, with many parallels; Lamm, as in n. 67, pl. 50; Harden, as in n. 67, 80.

Fig. 4–20. Bowls with solid base ring. 1:2.

144 (70–66). D rim .19

Light green with yellow streaks, white weathering. Rounded rim, pinched or tong-impressed decoration—two rows of zigzags forming a pattern of opposed triangles. **Fig. 4–19.**

58–66, PH .025, deep blue, tong-impressed, pattern uncertain. Fragment of rim and body, probably a bowl.

399–66, Max dim .022, greenish blue, tong-impressed, pattern uncertain. Fragment, no edge preserved.

498–66, Max dim .015, colorless, tong-impressed circle. Fragment, no edge preserved.

242–65, Max dim .014, light blue, incised geometric pattern. Fragment, no edge preserved.

Bases

Solid Base Ring (Nos. 145–51)

This type of base is comparatively rare at Jalame; all the examples are fragmentary. More than half the pieces were found in the factory dump.

Even among the few fragments there is considerable variation. One base is almost vertical; others are straight diagonals; still others splay outward. The diameters range from .06 to .095 (No. 145 is unusually large and heavy). The material is like that of other Jalame vessels: weathering is usually slight. Most of the fragments are greenish blue, a few green, one brown.

Bases of this kind that are contemporary with the factory are found elsewhere on both shallow and deep bowls.[69] They come mainly from Hanita and Nahariya and have also been found at Khirbet Shema.[70] But the type begins in the 2nd c., and is known in the Middle East, Anatolia, and Egypt.[71] Egyptian influence on our examples may be indicated by tool marks on some of the bases, but this feature may also be Palestinian, as Barag maintains with reference to the Hanita finds. None found in the West seem to be later than 2nd c.

69. Barag, "Glass Vessels," Types 2.12 (shallow), 3.16, 3.19 (deep).
70. Barag, *Hanita*, 15–17, no. 27 (shallow, with tooling), 21, nos. 40, 43 (deep, without tooling); Meyers, *Khirbet Shema*, pl. 8.7, nos. 18–21.
71. Clairmont, *Dura Glass*, 23, nos. 81–85, all colorless, dated "Early Imperial" but probably 2nd c.; Saldern, *Sardis Glass*, 29–30, nos. 188–92, all green, various dates; Harden, *Karanis*, nos. 221, 237, probably 4th c.

145 (87–64). D base .095

Greenish blue. Diagonal tool marks on exterior and interior of the base. Thick flat floor with pontil mark (D .017). Probably a large bowl. **Fig. 4–20; Pl. 4–8; Color Pl. 4A.**

146 (19–65). D base .082

Bluish green. Uneven base with tool marks on exterior. **Fig. 4–20; Pl. 4–8.**

147 (265–65). D base .06

Greenish blue. Shape like preceding. Tool marks on base, inside and out. **Pl. 4–8.**

148 (306–66). D base .086

Bluish green. No tool marks on base. Perhaps a deep bowl. **Fig. 4–20; Pl. 4–8.**

149 (322–66). D base ca. .06

Yellowish brown. No tool marks on base. **Fig. 4–20.**

150 (246–64). D base ca. .075

Light greenish blue, white weathering. Tool marks on base exterior. **Fig. 4–20.**

151 (329–64). D base .055

Yellowish green. Thick floor, irregular pad base. Tool marks inside and out, much deeper and cruder than on other examples. Pontil mark (D .01). **Pl. 4–8.**

Trail-wound Base (Nos. 152–56)

Not more than ten such bases have been identified at Jalame. The entire shape of only one could be restored, and it is doubtful whether the other bases belong to bowls, for published vessels with this kind of base are generally jugs. The fragments were found both in the factory dump and around the site; they must be contemporary with the factory. The base diameters range from .06 to .12; the average is about .08. The number of trail winds varies from two to five. The material is fairly good, with tiny bubbles (sometimes elongated) and, generally, slight weathering. The colors are yellowish green, green, and greenish blue.

These bases are rare not only at Jalame but elsewhere in the Syro-Palestinian area. They are not among Barag's Types, but similar vessels have been found near Beit

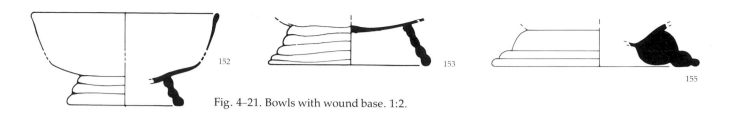

Fig. 4–21. Bowls with wound base. 1:2.

Govrin.[72] The only examples published from excavations appear to be bases of flasks or jugs from Karanis,[73] a jug from a tomb at Qustul (Nubia),[74] a base found at Corinth,[75] a fragment at Sardis,[76] and a number of bases from the Mithraeum under the church of Santa Prisca in Rome.[77] Vessels with this type of base (provenience unknown) are in the Vatican Museum,[78] in the Damascus Museum (one said to come from Homs, another from the Hauran),[79] and also some in French museums.[80] All of the bases illustrated resemble our No. 155. The wide spread of proveniences seems to be evidence for both Eastern and Western origins.

152 (209–65, 210–65). Est H .05; D rim .10; D base .06

Light green, long horizontal bubbles in base. Three fragments forming nearly complete profile. Thickened, rounded rim. Trailed base, three winds. **Fig. 4–21.**

153 (76 65). D base (uneven) .085

Light green. Nearly flat floor. Trailed base, five winds. Pontil mark (D .01). **Fig. 4–21; Pl. 4–8.**

154 (69–66). D base .07

Light greenish blue. Shape like preceding. Trailed base, four winds. **Pl. 4–8.**

155 (171–65). D base .12

Light green, long bubbles, thick white weathering. Fragment of base, floor and wall. Slightly concave floor. Trailed base, three winds. **Fig. 4–21; Pl. 4–8.**

72. Mentioned in *Israel Museum News* 9 (1972) 107: Tomb group—violet glass vessels and several lamps, 3rd–4th c.

73. Harden, *Karanis*, 217–18, nos. 647–71. No. 658 (D base ca. .06) is illustrated: the base is light green, the body yellow. Others also have bases of contrasting color. These vessels are classified under flasks but, as the author points out, might be jugs. They are 4th c. or later.

74. W. B. Emery, *The Royal Tombs of Ballana and Qustul* (Cairo, 1938) 377, no. 863, pl. 106 B. The height is .18. The jug is cobalt blue.

75. Davidson, *Corinth* 12, 99, no. 633, a base fragment, light green, D .08. The context is not datable.

76. Saldern, *Sardis Glass*, 31, no. 196, a greenish blue fragment (D base .07) in disturbed context.

77. Isings, *Roman Glass*, 6 for a full discussion; also Isings, "Some Late Glass Fragments from Rome," *Proceedings of the 7th International Congress on Glass* (Brussels, 1965) paper 262.

78. F. Fremersdorf, *Antikes, Islamisches und Mittelalterliches Glas, Catalogo del Museo Sacro* 5 (Vatican City, 1975) 79, nos. 770–73, pls. 36, 37. The first two are unusually large (D bases .10, .115) and high (H .055). No. 770 is blue-green, no. 771 deep green. The colors of nos. 772–73 (D bases .074, .086) are not mentioned.

79. Mentioned by E. Spartz, *Antike Gläser* Staatlichen Kunstsammlungen Kassel (Kassel, 1967), in commentary on a similar jug in Kassel, no. 98. Many references are given here.

80. Isings, *Roman Glass*, 6.

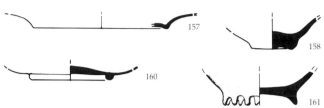

Fig. 4–22. Miscellaneous bowl bases. 1:2.

156 (112–65). D base ca. .08

Light greenish blue. Floor apparently flat. Base made of two flattened trails. Tool marks on exterior. **Pl. 4–8.**

Miscellaneous Bowl Bases (Nos. 157–61)

157 (269–66). PH .008, D bottom .07

Pale green, slight weathering. Fragment of bottom and body. Almost horizontal floor; wall spreads out to open form. From factory dump. **Fig. 4–22.**

158 (390 66). PH .018, D bottom .022

Light green, dark weathering. Fragment of bottom and body. Thickened bottom, convex on top, deep pontil scar (D .011). Wall spreads to open form, somewhat like preceding. From factory dump. **Fig. 4–22.**

159 (166–65). PH .008, D base .08

Light purple, dark weathering. Fragment of base. Tubular base-ring. Floor spreads downward, wall upward. From factory dump.

160 (215–65). PH .006; D base .046; Th wall .0015

Pale bluish green, iridescence, dark weathering. Base and fragment of body. Solid ring base, convex floor. Pontil mark (D .012). Wall spreads out and slightly upward. This may be the base for a bowl like Nos. 118–21; it certainly predates the factory. Found in eastern part of site, with other earlier glass and pottery. **Fig. 4–22.**

161 (215–64). PH .015; D base .04

Greenish blue, surface pitted. Fragment of base and body. Thickened base with pontil mark (D ca. .007). Twelve small "toes" pulled out from the bottom (two broken off). Found on surface. **Fig. 4–22; Color Pl. 4A.**

This is the only example of its kind at Jalame. A bowl found at Nahariya (Barag, *Glass Vessels*, Type 3.25) is dated 3rd–first half of 4th c. A number have been recorded at Dura (Clairmont, *Dura Glass*, 50–51), dated 2nd or early 3rd c.; references to both eastern and western examples are given. Clairmont believes the form to be eastern, imported to the west. In Portugal three fragments of such vessels are known: Alarcão, *Conimbriga* 6, 189, no. 193 and n. 36, 38.

Cups, Goblets, Beakers

Three types of cups are easily distinguishable: (1) cup with rounded rim, solid base, and trail decoration (Nos. 162–86); (2) cup with rounded rim, tapering wall, and pushed-in base (Nos. 187–94); (3) cup with rounded rim, tapering wall, and concave bottom (Nos. 195–200). The first variety is one of the factory's chief products, while the second and third may have been made at a nearby factory as yet unknown to us. These two types are relatively rare at Jalame, but they are fairly common elsewhere in northern Palestine.

The few goblet fragments (Nos. 201–2) undoubtedly were imported, as were conical vessels with rounded rims, possibly beakers (Nos. 203–5).

Cup with Solid Base (Nos. 162–86)

This type of drinking vessel (Pl. 4–9) was produced in quantity at Jalame: more than 350 fragments can be identified. About 80 percent were found in the factory dump, the rest around the central area, not concentrated in any one place.

The characteristic features are: rounded, slightly thickened rim, walls contracting, then flaring slightly near the bottom before turning into the thick, solid base (sometimes slightly concave), which invariably bears a pontil scar or remains of the knock-off (D of scar .01–.015). The floors are either flat or convex, occasionally domical (No. 177). The walls of some cups are almost straight, but the slightly concave profile is more common. The base is the most easily recognizable part of the vessel because of its solidity. More than 30 complete and at least 25 fragmentary bases were found. Their diameters range mostly from .03–.05.

The rim is more difficult to identify since usually only small sections are preserved. The diameters are chiefly .07–.08, with a few smaller or larger. The rim diameter is generally about 50 percent of the height of the cup, the base diameter 35–45 percent. The contrast between the solid base and the thin walls is quite striking: with few exceptions, the walls do not exceed .002 in thickness.

The material is of fairly good quality, with tiny bubbles scattered throughout the body. The weathering is usually moderate and whitish; dark weathering is the exception.

The colors, in order of frequency, are greenish blue, green, yellowish green, olive green, colorless with green tinge, and yellowish brown. The last two are comparatively rare. The decoration generally consists of a single trail of the same color wound once around the vessel wall, in a few cases two or three times. One fragment (No. 166) has a purple trail. Examples with colored decoration are known elsewhere, but at Jalame the numerous vessel fragments with deep greenish blue trails are more likely from small flasks. The trail around the cup may be fairly high on the wall or lower down; the placement is not necessarily proportionate to the size of the cup. In cups with similar rim diameters the trail may be as high as .023 below the rim or as low as .047, but most are .03–.04 below the rim. This variation perhaps indicates that a number of glassblowers were occupied in making these cups. One sees today in Hebron and other such factories that the workers acquire personal habits of making vessels.

The method of making the cups explains the contrast between body and base. A parison blown into a shape approximately that of the cup is pressed upon a hot, solid gob of glass previously dropped on a flat, often slightly rough, surface. The parison and gob are then picked up together on the blowpipe, a pontil is attached to the center of the gob and the blowpipe is cracked off. The whole is reheated, the vessel shaped with a wooden tool into its final form, the rim slightly thickened and rounded by reheating. Finally, a trail is wound around the body, the pontil is knocked off, and the vessel annealed.

This kind of cup is typical of the Syro-Palestinian region, but published examples with definite provenience are relatively few. Barag ("Glass Vessels") assigns the shape to his Types 4.6 and 4.7. At Samaria a considerable number were found; the dates assigned cover the 3rd–5th c.[81] Similar cups come from Nahariya tombs believed to have been in use during the 3rd and 4th c.[82] A tomb group from near Tyre, assigned to the 4th c., also contains such cups.[83] Mesad Tamar has produced fragments datable to the 4th c.[84]

It seems certain that the type was not produced in Egypt. The closest parallel at Karanis has a somewhat similar body but a tooled base.[85] A single example in the Cairo Museum was obtained by purchase; it is probably not Egyptian.[86] The type seems almost completely

---

81. Crowfoot, *Samaria* 3, 410, fig. 94.14, no. C697, a greenish beaker with blue trail, from Tomb E 220, dated 3rd c. Remains of ten more were found in the Ganymede House, dated 4th c. (p. 404) and four in the "glass factory" area, 4th–5th c. (p. 405). From the North Cemetery, Tomb I, dated 4th–5th c. (413, fig. 95.20), came a greenish cup with blue trail.

82. D. Barag, "Nahariya," 29, pl. 3.

83. Harden, "Tomb-groups," 153, nos. G26–28.

84. Erdmann, "Mezad Tamar," 100 and pl. 1, nos. 13–15. These are bases; the rims are discussed separately, and they are so fragmentary that any definite connection between the two seems impossible to ascertain. The many references quoted include western examples that are not quite similar.

85. Harden, *Karanis*, 133–34, nos. 362–64, pl. 15.

86. Edgar, *Glass*, 15, no. 32.467, pl. 3 (green). Harden mentions ("Tomb-groups," 153) that the cup is probably Syrian.

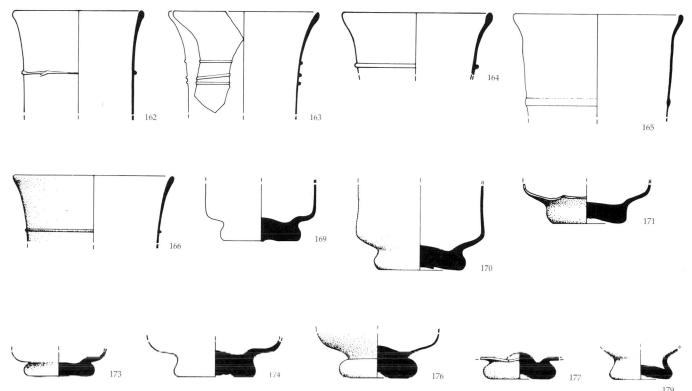

Fig. 4–23. Cups with solid base. 1:2.

absent from the West.[87] Numerous examples, supposedly Syro-Palestinian, are in public and private collections.[88]

Rim Fragments

162 (373–66). D rim .07

Pale yellowish green. Trail of same color. **Fig. 4–23; Pl. 4–9.**

163 (84–65). D rim .08

Yellowish green. Trail of same color wound several times. **Fig. 4–23.**

164 (331–64). D rim .08

Pale yellowish green. Rim splays out and turns inward at top. Trail of same color. **Fig. 4–23.**

165 (428–66). D rim .08

Yellowish green. Rim splays out and turns inward, as in preceding. Trail of same color, protruding slightly inside. **Fig. 4–23.**

87. A profile of a cup of this sort, found at Ibiza and now in Museo Arqueológico, Barcelona (no. 7.144) is shown by M. Vigil Pascual, *El Vidrio en el mundo antiguo* (Madrid, 1969) 168, fig. 156.
88. E.g., Israel Museum, from El-Bassa, El-Makr, Nahariya; Dept. Antiquities, from Nahariya, Even Menachem; Akko Museum, from various places; British Museum (no. 92-3-17-40), from near Nazareth; Hayes, *Toronto Glass*, 103–4, nos. 374–77, said to be from Palestine; two in the Museum of Art and Archaeology, University of Missouri-Columbia: No. 68.155, bluish green, trail of same color, H .09, D rim .065 (Pl. 4–9); No. 70.311, greenish blue, H .08, D rim .052; both purchased in Jerusalem.

166 (287–66). D rim ca. .08

Pale green. Purple trail. **Fig. 4–23; Pl. 4–9.**

167 (421–66). D rim .07

Light green. Trail of same color. **Pl. 4–9.**

168 (434–66). D rim .075

Pale greenish blue. Trail of same color. **Pl. 4–9.**

Base Fragments

169 (19–66). D base .043

Dark bluish green with yellow streak, unweathered. **Fig. 4–23; Pl. 4–9.**

170 (321–64, 324–64). D base .048

Yellowish green, interior unweathered, white weathering on exterior. Non-joining fragment preserves trail of same color. **Fig. 4–23; Pl. 4–9; Color Pl. 4A.**

171 (464–64). D base .04

Olive green. **Fig. 4–23.**

172 (64–65). D base .049

Greenish blue, unusually heavy white weathering. **Pl. 4–9.**

173 (211–65). D base .032

Light greenish blue. **Fig. 4–23; Pl. 4–9.**

174 (164–65). D base .043

Olive green. The color plate shows cup base of same

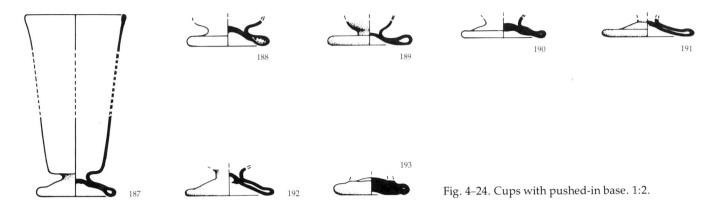

Fig. 4–24. Cups with pushed-in base. 1:2.

color, size, and profile (255–64, uncatalogued). **Fig. 4–23; Color Pl. 4A.**

175 (473–66). D base .039

Colorless, faint greenish tinge. Surface pitted, dark weathering. **Pl. 4–9.**

176 (219–65). D .042

Yellowish green, large bubble in base, blowing spirals. **Fig. 4–23.**

177 (248–64). D base .038

Yellowish green. **Fig. 4–23.**

178 (160–65). D base .046

Bluish green, yellow streak. **Pl. 4–9** (2 views).

179 (210–64). D base .032

Pale yellowish green. The shape differs from others: base and wall join without constriction. **Fig. 4–23; Pl. 4–9.**

180 (167–64). D base .037

Greenish blue. **Pl. 4–9.**

181 (196–65). D base .05

Olive green. **Pl. 4–9.**

182 (5–66). D base .043

Greenish blue. **Pl. 4–9.**

183 (54–66). D base .043

Dark greenish blue. **Pl. 4–9.**

184 (243–66). D base .046

Dark greenish blue. **Pl. 4–9.**

185 (461–66). D base .046

Dark greenish blue. **Pl. 4–9** (2 views).

186 (313–66). D base .053

Green. **Pl. 4–9.**

Cup with Pushed-in Base (Nos. 187–94)

Some 60 bases of this type have been identified, but since relatively few were found in the dump and a number in the fill of the wine press tank it is possible that they were not made in the factory. They are smaller than the cups with solid bases and suggest a relationship like that of the modern "wineglass" to "tumbler." The only nearly complete specimen is No. 187, which can serve to represent the entire group. It has a thickened, rounded rim tapering downward to a sharp constriction above the base, which is formed by pushing up the center of the bottom. The constricted portion separating body and base is not high enough to be called a stem; in this respect the cup is easily distinguished from the stemmed goblet (see below).

The diameter of the base is generally greater than the lowest part of the body. A pontil mark (D .008–.02) is invariably present, and sometimes part of the pontil knock-off. The base-ring may be circular in form or elongated. The shape of the body is difficult to determine when little of the wall remains, but an approximately cylindrical form, splaying at the rim, is probably to be assumed. The heights of the cups seem to have been between .08 and .10, with rim diameters varying from .04 to .07 and bases from .03 to .06. Most of the bases are about .045 in diameter.

The cups are generally greenish blue or green, and have the usual kind of weathering. An exception is No. 193, a base, which is ruby red in color and entirely unweathered. This cannot have been a product of the factory.

The type is Barag's 4.5, found at Samaria.[89] There are quite a few examples in museums, both in Israel and elsewhere, but the Samaria cup seems to be the only published piece from a controlled excavation. On the whole, the type is not common and seems soon to have given way to the stemmed goblet, which became popular in late 4th c. and continued for a long time thereafter. Of the latter there is not even one fragment at Jalame.

187 (385–64). Est H .098; D base .042; D rim ca. .052; Th wall .015

Light green. Fragments of base, rim, and body. From wine press tank. **Fig. 4–24; Pl. 4–9.**

89. Crowfoot, *Samaria* 3, 416 and fig. 96, 10 (the town site) dated 4th–5th c.

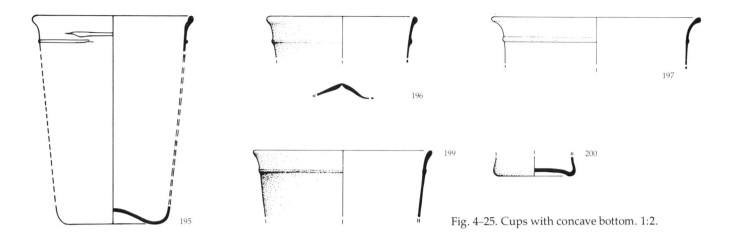

Fig. 4–25. Cups with concave bottom. 1:2.

188 (166–64). D base .043

Greenish blue. **Fig. 4–24.**

189 (99–64). D base .043

Greenish blue. **Fig. 4–24.**

190 (77–64). D base .042

Greenish blue. **Fig. 4–24; Pl. 4–9.**

191 (457–64). D base .05

Light greenish blue. From wine press tank. **Fig. 4–24; Pl. 4–9.**

192 (458–64). D base .045

Light greenish blue. From wine press tank. **Fig. 4–24; Pl. 4–9** (2 views).

193 (393–64). D base .04

Ruby red, tiny bubbles, no weathering. **Fig. 4–24.**
This fragment was submitted to the Brookhaven National Laboratory (courtesy of Dr. Edward V. Sayre), where it was determined that it is different in composition from other Jalame glass and may have been of foreign origin. The evidence was, however, thought inconclusive.

194 (189–64). D base .041

Light greenish blue. **Pl. 4–9.**

Cup with Concave Bottom (Nos. 195–200)

Some 37 rim fragments were identified, ranging in size from .06 to .095, nine of them too small to measure.

The cup has a rounded, thickened rim, slightly flaring. The wall tapers somewhat, forming an almost cylindrical body. The bottom is concave, without a defined base, sometimes with a sharp kick and a pontil mark (D ca. .01). A single horizontal trail of the same color is applied not far below the rim (.01–.014). The placement of the trail, unlike the cups with solid base, emphasizes the rim rather than the body. On some examples the trail protrudes inside as well as out (see No. 199).

The shape can be recognized mainly by rim frag-

ments, as the kicked base may also be associated with other kinds of vessels.

Most of the specimens are greenish blue, both light and dark. Except for a few (Nos. 196, 198), they exhibit the usual type of material and weathering.

The type is well documented in northern Palestine. One example was found in a tomb at Yehiam in western Galilee and another at Peqi'in, within the same general area. Both these tombs are dated by the excavator to the first part of the 4th c.[90] At least one such cup was found at Nahariya,[91] one is published from Khirbet Shema,[92] and one is in a group of glass vessels said to be from Tyre.[93] Cups of similar shape but without trails have been found at Samaria and at Hanita.[94] A single example with a trail from Mit Rahineh, Egypt, is illustrated by Edgar, who mentions that it has a green tinge.[95] There seem to be no such cups at Karanis, and one may assume the type came from the north. It is not sure, however, that it was a Jalame product.

No. 200, a fragmentary cup unique at Jalame, lacks a pontil mark. The body may have been cylindrical or had a concave wall. A base fragment from Mesad Tamar[96] is comparable; many complete specimens come from Cyprus, where they generally have concave walls.[97] The dates assigned to such cups range through the 3rd and 4th c.; our fragment was found in fill at the eastern edge of the area and is probably later than the factory.

90. V. Tsaferis, "Tombs in Western Galilee," *Atiqot* 5 (1969) 74, fig. 2.7, pl. 16:13 (Yehiam); 77, no. 3, fig. 5, pl. 17:14 (Peqi'in).
91. Barag, "Nahariya," 29, pl. 3.
92. Meyers, *Khirbet Shema*, pl. 8.6, no. 6, dated late 3rd, 4th c.
93. Harden "Tomb-groups," 152, no. G24, fig. 1. It seems to have trail decoration, though this is not mentioned.
94. Crowfoot, *Samaria* 3, 413, fig. 95, no. 22, from North Cemetery, dated 4th–5th c. Barag, *Hanita*, 28, no. 66. He gives parallels mentioned above, as well as western examples, referring to Isings Form 106c. The proportions are somewhat different, and there need not be a close connection with eastern examples.
95. Edgar, *Glass*, no. 32463, pl. 2.
96. Erdmann, "Mezad Tamar," 103, no. 102, pl. 2.
97. Vessberg, "Cyprus Glass," 122, pl. 3, no. 30. See also Hayes, *Toronto Glass*, 65, no. 190.

195   (152–65). Est H .11; D rim .085

Light greenish blue. Two fragments, not joining. **Fig. 4–25.**

196   (303–65). D rim ca. .09

Dark greenish blue, black impurities and dark enamel-like weathering. Seven rim fragments (two joining). This kind of material is uncommon at Jalame. Possibly these fragments all belong to one vessel. **Fig. 4–25.**

197   (138–65). D rim .10

Light greenish blue. Rim flares more than usual from the almost vertical wall. **Fig. 4–25.**

198   (414–66). D of three rims .09, fourth ca. .10

Pale greenish blue, dark weathering, except one unweathered. Four fragments of different vessels. **Pl. 4–10.**

199   (464–66). D rim .095

Pale greenish blue, tiny bubbles, blowing spirals, black impurities. Very little weathering. **Fig. 4–25.**

200   (295–66). D bottom .042

Olive green, slight weathering. No pontil mark. **Fig. 4–25.**

Goblets (?) (Nos. 201–2)

A few fragments, probably of goblets, were found in places that indicate an early 5th c. date. The closest parallels seem to be fragments found at Sardis,[98] dated by context to 5th and early 6th c. As mentioned by Saldern, these might be lamps, but our fragments are too incomplete for certain identification.

201   (307–64). PH .032; Max dim .043

Deep blue, patches of dark weathering. Part of base and body, no edge preserved. Solid base formed of a separate gather pushed into the bowl, forming a slightly convex floor. Body probably globular. **Fig. 4–26.**

202   (8–65). PH .018; Max dim .032

Light green, patches of white weathering. Part of base and body, no edge preserved. Shape like preceding except that vessel floor is flat and shape of body uncertain. Pontil mark (D .013). **Fig. 4–26.**

Conical Vessels (Lamps or Beakers) (Nos. 203–5)

Conical vessels[99] with rounded rims are rare at Jalame, and not very common in general. The few examples that could be identified have applied deep greenish blue bases (Nos. 203–4). Others may not have been recognized. Some were found in the factory dump, others

not far from the furnace, but their scarcity makes it unlikely that they are products of the factory.

The type to which No. 203 belongs is shown on Pl. 4–10.[100] Others from the Palestinian area are in museums, but none from excavations seem to have been published. In Egypt there are similar vessels,[101] apparently much less common than those with cracked-off rim. No. 205, with a base knob, is also paralleled in Egypt.[102]

203   (42–65). PH .012; D base .027; Th wall .0035

Pale green. Base and small portion of body. Circular base formed of a deep greenish blue trail (with bubbles and swirls). Body apparently conical, bottom flat. **Fig. 4–26.**

204   (171–64). Ph .036; Th wall .001

Colorless, slight greenish blue tinge. Fragment of wall, no finished edge. Deep greenish blue trails applied in zigzag pattern. **Color Pl. 3C.**

205   (25–66). PH .031; D base knob .014

Pale green, rounded and flattened deep greenish blue blob forming base knob. Fragment of base and body. Pontil mark (D .008). Body apparently conical. **Fig. 4–26; Color Pl. 3C.**

Lid for Beaker (No. 206)

One fragment has been identified: it was found at the eastern edge of the excavated area. Such lids have been found with beaker-like vessels in tombs at northern sites such as Nahariya and Hanita,[103] and many were found in Cyprus.[104] The profiles show concave centers like ours but the rims bend much farther downward. Many bear painted figures, more rarely, painted inscriptions. Beakers for which such lids served have not been found at Jalame.

206   (306–65). D .08; Th at center .0015, at edge .001

Pale greenish blue, white weathering. Fragment preserving complete profile. Cut edge, slightly wheel-polished, no trace of decoration. **Fig. 4–26.**

Jugs and Bottles

Fragments of bottles and jugs are probably more numerous than those of any other kind of vessel, even

---

98. Saldern, *Sardis Glass*, 57, no. 323; 62, no. 384. Other examples shown do not have a spreading body like our fragments.
99. The reasons for calling these lamps rather than beakers is explained in Harden, *Karanis*, 155, and in a previous article, Crowfoot-Harden, "Lamps." There is also evidence for their use as beakers (see discussion below in connection with conical vessels with cracked-off rim).

100. Museum of Art and Archaeology, University of Missouri-Columbia, No. 70.186. Complete, mended. Pale green, deep greenish blue zigzag trail. H .16, D rim .087. Photo courtesy of the museum.
101. Harden, *Karanis*, 164, no. 465 (brownish yellow, with greenish base coil).
102. Ibid., nos. 466–68.
103. For Nahariya see Barag, "Nahariya Congress"; for Hanita see Barag, *Hanita*, 31–32 (nos. 68–69), including an extensive discussion of the origin of such lids (preferring the Phoenician coast as opposed to Cyprus) and offering a 3rd to mid-4th c. date.
104. Vessberg, "Cyprus Glass," 149–50, Type 1.

Fig. 4–26. Goblets, beakers, beaker lid. 1:2.

bowls. Ranging widely in size, they obviously had various uses. In view of the huge quantities of fragments and of the many ways in which rims, bodies, bases, and handles might be assembled, shapes can be reconstructed only tentatively. Wherever possible, complete vessels found in tombs at neighboring sites are cited as parallels. In many cases it is pointless to insist on definite resemblances; they may be valid or, on the contrary, misleading. A representative selection of the component parts of these vessels is offered here; few generalizations can be made.

In distinguishing jugs from bottles, the usual criteria—shape of body, base, and rim—are not sufficient. In general, only one feature is valid—a handle, as on a jug, or the absence of one, as on a bottle. When a handle is preserved or the rim broken in a way that suggests a handle had been present, the vessel is called a jug; when the rim is complete without a trace of a handle, the vessel is considered a bottle.

One kind of rim almost always belongs to a type of jug that is not common at the site. Few were found in the factory dump and some came from the wine press tank. A jug from Samaria shows the shape (Fig. 4–27).[105] The rim is rounded, sometimes slightly thickened or folded inward. The "funnel mouth" is decorated with a spiral thread (Nos. 207–16). The cylindrical neck spreads at the bottom, usually into a globular body (no complete profile is preserved). Long vertical bubbles in the neck show that it was pulled out from the parison. The handle is either a thick trail, circular in section, or a flat strap with ribbed outer surface (see Handles, below). The bottom seems to have been concave, without a definite base.

The material is in general quite good, the walls thin. The only impurities are in the handles and trails. Rim diameters vary from .045 to ca. .075 (some impossible to measure). The colors, in order of frequency, are greenish blue, green, olive green, colorless, and purple (the last three rare). The decorative trails are usually of the same color as the vessel. Exceptional are rims with dark greenish blue trails (No. 214). In some cases (possibly all) there is a thick trail around the lower part of the neck, and one

piece (No. 216)[106] has a trail wound around the entire length of rim and neck.

Jugs with a single thick trail beneath the rim (Nos. 217–28; for a complete example see Pl. 4–10)[107] are more numerous, and most were found in the factory dump. The rims, necks, and bodies are similar to those with spiral trails, but these jugs usually had bases rather than rounded bottoms. The rim diameters vary from .035 to .09. The colors are mainly green of various shades, fewer greenish blue, rarely brown, and, exceptionally, purple. The trails are usually the same color as the vessel, but some have dark greenish blue trails (Nos. 221–22) and one olive green rim has a light green trail (No. 227). There is also one purple rim with remains of a handle of the same color (No. 223; see also purple handles, Nos. 250–51). Two fragmentary jugs with single trail come from a tomb on the Mount of Olives.[108] Many jugs in museums are said to be from Syro-Palestinian sites; the dates assigned fit in well enough with our evidence. Some are from tombs that were in use for many years; others are attributed to definite periods on the basis of associated finds. Most of them are thought to be 4th c. products.[109]

Bases that can be attributed to jugs are of the folded or "pushed-in" variety. They may be formed from the first parison—that used to make the entire vessel—or from an added parison. In both cases a foot of some height is produced, with a hollow base-ring at the bottom. Most of the fragments came from the factory dump; a few were found in the wine press tank. The method of making a base by folding the first parison is shown in Fig. 3–11. When a second parison is added, the vessel floor is usually rather flat, while it is more likely to be convex when a single parison is used. There is considerable variation in the forms produced (compare Nos. 242–49 with Nos. 229–41), and it is impossible to be certain of the body and rim shape even by comparison with complete vessels.

105. Crowfoot, *Samaria 3*, 416, fig. 96,9 (H ca. .10). Barag, "Glass Vessels," Type 8.14–1, cites this jug as well as another (Iliffe, "El Bassa," 89, fig. 24) that Barag dates late 4th–early 5th c.

106. This kind of trailing is found on medieval glasses: see, e.g., Saldern, *Sardis Glass*, 102, no. 790, pls. 18, 28, and references given there. Our No. 216, however, is of the same material as other Jalame glass and is probably not later than the 5th c. Its context is not informative.

107. Corning Museum of Glass, no. 54.1.96. H .235. Photo courtesy of the museum.

108. Bagatti-Milik, 146, fig. 34, 15 and 17.

109. See, e.g., Hayes, *Toronto Glass*, 107–8, no. 397, said to be from Beth Shan; Auth, *Newark Glass*, no. 121, "from Syria."

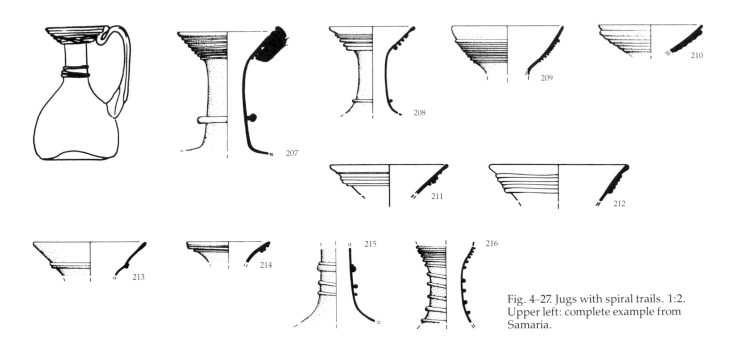

Fig. 4–27. Jugs with spiral trails. 1:2. Upper left: complete example from Samaria.

Jug Handles

The handles are of two kinds: ribbed strap handle (Nos. 250–56) and handle made of a thick trail, circular in section (Nos. 257–61). Strap handle fragments are numerous; some 25 were inventoried. Most were found scattered, not in the factory dump. Of various sizes, they are all essentially the same—a broad strip of glass drawn across a comb-like device to form vertical ribbing on the exterior. (The inside of the handle is always flat.) The bottom of the handle was first attached to the vessel at the shoulder or, if the shoulder is not well defined, above the widest part of the vessel. The strip is drawn up to the rim and attached to it or beneath it. At the upper end it is often looped back and forth several times so that it becomes thinner and trails off to a point. This elaborate finishing method obviates the need of shears to clip off the end (see Chap. 3). The lower ends of the handles range in width from .02 to .055.

The handles are of poorer quality glass than the vessels. They contain many long bubbles; there are also more impurities and the glass is sometimes streaked with another color. When part of the vessel wall is still attached to the bottom of the handle, its curve indicates that the jug was more or less globular. The colors of the handles are green (pale to light, sometimes streaked with yellow), greenish blue, dark greenish blue (two fragments), yellowish brown (one fragment), and purple (two examples, one attached to a purple body).

Trail handles were also found in quantity; most are incomplete. They were attached, like the strap handles, to the body of the jug and drawn up to the rim, which is presumed to have had a rounded lip and probably a funnel mouth. Most of the fragments were not found in the factory dump. In addition to the trail handles catalogued (Nos. 257–61) there are examples with other color combinations: dark greenish blue handle on a yellowish green body (90–66), olive green handle and body (125–64), pale green handle on a colorless body (191–64).

Jug Rims with Spiral Trail (Nos. 207–16)

207   (403–64). D rim .052

Light bluish green. Large black impurities in applied trails. Rounded, infolded rim. Trail of same color starting just below the lip, wound seven times around mouth. Thick, single trail around lower part of neck. Trail handle (probably circular in section) of same color. Found in wine press tank. **Fig. 4–27; Pl. 4–10.**

208   (39–64). D rim .046

Pale green. Rounded rim. Trail of same color wound seven times, starting at top. Single trail around base of neck. Large chip in rim suggests a wide strap handle. **Fig. 4–27; Pl. 4–10.**

209   (298–64). D rim .05

Pale green. Rounded rim. Trail of same color wound ten times, beginning at top. **Fig. 4–27; Pl. 4–10.**

210   (135A–64). D rim .052

Pale olive green. Rounded rim, trail of same color wound six times. **Fig. 4–27.**

211   (208–64). D rim .062

Light olive green. Rounded rim, trail of same color wound four times, starting at bottom. **Fig. 4–27.**

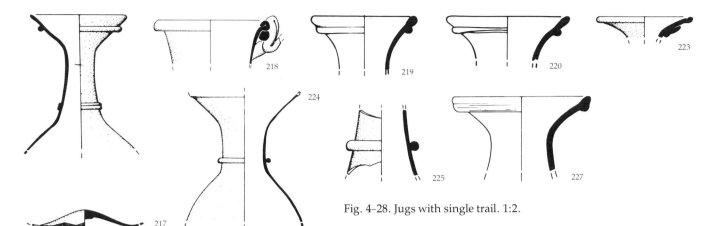

Fig. 4–28. Jugs with single trail. 1:2.

212 (155–64). D rim .07

Light greenish blue. Rounded rim. Trail of same color wound five times. Found near glass furnace. **Fig. 4–27.**

213 (156–64). D rim .06

Light greenish blue. Rounded rim, trail of same color wound twice around lower part of mouth. Found near furnace. **Fig. 4–27.**

214 (230–64). D rim .045

Light green. Rounded rim. Thin dark greenish blue trail wound twice just below the upper edge. A small fragment (442–64) has a dark greenish blue trail wound four times (D rim .045). **Fig. 4–27; Color Pl. 3C.**

215 (289–66). PH .037

Greenish blue. Cylindrical neck (rim missing) spreading into globular body. Trail of same color wound several times around neck. **Fig. 4–27.**

216 (79–65). PH .04

Light greenish blue. Funnel mouth, cylindrical neck (rim missing). Trail of same color wound around both, starting at base of neck. Probably globular body. **Fig. 4–27; Pl. 4–10.**

Single Trail (Nos. 217–28)

217 (22–66). D rim .05

Ten fragments of rim, body, and bottom. Yellowish brown. Rounded rim, funnel-shaped mouth, cylindrical neck spreading to globular body. Thickened floor with pontil mark (D .01). Trail of same color below the rim, double trail around base of neck. Break in rim suggests a handle. **Fig. 4–28; Pl. 4–10.**

218 (201–64). D rim ca. .05

Light yellowish green. Infolded rim, handle formed by thick trail of same color. **Fig. 4–28.**

219 (177–64). D rim ca. .056

Light green. Thickened, infolded rim. Trail of same color. Bit of handle preserved. **Fig. 4–28.**

220 (82–65). D rim .063

Light greenish blue. Trail of same color. This exceptionally thick fragment must come from an unusually large vessel. Breakage indicates a handle. **Fig. 4–28.**

221 (275–66). D rim .08

Pale bluish green. Rounded rim, dark greenish blue trail. From factory dump. **Pl. 4–10.**

222 (109–64). D rim .05

Pale bluish green. Rounded rim, dark greenish blue trail. **Pl. 4–10.**

223 (316–66). D rim .05

Dark purple. Infolded rim, trail of same color. This trail seems part of a handle. From factory dump. **Fig. 4–28.**

224 (100–64). D top .06

Pale greenish blue. Trace of trail at top, rim missing. Single trail of same color around base of neck. **Fig. 4–28.**

225 (197–64). PH .035

Light greenish blue. No finished edge, thick trail of same color near base of neck. **Fig. 4–28.**

226 (209–64). PH .035

Light bluish green. Thick dark greenish blue trail around lower part of neck. Body begins to spread out below. No edge preserved. **Pl. 4–10.**

227 (281–66). D rim .067

Olive green. Unweathered inside, white weathering outside. Thickened rim with light green trail. From factory dump. **Fig. 4–28.**

228 (240–64). D rim ca. .06

Pale olive green, handle light bluish green. Rounded rim with funnel mouth, single trail of same color. Fragment of handle, probably ribbed, attached to rim, looped down and up before descending to shoulder. **Pl. 4–10.**

Bases (Nos. 229–49)

229 (382–64). D base .062

Greenish blue. From wine press tank. **Fig. 4–29.**

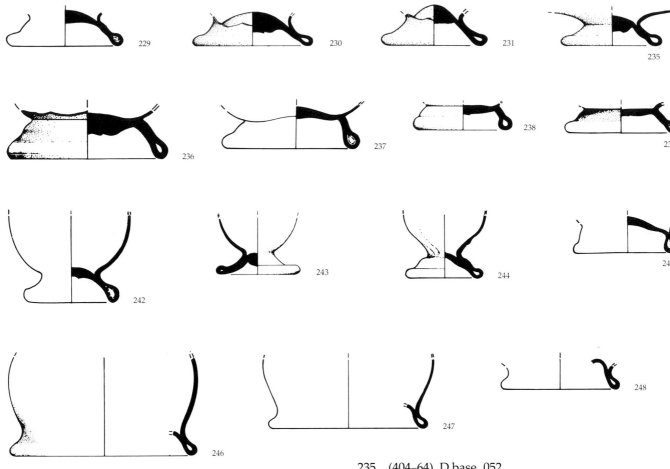

Fig. 4–29. Jugs—bases. 1:2.

230 (460–64). D base .061

Dark green, yellow streak. From wine press tank.
Fig. 4–29; Pl. 4–11.

231 (51–64). D base .055

Light green. Pontil scar (D .012) is dark greenish blue.
Fig. 4–29.

232 (436–66). D base .042

Colorless with green tinge. Dark weathering. Base
unusually high.

233 (63–65). D base .053

Green. Floor is convex. **Pl. 4–11.**

234 (365–64). D base .049

Yellowish brown, almost unweathered. **Pl. 4–11; Color
Pl. 4A.**

235 (404–64). D base .052

Light green with yellow streaks. From wine press tank.
Fig. 4–29; Pl. 4–11; Color Pl. 4A.

236 (80–64). D base .081

Light green with yellow streaks. Unusually thick floor
with circular protrusion beneath, large pontil mark (D
.0165). **Fig. 4–29.**

237 (102–64). D base .071

Olive green with yellow streaks. **Fig. 4–29; Color Pl.
4A.**

238 (377–64). D base .053

Light bluish green. **Fig. 4–29.**

239 (69–64). D base .06

Yellowish green. **Fig. 4–29.**

240 (114–66). D base .056

Greenish blue. The wall spreads widely and, at one
point, downward, showing distortion while vessel was
held on the pontil. Base is symmetrical. **Pl. 4–11.**

241 (144–65). D base .04

Light green. Pontil scar (D .01) is dark greenish blue.

242 (83–65). D base .05

Olive green. From factory dump. **Fig. 4–29; Pl. 4–11.**

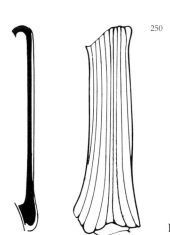
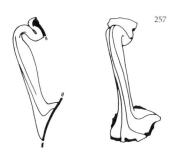

Fig. 4–30. No. 250, strap handle. Nos. 257–58, trail handles. 1:2.

243   (355–66). D base .043

Light bluish green. The base curves down and outward, unlike others of this type, where the base is convex and much narrower in proportion to the body. Pontil knock-off (D .014) with traces of iron oxide fills center of base. From factory dump. **Fig. 4–29; Pl. 4–11.**

244   (103–65). D base .042

Green. **Fig. 4–29; Pl. 4–11.**

245   (226–65). D base .05

Olive green. (Also Chap. 3, No. 8.) **Fig. 4–29.**

246   (64–66). D base ca. .10

Light green. **Fig. 4–29.**

247   (72–66). D base .086

Olive green. **Fig. 4–29.**

248   (380–66). D base .063

Light greenish blue. **Fig. 4–29.**

249   (65–66). D base ca. .075

Light olive green. **Fig. 4–29.**

Strap Handles (Nos. 250–56)

250   (433–64). PL .11

Purple. Flat, multiple-ribbed handle, top broken off. Bottom finished, still attached to globular body fragment of same color. **Fig. 4–30; Pl. 4–11.**

251   (329–66). PL .068

Streaky purple. Same as preceding, top broken off. Bottom finished, still attached to globular body fragment of same color. **Pl. 4–11.**

252   (20–66). PL .036

Streaky dark greenish blue. Same as preceding. None of body preserved. **Pl. 4–11.**

253   (154–65). PL .07

Light green. Same as preceding, top broken off. Bottom finished, attached to globular body fragment of same color. **Pl. 4–11.**

254   (9–66). PL .051

Greenish blue with yellow streak. Same as preceding. Bottom finished, attached to quite large globular body of same color. **Pl. 4–11.**

255   (158–64). PL .042

Light green. Same as preceding. Bottom finished, attached to large globular body of same color. **Pl. 4–11.**

256   (7–65). PL .039

Light greenish blue. Similar to preceding. **Pl. 4–11.**

Trail Handles (Nos. 257–61)

257   (371–64). PH .067

Greenish blue with yellow streak. Traces of infolded rim, funnel mouth, globular body. Trail handle attached to body, pulled up to rim and folded (see discussions above for inventoried pieces). **Fig. 4–30; Pl. 4–12.**

258   (100–65). PH .057

Greenish blue with yellow streaks. Trail, circular in section, attached to body, pulled up and folded (end broken off). **Fig. 4–30; Pl. 4–12** (2 views).

259   (145–65). PL .057

Light and dark greenish blue with red streak. Trail drawn up toward rim from pale greenish blue globular body. **Pl. 4–12.**

260   (105–66). PL .065

Greenish blue with yellow streak. Trail attached to globular body and drawn up toward rim. **Pl. 4–12.**

261   (421–64). PL .065

Light greenish blue. Trail drawn up toward rim from globular body of same color. From wine press tank. **Pl. 4–12.**

Bottles with Globular Body, Single Trail (Nos. 262–71)

Fragments of these have been found in quantity, but only the rims are easily recognized. There are several

Fig. 4–31. Bottles, funnel mouth, single trail. 1:2.

varieties. Pl. 4–12[110] shows the type with rounded rim and single trail beneath it (Nos. 262–71). The long cylindrical neck joins the presumably globular body without a constriction. There is no base; the bottom usually has a kick (see n. 112 below).

Fragments were found mostly in the factory dump. The rim sizes extend from .04 to .09, with concentration around .06–.07. The colors are as usual, but in somewhat different proportions from vessels of other shapes. There are a considerable number of colorless fragments, and more green (yellowish, olive, light green) than bluish green. Purple and brown are rare.

Slight variations in the rim can be noted: No. 262 is partly folded inward; this may have been unintentional. The type is found in Samaria, but identical bottles do not seem plentiful.[111] No. 271, with a vertical rim, is an odd variation.

The bottoms that can be assigned to large globular bottles range in diameter from .05 to .10, but these measurements are rather meaningless, since the angle of the wall determines the size of the bottle. The bottoms are generally concave and thickened in the middle. The walls, insofar as they are preserved, are extremely thin; it is impossible to restore an entire vessel unless the fragments are found in a relatively confined area (as in No. 273, from the wine press tank). Where the middle of the bottom is preserved, there is generally a pontil mark (D .009–.015). Since these fragments are nearly impossible to photograph or draw, a few representative pieces are listed.[112]

262   (27–64). D rim .07

Pale green. Rounded rim, partly folded inward, funnel

mouth, trace of cylindrical neck. Single trail of same color. **Fig. 4–31; Pl. 4–12.**

263   (192–64). D rim .054

Light green. Rounded, thickened rim, funnel mouth. Single trail of same color. **Fig. 4–31; Pl. 4–12.**

264   (164–64). D rim .052

Pale bluish green. Rounded, outsplayed rim, funnel mouth, probably cylindrical neck. Trail of same color wound twice. **Fig. 4–31; Pl. 4–12.**

265   (481–66). D rim .085

Three joining fragments. Greenish blue, small horizontal bubbles in rim. Weathered inside only. Single trail of same color. Broken edge below trail seems finished—probably cracked in annealing. From factory dump, near bedrock. **Fig. 4–31.**

266   (29–65). D rim .06

Light green. Infolded rim, funnel mouth, single trail of same color. **Pl. 4–12.**

267   (502–65). D rim ca. .06

Greenish blue body; light green trail. From factory dump. **Pl. 4–12.**

268   (315–66). D rim unknown

Yellowish green. Single trail of same color. **Pl. 4–12.**

269   (416–66). D rim .09

Yellowish green. Single trail of same color. From factory dump. **Pl. 4–12.**

270   (359–66). D rim ca. .11

Light bluish green. Single trail, vessel and trail both thin. From factory dump. **Pl. 4–12.**

271   (453–64). D rim .046

Light green. Rounded rim bending in sharply. Thick trail of same color just below rim. An unusually small specimen. **Fig. 4–31.**

Globular Bottles with Conical Neck (Nos. 272–83)

The number of examples found is hard to calculate; while the rim and neck are distinctive, the countless body fragments may belong to various shapes.

The typical bottle has a rounded rim, sometimes thickened, a long conical neck, and a globular body with rounded bottom, often slightly concave. There is sometimes a constriction at the base of the neck (perhaps more common on small bottles) or the transition from neck to body may lack a distinct division. There is no

110. Rockefeller Museum, Jerusalem, No. 1094. H. .295. Provenience not recorded. Photo courtesy of the museum.
111. Barag, "Glass Vessels," Type 15.17–1. The Samaria example cited by Barag (Crowfoot, *Samaria* 3, 409, fig. 94,8) was restored from nearly a hundred fragments. The height is not recorded, but a similar one from Hebron, .25 high, is mentioned. The Samaria bottle was dated 3rd c., but Barag believes the type is late 3rd c. or early 4th, and the Jalame evidence extends the date into the second half of the 4th c. Similar evidence is provided by a fragmentary bottle found in Portugal: Alarcão, *Conimbriga* 6, 197, no. 234, pl. 43, "moss green," from a 350–400 context.
112. Bottoms of large globular bottles: 67–65, D ca. .10, concave, pontil D .013, brown; 295–64, Max dim .08, concave, pontil D .01, light greenish blue; 114–64, D ca. .075, concave, pontil D .011, light yellowish green; 424–66, D ca. .075, concave, pontil D .009, light greenish blue (from factory dump); 368–64, D ca. .05, slightly concave, pontil D .015, light green, tiny dark greenish blue blob on exterior (from factory dump); 326–64, D .055, flat bottom, thickened convex floor, pontil D .012, light green; 162–65, D ca. .06, slightly concave, no pontil, pale greenish blue (very large bottle); 454–64, D ca. .07, concave, no pontil, uniform thickness throughout (.0015).

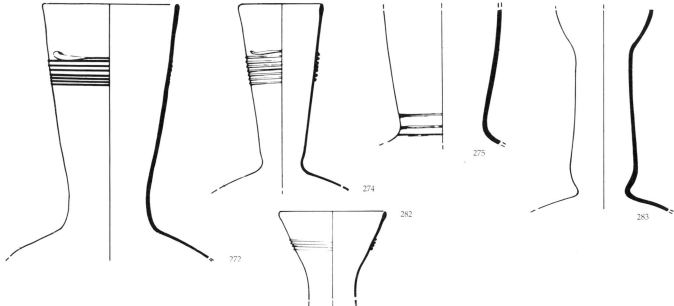

Fig. 4-32. Bottles with conical neck. 1:2.

added base. The sizes of these bottles have been calculated as between .20 and .30 or as much as .40 in height. The rim diameters range from .024 to .08, concentrated between .055 and .07.

The quality of the glass is like that of common Jalame products, but the walls are especially thin, and white weathering is usually seen. The colors are greenish blue or yellowish green, green, olive green, and less often, colorless.

Decoration, when present, consists of a fine trail of the same color wound around the neck fairly near the top. The number of winds varies between four and ten. When decoration is absent or not preserved on the rim fragment, it is possible that the bottle may have been of a different shape, or the vessel may have been a cup. The rim diameters of small cups and large bottles are very close.

Many more rims and necks without trails were noted than those so decorated. Those with trails are usually of thin greenish blue glass. Comparatively few of these were found in the factory dump, while a considerable number came from the wine press tank, possibly indicating that they were not made at the site. In the factory dump were numerous rims and necks of slightly thicker glass, more often yellowish green and green than greenish blue, many apparently undecorated. In the general area (neither dump nor tank) the various kinds seemed to appear at random.

The shape is not frequently found in publications. The closest parallels come from Beth Shearim catacombs.[113]

Other more or less similar bottles have been found at Nazareth, Samaria, Jerusalem, and Gezer, while still others from Egypt and Cyprus resemble this Jalame type in a general way.[114]

Bottles with a cylindrical trail-decorated neck contracting sharply at the lower part have appeared at a number of sites,[115] but none has been found at Jalame. While the body and bottom are like our bottles, the upper part is quite different. This shape has been dated very late 4th and 5th c. Nos. 282–83 vary from the usual Jalame type.[116]

272 (435–64). D rim .07

Light bluish green. Rounded rim. Trail of same color wound eight times around neck starting at top. **Fig. 4–32; Pl. 4–13.**

273 (413–64). D bottom ca. .13

Rim missing. Pale greenish blue. From wine press tank. **Pl. 4–13.**

274 (260–64). D rim .045

Light bluish green. Rounded rim. Trail of same color wound around neck eight times starting at top. **Fig. 4–32; Pl. 4–13.**

114. References to all these are given in Avigad as in n. 113 above. None seems exactly like the Jalame examples.

115. Barag, "Glass Vessels," Type 15.29–1, found at Beth Shan, Gerasa, Bet Yerah, and other sites.

116. No. 282 resembles Barag, "Glass Vessels," Type 15.20, from the Mount of Olives (Bagatti-Milik, 143, fig. 33, no. 24) and is believed by Barag to date late 4th or early 5th c. For No. 283 see Barag, "Glass Vessels," Type 15.17. Examples are cited from Kfar Dikhrin (L. Y. Rahmani, "Mirror-Plaques," 52, fig. 2:1), Gerasa, Bet Yerah, and Shavei Zion. They are all thought to date, at earliest, 5th c. A fragment from Khirbet Shema (Meyers, *Khirbet Shema*, pl. 8.6, no. 7) is dated by context as late 1st to mid-3rd c.

113. See Barag in Avigad, *Beth Shearim* 3, 203, nos. 32–34, fig. 98; also Barag, "Glass Vessels," Type 15.13.

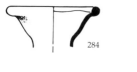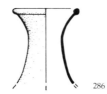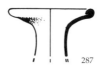

Fig. 4–33. Bottles with infolded rim. 1:2.

275   (339–64). PH .075

Pale greenish blue. Rim not preserved. A very large bottle, probably more than .30 high. **Fig. 4–32.**

276   (335–64). D rim .062

Light greenish blue. Rounded rim. Trail of same color starting .044 below rim, wound nine times. From wine press tank. **Pl. 4–13.**

277   (376–64). D rim ca. .065

Light greenish blue. Rounded rim. Single trail of same color .051 below rim. **Pl. 4–13.**

278   (185–64). D of rims .057, .06, .07; Th rims .001–.002; D of pontil mark on fragment of bottom .01

Fragments of at least four bottles: rims and necks, bodies, one fragment of bottom. All pale greenish blue. Rounded rims, trails of same color wound six or eight times. **Pl. 4–13.**

279   (22–64, 338–64). D rim .051

Light greenish blue. Rounded rim. Trail of same color wound six times around neck, starting at top. **Pl. 4–13.**

280   (247–64). D rim .05

Pale green. Thickened, rounded rim. Trail of same color around neck. **Pl. 4–13.**

281   (98–65). D rim .05

Pale greenish blue. Rounded rim. Trail of same color wound around neck five times. **Pl. 4–13.**

282   (227–65). D rim .055

Pale yellowish green. Tiny bubbles. Rounded rim, long funnel mouth, short cylindrical neck beginning to spread into body. Trail of same color wound four times. **Fig. 4–32.**

283   (115–65). PH .11; Th wall .002 -.003

No edge preserved. Greenish blue, small elongated bubbles in neck, little weathering; limey encrustation inside. Funnel mouth, long cylindrical neck flaring and then contracting before spreading into globular form. **Fig. 4–32; Pl. 4–13.**

Bottles with Infolded Rim (Nos. 284–88)

This rim type occurs in some quantity, but the vessel shapes cannot be reconstructed. The examples shown have flaring rims from .03 to .05 in diameter; the body shapes undoubtedly varied greatly. A bottle from a Samaria tomb is globular,[117] but other shapes could be cited: tall flasks, some possibly with mold-blown ribbing on the body. The infolded rim occurs both early and late, and in many areas, east and west.

Our fragments were found both in the factory dump and in other parts of the site; No. 288 is dated by context to the pre-factory period.

284   (371–66). D rim .05

Light green, heavy brownish weathering. Infolded rim, funnel mouth. From factory dump. **Fig. 4–33.**

285   (102–65). D rim .04

Pale green, tiny bubbles, white weathering. Infolded rim, funnel mouth. From factory dump. **Fig. 4–33.**

286   (270–65). D rim .035

Greenish blue. Tiny bubbles and black impurities. Infolded rim, funnel mouth, short neck spreading to rounded body. **Fig. 4–33.**

287   (82–64). D rim .045

Greenish blue. Infolded rim flaring from cylindrical neck. **Fig. 4–33.**

288   (350–66). Est D rim .062

Purple. Long horizontal bubble in rim, dark weathering. Infolded, flaring rim. Context before 351. **Fig. 4–33.**

Cf. No. 93, a bowl with similar rim, from pre–351 context.

Bottles with Ribbed Rim (Nos. 289–92)

Only six fragments with this distinctive type of rim were found, all but No. 289 in the factory dump. The measurable rim diameters range from .075 to .086; these vessels are quite large.

A number were found at Beth Shearim;[118] complete examples have long cylindrical necks, piriform or conical bodies, and are .20 or more in height. A similar bottle of about the same height with a more pronounced rib was found at Rosh Ha-ayin in a 250–350 context.[119] Possibly this type of rim antedates the Jalame factory, but there is not enough evidence from the find spots of the fragments to verify this supposition.

117. Crowfoot, *Samaria* 3, 410, fig. 94, 10, assigned to the 3rd c. but probably 4th.

118. Barag in Avigad, *Beth Shearim* 3, 198, 200, nos. 1–10, all from Catacomb 20.

119. Eitan, "Rosh Ha-ayin," fig. 13,9.

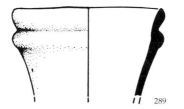  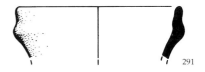 

Fig. 4–34. Bottles with ribbed rim. 1:2.

289 (109–65). D rim .08

Light green, large, long bubbles, white weathering. **Fig. 4–34; Pl. 4–14.**

290 (478–66). D rim .075

Pale green, a few bubbles, blowing spirals, no weathering. **Fig. 4–34.**

291 (460–66). D rim ca. .086

Light olive green, tiny bubbles, very little weathering. **Fig. 4–34.**

292 (191–65). D uncertain

Light greenish blue, tiny bubbles, some impurities, white weathering. **Fig. 4–34.**

Large Bottles (Nos. 293–301)

Large bottles with only rim fragments preserved (D .06–.09), although found in quantity, are impossible to restore with certainty. Nos. 293–301 are representative. Some were found in the factory dump, others around the site, none in the wine press tank. The rims are usually rounded, sometimes thickened, occasionally folded inward (Nos. 296, 299). The only indication of the form of the body is afforded by No. 301. Quite a few fragments of this kind were found, some in the factory dump. A parallel is offered by an incomplete bottle from Beth Shearim,[120] which has the ribbed rim seen on Nos. 289–92. No. 301 probably had such a rim.

In color, quality of material, and weathering, there is nothing notable about these large bottles; probably they were produced in the factory. The quantities of body fragments that cannot be assigned to any shape are sufficient to restore hundreds of such bottles.

293 (120–65). D rim .07

Yellowish green, a few tiny bubbles, blowing spirals, patches of white weathering. Thickened, rounded rim; nearly vertical wall tapering slightly. Another (402–66) is almost identical; both come from the factory dump. **Fig. 4–35.**

294 (305–65). D rim ca. .09

Pale greenish blue, tiny bubbles, blowing spirals, slight weathering. Thickened, rounded rim; nearly vertical wall tapering slightly. **Fig. 4–35.**

295 (284–65). D rim .07

Light greenish blue, many bubbles, white weathering. Thickened rim, wall tapering slightly. **Fig. 4–35.**

296 (431–64). D rim .078

Light greenish blue, tiny bubbles, surface dulled. Uneven infolded rim, neck tapering slightly. **Fig. 4–35.**

297 (78–65). D rim .06

Greenish blue, a few impurities, blowing spirals, some white weathering. Rounded rim, almost vertical wall bulging slightly. Trail of same color .032 below rim. **Fig. 4–35; Pl. 4–14.**

298 (272, 303–64). D rim .07

Yellowish green, many large bubbles. Thickened, rounded rim, conical neck. **Fig. 4–35; Pl. 4–14.**

299 (23–65). D rim .06

Light green, blowing spirals. Slightly flaring infolded rim, long tapering neck spreading to bulbous body. **Fig. 4–35; Pl. 4–14.**

300 (14–64). D rim .06

Yellowish green, small bubbles, blowing spirals, white weathering. Rounded rim, tapering wall. An identical fragment (360–64) comes from the factory dump. **Fig. 4–35.**

301 (451–66). PH .05

Five fragments, two joining (some possibly from another bottle). Light olive green, a few bubbles, blowing spirals, slight weathering and pitting. Small part of neck, rounded shoulder and slightly tapering body. From the factory dump. **Fig. 4–35; Pl. 4–14.**

Small Bottles and Flasks (Nos. 302–40)

Small globular bottles are difficult to recognize because few restorable pieces were found. Bottles with flared and infolded rims (Nos. 302–5) occur throughout the first four centuries A.C. No. 305 is datable to the 1st c. because of its dark blue color, and No. 304 also seems of that period.[121] Hardly any such rim fragments were found in the factory dump. Nos. 307–8, lacking rims, may be of somewhat different shape, but the bottom of No. 307 is presumably the norm for most globular and piriform bottles. While rim fragments are few, bottoms

120. Barag in Avigad, *Beth Shearim* 3, 200, no. 10, fig. 97, 14, from Catacomb 20.

121. Perhaps from long-necked unguentaria. See Barag, "Glass Vessels," Type 21.1; Eitan, "Rosh Ha-ayin," fig. 12,1.

of these bottles are numerous (at least 100), the great majority found in the factory dump. Various kinds of rims must have been used, mostly the simple rounded rim that is hard to identify. The colors are usually bluish green, yellowish green, and olive green, but 18 of them, with diameters .03–.04, are colorless, and 4 are purple. Among those catalogued, Nos. 313–16 may be late 1st to early 2nd c., and No. 317 is certainly 1st c.

A few fragmentary small bottles that were not globular are Nos. 318–20. The first two are typical of the 1st c. in material and form; the last may also be earlier than the factory. None was found in a helpful context.

Of long tubular flasks only bottoms (about 15 in all) were identified. Nos. 321–24 are characteristic. The form is simple, finishing with a slightly flared rim, sometimes folded but not carefully finished, most without a pontil mark. Such flasks were made from the 1st c. onward:[122] No. 324 comes from a pre–351 context; almost all the others are from the factory dump. The fragments are too few to assume they were made at Jalame.

Another kind of tubular flask, ending in a long solid drop, is rare at Jalame. The type is usually ascribed to the 1st or 2nd c.; a longer life seems doubtful. Only bottoms have been identified (Nos. 325–26). The long graceful body may rise to a rounded, folded, or cracked-off rim— these varieties have been found at various places: Cyprus,[123] Greece,[124] and the Black Sea coast.[125] The Jalame fragments indicate a body spreading evenly upward, while others are more bulbous. Still other such fragments are from amphoriskoi,[126] but this shape seems unlikely for our fragments.

The spindle- or pipette-shaped flask is a common 4th c. form in both East and West.[127] The type is well described by Harden,[128] who considers it Syrian rather than Egyptian, although it has been found in Egypt (not at Karanis).

A variation on this shape is No. 327, unique at the site. This flask has a large bulb at the bottom and expands at the middle; the top is missing. Similar flasks show a roughly cracked-off top (Fig. 4–37). Published examples (none with any context) are: one (and a fragment) in Cairo,[129] four (two fragmentary) in Aquileia,[130] one in

Newark,[131] two in Pittsburgh.[132] Sixteen such flasks (unpublished) were found in a grave at El Makr (east of Akko). The curious way in which the tops of the vessels are broken (unlike the more common pipette-shaped flasks) suggests these may have been sealed, then broken to release the contents. The contents may have been a medicinal liquid of a measured quantity, as the flasks are all approximately the same height. No. 327, if complete, would be about .30 high.

Nos. 328–29, although quite different from each other, may both be bottoms of amphoriskoi. Too little of either is preserved for certainty, and neither comes from a significant context.[133] No. 330, similar in shape to No. 329, has two applied trails; no parallel has been noted. It was found near the furnace in a context contemporary with the factory.

For No. 331 the only parallel thus far noted is a jug auctioned in 1979, dated 2nd–3rd c.[134]

No. 332 is one of a number of early rims that turned up on the site—one of the tall unguentaria common in the 2nd c.[135] Two others (479–66, 429–66, uncatalogued) are of greenish blue glass; the first was on the surface, the second in a pre–351 context.

No. 333, a small folded base, also is from an early vessel, perhaps a jug.

No. 334 is unique, the complete shape uncertain. No parallel has been found.

Fragments of vessels with tooled indentations have been found at Jalame in some quantity, but most of them are very small. The technique was common all over the ancient world from the 1st c. onward,[136] used to decorate beakers, jars, and bottles. Two partly restorable bottles (Nos. 335–36) were found, and other fragments perhaps from beakers (e.g., 160–64, olive green), but it is unlikely that any were made at Jalame. Exact parallels are few and the dates given do not correspond with ours.[137]

Cosmetic flasks were not in the factory's repertory, but various types were found. No. 337, of which only the base

122. E.g., Eitan, "Rosh Ha-ayin," fig. 13,5.

123. Vessberg, "Cyprus Glass," 141, pl. 9, no. 30.

124. E. Dusenbery, "Ancient Glass from the Cemeteries of Samothrace," *JGS* 9 (1967) 44, no. 32, "Augustan context"; Davidson, *Corinth* 12, 106, no. 673, 1st c. context.

125. Bucovală, *Sticlă*, 132–33, no. 274, assigned to 1st c.; B. Filarska, Skła *Starozytne* (Warsaw, 1952) 212, no. 294, pl. 49,1 (found at Phanagoria).

126. Barag, "Glass Vessels," Type 10.1, from Sidon, 1st–2nd c.

127. Ibid., Type 22.4; Isings, *Roman Glass*, Form 105.

128. Harden, *Karanis*, 268: "roughly the shape of a pipette with a biconical or bulbous widening in the centre of a tubular body. The rim is plain or folded, and at the bottom of the vase there is usually a slight bulb."

129. Edgar, *Glass*, 60, no. 32691, pl. 8, almost colorless, H .315. No. 32692 preserves only the bulb at the bottom.

130. M. C. Calvi, *I Vetri romani del Museo di Aquileia* (Aquileia, 1968) 152, no. 325, pl. O, no. 2; 24, no. 5 (grayish blue, H .33, .26). These flasks are in

the Pucailovich Collection, donated to the museum in 1955. No information is given concerning this collection. Calvi remarks that she knows no other examples of this shape.

131. Auth, *Newark Glass*, 117, no. 141, colorless with blue tinge, H .356.

132. A. Oliver, Jr., *Ancient Glass in the Carnegie Museum of Natural History, Pittsburgh* (Pittsburgh, 1980) 85, nos. 112–13, both pale green, H. .32, .31.

133. For a possible parallel see Barag, "Glass Vessels," Type 10.2 (from Emesa). For a full discussion of amphoriskos types see Stern, *Custodia*, 82–86, no. 23, pl. 8. For no. 329 see Barag, "Glass Vessels," Type 10.4–1, from Beit Fajjar (*QDAP* 4, pl. 85, 4).

134. *Catalogue of the Constable-Maxwell Collection of Ancient Glass* (London, 1979) 98, no. 160 (H .063, "a pale aubergine glass jug . . . with spherical body, tapering neck, wide trefoil lip and straight handle, with narrow pointed base, the handle and rim in pale green glass."

135. Barag, "Glass Vessels," Type 21.

136. Isings, *Roman Glass*, Form 32 (beakers) and references given there to vessels found in Cyprus, at Karanis, and in the West.

137. For No. 335 cf. Vessberg, "Cyprus Glass," 135, pl. 7, no. 42; Bagatti, "Museo Francescano," 229, fig. 4,104, from Beth Shan. For No. 336 the nearest parallel seems to be a bottle found at Amman, dated 3rd c. by context: Harding, "Jebel Jofeh," 91, no. 340, pl. 29.

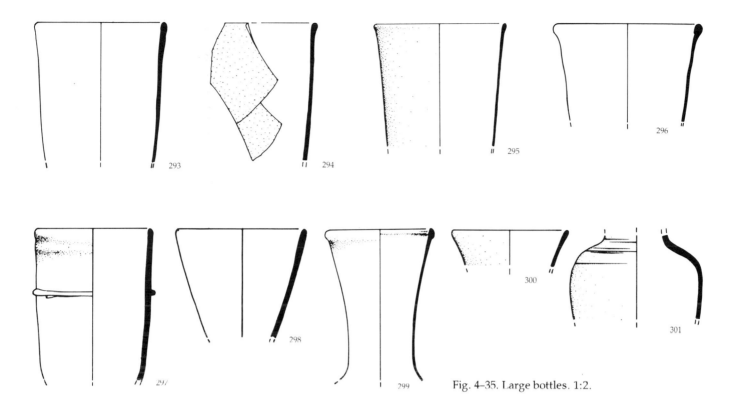

Fig. 4-35. Large bottles. 1:2.

was found, is quite common in the region but rare at Jalame.[138]

Of the double tube flasks, only two fragments were found: part of a rim (No. 338, near the surface) and part of a bottom (No. 339, in the factory dump). It is impossible to tell whether either had handles or decorative trails. The type has been discussed exhaustively by E. Stern,[139] who demonstrates that it was exclusively a Palestinian product, not manufactured in Syria. Two fragments were found in the Beth Shearim catacombs; in connection with these Barag discusses the development of the type from the early 4th through the 6th c.[140] It is interesting that none has been found in the tombs of Hanita or Nahariya,[141] and not many on the coast. Inland and in Transjordan they are common: Megiddo, Samaria, Beth Shan, Gezer, and other sites have produced examples.[142]

One fragment of a lentoid flask was found (No. 340) in a context not closely datable. Such flasks had short narrow necks and often two handles, like the pottery flasks

from which they were derived. Barag has collected the published examples from excavations;[143] the earliest is from Huqoq, found in a late 1st- early 2nd c. context;[144] others date to the 3rd or 4th c. They occur at various Palestinian sites but are not common.[145] Barag notes a resemblance to a flask engraved on the large Beth Shearim plate.[146]

Rims and Bodies

302 (25-64). D rim .021

Dark greenish blue, long bubbles, blowing spirals, white weathering. Slightly flaring rim folded inward, long neck spreading toward body. **Fig. 4-36; Pl. 4-14.**

303 (75-66). D rim .025

Pale green, heavy black weathering. Fragment of rim and neck. Slightly flaring rim folded inward, short cylindrical neck spreading to body. From factory dump. **Fig. 4-36.**

304 (59-66). D rim .015

Pale green. Rim and fragment of neck. Flaring rim folded inward. 1st c. **Fig. 4-36.**

138. See Barag in Avigad, *Beth Shearim* 3, 202, fig. 97, no. 26, and references to others from Palestine. Barag mentions a flask found at Dura that establishes the beginning of this type as not later than mid-3rd c.

139. Stern, *Custodia*, 115–18, no. 35.

140. Barag in Avigad, *Beth Shearim* 3, 201, nos. 22–23. No. 22 was found in the same context as the engraved plate (ibid., 207, 209–13).

141. See Barag, "Glass Vessels," Type 12.

142. See Stern, as in n. 139, for references. In Transjordan two undecorated double flasks, with their spatulas, were found in tombs: see J. B. Hennessy in "Preliminary Report on the 1979 Season of the Sydney-Wooster Joint Expedition to Pella," *ADAJ* 24 (1980) 33, pl. 14.

143. Barag, "Glass Vessels," Type 9. To these can now be added Erdmann, "Mezad Tamar," 103, no. 98. Eastern and Western parallels are given in Barag's n. 52.

144. Kahane, "Huqoq," 135, no. 21.

145. For a flask without handles see Bagatti-Milik, 144, fig. 34, no. 6. The tomb in which it was found is dated by lamps mid-3rd to mid-4th c.

146. Avigad, *Beth Shearim* 3, 211, fig. 100, but it may not be of lentoid shape.

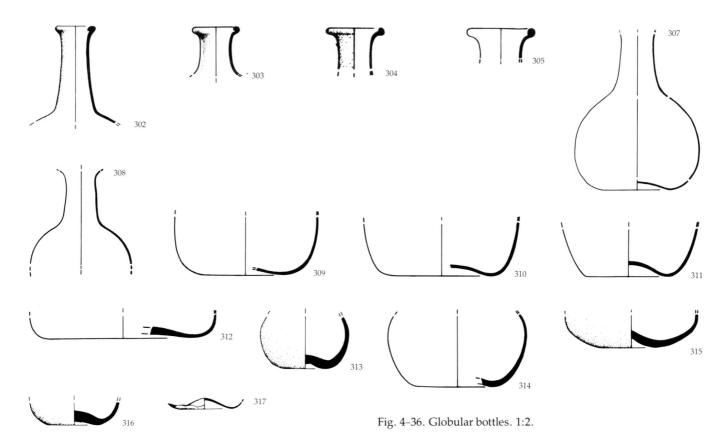

Fig. 4–36. Globular bottles. 1:2.

305 (323–66). D rim .035

Dark blue, dark weathering. Fragment of rim and neck. Flaring rim folded inward. From factory dump. 1st c. **Fig. 4–36.**

One other dark blue rim fragment (366–66), Est D .05, probably dates to the 1st c.

306 (207–64). D at base of neck .023

Greenish blue, blowing spirals. Short cylindrical neck, flaring slightly toward the rim (not preserved) spreading at bottom. Rim probably like preceding. **Pl. 4–14.**

307 (516–64). PH .085

Pale greenish blue with yellow streak. Long bubbles in neck, slight weathering. Almost entire profile. Cylindrical neck, splaying toward rim (not preserved), globular body, concave bottom, no pontil mark. **Fig. 4–36.**

308 (111–64, 251–64). PH .052

Greenish blue, white weathering. Flaring rim (lip not preserved), cylindrical neck, globular body, very thin wall. **Fig. 4–36.**

Bottoms

309 (218–65). D bottom ca. .05

Light green, many bubbles, slight white weathering.

Slightly concave bottom. Pontil mark not preserved. **Fig. 4–36.**

310 (378–66). D bottom ca. .06

Pale green with yellow streak. Blowing spirals, white weathering and pitting. Concave bottom, no pontil mark. From factory dump. **Fig. 4–36.**

311 (312–64). D bottom ca. .045

Pale green, few bubbles, slight weathering. Concave bottom, no pontil mark. From wine press tank. **Fig. 4–36.**

312 (376a–66). D base ca. .08

Light olive green, white weathering. Slightly concave base, no pontil mark preserved. From factory dump. **Fig. 4–36.**

313 (268–64). D bottom ca. .036

Partly light green, partly yellowish brown, tiny bubbles, white weathering. Concave bottom, quite thick, pontil mark (D .008). Wall thins toward top of fragment. 1st or 2nd c. **Fig. 4–36.**

314 (379–66). D bottom ca. .044

Light greenish blue, many tiny bubbles, white weathering. Slightly concave, thickened bottom. Pontil mark not preserved. Wall thins as it curves upward. 1st or 2nd c. **Fig. 4–36.**

315   (382–66). D bottom ca. .035

Dark greenish blue, a few tiny bubbles, dark weathering. Thickened base with kick. Pontil mark (D .009). From pre–351 context, 1st or 2nd c. **Fig. 4–36.**

316   (433–66). D bottom ca. .03

Light green, tiny bubbles, white weathering. Thickened bottom, slightly concave, with pontil mark (D .01). 1st or 2nd c. **Fig. 4–36.**

317   (98–64). D bottom ca. .035

Dark blue, white weathering and pitting. Bottom and part of body. Bottom slightly concave, no pontil mark. Probably globular body. 1st c. **Fig. 4–36.**

318   (236–64). PH .03

Deep blue, tiny bubbles, white weathering. Fragment of bottom and body. Slightly flattened bottom; wall curves into rounded form. Trace of pontil mark. 1st c. **Fig. 4–37.**

319   (140–64). Th bottom .007

Olive green, tiny bubbles. Bottom and part of body. Thickened, flattened bottom with remains of pontil wad. Body probably piriform. **Fig. 4–37.**

320   (90–64). Th wall .003

Light green. Fragment of bottom and body. Thickened bottom, concave, pontil mark. Body probably piriform. **Fig. 4–37.**

Tubular Flasks

321   (92–65). PH .06

Light green, long vertical bubbles, small impurities, iridescence. No pontil mark. From factory dump. **Fig. 4–37; Pl. 4–14.**

322   (292–66). PH .049

Yellowish brown, tiny long bubbles, white weathering. Similar to preceding. From factory dump. **Pl. 4–14.**

323   (114–65). PH .025; Th of wall .003 (thicker than the others)

Greenish blue, long bubbles, slight iridescence. No pontil mark. From factory dump. **Fig. 4–37.**

324   (375–66). PH .03

Light greenish blue, white weathering. No pontil mark. Pre–351 context. **Fig. 4–37.**

Miscellaneous Flasks

325   (95–65). PH .045

Light green, iridescence, pitting. No pontil mark. **Fig. 4–37; Pl. 4–14.**

326   (351–64). PH .04

Colorless, green tinge, dark weathering. No pontil mark. **Fig. 4–37.**

327   (390–64). PH .135

Pale greenish blue, long vertical bubbles. Nine joining

fragments of body. Bulb-like bottom (no pontil mark) constricting and then spreading upward. From wine press tank. **Fig. 4–37; Pl. 4–14.**

328   (62–65). PH .056

Pale green, small bubbles, heavy white weathering. Two joining fragments. Thickened bottom, slightly flattened, pontil mark (D ca. .01). Wall spreads into conical form. **Fig. 4–37.**

329   (86–65). PH .031; Th wall .005

Light green, large and small bubbles. Solid conical bottom contracting to somewhat thinner wall, no pontil mark. This may be an amphoriskos, a fairly large vessel since bottom is heavy. **Fig. 4–37.**

330   (311–64). PH .032

Pale green. Fragment, no finished edge. Pointed bottom spreading upward into uncertain form. Two dark greenish blue horizontal trails. **Fig. 4–37; Color Pl. 3C.**

331   (1–65). PH .029; Th at top of fragment .008

Fragment of bottom and wall. Olive green, solid material, white weathering. Pointed bottom, body globular. Found on surface. **Fig. 4–37.**

332   (128–66). D rim .053

Colorless with faint green tinge, unweathered. Fragment of rim and neck. Rounded rim folded in (with air space) and flattened to form horizontal surface. Neck probably cylindrical. From factory dump. 2nd c. **Fig. 4–37.**

333   (447–66). D base .037

Pale bluish green. Fragment of base and body. Pushed-out base, somewhat irregular, concave bottom. From factory dump. Pre–351 context. **Fig. 4–37.**

334   (349–66). PH .007, D rim .035

Pale green. Fragment, rim and neck. Hollow rim formed by dark greenish blue tube applied to rim. Neck probably cylindrical. Pre–351 context. **Fig. 4–37.**

Bottles with Indents

335   (182–64). PH .073; D bottom .05

Greenish blue, small bubbles. Bottom and part of body. Concave bottom, thickened at center. Pontil mark (D .01). Series of tooled indentations (perhaps ten) on lower part of body. A fragment (160–64) is similar but may be from a beaker. **Fig. 4–37.**

336   (429–64). PH .058

Pale greenish blue. Many joining fragments of neck and body, no finished edge. Cylindrical neck spreading into ovoid body with extremely thin walls. Five shallow indentations, irregularly placed. From wine press tank. **Fig. 4–37.**

337   (373–64). D base .045

Light greenish blue, a few tiny bubbles, bottom unweathered, white weathering on top. Pushed-in base with air space. Pontil mark (D .01). **Fig. 4–37.**

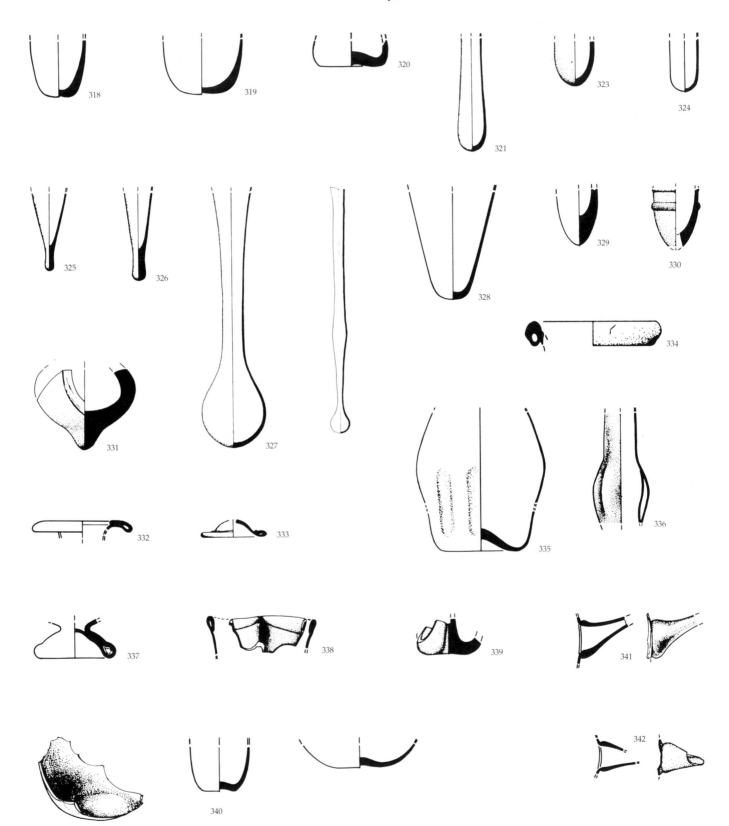

Fig. 4–37. Miscellaneous bottles. No. 334, 1:1; complete flask (not found at Jalame) to right of No. 327, 1:3; others 1:2.

338 (223–64). PH .02

Light green. Rim folded inward and pinched to form two tubes. From topsoil. **Fig. 4–37.**

339 (19–67). PH .025

Dark yellowish brown. Flattened bottom, traces of pontil mark. Body pinched to form two tubes. From factory dump, pre–351 context. **Fig. 4–37.**

340 (13–67). PH .031; D .02 x .035

Light brown, patches of white weathering. Thickened oval bottom, slightly concave, no pontil mark. Flattened body. **Fig. 4–37.**

Spouted vessels (Nos. 341–42)

Spouted jugs and bottles are fairly common all over the Mediterranean world, from the 1st c. to the Byzantine period. They were not made at Jalame: only two spouts were found, both in the eastern part of the excavated area and probably to be associated with early 2nd c. tombs (see Chap. 2). The shape of such a vessel is shown on Pl. 4–15.[147]

Syro-Palestinian examples are recorded at Huqoq, in a Judean Desert Cave, and at Jebel Amman. These can be dated chiefly to the 2nd c.[148] Others, without context, are in various museums.

For the West, Isings Form 99 shows the shape.[149] An extensive discussion of a spouted jug found in western Germany includes the long mooted question of the purpose of these vessels—now believed not baby feeders or lamp fillers but rather intended for medical purposes and hence best called "droppers."[150]

341 (228–65). PL of spout .027

Greenish blue. Curving vessel wall, conical spout, tip broken off. **Fig. 4–37.**

342 (153–65). PL of spout .022

Light green. Similar to preceding, tip of spout broken off. **Fig. 4–37.**

Mold-Blown Vessels

In the case of these vessels the shapes are often so doubtful that the technique rather than the form must be used for classification. When possible, shapes are identified.

Nos. 343–45 are from small bottles or jars like that on Pl. 4–15[151] or from other forms such as jugs. There are similar bottles in Egypt[152] and a few from Palestine,[153] but they are not common. Those at Jalame probably postdate the factory. Only No. 343 comes from a significant context—the wine press tank.

Fragments of a large bottle with mold-blown spiral ribbing (No. 346), a fairly common type of decoration on bottles like that in Fig. 4–38,[154] is interesting chiefly because it provides evidence that the wine press tank was filled all at one time. Its 13 fragments were found at various depths in the tank, which was abandoned after the factory had stopped working (see Chap. 2). Bottles with similar ribbing have been found at Hanita, Nahariya,[155] and elsewhere in the region, but few are dated by context.[156] Various techniques of producing this effect and the question of date are discussed in connection with a spirally ribbed bottle from Kerch.[157] The Jalame vessels seem to have been blown into a mold and then twisted after removal, without going through a stage of reblowing, as was commonly done in later times.

No. 347 has two parallels, one from Kerch, the other found in Cologne.[158] Each has a long strap handle with a lion mask appliqué at the lower end. A 4th c. date is assigned the Kerch example. Similar jugs without trail or appliqué have been found at Kfar Dikhrin; these are dated 5th c.[159]

Globular bottles with vertical ribs, common all over the area and in Cyprus as well, appeared at Jalame only as small body fragments. In many cases it is difficult to determine whether the ribs were mold-blown, pinched out from the parison, or were trails marvered into the surface. In most cases tooling or pinching has been assumed. For this reason our fragments are included in that section (see below).

A single fragment of a "honeycomb bowl," a type common in the 4th c., was found in a context later than the factory (No. 350). In any case, the vessel was obviously not made there. Characteristic is the slightly

147. Museum of Art and Archaeology, University of Missouri-Columbia, No. 71.103, handle missing. Pale olive green, pad base. H .112, D rim .029. Gift of Israel Department of Antiquities.

148. Barag, "Glass Vessels," Type 23.1. Kahane, "Huqoq," 123, pl. 18, 2, fig. 2.14; Harding, "A Roman Tomb in Amman," *ADAJ* 1 (1951) 31, no. 28, pl. 9. The Judean Desert Cave example (spout only) is illustrated in Barag, "Glass Vessels," pl. 24, but not mentioned or described.

149. Isings, *Roman Glass*, 118. Examples mentioned are dated 2nd–5th c.

150. E. Welker, "Die römischen Gläser von Nida-Heddernheim," *Schriften des Frankfurter Museums für vor-und Frühgeschichte* 3 (Frankfurt, 1974) 95–98. The dates given are 2nd–4th c., but she mentions that most examples can be dated 3rd c.

151. Museum of Art and Archaeology, University of Missouri-Columbia, No. 65.3, light green, H .13, D rim .052. Photo courtesy of the museum.

152. Harden, *Karanis*, 220 ff, nos. 700–1, dated not earlier than 4th c.

153. Baramki, "Karm al-Shaikh," 3, pl. 5, 19, without definite date; Hayes, *Toronto Glass*, 113, nos. 428–29 (jugs), 433 (bottle). All are said to be from Tubas (northeast of Samaria).

154. Reproduced from Bagatti, "Museo Francescano," 229, fig. 4, no. 103, from Beit Ras (Transjordan).

155. Barag, *Hanita*, 26–27, no. 52, and "Nahariya Congress," fig. 1.

156. A jug with spiral ribbing: Iliffe, "El-Bassa," 88, fig. 24, can be assigned to second half of 4th c.

157. Stern, *Custodia*, 107–10, no. 33, pl. 7. Parallels from both East and West are cited, with dates 3rd–4th c. in the East. Stern's personal observation of methods used in a Damascus glass factory is of interest.

158. B. A. Shelkovnikov, ed., *Artistic Glass, an Album . . . Hermitage Museum* (in Russian) (Leningrad, 1967) no. 23, H .30; Kisa, *Glas*, 432, fig. 93, H .38.

159. L. Y. Rahmani, "Mirror-Plaques," 53, Fig. 2; 6.

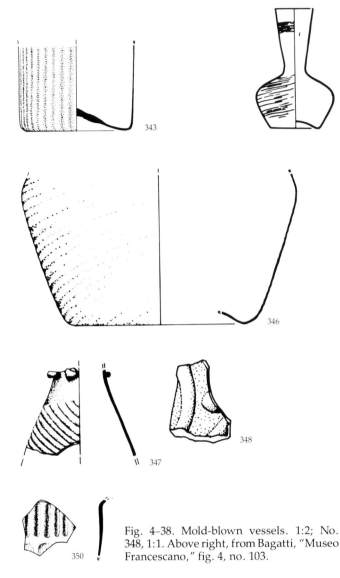

Fig. 4-38. Mold-blown vessels. 1:2; No. 348, 1:1. Above right, from Bagatti, "Museo Francescano," fig. 4, no. 103.

flaring, cracked-off rim (not preserved) above a row of vertical ribs. Below that the design seems slightly different from the usual one, but so little remains that certainty is impossible.[160]

A few early mold-blown fragments were found in the factory dump. Nos. 348–49 are from the bottoms of typical 2nd c. square jugs.

343 (383–64). PH .053; D bottom .06

Greenish blue. Four joining fragments. Bottom kicked, thickened at center. Pontil mark (D ca. .009). Nearly cylindrical body with vertical mold-blown ribs extending to the bottom. From wine press tank. **Fig. 4-38.**

344 (71–66). PH .037; D bottom ca. .05

Pale purple, iridescent, dark weathering. Fragment of bottom and wall. Similar to preceding. **Pl. 4-15.**

345 (43–64). PH .027

Light greenish blue, white weathering outside, unweathered inside. Fragment of bottom and wall. Cylindrical body with mold-blown vertical ribs beginning .01 above the bottom. **Pl. 4-15.**

346 (391, 438–64). PH .076; D bottom ca. .08; Th wall .001+

Pale green, a few large bubbles. Nine joining fragments, four not joining. Concave bottom; wall spreading out and turning in to form piriform body. Mold-blown spiral ribbing, extending to ca. .02 from bottom. Found at various depths in wine press tank. **Fig. 4-38; Pl. 4-15.**

Four pieces possibly of similar vessels were found in the factory dump; they are fragmentary but seem to exhibit spiral mold-blown ribbing (190–65, yellowish green, with concave bottom; 76–66, yellowish green; 42–66, light yellowish green; 120–66, yellowish green). The walls of these fragments are slightly thicker than those of No. 346.

Ten fragments (17–67) of an extremely thin greenish blue vessel (shape uncertain; th of wall less than .001) were found in the "sorting floors." It seems to have mold-blown spiral ribbing.

347 (94–65). PH .043; D neck ca. .026

Light greenish blue, large bubbles. Fragment of body and neck, no finished edge. Cylindrical neck, pear-shaped body with mold-blown slanting ribs (not in relief inside). Trail of same color around base of neck. **Fig. 4-38; Pl. 4-15.**

348 (198–66). Max dim .021; Th .004

Pale green. Fragment of bottom of square jug. Mold-blown pattern—part of two circles and a boss. **Fig. 4-38.**

349 (207–66). Max dim .028, .025; Th .002–.004

Pale greenish blue. Two non-joining fragments of bottom of square jug. Each fragment has an oval petal (deformed?) in sharp relief. **Pl. 4-15.**

350 (305–66). PH .029

Yellowish green, iridescence and dark weathering. Two fragments (not joining), no edge preserved. Cracked-off rim, mold-blown pattern. **Fig. 4-38; Pl. 4-15.**

Vessels with Pinched Ribs (Nos. 351–55)

Bifurcated Ribs

A type of decoration found on various shapes of vessels is represented at Jalame only by a few fragments (Nos. 351–53). To form the bifurcated ribs, the parison is pinched during the initial stage of blowing, before the vessel reaches its full size.[161] No. 351, the most complete

---

160. For the shape see Isings, *Roman Glass*, Form 107a. To the thorough discussion of the type by Stern, *Custodia*, 90–95 (No. 26), referring to examples found from Syria to western Europe, may be added some fragments found in southern Palestine (Erdmann, "Mezad Tamar," 110, nos. 919–22).

161. In some publications it is stated that trails were applied to the surface and then pinched together, or that the vessel was first blown into a mold, but actual experimentation has proved these notions wrong.

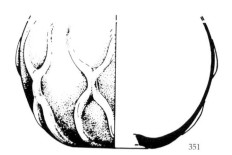

Fig. 4-39. Vessel with bifurcated ribs. 1:2.

vessel with this decoration at Jalame, is a globular bottle that probably had a cylindrical neck and was about the same height as one found at Hanita (est H .143). The latter has a squatter body and the bottom is not thickened, but the general resemblance to ours is obvious.[162]

Nos. 352–53 are probably from bowls rather than bottles, and another small fragment (345-66, uncatalogued, pale greenish blue) is probably also from a bowl. Two of these were found in a pre-factory context; No. 351 was near the furnace.

Possibly the best evidence for dating the decoration is furnished by fragments found at Dura, where it is thought to have begun in the 2nd c.,[163] but there is other evidence for an early date in a modiolus decorated with bifurcated ribs, said to have come from Palestrina.[164] This is the only instance of such decoration on a modiolus, which is generally considered a 1st or 2nd c. form.[165]

351 (398-64, 259-64, 322-64). PH .07; D bottom ca. .05

Light greenish blue, tiny bubbles. Globular bottle, three joining fragments of body and bottom. Thickened, slightly concave bottom, pontil mark not preserved. Walls pinched into bifurcated pattern. **Fig. 4-39; Pl. 4-15.**

352 (304-66). Max dim .05; Th wall .002

Yellowish green. Fragment of body, globular form, no finished edge. Triple loop pattern pinched out of wall. **Pl. 4-15.**

353 (311-66). D of body ca. .05; Th .0015

Pale green. Fragment of wall, no edge preserved. Loop pattern pinched out from vessel wall.

Vertical Ribs

Fragments of bottles with vertically pinched ribs are fairly numerous at Jalame, but in no case can a shape be restored even partially. The ribs are sometimes so faint as to appear mold-blown; others seem like applied trails. Probably, however, the ribs were all pinched at an early stage of blowing, as in the case of the bifurcated ribs. Some may have been marvered later, thus producing ridges on the vessel's interior.

Most of the fragments are bluish green or other shades of green. Many were found in the dump, but not in such quantities as other types, and most of the fragments are so small that it is doubtful whether vertically ribbed vessels were made in the factory.

This form of decoration was used for bottles with more or less globular bodies and long necks, sometimes flaring toward the rim. Such a bottle, from a Beth Shearim catacomb, is published with references to others of the 3rd and 4th c.[166] Vessels with ribbing are also found in Cyprus,[167] and on the north coast of the Black Sea.[168]

354 (520-64). PH .016; Th wall .0015-.001

Pale green. Fragment of shoulder and body, no finished edge. Two raised ribs beginning at junction of neck and shoulder, radiating to globular(?) body.

355 (519-64). PH of largest fragment .075; Th wall .0005-.001

Pale yellow. Numerous fragments, some joining, of a bottle (probably globular). No finished edge. The walls are extraordinarily thin.

Other fragments with vertical pinched ribs, found in the dump, are 267-66: five pale green and greenish blue; 154-66, light yellowish green; 188-66, pale green. Examples of similar bottles, scattered around the site, are 364-66, pale olive green; 148-65, light bluish green, from a very large bottle; 278-64, yellowish green; 340-66, greenish blue, probably from a large bottle. Many other fragments were not inventoried.

Vessels with Applied Trails (No. 356)

This sort of decoration is extremely rare at Jalame; no fragment with a finished edge has been identified.

162. Barag, *Hanita*, 26–27, no. 50.
163. Clairmont, *Dura Glass*, 48–50. The fragments are classified in four groups on the basis of the pattern forms. This type of decoration is thought to have begun at Dura in the 2nd c. and continued there until the year 256, while going on elsewhere in later times. The references to examples found in Egypt, Cyprus, Syria, and elsewhere (Clairmont, 48, nn. 89–93) may be supplemented by finds in the Palestinian area: Hanita (n. 162 above); Samaria (Crowfoot, *Samaria* 3, 410, fig. 94.12); Beth Shan (Bagatti, "Museo Francescano," 229, fig. 3,78); Nahariya (Barag, "Nahariya Congress," 3, 2, 243, fig. 1). At Sardis two fragments were found, one with coins, the latest of Constantius II (Saldern, *Sardis Glass*, 20–21, nos. 92–93). A bottle in the Hermitage Museum, found at Kerch, is very like the Jalame example but has a wound base (Shelkovnikov, as in n. 158, no. 22, H .303. Other forms with similar decoration from Cologne (Fremersdorf, *Denkmäler* 5, pls. 110–11) are dated 3rd c.
164. T. E. Haevernick, "Modioli," *Glastechnische Berichte* 51 (1978) 328–30, fig. 3a, in the Field Museum of Natural History, Chicago (No. 26146, H .18, D rim .191).
165. Isings, *Roman Glass*, Form 37.
166. Barag in Avigad, *Beth Shearim* 3, 203, no. 31 (bluish green, H .202, bottom missing, thickened rounded rim). Similar bottles referred to here are from Yehiam, Huqoq, and Beth Shan. See also Barag, *Hanita*, 23, 26–27, no. 49; 28, no. 60.
167. Vessberg, "Cyprus Glass," 133, pl. 7, no. 17; Harden, "Vasa," 53, no. 8, fig. 22f.
168. Sorokina, "Das antike Glas der Nordschwarzmeerküste," *Annales JIV* 4 (Ravenna-Venice, 1967) 67–79, offers a wide variety of glass vessels, many of which have Syro-Palestinian parallels. The descriptions are necessarily brief, so for valid comparisons in form and date one must consult the original Russian publications.

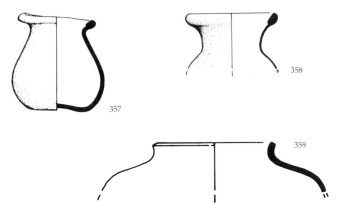

Fig. 4–40. Small jars. 1:2.

356   (29–64). Max dim .05; Th wall .001

Pale greenish blue, dark weathering on exterior. Fragment of wall, no finished edge. Probably globular with four thin trails of same color in a radiating pattern. **Pl. 4–15.**

Jars (Nos. 357–85)

Jars are characterized by a short neck and globular body. The simplest shape is represented by the only vessel discovered intact—a tiny jar (No. 357) found embedded in an upper layer of the conglomerate mass in the factory dump (see Chap. 2). Few fragments of such jars were recorded, but some may have been overlooked. The find spot of No. 357 and the fact that it is deformed indicate that it was made in the factory and discarded. Curiously, some jars of the same shape found elsewhere exhibit a similar deformity, e.g., a slightly taller one from a tomb at Hanita, with a flaring rim, rounded but not folded.[169] Others come from Amman and Gerasa.[170] A jar in Toronto is said to be from Nazareth, and another was found in Britain.[171] Although these are generally dated earlier than the Jalame piece, there is no doubt that ours is contemporary with the factory and probably of the decade 370–380.

No. 358, with a longer neck, may be compared to a jar from Samaria and another from Beit Fajjar, both with indented walls.[172] For No. 359, a jar with rounded rim,

very short neck and apparently globular body, a parallel has not appeared. A few other fragments at Jalame might be from such a vessel.

The jar with zigzag trail between rim and shoulder was not a Jalame product; only four examples could be identified (Nos. 360–63), each with a different kind of rim. One was found in the factory dump.

Two trail fragments not attached to vessels (Pl. 4–16) complete the meager evidence for such jars.[173] This kind of decoration is widespread in the Palestinian area and in Egypt[174] but seems unknown in the West.

The vessel with trails (usually dark greenish blue) applied to the body (see Pl. 4–16)[175] is represented at Jalame only by small fragments. Those that may be jars (Nos. 364–68) were found in the factory dump.

A basket handle is sometimes attached to jars like that just mentioned; one fragment (No. 369) was found. Such handles are not very common; some in collections are assumed to be Syro-Palestinian.[176] Ours can be dated 4th c.

A few fragments of vessel walls with small pinches as decoration probably belong to jars (Nos. 370–72), and a bowl rim (No. 143) has similar decoration. This type of pinching is not very common; most published vessels with pinches are small jars,[177] but there are also bottles (Fig. 4–43).[178] Examples have been found in Cyprus and at Gerasa, others are said to have come from Syria. They have been dated from the 3rd to the 6th and even the 7th c., but since all the Jalame fragments were found in the factory dump, these, at least, are likely to be from the second half of the 4th c. No. 373, a wall fragment, has an unusual, long pinched rib, for which no parallel has been found. It, too, was found in the factory dump and can be similarly dated.

Possibly belonging to "poppy-head jars" are the handles Nos. 374–75. A few of these globular jars were found at Karanis;[179] they are not common, and may well be later than the factory. Nos. 376–77 are loop handles from open vessels. No. 378 may have come from a jar such as that shown on Pl. 4–16. An undecorated jar of this kind

169. Barag, *Hanita*, 32–33, no. 70.

170. Harding, "Jebel Jofeh," 92, no. 377, pl. 29, dated 3rd c.; Baur, *Gerasa Glass*, 536, no. 72, fig. 25. Pale green, H .065, assigned to the 5th c. without any reason offered.

171. Hayes, *Toronto Glass*, 57, no. 141, bluish green, H .045–.049, deformed like ours, dated 2nd c.; D. Charlesworth, "A Group of Vessels from the Commandant's House, Housesteads," *JGS* 13 (1971) 35, no. 10. This jar is even more tipsy than ours, of "poor green bubbly glass," H .055. It is remarked that jars of this kind were common only in the 1st and early 2nd c. See also Isings, *Roman Glass*, 88, Form 68, with many references, all dated 1st–3rd c.

172. Crowfoot, *Samaria* 3, 409, pl. 94.5, dated 3rd c. but probably later; Husseini, "Beit Fajjar," 176, pl. 85.5, from a 4th c. grave.

173. Not catalogued: G510–64, PL .019, light greenish blue, from factory dump; G148–66, PL .029, pale greenish blue.

174. Barag in Avigad, *Beth Shearim* 3, 203, fig. 97, 30, refers to such vessels from Megiddo, Samaria, sites around Jerusalem, and Amman. All are dated 3rd or 4th c. Harden, *Karanis*, 179–80, nos. 493–98, dated 4th or 5th c.

175. Museum of Art and Archaeology, University of Missouri-Columbia, No. 70.108. Greenish blue, dark greenish blue trails. H .079, D rim .058. Purchased in Israel. Photo courtesy of the museum.

176. E.g., *Bomford Coll.*, 34, no. 161; Auth, *Newark Glass*, 139, no. 176.

177. Delougaz-Haines, pl. 50, no. 9; Baur, *Gerasa Glass*, 536, no. 67, fig. 18,244; Vessberg, "Cyprus Glass," 146, pl. 4,22; E. Spartz, *Antike Gläser*, Staatlichen Kunstsammlungen Kassel (Kassel, 1967) no. 149, pl. 36, "from Syria"; Auth, *Newark Glass*, 138, no. 175.

178. Museum of Art and Archaeology, University of Missouri-Columbia, No. 68.157, pale bluish green, H .128, D rim .039. Acquired in Jerusalem. Drawing courtesy of the museum.

179. Harden, *Karanis*, 182–83, nos. 509, 511, dated 4th–5th c.

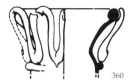 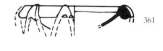 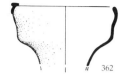 

Fig. 4–41. Jars with trail decoration. 1:2.

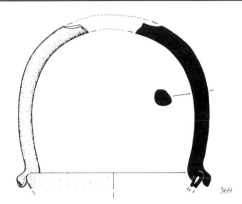

Fig. 4–42. Jar with basket handle. 1:2.

was found at Beth Shearim as well as in Egypt and Cyprus.[180] The vessels to which Nos. 379–80 belong have not been identified; No. 381 is reminiscent of the handles of "dolphin jugs," usually dated 2nd c. or 3rd at latest. Some examples may be as late as 4th c.[181]

Remnants of the scalloped trails descending the sides of amphoriskoi like that shown in Pl. 4–16[182] are represented by Nos. 383–85. A few others are even more fragmentary.

357 (133–66). H .05; D rim .04

Pale bluish green, blowing spirals, impurities, white weathering. Intact, cracked. Irregular infolded rim, short concave neck, globular body. Bottom slightly concave, pontil mark (D .023). Body deformed. From factory dump. **Fig. 4–40; Pls. 2–9C, 4 16; Color Pl. 3D.**

358 (172–64). D rim ca. .048

Pale green, small impurities in rim. Thickened flaring rim, infolded, globular body. A similar piece (419–66, D rim .045) came from the factory dump. **Fig. 4–40.**

359 (296–66). PH .011; D rim .03

Pale green, dark weathering. Rounded rim, very short neck, probably squat globular body, concave bottom. From factory dump. **Fig. 4–40.**

Jars with Zigzag Trail

360 (216–65). D rim ca. .03

Light green, good material, no weathering. Infolded rim, funnel mouth, globular body. Thick trail of same color applied to rim and shoulder, the lower ends resting on a horizontal trail applied around the shoulder. **Fig. 4–41; Pl. 4–16.**

361 (225–65). D rim .054

Greenish blue, dark weathering, pitting. Infolded rim, funnel mouth, traces of zigzag trail of same color. **Fig. 4–41.**

362 (40–66). D rim .06 (slightly deformed)

Pale green, thick white weathering. Rounded rim, high collar, cylindrical neck. Bit of dark greenish blue trail preserved on rim. From factory dump. **Fig. 4–41.**

363 (149–64). D rim .06

Yellowish green, slight weathering. Thickened, rounded rim with low collar curving in at bottom to cylindrical neck. Fragments of trail of same color preserved. **Fig. 4–41.**

364 (420–64). Max dim .02; Th wall .002

Pale green. Fragment, no finished edge. Dark greenish blue trail in zigzag pattern. **Color Pl. 3C.**

365 (2–67). Max dim of largest fragment .021; Th wall .0015

Pale yellow. Four non-joining fragments, no finished edge. Dark greenish blue zigzag trail on one fragment. The others have straight trails, no pattern discernible.

366 (168–65). Max dim of larger fragment .036; Th wall .002

Pale yellowish green. Two fragments, not joining, no finished edge. Curving body, probably globular. Zigzag dark greenish blue trail.

367 (84–66). Max dim .025; Th wall .002

Yellowish green, a few bubbles and striations. Fragment of wall, no finished edge. Thick dark greenish blue zigzag trail. **Color Pl. 3C.**

368 (130–66). Max dim .03; Th wall .001–.002

Pale green. Vessel fragment, no finished edge. Body probably globular, dark greenish blue curving zigzag trail. Body unweathered, white weathering on trail. **Color Pl. 3C.**

180. Barag in Avigad, *Beth Shearim* 3, 202, no. 27. References are given to Harden, *Karanis*, nos. 789–90, Vessberg, "Cyprus Glass," 146, pl. 4:32 and others.
181. For handles in general, see Kisa, *Glas*, 493ff, fig. 156. For a possible 4th c. date see Isings, *Roman Glass*, 79, Form 61.
182. Museum of Art and Archaeology, University of Missouri-Columbia, No. 62.2, brown, H .177, D rim .036, said to have come from near Hebron. Photo courtesy of the museum. Cf. Barag, "Glass Vessels," Type 10.3, from Tarshiha (Iliffe, "Tarshiha," *QDAP* 3 [1934], pl. 8). The amphoriskos is considered late 4th c. or even later.

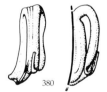

Bottle with pinched walls
(n. 178). 1:2.

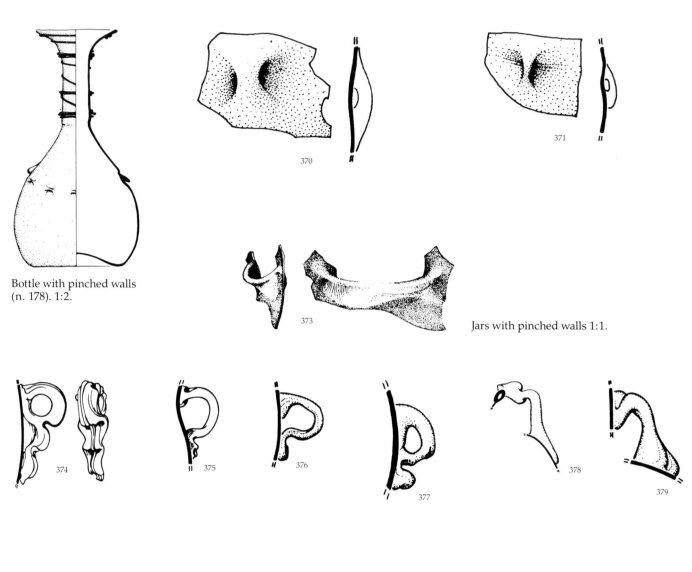

Jars with pinched walls 1:1.

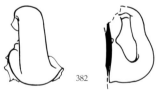

Fig. 4–43. Various jar handles. Nos. 376–77, 379, 1:1; others, 1:2.

Jar with Basket Handle

369 (81–65). PL .09; D of handle ca. .01

Light green, long bubbles, slight weathering. Folded vessel rim with part of basket handle, a thick trail circular in section. **Fig. 4–42.**

Jars with Pinched Walls

370 (139–66). Th wall .001

Pale green, slight weathering. Fragment of globular vessel wall. Horizontal pinch. From factory dump. **Fig. 4–43.**

371 (110–65). Max dim .026; Th wall .001

Pale green, striations, a few bubbles. Fragment of convex vessel wall. Horizontal pinch. From factory dump. **Fig. 4–43.**

372 (82–66). Max dim .035; Th .001–.0025

Light bluish green. Fragment of body, no finished edge. The piece is strongly curved, with a "strap" of the same color drawn horizontally across the concave side. From factory dump. **Pl. 4–16.**

373 (66–66). Th wall .001

Pale green. Fragment of vessel wall (no finished edge).

Wall convex with long rib pinched out, forming a small air space. Shape of the vessel unknown; it may be deformed. From factory dump. **Fig. 4–43.**

Jar Handles

374 (94–66). PH .049; Th body .001
Colorless, grayish green tinge. Trail of same color forming handle with one open loop and two closed loops. Additional loops probably continued down the wall. **Fig. 4–43.**

375 (97–64). PH .038
Pale greenish blue. Wall splays upward from neck and downward to globular body. Handle a dark greenish blue trail attached to neck and body. **Fig. 4–43.**

376 (169–65). PH .018; Th wall .001
Pale green. Thin-walled open vessel (no finished edge). Handle a trail of same color attached to the body. **Fig. 4–43.**

377 (203–65). PH .026; Th wall ca. .0015
Pale green, small bubbles. Globular vessel (no finished edge). Trail of same color attached to wall. Bottom of handle broken; the trail may have continued below. From factory dump. **Fig. 4–43.**

378 (110–64). PH .053
Light green, small black impurities. Infolded rim. Handle of same color attached at rim and shoulder. **Fig. 4–43; Pl. 4–16.**

379 (419–64). PH .025; Th wall .001
Colorless, green tinge, tiny bubbles, dark weathering. Thin wall (no finished edge), handle attached to neck and shoulder. **Fig. 4–43; Pl. 4–16.**

Miscellaneous Handles

380 (26–66). PL .042
Pale green body, probably globular. Handle a trail of same color. From factory dump. **Fig. 4–43.**

381 (56–66). PL .046
Greenish blue body, trail of same color forming a loop handle. **Pl. 4–16.**
A similar handle (108–65) is purple, attached to a colorless body. Both from the factory dump.

382 (3–67). PH .043
Pale green, heavy dark weathering. Thick trail of same color forms a handle (top broken off). **Fig. 4–43.**

Amphoriskos Fragments (Nos. 383–85)

383 (163–66). PH .037; Th wall .001
Pale yellow (no finished edge). Thick light green trail with dark greenish blue streak on wall, tooled to form a ribbon down the side. From factory dump. **Pl. 4–16.**

384 (183–65). PH .044; Th wall .002

Pale green. Trail of same color on wall, tooled to form a scalloped ribbon. From factory dump. **Pl. 4–16.**

385 (180–65). PH .038; Th wall .0015
Colorless with yellow tinge. Light green trail on body, tooled to form a ribbon. From factory dump. **Pl. 4–16.**

Lamps (Nos. 386–403)

A few fragments of glass lamps represent types that are obviously not products of the factory.

Of the pieces catalogued, only Nos. 391, 398–99, and 403 were found in the factory dump. Where weathering is not mentioned, it is of the usual whitish kind. There is no unity in this group, nor any certainty that all must date from the period of the factory; some are probably later.

Nos. 386–87 are central wick-tubes from cup-shaped lamps. These are quite common on Palestinian sites, where they are dated variously to the 4th, 5th, or 6th c.[183]

Nos. 388–90 are probably from stemmed lamps that fitted into polycandela.[184] Nos. 391–96 display other forms of feet; these may or may not be parts of lamps.[185] No. 397, unique at the site, is possibly a lamp. No. 398 looks rather like the conical vessels discussed below, but it may have a pontil mark. No. 399, a handle and wall fragment, seems to belong to a large globular lamp like one from the Mount of Olives, compared by Barag to an example from a 4th c. tomb at Yavne (unpublished).[186] He dates the whole group late 3rd c. to 350.

386 (122–65). H .059, D rim .019
Light green, long vertical bubbles. Wick-tube from beaker-type lamp. Rounded rim unevenly folded inward. Sharp fracture where tube bottom is broken from vessel of same color. **Fig. 4–44; Pl. 4–16.**

387 (33–65). D bottom ca. .022
Greenish blue. Fragment of wick-tube for lamp (?). Irregular bottom, probably discarded for this reason. Pontil mark (D ca. .01). **Fig. 4–44.**

388 (135–66). D .022, Th wall .004
Light greenish blue, long vertical bubbles. Flat bottom, pontil mark (D .013). Wall tapers slightly. This might be the central tube from a beaker-type lamp, but it is rather large for this purpose. **Pl. 4–16.**

183. Bagatti-Milik, 148 and fig. 35, no. 11; Crowfoot, *Samaria* 3, 418, fig. 99, nos. 2, 3; Rahmani, "Maon Synagogue," 16 and fig. 9, no. 2.
184. These are found in many regions: Asia Minor, Syria, Egypt, Cyprus, etc. See, e.g., Saldern, *Sardis Glass,* 49–52 (Type 3, dated "early Byzantine") with discussion and many references; Chavane, *Salamine,* 65, nos. 171–73; Harden in Colt, *Nessana* 1, 83–85, nos. 51–54 (5th–7th c.).
185. For a great variety of lamp foot fragments (but no wick-tubes) see R. Pirling, "Die römische und byzantinische Glasfunde von Apamea in Syrien," *Annales AIHV* 7 (1977), 146, fig. 5, dating 4th c. or later.
186. Bagatti-Milik, 148 and fig. 35, no. 12; Barag, "Glass Vessels," Type 13.10.

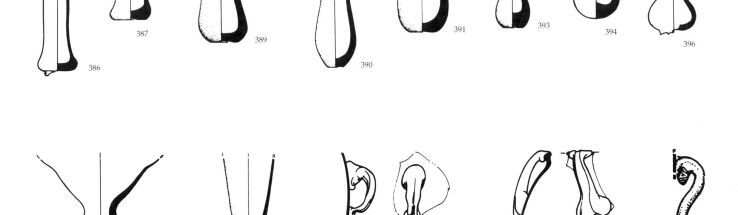

Fig. 4–44. Lamps. No. 403, 1:1; others, 1:2.

389 (28–66). PH .04

Yellowish brown, spherical and oval bubbles, slight dark weathering. Thickened bottom, pontil mark (D .011). Uneven form suggests this is deformed. **Fig. 4–44; Pl. 4–16.**

390 (33–64). PH .053

Pale green, dark weathering. Flat bottom, pontil mark (D .012). **Fig. 4–44; Pl. 4–16.**

391 (391–66). D bottom .015

Greenish blue, a few spherical and vertical bubbles, almost unweathered. Trace of pontil mark. **Fig. 4–44.**

392 (38–65). PH .032; Th of wall at top .004

Colorless, small spherical bubbles, pitting and weathering. Slightly concave bottom, pontil mark (D .01). Piriform body. **Pl. 4–16.**

393 (60–65). PH .032

Light green, dark weathering. Thickened bottom, flattened, with pontil mark. **Fig. 4–44; Pl. 4–16.**

394 (301–66). PH .027

Pale green, dark weathering. Thick bottom, trace of pontil mark. **Fig. 4–44.**

395 (28–64). PH .025; Th of wall at top .002

Light green, pitting and dark weathering. Piriform body, thick concave bottom, traces of pontil mark (D .012). **Pl. 4–16.**

396 (123–65). PH .034

Light greenish blue. Pontil scar (D .015). **Fig. 4–44.**

397 (212–65). PH .035

Pale green, a few tiny bubbles, dark weathering. Similar to preceding (upper part). Constricted neck, flaring rim. **Fig. 4–44.**

398 (446–66). PH .042

Light bluish green, tiny bubbles. Bottom thickened. Pontil mark? **Fig. 4–44.**

399 (53–66). Th vessel wall .002

Light green, black impurities and bubbles in handle. Handle and part of body. Globular lamp or bowl, trail of same color (with yellowish green streak) applied to wall and pulled down to form short, flattened handle. **Fig. 4–44; Pl. 4–16.** (2 views).

400 (179–65). PH .034; Th wall .0005

Light green, small black impurities. Handle and small portion of thin-walled body. Applied trail of same color pulled upward to rim. **Pl. 4–16.**

401 (111–65). PH .037; Th wall .001; W handle .015

Light greenish blue, bubbles in handle. Fragment of handle and thin-walled body of open vessel, possibly a lamp. Heavy trail of same color attached to wall, then looped out and down to form handle (broken at bottom, probably continued in a trail below). **Pl. 4–16.**

402 (141–65). PH .042; Th wall .001+

Pale greenish blue. Handle and fragment of body. Trail of yellowish green applied to wall and pulled up over thickened, rounded rim. **Fig. 4–44; Pl. 4–16.**

403 (400–66). PL .012

Handle: dark greenish blue trail attached to rounded body. **Fig. 4–44.**

Vessels with Cracked-off Rims

Certain features are characteristic of vessels with cracked-off rims. These are made with the blowpipe (not using the pontil). The types of bases are limited (at

Jalame most do not have bases),[187] and none of the Jalame examples has a handle. Most of these vessels are bowls, cups, and beakers.

The earliest blown vessels, of the 1st c. B.C., were made with the blowpipe alone. These are generally small flasks, the rims cracked off, unworked and often uneven.[188] More developed forms, usually with very thin walls, were produced in the 1st c. A.C. The shapes are quite varied.[189]

Examples from the 2nd and 3rd c. have the same kind of rim,[190] and very little difference can be noted in 4th c. vessels. Often earlier and later pieces can hardly be differentiated. There is, however, one type of vessel that seems to have been manufactured only in the 4th c.: a conical vessel that may be either a lamp or a beaker (see below).

Conical Vessels (Nos. 404–58)

The shape is a true cone except for a rounded or flattened bottom. The rim is cracked off and wheel-polished; horizontal wheel-cut grooves or abraded bands are usually found at intervals on the wall. Blobs of cobalt blue glass (see Chap. 9) are often applied to the exterior, either in a horizontal row or in groups (Pl. 4–17 and Color Pl. 4B).[191] Rarely, there are intense greenish blue blobs (see No. 438). The essential features are (1) the cracked-off and wheel-polished rim and (2) the absence of a pontil mark. Grooves and blobs are variable elements.

About 100 fragments of such conical vessels were excavated, at least three-fourths from the factory dump. The rim diameters range from ca. .08 to ca. .13.

The material is generally of good quality, without bubbles. The color range is small: some are pale green but most are colorless with a green or yellow tinge, and others seem entirely colorless. The thickness of the fragments varies, since the walls are always thinner in the middle part of the vessel.

Weathering is usually white, but some fragments have an outer black crust. In no case has weathering seriously damaged the glass.

The blue blobs vary in size as well as in thickness and in intensity of color. Some are prominent and of irregular shape; others are flat. Some protrude on the interior; in other examples the wall is smooth. In addition to fragments of rims and bottoms, there are many small pieces without a finished edge on which blobs are preserved (Pl. 4–18). Conical vessels without blobs are essentially the same (as far as can be determined) in material, colors, measurements, and weathering.

The fragments found at Jalame offer a unique opportunity to study the manufacturing method, for there are not only vessel fragments but quantities of material discarded during the process. The crucial fragments are the moils or overblows—pieces cracked off from the tops of the vessels. (For description and catalogue see below).[192]

Study of these fragments was first systematically undertaken by S. M. Goldstein.[193] He examined them with a binocular microscope and studied them statistically. A simple computer sorting program revealed that there was a direct relationship between the diameter and thickness of the vessel rims and the cracked-off moils, even though no actual joins could be found. Microscopic examination confirmed that scratched lines and chipping existed at the outer edges both of the vessel rims and of the moils. Thus Goldstein proposed that the conical vessels were blown into full-sized molds, then annealed, and the excess glass removed by scoring a ring around the circumference of the vessel and cracking it off the blowpipe.[194] However, subsequent observation of glassmakers at work in different circumstances, along with examination of additional ancient objects, convinced him otherwise—that the vessels were probably cracked off at the rim before annealing.[195]

Following Goldstein's original assumption, G. D. Weinberg presented the problem to Dominick Labino in the autumn of 1978. Labino experimented with various methods of producing a conical vessel like those from Jalame and, as a result, a method that could have been used in making such vessels was determined. The steps in the process were as follows:

(A) A gather of glass was taken from the furnace on a blowpipe (Fig. 4–45A).

(B) The gather was shaped into a sphere by rotating it in a wet wooden "block" (Fig. 4–45B).

187. Bases on bowls with cracked-off rims are mentioned as exceptional by Fremersdorf, *Denkmäler* 7, 41, pl. 70; 42, pl. 71; 52, pl. 99.

188. Avigad, "Excavations in the Jewish Quarter of the Old City of Jerusalem, 1971," *IEJ* 22 (1972) 200, pl. 46B; Avigad, *Discovering Jerusalem* (New York, 1983) 189–90.

189. At Corinth a number of beakers with cracked-off rims (Davidson, *Corinth* 12, nos. 637, 638, 651, 653) were found in 1st c. deposits. Isings, *Roman Glass*, cites many western bowls (Forms 12, 17), flasks (Forms 27, 28), and beakers (Forms 29, 31, 32).

190. Isings, *Roman Glass*, Forms 96, 103, 104, all dated 3rd c.

191. Museum of Art and Archaeology, University of Missouri-Columbia, No. 68.415. Colorless with green tinge. H .163, D rim .141. Photo courtesy of the museum.

192. The only other recorded objects of this kind were found at Merida, Spain, in 1948, but published only after the Jalame excavation was concluded. See J. Price, "Some Roman Glass from Spain," *Annales AIHV* 6 (1973) 80–84, fig. 4.

193. S. M. Goldstein, "A Preliminary Study of the Glass Manufactured at Jalame in Israel," Ph.D. diss., Harvard University, 1970, 112–16.

194. Ibid., 113–14.

195. During Goldstein's visit to the Tahan glass factory in Cairo in 1979, he observed the manufacture of conical lamp inserts. These objects were not quite so thick as the Jalame vessels and the quality of the glass was inferior. The completed form resembled a modern hurricane shade, open at both ends. The rim was rounded by reheating on the pontil rod, then removed still retaining a heavy button base, and put aside. This button and a portion of the base was subsequently cracked off by an assistant who rotated the body against a red-hot iron implement. It was unclear whether or not these lamps were partially annealed before this process. However, after the excess glass was removed, they were returned to the annealing chamber.

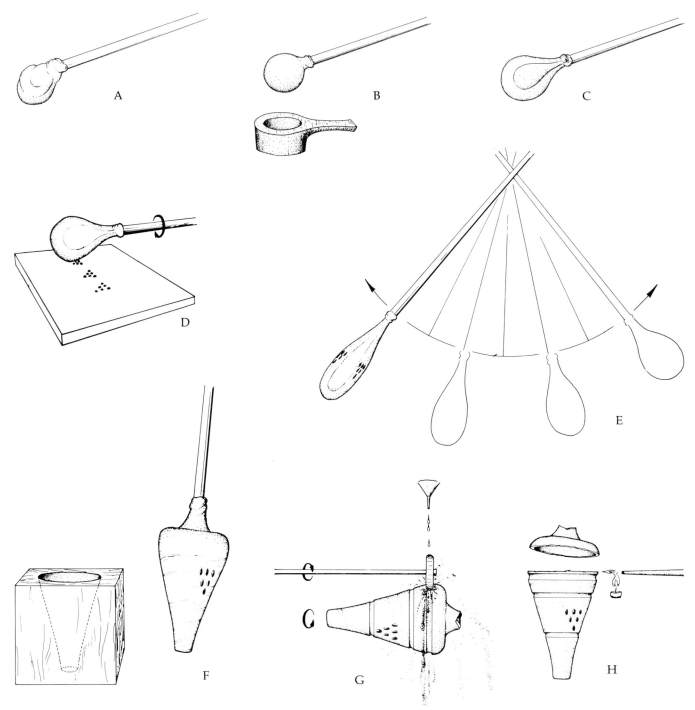

Fig. 4–45. Method of making conical beakers: (A) gather taken from furnace on blowpipe; (B) gather shaped with wooden block; (C) bulb blown into pear shape; (D) cold chips picked up; (E) bulb swung to lengthen form; (F) vessel blown into mold; (G) grooves made with grinding wheel; (H) moil removed with torch.

Each time, between this step and those following, the gather was reheated.

(C) The sphere was blown into a slightly elongated pear shape (Fig. 4–45C).

(D) Decorative blobs were now added—cold glass chips that were picked up on the hot vessel (Fig. 4–45D).

(E) The glass bulb was then swung to and fro in order

to lengthen the shape (Fig. 4–45E). The motion tends to lengthen the blobs as well, and on conical vessels the blobs are usually elliptical.

(F) To make the vessel assume a conical form, it was rotated upon a marver, but a mold (which was not available at the time) would have been preferable. This would be a wooden block (always kept moist) into which the vessel could be blown and rotated and thus formed into a cone (Fig. 4–45F). The pressure applied by marvering or molding flattens the blobs and sometimes causes them to protrude slightly on the interior. Pressing the vessel into a mold produces an overblow or moil.

The vessel, with the moil still attached, was then cracked off from the blowpipe and was annealed.

(G) When the vessel was cold, horizontal grooves (present on almost all the Jalame vessels) were engraved with a wheel. Labino used a stone wheel upon which water dripped, guiding the vessel with his hand, bracing it against the machine. The wheel was of course electrically driven, but the same result could be obtained by having an assistant turn it.

With the decoration—grooves and blobs—now complete, the moil had to be removed. The first method tried was placing the vessel upon a revolving stand and applying a small torch with pinpoint flame to the point where the separation was desired. After a few revolutions, the top cracked off evenly. This produced an intact moil, as seen in Fig. 4–45I I.

Presuming that Roman glassmakers might not have been able to produce a pinpoint flame, a second method was tried. A string was fastened around a modern jar at the point where the moil was to be cracked off; the string, soaked in kerosene, was set alight. This worked well, and the moil cracked off at an oblique angle rather than horizontally, as when the torch was used. Most of the Jalame moil fragments have this oblique angle (see Nos. 501–5). Instead of kerosene, pitch could have been used for this purpose.

A third method involved pulling out a trail from a gob of hot glass with a pointed tool and wrapping it around a vessel scored to mark the desired point of fracture. This resulted in breaking the moil into fragments that looked much like those found at Jalame. Remains of trails perhaps used to wrap around the vessel and crack off the moil can be identified by comparison with fragments produced by Labino's experiment. The old and new trails (Pl. 4–23) are similar except for weathering on the former.

After the moil was removed, the vessel rim was finished by grinding and polishing. Every Jalame vessel of this kind has a ground rim except one fragment with an uneven edge (No. 404); perhaps indicating that in this case the moil was cracked off without the use of heat, by scoring the point of fracture. This method could work satisfactorily only on thin-walled vessels.

While the vessel glass is clear, with few impurities, the moils are generally bubbly and muddy-looking, containing dark flecks of iron rust.[196] Such flecks tend to collect in the area nearest the blowpipe, especially when the pipe is overheated, possibly because the tip is too nar-

row.[197] Thus iron oxide particles do not appear in the vessel itself.

Conical glass vessels have been found all the way from the Middle East to western Europe. The differences between eastern and western forms are remarkably slight, but there is recognizable diversity in material and appearance. Syro-Palestinian vessels are generally light green or almost colorless and usually thick-walled. Relatively few excavated in this region have been published,[198] but there are many in collections, some with more or less accurate proveniences. Jalame is the only place where production of these vessels has been verified.

Egyptian examples are chiefly of dark green glass; they are thin-walled and many have dark cobalt blue blobs.[199] Similar vessels have been found in Nubian tombs; among them at least one, with blue blobs and horizontal grooves, seems to be a Syro-Palestinian type.[200]

Many conical vessels, olive brown with blue blobs, have been found in South Russia.[201] More study is needed to establish where these fit into the picture. It is worth noting that a vessel with rounded bottom, blobs, and abraded bands, found at Hanita, seems like some from the northern Black Sea region.[202]

In western Europe conical vessels are plentiful; probably they were made in one or several centers there. In Germany their high period is the turn of the 3rd and 4th c.[203] Some western examples have blobs of other colors in addition to blue, a feature that seems absent in the East.

Conical vessels have been identified both as beakers and as lamps, and there is evidence that they could be used for each of these purposes under varying circumstances. At Karanis some were noted as having oily stains or an oily feel, and Harden also cites an example found in the West with oily stains inside.[204] A wooden tripod from Karanis, found not far from a conical vessel, is shown here (Pl. 4–17).[205] Since the stand must have

196. See Chap. 3, n. 13, and Chap. 9 for further discussion.

197. F. W. Hodkin and A. Cousen, *Textbook of Glass Technology* (New York, 1925) 403.

198. Iliffe, "El Bassa," 89, fig. 22 (more pointed than ours); S. Yeivin, "A Year's Work in Israel," *Archaeology* 11 (1958) 239, 241, from Khirbet Manawat.

199. Harden, *Karanis*, nos. 457–63, pls. 5 and 16.

200. See W. B. Emery, *The Royal Tombs of Ballana and Qustul* (Cairo, 1938) Tomb Q 14–75, 377, pl. 106d, now in Egyptian Museum, Cairo, No. 71145, H .158. From other tombs came two brown conical beakers (Nos. 71143, 71146) with darker blue blobs; No. 71148 is dark green, undecorated; No. 71144, light green, has a definite foot. The last four are probably of Egyptian origin.

201. Sorokina, "Nuppengläser," 71–79.

202. Barag, *Hanita*, 28–30, no. 67. Cf. Sorokina, as in note 201, fig. 2, Type 1.

203. Fremersdorf, *Denkmäler* 7, passim.

204. Harden, *Karanis*, 155. The western piece is shown in Morin-Jean, *La Verrerie en Gaule sous l'empire romain* (Paris, 1922–1923) pl. 10.

205. Wooden tripod holding glass lamp, from *Karanis: An Egyptian Town in Roman Times*, ed. E. K. Gazda (Ann Arbor, 1983) 25, fig. 41. Photo courtesy of Kelsey Museum of Archaeology, University of Michigan, Ann Arbor.

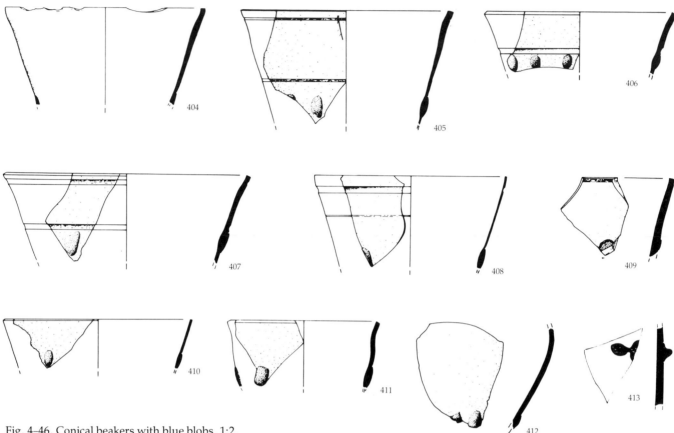

Fig. 4–46. Conical beakers with blue blobs. 1:2.

been intended to hold something of conical form, a glass lamp would seem a natural candidate. (The stand might, however, have held a beaker during a drinking party.) An engraved representation of two suspended conical vessels on a tombstone in Rome also argues for their use as lamps.[206] The notion that they could have been inserted into the polycandela of Byzantine times has not been substantiated.[207]

The most convincing evidence for the use of these vessels as lamps is furnished by representations of the menorah on a mosaic in the synagogue at Hammat Tiberias.[208] Color Pl. 4C shows a detail of one of the two menorahs that flank the Torah shrine. A conical vessel is fixed (by what means is not clearly shown) on the top of each of the branches, each vessel bearing a wick with a red flame. The vessels pictured are light blue with dark rims, meant to represent transparent glass, as the white

highlight on each vessel wall surely indicates. This synagogue was functioning at the same time as the Jalame factory; and while a connection between the two cannot, of course, be proved, it is not impossible that lamps for the Tiberias synagogue were manufactured at Jalame. At least two other synagogue mosaics show menorahs with conical vessels used as lamps, but it is not clear whether they are meant to be of glass.[209] In general, menorahs represented on mosaics (and on gold-glass vessels) show lamps of Roman types—bronze or terracotta—crowning the branches. The tradition of conical glass lamps for menorahs still existed in the Middle Ages, as a 14th c. manuscript shows. A menorah is illustrated with conical glass lamps fixed in metal (?) holders on the ends of the branches.[210]

There is also evidence for the use of conical vessels as beakers. A drinking inscription on a vessel found in Hungary is not convincing, since the letters were scratched over previously applied blobs.[211] Better evi-

206. Goodenough, *Symbols* 3, fig. 784. They are suspended; the author calls them (vol. 2, 24) "baskets probably containing grain," presumably because diagonal lines are shown on the vessel bodies.

207. A polycandelon supporting three conical beakers was illustrated in *JGS* 16 (1974) 126, no. 9 as an acquisition of the Gemeente Museum, The Hague. A query to the museum elicited the information that there is no basis for associating these objects.

208. Dothan, *Hammath Tiberias*. The menorahs are described on 37–38 and shown on a number of plates (both color and black and white). Our illustration is by courtesy of the author. (I am indebted to Gusta Lehrer-Jacobson for calling my attention to the menorahs on this mosaic.)

209. Ibid., 37–38.

210. F. Rademacher, *Die deutschen Gläser des Mittelalters* (Berlin, 1933) 86, n. 3, pl. 19,e. The menorah bears the caption: "candelabrum templi aureum." This manuscript is dated ca. 1370; another of somewhat later date is mentioned by Rademacher as having the same representation, with conical green glass lamps.

211. Fremersdorf, *Denkmäler* 7, 51, pls. 96/97.

dence is supplied by the engraved representation on the large plate found in a Beth Shearim catacomb. Here a conical vessel is shown in conjunction with a jug and a pitcher, while hanging lamps are portrayed as having a different shape.[212]

It is quite likely that conical vessels were used for various purposes—one found at Karanis contained four dice.[213]

Conical Vessels with Blue Blobs (Nos. 404–38)

Rim Fragments

404 (278–66). D rim .108; Th rim .0035

Colorless, green tinge, slight weathering. Three joining fragments of rim and body. Roughly ground rim. Small cobalt blue blob at lowest preserved point. **Fig. 4–46; Pl. 4–17.**

405 (132–66). D rim ca. .105; Th rim .003

Colorless, green tinge, dark weathering, particularly on rim. Bubbles in the blobs. Wheel-polished rim; wall thins as it tapers. Lightly abraded horizontal lines below rim outside, another set farther down. One cobalt blue blob and part of another. **Fig. 4–46; Pl. 4–17; Color Pl. 4B.**

406 (137–66). D rim ca. .10; Th rim .003

Pale green, blowing spirals, slightly pitted outside, dark weathering. Interior shiny, exterior dull. Wheel-polished rim; wheel-cut groove above three small cobalt blue blobs. **Fig. 4–46; Color Pl. 4B.**

407 (107–66). D rim ca. .13; Th rim .003

Light green, patches of dark weathering. Wheel-polished rim, flaring slightly. One irregularly shaped cobalt blue blob. Two sets of shallow grooves. **Fig. 4–46; Pl. 4–17; Color Pl. 4B.**

408 (288–66). Est D rim .10; Th rim .0015

Colorless, green tinge, dark weathering, especially in groove and on blob. Wheel-polished rim, extremely thin wall. Shallow wheel-cut groove near rim, narrow abraded line lower down. Slight irregular abrasions just below edge of rim. Part of one dark greenish blue blob. **Fig. 4–46.**

409 (398–66). D rim uncertain; Th rim .0035

Pale yellowish green, dark weathering, especially on blob. Rim wheel-polished inside and out to .002 below edge. One cobalt blue blob. **Fig. 4–46.**

410 (285–65). D rim ca. .10; Th rim .002

Colorless, faint green tinge, white and dark weathering. Rim wheel-polished inside and out to .002 below edge. One pale cobalt blue blob. **Fig. 4–46.**

411 (165–65). D rim ca. .08; Th rim .003

Pale green, patches of dark weathering. Wheel-polished, slightly flaring rim. Exterior possibly polished. One cobalt blue blob. Three rim fragments of same shape (308–66) found in factory dump. **Fig. 4–46; Pl. 4–17.**

412 (440–64). Th at top of fragment .003

Bowl (?), fragment of body, no finished edge. Pale green, dark weathering, pitting. Convex wall. Parts of two oval cobalt blue blobs at bottom. Another pale green fragment with curving wall preserves part of a blue blob (465–64). **Fig. 4–46; Pl. 4–17.**

Wall Fragments

None of the fragments has a finished edge. The thickness of the walls varies, as the middle part of the vessels is always thinner than top and bottom. Thus the wall thickness indicates to some extent where a fragment belongs.

There is great variety in the sizes of the blobs as well as in their shapes, thicknesses, and intensity of color. All but No. 438 are cobalt blue. Some fragments may belong to bowls, but all those that preserve enough of the wall to determine the shape seem to be from conical vessels.

413 (151–66). Max th .0045

Fragment of vessel, no finished edge. Colorless, green tinge, one large elliptical bubble. Two cobalt blue blobs irregularly placed, one running into the other. Probably a discarded fragment. **Fig. 4–46; Pl. 4–18; Color Pl. 4B.**

414 (138–66). Th .002–.004

Colorless, green tinge. Slight weathering outside, interior unweathered. Three small blobs. The wall thickness indicates that the rim was just above the preserved edge. **Pl. 4–18; Color Pl. 4B.**

415 (10–67). Th .002–.003

Colorless, green tinge, dark weathering. Three small blobs. **Pl. 4–18.**

416 (117–66). Th .003–.0015

Pale green, dark weathering. Two long blobs, wheel-abraded band above. **Pl. 4–18; Color Pl. 4B.**

417 (212–66). Th .0025

Colorless, yellow tinge, dark weathering. Parts of two oval blobs. Wheel-abraded band above. **Pl. 4–18.**

418 (504–64). Th .0015–.003

Colorless, green tinge, dark weathering. Two long blobs. **Pl. 4–18.**

419 (126–66). Th .0015

Colorless, green tinge, slight weathering. Parts of two long blobs. **Pl. 4–18; Color Pl. 4B.**

420 (1–67). Th .0015

Colorless, slight dark weathering. Two small oval blobs. **Pl. 4–18; Color Pl. 4B.**

---

212. Avigad, *Beth Shearim* 3, 210, fig. 100. It is pointed out in Zevulun-Olenik, *Talmudic Period*, 34, 35 (Hebrew), that these three vessels may be the "kos of benediction," the "lagin of wine," and the "kiton of water"—all required for the ritual blessing over wine.
213. Harden, *Karanis*, 155, no. 460.

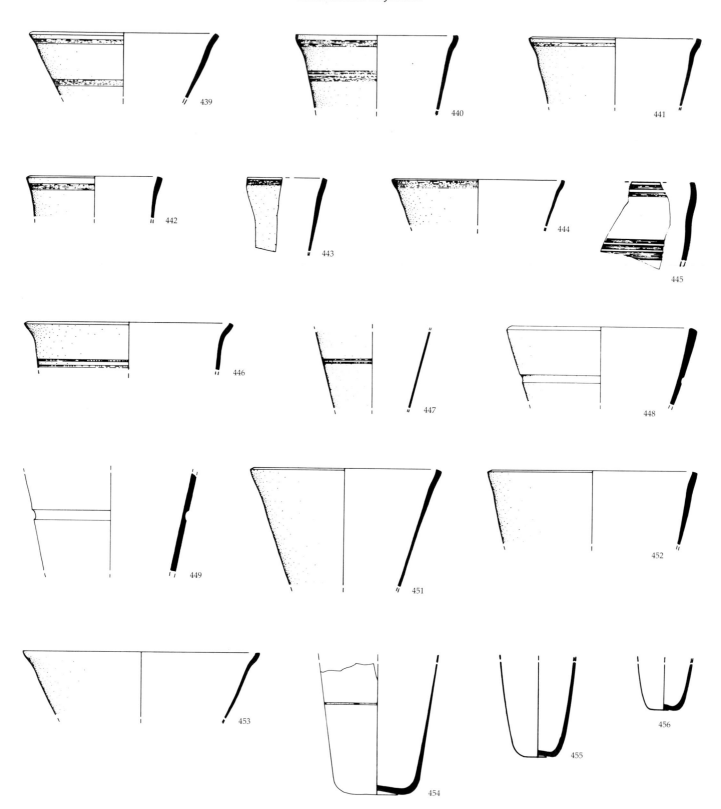

Fig. 4–47. Conical beakers, grooved and plain. 1:2.

421 (240–65). Th .002

Colorless, green tinge, slight weathering. Part of one long blob, wheel-abraded band above. **Pl. 4–18.**

422 (111–66). Th .002

Colorless, green tinge, almost no weathering. Oval blob, wide band of lightly abraded lines above. **Pl. 4–18; Color Pl. 4B.**

423 (113–66). Th ca. .003

Colorless, yellow tinge, dark weathering. Part of one large oval blob. Horizontal wheel-abrasions show that blob was applied incorrectly in a slanting position. **Pl. 4–18; Color Pl. 4B**

424 (3–66). Th .0015

Colorless, dark weathering. Oval blob, fine abraded lines above it. **Pl. 4–18; Color Pl. 4B.**

425 (241–65). Th .0024 +

Very pale green, dark weathering and pitting. Small circular blob. **Pl. 4–18.**

426 (441–64). Th .002

Pale green, dark weathering. Part of one oval blob, trace of another. **Pl. 4–18.**

427 (118–65). Th .002–.0025

Pale green, dark weathering. Irregular round blob containing large bubbles. **Pl. 4–18.**

428 (129–66). Th .001

Colorless, green tinge, dark weathering. Large oval blob. **Pl. 4–18; Color Pl. 4B.**

429 (108–66). Th .0015

Colorless, no weathering. Long irregular blob. **Pl. 4–18; Color Pl. 4B.**

430 (195–66). Th .0024

Pale green, dark weathering. Part of one oval blob. **Pl. 4–18.**

431 (425–64). Th .001

Colorless. Small oval blob, long vertical bubbles, also in vessel wall. **Pl. 4–18.**

432 (4–66). Th .001

Colorless, green tinge, white weathering. Long oval blob. **Pl. 4–18; Color Pl. 4B.**

433 (140–66). Th .001 +

Pale green, surface roughened and pitted. Long narrow blob with tiny bubbles. **Pl. 4–18; Color Pl. 4B.**

434 (256–66). Th .002

Pale green, slight iridescence. Long oval blob with many small bubbles. **Pl. 4–18.**

435 (110–66). Th .0015

Colorless, green tinge, dark weathering. Small oval blob. **Pl. 4–18; Color Pl. 4B.**

436 (439–64). Th .0015

Colorless, white weathering. Large oval blob with many small bubbles. **Pl. 4–18.**

437 (264c–64). Th .0015

Colorless, faint green tinge, dark weathering. Small oval blob. **Pl. 4–18.**

438 (105–65). Th .001

Pale yellow. Tapering wall, part of dark greenish blue blob partially marvered into surface. **Pl. 4–18.**

Conical Vessels, Grooved and Plain (Nos. 439–53)

439 (283–66). D rim .10; Th rim .003

Colorless, faint green tinge, dark weathering inside only. Rim wheel-polished on both sides. Two bands of lightly abraded lines. **Fig. 4–47; Pl. 4–19.**

440 (405–66). D rim .084; Th rim .0035

Greenish blue, white weathering outside, interior unweathered. Rim spreads out and contracts to the lip, wheel-polished. Two abraded bands of fine lines. (Material different from others of same shape.) **Fig. 4–47; Pl. 4–19.**

441 (275–65). D rim .09; Th rim .003

Colorless, yellow tinge, patches of dark weathering. Wheel-polished, slightly flaring rim. Fine abraded lines below the rim inside and out. **Fig. 4–47.**

442 (183–66). D rim .074; Th rim .0035

Pale green, slight weathering. Wheel-polished rim, slightly flaring, wide band of lightly abraded lines. **Fig. 4–47.**

443 (186–66). D rim uncertain; Th rim .003

Pale green, slight pitting. Wheel-polished rim, band of abraded lines. **Fig. 4–47.**

444 (467–66). D rim .092; Th rim .0025

Colorless, green tinge, slight weathering. Rim wheel-polished on both sides, band of abraded lines. **Fig. 4–47.**

445 (145–66). D rim uncertain; Th (uniform) .003

Pale green, surface dulled, dark weathering. Wheel-polished rim, bending inward. Two wide, abraded bands below rim, three lower down. **Fig. 4–47.**

446 (468–66). D rim .102; Th rim .003

Pale yellow, blowing spirals, dark weathering. Wheel-polished rim, two abraded bands on body. **Fig. 4–47.**

447 (334–66). No edge preserved; Th ca. .002

Colorless, green tinge, dark weathering, pitting. Two lightly engraved lines around mid-body. **Fig. 4–47.**

448 (91–66). D rim ca. .10; Th rim .0045

Pale green, dark weathering. Wheel-polished rim. Shallow wheel-cut groove on body. **Fig. 4–47; Pl. 4–19.**

449 (134–66). No edge preserved; Th wall .003

Pale yellow, clinging brown weathering. Section of conical body, one wide wheel-cut groove like preceding. **Fig. 4–47; Pl. 4–19.**

450 (368–66). D rim ca. .085; Th rim .004

Pale green. Severe pitting, dark weathering. Wheel-polished rim, tapering wall. Material like preceding. **Pl. 4–19.**

451 (278–65). D rim .10; Th .003

Colorless, green tinge, patches of dark weathering, pitting. Wheel-polished rim; lightly abraded lines just below rim on both sides. **Fig. 4–47; Pl. 4–19.**

452 (426–66). D rim .11; Th rim .004

Colorless, yellow tinge, dark weathering and pitting outside, none inside. Wheel-polished, slightly flaring rim. **Fig. 4–47.**

453 (445–66). D rim ca. .13; Th rim .003

Colorless, green tinge, slight weathering and pitting. Rim wheel-polished. **Fig. 4–47.**

Conical Vessels, Bottoms (Nos. 454–58)

454 (107–65). Th at broken edge .001; near bottom .003

Pale green, pitting and dark weathering. A few small spherical bubbles near bottom, vertical bubbles farther up the wall. Thickened, concave bottom, no pontil mark. Narrow abraded band about mid-body. **Fig. 4–47; Pl. 4–19.**

455 (92–66). Th wall .0015; bottom .0025

Pale green, streak of purple in bottom, little weathering. Slightly concave bottom, no pontil mark. **Fig. 4–47; Pl. 4–19.**

456 (376–66). Th wall .0015

Light green. Thickened, slightly concave bottom with roughened surface, no pontil mark. **Fig. 4–47; Pl. 4–19.**

457 (6–66). PH .032; Th wall .002

Colorless, green tinge, thick dark weathering. Slightly concave bottom, no pontil mark.

458 (86–66). PH .031; Th wall .0015

Colorless, faint yellow tinge, dark weathering and pitting. Slightly concave bottom, no pontil mark.

Bowls and Cups (Nos. 459–96)

Many bowls and cups are decorated like the beakers, with grooves or abraded lines. Of the 36 catalogued fragments, 24 came from the factory dump; 8 were from the extreme eastern part of the excavated area, where lamps and pottery datable to the 2nd c. were also found. This suggests that some of the glass bowls (Nos. 465–68, 474–76) may date to the same time. Since techniques changed little during several hundred years, it is difficult to determine dates unless other criteria can be adduced. Some differences do exist: for example the grooved

bowls thought to be 2nd c. have thinner walls than those from the dump, and their rims do not flare; and fragments with abraded decoration, considered 4th c., have been found only in the factory dump.

The two joining fragments of No. 469 were found widely separated—one in the dump, the other 30 m distant, in the central part of the excavated area. If the criterion of wall thickness is applied (the rim is missing), the bowl fits into the later category. How these two fragments became so widely dispersed is puzzling; this also occurs with pottery (Chap. 7, No. 153).

The bowls have been arranged according to shape: shallow, hemispherical, deep. It has been assumed that they are rounded on the bottom, without distinct bases. All the rims are ground and wheel-polished. The material is generally very compact, seldom having even tiny bubbles.

The colors are limited to colorless with green or yellow tinge (20 examples), pale green (10), pale bluish green (6), a few yellowish green, one colorless with a purple streak. The weathering seems to follow the coloration; pale green fragments often have dark weathering, while colorless pieces are weathered white.

Decoration, when present, almost invariably consists of grooves or lightly abraded bands. Thin-walled bowls, including those presumed to be 2nd c., may have grooves as deep as those of thick-walled bowls.

Many tiny, delicate fragments, colorless or nearly colorless, from vessels of indeterminate shape, were found in sifting earth from the factory dump. Most are unweathered or nearly so. All preserved rims are cracked-off, some polished, some not. It is doubtful whether these are from vessels made at the site; they might have been brought in for use as cullet.[214]

Parallels from nearby sites for contemporary bowls with grooved decoration are rare. For shallow bowls such as Nos. 459–64 there is one comparable fragment from Sardis[215] and several from Sirmium, Yugoslavia;[216] in western Europe there are many more.[217] For the hemispherical bowls (Nos. 465–69) and the deep bowls with vertical walls (Nos. 470–76) parallels from dated contexts are elusive. For the bowls with flaring rim, both shallow and deep, thin-walled and thick-walled, more comparative material is available. Thin

---

214. Examples of these fragments are 224–66, 7 rim fragments, each with fine engraved horizontal lines; 223–66, 13 fragments without finished edges, all with abraded horizontal lines; 222–66, 4 fragments, one with unworked rim, others without finished edge, all with abraded horizontal lines; 221–66, 3 fragments (one with rim?) with a series of horizontal abraded lines; 127–65, without finished edge, four bands of abraded lines, possibly from a cup; 245–66, 226–66, 279–66, cup rims (cracked-off) with abraded horizontal lines.

215. Saldern, *Sardis Glass*, 32, no. 206, pl. 22 (without context).

216. M. Parović-Pešikan, "Excavations of a Late Roman Villa at Sirmium," *Sirmium* 2 (Belgrade, 1971) 38, pl. 27, 1–4.

217. Isings, *Roman Glass*, Form 116 and references given there.

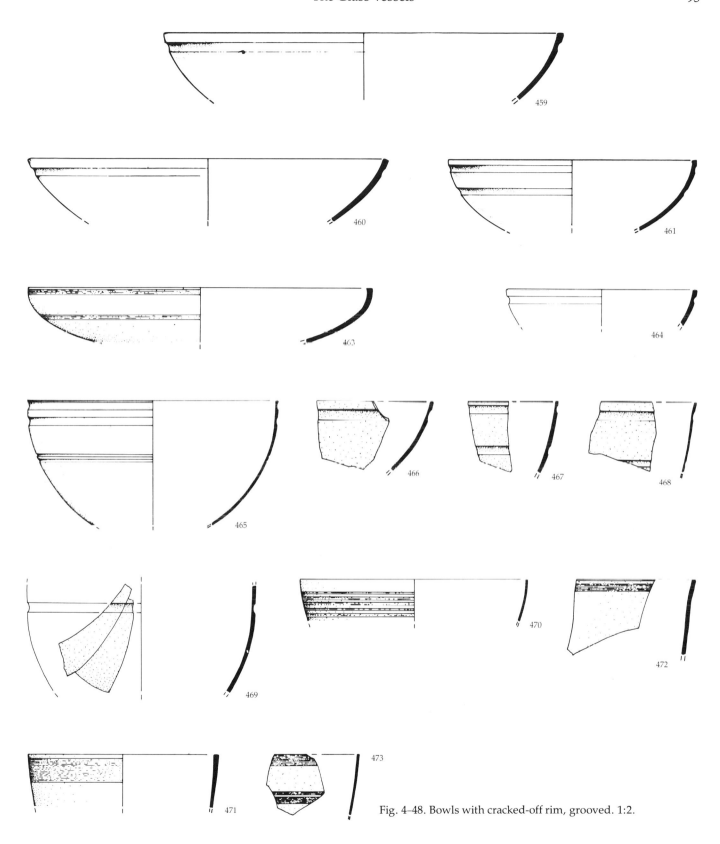

Fig. 4–48. Bowls with cracked-off rim, grooved. 1:2.

bowls have been found at Tyre,[218] in Cyprus,[219] and extensively in the West.[220] Bowls with thicker walls (Nos. 483–84) have been found in Jerusalem and at Mesad Tamar.[221] One fragment found at Jalame has decoration other than simple engraved or abraded horizontal lines (see No. 518).

Shallow Bowls

459 (20–67). D rim .21; Th .0035

Colorless, white weathering, surface dulled and pitted. Wheel-polished rim, broad groove slightly below. **Fig. 4–48; Pl. 4–19.**

460 (144–66). D rim .019; Th .0035

Colorless, green tinge, many tiny bubbles, dark weathering only where polished, iridescence. Wheel-polished rim, broad groove just below. **Fig. 4–48; Pl. 4–19.**

461 (85–65). D rim ca. .13; Th .003

Pale green, dark weathering, iridescence. Wheel-polished rim, two broad grooves, one just under the rim, another below. **Fig. 4–48; Pl. 4–19.**

462 (486–66). D rim .16; Th rim .0025

Pale greenish blue, a few bubbles. Heavy white weathering and pitting. Faint polishing marks, obscured by weathering. **Pl. 4–19.**

463 (475–65). D rim .184; Th .004

Pale bluish green, white weathering, surface pitted and dulled. Rim wheel-polished but uneven. Two broad bands of wheel-abraded lines, one at rim, another lower down. **Fig. 4–48; Pl. 4–19.**

464 (191–66). D rim ca. .10; Th .0025

Colorless, green tinge, slight dark weathering, pitting. Wheel-polished rim, lightly abraded lines and shallow groove below. **Fig. 4–48; Pl. 4–19.**

Hemispherical Bowls

465 (150–65). D rim .134; Th rim .0024

Colorless, green tinge, patches of white weathering. All exterior wheel-polished, two wide grooves below rim, two narrower grooves lower down. From Trench J. 91–65 and 93–65, colorless fragments with abraded lines, were found nearby and may date to the 2nd c. **Fig. 4–48; Pl. 4–19.**

466 (146–65). D rim ca. .17; Th rim .0025

Colorless, green tinge, slight dark weathering,

especially in groove. Wheel-polished rim, wide groove below. From Trench J. **Fig. 4–48.**

467 (294–66). D rim ca. .17; Th rim .002

Colorless, green tinge, slight weathering and pitting. Rim and exterior wheel-polished. Wide grooves below the rim, another lower down. From Trench J. **Fig. 4–48.**

468 (276–65). D rim ca. .12; Th rim .0015

Colorless, green tinge, slight weathering and pitting. Rim and part of exterior wheel-polished, wide shallow groove below rim and another farther down. From Trench J. **Fig. 4–48.**

469 (8–66). Max dim ca. .12; Th .003

Two joining fragments, no finished edge. Pale green, dark weathering, iridescence. Wide wheel-cut groove near top of fragment, which cannot be far below the rim. The two pieces were found about 30 m distant from each other. Probably 2nd c. **Fig. 4–48; Pl. 4–20.**

Deep Bowls

470 (455–66). D rim .124; Th rim .002

Colorless, green tinge, slight weathering. Rim slightly wheel-polished, lightly abraded bands. **Fig. 4–48.**

471 (184–66). Est D ca. .10; Th rim .0035

Colorless, yellow tinge, slight weathering, surface dulled. Wheel-polished rim, wide abraded band. **Fig. 4–48.**

472 (462–66). D rim ca. .20; Th rim .003

Pale bluish green, white weathering, pitting. Rim ground, not much polished. Wheel-abraded lines below rim. **Fig. 4–48.**

473 (201–65). D rim ca. .08–.10; Th rim .002

Colorless, greenish blue tinge, a few bubbles, slight weathering. Wheel-polished rim. Two bands of fine abraded lines. **Fig. 4–48.**

474 (151–65). D rim .11; Th rim .002

Colorless, green tinge, white and dark weathering, pitting. Wide groove, exterior wheel-polished above groove. From Trench J. **Fig. 4–49; Pl. 4–20.**

475 (224–65). D rim .09; Th rim .0015

Colorless, green tinge, dark weathering, pitting. Rim and part of exterior wheel-polished; shallow, wide groove. From Trench J. **Fig. 4–49.**

476 (223–65). D rim ca. .11; Th rim .0025

Colorless, green tinge, tiny bubbles, dark weathering. Rim and part of both faces wheel-polished; two wide shallow grooves. **Fig. 4–49.**

Bowls with Flaring Rim

477 (88–66). D rim .11; Th rim .0015

Colorless, green tinge, a few small bubbles, dark weathering. Rim slightly wheel-polished. Two bands of abraded lines. **Fig. 4–49; Pl. 4–20.**

218. Barag, "Glass Vessels," Type 3.21; Harden, "Tomb-groups," 152, No. G 23.
219. Harden, "Vasa," 49, no. 20, fig. 20m (dated 300–350).
220. Isings, *Roman Glass*, Form 96 and references there.
221. Bagatti-Milik, 148, fig. 35, no. 18; Erdmann, "Mezad Tamar," 106, nos. 431–35. The author suggests these may be early Arab lamps, which seems unlikely unless the material differs from ours. This confusion is probably due to the fact that few examples have been found in the Palestinian region. Comparative material, the author remarks (n. 72), is more plentiful in the West. She offers numerous references.

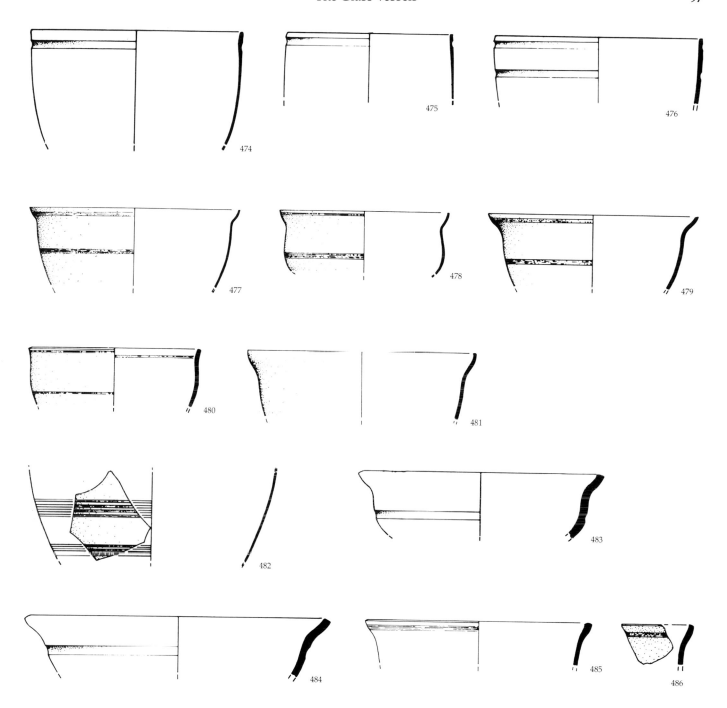

Fig. 4–49. Bowls with cracked-off rim, grooved. 1:2.

478 (170–66). D rim .092; Th rim .0015

Colorless, green tinge, slight dark weathering and pitting, iridescence. Wheel-polished rim, two abraded bands. **Fig. 4–49.**

479 (448–66). D rim .11; Th rim .0025

Pale green, slight dark weathering. Wheel-polished rim, two abraded bands. Wall somewhat thicker than in similar vessels. **Fig. 4–49.**

480 (193–66). D rim .092; Th rim .003

Pale green, a few bubbles, slight weathering, pitting. Slightly wheel-polished rim, two abraded bands outside, one inside. **Fig. 4–49.**

481 (13–65). D rim .12; Th rim .002

Yellowish green. Slightly wheel-polished rim, not quite even. **Fig. 4–49; Pl. 4–20.**

Fig. 4–50. Bowls with cracked-off rim. 1:2.

482 (30–66). Max dim .11; Th wall .002

Colorless, green tinge, slight dark weathering on exterior only. Fragment of body, no edge preserved. Two bands of lightly abraded lines. **Fig. 4–49.**

483 (131–66). D rim .134; Th rim .004

Pale green, dark weathering, pitting. Wheel-polished rim. Wide wheel-cut groove around body. Bottom probably rounded. **Fig. 4–49.**

484 (27–66). D rim ca. .164; Th rim .004+

Pale green, a few tiny bubbles, dark weathering. Wheel-polished inside and out. Wide wheel-cut groove. **Fig. 4–49; Pl. 4–20.**

485 (466–64). D rim ca. .12

Light greenish blue. Wheel-polished rim, band of lightly abraded lines. **Fig. 4–49.**

486 (470–66). D rim uncertain

Pale green. Rim wheel-polished, with a groove along the top caused by a slip of the tool (?). Wide abraded band. Shape similar to preceding. **Fig. 4–49.**

Cups with Slightly Flaring Rims

487 (402–64). D rim .08

Colorless, green tinge, a few tiny bubbles, slight weathering. Wheel-polished rim, series of narrow abraded bands. **Fig. 4–50.**

488 (399–64). D rim .09

Colorless, yellow tinge, many tiny bubbles, dark weathering, pitting. Rim cut rather roughly. Lightly abraded lines immediately below it. **Fig. 4–50.**

489 (469–66). D rim uncertain

Colorless, green tinge. Polished rim, abraded band just below it. **Fig. 4–50.**

490 (59–64). D rim .08

Colorless, purple tinge and dark purple streak, blowing spirals. Pitted inside, dark weathering outside. Rim slightly wheel-polished. **Fig. 4–50.**

491 (501–64). D rim .052

Pale green. Bands of lightly abraded lines inside and out. Wall tapers inward, perhaps forming a conical shape. **Fig. 4–50.**

492 (476–65). D rim .09

Pale bluish green, blowing spirals. Several bands of lightly abraded lines. **Fig. 4–50.**

Cups with Wall Indents

493 (159–65). D rim .10

Pale yellowish green, a few tiny bubbles, dark weathering. Slightly flaring rim, wheel-polished. Large indent; there were probably five or six around the body. **Fig. 4–51.**

494 (89–66). PH .032

Colorless, green tinge, dark weathering. No finished edge preserved. Flaring toward rim, indent at lower edge. Lightly abraded lines around body. **Fig. 4–51.**

Bowl Bottoms

495 (513–64). Max dim .025

Colorless, green tinge. Weathered outside only. Two concentric circles lightly engraved inside (D ca. .04), within these a circle (D .02) of scratched lines. **Fig. 4–51.**

496 (37–66). PH .023

Light green. Rounded bottom, no pontil mark. This might be a conical lamp, but the wall is very thin, and the shape spreads out more than is usual. **Fig. 4–51.**

Moils (Nos. 497–516)

These waste products, resulting from the manufacture of vessels with cracked-off rims, were found in great numbers, most of them in the factory dump. Their lower edges vary in thickness from .001 to .005 and the bottom diameters from .06 to .20. This wide range indicates that

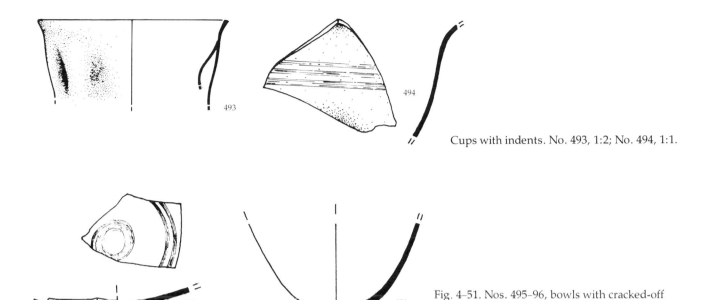

Cups with indents. No. 493, 1:2; No. 494, 1:1.

Fig. 4–51. Nos. 495–96, bowls with cracked-off rims (bottoms). 1:1.

many different vessels were made in this technique (described above).

Statistics have been compiled for 359 moils; probably there are still more among the debris recovered.

A general summary produced the following information:

Moils .0045–.0055 thick are rare (8) and range from .11 to .14 in diameter.

Moils .004 thick are not common (24); their diameters are mostly between .105 and .15. **Pl. 4-22D.**

Moils .0035 thick (24) are mostly .095 to .14 in diameter.

Moils .003 thick are more numerous (58); the diameters range from .06 to .20, with a concentration between .065 and .12. **Pl. 4-22C.**

Moils .0025 thick are fewer (39); their diameters are chiefly between .09 and .13. **Pl. 4-22B.**

Moils .002 thick are more plentiful (86), their diameters between .06 and .20, with a concentration from .07 to .13. **Pl. 4-22A.**

Moils .0015 thick (56) have diameters from .075 to .20, the greatest concentration from .08 to .11. **Pl. 4-21E.**

Moils .001 thick (64) have diameters from .06 to .20, the greatest concentration from .075 to .11. **Pl. 4-21D.**

Matching up vessels with moils is difficult: one attempt is shown here (Pl. 4–21A). The two do not fit exactly, but the diameters are quite close.

Tops of moils are hard to identify as they are usually extremely fragmentary. Nos. 497–99 (Fig. 4–52) are the best preserved tops. On Pl. 4–21B,C are shown fragments of moil tops of various thicknesses. These are green, yellowish green, and colorless; all exhibit impurities and bubbles.

Most of the fragments are from the lower part of the moils. All those shown in profile (Nos. 500–509) are either pale green or colorless with a green tinge. These are the predominating colors; there are a few greenish blue, yellowish green, etc. Almost all have bubbles, swirls made by rotating the parison while blowing, black impurities, and weathering of various sorts, often quite dark in color. Nos. 502 and 510 have fine abraded lines around the outside edge; there are quite a number of such pieces, most of them very small. These lines indicate either the scoring of the rim before cutting off the moil, or the extension of the decorative lines to a point higher than was intended. In any case, they show that abrasion and engraving were accomplished before separating the moil. Nos. 500, 502, and 504 display the rough edge produced by the removal of the moil (see also conical vessel No. 404). The features seen on these profiles can be checked by referring to Fig. 4–45.

497 (396–66). D top ca. .03; Th of lowest preserved portion .004

Light green. Fragment of top and side. Blowing spirals, elongated bubbles, black impurities. Dark weathering outside. **Fig. 4–52.**

498 (258–66). D top exterior .028, interior .019

Colorless with purple streaks. Three joining fragments of top and side. The top is flat, broken off smoothly. Vertical oval bubbles, a few small impurities, slight iridescence. **Fig. 4–52.**

499 (482–66). Th at top .0035; Th at bottom .002

Colorless, green tinge. Many small bubbles near bottom, dark weathering. Fragment of central part, no edge preserved. Horizontal tool marks (?) on exterior. The top of

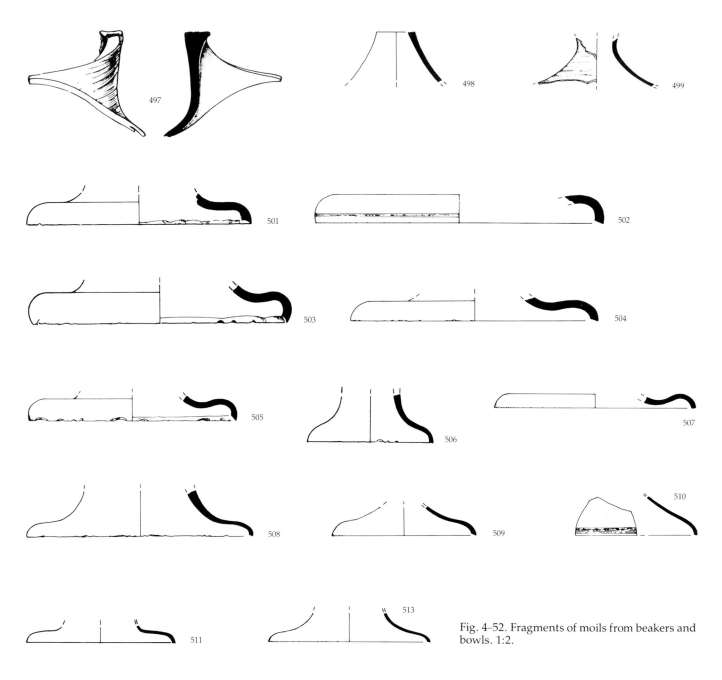

Fig. 4–52. Fragments of moils from beakers and bowls. 1:2.

the fragment must be very near the blowpipe (D of pipe end ca. .025). **Fig. 4–52.**

500   (307–66). Outer D of ring .021, inner .01

Pale bluish green. Blowing spirals, dark weathering. Perhaps the top of a moil, preserving entire ring formed by blowpipe. Top and bottom of the fragment are rough.

501   (5–64). D rim .12; Th at edge .0055

Colorless, green tinge. Fragment of bottom and side. Note chipped edge. Small bubbles, few black impurities, dark weathering. **Fig. 4–52.**

502   (338–66). Est D .152; Th at edge .005

Pale green. Many small bubbles, almost no weathering.

Fragment of bottom and side. Evenly cut rim. Lightly abraded lines around exterior just above edge. **Fig. 4–52.**

503   (395–66). D rim .135; Th at edge .005

Pale green. Clear glass, few impurities and bubbles, slight weathering outside. Fragment of body and side. **Fig. 4–52.**

504   (493–66). D bottom unknown, probably .12; Th .005

Pale green, bubbly, blowing spirals, dark weathering. Fragment of body and side. **Fig. 4–52.**

505   (106–66). D rim .11; Th at edge .004

Pale green, long bubbles, black impurities, almost no weathering. Fragment of bottom and side. Bottom edge rough. **Fig. 4–52.**

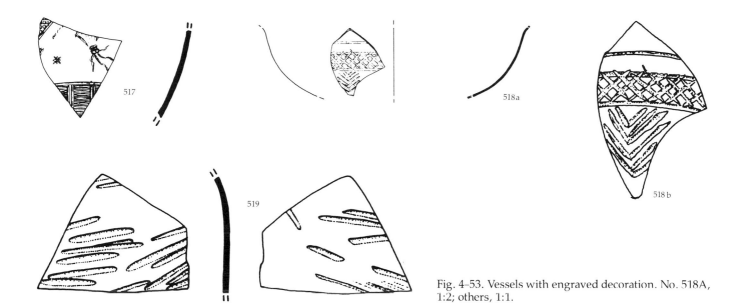

Fig. 4–53. Vessels with engraved decoration. No. 518A,
1:2; others, 1:1.

506   (77–66). D rim .065; Th at edge .0035

Pale green, large and small bubbles, few dark impurities, dark weathering outside, interior unweathered. Fragment of bottom and side. Edge rather rough. **Fig. 4–52.**

507   (157–65). D rim .104; Th at edge .003

Pale green, many large and small bubbles, few impurities. Iridescence and dark weathering. Fragment of bottom and side. Rim somewhat rough. **Fig. 4–52.**

508   (492–66). D rim unknown; Th at edge .0025

Pale green, muddy appearance, impurities, large bubbles. Fragment of bottom and side. Edge unevenly cut. **Fig. 4–52.**

509   (472–66). D rim ca. .076; Th at edge .0025

Pale green, many small bubbles, dark weathering, surface dulled. Fragment of bottom and side. Uneven, slightly rough edge. **Fig. 4–52.**

510   (477–66). D rim ca. .16; Th at edge .002+

Pale green, dark weathering, pitting. Fragment of bottom and side. Smooth edge, band of fine abraded lines just above. **Fig. 4–52.**

511   (394–66). D rim .08; Th at edge .002

Colorless, green tinge, tiny bubbles, a few black impurities, slight weathering. Fragment of bottom and side. Edge somewhat rough. **Fig. 4–52.**

512   (262–66). D rim .13; Th at edge .0015

Pale greenish blue, excellent material, no weathering. Fragment of bottom and side. Wheel-polished edge, band of fine abraded lines just above.

513   (474–66). D rim .085; Th at edge .0015

Colorless, yellow tinge, one impurity, brown weather-

ing following line of blowing spirals. Fragment of bottom and side. Edge slightly rough. **Fig. 4–52.**

514   (156–65). D ca. .13; Th at edge .0045

Pale green. Long horizontal bubbles, a few impurities, slight dark weathering. Fragment of bottom and side, bottom edge rough.

515   (101–64). D .15; Th at edge .004

Pale green. Tiny bubbles, iridescence, dark weathering, pitting. Fragment of bottom and side, edge quite smooth.

516   (509–65). Th at lower edge .002; upper edge .0035

Colorless, yellow tinge, many bubbles in swirling pattern. Iridescent. Fragment, no finished edge.

Vessels with Engraved Designs (Nos. 517–19)

Only three fragments with engraved designs were found; it is obvious that such were not made in the factory.

No. 517 (shape uncertain) is of extraordinarily fine quality. The only parallel for the design that has come to my attention is a partly preserved bowl and some fragments that have eight-pointed stars like those of our piece. These were found at Samaria in a 4th-c. context.[222] The quality of the material and the execution of the latter are, however, far inferior.

No. 518, although unique at Jalame, is representative of a common type of bowl widespread in the 4th c. in the West. In the East it was much rarer. The best examples are one found at Tyre and another in the Ashmolean

222. Crowfoot, *Samaria* 3, 416–17, fig. 97.

Museum, undoubtedly of Syro-Palestinian origin.[223] The most detailed discussion of the shape and decoration is Harden's article on the Wint Hill bowl, found in England.[224] He determined that the center for making these bowls was Cologne, and since the time of his publication others have been found that confirm this theory. The two bowls from the Syro-Palestinian area are believed by Harden to have originated there, even though they are extremely like the Western examples. Two fragments found at Corinth seem to be closely related to such bowls.[225]

No. 519 is a curious piece of indefinite shape for which only one possible parallel has thus far been noted: a bowl found in Portchester Castle, in a late 3rd or early 4th c. context.[226]

517   (118–66). PH .026; Th .0015

Colorless, green tinge, a little white weathering. Fragment of body, no finished edge. Perhaps a shallow bowl. Very fine wheel-cut engraving: at upper left, part of a sec-

223. Iliffe, "El Bassa," 88, fig. 17 (D rim .14); Harden, "Tomb-groups," 156–58, fig. 3 (D rim .137). The dating of the El Bassa bowl has been revised by Barag to second half of 4th c., instead of the year 396.
224. D. B. Harden, "The Wint Hill Hunting Bowl and Related Glasses," *JGS* 2 (1960) 45–81.
225. Davidson, *Corinth* 12, 95, nos. 593–94, fig. 6.
226. Harden, "The Glass," in Cunliffe, *Portchester,* 369, fig. 197,3.

tion with tiny squares bounded by a diagonal line; below this five short strokes in the same diagonal line. At upper right a squid (?), the body outlined with engraved lines, very fine scratched lines in the interior, two large eyes in the "face," from which extend four wavy tentacles made by short scratched lines. At left center, an eight-pointed star—a starfish (?). At extreme left two slanting lines extending into the broken edge. Filling the bottom of the fragment is an engraved basket (?): a horizontal groove with two sets of double vertical grooves depending from it, the spaces between them filled with short horizontal grooves. From factory dump. **Fig. 4–53; Pl. 4–23.**

518   (500–64). PH .043; Max dim .144; Th ca. .002

Light greenish blue, one large bubble. Fragment of body, no finished edge. Shallow bowl with outsplayed rim (not preserved). On exterior, three sets of fine wheel-abraded lines; on top of the two lower sets of lines are coarse hand-abraded patterns—checkerboard above, chevron below. From wine press tank. **Fig. 4–53A and B (detail); Pl. 4–23.**

519   (56–64). Max dim .04; Th .002

Pale green, dark weathering, pitting on exterior. Fragment with slight curve, no edge preserved, perhaps a dish. Well cut, apparently random pattern of long lines, many on convex exterior (?), fewer on interior (?). From factory dump. **Fig. 4–53; Pl. 4–23.**

5

GLORIA S. MERKER

The Coins

During the four seasons of excavation at Jalame, 403 coins were found.[1] Of these, 207 proved to be identifiable beyond reasonable doubt and are described in the catalogue.[2] The earliest are seven local city coins of the 1st–3rd centuries (Nos. 1–7), including issues of Tyre and Ptolemais-Ace. However, most of the preserved coins are bronzes issued at Roman Imperial mints from the mid–3rd to the 5th century (Nos. 8–114, 116–207). The mints of Antioch, Constantinople, Alexandria, Cyzicus, Nicomedia, Thessalonica, Rome, and Arles are represented. In addition to the Imperial bronzes, there is one gold coin, a solidus of Valens (No. 115). No recognizable hoards were found; all the coins were single finds scattered throughout the site.

The chronological distribution of the identifiable Roman Imperial coinage should provide evidence for dating the glass factory, assuming that the number of preserved coins of different periods reflects in a general way the rise and decline of commercial activity at the site. This chronological distribution is summarized in Fig. 5-1, dividing the material into convenient periods. Of coins issued during the second half of the 3rd century and the early years of the 4th there are only eleven examples (Nos. 8–18). For the two decades 314–ca. 335, the finds remain few—only eight coins are preserved (Nos. 19–26). The number increases slightly for the period 333–ca. 350, with seventeen coins (Nos. 27–33, 67–72, 83–86). A very sharp increase in the number of identifiable coins can be observed beginning with issues of the later years of the reign of Constantius II, dating 351–361 (Nos. 34–66). If to these are added the contemporary coins of Julian issued in 355–363 (Nos. 73–82), and other, not completely identifiable coins of the House of Con-

stantine from the period 351–363 (Nos. 87–108), the total number of preserved coins issued during the brief period 351–363 grows to sixty-five, nearly one-third of all the identifiable coins from Jalame. A slight decrease to sixty-two coins can be noted for the somewhat longer period 364–383 (Nos. 109–28, 132–35, 148–85). Issues belonging to the late years of the 4th century and the first years of the 5th gradually decrease in number. For the quarter-century 383–408 there are thirty identifiable coins (Nos. 129–31, 136–45, 186–202). Only seven coins represent the second and third quarters of the 5th century (Nos. 146–47, 203–7); the latest of these was issued during the reign of Leo I.

The chronological distribution of the coins suggests that the glass factory was established about 351. The relatively small number of coins issued before this date that were found at the site probably are remains of the non-commercial occupation that predated the factory. The factory appears to have flourished until 383. Industrial activity at the site appears to have come to an end altogether during the late years of the 4th century. The few coins belonging to the 5th century probably represent the later habitation of the site.

Abbreviations used in the catalogue:

BMC Palestine: G. F. Hill, *A Catalogue of the Greek Coins in the British Museum . . . Palestine* (London, 1914).
BMC Phoenicia: G. F. Hill, *A Catalogue of the Greek Coins in the British Museum . . . Phoenicia* (London, 1910).
Bruck: Guido Bruck, *Die Spätrömische Kupferprägung* (Graz, 1961).
JIAN: *Journal International d'Archéologie Numismatique*.
LRBC: P. V. Hill, J. P. C. Kent, and R. A. G. Carson, *Late Roman Bronze Coinage* (London, 1960).
RIC: H. Mattingly et al., eds., *The Roman Imperial Coinage* (London, 1923–   ). Vol. VIII of *RIC* appeared after this chapter had been completed. References to this volume have been added for coins with legible mintmarks; when needed, revised dates have been given in parentheses.

---

1. The following coins were taken by the Department of Antiquities, State of Israel, to complete its collections: Catalogue Nos. 10, 11, 13, 17, 19, 21, 26, 32, 69, 78, 115, 139, 148, 166. The remaining coins are stored in the Museum of Art and Archaeology, University of Missouri–Columbia.

2. Neither the precise forms of dress worn nor the breaks in the legends have been recorded because of the rather poor preservation of many of the coins. Thanks are due to Homer Athanassiou, Barbara L. Johnson, and Irwin L. Merker, for their participation in the identification and inventory of the coins.

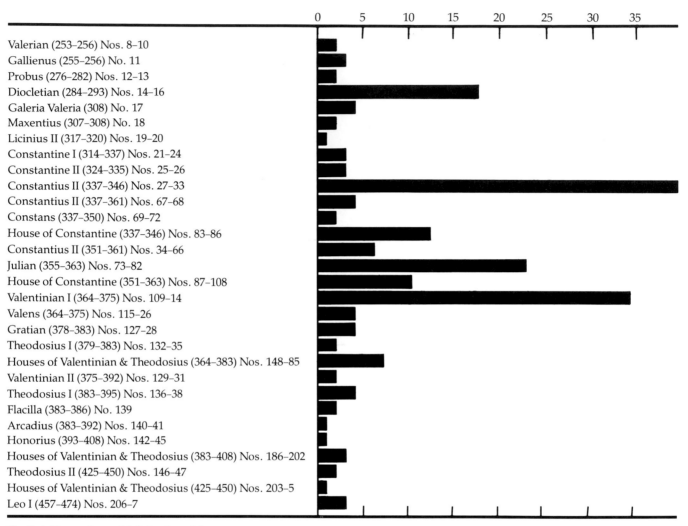

Fig. 5–1. Roman Imperial Coins from Jalame

Local City Coinage

1 (9–65).   Obv. Bust of Tyche r., wearing turreted crown, veil. In l. field palm branch.
Rev. Palm tree. In r. field monogram ⳤ, below . . . A Σ Date illegible.
AE Tyre 18/17 B.C.-A.D. 114/115 *BMC Phoenicia* nos. 275–87. Issues of the mint of Tyre are predominant among the city coins from sites in the Galilee; see D. Barag, "Tyrian Currency in Galilee," *Israel Numismatic Journal* 6–7 (1982–1983) 7–13.
From h–i:35–36 (Trench F–2) depth .80.[3]

2 (43–64).   Obv. Laureate bust of emperor r. [IMP]MAVRANT[ONINVS]
Rev. Bull r., standard behind. In r. field murex shell.

3. Depths for coins are below surface at points mentioned.

AE Tyre 211–217 (Caracalla) *BMC Phoenicia* nos. 377–78.
From b–c:43 (Trench D) depth ca. .45.

3 (97–65).   Obv. Draped and laureate bust of emperor r. [IMPCGVIBIVSTR]EBOGA[LLVSAVG]
Rev. Astarte with r. hand on trophy, crowned by Nike on column, all within hexastyle temple. [COL]TVROME[T]
AE Tyre 251–253 (Trebonianus Gallus) *BMC Phoenicia* no. 476 (Gallienus); *JIAN* 7 (1904) 92, no. 2462.
From FF:33 (Trench P) depth .35.

4 (8–66).   Obv. Laureate head of emperor r. [IMPCGV]IBVO[LVSIANVSAVG]
Rev. Tree between two baetyls. In ex. dog r., finding murex shell.
AE Tyre 251–253 (Volusian) *BMC Phoenicia* no. 442 (Trebonianus Gallus).

From GG, along north scarp of Trench OP, depth ca. .10.

5 (89–65).   Obv. Draped and laureate bust of emperor r. IMPCAESMA[VANTONINVSAVG]
Rev. Tyche holding rudder and cornucopiae, crowned by Nike on column, all within tetrastyle temple. COL[PTO]
AE Ptolemais-Ace 218–222 (Elagabalus) *BMC Phoenicia* nos. 37–40; L. Kadman, *The Coins of Akko-Ptolemais* (Jerusalem, 1961) no. 166.
From factory dump (Trench L) depth ca. 1.10.

6 (65–64).   Obv. Draped and laureate bust of emperor r.
Rev. Founder plowing r. with bull and cow yoked.
AE Caesarea or Sebaste 211–217 (Caracalla) *BMC Palestine* p. 26 no. 108, p. 80 no. 14.
From Trench H, depth ca. 1.50.

7 (84–65).   Obv. Bust of emperor r.
Rev. Bust of Sarapis r.
AE Caesarea, Neapolis, or Eleutheropolis 218–222 (Elagabalus) *BMC Palestine* p. 27 nos. 116–17, p. 62 nos. 106–8, p. 142 no. 6.
From t:9 (Trench A–6) depth 1.25.

Roman Imperial Coinage

Valerian

8 (107–65).   Obv. Draped and radiate bust of emperor r. IMPCPLICVALERIANVSAVG
Rev. Aequitas holding scale and cornucopia [AEQ]VITASAVGG
Antoninianus 253–254 Antioch *RIC* V, 1 no. 278.
From south part of Trench F–5, depth 1.00.

9 (68–64).   Obv. Draped and radiate bust of emperor r. [IMPC]PLICVALE[RIANVS]AV[G]
Rev. Emperor holding scepter, sacrificing l. over altar. [P]MTRPIICOSPP
Antoninianus 254 *RIC* V, 1 no. 208.
From Trench I, surface.

10 (59–65).   Obv. Draped and radiate bust of emperor r. IMPCPLICVALERIANVSAVG
Rev. Roma seated l. on shield, holding Victory and spear. ROMAEAETERNAE
Antoninianus 256 *RIC* V, 1 no. 221.
From S:33 (Trench M) just below surface. **Pl. 5–1.**

Gallienus

11 (81–65).   Obv. Draped and radiate bust of emperor r. IMPCPLICGALLIENVSPFAVG

Rev. Emperors sacrificing at altar. PI[ET]ASAVGG
Antoninianus 255–256 Antioch *RIC* V, 1 no. 447.
From w–x:4–5 (Trench A–6) depth 1.35. **Pl. 5–1.**

Probus

12 (40–66).   Obv. Draped and radiate bust of emperor r. IMPCMAVRPROBVSP[FAVG]
Rev. Emperor r., receiving Victory from Jupiter. CLEMENTIATEMP In center field S· In ex. XXI
Antoninianus 276–282 Antioch *RIC* V, 2 no. 922.
From bb:8 (Trench J–6) near surface.

13 (125–66).   Same obv. and rev. types as No. 12. In center field Γ
Antoninianus 276–282.
From west part of Trench Y–3S, dark fill near bedrock, from sifting, with Nos. 16, 30, 73, 77, 108.

Diocletian

14 (108–66).   Obv. Draped and radiate bust of emperor r. IMPCCVALDIOCLETIANVSPFAVG
Rev. Victory holding palm, offering wreath to emperor holding globe and scepter. VICTORIAAVG In center field Z In ex. XXI
Antoninianus 284 Antioch *RIC* V, 2 no. 326.
From Trench X–1, depth ca. .15–.20.

15 (9–67).   Obv. Draped and radiate bust of emperor r. IMPCCVALDIOCLETIANVSPFAVG
Rev. Jupiter holding globe and scepter, facing Hercules holding Victory, club, and lion skin. IOVETHERCVCONSERAVGG In center field Z In ex. XXI
Antoninianus 293 Antioch *RIC* V, 2 no. 323.
From b:41 in dark fill just above bedrock (see Chap. 2, glass-sorting floors). **Pl. 5–1.**

16 (126–66).   Same obv. and rev. types as No. 15.
Antoninianus 285 or 293 Mintmark illegible *RIC* V, 2 no. 323.
Found with Nos. 13, 30, 73, 77, 108.

Galeria Valeria

17 (86–66).   Obv. Draped and diademed bust of empress r. GALVALERIAAVG
Rev. Venus l., holding apple and raising her veil. VENERIVICTRICI In l. field P In r. field R In ex. ALE (?)
Follis 308 Alexandria (?) *RIC* VI no. 74.
From qq:61 (Trench J–11) depth .55.

Maxentius

18 (1–65).   Obv. Laureate bust of emperor r.
IMPCMAXENTIVSPFAVG
Rev. Roma seated in hexastyle temple. CON-
SERV[VRB]SVAE In l. field H In ex. RP
Follis 307–308 Rome *RIC* VI no. 202a.
From i–j:4–5 (Trench A–4) depth .40. **Pl. 5–1.**

Licinius II

19 (41–65).   Obv. Draped and laureate bust of Licinius l.,
holding mappa and scepter.
DNVALLICINLICINIVSNOBC
Rev. Jupiter l., holding Victory on globe and
scepter, captive kneeling at l. IOVICON-
SERVATORICAESS In r. field Δ I In ex.
SMANT
Follis 317–320 Antioch *RIC* VII no. 29.
From II:33–34 (Trench P) depth .35. **Pl. 5–1.**

20 (21–66).   Same obv. and rev. types as No. 19, but cap-
tive standing. In r. field A (?) In ex.
SMANT
Follis 317–320 Antioch *RIC* VII no. 29.
From AA:16 (Trench S–1) depth 1.30.

Constantine I

21 (77–65).   Obv. Draped and laureate bust of emperor r.
[IMP]CONSTANTINVSPFAVG
Rev. Sol. l. holding globe. SOLIIN-
VICTO[COMITI] In l. field R In r. field F
X
Follis 314–315 Rome *RIC* VII no. 27.
From P:28 (Trench M–1) on bedrock.

22 (6–65).   Obv. Laureate head of emperor r. CON-
STANTINVSAVG
Rev. Camp gate with two towers, star above.
PROVIDENTIAEAVGG In ex. SMKT·
Follis 325–326 Cyzicus *LRBC* I 1187; *RIC* VII
no. 34.
From RR:37–38 (Trench J–1) near surface.
Pl. 5–1.

23 (87–65).   Obv. Helmeted bust of Constantinople l.
CONSTANTINOPOLIS
Rev. Victory l. on prow, holding shield. In
ex. SMALA·
Follis 335–337 Alexandria *LRBC* I 1444; *RIC*
VII no. 71.
From GG:47 (Trench Q) depth 1.20. **Pl. 5–1.**

24 (96–65).   Obv. Helmeted bust of Constantinople l.
CONSTANTINOPOLIS
Rev. Standard between two soldiers.
GLORIAEXERCITVS In ex. CONSA
Follis 336–337 Constantinople *LRBC* I
1039–40; *RIC* VII no. 144.
From aa:32 (Trench J–2) .50 below top of wall
of south wine press vat.

Constantine II

25 (16–65).   Obv. Draped and laureate bust of Con-
stantine r. CONSTANTINVSIV[NNOB]C
Rev. Camp gate with two towers, star above.
PROV[IDEN]TIAECAESS In ex. SMKΓ
Follis 324–325 Cyzicus *LRBC* I 1203; *RIC* VII
no. 26.
Found on surface.

26 (67–64).   Obv. Draped and laureate bust of Constantine r. CONSTANTINVSIVNNOBC
Rev. Two standards between two soldiers
holding spears. GLORIAEXERCITVS In
ex. SMANΘ
Follis 330–335 Antioch *LRBC* I 1357; *RIC* VII
no. 87.
Found on surface.

Constantius II

27 (156–66).   Obv. Draped and laureate bust of Con-
stantius r. FLIVLCONSTANTIVSNOBC
Rev. Two standards between two soldiers
holding spears. GLORIAEXERCITVS In
ex. SMALA
Follis 333–335 Alexandria *LRBC* I 1430; *RIC*
VII no. 60.
From Trench K, under kitchen floor.

28 (182–66).   Obv. Diademed head of emperor r. CON-
STANTIVSAVG
Rev. Standard between two soldiers holding
spears. GLORIAEXERCITVS In ex. . . . .
AN . . .
AE3 337–341 Antioch *LRBC* I 1391; *RIC VIII*
no. 56 (337–347).
From Trench OP–3, depth .20.

29 (88–65).   Obv. Draped and laureate bust of emperor r.
DNFLCONSTA[NTIV]SAVG
Rev. Securitas leaning on pillar, holding
scepter. [SECURIT]ASREIP
AE3 337–341 Rome *LRBC* I 591, 598, 603; *RIC
VIII* nos. 15, 22, 33, 44 (337–340).
From Q:35 (Trench M–1) on hard lime floor,
depth .40.

30 (124–66).   Obv. Diademed head of emperor r.
[DN]CONSTANTIVSPFA[VG]
Rev. In four lines within wreath, VOT XX
MVLT XXX In ex. SMAN . . .
AE3 341–346 Antioch *LRBC* I 1398; *RIC VIII*
no. 113 (347–348)
Found with Nos. 13, 16, 73, 77, 108.

31 (38–64).   Same obv. and rev. types as No. 30, but head
laureate.
AE3 341–346 Cyzicus (?) *LRBC* I 1305.
From factory dump, near surface.

32 (56–64).   Same obv. and rev. types as No. 30.

Mintmark illegible.
AE3 341–346 *LRBC* I, e.g. 1398.
From glass deposit at Q–5:21–23 (Trench I)
.50 below top of wall, with No. 106.

33 (87–66). Same as preceding.
From dump (Trench Y–3S), sifting in conglomerate mass, with Nos. 123, 158, 180,
186.

34 (51–66). Obv. Draped and diademed bust of emperor
r. DNCONSTAN[TIVS]PFAVG
Rev. Virtus l., spearing falling horseman
who raises both arms (FH3 type). FEL-
TEMPREPARATIO In center field dot In
ex. CONSΓ
AE3 351–354 Constantinople *LRBC* II 2043;
Bruck p. 21; *RIC VIII* no. 121 (351–355).
From dump (Trench Y–3) above conglome-
rate mass, depth .80.

35 (66–64). Same obv. and rev. types as No. 34. In ex.
ΛLEΛ
AE3 351–361 Alexandria *LRBC* II 2844, 2846;
RIC VIII nos. 80, 82 (351–355).
Found on surface.

36 (82–65). Same as preceding.
From w–x:4–5 (Trench A–6) depth 1.35.

37 (184–66). Same obv. and rev. types as No. 34. In ex.
R*P
AE3 352–354 Rome *LRBC* II 674–76; *RIC VIII*
nos. 276, 279 (352–355).
From Trench X–1 (sifting), depth 1.00—soft
fill below hard conglomerate.

38 (139–66). Same obv. and rev. types as No. 34. In ex.
AN . . .
AE3 351–354 Antioch *LRBC* II 2632; *RIC VIII*
no. 153 (350–355).
From T:46 (Trench X–2 balk) depth .50,
above hard floor, with Nos. 74, 93.

39 (27–64). Same obv. and rev. types as No. 34. In center
field M In ex. . . . CO . . .
AE3 355–360 Arles (?) *LRBC* II 458; Bruck p.
21.
From dump (Trench L) depth .10, near No.
190.

40 (37–66). Same obv. and rev. types as No. 34. In l.
field D In ex. . . . CON
AE3 353–354 Arles (?) *LRBC* II 455; Bruck p.
21.
From Z:12, slightly below level of stone
basin next to kitchen wall.

41 (178–66). Same obv. and rev. types as No. 34. In l.
field D In ex. ·TCON
AE3 353–354 Arles (?) *LRBC* II 455; Bruck p.
65 for mintmark.

From Trench X–1 (sifting), above third conglomerate layer, depth 1.00.

42 (103–66). Same obv. and rev. types as No. 34. In l.
field M
AE3 351–361 Mintmark illegible.
From Trench Y–3S between two conglomerate layers (sifting).

43 (42–66). Same obv. and rev. types as No. 34, but bust
bareheaded. In l. field S (?)
AE3 351–361 Mintmark illegible.
From PP:19 (Trench S–2) depth .50.

44 (84–66). Same obv. and rev. types as No. 34. In l.
field A
AE3 351–361 Mintmark illegible.
From dump (Trench Y–3S) between two conglomerate layers (sifting).

45 (52–65). Same obv. and rev. types as No. 34.
AE3 351–361 Mintmark illegible.
From dump (west end of Trench L), sifting.

46 (102–66). Same as preceding.
Found on surface, northeast corner of Trench
J–12.

47 (4–67). Same as preceding.
From Y–b:41–55 over fourth floor (sifting)
with Nos. 63, 102, 116, 173. See Chap. 2,
glass-sorting floors.

48 (127–66). Obv. Draped and diademed bust of emperor
r. DNCONSTANTIVSPFAVG
Rev. Virtus l., spearing falling horseman,
who clutches horse's neck (FH4 type).
FELTEMPREPARATIO In l. field M In ex.
ALE . . .
AE3 355–361 Alexandria *LRBC* II 2848 (FH3);
RIC VIII no. 84.
From ll:43 (Trench J–13) depth .20, near Nos.
196, 202. **Pl. 5–1.**

49 (44–65). Same obv. and rev. types as No. 48. In ex.
ALE . . .
AE4 351–361 Alexandria *LRBC* II 2844, 2846
(AE3); *RIC VIII* nos. 80, 82.
From surface of dump (Trench L).

50 (105–65). Same obv. and rev. types as No. 48. In ex.
ANA
AE3 351–361 Antioch *LRBC* II 2634–35; *RIC
VIII* no. 155 (350–355).
From Y:42 (Trench M–2), hard floor, depth
.80.

51 (105–66). Same obv. and rev. types as No. 48. In obv. l.
field Δ In rev. l. field B In rev. center field
dot.
AE2 351–354 Constantinople *LRBC* II 2033;
Bruck p. 21; *RIC VIII* no. 112 (351–355).

Found on surface, southeast section of Trench J–12, near No. 195.

52 (40–64). Same obv. and rev. types as No. 48. In l. field M (?)
AE3 351–361 Mintmark illegible.
From Grave Q (Trench A–3).

53 (104–65). Obv. Draped and diademed bust of emperor r. DNCONSTANTIVSPFAVG
Rev. Unclear, either FH3 (No. 34) or FH4 (No. 48). In ex. AN . . . (?)
AE3 351–361 Antioch (?) *LRBC* II 2632, 2635.
From W:43 (Trench M–2) depth 1.20. See Chap. 2, glass-sorting floors.

54 (75–66). Same obv. and rev. types as No. 53. In l. field M
AE3 351–361 Mintmark illegible.
From dump (Trench Y–3S), sifting, with Nos. 88, 99.

55 (85–66). Same as preceding.
From wall at e:21 (Trench H), above lowest course.

56 (30–65). Same obv. and rev. types as No. 53. In l. field X (?)
AE3 351–361 Mintmark illegible.
From Trench A–3, cleaning.

57 (111–66). Same obv. and rev. types as No. 53.
AE3 351–361 Mintmark illegible.
From dump (Trench Y–3S) sifting, with Nos. 111, 157.

58 (158–66). Same as preceding.
From U:52 (Trench X–2) depth 1.50.

59 (172–66). Same as preceding.
From Trench X–1, sifting fill below conglomerate mass (depth 1.00), with No. 119.

60 (136–66). Same as preceding.
From dump (Trench Y–3S) sifting in lowest conglomerate mass.

61 (38a–65). Same as preceding.
From a:4–5 (Trench A–4) depth 1.25, with No. 75.

62 (70–65). Same as preceding.
From r–s:9–10 (Trench A–5) depth 1.50.

63 (1–67). Obv. Draped and diademed bust of emperor r. DNCONSTANTIVSPFAVG
Rev. Virtus l., holding globe and spear. SPESREIPVBLI[CE] In ex. A . . .
AE3 355–361 Antioch or Alexandria Bruck p. 69 (AE4); *LRBC* II, 2638, 2850 (AE4, Virtus r.).
Found with Nos. 47, 102, 116, 173.

64 (15–64). Same obv. and rev. types as No. 63. In l. field star. In ex. ANTA (?)
AE3 355–361 Antioch (?) *LRBC* II 2638 (AE4, Virtus r.).
From dump (Trench L) in hard gritty fill depth 1.90.

65 (8–64). Same obv. and rev. types as No. 63.
AE3 355–361 Mintmark illegible.
From dump (east end of Trench L) depth .40.

66 (99–66). Same obv. and rev. types as No. 63.
AE4 355–361 Mintmark illegible.
From dump (Trench Y–3S) sifting between conglomerate masses, with No. 171.

67 (18–65). Obv. Draped and diademed bust of emperor r. . . . . TIVSPFAVG
Rev. Illegible
AE3 337–361
From m:4–5 (Trench A–5) depth 1.05, with Nos. 154– 55.

68 (115–66). Obv. Draped and diademed bust of emperor r. DNCONSTAN . . .
Rev. Illegible
AE3 337–361.
From H:52 (Trench X–1) depth .30.

Constans

69 (52–66). Obv. Laureate head of emperor r. DNCONSTANSPFAVG
Rev. Standard between two soldiers holding spears. GLORIAEXER[CITVS] In ex. CON . . .
AE3 337–341 Constantinople *LRBC* I 1044–45; *RIC VIII* nos. 28, 44 (337–340).
From SS: +9 (Trench OP–1) depth .40.

70 (90–65). Obv. Diademed head of emperor r. DNCONSTANSPFAVG
Rev. In four lines within wreath, VOT XX MVLT XXX In ex. SMALB
AE3 341–346 Alexandria *LRBC* I 1476; *RIC VIII* no. 34 (347–348).
From L:29 (Trench M–1) depth .40. **Pl. 5–1.**

71 (14–66). Same obv. and rev. types as No. 70.
AE3 341–346 Mintmark illegible.
From y: +17 (Trench OP) depth .20.

72 (51–64). Obv. Draped and diademed bust of emperor l., holding globe. DNCONSTANSPFAVG
Rev. Emperor holding spear, leading captive r. from hut beneath tree. FELTEMPREPARATIO In ex. SMNA
AE2 346–350 Nicomedia *LRBC* II 2291; *RIC VIII* no. 70 (348–351).
From cut through hard red floor at U–V:5–12 (Trench A–3 extending into A–2), with Nos. 151–52.

Julian

73 (123–66). Obv. Draped bust of Julian r., bareheaded. DNCL[I]VLIAN[VSNOBC]AES
Rev. Virtus l., spearing falling horseman, who clutches horse's neck (FH4 type). FELTEMP[REPARATIO] In center field dot In l. field ·M·
AE3 355–360 Constantinople *LRBC* II 2052; *RIC VIII* no. 138 (FH3) (355–361)
Found with Nos. 13, 16, 30, 77, 108.

74 (140–66). Obv. Same type as No. 73.
Rev. Unclear, either FH3 or FH4.
AE3 355–360 Mintmark illegible *LRBC* II, e.g. 2049–52.
Found with Nos. 38, 93.

75 (38–65). Obv. Same type as No. 73, but [DNIVLIA]NVSNOBC
Rev. Unclear, either FH3 or FH4.
AE3 355–360 Mintmark illegible *LRBC* II, e.g. 1611.
Found with No. 61.

76 (29–65). Obv. Same type as No. 73, form of legend uncertain.
Rev. Unclear, either FH3 or FH4
AE3 355–360 Mintmark illegible *LRBC* II, e.g. 2049–52.
From R–U:31–34 (Trench M), black earth near surface.

77 (122–66). Obv. Bust of Julian r. . . . ANVS . . .
Rev. Virtus l., holding globe and spear. [SPESREIPVBLICE]
AE4 355–363 Mintmark illegible Bruck p. 69; *LRBC* II, e.g. 2850–52 (Virtus r.)
Found with Nos. 13, 16, 30, 73, 108.

78 (5–65). Obv. Draped and diademed bust of emperor r. DNFLCLIVLIANVSPFAVG
Rev. Bull r., two stars above. SECVRITASREIPVB In ex. TCONST In r. field eagle on wreath, holding another wreath in beak
AE1 361–363 Arles *LRBC* II 468; Bruck pp. 64–65; *RIC VIII* no. 318 (360–363).
From Q:20 (west of furnace) depth ca. .80.
Pl. 5–1.

79 (26–66). Same obv. and rev. types as No. 78. In ex. ANTΓ between branches.
AE1 361–363 Antioch *LRBC* II 2640–41; *RIC VIII* nos. 216–17.
From east side of wall at b–e:18–22 (Trench H) sifting.

80 (59–64). Same obv. and rev. types as No. 78. In ex. AN . . . between branches.
AE1 361–363 Antioch *LRBC* II 2640–41; *RIC VIII* nos. 216–17.
From d–e:15–17 (Trench H) below tumbled stones.

81 (59–66). Same obv. and rev. types as No. 78. In ex. CVZΓ
AE1 361–363 Cyzicus *LRBC* II 2511; *RIC VIII* no. 127.
From S:51 (Trench X–2, west half) depth .75.

82 (10–65). Obv. Type unclear . . . VLIANVS . . .
Rev. Illegible.
AE3 355–363
From yy:42 (Trench J–8) depth .30.

House of Constantine, Emperor Uncertain

83 (10–64). Obv. Laureate head of emperor r. DNCONSTAN . . . PFAVG
Rev. Standard between two soldiers holding spears. GLORIAEXERCITVS In ex. CONS(?)
AE3 337–341 (Constantine II or Constantius II) Constantinople (?) *LRBC* I 1042–43.
From O–P:14–15 (Trench A–1) .50 below top of wall at south.

84 (83–65). Same obv. and rev. types as No. 83.
AE3 335–341 Mintmark illegible *LRBC* I, e.g. 1024–33, 1042–45.
From I:25 (Trench M–1) depth .25.

85 (76–65). Same as preceding.
From r–s:9–10 (Trench A–6) depth 1.55, near Nos. 128, 168, 203.

86 (1a–64). Obv. Diademed head of emperor r.
Rev. In four lines within wreath [VOTA X]X MV[LT XX]X
AE3 341–346 (Constantius II or Constans) Mintmark illegible *LRBC* I, e.g. 1481–83.
From dump (Trench L).

87 (63–66). Obv. Draped bust of emperor r.
Rev. Virtus l., spearing falling horseman, who raises both arms (FH3 type). [FEL-TEMPREPARATIO]
AE3 351–361 (Constantius II, Gallus, or Julian Caesar) Mintmark illegible *LRBC* II, e.g. 2836, 2846.
From W:54 (Trench X–2) depth .75, in conglomerate.

88 (74–66). Same obv. and rev. types as No. 87. In l. field M
AE3 355–361 (Constantius II or Julian Caesar) Mintmark illegible Bruck p. 21; *LRBC* II, e.g. 2848–49.
Found with Nos. 54, 99.

89 (47–66). Obv. Draped bust of emperor r.
Rev. Virtus l., spearing falling horseman,

who clutches horse's neck (FH4 type).
[FELT]EMPRE[PARATIO] In l. field Γ In
center field dot In ex. CONS . . .
AE2 351–354 (Constantius II or Gallus) Constantinople *LRBC* II 2028–29.
From Trench Y–1 and east balk, beneath clay
floor, depth 1.00.

90 (25–65).   Obv. Draped bust of emperor r., bareheaded
(?).
Rev. Unclear, either FH3 (No. 87) or FH4
(No. 89).
AE3 351–361 (Constantius II, Gallus, or
Julian Caesar) Mintmark illegible *LRBC* II,
e.g. 2039– 52.
From O–P:41–42 (Trench M) depth .10.

91 (11–65).   Same as preceding.
From o–p:6 (Trench A–5) depth .90.

92 (185–66).   Same as preceding.
From Trench OP–3, surface.

93 (137–66).   Same obv. and rev. types as No. 90. In l.
field M
AE4 355–361 (Constantius II or Julian
Caesar) Mintmark illegible Bruck p. 21;
LRBC II, e.g. 2848–49 (AE3).
Found with Nos. 38, 74.

94 (13–65).   Same obv. and rev. types as No. 90.
. . . NOBCAES
AE3 351–360 (Gallus or Julian Caesar)
Mintmark illegible *LRBC* II, e.g. 2040,
2050.
From cc:41 (Trench J–2) depth .20.

95 (32–65).   Obv. Draped bust of emperor r., bareheaded
(?)
Rev. Virtus l., holding globe and spear.
SPESREIPVBLIC[E] In ex. ANA
AE3 355–361 (Constantius II or Julian
Caesar) Antioch Bruck p. 69 (AE4); *LRBC*
II 2638–39 (AE4, Virtus r.).
From dump (Trench L) just below topmost
conglomerate mass.

96 (130–66).   Same obv. and rev. types as No. 95, but form
of bust unclear. In ex. ALEA
AE3 355–363 (Constantius II or Julian) Alexandria *LRBC* II 2850–52 (AE4, Virtus r.).
From J:53 (Trench X–1) in crumbly fill, depth
.50.

97 (94–66).   Same as preceding.
From dump (Trench Y–3S) sifting below conglomerate mass, with Nos. 110, 156, 170.

98 (51–65).   Same obv. and rev. types as No. 95, but bust
diademed.
AE3 355–363 (Constantius II or Julian)

Mintmark illegible *LRBC* II, e.g. 2850–52
(AE4, Virtus r.).
From G:40 (Trench M–1) in topsoil.

99 (76–66).   Same as preceding.
Found with Nos. 54, 88.

100 (131–66). Same as preceding.
From I:52 (Trench X–1) depth .50, near No.
96.

101 (161–66). Same as preceding.
From G:49 (Trench X–1) in white conglomerate mass, depth 1.45.

102 (2–67).   Same as preceding.
Found with Nos. 47, 63, 116, 173.

103 (14–64).   Same obv. and rev. types as No. 95, but bust
diademed.
AE4 355–363 (Constantius II or Julian)
Mintmark illegible *LRBC* II, e.g. 2850–52
(Virtus r.).
From S–W:12–14 (under calcined block in
north wall of furnace).

104 (25–64).   Same as preceding.
From surface.

105 (52–64).   Same as preceding.
From north part of Trench A–3, black earth
under hard floor, below Nos. 72, 152.

106 (57–64).   Same as preceding.
Found with No. 32.

107 (106–65). Same as preceding.
From T:44 (Trench M–2) on hard floor, depth
1.10.

108 (121–66). Same as preceding.
Found with Nos. 13, 16, 30, 73, 77.

Valentinian I

109 (95–65).   Obv. Draped and diademed bust of emperor
r. DNVALENTINIANVSPFAVG
Rev. Emperor dragging captive r., holding
labarum. GLORIAROMANORVM In ex.
ANTΓ
AE3 364–375 Antioch *LRBC* II 2653, 2658.
From R:44–45 (Trench M–2) above conglome-
rate mass, depth .70. **Pl. 5–1.**

110 (98–66).   Same obv. and rev. types as No. 109. In ex.
. . . NT . . .
AE3 364–375 Antioch *LRBC* II 2653, 2658.
Found with Nos. 97, 156, 170.

111 (112–66). Obv. Draped and diademed bust of emperor
r. DNVALENTIN[IANVSPF]AVG
Rev. Victory l., holding wreath and palm.
SECVRITASREI[PVBLICAE]

In ex. ·C . . . (?)
AE3 364–375 Constantinople (?) *LRBC* II
2071, 2087, 2094.
Found with Nos. 57, 157. **Pl. 5–1.**

112 (53a–65). Same obv. and rev. types as No. 111. In ex.
SMKB
AE3 367–375 Cyzicus *LRBC* II 2529.
From dump (Trench L, west end), sifting,
depth 1.00, with No. 167.

113 (67–66). Same obv. and rev. types as No. 111. In l.
field A In r. field wreath In ex. TES(?)
AE3 367–375 Thessalonica (?) *LRBC* II 1721;
Bruck, p. 67.
From dump, surface.

114 (181–66). Same obv. and rev. types as No. 111.
AE3 364–375 Mintmark illegible.
From W:31–32 (Trench F) in wall, depth .60.

Valens

115 (1–64). Obv. Draped and diademed bust of emperor
r. DNVALENSPERFAVG
Rev. Emperor standing, holding standard
with cross and Victory on globe. RES-
TITVTORREIPVBLICAE In l. field cross.
In ex. *ANTB*
Solidus 364–367 Antioch *RIC* IX, 272, no.
2(d).
From Trench C, surface. **Pl. 5–1.**

116 (3–67). Obv. Draped and diademed bust of emperor
r. . . . VALEN . . .
Rev. Emperor dragging captive r., holding
labarum. [GLO]RIARO[MANORVM]
AE3 364–375 Mintmark illegible *LRBC* II, e.g.
2070, 2086, 2091.
Found with Nos. 47, 63, 102, 173.

117 (61–66). Obv. Draped and diademed bust of emperor
r. DNVALEN[SPFAVG]
Rev. Victory l., holding wreath and palm.
SECVRITASR[EIPVBLICAE] In ex.
R·PRI . . .
AE3 367–375 Rome *LRBC* II 719.
From QQ:+5 (Trench OP–1) depth .85, near
No. 187.

118 (67–65). Same obv. and rev. types as No. 117. In ex.
ALEA
AE3 364–375 Alexandria *LRBC* II 2861, 2863.
From G:42 (Trench M–1) depth .15.

119 (173–66). Same obv. and rev. types as No. 117. In ex.
SMNA(?)
AE3 364–375 Nicomedia (?) *LRBC* II 2329–30,
2337.
Found with No. 59.

120 (2–64). Same obv. and rev. types as No. 117.
AE3 364–375 Mintmark illegible *LRBC* II, e.g.
2073, 2088, 2095.
From dump (Trench L) depth 1.70.

121 (27–65). Same as preceding.
From outside west wall of furnace.

122 (60–65). Same as preceding.
From dump (Trench L) sifting, depth 1.10.

123 (90–66). Same as preceding.
Found with Nos. 33, 158, 180, 186.

124 (93–66). Same as preceding.
From V:48 (Trench X–2) depth 1.35, with No.
181.

125 (119–66). Same as preceding.
From N:50–51 (Trench X–1) depth .50.

126 (10–66). Obv. Draped and diademed bust of emperor
r. . . . ENS . . .
Rev. Illegible
AE3 364–375
From surface.

Gratian

127 (22–65). Obv. Draped and diademed bust of emperor
r. DNGRATIANVSPFAVG
Rev. Roma seated, holding globe and spear,
right leg bare. CONCOR[DIA]AVGGG In
r. field O In ex. CONSΓ
AE3 378–383 Constantinople *LRBC* II 2123.
From ee–ff:42 (southeast corner Trench J–3)
depth .30. **Pl. 5–1.**

128 (73–65). Obv. Draped and diademed bust of emperor
r. DNGRAT[IANVSPFAVG]
Rev. In four lines within wreath, VOT X[X
M]V[LT XXX]
AE4 383 Mintmark illegible *LRBC* II, e.g.
2156.
From Trench A–6, near Nos. 85, 168, 203.

Valentinian II

129 (134–66). Obv. Draped and diademed bust of emperor
r. [D]NVALENTIN[IANVSPFAVG] In l.
field T
Rev. In four lines within wreath, VOT X
MVLT XX In ex. ALEA
AE4 383–392 Alexandria *LRBC* II 2889.
From vv:40 (Trench J–8) depth .40.

130 (164–66). Obv. Draped and diademed bust of emperor
r. [DNVA]LENTINIANVSPFAVG
Rev. Victory dragging captive l., carrying
trophy. SALVSREIPVBLICAE In l. field ⚹
In ex. CONSD

AE4 383–392 Constantinople *LRBC* II 2183.
From P:10 (Trench A–1) on surface.

131 (60–66). Obv. Draped and diademed bust of emperor
r. . . . ENTINIAN . . .
Rev. Illegible
AE4 375–392.
From RR:+12 (Trench OP–1) depth .80.

Theodosius I

132 (99–65). Obv. Draped and diademed bust of emperor
r. [DNTHEO]DOSIVSPFAVG
Rev. In four lines within wreath, VOT X
MVLT XX In ex. ALEΓ
AE4 383 Alexandria *LRBC* II 2882.
From x–y:19–20 (Trench A–6) depth .90.

133 (35–66). Same obv. and rev. types as preceding. In
ex. ANA
AE4 383 Antioch *LRBC* II 2741.
From HH:2 (Trench S–3) depth .50.

134 (78–66). Same as preceding.
From Trench J–11, northeast corner, near
surface.

135 (148–66). Same obv. and rev. types as preceding. In
ex. . . . RP(?)
AE4 379–383 Rome (?) *LRBC* II 767.
From e:47 (Trench X–3) below topmost floor
(see Chap. 2, glass-sorting floors).

136 (186–66). Obv. Draped and diademed bust of emperor
r. DNTHEODOSIVSPFAVG
Rev. Victory dragging captive l., carrying
trophy. SALVSREIPVBLICAE
In l. field ⯑
AE4 383–395 Mintmark illegible *LRBC* II, e.g.
2184, 2192.
From c:49 (Trench X–3) depth .80 in tumble
of brick and stone. **Pl. 5–1.**

137 (162–66). Same as preceding.
From Trench OP–2, depth 1.05, on bedrock.

138 (8–67). Same as preceding.
From Trench X–3 balk, soft fill under intrusive late burial.

Flacilla

139 (12–64). Obv. Draped and diademed bust of empress
r. AELFLACILLAAVG
Rev. Victory seated r., writing on shield.
SALV[SREIPVBLICAE]
AE4 383–386 Mintmark illegible *LRBC* II, e.g.
1844.
From Trench H, stuck on the vertical surface
of a period 4 wall.

Arcadius

140 (40–65). Obv. Draped and diademed bust of emperor
r. [DNARC]ADIVSPFAVG
Rev. Victory dragging captive l., carrying
trophy. [SALVSREI]PVBLICAE
In l. field ⯑
AE4 383–392 Mintmark illegible *LRBC* II, e.g.
2185.
From a–b:12–14 (Trench A–2, just outside
furnace).

141 (94a–65). Same as preceding.
From f–g:27 (small trial trench) in hard floor
full of glass fragments, with No. 144.

Honorius

142 (16–66). Obv. Draped and diademed bust of emperor
r. [DNHO]NORIVSPF[AVG]
Rev. Victory dragging captive l., carrying
trophy. [SALVSREI]PVBLICA[E]
AE4 393–395 Mintmark illegible *LRBC* II, e.g.
2194.
Found on surface outside excavation area.

143 (15–65). Obv. Draped and diademed bust of emperor
r. DNHONORI[VSPFAVG] In l. field star.
Rev. Three emperors.
GLORI[AROMANORVM] In ex. S . . .
AE3 402–408 Nicomedia or Cyzicus *LRBC* II
2447, 2591.
From i:27–28 (Trench F–2) depth 1.25.

144 (94–65). Same obv. and rev. types as No. 143.
AE3 402–408 Mintmark illegible.
Found with No. 141.

145 (141–66). Same as preceding.
From X:45 (Trench X–2) same place as No.
74, but where floor is broken.

Theodosius II

146 (69–65). Obv. Bust of emperor r. [DN]THE-
ODO[SIVSPFAVG]
Rev. Cross in wreath.
AE4 425–450 Mintmark illegible *LRBC* II, e.g.
2234.
From p–q:10–11 (Trench A–5) depth 1.50.

147 (190–66). Same as preceding.
From N:9 (Trench A–3) depth .55.

Houses of Valentinian and Theodosius,
Emperors Uncertain

148 (39–64). Obv. Draped and diademed bust of emperor
r.
Rev. Emperor dragging captive r., holding

labarum. GLOR[IAROMANORVM] In ex.
ANTΓ
AE3 364–375 (Valentinian I, Valens, or Grat-
ian) Antioch *LRBC* II 2653–55, 2658–62.
From Trench I, near surface.

149 (2–65).   Same obv. and rev. types as No. 148. In ex.
ANTA
AE3 364–375 (Valentinian I, Valens, or Grat-
ian) Antioch *LRBC* II 2653–55, 2658–62.
From Trench L, surface.

150 (86–65).   Same as preceding.
Found at L–M:36–37 (Trench M–1) on white
floor, depth .30–.40.

151 (46–64).   Same obv. and rev. types as No. 148.
AE3 364–375 (Valentinian I, Valens, or Grat-
ian) Mintmark illegible.
Found with Nos. 72, 152.

152 (47–64).   Same as preceding.
Found with Nos. 72, 151.

153 (3–65).   Same as preceding.
From l m:1 2 (Trench Λ 4) depth .75.

154 (17–65).   Same as preceding.
Found with Nos. 67, 155.

155 (20–65).   Same as preceding.
Found with Nos. 67, 154.

156 (96–66).   Same as preceding.
Found with Nos. 97, 110, 170.

157 (110–66).   Same as preceding.
Found with Nos. 57, 111.

158 (89–66).   Obv. Draped and diademed bust of emperor
r.
Rev. Victory l., holding wreath and palm.
SECVRITASREI[PVBLICAE] In ex.
ANT . . .
AE3 364–383 (Valentinian I, Valens, or Grat-
ian) Antioch *LRBC* II 2656–57, 2663–67,
2709.
Found with Nos. 33, 123, 180, 186.

159 (6–64).   Same obv. and rev. types as No. 158. In ex.
ALEΓ
AE3 364–375 (Valentinian I, Valens, or Grat-
ian) Alexandria *LRBC* II 2860–64.
Found in Trench K, ca. .15 below hard floor.

160 (145–66).   Same obv. and rev. types as No. 158. In ex.
A . . .
AE4 364–383 (Valentinian I, Valens, or Gratian) Antioch or Alexandria *LRBC* II
2656–57, 2663–67, 2709, 2860–64 (AE3).
From D:55 (Trench Y–3S) in conglomerate,
depth 1.20.

161 (53–66).   Same obv. and rev. types as No. 158. In ex.
TES
AE3 364–378 (Valentinian I or II, Valens, or
Gratian) Thessalonica *LRBC* II 1706–7,
1721–23, 1811–12, 1814–15.
From R:54 (Trench X–2) depth .70.

162 (117–66).   Same obv. and rev. types as No. 158. In ex.
CON . . . (?)
AE3 364–375 (Valentinian I, Valens, or Gratian) Constantinople (?) *LRBC* II 2071–73,
2087–88, 2094–96.
From west edge of dump (Trench Y–3S) sifting.

163 (69–66).   Same obv. and rev. types as No. 158.
AE3 364–383 (Valentinian I or II, Valens, or
Gratian) Mintmark illegible *LRBC* II, e.g.
2656–57, 2663–67, 2709, 2860–64.
From dump (Trench Y–3S) sifting between
conglomerate layers, with No. 179.

164 (39–66).   Same as preceding.
From dump (Trench Y–3S) depth .40, on topmost conglomerate layer.

165 (133–66).   Same as preceding.
From J:47 (Trench X–1) depth .70, under No.
100.

166 (11–64).   Same obv. and rev. types as No. 158.
AE4 364–383 (Valentinian I or II, Valens, or
Gratian) Mintmark illegible *LRBC* II, e.g.
2656–57, 2663–67, 2709, 2860–64 (AE3).
From dump (Trench L) depth ca. 1.20, on
hard sloping "floor" containing many
glass fragments.

167 (53b–65).   Same as preceding.
Found with No. 112.

168 (74–65).   Same as preceding.
From Trench A–6, near Nos. 85, 128, 203.

169 (56–66).   Same as preceding.
From V:48 (Trench X–2) depth .85.

170 (97–66).   Same as preceding.
Found with Nos. 97, 110, 156.

171 (100–66).   Same as preceding.
Found with No. 66.

172 (179–66).   Same as preceding.
From e:22 (Trench H), cleaning.

173 (5–67).   Same as preceding.
Found with Nos. 47, 63, 102, 116.

174 (58–64).   Probably same obv. and rev. types as No.
158.
AE4 364–383 (Valentinian I or II, Valens, or

Gratian) Mintmark illegible.
Found with No. 175.

175 (61–64). Same as preceding.
From dump (Trench L) with No. 174.

176 (4–65). Same as preceding.
From e:2–3 (Trench A-4) depth 1.00.

177 (12–65). Same as preceding.
From north end of Trench F-2 on bedrock.

178 (68–65). Same as preceding.
From dump (Trench L, west end) depth 1.20.

179 (73–66). Same as preceding.
Found with No. 163.

180 (91–66). Same as preceding.
Found with Nos. 33, 123, 158, 186.

181 (92–66). Same as preceding.
Found with No. 124.

182 (35–65). Obv. Draped and diademed bust of emperor r. . . . IVSPFAVG
Rev. In four lines within wreath, VOT X MVLT XX
AE4 383 (Theodosius I or Arcadius) Mintmark illegible *LRBC* II, e.g. 2741, 2743.
From Trench M, cleaning over topmost conglomerate layer.

183 (8–65). Same obv. and rev. types as No. 182.
AE4 383 (Valentinian II, Theodosius I, or Arcadius) Mintmark illegible *LRBC* II, e.g. 2740–43.
Found with No. 182.

184 (26–65). Same as preceding.
From m:13 (Trench A-5) depth 1.20.

185 (46–65). Same as preceding.
From w-x:16–17 (Trench A-6) depth .65.

186 (88–66). Obv. Illegible
Rev. Two Victories facing one another, holding wreaths. [VICTORIAAVGGG] In ex. . . . P(?)
AE3 383–387 (Valentinian II, Theodosius I, or Arcadius) Rome (?) *LRBC* II 782–793 (AE4).
Found Nos. 33, 123, 158, 180.

187 (62–66). Obv. Draped and diademed bust of emperor r.
Rev. Victory dragging captive l., holding trophy. SALVSREIPVBLICAE In l. field ⳨ In ex. SMKΓ
AE4 393–395 (Theodosius I, Arcadius, or Honorius) Cyzicus *LRBC* II 2577–79.
Found near No. 117.

188 (79–66). Same obv. and rev. types as No. 187. In l. field + In ex. ANT . . .
AE4 383–395 (Valentinian II, Theodosius I, Arcadius, or Honorius) Antioch *LRBC* II 2763–67, 2772–75.
From Trench J-11, southwest part, on surface.

189 (23–65). Same obv. and rev. types as No. 187. In l. field ⳨
AE4 383–408 (Valentinian II, Theodosius I, Arcadius, or Honorius) Mintmark illegible *LRBC* II, e.g. 2183–85, 2192–94, 807–11.
From PP:34 (Trench P) near surface.

190 (26–64). Same as preceding.
Found near No. 39.

191 (63–64). Same as preceding.
From dump (Trench L) depth ca. 1.55.

192 (36–65). Same as preceding.
From M:41 (Trench M) depth .10.

193 (80–65). Same as preceding.
From G:42 (Trench M-1) in hard red fill, depth .35.

194 (50–66). Same as preceding.
From east part of Trench J-6, surface.

195 (106–66). Same as preceding.
Found near No. 51.

196 (128–66). Same as preceding.
From kk:42 (Trench J-13) near Nos. 48, 202.

197 (180–66). Obv. Draped and laureate bust of emperor r.
Rev. Emperor riding r. [GLORIA ROMANORVM]
AE3 393–395 (Theodosius I, Arcadius, or Honorius) Mintmark illegible *LRBC* II, e.g. 2189–91.
From Trench J-14, on surface.

198 (32–66). Obv. Draped and diademed bust of emperor r. DN . . . VSPFAVG
Rev. Emperor being crowned by Victory. VIRTVSEXERCITI In ex. CONSA
AE3 395–408 (Arcadius or Honorius) Constantinople *LRBC* II 2205–6.
From mm:39 (Trench J-5), cleaning wall.

199 (42–64). Same obv. and rev. types as No. 198.
AE3 395–408 (Arcadius or Honorius) Mintmark illegible.
From I-K:20–21 (Trench A-1, southwest corner) in red earth.

200 (31–65). Obv. Draped and diademed bust of emperor r. In l. field star.
Rev. Three emperors.

GLORIARO[MANORVM] In ex. ANTA
AE3 402–408 (Arcadius, Honorius, or Theodosius II) Antioch *LRBC* II 2801–4.
Found west of furnace room (Trench A–2) in
red earth.

201 (29–66). Same obv. and rev. types as No. 200.
AE3 402–408 (Arcadius, Honorius, or Theodosius II) Mintmark illegible.
From northeast part of Trench S–3, depth not
recorded.

202 (129–66). Same as preceding.
From nn:43 (Trench J–13) near Nos. 48, 196.

203 (75–65). Obv. Draped and diademed bust of emperor
r.
Rev. Cross within wreath.
AE4 (small) 425–450 (Theodosius II or Valentinian III) Mintmark illegible *LRBC* II, e.g.
2604–6.
From Trench A–6, near Nos. 85, 128, 168.

204 (165–66). Same as preceding.
From N:8 (Trench A–1) depth .10.

205 (151–66). Same as preceding.
From d-e:12 (Trench K), just below level of
plaster floor, with six illegible coins.

Leo I

206 (41–64). Obv. Head of emperor r. [DNLEO]SPFAV[G]
(?)
Rev. Illegible.
AE4 (small) 457–474 Mintmark illegible
LRBC II, e.g. 2258–76, p. 44.
From northern part of Trench A, depth .20.

207 (19–64). Obv. Illegible
Rev. Monogram of Leo
AE4 (small) 457–474 Mintmark illegible
LRBC II, e.g. 2262.
From Trench K, depth ca. 1.10.

6

ANNA MANZONI MACDONNELL

The Terracotta Lamps

The study of the lamps has proved difficult since the main publications are based on public or private collections of Palestinian lamps, mostly without definite proveniences. Those from excavations are seldom firmly dated as they often come from tombs sometimes used for several centuries or partially plundered. A thorough study of the lamps of Palestine of all periods is still to be written.[1]

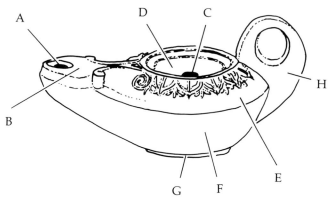

Parts of the Lamp
A. wick hole; B. nozzle; C. filling hole; D. discus; E. shoulder; F. side; G. base; H. handle.

Fragments of about four hundred terracotta lamps were excavated at Jalame, but only a few are intact or nearly complete. A selection is presented here, omitting many pieces that are small and uninformative. Despite the lack of secure stratification in many parts of the site, the lamps are of value not only in helping to provide a picture of the material equipment but also in dating the periods of occupation and in showing considerable importation from other parts of the Near East. It is also valuable to have a group of lamps, however fragmentary, that derive from a single settlement and thus constitute a regional group. Few such assemblages have been published. Most of the lamps are from the time of the glass factory, a few earlier or later.

Hellenistic Period (No. 1)

There is a single fragmentary lamp of the Hellenistic period, probably of the 2nd century B.C.

First and Second Centuries

About one hundred specimens of the 1st and 2nd centuries were found on the site. Some of these are local Palestinian, others were imported, their origins often indeterminable.

"Herodian Lamps" (Nos. 2–6)

Two techniques of lamp manufacture existed at this time: wheel-making and molding. Wheel-made lamps of the variety shown here (Nos. 2–3) were produced in Palestine during about 150 years, beginning in the late 1st century B.C. These form a group separate from the preceding Hellenistic molded lamps and the molded discus lamps of Roman times that gradually replaced them. It is now believed that the wheel-made variety extended into the first half of the 2nd century, co-existing with the molded lamps (No. 4).[2]

After the 1st century molded lamps were used almost exclusively in Palestine. Whereas later lamps (4th century) are of types found mainly in northern Palestine, the lamps of the 1st–2nd centuries cannot be differentiated from those found throughout the country.

The term *Herodian* refers to the reigns of all the Herods, from 37 B.C. to the end of the 1st century A.C.[3] Recent

1. This chapter has been adapted from the M.A. thesis of Anna Manzoni, University of Missouri–Columbia, 1972. The editor has condensed the manuscript and added later references, with assistance from Prof. Dan Barag. The author had the advantage of advice from the late Prof. P. P. Kahane, Visiting Professor at the University of Missouri-Columbia, 1969–1972. She was also assisted by Mrs. Varda Sussman of the Israel Department of Antiquities.

2. Since Kahane, "Huqoq," 137–39, presents a comprehensive discussion of the "Herodian" lamps and their immediate successors, detailed comments are unnecessary; generally only material found later will be cited. See e.g., Aharoni, "Cave of Horror," 192 and fig. 4.
3. Smith, "Household Lamps," 2.

discoveries in Jerusalem indicate that the wheel-made variety began "after the time of Herod I or, more probably, in the later years of his reign."[4] Kahane suggested that the Herodian wheel-made type was derived from Broneer's Type XVII.[5] This seems logical because in Greece, as well, these are the only wheel-made lamps that continued after the introduction of molded lamps.[6]

Examples of the "Herodian" lamp have been found throughout Palestine and Transjordan, perhaps originating in the vicinity of Jerusalem.[7] After 70 A.C. the wheel-made type is found in small quantities in the south and in Galilee, two places of Jewish refuge, and it continued in these regions until the end of the Bar Kokhba revolt, in the year 135.

The earlier examples have wheel-made bodies to which were added hand-made nozzles. Later "Herodian" lamps were made in two-part molds (Nos. 4–6). On the wheel-made variety the bases are generally merely a flattened, slightly convex portion of the body, whereas the mold-made lamps have low, defined bases. Handles occur occasionally on both kinds. The earliest wheel-made lamps are undecorated, while the later ones have stamped circles on the nozzle and/or horizontal incisions.[8] These details appear on the earliest mold-made lamps; later the decoration became more elaborate, including pictorial relief representations around the filling hole.[9]

These molded, decorated lamps were discussed by Kahane, who called them "successors of the 'Herodian' lamp" and assigned them to A.C. 50–70.[10] The dates for the type have subsequently been fixed, on the basis of excavations in the Judean Desert, to the years between 70 and 135.[11]

Much experimentation was taking place in lamp manufacture in Palestine during the early 1st century, making a chronology of "Herodian" lamps difficult to establish. Kahane defined a chronology linking the wheel- and mold-made varieties,[12] and the finds from Jalame seem to agree with his conclusions. No. 2, a nozzle, has an oval wick hole and the knife-paring common to wheel-made "Herodian" lamps. No. 3, an intact specimen with a round filling hole, corresponds to Smith's Type II and is dated slightly later.[13]

The two mold-made "Herodian" specimens from Jalame are worth noting. No. 4 corresponds to Kahane's type (d), characterized as "plain or simply decorated" like the wheel-made varieties "but made in a mold."[14] Few examples of this type are published: of the five listed by Kahane, three are from the Dead Sea area, two from northern Palestine.[15] A fragmentary lamp almost exactly like our No. 4 was excavated at Nazareth, unfortunately in undatable context.[16] No. 4 indicates that during this phase the plain or simply decorated wheel-made and the more elaborately decorated mold-made "Herodian" lamps were both in use.

No. 5 has relief circlets on the nozzle, as do many of the later mold-made "Herodian" lamps. Since only a fragmentary example remains, little but the technique can be determined. No. 6 is particularly important for the history of the site, since it was found below an ashlar block at the edge of the furnace room. This block was in place before the glass factory was established (see Chap. 2, Period 1). The lamp is of a rare type, related to the "Herodian" lamps.

Discus Lamps (Nos. 7–17)

The so-called discus type is the most common of the late 1st-century and early 2nd-century lamps. There is no standard base; the forms range from a simple disc to a flat single or double ring. The nozzle is short and rounded. Decoration in a variety of motives may appear on the shoulder and discus, but some lamps are undecorated. It is presumed that none had a handle, although in the case of fragments this is not always possible to prove. The lamps are all rather thin-walled, with a depressed discus and red or black glaze on the exterior. In instances where identification of a fragment is doubtful, the type of clay is important for dating, because at Jalame the lamps of the 1st and 2nd centuries are thin-walled and usually slipped or glazed, while those of the 3rd and later are thick-walled and of a coarser fabric.[17]

The use of glaze seems to coincide at least in part with that on Attic lamps. Perlzweig was able to establish that in Athens glaze was given up at the end of the 2nd century and reintroduced for a short time in the 4th.[18] The

4. Avigad, "Jewish Quarter 1970," 140.

5. Kahane, "Huqoq," 135–36. Cf. Broneer, *Corinth Lamps*, pl. 6, nos. 296, 300.

6. Broneer, *Corinth Lamps*, 61. He mentions that the clay is gritty red or grayish brown, unlike that of the Jalame specimens.

7. Smith, "Herodian Lamp," 53, n. 2.

8. Ibid., 54.

9. Sussman, *Jewish Lamps*, passim.

10. Kahane, "Huqoq," 138–39.

11. Aharoni, "Cave of Horror," 194, fig. 4, nos. 1 and 3, with features very like our No. 5. See also D. Barag, "Lamps of the Bar Kokhba Period from Caves in the Judean Desert," *Proceedings of the 5th World Congress of Jewish Studies* (1969) 87–91, English summary 232 f.

12. Kahane, "Huqoq," 135–39, divides the "Herodian" lamps into five groups, ranging in date from the time of Herod I to the 2nd c. These dates have been somewhat modified in the light of subsequent work by Avigad ("Jewish Quarter 1970") and Sussman (*Jewish Lamps*), but the basic development of the various types remains unchanged. Smith's "Herodian Lamp" is helpful in its treatment of the wheel-made varieties.

13. Smith, "Herodian Lamp," 61, fig. 2.

14. Kahane, "Huqoq," 138.

15. Ibid.

16. Bagatti, *Nazareth*, 300, fig. 233, no. 4.

17. Avigad, *Beth Shearim* 3, 185, states that the discus type began in the Roman Empire in the 1st c., became widespread in the 2nd, in Palestine appeared as a local product at the beginning of the 2nd c., but became common mainly in the 3rd.

18. Perlzweig, *Agora Lamps*, 21, 64. From a study of shop sequences in the Agora lamps it was concluded that glaze reappeared toward 325 and was abandoned around 360.

Jalame lamps seem to follow this general pattern, glaze being used during the 1st and 2nd centuries and again in the 4th, specifically on the Beit Nattif types (see below). Discus lamps have been found throughout Palestine.[19] According to Kahane, this type has its origins in Broneer's Type XXV and Loeschcke's Type VIII.[20] Dating for this type at Jalame concurs with Kahane's at Huqoq: the second half of the 1st century, with a possible extension into the 2nd.[21] The only nearly complete specimen from Jalame, No. 7, shows the basic form of these lamps.

The undecorated lamps include No. 7 and numerous uncatalogued fragments. These have only a relief band encircling the depressed discus. No. 8, somewhat more elaborate, may be the base of such a lamp. Although few Palestinian lamps with plain disci are published, this is not evidence of rarity. Such lamps are found in Cyprus[22] and at Dura.[23] A lamp of similar shape and fabric is among the imported lamps found in the Athenian Agora; its lightness is characterized as that of Syrian ware.[24] This hypothesis fits the Jalame material very well, establishing the site's connection with northern as well as southern Palestine during its late 1st- and 2nd-century occupation.

Various patterns appear on the decorated discus lamps, but in the case of the Jalame fragments, it is often impossible to know if the discus was decorated. The patterns and their parallels are discussed in the catalogue.

One of the commonest shoulder patterns is the ovolo (Nos. 9–12); these lamps may either have plain disci or designs in relief. No. 13 has a double ax on the shoulder and concentric circles on the base. A lamp said to be from Hebron, combining ovolo, scroll, and double ax on the shoulder, with a bunch of grapes in relief on the discus, is shown on Pl. 6–5.[25] The letters **alpha** and **lambda** are incised on the base.

Discus lamp fragments with pointed leaves on the shoulder are common at Jalame (Nos. 14–17), but there is considerable variation in both pattern and date. No. 14 seems entirely different from the other examples and has an exact parallel found in Hungary. It is unlikely that our lamp was imported from Hungary; probably both were imports from somewhere else. Nos. 15–17, with a different but distinctive leaf pattern (much worn), seems to be a Syro-Palestinian type that does not appear elsewhere. Examples have been found in Syria and as far south as

the Dead Sea Caves (see No. 15). A lamp in Missouri is said to be from Ain Samiyah (Pl. 6–5).[26] The discus shows a basket in relief containing fruits and leaves. The Greek letters **ZOH** [*sic*], with serifs, were inscribed on the base before firing. The pattern apparently continued into the 3rd century (see note with No. 15), and it also appears among the Beth Shearim lamps, where the leaves seem more like palmettes (see No. 45, a small fragment of a similar lamp).[27]

Other Late First- or Early Second-Century Lamps (Nos. 18–26)

Other lamp fragments of the same period are different from the discus type. The most nearly complete lamp in this group is No. 18, a fine piece that resembles no other published example from the Syro-Palestinian area. The only similar lamp noted thus far is said to be from Carthage. That lamp is signed by the maker; ours has only the *planta pedis*, a stamp common all over the Mediterranean. No. 19, while probably imported, is difficult to identify because the fragment is small. The identical figure (a dolphin) has not appeared elsewhere, but there is some resemblance to the fabric of a lamp fragment from Tarsus (showing a goose), and ours may be from Asia Minor. The rather metallic appearance of No. 20 resembles that of lamps from a burial cave at Tel Halif (southeast of Hebron), at Tyre, and at Beth Shearim, but the fabric and delicate detail of our lamp suggest an earlier date. A single ring handle, without the rest of the lamp, was found (No. 21). Such handles appear on lamps from Samaria, Nazareth, and other sites. Another type of handle of the same period is represented by No. 22. This was undoubtedly imported, but parallels can be drawn from both east and west. Nos. 23–26 are unique at Jalame, and convincing parallels have not been located.

Between the middle of the 2nd century and the last quarter of the 3rd there seems to be a gap in the sequence of lamps. There are also only ten coins from this period, a very small amount compared to later times.

Third- and Fourth-Century Lamps

Late Third-Century to Mid Fourth-Century Lamps (Nos. 27–39)

Beginning in the late 3rd century there seems to have been somewhat more occupation of the site, but lamps

19. Kahane, "Huqoq," 129–30. For a complete list of the areas where these lamps were found, see 134–35.
20. Ibid., 129. See also Vessberg, "Cyprus Lamps," Type 13, 126 f, 189, fig. 39:1.
21. Kahane, "Huqoq," 130.
22. See n. 20 above.
23. Baur, *Dura Lamps*, pl. 7, no. 394.
24. Perlzweig, *Agora Lamps*, 4, referring to no. 135.
25. Museum of Art and Archaeology, University of Missouri-Columbia, No. 68.146c. L .086; W .073; H .024. Buff clay, red and black glaze. Photo courtesy of the museum.

26. Museum of Art and Archaeology, University of Missouri-Columbia, No. 68.301. L .076; W .061; H .02. Buff clay with matt red glaze. Photo courtesy of the museum. An apparently identical lamp (part of discus missing) was found in a tomb near Tyre dated 2nd c. Part of a signature on the base, restored, reads **[Z]OH**: See Maurice Dunand, "Tombe peinte dans la campagne de Tyr," *BMBeyrouth* 18 (1965) 47 and 48, fig. 11. Still another, exactly like ours, was found in a tomb in the same region and assigned to the same date. Unfortunately, the base is missing. See J. Hajjar, "Un hypogée romain à Deb'aal dans la région de Tyr," *BMBeyrouth* 18 (1965) 72 F.374a, pl. 20.
27. Cf. Avigad, *Beth Shearim* 3, 187–88, nos. 17 and 19, pl. 70.

are still rather scarce. In most cases they are extremely fragmentary and therefore difficult to assign to definite dates.[28] During this period there are both Palestinian lamps and imported ones. The latter give evidence that Jalame was involved in commerce to some extent.

Two deposits of lamps found in cisterns at Beit Nattif, southwest of Jerusalem, contained material that has been dated to this general period. While some comparisons may be drawn between these and the Jalame fragments, the resemblances are not striking.

Lamps apparently of local make are Nos. 27–31A. For none of these fragments has it been possible to find identical parallels, but the type of clay and the various forms of decoration are found on Palestinian lamps of the period. Possibly not later than the middle of the 4th century and also of local manufacture are Nos. 32–35. These likewise have uncertain parallels, and it is possible that they (particularly No. 35) are somewhat later.

Nos. 36–39 were imported and probably are not later than the mid 4th century. No. 36 is probably an Attic lamp. No. 37 is Cypriote. No. 38 is difficult to assign to a specific place. The chain of impressed, dot-centered lozenges on the shoulder is also found on the shoulder of No. 42, and a single lozenge is a nozzle ornament on No. 87. There has been much speculation about the nature of this decoration. The lozenge appears as both a Jewish and a Christian religious symbol during the Byzantine period.[29] Because the two examples from Jalame (Nos. 38 and 42, the latter a Beth Shearim type) employ this pattern not as a focal point but rather as a decorative motive on the shoulder in exactly the same manner as the common ovolo or geometric designs, it is likely that here the intent is purely ornamental. Finally, No. 39, which has been impossible to place, seems to have some connection with Corinth.

Lamps of the Beth Shearim Type (Nos. 40–68)

The publication of Avigad's *Beth Shearim* 3 in an English version (1976) made available to a wider audience the important material originally published in 1971. The lamps found at Beth Shearim are the most common and most characteristic examples that existed during the period of the glass factory. As mentioned in n. 28, these

lamps (except for some found in Beth Shearim Catacomb 20) are considered to date not later than 352.

The type of Beth Shearim lamp with which we are chiefly concerned is included in Avigad's nos. 14–26.[30] These lamps are more or less piriform, with conical knob handle. There are usually deeply impressed floral or geometric motives on the shoulder and occasionally on the discus. Incised designs, often simple lines or herringbones, occur frequently, either independently or together with impressed motives. In general, the workmanship is crude, the buff or reddish brown clay is thick and usually without slip or glaze. Often there is a depressed discus in the form of an asymmetrical oval, either plain or decorated with a simple design. The bases are usually flat, their elongated outlines corresponding to the form of the lamp.[31] Avigad states that lamps of this type have been found in many parts of Galilee as well as at Caesarea. He emphasizes that their distribution "was restricted almost entirely to the northern part of the country" and that "they are indisputably a Galilean product which apparently was manufactured in a number of major workshops."[32]

Nos. 59–61 are of the general Beth Shearim type just mentioned, but no exact parallels have been noted. Lamps of the same general shape as No. 62 have appeared at Beth Shearim, Nazareth, Beth Shan, and Pella, but our example is much larger and better made than any of these. Nos. 63–64, fragments probably from similar lamps, are exactly paralleled at Beth Shearim.[33] Avigad mentions that this is an uncommon type probably of later date, quoting a similar one (unpublished) found in a 6th-century context in another catacomb.

Finally, Nos. 65–68, the first three fragments only of nozzle and shoulder, the last preserving a slightly larger portion of the lamp, are reminiscent of the Beth Shearim type. They do not seem, however, to be exactly the same, and they show possible relationship with Greek lamps.

Other Fourth-Century Lamps (Nos. 69–101)

While a Beth Shearim type of lamp is fairly easy to identify, other fragmentary lamps of this period cannot be so well categorized.

Nos. 69–72 are reminiscent of Beth Shearim lamps, but there are notable differences such as the rudimentary handle of No. 70, the unusual profile of No. 71, and the extremely poor workmanship of No. 72 (the drawing, Fig. 6-6, shows more detail than can be seen in a photograph). Nos. 73–75 do not seem to correspond

---

28. A factor complicating the problem of dating is that the type known as the "Beth Shearim lamp" because of its extensive use for burials in the catacombs there, is thought to have ceased in 352 when Beth Shearim was destroyed (see Avigad, *Beth Shearim* 3, 184 and 188–89, where the reason for giving this name to the type is discussed and parallels to these lamps at other sites are mentioned). While this *terminus ante quem* is reasonable for the burial site, it is evident that at Jalame (slightly less than 6.5 km from Beth Shearim), these lamps continued in use throughout the period of the glass factory, ca. 352–383. For this reason the lamps of the so called Beth Shearim type are included in a following section, without an exact date being specified for each lamp.

29. For the persistence of the lozenge pattern on lamps see Avigad, *Beth Shearim* 3, 189, no. 27, pl. 71. It is also found on glass jugs: see Barag, "Glass Pilgrim Vessels from Jerusalem—Part 1," *JGS* 12 (1970) 42–44, where the possible religious significance of the design is discussed.

30. Avigad, *Beth Shearim* 3, 188–89.

31. See ibid., 186, fig. 92, for the main types of lamp profiles from all periods represented at the site. Since the Jalame lamps seldom preserve both top and base, it is difficult to correlate these with the types of bases mentioned by Avigad.

32. Ibid., 189.

33. Ibid., 190, no. 32, pl. 71.

with any of the normal 4th-century types, but their fabric and decoration suggest a Syrian or Palestinian origin. No. 76, with the top almost complete, seems a crude development of the Beth Shearim lamp and must date somewhat later. Nos. 77–78, base fragments, are not informative in themselves, but they come from contexts within the period of the glass factory's activity. Nos. 79–82 may have been imported from Greece, possibly from Athens. No. 80 has a convincing parallel in Argos, and No. 82 seems to have existed both in Cyprus and in Athens.

Four lamps bear religious emblems (Nos. 83–86). Two have Jewish motives on the discus, two Christian. It is possible that both religions were practiced at Jalame or that the designs were not of particular interest to the owners of the lamps. Nos. 83–84 show menorahs of different types but apparently of similar date. According to Goodenough, "In shape and design these two conform to a fourth-century type of which numerous examples were discovered in Alexandria."[34] He does not explain the difference between the two representations or their possible significance. From our small fragments it is impossible to determine whether the lights on the menorah face toward or away from the nozzle; they neither confirm nor deny an observation that on Palestinian lamps the lights face the nozzle (with few exceptions), while on those from elsewhere they face the opposite way.[35] The Christian lamps are also of different kinds. No. 85, a fragment of discus and shoulder, with **chi rho** on the discus, is too small to determine the lamp's shape, but a North African lamp seems a close parallel. No. 86, with a shrine shown in relief on the discus (central portion missing), resembles other representations of Christian shrines, but an exact parallel is elusive.

No. 87 is of a type well known in northern Palestine. The lozenge with central dot was associated with both Jewish and Christian symbolism, but whether it had assumed religious meaning as early as the 4th century is uncertain.[36]

Nos. 88–89 are examples of a type common in Samaria, Beit Nattif, and elsewhere. They are characteristic of this period and have certain features that do not appear at other times, for example, the so-called star-knob handle. There is a great variety of patterns on these lamps, all molded, with relief decoration.[37] No. 90 is

somewhat the same but is much coarser and has an almost square handle. No. 91 is unique at Jalame, in both clay and design, but the type is probably much like Nos. 88–89; not enough is preserved for certainty. The last definitely Palestinian type (No. 92) is fragmentary and out of context.

No. 93 resembles Palestinian lamps except for the crude animal figure on the discus. Possibly the lamp came from Greece, although the clay does not seem like that of contemporary Athenian or Corinthian lamps.

Nos. 94–96 are fragments for which parallels have been elusive in the Palestinian area but which seem to have relations with Greece, and were either exported from there or influenced by Greek models.

The remaining lamps of this period (Nos. 97–101) are presented here simply because they were found on the site. For none of them could similar examples or a plausible origin be found.

Late Lamps (Nos. 102–6)

These extremely fragmentary lamps are not easily categorized. It is certain only that they postdate the late–4th–5th-century occupation of the site. They were found widely separated, as their recorded proveniences show.

Catalogue

The information that can be drawn from the lamp fragments corresponds well with the numismatic evidence. While many lamps, or fragments, can be dated with considerable accuracy by their context, in most cases this is not so. More reliable evidence is furnished by the *quantity* of lamps of each period.

The few 1st- and 2nd-century (Period 1) lamps (Nos. 2–26) show connections with both southern Palestine and Syria, as well as other Mediterranean regions. As a whole, they reflect types popular in most of Palestine during the early centuries of the Christian era.

The lack of late 2nd- and early 3rd-century lamps is conspicuous. Nos. 27–39, datable to the late 3rd century and the first half of the 4th (Period 2), indicate occupation of the site immediately prior to the establishment of the glass factory in the mid–4th century. Some of these lamps are of a type that originated in southern Palestine, while a few are certainly imports.

The most common form of lamp at Jalame is that found at nearby Beth Shearim. This variety and related lamps seem to have been restricted to the north, indicating that during the operation of the glass factory there was a stronger connection with Galilee than with southern Palestine.

1 (76-66). Part of base and wall
   PH .016; D base .05. Buff-gray clay (10YR 7/1),[38] dull

34. Goodenough, *Symbols*, 1, 160.
35. A. Levy, "An Observation on the Direction of the Decoration on Palestinian Oil Lamps," *IEJ* 23 (1973) 48–49. See, however, two examples in the Nicosia Museum, in T. Oziol, *Les Lampes du Musée de Chypre*, Salamine de Chypre 7 (Paris, 1977) 237, nos. 703–4, pl. 39—lamps with the menorah sideways. Seven other similar lamps are mentioned here, some definitely Cypriote, others presumed to be so.
36. For earlier examples, see the discussion of No. 38.
37. This type has been identified as peculiarly Samaritan: see V. Sussman, "Samaritan Lamps of the Third-Fourth Centuries A.D.," *IEJ* 28 (1978) 238–50. Many of the examples shown have Samaritan inscriptions, while others bear menorahs and other symbols associated with the Samaritan religion.

38. Munsell Chart readings are given only where they seem essential to understanding the fabric of a lamp, or where the clay is unusual. The color descriptions are the author's, not as given in the Munsell Chart.

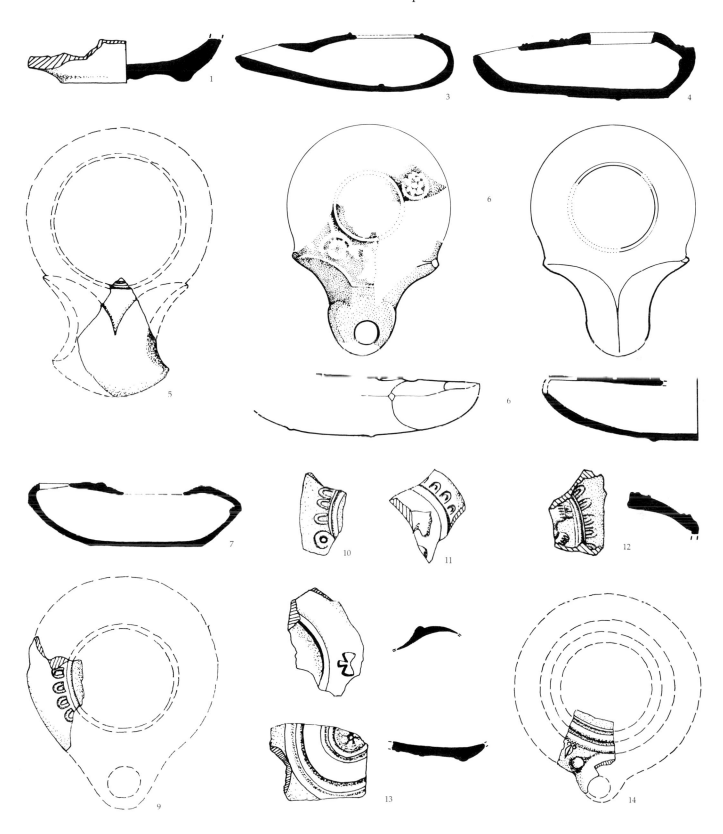

Fig. 6–1. No. 1, Hellenistic; Nos. –14, First and Second Centuries. Ca. 1:2.

black slip (N 3/0). High ring base, circular concavity in center enclosing incised circle. 2nd c. B.C. (?). From E–F:23–27 (Trench Y–1B), depth ca. 5.25, almost at bedrock, very little glass in fill. **Fig. 6–1; Pl. 6–1.**

2   (32–65). Nozzle and part of body

PL .048; PH .02. Orange clay, unslipped. Bow-spouted, wheel-made, knife-pared. Burning at wick hole. Mid–1st c. From cc:19 (Trench J–4), depth 1.30. **Pl. 6–1.**

Cf. Smith, "Herodian Lamp," 61, fig. 1 (Type 1); Kahane, "Huqoq," 126, fig. 3,18; 134–39 for an extensive list of parallels.

3   (21–65). Intact

L .086; W .055; H .023. Orange clay, unslipped. Bow-spouted, wheel-made, knife-pared, undecorated. Burning at wick hole. Third quarter of 1st c. From aa:15 (Trench J–4), depth 1.00. **Fig. 6–1; Pl. 6–1.**

Cf. Smith, "Herodian Lamp," 61, fig. 2 (Type 2) dated 50–135; see P. W. Lapp, *Palestinian Ceramic Chronology 200 B.C.–A.D. 70* (New Haven, Conn., 1961), 193 (Type 82), fig. c; Kahane, "Huqoq," as in No. 2.

4   (20–65). Complete

L .086; W .058; H .025. Orange clay, slip of same. Relief lines across nozzle, double relief circle around filling hole. Slightly raised round base, raised dot in center. Burning at wick hole. Probably late 1st or early 2nd c. From gg:21 (Trench J–4), depth 1.10. **Fig. 6–1; Pl. 6–1.**

Cf. Kahane, "Huqoq," Type (d), 138, dated mid–1st to early 2nd c.; numerous parallels are cited.

5   (140–65). Fragment of nozzle

PL .04; PW .025; PH .014. Buff and orange clay, burning at wick hole. Mold-made. One circlet in relief preserved. Ridge around nozzle. Late 1st or early 2nd c. From ee:19 (Trench J–4), depth 1.26. **Fig. 6–1; Pl. 6–1.**

Cf. Smith, "Household Lamps," 12, fig. 3, dated 1st c. The relief circlets are similar and base markings identical to those on our fragment; there is a pierced round handle. See also Kahane, "Huqoq," 126, fig. 3, no. 19, a somewhat similar piece that he dates second half of 1st c. Sussman, *Jewish Lamps*, shows lamps with similar nozzles, e.g., figs. 6, 27, 29, 37. See Aharoni, "Cave of Horror," fig. 4, no. 1, with similar bottom but no circlet on nozzle. See also Yadin, *Cave of Letters*, 114 and fig. 42 (CD.1), pl. 35.

6   (1–68). Many fragments forming almost complete profile

Est L .093; Est W .065; Est H .024. Fine buff clay (10YR 8/3), mottled red (2.5YR 5/6) and dark brown matt glaze (5YR 4/2). Burning at wick hole. Small discus, probably plain, surrounded by a ridge; central filling hole. Shoulder has rosettes in relief, possibly joined with relief lines. There was probably an added pierced handle. The nozzle bulges; above it a relief line separates it from the shoulder and ends in a small boss at each side. Relief ring on base. First half of 2nd c. From b:21–22 (Trench H) in dark earth just above bedrock, 4.05 below the datum. See plan of furnace, Fig. 3–3. **Fig. 6–1; Pl. 6–1.**

The base is characteristic of "Herodian" lamps (see No. 5), but the nozzle is quite different. A close parallel to this lamp is a fragment from a Judean Desert cave (Aharoni, "Cave of Horror," 192 and fig. 3, no. 13). Even though a small fragment, preserving little more than the nozzle, it shows distinctive features that seem not to appear elsewhere. The context gives a final date of 135; with this lamp are others of the more common variety (Aharoni's fig. 4, our No. 5). Aharoni mentions that the rounded nozzle belongs to "a later type which began to be produced in this period." The parallels he offers (his n. 14) are, however, not quite convincing. Several rather similar examples appear in Sussman, *Jewish Lamps*, esp. nos. 24, 145, 157, and 160. None of these is later than 135. Broneer's Type XXV (dated 50–100 and believed to come from Italy) shows a certain resemblance. It would seem that this is a fairly rare variation on the "Herodian" lamp, dating not much before 135.

7   (73–66). Complete except for broken discus

L .084; W .071; H .024. Fine buff clay (10YR 7/2), worn matt black glaze (10YR 3/1). Thin-walled. Circular body, ridge around discus, apparently undecorated. Raised nozzle defined by incised line and relief dot on each side. Flat base bordered by incised line. Late 1st or 2nd c. From γγ:36 (Trench J–12), depth .40. **Fig. 6–1; Pl. 6–1.**

For general type see Avigad, *Beth Shearim* 3, 185, nos. 2–7; also Perlzweig, *Agora Lamps*, pl. 5, no. 135, first half of 2nd c.

8   (16–66). Fragment of base and side

Max dim .045; D .04. Buff clay (5Y 7/2), matt black glaze (10YR 3/2) inside and out. Flat, double-ridged base with raised dot in center. Nine similar fragments found. Late 1st or 2nd c. From B–C:23–25 (Trench Y–1) ca. .30 above bedrock. **Pl. 6–1.**

9   (113–65). Fragment of discus, shoulder, and side

Max dim .044. Surface worn. Buff clay (10YR 8/4, inside; 2.5Y 8/2, outside), traces of black glaze (10YR 3/1). Stamped ovolo pattern surrounding discus. Late 1st or early 2nd c. From central part of Trench F–5, depth 1.50. **Fig. 6–1.**

These lamps were popular both in Palestine and elsewhere. For the ovolos see Kennedy, *Berytus* 14, 75, pl. 22, no. 507 (type 5), dated 2nd or 3rd c.; Broneer, *Corinth Lamps*, from Type XXI through Type XXVII—in other words, a common pattern that lasted a long time. See Yadin, *Cave of Letters*, 114, fig. 42, no. 3.1, dated late 1st or early 2nd c., and also a fragment in Nahal Mishmar: see P. Bar-Adon, "Expedition C," 28, fig. 1, no. 8; Iliffe, "Imperial Art in Trans-Jordan," *QDAP* 11 (1945) 1, pls. 8 and 9, nos. 134–36, 144, 145 (from Gerasa). Perlzweig, *Agora Lamps*, 84, pl. 5, no. 133, dated 2nd c. R. Noll discusses a North Italian lamp factory (*ÖJh* 30 [1936] 110–19); his fig. 51, no. 4 is a discus lamp with stamped ovolos around the shoulder and a ridge around the plain discus. This is probably what our fragment once looked like; but Loeschcke (*Vindonissa*) shows many lamps with similar shoulder decoration, some with handles and various kinds of nozzles;

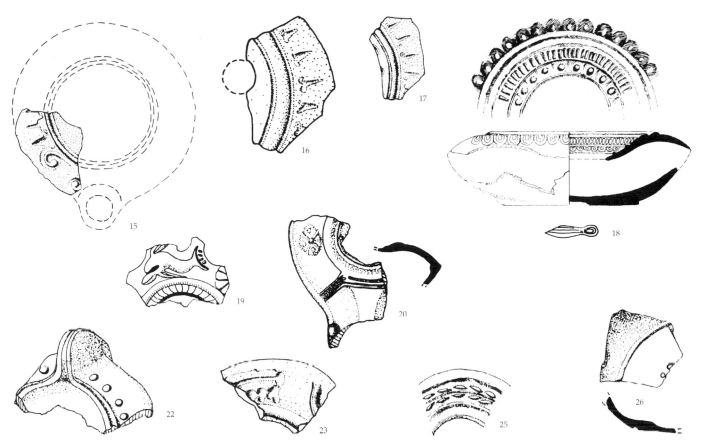

Fig. 6–2. First and Second Centuries. Ca. 1:2.

any of these might correspond with the Jalame piece, since the fragment is so small. See also Ben-Tor, "Horvat Usa," 24 and pl. 4, dated 2nd or 3rd c.

10   (54–66). Fragment of discus and shoulder

Max dim .029. Light buff clay, traces of red glaze. Ovolo on shoulder, scroll near nozzle. One similar fragment found. 1st or early 2nd c. From west section of Trench OP–2, surface to depth of .45. **Fig. 6–1.**

Cf. for a combination of ovolo and scroll a lamp in Missouri (Pl. 6–5 and n. 25.)

11   (23–66). Fragment of discus and shoulder

Max dim .035. Pale orange clay, traces of red glaze. On discus, forepart of a horse (?), much worn. Late 1st or early 2nd c. From southwest section of Trench OP, surface to depth of .50. **Fig. 6–1.**

For this general kind of lamp with a vague figure (a stag) see Goldman, *Tarsus* 1, 119 and pl. 103, no. 255, dated late 1st or 2nd c.

12   (50–65). Fragment of discus and shoulder

Max dim .031. Orange clay (5YR 7/4), black glaze outside (5YR 3/1), red inside (2.5YR 7/4). Ovolo on shoulder, part of animal (bear?) in relief on discus. 2nd c. From w–x:35–36 (Trench F–4), depth 1.30. **Fig. 6–1.**

Cf. for the same kind of lamp with figure of a bear, Goldman, *Tarsus* 1, 115, and pl. 102, no. 207; Loeschcke,

Vindonissa, pl. 12, no. 233; Ivanyi, *Pannonische Lampen*, pl. 9, no. 8.

13   (83–65). Two non-joining fragments of shoulder and base

(a) Max dim .041. Fine orange clay (5YR 7/6), matt red glaze (10R 4/8). Fragment of shoulder and discus, "double ax" motive in relief on shoulder. (b) D base .044. Flat base with two concentric relief circles and indistinct central design. Small part of side preserved. Late 1st or 2nd c. From I–J:31–32 (Trench M–1), depth 2.05. **Fig. 6–1.**

Cf. Kahane, "Huqoq," 126, fig. 3, no. 23, discussed on 129–30; also 127, fig. 4, no. 5, and 142. An extensive list of parallels is given. In addition see Smith, "Household Lamps," 25, fig. 16, from Samaria, with a bust of Helios on the discus, dated late 1st or early 2nd c. Also Kennedy, *Berytus* 14, no. 502, pl. 21. The double ax is also combined with representations other than Helios: see Kennedy, *Berytus* 14, no. 503; Crowfoot, *Samaria* 3, 373, fig. 88, no. 8. See Pl. 6–5 and n. 25 for a lamp with ovolo and double ax patterns on the shoulder. A similar lamp was found in Catacomb 20 at Beth Shearim: Avigad, *Beth Shearim* 3, 185, no. 4, pl. 70, dated 2nd c. Identical is a 2nd-c. lamp from the Temple Mount: see B. Mazar, "The Excavations in the Old City of Jerusalem Near the Temple Mount, Preliminary Report . . . 1969–70" (Institute of Archaeology, Hebrew University, Jerusalem, 1971) fig. 9, 3.

14 (105–66). Fragment of discus, shoulder, and nozzle

Max dim .029. Buff clay (7.5YR 7/4), matt red glaze (5YR 4/6) outside and in. Nozzle set off from shoulder with raised circle. Triple row of grooves surrounding filling hole. Pointed leaf (?) on shoulder. Late 1st or early 2nd c. From east section of Trench J–13, depth .35–.45. **Fig. 6–1.**

Cf. Ivanyi, *Pannonische Lampen,* no. 743, pl. 27, no. 5 (her type VII, 12), which seems an exact parallel, dated 1st c.

15 (91–66). Fragment of discus and shoulder

Max dim .037. Buff clay (2.5Y 7/2), black glaze inside and out (10YR 4/2). Shoulder with relief volutes and radial floral design. Three similar fragments found. Late 1st or early 2nd c. From west section of Trench J–13, depth .35, near No. 71. **Fig. 6–2.**

Cf. Yadin, *Cave of Letters,* 114, fig. 42:II.12; Kennedy, *Berytus* 14, 73, no. 505 (Type 5), pl. 22, which seems quite similar and is dated 2nd–3rd c.; Kahane, "Huqoq," 134, no. 15, fig. 3.21 and pl. 18.5 (right) is of Type VI, group 1, dated mid–3rd c. If the date is correct, this shows a later use of the scroll and leaf pattern.

16 (40–64). Fragment of discus, shoulder, and filling hole

Max dim .028. Pale orange clay (7.5YR 7/6), matt red glaze (2.5YR 4/8). Depressed discus with filling hole. Radial floral design on shoulder. Three similar fragments (not catalogued) found. Late 1st or 2nd c. From the wine press tank (Trench J), unstratified. **Fig. 6–2.**

17 (86–66). Fragment of discus and shoulder

Max dim .03. Buff (10YR 8/4) to orange clay (7.5YR 7/6), matt black glaze outside (10YR 3/1), red inside (10YR 4/6). Stylized leaves stamped on shoulder; traces of design on discus. Late 1st or early 2nd c. From Trench J–10, depth .60–.95 (bedrock). **Fig. 6–2.**

18 (28–65). Parts of discus, shoulder, base, and body.

(a) Shoulder and discus. Max dim .085. Fine thin orange clay (7.5YR 7/4), red and black glaze (2.5YR 4/6 and 10YR 3/1). Geometric relief design of lines and dots divided by raised rings, on depressed discus; stamped ovolos on shoulder, surrounding two ridges. (b) Complete, slightly raised base and part of side. PH .015; D base .053. Stamp on base: *planta pedis.* 2nd c. From VV–bb:31 (Trench J–2), depth .90. A tiny fragment of a similar lamp was found at ee:22 (Trench J–4), depth 1.55 (bedrock). Another tiny fragment (125–66) was found in Trench OP, cleaning. **Fig. 6–2; Pl. 6–2.**

Cf. a similar lamp in Szentléleky, *Lamps,* 105, no. 169 (fig.), top of lamp also shown on a plate (not numbered). This lamp, with a vertical pierced handle, is said to be from Carthage. The center of the discus (missing on the Jalame lamp) has a raised ring decorated with radial incisions, and a hole in the middle. A second hole is just outside this ring. The base bears the signature MNOVIVSTI. The author relates it to Broneer's Type XXVII, group 1, and dates it end of 2nd c. (p. 107), but this does not seem a good parallel. See possibly Loeschcke, *Vindonissa,* 242, Type VIII A 1, dated second third of 1st c., which is less elaborate. For the *planta pedis* cf. Ivanyi, *Pannonische Lampen,* no. 746, pl. 78,

no. 16, a similar stamp on the base of a slightly different lamp (pl. 27, no. 11) found at Ptuj, Yugoslavia.

19 (1–64). Fragment of shoulder and discus

Max dim .038. Fine buff clay (10YR 8/3), red and black glaze (2.5YR 5/6 and 5YR 4/1). Discus depressed and encircled with a relief band; shoulder with dolphin and rosette (?) in relief. One similar fragment found. Probably 1st or 2nd c. From Trench A, depth .15–.20. Found with No. 99. **Fig. 6–2.**

Cf. Walters, *Lamps,* 93, no. 616, pl. 18 and pl. 42, Form 79, with two similar dolphins. See Goldman, *Tarsus* 1, fig. 105, no. 317. This fragment of Group XXIII has a goose and a rosette on the rim. It is dated 1st or 2nd c.

20 (92–66). Fragment of shoulder, side, discus, and nozzle

PL .051; PW .031; PH .017. Fine buff clay (10YR 8/3) with matt brown and red glaze (5YR 3/1 and 2.5YR 5/4); red glaze inside. Thin-walled. Depressed discus, relief rosette on shoulder, nozzle crossed with two relief bands joining dotted band across shoulder. Raised circle at edge of wick hole. 3rd c. From e–f:41 (Trench D) depth .30. **Fig. 6–2.**

See Avigad, *Beth Shearim* 3, 186–87, nos. 9–11, pl. 70 with similar nozzles (especially no. 11); he dates these mid–3rd c., arguing that earlier and later dates assigned to similar lamps from other sites are incorrect. He points out that the geographical distribution of this type is extensive. Our lamp is not exactly like any he cites.

21 (77–66). Handle

Max dim .025. Reddish buff clay (7.5YR 7/4), red glaze (10R 4/6). Ring handle made by piercing; three faintly incised grooves along the edge. Late 1st or 2nd c. From dd:37 (Trench J–12), depth .45. **Pl. 6–2.**

Cf. Crowfoot in *Samaria* 3, 371, fig. 88, no. 2. Reference is made to *QDAP* 1 (1932) pl. 34, 2 (bottom right). Both of these are dated late 1st or early 2nd c.

22 (11–64). Handle, parts of shoulder and discus

PH .023; Max dim .043. Fine buff clay (5YR 7/3), brown and red glaze (5YR 3/1 and 5YR 6/6). Double groove on solid vertical handle and double ring surrounding depressed discus. Relief dots on shoulder. Late 1st or 2nd c. From W:3–4 (Trench A–3) depth .60, with much pottery and plaster containing glass slivers. **Fig. 6–2.**

A perfect parallel is from Constanza, Romania: see C. Iconomu, *Opaiţe greco-romane* (Muzeul Regional de Arheologie Dobrogea) 129, no. 666, and fig. 150; no date mentioned. Walters, *Lamps,* 181, no. 1201, fig. 255, shows a similar lamp from Ephesus with a rosette in the center of the discus.

23 (107–65). Fragment of shoulder, trace of handle

PL .036; PW .026. Buff clay (10YR 7/3), trace of burning. Shoulder has relief pattern difficult to interpret. Ridge around discus, which seems to have a broken edge. 2nd c. From Trench A–6, surface to depth of .80. **Fig. 6–2.**

24 (133–66). Fragment of discus and shoulder

Max dim .022. Pale orange clay (7.5YR 7/4), red glaze

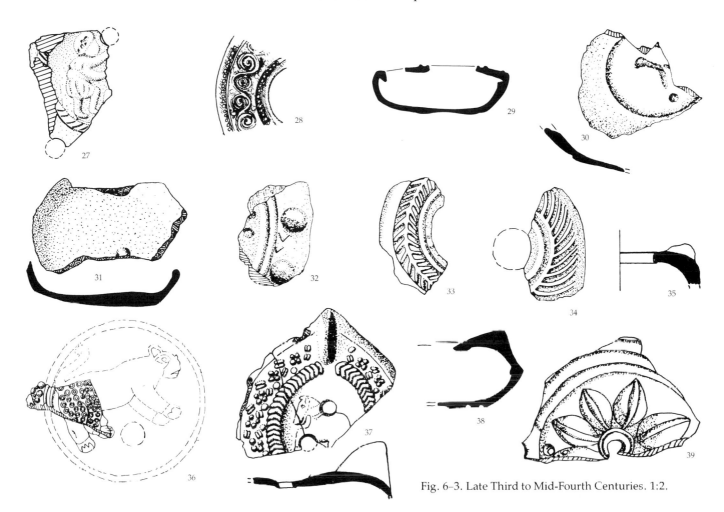

Fig. 6–3. Late Third to Mid-Fourth Centuries. 1:2.

(2.5YR 4/8). Vestige of volute and leaves on shoulder. Discus with floral relief design. Late 1st or 2nd c. From Trench J–10, depth .40 (above east-west wall). **Pl. 6–2.**

25 (29–65). Fragment of shoulder and large filling hole

Max dim .037; W of shoulder .018. Fine orange-buff clay (5YR 7/4, 10YR 7/3), burned around part of edge, probably near nozzle. Wreath in relief on shoulder between ridges. Probably 2nd c. From cc-dd:19 (Trench J–4), depth 1.35. **Fig. 6–2.**

Cf. Sussman, *Jewish Lamps*, 110, no. 208.

26 (95–66). Fragment of base and side

Max dim .029. Buff clay, traces of red glaze. Thin-walled. Base defined by incised lines, two stamped circles in center. Probably 2nd c. From west section of Trench OP–2, depth .40. **Fig. 6–2.**

Cf. Bovon, *Lampes*, 95, no. 669, pl. 18, dated 2nd c., signed in Greek **[Po]upliou**; Perlzweig, *Agora Lamps*, 96–97, pl. 9, nos. 288, 296, 298, 304, all signed Corinthian bases, dated 2nd c. Incised lines around bases appear to have been used alternately with the low ring base.

27 (41–65). Fragment of discus, shoulder, nozzle, and wick hole

Max dim .047. Fine clay, buff inside (10YR 7/2), orange

outside (5YR 7/6). On discus a male (?) figure with cap and tunic, facing right, within border of oblique ridges. Trace of filling hole above figure's head. Late 3rd or early 4th c. From I-M:32–36 (Trench M–1), depth 1.20. **Fig. 6–3.**

The crude representation, plus the absence of glaze, indicates a local copy of Roman works popular in Palestine during the 3rd and 4th c.

28 (45–65). Fragment of shoulder, nozzle, filling hole, and wick hole

PL .042; PW .028. Fine buff clay (10YR 8/3), red glaze (2.5YR 3/6). Traces of burning at filling hole. On shoulder, relief spiral, dots, and lines. First half of 4th c. From Trench M–1, cleaning. **Fig. 6–3; Pl. 6–2.**

Cf. Mader, *Mambre*, 154 and pls. 90,f and 94,i, dated 4th or 5th c. The nozzle is very like some examples from Beit Nattif, Cistern I: see Baramki, "Beit Nattif," pl. 6, nos. 10 and 13, but the scroll pattern on the shoulder is not illustrated. These lamps are dated ca. 300–350.

29 (8–64). Intact except for discus

L .072; W .059; H .026. Coarse orange clay (7.5YR 7/6), traces of red paint (2.5YR 5/6). Burning around wick hole. Base slightly concave, defined by low ridge. Irregular geometric relief pattern on shoulder. Discus, surrounded by double ridge, almost entirely broken out. Late 3rd-early

4th c. From S-T:21–22 (Trench A–2), just outside west wall of furnace, .40 below top of wall. **Fig. 6–3; Pl. 6–2.**

This lamp resembles the discus type, but the shoulder decoration is unlike other examples. Cf. Baur, *Dura Lamps*, 26, Type V. The pattern is much like a lamp of the early 2nd c.: Sussman, *Jewish Lamps*, 101, no. 182, but the shape is different.

30　(117–65). Part of side and base

D of base .035; Max dim .044. Reddish clay. Thin-walled. Round base set off from side by single groove. Impressed design or letter on base. Late 3rd c. to mid–4th. From Trench A–6, near surface. **Fig. 6–3.**

31　(146–65). Base and part of side

D of base .047. Fine buff clay. Part of stamped circle on flat bottom. Mid–4th c. From Trench Q, depth .65, below water jar deposit, with No. 70. **Fig. 6–3.**

31A　(48–65). Fragment of shoulder and discus

Max dim .038. Fine brown clay (5YR 5/3), burned. Two relief ridges around discus. Large globules on shoulder, with herringbones lightly incised between; stamped circles (?) on discus. Late 3rd c. From Trench P, depth 2.20, just outside wine press tank, near bedrock. **Fig. 6–3.**

Cf. Avigad, *Beth Shearim* 3, 185–90, no. 8, pl. 70, dated ca. 3rd c.; see also Harding, "Jebel Jofeh," pl. 25, nos. 51, 54, and possibly others. The tomb contents date, in general, to the 3rd c.

32　(13–64). Fragment of shoulder, small bit of side and filling hole

Max dim .04. Fine buff-yellow clay (7.5YR 7/4). Raised lines around large filling hole and row of dots at edge of ridged shoulder. 4th c. From west half of Trench A–3, depth .60–.70. **Pl. 6–2.**

The shoulder type appears in the 2nd c., e.g., Sussman, *Jewish Art*, no. 55. The lamp may be dated 4th c. as well: see Baramki, "Beit Nattif," pl. 10, nos. 2, 3, 25 (Cistern II).

33　(79–65). Fragment of shoulder

PL .043. Fine orange clay (5YR 6/6), traces of red glaze (10R 4/6). Herringbone design in low relief on shoulder. Not later than 350 (from context). From southern vat of wine press (Trench J–2), depth ca. 1.00. **Fig. 6–3.**

A lamp with similar shoulder pattern was found near Jerusalem; it is said to be "a familiar late third century type": Rahmani, "Raqafot," 79, fig. 3.

34　(91–65). Fragment of shoulder and discus, part of filling hole

Max dim .043. Fine orange clay, worn black glaze. Curving relief lines around shoulder. Groove and ridge around discus, which may have had a design. 4th c. From Trench M–1, north half, soft brown fill above bedrock. **Fig. 6–3.**

Cf. McCown, *Nasbeh* 1, 125, fig. 21, no. 4 (tomb 14), dated 3rd c. (p. 124); Szentléleky, *Lamps*, 100, no. 163, with a smaller filling hole.

35　(25–65). About half of shoulder, handle, part of side (three joining fragments)

D .05; W of shoulder .015. Pale orange clay, traces of burning. Stylized vine in relief around shoulder, knob handle. 4th c. From middle of Trench J–7, various depths. **Fig. 6–3; Pl. 6–2.**

Cf. Sussman, "Rehovot," 69–71, pl. 15, no. 12, a lamp from Qatra (10 km from Rehovot) of her type 3, group 2. She dates these to "the end of the Roman period" and believes all such lamps were made in the Yavne district.

36　(93–66). Fragment of discus and shoulder

Max dim .035. Fine pale orange clay (5YR 7/3), red glaze (10R 5/6). Part of a panther (?) in relief on discus, punched dots representing spots. Relief dots (grapes?) on shoulder. Mid–4th c. From c-f:9–12 (Trench K) below kitchen floor. Dated by context before 383. **Fig. 6–3; Pl. 6–2.**

Cf. Perlzweig, *Agora Lamps*, 130, pl. 21, no. 989, an Attic lamp of mid–4th c. with Greek inscription on discus: **Apektos.** See also Walters, *Lamps*, 199, no. 1328, a lamp from Ephesus with border of grapevines on shoulder.

37　(65–66). Two joining fragments preserving handle, part of shoulder and discus, filling hole, and part of another hole

PH (with handle) .019; PW .063; PL .058. Fine buff clay (10YR 7/3), no slip. Wreath of flowers in relief around shoulder, herringbone border within; on discus a horse facing left. Mold extremely worn, relief indistinct. 4th c. From Trench J–11, depth .35, just above bedrock. A similar shoulder fragment (103–66, not catalogued) was found in Trench X–2, south half, depth 1.50. **Fig. 6–3.**

A Cypriote lamp, as is amply proved by the publication of the lamps in the Nicosia Museum: T. Oziol, *Les Lampes du Musée de Chypre,* Salamine de Chypre 7 (Paris, 1977). The decoration on the shoulder of the Jalame lamp is almost exactly like that on 220 (fig. 8, extreme right) of this volume. The author considers it the latest phase of this type of shoulder ornament, which appears with various patterns on the discus.

Nos. 717–38 of the Salamis volume have a horse on the discus, but the type varies considerably. Nos. 717–24 show a galloping horse and have an inscription on the discus (the meaning of which is discussed at length on 243) and are signed in Greek on the bottom: **Eutychytos.** On nos. 725–38—the series to which the Jalame lamp belongs—is shown a standing horse with one forefoot raised. There is no inscription or signature. To judge from the photographs, no. 731 appears most like the Jalame example, but the molds are worn and the figures unclear.

A degenerate example of the type in the Museum of Art and Archaeology of the University of Missouri-Columbia (No. 59.72.21: see Pl. 6–5) was acquired by exchange with the Cyprus Department of Antiquities. It is almost the same color (7.5YR 7/4) as the Jalame fragment but smaller (L .072, W .05, H .023) and has a flower wreath on the shoulder, a horse (and possibly rider) on the discus. For its publication see P. Aström, Jane C. Biers, et al., *Corpus of Cypriote Antiquities* 2, *The Cypriote Collection of the Museum of Art and Archaeology, University of Missouri-Columbia, Studies in Mediterranean Archaeology* XX:2, no. 76. It may be compared with nos. 739–41 in Oziol's publication.

Oziol provides essential references in discussing the Cyprus lamps, but the following may be added: M. A. Dazsewski, "Polish Excavations at Kato (Nea) Paphos 1968–1969," *RDAC* 1969, 136–37, fig. 6, like the Jalame example and dated by the author to late 4th or early 5th c.; Heinz Menzel, *Antike Lampen* (Mainz, 1969) 85, no. 533 and fig. 80, no. 8, which appears similar to the Jalame fragment; Waagé, *Antioch* 3, 76, fig. 79, no. 50e:149, with unclear figure on the discus.

38 (17–66). Fragment of shoulder, side and base, handle and edge of discus

PH (with handle) .03; Est D .075, base .032. Gray core (10YR 4/1), buff (10YR 6/2) and orange clay (5YR 6/6). Very thin wall. Depressed discus surrounded by single ridge. Stamped lozenges with central dot on shoulder; solid triangular single-grooved handle with stamped circle at its base. Base has concentric grooves and stamped rosette in center. The fabric and workmanship are of finer quality than most of the lamps found at Jalame; it may be Syrian. 4th c. From B:31 (balk between Trenches Y–1 and Y–2), depth 1.50. **Fig. 6-3; Pl. 6-2.**

For the shoulder design only, cf. Baramki, "Beit Nattif," pl. 11, no. 11, and Iliffe, "El Bassa," 86, fig. 8. See also our No. 42, and the same design on a Beth Shearim lamp: Avigad, *Beth Shearim* 3, 187, no. 14 (group *a*) and pl. 70.

39 (35–64). Half of discus: part of shoulder and filling hole; air hole above a bit of nozzle (burned)

D discus .06. Fine dark orange clay (5YR 5/6), red matt glaze (2.5YR 4/6). Eight-petaled relief rosette on discus, concentric ridges on shoulder. Probably mid–4th c. From dump (west end of Trench L) depth .25–.50, with coins Nos. 39 and 190. **Fig. 6-3.**

Cf. Broneer, *Corinth Lamps*, pl. 14, no. 1085, Type XXVIII, of red clay, with red-brown glaze. Broneer says of this type (p. 107): "A few rare examples have large raised rosettes on which the veins are indicated on the petals." No. 39, probably imported, seems to be of this variety.

40 (43–66). Nozzle and part of discus

PL .046. Pale orange clay, burning at wick hole. Ridge around discus, incised geometric design on nozzle, stamped concentric circles flanking wick hole. Early 4th c. From west end of Trench S–3, depth .65. **Fig. 6-4; Pl. 6-2.**

Cf. Avigad, *Beth Shearim* 3, 187, no. 13, pl. 70, considered a transitional type. For the nozzle design see also Dunand-Duru, *Oumn el-Amed*, 217, fig. 89, a.

41 (34–66). Fragment of shoulder and discus, handle

PH (with handle) .018. Pale orange clay (7.5YR 7/4), traces of red glaze (2.5YR 5/8). Solid trapezoidal handle with raised dot at its base. Stamped ovolos on shoulder, ridge around discus. Late 4th c. From T:14–15 (Trench A–2), cleaning in north "door" of furnace (see Chap. 3). **Fig. 6-4.**

This resembles No. 42 except for the shoulder pattern. The ovolo is a very common pattern beginning, according to Perlzweig (*Agora Lamps*, 24), at Corinth and having its

floruit in Athens before 267 (Vandal invasion). In the Palestinian area it obviously lasted much longer: Bagatti, *Nazareth*, 304, fig. 235, no. 16. Cf. also Avigad, *Beth Shearim* 3, 187, no. 13, pl. 70.

42 (46–66). Fragment of shoulder and discus, handle

PH (with handle) .017. Pale orange clay (7.5YR 7/4). Depressed oval discus (broken) surrounded by double ridge, stamped lozenges with central dot on shoulder. Solid triangular handle with central groove, raised dot at base. Almost identical to No. 38. Another shoulder fragment (108–66, not catalogued) is similar. 4th c. From Trench Y–1 balk, to depth of 1.00. **Fig. 6-4.**

Cf. Avigad, *Beth Shearim* 3, 187, no. 14, pl. 70.

43 (22–65). Nozzle and part of body missing

PH (with handle) .041; W .065; PL .059. Orange-buff clay (5YR 7/4, bottom; 7.5YR 7/4, top). Depressed discus with filling hole. Single-grooved solid conical handle; crude leaves and dots stamped on shoulder. 4th c. From factory dump (Trench L, west end), embedded in plaster, a lump of which remains inside the lamp. Found just beneath the uppermost layer of plaster and glass, suggesting a date before 383. **Fig. 6-4; Pl. 6-2.**

Cf. Avigad, *Beth Shearim* 3, 187, nos. 17–18, pl. 70.

44 (67–66). Nozzle and small part of discus

PL .048. Buff-orange clay, burning at wick hole. Incised geometric design on nozzle, groove around discus. Mid–4th c. From U:53 (Trench X–2), depth 1.10. **Fig. 6-4.**

Cf. Dunand-Duru, *Oumn el-Amed*, 217, fig. 89,g; also Avigad, *Beth Shearim* 3, 187, no. 17, pl. 70.

45 (13–66). Fragment of discus, shoulder, and filling hole

Max dim .035. Orange clay interior (5YR 7/6), buff exterior (10YR 8/3). Depressed discus with encircling ridge. On the shoulder deeply stamped leaves, circles, short oblique strokes, and running loop design. Mid–4th c. From Trench Y–1, depth .60–.80. **Fig. 6-4.**

Cf. Avigad, as in No. 44. See also Dunand-Duru, *Oumn el-Amed*, 217, fig. 89,g, with same stamped leaves as well as circles and two small lozenges.

46 (7–65). Fragment of shoulder, discus, filling hole, and handle

PH (with handle) .02. Pale orange clay. Thick-walled. Oval, depressed discus, outlined by groove. Shoulder has crude stamped rosette; solid grooved handle with deeply stamped circle at its base. 4th c. From factory dump (Trench L) near surface. **Fig. 6-4.**

The lamp resembles Avigad, *Beth Shearim* 3, 187, no. 18, pl. 70, and others (group *a*), but no exact parallel appears.

47 (39–65). Fragment of shoulder and side

Max dim .024. Pale orange clay. Thin-walled. Stamped palmettes on shoulder. Mid–4th c. From Trench Y, depth 1.40. **Fig. 6-4.**

Cf. Baur, *Dura Lamps*, 44, pl. 7, no. 283 (Type VI). Stamped palmettes are found at Dura from mid–3rd c.

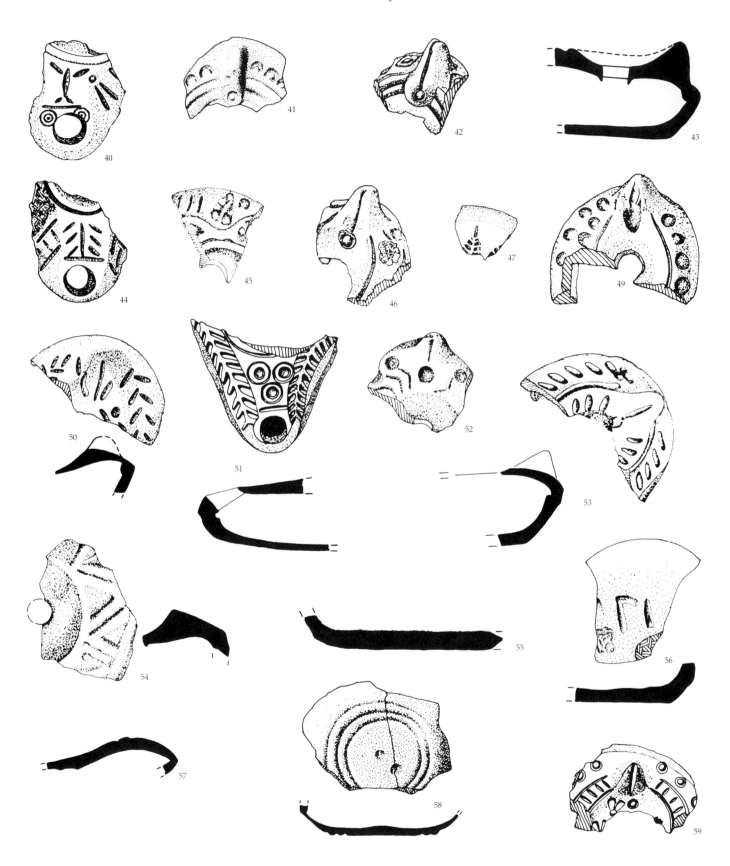

Fig. 6–4. Lamps of Beth Shearim Type. Ca. 2:3.

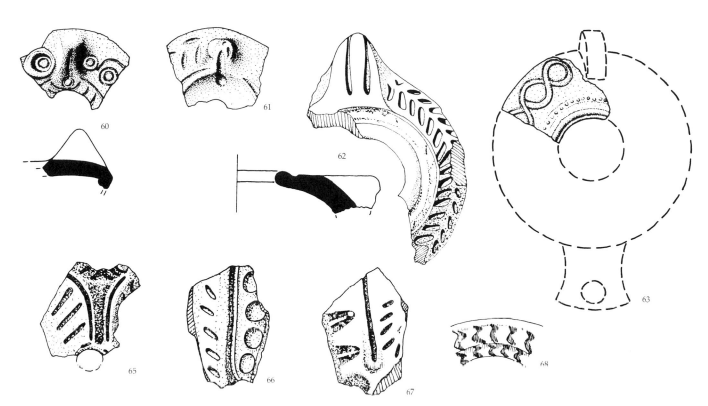

Fig. 6–5. Lamps of Beth Shearim Type. Ca. 2:3.

onward. See also Avigad, *Beth Shearim* 3, 187–88, no. 19, pl. 70, with rather fuller leaves resembling palmettes.

48   (12–65). Fragment of shoulder, discus, and handle

PH (with handle) .02. Buff clay. Handle with single groove, grooves on discus, small filling hole. Stamped circles on shoulder. 4th c. From m–s:8–17 (Trench A–5, south section), depth 1.10–1.30. **Pl. 6–2.**

Cf. for shoulder pattern Avigad, *Beth Shearim* 3, 188, no. 20, pl. 70.

49   (50–66). Fragment of shoulder, discus, filling hole, and handle

PH (with handle) .019; PL .048; W .054. Fine orange clay. Thick-walled. Depressed oval discus, outlined with ridge; shoulder has two rows of stamped ovolos on one side, one row on the other; solid conical handle, with ridge in center, stamped circle at base. The lamp appears somewhat lopsided. 4th c. From Trench X–2, depth .50–.60, with No. 51. **Fig. 6–4; Pl. 6–3.**

Cf. Avigad, *Beth Shearim* 3, 188, no. 20—not exactly similar.

50   (40–65). Fragment of shoulder, side, and handle

PH (with handle) .026. Orange clay. Rudimentary, triple-grooved conical handle; crude herringbone pattern stamped on shoulder. Mid–4th c. From Trench Y, depth 1.10–1.20. **Fig. 6–4.**

Cf. for herringbone pattern, Avigad, *Beth Shearim* 3, 188, no. 21, pl. 70.

51   (49 66). Nozzle, part of base

PH .027; PW .054; PL .058. Buff clay. Impressed concentric circles flanked by herringbone pattern. Groove around discus. 4th c. From Trench X–2, depth .50–.60, with No. 49. **Fig. 6–4; Pl. 6–3.**

Cf. Smith, *Pella*, 219 and pl. 65, nos. 225 and 253, not identical but related (dated 4th–6th c.). The nozzle is somewhat like Avigad, *Beth Shearim* 3, 188, no. 22, pl. 70.

52   (6–65). Fragment of shoulder, discus, handle, and filling hole

PH (with handle) .019. Fine buff clay. Crude stamped circles and herringbone design on shoulder. Solid handle, single ridged, with depression at base. 4th c. From a–e:1–4 (north section, Trench A–4) depth .80. **Fig. 6–4.**

Cf. Avigad, *Beth Shearim* 3, 188, no. 22, pl. 70, with positions of circles and herringbone pattern reversed.

53   (9–64). Fragment including parts of discus, shoulder, base, and handle

H (without handle) .028; Est W .065. Gritty buff clay, no slip. Grooves on shoulder and discus forming crude herringbone pattern; depressed discus. Solid conical handle with single vertical groove. Base flat as far as preserved. 4th c. From I–K:12–13 (Trench A–1) red earth just above clay floor. **Fig. 6–4.**

Although resembling Beth Shearim lamps, e.g. Avigad,

Beth Shearim 3, 188, no. 24, pl. 70, there seems to be none exactly the same.

54 (7–66). Fragment of shoulder and discus

Max dim .054. Orange clay, partly burned. Very thick-walled. Depressed discus, small filling hole, triangles and dots in relief on shoulder. 4th c. From MM:17 (Trench S–1) near surface. **Fig. 6–4.**

Cf. Avigad, *Beth Shearim* 3, 188, no. 25, pl. 70.

55 (20–64). Part of bottom and side

PW .044; PL .073. Friable pale orange clay. Thick wall, flat, elongated bottom, with small circle stamped on it. 4th c. From L-P:10–11 (Trench A–1) in deep trench with many glass fragments. **Fig. 6–4; Pl. 6–3.**

Cf. Avigad, *Beth Shearim* 3, 186, fig. 92, no. 6.

56 (23–64). Part of base and side

PH .015; Est D .07. Pale orange clay. Thick-walled, flat bottom. Two deeply incised letters: Γ I. 4th c. From I–K:20–21 (Trench A–1, southwest corner) with coin No. 199. **Fig. 6–4; Pl. 6–3.**

Cf. Avigad, *Beth Shearim* 3, 188, fig. 92, no. 6.

57 (101–66). Almost entire base and side up to shoulder

PH .017; D base .04. Pale orange clay. Fairly thin-walled. Low ridge around base, small dot in center. 4th c. From Trench S–3, depth .75. **Fig. 6–4; Pl. 6–3.**

The same profile and base are found on earlier lamps, but this example is rather coarse and seems to be not before 4th c.

58 (75–65). Almost entire base and side up to shoulder

PH .013; D of base .043. Orange clay. Thin-walled. Low base defined by double ridge. Two stamped circles near center. Two similar fragments (24–65, 24–66, not catalogued) without base markings. 4th c. From Trench Y, depth 1.75. **Fig. 6–4.**

59 (10–66). Fragment of discus, shoulder, and handle

PH (with handle) .017; PW .047. Fine buff clay. Thick-walled. Design on shoulder: incised lines between grooves, stamped circles around edge. Stamped leaves on discus; solid handle with single groove. 4th c. From E:23 (Trench Y–1) depth .40. **Fig. 6–4; Pl. 6–3.**

This and the following two lamps (Nos. 60–61) resemble Beth Shearim lamps in general, but no exact parallels are illustrated (Avigad, *Beth Shearim* 3, pl. 70).

60 (15–64). Fragment of discus, shoulder, and handle

PH (without handle) .022. Pale orange clay, buff slip. Shoulder has stamped concentric circles; discus (broken) has incised lines; conical, grooved handle. 4th c. From I–T:1–9 (Trench A–3) from cleaning, with No. 65. **Fig. 6–5.**

See No. 59.

61 (31–64). Fragment of discus, shoulder, handle, and filling hole

PH (with handle) .018. Orange and buff clay. Depressed oval discus outlined with ridge; shoulder has stamped radial strokes within border of strokes; conical handle with incised line and stamped circle below. Late 4th c. From dump (Trench L) near surface. **Fig. 6–5.**

See No. 59.

62 (33–66). Handle, part of shoulder, and filling hole

PH (with handle) .015; Est W .08; PL .09. Soft buff clay (10YR 7/3), burned at handle and filling hole; traces of matt red glaze (2.5YR 5/4). Solid flat triangular handle, double-grooved; large filling hole surrounded by ridge. Traces of relief pattern between ridge and shoulder. Stamped herringbone pattern on shoulder. 4th c. From Trench J–5, depth .50. **Fig. 6–5.**

Cf. Smith, *Pella*, 215–16, no. 35, pl. 83, dated from tomb contents to 3rd or 4th c. For lamps of this general kind see Avigad, *Beth Shearim* 3, 189, nos. 27–29, pl. 71, said to be an uncommon type; also FitzGerald, *Beth-Shan* 3, 41 and pl. 36, nos. 15–16, found with lamps of first half of 4th c.; Bagatti, *Nazareth*, 136, fig. 81, no. 1, found under mosaic pavement of Byzantine church.

63 (5–65). Fragment of shoulder and filling hole

Max dim .036; D filling hole ca. .022. Fine buff clay (2.5Y 7/2), traces of orange glaze (7.5YR 7/4). Ridge and row of small dots around large filling hole. Guilloche pattern around shoulder. 4th or early 5th c. From a–i:1–7 (Trench A–4), depth .50–.60. A pyramidal handle of similar clay (90–65, not catalogued) was found in Trench Q, near water jar deposit (see Chaps. 2 and 7). **Fig. 6–5.**

Cf. Avigad, *Beth Shearim* 3, 190, no. 32, pl. 71, exactly like our piece except for clay and glaze. The type is said to be uncommon and the date uncertain, possibly intrusive in Catacomb 17. A similar lamp (unpublished) was found in Catacomb 24 in 6th c. context (ibid., 190, n. 206).

64 (15–65). Fragment of nozzle and wick hole

PL .035; PW .017; PH .017. Fine buff clay (10YR 7/3), traces of red glaze (2.5YR 4/6). Nozzle outlined with relief line. 4th or 5th c. From Trench F–3, near surface. **Pl. 6–3.**

Cf. Avigad, *Beth Shearim* 3, 190, no. 32, pl. 71. This may be a nozzle from a lamp like No. 63.

65 (12–64). Fragment of nozzle, shoulder, and discus

PL .036. Orange-buff clay, burning at wick hole. Central channel bordered by grooves extending around discus to wick hole; incised lines on sides of nozzle and on discus. Second half of 4th c. From I–T:1–9 (Trench A–3) from cleaning, with No. 60. **Fig. 6–5.**

This seems rather like Avigad, *Beth Shearim* 3, 190, pl. 71, no. 34, said to be the only example of its kind at this site and to date mid–6th c. at earliest. Actually it has a different type of discus reminiscent of some Corinthian lamps (Broneer, *Corinth Lamps*, Type XXVIII, 105, fig. 49, nos. 9–11, dated 4th or 5th c.). The clay of our fragment, however, is not Corinthian.

66 (111–65). Fragment of shoulder, nozzle, and wick hole

PL .046. Fine buff-orange clay. Very thick-walled. Oblique grooves on nozzle, stamped circles on shoulder. 4th c. From Trench A–5, depth .90–1.10. **Fig. 6–5.**

The fabric and general appearance resemble the later Beth Shearim lamps, but no exact parallel is illustrated in Avigad, *Beth Shearim* 3.

67 (68–66). Fragment of shoulder and nozzle

PW .0315; PL .047. Fine orange clay. Thick-walled. Stamped triangular leaves on shoulder, short oblique lines incised on nozzle, with long incised groove separating the two parts. Edge of shoulder appears unbroken, as if top and bottom had separated. Late 4th c. From south half of Trench X–2, near bedrock. **Fig. 6–5.**

Cf. Iliffe, "El Bassa," 86, fig. 11, a slipper-shaped lamp with thick walls and apparently similar decoration, probably late 4th c.

68 (131–65). Fragment of discus, shoulder, side, nozzle, and wick hole

PH .023. Very soft orange clay. Stamped zigzag pattern on shoulder. Discus much worn; may have same pattern. Mid-4th c. From Trench M–1, rock cutting with stony fill, depth .90. **Fig. 6–5; Pl. 6–3.**

Perhaps related to Beth Shearim lamps, although no identical specimen is illustrated. Cf. Perlzweig, *Agora Lamps*, 134, no. 1116 (pl. 22), dated late 4th c. Although there is probably no connection with this Attic lamp, there is a definite resemblance.

69 (106–66). Handle and fragment of shoulder and side

PH (with handle) .033. Fine orange clay, buff slip. Solid handle with double groove. Lightly incised line defining discus. Stamped concentric circles on shoulder. Late 4th c. From Trench OP–3, near surface. **Fig. 6–6.**

A lamp with similar concentric circles and a channel leading to the nozzle comes from a tomb at Sidon: M. Meurdrac, "Une sépulture chrétienne à Sidon," *Berytus* 4 (1937) 134, no. 2, pl. 25. It is dated 4th c. A lamp from the Athenian Agora (Perlzweig, *Agora Lamps*, 103, no. 376, pl. 11), dated 6th–7th c., is very like ours. The stamped circles seem identical; the handle has small circles instead of vertical grooves.

70 (145–65). Fragment of discus, shoulder, filling hole, and handle

PH (with handle) .016; Est W .055. Orange-buff clay. Crude, single-grooved handle. Stamped rosettes of various sizes on shoulder. 4th c. From Trench Q, depth .65, below water jar deposit, with No. 31. **Fig. 6–6.**

71 (90–66). Fragment of shoulder and side.

PL .044. Fine orange clay (5YR 7/6), buff slip (10YR 8/3). Stylized leaves stamped on top; circles stamped around edge of shoulder, which is beveled. 4th c. From Trench J–13, depth .35, near No. 15. **Fig. 6–6.**

72 (58–66). Fragment of shoulder, discus, and nozzle

PL .037. Pale orange clay. Faintly stamped ovolo pattern on shoulder; nozzle has ridge on each side, with stamped circles as shown on Fig. Late 4th c. From Trench Y–1 balk, nearly on bedrock. **Fig. 6–6.**

The decoration reminds one of earlier lamps, e.g., No. 20 and Avigad, *Beth Shearim* 3, 186–87, nos. 9–11, but the clay and workmanship are very poor and suggest a late

date. Another similar piece (154–66) is too fragmentary for inclusion.

73 (67–65). Two non-joining fragments of shoulder, nozzle and part of wick hole

Max dim (a) .04, (b) .034. Fine buff-orange clay. Thick-walled. Deeply impressed rosettes of different sizes and raised oblique strokes beside central groove on nozzle. Burning at wick hole. Late 4th c. From w-x:16–17 (Trench A–6) depth .80. **Fig. 6–6.**

74 (26–66). Nozzle and part of base

PH .031; PL .041. Friable orange clay, burning at wick hole. Stamped rosettes, circles, and lines. Rather deep body; bottom flat. Second half of 4th c. From β:44 (Trench Y–3), depth ca. 1.00. **Fig. 6–6.**

75 (35–66). Fragment of nozzle and wick hole

PL .031; PW .025. Buff clay, burned. Short incised strokes on sides of nozzle, which has two long grooves. Second half of 4th c. From west side of Trench Y–1, depth 1.60–1.80. **Fig. 6–6.**

Cf. Bagatti, *Nazareth*, 136, fig. 81, nos. 10–11. These were found under the mosaic pavement of the Byzantine church.

76 (32–64). Three joining fragments forming most of shoulder, discus, part of sides and nozzle; one small non-joining fragment of side

PH (with handle) .021; PL .081; Est W .064. Buff clay (10YR 8/4), burning at wick hole. Depressed discus with central filling hole. Crude stamped leaves and circles on shoulder; two rows of stamped circles above nozzle. Late 4th c. From inside wall at g:22 (Trench H). **Fig. 6–6; Pl. 6–3.**

77 (107–66). Two joining fragments of base, side, and nozzle.

PH .011; PL .034; D base .031. Fine dark red clay (10R 4/6), slight burning at nozzle. Low ridge around base and traces of incised design on bottom, possibly a letter. Two slanting grooves on either side of nozzle. Date: 351–383. From dump (Trench Y–3S), with three coins of Period 3 (Nos. 57, 111, 112). One other base fragment from same place (81–66) may join. **Fig. 6–6.**

Possibly related to Avigad, *Beth Shearim* 3, 189–90, no. 31, pl. 71.

78 (72–66). Fragment of base (?)

PL .038; PW .031. Buff clay. Thick-walled. Two lines of three stamped circles separated by groove. Date: 351–383. From dump (Trench Y–3S) in fill between conglomerate layers, with many coins (Nos. 33, 123, 150, 158, 186). **Pl. 6–3.**

If this is indeed part of a base, cf. Iliffe, "El Bassa," 87, fig. 16, with short strokes rather than circles.

79 (127–65). Handle and part of side

PH .047. Fine reddish clay (2.5YR 6/4), matt red glaze (2.5YR 4/4). Solid handle with two vertical grooves. 4th c. From south half of Trench M–1, depth .25. **Pl. 6–3.**

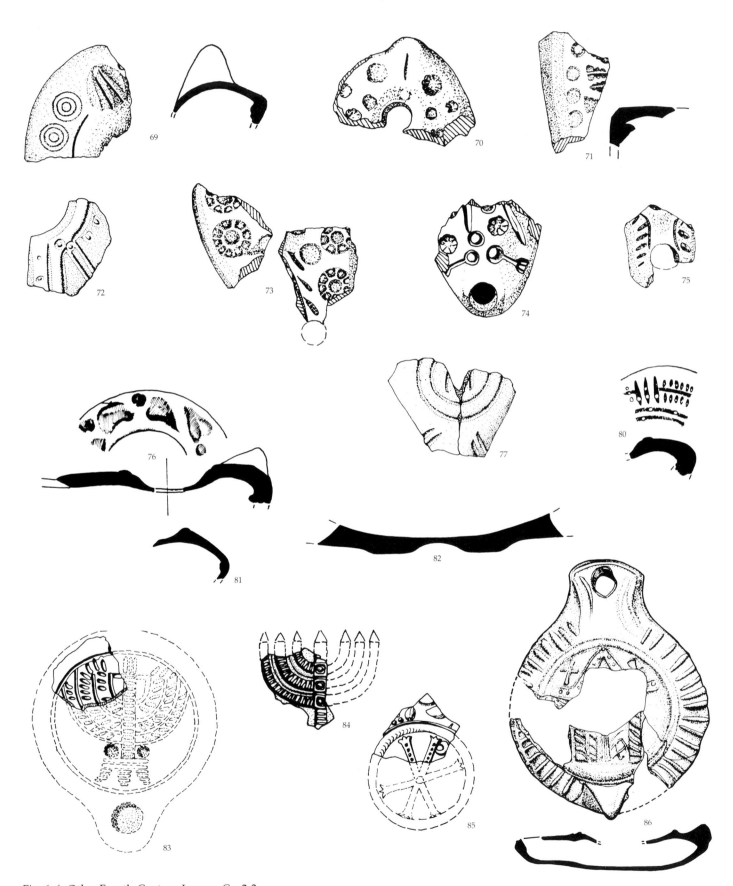

Fig. 6–6. Other Fourth-Century Lamps. Ca. 2:3.

Cf. an Attic lamp of second half of 4th c. (Perlzweig, *Agora Lamps*, pl. 25, no. 1303).

80 (66–66). Fragment of shoulder, discus, and side

Max dim .029. Fine orange clay (10R 5/6), darker slip (10R 4/6). Thick-walled. Impressed and relief geometric design on shoulder; ridge around plain, depressed discus. 4th c. From Trench J–11, near surface. **Fig. 6–6; Pl. 6–3.**

Cf. Perlzweig, *Agora Lamps*, 98, no. 321, pl. 9, of dark orange clay, dated late 4th into 5th c. The shoulder appears similar; the discus has rays in relief. See also Bovon, *Lampes*, 67, nos. 438 (brick-red), 439, pl. 11, both signed **Ilarou,** dated 4th c.

81 (8–65). Fragment of shoulder, side, discus, and filling hole

Max dim .048. Fine buff clay. Stamped herringbone pattern on shoulder; depressed discus, undecorated, with small filling hole. The lamp may be circular. This type was produced during the 4th c. in Palestine and elsewhere. One similar fragment found. 4th c. From Trench J–3, southeast corner, near surface. **Fig. 6–6; Pl. 6–3.**

Cf. rather similar lamps from Athens (Perlzweig, *Agora Lamps*, 141, nos. 1365 and 1373, pl. 26), the former dated first half of 4th c., the latter late 4th c.

82 (26–64). Base and part of sides

PH .014; PW .041; PL .091. Orange clay. Thick-walled. Deep indentation in center of base. Both ends elongated like double-spouted lamps. Probably before 383. From Q-T:7–9 (Trench A–3) under hard floor (see Chap. 2). **Fig. 6–6; Pl. 6–3.**

Cf. Perlzweig, *Agora Lamps*, 157, no. 2009, pl. 32, dated second half of 4th c. See also J. Oziol and J. Pouilloux, *Salamine de Chypre*, vol. 1 (Paris, 1977) no. 430, pl. 19, similar in shape, date not mentioned.

83 (118–65). Fragment of discus and shoulder

PL .027. Orange clay (7.5YR 6/4). Thin-walled. Incised lines forming three branches of a seven-branched candelabrum and part of central support, each branch with incised oblique lines, those at the top representing flames. Groove dividing discus from sloping shoulder. 4th c. From Trench A–6, north section, depth .90. **Fig. 6–6.**

Cf. A. Reifenberg, *Ancient Hebrew Arts* (New York, 1950) 147, no. 1, fig. on p. 146, dated 4th c. and said to be from Alexandria. Our figure is restored from Reifenberg's example. For another similar lamp from Caesarea, see Goodenough, *Symbols*, 3, fig. 344. He believes it to show "Alexandrian sources or influences" (ibid., 1, 160).

84 (3–67). Fragment of discus

PL .03. Orange clay (5YR 6/4). Thin-walled. Central support and three branches of seven-branched candelabrum, all in relief, decorated with incised lines, and relief squares on central support, enclosing raised dots. 4th c. From trench at Y-b:45–47, cleaning fourth hard floor (see Chap. 2, Period 3). **Fig. 6–6; Pl. 6–3.**

For the type of menorah, see one found on Mt. Carmel: Goodenough, *Symbols* 3, fig. 345. Cf. also Reifenberg,

Ancient Hebrew Arts, 146, no. 2, in the collection of the American University, Beirut (from which our restoration of the lights has been taken). The squares enclosing the circles on the central support seem not to appear on other lamps.

85 (34–65). Fragment of discus and shoulder

Max dim .033. Buff clay, unslipped. Thin-walled. Depressed discus, bordered by relief ring. Parts of **chi** and **rho** with rows of relief dots. Floral relief decoration on shoulder. 4th c. From dump (Trench L, west end), depth .50–1.00, with coin No. 45, dating 351–361. **Fig. 6–6; Pl. 6–3.**

A North African lamp has a discus and surrounding pattern much like our example (Menzel, *Antike Lampen*, 94, no. 615 and fig. 79, no. 4). The clay is described as yellow-brown. Although the date is not mentioned, the shape and decoration do not resemble those of the typical 5th-c. North African Christian lamp, suggesting that this example as well as ours may be earlier. Cf. also C. von Praschniker, F. Miltner, H. Gerstinger, *Forschungen in Ephesus* 4, part 2, *Das Coemeterium der sieben Schläfer*, pl. 4, no. 568 (dated 4th or 5th c.); Broneer, *Corinth Lamps*, 110, Type XXVIII, fig. 52, for general parallels.

86 (33–64). Parts of discus and body missing

L .102; W .078; H (without handle) .02. Brown, somewhat gritty clay (2.5YR 5/4). Solid, conical handle. Radial ridges on shoulder; two relief lines on each side of wick hole. On the discus a shrine in relief, supported on two spiraliform columns. Oblique and straight lines between columns indicate closed doors. Gabled roof, with cross above at one side, the other cross only partly preserved. From west side of Trench K, near the wall, with Cypriote Red Slip Ware (see Chap. 7), dated to second half of 4th c. This type of lamp is usually dated 6th c. **Fig. 6–6; Pl. 6–4.**

For two lamps with representations of shrines with columns and gabled roofs, one with vases, the other with concentric circles (no indication of religious affiliation), see Goodenough, *Symbols* 1, 153; 3, 286–87.

A lamp of similar shape, but having a conventional leaf pattern on the discus, was found in the synagogue at En-Gedi (D. Barag and Y. Porat, "The Synagogue at En-Gedi," *Qadmoniot* 11 (1970) 100 (in Hebrew).

87 (1–65). Intact except for chipped handle and holes in bottom

L .091; W .059; H .031. Friable red-buff clay (7.5YR 5/6), burned at wick hole. Large filling hole. Rings of relief dots and oblique lines on shoulder. Nozzle has lozenge with central dot, all in relief in square bordered by double ridges. Lug handle. Crude flat base ring, one relief dot preserved. Third quarter of 4th c. From m:4–5 (Trench A–5), depth 1.05, with coins Nos. 67 (337–361) and 154 and 155 (364–375). **Fig. 6–7; Pl. 6–4.**

No exactly similar lamps seem to be known, but for related specimens (none closely dated) see Sellers-Baramki, 41, fig. 43, no. 318 (Type X) dated tentatively 4th–6th c.; Kennedy, *Berytus* 14, pl. 24, no. 606, similar except for

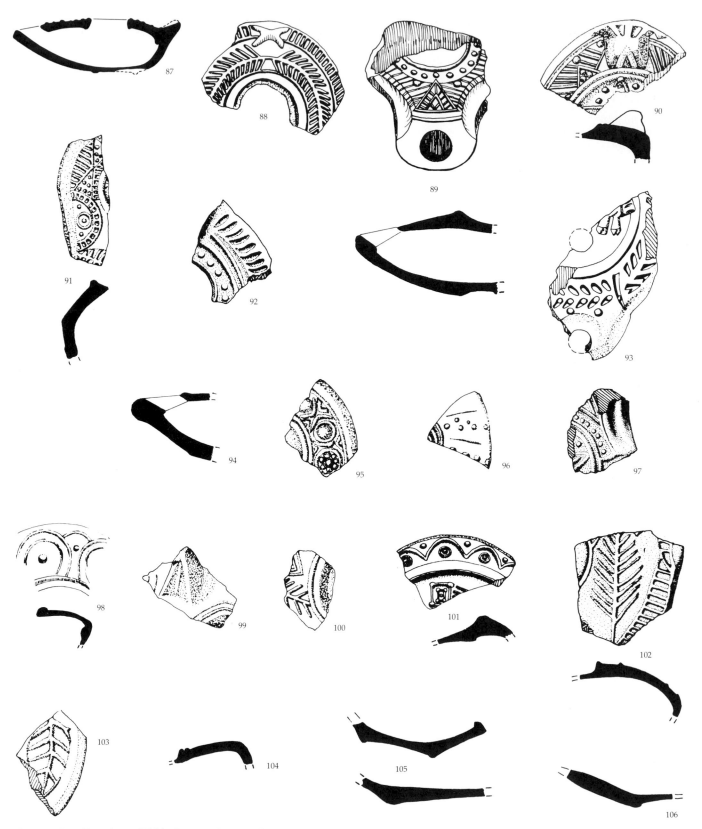

Fig. 6–7. Late Fourth- and Fifth-Century Lamps. Ca. 2:3.

nozzle; Smith, *Pella*, pl. 83, no. 150, somewhat similar, with a lozenge (not enclosed) on the nozzle (Tomb 5, dated 4th–6th c.); Goodenough, *Symbols* 1, 152; 3, nos. 301–2, from Beth Shan. These have lozenges on the nozzle, placed differently.

88   (10–64). Fragment of shoulder with handle and part of discus

Max dim .054. Orange-buff clay. Herringbone pattern on shoulder, star-knob handle. 4th c. From X–Z:8–12 (Trench A–2), depth 1.30. **Fig. 6–7; Pl. 6–4.**

This appears to have been a common type in Samaria: see Crowfoot in *Samaria* 3, 375, no. 3, fig. 89 (similar handle); Sellers-Baramki, 36–37, fig. 39, no. 312 and fig. 40, no. 338, dated 4th or early 5th c. Husseini, "Beit Fajjar," pl. 86, 2, no. 8 shows a star-knob-handled lamp with identical shoulder pattern. See also Mader, *Mambre*, 151ff, pl. 88, b. Beit Nattif I lamps have the star-knob handle but a different nozzle (see Baramki, "Beit Nattif," pl. 6).

89   (18–65). Nozzle and parts of discus and base

Pl .058; PW .048; PH .032, Est D base .03. Coarse orange-buff clay. Depressed discus surrounded by ridge and ring of relief dots. Nozzle has hatched relief triangle, relief lines on shoulder. Concave base, low ring in relief and small knob in center. Late 4th c. From t–v:7–8 (Trench A–6), depth 1.10. **Fig. 6–7.**

This nozzle belongs to a lamp like the preceding. With it were two fragments of a lamp with a more prominent star-knob handle and a small piece of the base (100–65). See n. 37 above for discussion of possible Samaritan connections.

90   (30–64). Fragment of discus and shoulder, with stublike handle

PH .019; Max dim .054. Coarse red-brown clay (2.5YR 6/4), no slip. Relief decoration: groups of oblique lines and raised dots on shoulder; similar pattern on discus. From d–e:15–17 (Trench H) with a coin of Julian (360–363). **Fig. 6–7; Pl. 6–4.**

For a nearly similar shoulder pattern see a discus lamp from Beit Nattif (Cistern I): Baramki, "Beit Nattif," 5, pl. 7, no. 2, dated 3rd c. For the handle, cf. Kennedy, *Berytus* 14, 79 and pl. 24, no. 606 (Type 12), dated late 4th or 5th c.

91   (99–66). Fragment of shoulder, discus, and nozzle

PL .049. Gritty light brown clay (5YR 6/6), nozzle burned. Discus bordered by ridge. Molded relief design of circles, semicircles, lines, and dots on nozzle and shoulder. Late 4th–5th c. From LL–UU:5–20 (Trench S–3), depth .75. **Fig. 6–7; Pl. 6–4.**

Cf. for the pattern Sellers-Baramki, fig. 40, no. 325 (Type VII), dated 4th–5th c.; also Crowfoot in *Samaria* 3, 374, no. 2, fig. 89, dated 3rd–4th c. (too early). The profile of our lamp is different.

92   (69–65). Fragment of shoulder, discus, filling hole, and handle

Max dim .031. Orange clay. Thick-walled. Shoulder has ring of relief dots, separated by double groove from row of short curved lines. Ridge around large filling hole. Handle rises sharply from shoulder. Context before 351—Trench Y, depth 2.00, near bedrock. Date of lamp mid–4th-early 5th c. **Fig. 6–7.**

Cf. Saller, *Bethany*, 183, pl. 109, no. 14, dated to Byzantine period, apparently 6th c.

93   (36–66). Fragment of shoulder, discus, and nozzle

PL .063. Buff clay, nozzle burned. Depressed discus bounded by ridge, animal in relief molded and incised, forepaws and muzzle preserved. Filling hole (broken) below animal's feet. Late 4th–5th c. From β:44 (Trench Y–3), depth .30–.50, with No. 95. **Fig. 6–7; Pl. 6–4.**

Cf. Perlzweig, *Agora Lamps*, 64, no. 2420, pl. 38, and others dated 5th and 6th c., "derived from 3rd century archetypes."

94   (17–65). Nozzle, parts of shoulder and base

PH .026; PW .059. Coarse gray clay (10YR 5/1), burned at wick hole. Undecorated. 4th c. or later. From K:41 (Trench M–1), depth .40. **Fig. 6–7; Pl. 6–4.**

Cf. a possibly similar lamp, perhaps from Syracuse: M. Bernhard, *Lampki Starozytne* (Warsaw, 1955) 348, no. 392 and pl. 122, dated 4th–6th c. Also cf. Bovon, *Lampes*, 85, no. 598, pl. 14, with raised ring around fairly large central hole. Here also references to lamps from Piazza Armerina, Volubilis, and Hungary.

95   (37–66). Fragment of shoulder and discus

Max dim .034. Gritty buff clay. Shoulder has relief design of circles and rosettes ringed with ridges; relief bands around depressed discus. Late 4th c. From Trench Y–3, among discarded bricks and conglomerate, with No. 93. **Fig. 6–7.**

A lamp of 4th or 5th c. with similar circles in lower relief and incised crosses between them was found at Argos. The discus is depressed and undecorated: Bovon, *Lampes*, 74, no. 514, pl. 13. For a somewhat similar pattern cf. Saller, *Bethany*, 52 and fig. 17, no. 6, in a tomb of the Second Church, dated 4th–6th c.

96   (112–65). Fragment of shoulder

PL .029; PW .023. Fine gray clay (10YR 7/1), traces of red glaze (10R 4/4). Groups of relief dots separated by ridges. Three ridges around discus or filling hole. 4th or early 5th c. From m–p:1–5 (Trench A–5), depth 1.10. **Fig. 6–7.**

Cf. Bovon, *Lampes*, 70, no. 478 and pl. 12, a lamp from Argos dated 1st half of 5th c. with tiny raised dots around shoulder, but no dividing lines between. The discus is surrounded by three ridges as in our specimen. The clay is described as "gris violacé."

97   (2–65). Fragment of discus and nozzle, broken all around

Max dim .033. Orange clay, burned. Discus has molded geometric design in relief, bordered with ring of relief dots. 4th or 5th c. From dump (Trench L), cleaning. **Fig. 6–7; Pl. 6–4.**

98   (108–65). Fragment of shoulder, side, and filling hole

Max dim .035; PH .012. Fine gray clay. Shoulder has double arches molded in relief, joined by small single arches, each with a central relief dot. Ridge around large filling hole. 4th c. From Trench A–6, depth .60, with No. 23. **Fig. 6–7; Pl. 6–4.**

99 (2–64). Handle and part of shoulder

Max dim .039; L of handle .019. Fine buff clay, traces of matt red glaze. Pyramidal handle; parallel molded relief lines on shoulder. Mid–4th to mid–5th c. From Trench A, depth .15– .20, with No. 19. **Fig. 6–7.**

100 (8–66). Fragment of discus and shoulder

Max dim .03. Gritty buff-orange clay. Discus depressed and surrounded by double ridge; relief branch and triangles or lozenges on shoulder. Late 4th–5th c. From Trench Y–2, top soil. **Fig. 6–7.**

101 (30–65). Fragment of discus and shoulder

Max dim .045; PH .011. Fine buff clay. Scallops with dotted circles in relief on shoulder. Geometric design in relief on discus. Late 4th c. From d:24 (Trench F–1) below hard clay floor, near coins of Arcadius and Honorius. **Fig. 6–7; Pl. 6–4.**

102 (19–65). Fragment of discus, shoulder, and side

PL .044. Gritty orange clay. Discus depressed, ridge around it. Branch in relief on shoulder, bordered with short ridges. Probably late Byzantine or early Arab. Provenience not recorded. **Fig. 6–7; Pl. 6–4.**

Cf. Sussman, "Kefar Ara," 98 (Group C, end of Byzantine period), figs. 2:7, 3:1–4. Also Crowfoot, *Samaria* 3, 376, no. 8, fig. 89, dated to early Arab period.

103 (16–64). Fragment of shoulder

PL .04; PW .025. Coarse buff clay. Thick-walled. Branch design in relief. 5th–6th c. From J–Q:3–10 (Trench A–3) below lamp No. 32. **Fig. 6–7.**

Cf. Saller, *Bethany,* 52, fig. 16, no. 13, dated early Byzantine (4th–6th c.); Wampler, *Nasbeh* 2, pl. 73, no. 1671, similarly dated; also Mader, *Mambre,* pl. 89, c.

104 (4–64). Fragment of shoulder, side, and discus

Max dim .032; PW .028. Gritty orange clay (5YR 6/6). Geometric relief design on shoulder, two ridges around discus (broken). 5th c. or later. From D-I:8–12 (Trench A), depth .40–.50. **Fig. 6–7; Pl. 6–4.**

105 (85–65). Base, part of sides

H to shoulder .016. Reddish clay, burned inside. Oval, slightly concave base with slight ridge around it. 6th–8th c. From Trench P, depth .35–.50. **Fig. 6–7; Pl. 6–4.**

Cf. F. E. Day, "Early Islamic and Christian Lamps," *Berytus* 7 (1942) 72, pl. 12, no. 2.

106 (68–65). Fragment of base, side, and bottom of nozzle

PH .011. Rather coarse buff-orange clay; traces of burning at nozzle. Raised base. 6th c. From north half of Trench M–1, in brown fill. **Fig. 6–7; Pl. 6–4.**

7

BARBARA L. JOHNSON

The Pottery

Introduction

An unexpected product of the excavations was the enormous quantity of pottery recovered. Though most of it is Late Roman, both earlier and later material was found. Several hundred sherds ranging in date from the Early Bronze Age to Persian times indicate pre-Hellenistic occupation. Hellenistic and Early Roman material is represented by a few small pieces. Although none of the well-known painted Nabataean vessels was recovered, a quantity of Nabataean plain ware appeared.

Outstanding among the Late Roman pottery is the fine tableware. Each of the three major products of the period was found. Readily identifiable but few in numbers and shapes was the African Red Slip Ware (ARSW). Greatly overshadowing (in quantity) the North African material was the Late Roman C Ware ("Phocaean Red Slip Ware"; LRCW) and Cypriote Red Slip Ware (CRSW). This proportion is repeated at virtually all Late Roman sites in Palestine. The number of forms is smaller in both LRCW and CRSW than in ARSW, but the variety of detail within a given form is greater. This is seen especially in LRCW Form 3 and CRSW Forms 2 and 9. In addition, several heretofore unclassified shapes have been added to the repertory of each of these wares.

A fragment of the lower rim and body of a bowl imitates a shape common to Local Athenian Late Roman D Ware (see below). Two things are worth noting about the fine tablewares found at Jalame. First, it is evident that the flow of trade was from Cyprus and Asia Minor, not from North Africa.

Second, the amount of fine ware found is extremely large for a relatively small site; the reason for this is not clear. Cooking and serving wares are also plentiful. Their parallels come from the Galilee area, showing that Jalame falls into that sphere of influence. Examples of storage and/or transport amphoras were common, most in quite fragmentary state (an exception is the local Pal-estinian Baggy Jar, see Nos. 762–827, below). Too little is known about amphoras of the eastern Mediterranean in the Roman period for detailed comment. It may be noted that well-known shapes, the Micaceous Water Jar (Amphora Form 2), the Gaza Amphora (Amphora Form 3), and the "Panel" Amphora (Amphora Form 4), though distinctive and of wide distribution, are not common at Jalame. The examples listed under "Miscellaneous Amphoras" mainly illustrate the variety found at the site.

The importance of the ceramic material from Jalame is to show the types (and variations within them) and the quantities of pottery that may be recovered from a Late Roman site in Palestine.

* * *

The pottery is presented chronologically, from the Bronze Age to Crusader times. The order of presentation is basically from open to closed shapes.

Only grits and inclusions that are not minute are commented on specifically, that is, as small and large.

Color references are according to the *Munsell Soil Color Charts* unless it was impossible to read them. For the pottery the verbal descriptions as well as the numerical are those of the Charts.

The Late Roman Fine Wares begin with ARSW, followed by the LRCW ("Phocaean Red Slip Ware") and CRSW. Previously unclassified forms are placed at the end of the specific class of pottery to which they belong.

Next are the other open shapes—bowls, basins, and cooking wares and cooking pot lids. Jugs are presented in a single unit, except for those that clearly belong to an earlier or later period. Amphoras are presented immediately before the bell-shaped lids. These were probably used as covers for large jars.

Pre-Hellenistic Pottery

The pre-Hellenistic pottery is fragmentary and without meaningful contexts; thus only a small selection is pre-

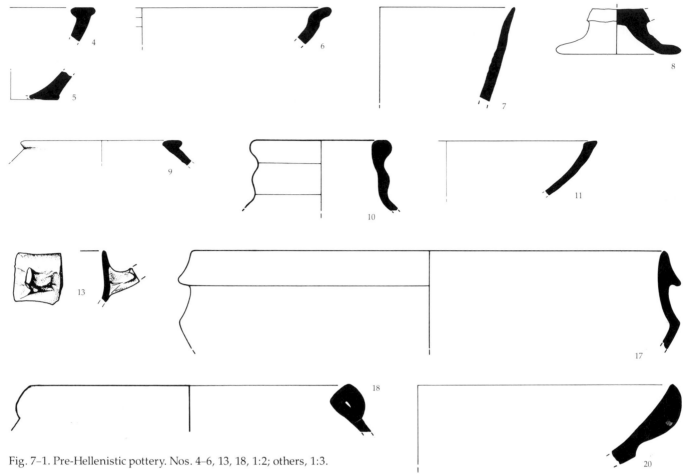

Fig. 7–1. Pre-Hellenistic pottery. Nos. 4–6, 13, 18, 1:2; others, 1:3.

sented. It dates from the Early Bronze Age to the Persian period and includes both local and imported products.[1]

Early Bronze Age

Hole Mouth Jar (No. 1)

1   (376–65). PH .03; Est D rim .27

Fine clay, dark gray core (5YR 4/1), outer bands light reddish brown (5YR 6/3), a few white and black grits and mineral inclusions, occasional small ones. Remains of reddish brown slip on exterior.

Middle Bronze Age

Vessels with Burnished Red Slip (Nos. 2–5)

2   (679–66). PH .034

Coarse clay, very dark gray core (5YR 3/1), outer bands light reddish brown (5YR 6/4), a few minute to large white grits; red slip (2.5YR 5/6).

3   (3–67). PH .027; D rim .37

Coarse clay, gray core (5YR 5/1), outer bands light reddish brown (5YR 6/4), some white and black grits; red slip (2.5YR 4/6).

4   (183–65). PH .028

Coarse clay, dark gray core (5YR 4/1), outer bands pink (7.5YR 7/4), some minute to large white and gray grits; red slip (2.5YR 4/8). **Fig. 7–1.**

5   (911–66). PH .025; D base .08

Coarse clay, gray core (5YR 5/1), outer bands light brown (7.5YR 6/4), some minute to small white and gray grits; red slip (10R 5/6) on exterior. **Fig. 7–1.**

Cooking Pot (No. 6)

6   (132–66). PH .042; D rim .398

Coarse clay, dark gray core (5YR 4/1), outer bands light brown (7.5YR 6/4), many minute to small black and white grits. **Fig. 7–1.**

1. For similar jars see R. Amiran, *Ancient Pottery of the Holy Land* (Jerusalem, 1969) 59, pl. 16.6. I wish to thank Prof. Amiran for advising on the pre-Hellenistic pottery; any errors of attribution are my own. For Nos. 2–5 see ibid., 90–93, pls. 25–26. The identification of Nos. 6–11 as Middle Bronze is based on their general characteristics and similarity to pottery of this period. For No. 12, see ibid., 116–20, pl. 36, esp. no. 15. The Late Bronze Cypriote Wares appear in ibid., 172–78, pls. 53–55; for the Iron Age see ibid., 227–32, especially pl. 76.9. For No. 18 see Crowfoot, *Samaria*

3, 114–15, fig. 6.13. No. 19 is dated to the Iron Age on the basis of its similarity to other examples of the period. The mortar (No. 20) is a common type of the Persian period that apparently continued into Hellenistic times. See, for example, Briend, "Annexe-Khirbet Kinniyeh," in J. Briend and J. B. Humbert, *Tell Keisan (1971–1976)* (Göttingen, 1980) 113, pl. 7.1–3, and E. Nodet in the same volume ("Le Niveau 3 [Periode Perse]") 122, pl. 20.15–21.

Chalice (?) (No. 7)

7   (509–66). PH .051; D rim .144

Fine strong brown clay (7.5YR 5/8), some white and black grits. Two painted pinkish white (7.5YR 8/2) dots set vertically on exterior. **Fig. 7–1.**

Pedestal Foot (No. 8)

8   (909–66). PH .038; D foot .10

Coarse clay, dark gray core (5YR 4/1), outer bands reddish yellow (5YR 6/6), some white and black grits, occasional small ones. Traces of red painted decoration on upper surface of foot. **Fig. 7–1.**

Jars (Nos. 9–11)

9   (352–65). PH .042; D rim .26

Coarse clay, dark gray core (5YR 4/1), outer bands light reddish brown (5YR 6/4), minute to small white and gray grits. **Fig. 7–1.**

10   (134–66). PH .057; D rim .12

Coarse clay variegated reddish brown (5YR 4/4) and yellowish red (5YR 5/6), many minute to small red, white, and gray grits. **Fig. 7–1.**

11   (125–66). PH .045; D rim .24

Coarse clay, gray core (5YR 5/1), outer bands brown (7.5YR 5/3), many minute to small white and black grits. Traces of reddish brown slip or painted decoration inside. **Fig. 7–1.**

Tel el-Yahudiyeh Ware Jug (No. 12)

12   (20–65). PH .017; D bottom .17

Fine clay variegated very dark gray (2.5YR N3/) and light brown (7.5YR 6/4), some white grits. Burnished very dark gray slip (2.5YR N3/). Incised decoration outside.

Late Bronze Cypriote Wares

Monochrome Ware Bowl (No. 13)

13   (898–66). PH .028

Fine reddish brown clay (2.5YR 5/4), occasional white grits; variegated red (2.5YR 4/6) and weak red (2.5YR 4/2) slip. **Fig. 7–1.**

"Milk Bowl" (White Slip Ware) (No. 14)

14   (39–65). PH .03

Burnished white slip (10YR 8/1), reddish brown (2.5YR 4/4) band around rim.

An uncatalogued body fragment (385–66) shows the characteristic painted lattice pattern.

Base-Ring Ware Jug (No. 15)

15   (1046–66). Max dim .04

Part of body and lower end of inserted handle. Fine clay banded red (2.5YR 5/6) and dark gray (2.5YR N4/), some white inclusions. Variegated gray and reddish brown slip on exterior.

Knife-Shaved Jug (No. 16)

16   (890–66). PH .028

Fine light gray clay (2.5YR N7/). Traces of red slip on exterior.

Iron Age

Cooking Pot (No. 17)

17   (49–66). PH .078; D rim .371

Coarse clay banded dark gray (5YR 3/1) and light brown (7.5YR 6/4), many white grits and mineral inclusions. Remains of pink slip (7.5YR 7/4). **Fig. 7–1.**

Jars (Nos. 18–19)

18   (416–66). PH .026; D rim .34

Coarse clay, dark gray core (5YR 4/1), outer bands reddish brown (7.5YR 4/3), many mineral inclusions. **Fig. 7–1.**

19   (502–65). PH .033

Coarse clay banded very dark gray (2.5YR N3/), reddish brown (5YR 5/3) and red (2.5YR 4/6), many white grits and mineral inclusions.

Persian Period

Mortar (No. 20)

20   (227–65). PH .043; D rim .27

Fine pale brown clay (10YR 8/4), a few white grits. **Fig. 7–1.**

Hellenistic and Early Roman Wares

Hellenistic/Early Roman pottery (Nos. 21–45) is represented mainly by single examples. Jugs similar in shape to No. 23 are known from Capernaum, where they are dated to the Early Roman period (63 B.C.–A.D. 135).[2] No. 22 is made from a mold with two different halves. A band of oblique relief lines decorates the upper neck on one side. The process of manufacture has given this jug an oval mouth and a two-part vertical handle not completely trimmed.

On the basis of shape, clay, and slip, Nos. 27–36 have been grouped together as probable examples of Eastern Sigillata A,[3] while Nos. 37–41 are unclassified red-slip wares.

The two fragments of "Cypriot Sigillata" (Nos. 42–43) belong to Hayes Form 11, for which he suggests a date of "second half of the 1st c. onwards; probably mainly 2nd c."[4]

2. Loffreda, *Cafarnao* 2, 34, 165, fig. 4.1–5.
3. No study of Eastern Sigillata A in all its forms and variations has been published; it has, however, been treated rather fully in F. O. Waagé, *Antioch-on-the-Orontes* 4, Part 1, *Ceramics and Islamic Coins* (Princeton, 1948) 18–38, and Crowfoot, *Samaria* 3, 306–57.
4. J. W. Hayes, "Cypriot Sigillata," *RDAC* 1967, 65–77. For Form 11 see 71, 72, and parallels cited. A. Negev, *The Late Hellenistic and Early Roman Pottery of Nabatean Oboda, Final Report*, QEDEM, Monographs of the Institute of Archaeology, The Hebrew University of Jerusalem, 22 (Jerusalem, 1986), appeared too late for use in this chapter.

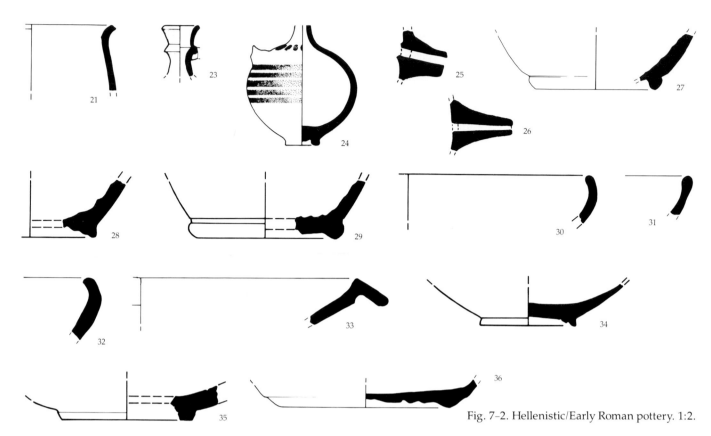

Fig. 7–2. Hellenistic/Early Roman pottery. 1:2.

The Rhodian amphora handle and toe (Nos. 44–45) represent a common transport container of this period. They date to the 1st c. B.C.[5]

Jugs (Nos. 21–24)

21   (327–65). PH .036; D rim .09

Fine light red clay (2.5YR 6/6), many white and black grits; reddish brown (2.5YR 5/4) and weak red (2.5YR 4/2) slip inside and out. **Fig. 7–2.**

22   (108–64). PH .029; D rim .03–.033

Fine very pale brown clay (10YR 8/4), a few white and black grits. Traces of light red slip. Moldmade. Band of relief oblique lines decorates one side of neck below rim. Soft fabric. **Pl. 7–1.**

23   (240–66). PH .041; D rim .031

Fine clay, dark gray core (2.5YR N4/), narrow outer bands red (2.5YR 5/6), a few white and black grits, occasional small white ones. **Fig. 7–2.**

24   (4–66). PH .065; D foot .019

Fine very pale brown clay (10YR 8/4), a few minute and small white and black grits. Traces of red painted dots around base of neck, four bands around body. Soft fabric. **Fig. 7–2; Pl. 7–1.**

5. I wish to thank Dr. Virginia Grace for consultation and for access to her unpublished records in identifying these fragments.

Spouts (Nos. 25–26)

25   (560–64). L .026

Fine very pale brown clay (10YR 8/4), a few black grits; traces of red slip. Soft fabric. **Fig. 7–2.**

26   (188–64). L .034

Fine light brown clay (7.5YR 6/4), occasional black grits and mineral inclusions; traces of red slip. Soft fabric. **Fig. 7–2.**

Eastern Sigillata A (?)

Jugs (Nos. 27–29)

27   (1019–65). PH .03; D foot .065

Fine reddish yellow clay (7.5YR 7/6); red slip (2.5YR 4/8) on exterior. **Fig. 7–2.**

28   (1022–65). PH .03; D foot .071

Fine reddish yellow clay (7.5YR 7/6); red slip (2.5YR 4/8) on exterior. **Fig. 7–2.**

29   (1210–66). PH .03; D foot .076

Fine reddish yellow clay (7.5YR 7/6); red slip (2.5YR 4/8) on exterior. **Fig. 7–2.**

Plates with Incurved Rim (Nos. 30–32)

30   (1211–66). PH .027; D rim .192

Fine reddish yellow clay (7.5YR 7/6); mottled light red (2.5YR 6/6) and red (2.5YR 4/6) slip. **Fig. 7–2.**

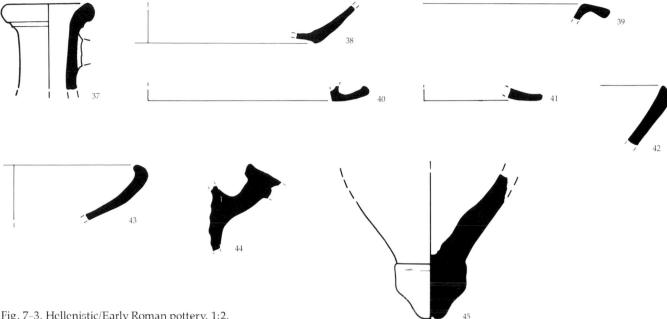

Fig. 7–3. Hellenistic/Early Roman pottery. 1:2.

31   (1214–66). PH .022
   Fine pink clay (7.5YR 8/4); red slip (2.5YR 4/8). **Fig. 7–2.**

32   (561–64). PH .034
   Fine pink clay (7.5YR 7/4); red slip (2.5YR 4/8). **Fig. 7–2.**

Plate with Wide Rim (No. 33)

33   (1215–66). PH .026; D rim .26
   Fine reddish yellow clay (7.5YR 7/6); red slip (2.5YR 4/8). **Fig. 7–2.**

Bases (Nos. 34–36)

34   (1209–66). PH .022; D foot .052
   Fine reddish yellow clay (7.5YR 7/6); red slip (2.5YR 4/8). **Fig. 7–2.**

35   (1021–65). PH .016; D foot .07
   Fine reddish yellow clay (7.5YR 7/6); red slip (2.5YR 4/8). **Fig. 7–2.**

36   (1026–65). PH .015; D bottom .09
   Fine reddish yellow clay (5YR 6/6); red slip (2.5YR 5/8). Trimming marks on floor; center of bottom smeared. **Fig. 7–2.**

Unclassified Red Slip Wares

Jug (No. 37)

37   (1020–65). PH .048; D rim .05
   Fine reddish yellow clay (5YR 7/6), occasional black and white grits; red slip (2.5YR 4/8). **Fig. 7–3.**

Base and Lower Body (No. 38)

38   (562–64). PH .02; D bottom .18

   Fine light brown clay (7.5YR 6/4); red slip (2.5YR 4/8), occasional mica. **Fig. 7–3.**

Bowl with Wide Rim (No. 39)

39   (1027–65). PH .009; D rim .221
   Fine light brown clay (7.5YR 6/4), a few white and black grits; red slip (2.5YR 4/8). **Fig. 7–3.**

Lids (?) (Nos. 40–41)

40   (1216–66). PH .01; D rim .214
   Fine reddish yellow clay (5YR 6/6), occasional white and black grits; red slip (2.5YR 5/8). Rim smeared out of shape at one point. **Fig. 7–3.**

41   (1217–66). PH .007; D rim .126
   Fine light reddish brown clay (5YR 6/4), occasional white and black grits; red slip (2.5YR 4/8). **Fig. 7–3.**

Cypriot Sigillata (Nos. 42–43)

42   (1029–65). PH .033
   Fine reddish yellow clay (5YR 6/6); yellowish red slip (5YR 5/6), dark gray (5YR 4/1) at rim. **Fig. 7–3.**

43   (1028–65). PH .03; D rim .14
   Fine strong brown clay (7.5YR 5/6), some white grits. Brown/strong brown slip (7.5YR 4/2) on interior and upper part of exterior, outside of rim and below it very dark gray (7.5YR N3/). **Fig. 7–3.**

Rhodian Amphoras (Nos. 44–45)

44   (145–66). Max dim .086
   Fine light red clay (2.5YR 6/6), a few white grits. **Fig. 7–3.**

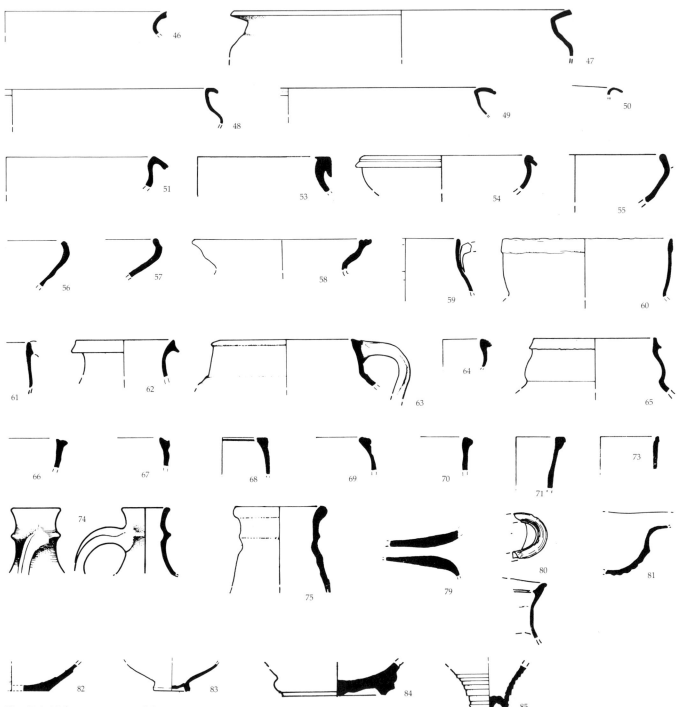

Fig. 7–4. Nabataean wares. 1:2.

45   (177–66). PH .078

Fine light red clay (2.5YR 6/6), a few white and black grits; very pale brown slip (10YR 8/3). **Fig. 7–3.**

Nabataean Wares

Since a comprehensive study of Nabataean pottery remains to be published, few parallels can be cited.[6] All

Jalame examples are plain wares. The basis for including some of the fragments in this section is their similarity to known Nabataean types. Because this pottery is believed to have been produced not later than the 2nd c., the Jalame

6. For bowls like Nos. 46–52 see P. C. Hammond, *The Excavation of the Main Theater at Petra, 1961–1962. Final Report* (London, 1965) pl. 54, I, middle row, first on left. For bowls like Nos. 55–57 see 358–60, fig. 4.42 in P. J. Parr, "A Sequence of Pottery from Petra," in J. A. Sanders, ed., *Near Eastern Archaeology in the Twentieth Century, Essays in Honor of Nelson Glueck* (New York, 1970) 348–81.

contexts are not meaningful. However, 18 come from pre–351 contexts, often just above bedrock, and many of these may date to Period 1 (see Chap. 2). It may also be significant that 23 sherds were found along the ridge or on the slopes just below the top of the ridge, an area that in Period 1 may have been occupied by a cemetery; it was not used for living quarters until the 2nd quarter of the 4th c., late in Period 2.

Carinated Bowls (Nos. 46–52). 13 examples.

46   (314–64). PH .013; D rim .174
 Fine clay, very dark gray core (2.5YR N3/), outer bands reddish brown (2.5YR 5/4). **Fig. 7–4.**

47   (363–65). PH .026; D rim .18
 Fine clay, dark gray core (5YR 4/1), outer bands light red (2.5YR 6/6). **Fig. 7–4.**

48   (680–66). PH .02; D rim .22
 Fine clay, very dark gray core (2.5YR N3/), outer bands yellowish red (5YR 4/6). **Fig. 7–4.**

49   (704–66). PH .015; D rim .218
 Fine clay, very dark gray core (2.5YR N3/), outer bands reddish brown (2.5YR 5/4). **Fig. 7–4.**

50   (315–64). PH .005; Est D rim .158
 Fine clay, very dark gray core (2.5YR N3/), outer bands reddish brown (2.5YR 5/4). **Fig. 7–4.**

51   (18–67). PH .016; Est D rim .172
 Fine clay, very dark gray core (2.5YR N3/), outer bands reddish brown (2.5YR 5/4). **Fig. 7–4.**

52   (440–65). PH .048; Max dim .279
 Fine clay, very dark gray core (2.5YR N3/), outer bands yellowish red (5YR 4/6).

Bowl with Downward Folded Rim (Nos. 53–54). One fragment of each form. Form 1 is close to the carinated bowls above, except for shape.

Form 1

53   (483–65). PH .019; D rim .144
 Fine red clay (2.5YR 4/6), a few white and black grits and mineral inclusions. **Fig. 7–4.**

Form 2

54   (598–66). PH .019; D rim .09
 Fine clay, dark gray core (2.5YR N4/), outer bands red (2.5YR 5/6), a few white and black grits. **Fig. 7–4.**

Bowl with Inward-curved Rim (Nos. 55–57). Five pieces.

55   (326–65). PH .026; D rim .095
 Fine red clay (2.5YR 5/6), a few white and black grits; occasionally white ones have erupted through surfaces. Surfaces reddish brown (2.5YR 5/4); top of rim and upper exterior weak red (2.5YR 4/2). **Fig. 7–4.**

56   (407–65). PH .025; D rim .10
 Fine clay, very dark gray core (2.5YR N3/), outer bands

reddish brown (2.5YR 4/4), a few white and black grits. Surfaces reddish brown (2.5YR 5/4); exterior rim and below weak red (2.5YR 4/2). **Fig. 7–4.**

57   (10–67). PH .023; D rim .101
 Fine clay, dark gray core (2.5YR N4/), thin outer bands reddish brown (2.5YR 5/4), a few white and black grits and mineral inclusions. **Fig. 7–4.**

Vessel with Wide Grooved Rim (No. 58). One example.

58   (594–66). PH .017; D rim .095
 Fine clay, dark gray core (2.5YR N4/), outer bands reddish brown (2.5YR 5/4), a few white and black grits. **Fig. 7–4.**

Jug with Rounded-Off Rim (No. 59). One fragment.

59   (200–64). PH .028; D rim .06
 Fine light red clay (2.5YR 6/8), a few white and black grits. **Fig. 7–4.**

Jug with Folded Rim (Nos. 60–61). Seven fragments.

60   (271–64). PH .031; D rim .09
 Fine clay, very dark gray core (2.5YR N3/), outer bands reddish brown (2.5YR 4/4), occasional white grits. **Fig. 7–4.**

61   (592–66). PH .025
 Fine clay, dark gray core (2.5YR N4/), thin outer bands weak red (2.5YR 5/2), occasional white grits. Bit of handle preserved on rim. **Fig. 7–4.**

Jug with Triangular Rim (Nos. 62–65). Two examples of Form 1; other forms represented by one piece each.

Form 1

62   (733–66). PH .02; D rim .053
 Fine reddish brown clay (2.5YR 4/4), occasional white and black grits. **Fig. 7–4.**

Form 2

63   (536–66). PH with handle .035; D rim .085
 Fine light red clay (2.5YR 6/6), a few white and black grits. **Fig. 7–4.**

Form 3

64   (417–65). PH .016; D rim .05
 Fine light red clay (2.5YR 6/6), a few white grits. **Fig. 7–4.**

Form 4

65   (847–65). PH .03; D rim .065
 Fine red clay (2.5YR 5/6), a few white and black grits; occasionally white ones have pitted the surfaces. **Fig. 7–4.**

Jug with Ridged Rim (Nos. 66–67). One example of each form.

Form 1: Inner Edge Ridged

66   (603–66). PH .017; D rim .07
 Fine clay, dark gray core (2.5YR N4/), outer bands light

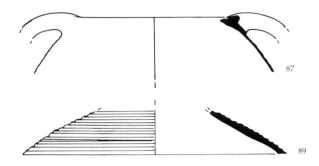

Fig. 7–5. Nabataean wares. 1:2.

red (2.5YR 6/8), a few white and black grits; occasionally white ones have pitted the surfaces. **Fig. 7–4.**

Form 2: Outer Edge Ridged

67   (425–65). PH .016; D rim .11
Fine clay, dark gray core (2.5YR N4/), outer bands red (2.5YR 5/6), occasional white grits. **Fig. 7–4.**

Jug with Thickened Rim (Nos. 68–71). Two fragments of Form 1; One each of Forms 2 and 3.

Form 1

68   (601–66). PH .02; D rim .05
Fine red clay (2.5YR 5/6), a few white and black grits. **Fig. 7–4.**

69   (611–66). PH .018; D rim .04
Fine red clay (2.5YR 5/6), a few white grits, occasionally erupted through surfaces. Reddish brown slip (2.5YR 4/4) outside extending to inside of rim. **Fig. 7–4.**

Form 2

70   (11–67). PH .018
Fine dusky red clay (2.5YR 3/2), a few white and black grits. Reddish yellow slip (5YR 6/6) on exterior extending to inside of rim. **Fig. 7–4.**

Form 3

71   (1007–65). PH .028; D rim .052
Fine red clay (2.5YR 4/6), a few white and black grits. End of handle preserved on rim. **Fig. 7–4.**

Jug with Thickened Grooved Rim (No. 72). One fragment.

72   (543–65). PH .022
Fine reddish brown clay (5YR 5/3), a few white and black grits. Traces of reddish yellow slip (5YR 6/6) on exterior.

Jug with Rounded-Off Rim (No. 73). One example.

73   (593–66). PH .018; D rim .032
Fine clay, very dark gray core (2.5YR N3/), outer bands red (2.5YR 4/6), a few white and black grits. **Fig. 7–4.**

Jug with Out-Turned Rim (Nos. 74–75). One example of each form.

Form 1

74   (93–65). PH .037; D rim .028
Fine clay banded dark gray (2.5YR N4/) and red (2.5YR 5/6), a few white and black grits; occasionally they have pitted the surfaces. Very pale brown slip (10YR 8/3) on exterior. **Fig. 7–4.**

Form 2

75   (539–65). PH .042; D rim .051
Fine clay banded red (2.5YR 5/6) and very dark gray (2.5YR N3/), many white and black grits; a few have pitted the surfaces. **Fig. 7–4.**

Jug with Outwardly-Offset Rim (No. 76). One fragment.

76   (467–65). PH .026
Fine clay banded dark gray (2.5YR N4/) and light red (2.5YR 6/6), a few white and black grits.

Jug with Pinched Mouth (No. 77). One fragment.

77   (414–65). PH .016
Fine red clay (2.5YR 5/6), a few white and black grits.

Jug with Sloping Neck (No. 78). One example.

78   (213–64). PH .32; D rim .06
Fine light brown clay (7.5YR 6/4), incomplete reddish brown (5YR 4/3) band, many white and black grits and mineral inclusions. Traces of red (2.5YR 5/6) slip (?) on neck.

Spouts (Nos. 79–80). One example of each.

79   (558–66). PL .039
Fine clay, gray core (2.5YR N5/), outer bands light red (2.5YR 6/6), some white and black grits; a few have pitted the surfaces. **Fig. 7–4.**

80   (283–66). PL .023
Fine clay, reddish brown core (2.5YR 4/4), outer bands dusky red (2.5YR 3/2), a few white grits, some erupted through surfaces. Traces of reddish yellow slip (5YR 6/6). **Fig. 7–4.**

Various Jug Fragments (Nos. 81–86). One example of each.

81   (200–66). PH .034
Fine weak red clay (2.5YR 5/2), some white and black grits, a few erupted, pitting the surfaces. **Fig. 7–4.**

82   (360–65). PH .015; D base .041
Fine weak red clay (2.5YR 4/2), a few white and black grits. **Fig. 7–4.**

83   (97–65). PH .024; D foot .03
Fine clay banded dark gray (2.5YR N4/) and reddish brown (2.5YR 4/4), some white and black grits; a few have pitted the surfaces. **Fig. 7–4.**

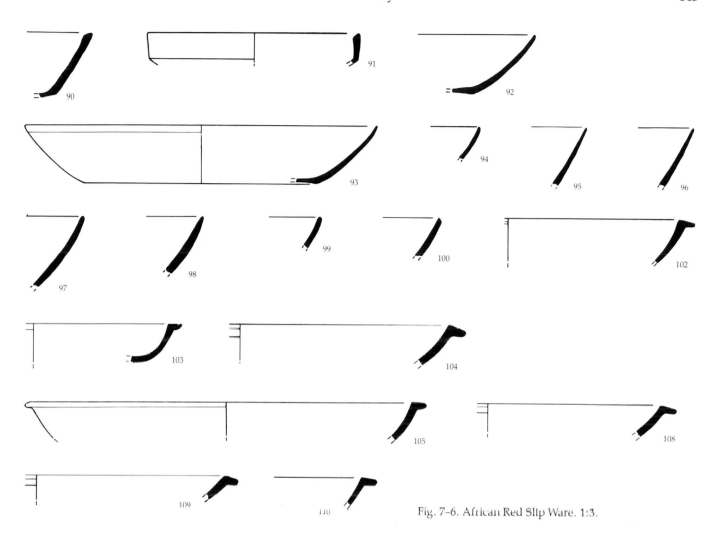

Fig. 7–6. African Red Slip Ware. 1:3.

84 (371–65). PH .008; D foot .029

Fine dark gray clay (2.5YR N4/), thin outer bands light reddish brown (2.5YR 6/4), some white grits, a few black. **Fig. 7–4** .

85 (366–65). PH .025; D base .022

Fine clay banded red (2.5YR 5/6) and dark reddish gray (10R 4/1), some white grits, a few black, occasional mineral inclusions. **Fig. 7–4.**

86 (1023 66). PH .02; D foot .029

Fine red clay (2.5YR 4/6), some minute to small white grits, a few have erupted through surfaces, a few black grits.

Cooking Pot (No. 87). Four fragments.

87 (103–66). PH .04; D rim .124

Fine clay banded dark gray (2.5YR N4/) and red (2.5YR 5/6), a few white and black grits and mineral inclusions. **Fig. 7–5.**

Cooking Pot Lids (Nos. 88–89). Nine examples.

88 (373–66). PH .041; D rim .25

Fine clay banded light red (2.5YR 6/8) and red (2.5YR 5/8), a few white and black grits.

89 (382–66). PH .024; D rim .14

Fine reddish brown clay (5YR 5/3), a few white and black grits and mineral inclusions. Outside of lid ribbed. **Fig. 7–5.**

Late Roman Fine Wares

Of the three major Late Roman Fine Wares,[7] ARSW is represented by the smallest number of sherds, while LRCW and CRSW (and specific shapes within them) are common.

African Red Slip Ware (ARSW)

Only 12 of the nearly 200 known shapes were found; all conform to the accepted characteristics of clay, slip, surface

7. The studies that today form the basis for examination of Late Roman Fine Wares are J. W. Hayes, *Late Roman Pottery* and *Supplement to Late Roman Pottery*. A summary of earlier work may be found in Hayes *LRP*, 2–8. The term *Phocaean Red Slip Ware* as a substitute for *Late Roman C* was proposed in Hayes, *LRP Suppl.* 1980; here it will be used only in combination with the more commonly accepted term, *Late Roman C*. Form numbers are those of Hayes in *LRP*.

treatment, and decoration. Their contexts date them to the second half of the 4th c.

Form 14 (Nos. 90–91). Five fragments. Though common in the ARSW repertory, the shape is rare in Palestine (an example is known from El Arish, unpublished).

90   (256–66). PH .053

Coarse light red clay (2.5YR 6/8); red slip (2.5YR 4/8) outside and in, except for large part of upper wall. **Fig. 7–6.**

91   (204–65). PH .025; D rim .169

Fine light red clay (2.5YR 6/8); red slip (2.5YR 4/8), partly matt. **Fig. 7–6.**

Form 50 (Nos. 92–101).[8] One of the two forms most frequently found (28 sherds). All belong to Type B (Hayes, *LRP*, 68–73, fig. 12). The clay is fine and usually red (2.5YR 5/8, 4/6, 5/6), sometimes light red (2.5YR 6/6, 6/8). The slip is also red (2.5YR 4/8, 5/8, 5/6; 10R 5/8).

92   (239–65). H .049; D rim .27

Slight offset forms transition from bottom to side. Slip on interior extending to outside of rim; exterior body has matt slip on upper part. **Fig. 7–6.**

93   (240–65). H .047; D rim .278, base .185

Offset forms transition from bottom to side. Slip dribbled onto exterior. **Fig. 7–6.**

94   (522–66). PH .024

Slip on upper part of exterior. **Fig. 7–6.**

95   (517–66). PH .047

Slip extends to .035 below rim on exterior. **Fig. 7–6.**

96   (518–66). PH .044

Typical clay and slip. **Fig. 7–6.**

97   (524–66). PH .056; D rim .33

Slip on interior and top of rim, dribbled onto exterior. **Fig. 7–6.**

98   (238–65). PH .046

Typical clay and slip. **Fig. 7–6.**

99   (516–66). PH .025

Typical clay and slip. **Fig. 7–6.**

100   (340–65). PH .03

Slip on interior, dribbled onto exterior. **Fig. 7–6.**

101   (236–65). Max dim .112

Narrow molding separates bottom and side, groove near center of bottom. Brush and turning marks on interior. Slip on interior only.

Form 58 (Nos. 102–10).[9] The second of the two forms most frequently found at Jalame (27 fragments). All belong to Type A or a variant thereof (Hayes, *LRP*, 92–96, fig. 14). The clay is usually fine but may be coarse; it is always a variety of red (2.5YR 4/8, 5/8; 10R 5/8). The slip is close to that of the clay (2.5YR 4/8, 5/8, 5/6); occasionally the red varies to reddish brown (No. 110).

102   (225–66). PH (a) .036 (b) .023; D rim .298

Typical clay and slip. **Fig. 7–6.**

103   (249–65). H .042; D rim .31

Typical clay and slip. Ridge separates bottom and side. Groove at outer edge of floor. **Fig. 7–6.**

104   (324–65). PH .32; D rim .338

Typical clay and slip. Slip extends onto upper part of exterior. **Fig. 7–6.**

105   (255–66). PH .031; D rim .317

Typical clay and slip. **Fig. 7–6.**

106   (246–65). PH .038; D rim .32

Typical clay and slip.

107   (348–65). PH .029; D rim .34

Typical clay and slip.

108   (244–65). PH .027; D rim .297

Coarse clay. Slip extends below rim on exterior. **Fig. 7–6.**

109   (248–65). PH .025; D rim .317

Coarse clay. Slip extends to underside of rim on exterior. **Fig. 7–6.**

110   (528–66). PH .023

Typical clay and slip. Slip variegated red and reddish brown (2.5YR 4/4). **Fig. 7–6.**

Form 59 (No. 111).[10] One of the two examples found. It belongs to Type A, while the other (533–65, uncatalogued) is of Type B (Hayes, *LRP*, 96–100, fig. 15).

111   (208–66). PH (a) .038 (b) .044; Max dim ca. .043; D rim .348

Coarse red clay (10R 5/8); red slip (2.5YR 5/8) on interior extending onto outside of body. Vertical gouges on exterior wall. Similar, but without gouges, is 533–65. **Fig. 7–7.**

Form 60 (No. 112). Three sherds of this uncommon shape were found (Hayes, *LRP*, 98, 100, fig. 15). No parallels are known in the Syro-Palestinian area.

112   (55–65). H .03; D rim .40

Fine red clay (2.5YR 5/8); red slip (2.5YR 5/8) on interior, exterior body unslipped. **Fig. 7–7.**

---

8. Avigad, "Beth Shearim, 1954," 210, fig. 3.18; Bagatti, *Nazareth*, 228, fig. 227.4; Ben Tor, "Tel Yoqneam," 72–73, fig. 8.10; Crowfoot, *Samaria* 3, 358, fig. 84.1–2; Iliffe, "Sigillata Wares," 5, fig. 1; Loffreda, *Cafarnao* 2, 168, 68, fig. 17.18–21; 102, fig. 30.12; 132–33, fig. 46.12; Meyers, "Meiron, 1976," 13–14, fig. 14.1; Riley, "Caesarea Hippodrome," 41–42, no. 69.

9. Bagatti, *Nazareth*, 228, fig. 227.1–3; Crowfoot, *Samaria* 3, 360, fig. 84.18; Loffreda, *Cafarnao* 2, 174, 75, fig. 17.28–33; Loffreda, *Sinagoga*, 77–80, fig. 3.4; Saller, *Bethany*, 260, no. 4957, fig. 49.

10. Bagatti, *Nazareth* 290, fig. 227, 14–18; Loffreda, *Cafarnao* 2, 172, 74, fig. 17.22, fig. 21.1–5; Loffreda, *Sinagoga*, 78, 80, fig. 3.13; Meyers, *Khirbet Shema*, 234, pl. 7.23.1; Saller, *Bethany*, 260, fig. 49.3081, 4039.

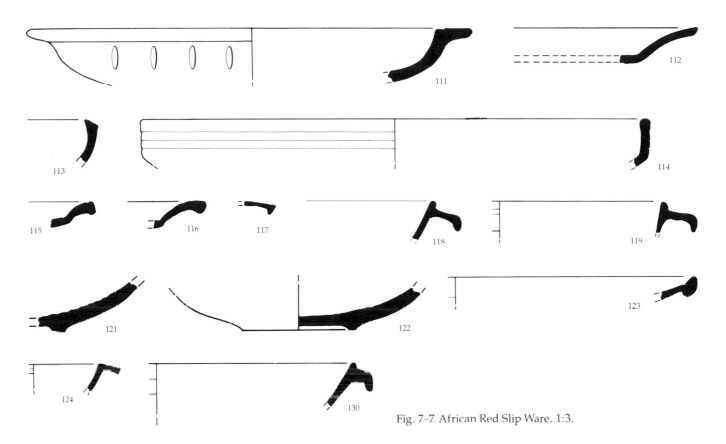

Fig. 7–7. African Red Slip Ware. 1:3.

Form 61 (No. 113).[11] Although common in the ARSW repertory (Hayes, *LRP*, 100–107, fig. 16), only one fragment was found.

113   (224–66). PH .035

Fine red clay (2.5YR 5/8); red slip (2.5YR 4/8). **Fig. 7–7.**

Form 63 (No. 114).[12] Two fragments. Hayes noted that this shape is rare in a large size (*LRP*, 109–10, fig. 18).

114   (52–64). PH .039; D rim .397

Fine light red clay (2.5YR 5/8); red slip (2.5YR 4/8). Two grooves around outside of body. **Fig. 7–7.**

Form 67 (Nos. 115–16).[13] Though common in the ARSW repertory (Hayes, *LRP*, 112–16, fig. 19; Hayes, *LRP Suppl.* 1980, 485) only two sherds were found.

115   (195–65). PH .02; D rim .34

Coarse red clay (2.5YR 5/8); red slip (2.5YR 5/8) around interior. Groove on top of rim at outer edge. **Fig. 7–7.**

116   (243–65). PH .022

Fine red clay (2.5YR 5/8); red slip (2.5YR 5/8) on interior extending over rim; matt red slip of same color on underside of rim. Groove around top of rim at outer edge. **Fig. 7–7.**

Form 70 (No. 117). One fragment. This small bowl is uncommon outside Tunisia (Hayes, *LRP*, 119, fig. 20.7). No others reported from Palestine.

117   (209 65). Max dim .041

Fine red clay (2.5YR 5/8); red slip (2.5YR 5/8) on upper and outer surface of rim. Two grooves on top of rim at outer edge, at least one more at inner edge. **Fig. 7–7.**

Form 91 (Nos. 118–22). Eight examples; both Type A (No. 118) and Type B (No. 119). The former is said to be uncommon, the latter fairly common (Hayes, *LRP*, 140–44, fig. 26; *LRP Suppl.* 1980, 486). It is reported from a number of Palestinian sites.[14]

118   (84–64). PH (a) .032 (b) .014; D rim .29

Underside of rim and body unslipped. Ridge on underside of rim at junction with body. Found in wine press tank. **Fig. 7–7.**

11. Crowfoot, *Samaria 3*, 361, fig. 84.20; Loffreda, *Cafarnao 2*, 167, 68, fig. 21.8–10; Meyers, "Meiron, 1976," 14–15, fig. 14.16.
12. An example of Form 63 is reported from Dibon. See Tushingham, *Dibon*, 153, fig. 11:16.
13. Aharoni, *Ramat Rahel 1959–1960*, fig. 18.9; Saller, *Bethany*, 260, fig. 49. 3486, 2419, 2418. Examples have also been found at Dibon. See Tushingham, *Dibon*, 74–76, 152, fig. 11.13, 14.
14. Bagatti, *Nazareth*, 290, fig. 227.13; Crowfoot, *Samaria 3*, 358–60, fig. 84.5, 6; Delougaz-Haines, 31–32, pl. 52.63; FitzGerald, *Beth Shan 3*, 38, pl. 30.18, 34.48; Landgraf, *Tell Keisan*, 54–64, fig. 16.1; Loffreda, *Cafarnao 2*, 173, 74, fig. 21.6; Meyers, "Meiron, 1976," 14, fig. 14.13, 15; Saller, *Bethany*, 260, fig. 49.3084; see Tushingham, *Dibon*, 74–76, 152, fig. 11.11.

119 (30–64). PH .025; D rim .307

Underside of rim and outside of vessel unslipped. **Fig. 7–7.**

120 (79–64). PH .03

Matt slip on exterior. Groove marks transition from bottom to body. Radial feather rouletting on interior.

121 (123–64). PH .031; D foot .08

Matt slip on exterior; radial feather rouletting on interior. Low ring foot. **Fig. 7–7.**

122 (216–66). PH .024; D foot .062

Slip on interior; radial feather rouletting. Low false ring foot. **Fig. 7–7; Pl. 7–1.**

Form 104 (No. 123).[15] Fragment belongs to Type A (Hayes, *LRP*, 160–66, figs. 29–31).

123 (50–65). PH .02; D rim .377

Fine red clay (2.5YR 5/8); polished red slip (2.5YR 4/8) on interior and on upper and outer rim. **Fig. 7–7.**

Unclassified ARSW Form (No. 124). One example.

124 (349–65). Max dim (a) .046; PH (b) .023 (c) .024; D rim .138

Fine red clay (10R 5/8), red slip (2.5YR 4/8) matt on exterior. Transition from rim to body marked by narrow ridge. **Fig. 7–7.**

Fragments without Rims (Nos. 125–27). Two specimens with stamped decoration; No. 125 has a stamp closely resembling Type 35 (Hayes, *LRP*, 236, fig. 40). No. 127 is of interest for the graffito on the floor.

125 (10–64). PH .04; D foot .10

Fine red clay (10R 5/8); red slip (2.5YR 5/8) on interior. Groove around underside inside foot. At center floor concentric circles with whirl fringe inside two concentric grooves. **Pl. 7–1.**

126 (254–66). Max dim .049

Coarse red clay (2.5YR 5/8); red slip of same color on interior. Leaf pattern on floor interrupting three concentric surrounding grooves. **Pl. 7–1.**

127 (270–66). PH .014; Max dim .063

Fine red clay (10R 5/8); red slip (10R 5/8), matt on exterior. Ridge separates bottom from side. Groove at edge of floor. Inside and interrupting it is a graffito. **Pl. 7–1.**

Imitations of African Red Slip Ware (Nos. 128–30). Three sherds are ARSW shapes but are unlike in clay or slip. No. 128 resembles Form 14, but its coarse pink clay and dull red slip preclude its being ARSW. No. 129 is like Form 61 in shape, but again the quality of clay and slip separate it

from ARSW products. They are probably Egyptian imitations.[16] No. 130 imitates Form 91, but its fabric is not Egyptian; it may be a Syro-Palestinian copy of this ARSW shape.

128 (155–64). PH .024; D rim .14

Thickened rim beveled inward. Coarse pink clay (5YR 7/4), a few white grits and small red inclusions; dull light red slip (2.5YR 6/8) on interior and top of rim, red (2.5YR 5/6) on exterior.

129 (4–67). PH .02; Max dim .031

Part of rim and side. Coarse light red clay (2.5YR 6/6), a few white grits and small red inclusions; red slip (2.5YR 4/6).

130 (215–66). PH .035; D rim .337

Fine reddish yellow clay (7.5YR 6/6); matt yellowish red (5YR 4/6, 5/6) and black (5YR 2/1) slip. **Fig. 7–7.**

Late Roman C (LRCW)

This ware, also called Phocaean Red Slip Ware, is common. Ten shapes are known, according to Hayes's typology; of these, Forms 1, 2, 3, 4, and 8 are represented; Form 3 is the most popular. In addition, several shapes not heretofore published as LRCW (Nos. 177–81) are presented without Form numbers.

The characteristics of clay, slip, surface treatment, and decoration are described by Hayes (*LRP*, 323–70, figs. 65–79; *LRP Suppl.* 1980, 525–27).

Contexts indicate a date of second half of 4th c. for the LRC pottery.

Form 1 (Nos. 131–38). With the exception of No. 138, the bowls (30 sherds in all) have a vertical rim that may curve inward (Hayes, *LRP*, 325–27, fig. 65). Two examples preserve the profile to the foot. On No. 131 this is a tall heavy ring foot; No. 138 has a false ring foot.

The clay is fine or coarse; the color is usually light red (2.5YR 6/6, 6/8), occasionally red (2.5YR 5/8) or reddish yellow (5YR 6/6). The slip is red (2.5YR 4/6, 5/6, 5/8); infrequently it runs to dark red (2.5YR 3/6).

Parallels, though rare, are known in Palestine.[17]

131 (234–65). H .061; D rim .16, foot .082

Some white and black grits and mineral inclusions. **Fig. 7–8.**

132 (52–65). PH .045; D rim .318

Many white and black grits and mineral inclusions. **Fig. 7–8.**

133 (127–64). PH .03; D rim .178

A few white grits, many mineral inclusions. **Fig. 7–8.**

134 (1051–66). PH .03; D rim .18

Inclusions as No. 131. **Fig. 7–8.**

---

15. Delougaz-Haines, 31–32, pl. 54.3; FitzGerald, *Beth Shan* 3, 38, pl. 24.47; Landgraf, *Tell Keisan*, 54–64, fig. 16.4, 5; Loffreda, *Cafarnao* 2, 172, 74, fig. 21.11–14, esp. fig. 21.11; Prausnitz, *Shavei Zion*, 41–43, fig. 12.1, 2, 4. A piece was also found at Dibon; see Tushingham, *Dibon*, 74–76, 152, fig. 11.12.

16. For Egyptian Red Slip Wares see Hayes, *LRP*, 387–401, esp. 387–97, and Hayes, *Toronto Pottery*, 24–27.

17. Loffreda, *Cafarnao* 2, 166–67, 67, fig. 21.18–25.

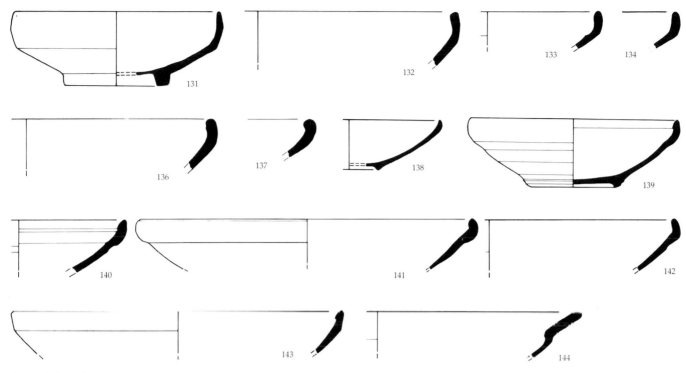

Fig. 7–8. Late Roman C pottery. 1:3.

135   (877–65). PH .023; D rim .15

Some white grits and mineral inclusions.

136   (878–65). PH .041; D rim .297

Some white and black grits, many mineral inclusions. **Fig. 7–8.**

137   (460–64). PH .031; D rim .27

Inclusions as No. 136. **Fig. 7–8.**

138   (26–66). H .042; D rim .15, foot .052

Some white grits, many mineral inclusions. **Fig. 7–8.**

Form 1 Variants (Nos. 139–43). These bowls with a shallow depression below the rim on both surfaces are related to Form 1. The clay is fine (rarely coarse), the characteristic color is red (2.5YR 5/6); one example is light red (2.5YR 6/6). The slip is red (10R 5/6; 2.5YR 4/6) except when the rim exterior fired very dark gray (2.5YR N3/) from stacking in the kiln.

139   (112–64). H .055; D rim .167, foot .068

Some white and black grits and mineral inclusions. **Fig. 7–8.**

140   (192–64). PH .042; D rim .17

Many white grits and mineral inclusions. **Fig. 7–8.**

141   (195–64). PH .04; D rim .265

Many white and black grits and mineral inclusions. **Fig. 7–8.**

142   (873–65). PH .04; D rim .292

Inclusions as No. 141. **Fig. 7–8.**

A bowl with infolded rim (No. 143) is like the previous group in shape but lacks the shallow depression.

143   (207–66). PH .034; D rim .259

Fine light red clay (2.5YR 6/8), some white grits and mineral inclusions; red slip (2.5YR 5/8). **Fig. 7–8.**

Form 2 (No. 144). Four fragments. Parallels are known (Hayes, *LRP*, 327–29, fig. 66).[18]

144   (192–65). PH .035; D rim .32

Fine light red clay (2.5YR 6/6), a few white grits and mineral inclusions; red slip (2.5YR 5/8), outside of rim dark red (2.5YR 3/6). **Fig. 7–8.**

Form 3 (Nos. 145–72). The most common LRCW shape at Jalame (101 fragments), in Palestine,[19] and, indeed, wher-

18. Ibid., 172–73, 74, fig. 21.15–17.
19. Form 3 parallels in Palestine: Adan, "Horvat Ammudim," 24–25, fig. 3.10, 12, 13; Baly, *Nessana* 1, Shape 14.A3; Bagatti, *Nazareth*, 290, fig. 228.1–4; Ben-Tor, "Tel Yoqneam," 73, fig. 8.7; Corbo, *Kh. Siyar el-Ghanam*, 68–69, fig. 20.4, 13, 19; Crowfoot, *Samaria* 3, 360, fig. 84.11–16; Delougaz-Haines, 31–32, pl. 52.10–22, pl. 54.7, 9; FitzGerald, *Beth Shan* 3, pl. 21.15, 16; Landgraf, *Tell Keisan*, 52–57, fig. 14a.1–31; Loffreda, *Cafarnao* 2, 170–71, 72, fig. 18.15–19; Loffreda, *et-Tabgha*, 133, fig. 49.203, fig. 50.7; Loffreda, *Sinagoga*, 77–80, fig. 3.5, 8; Meyers, "Gush Halav," fig. 15.10; Meyers, *Khirbet Shemu*, 235–36, pl. 7.23.2–4, Meyers, "Meiron 1976," 10–14, fig. 14.8–12; Riley, "Caesarea Hippodrome," 37, 39; Saller, *Bethany*, 257–59, fig. 49.1, 3384, 3330; Sellers-Baramki, 26–29, fig. 29.5, fig. 30.1, 3; Tsori, "Kyrios Leontis," fig. 6.5; Tushingham, *Dibon*, 74–76, 152, fig. 11.1–9. Aharoni, *Ramat Rahel 1961–1962*, fig. 7.22, from Stratum IIA, dated 6th–7th c.

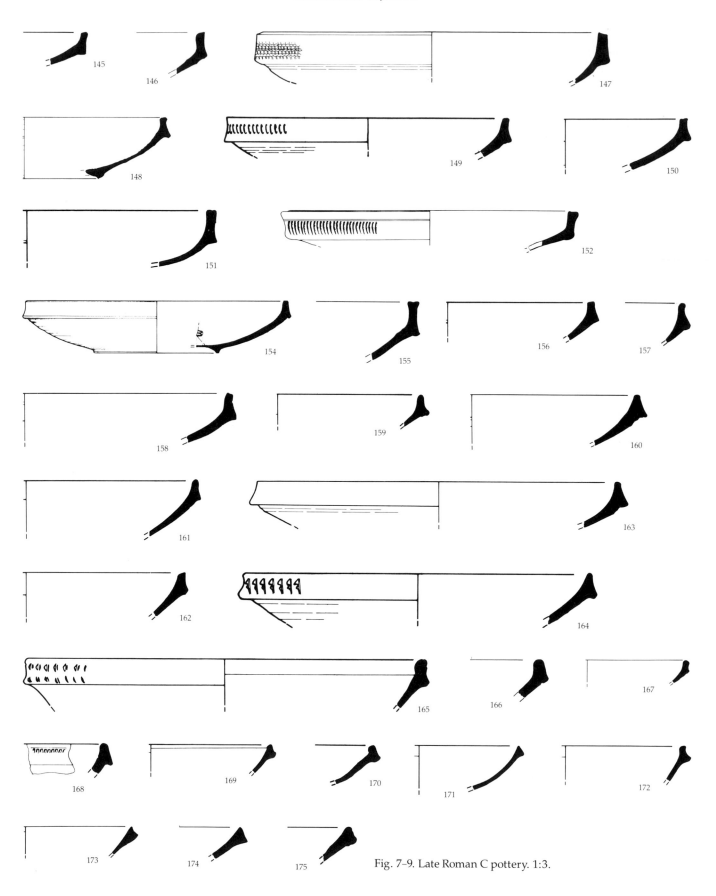

Fig. 7–9. Late Roman C pottery. 1:3.

ever the ware is found (Hayes, *LRP*, 328–38, figs. 67–69; *LRP Suppl.* 1980, 526).

Rarely is the clay less than fine. Most often the clay color is light red (2.5YR 6/6, 6/8) or red (2.5YR 5/6, 5/8; 10R 5/6); the range also includes yellowish red (5YR 5/8), reddish yellow (5YR 6/6), and reddish brown (2.5YR 5/4; 5YR 5/4). One sherd is pink (5YR 7/4).

The slip also shows single or combined colors; for example, light red (2.5YR 6/6), red (2.5YR 4/6, 4/8, 5/6, 5/8; 10R 4/6, 5/8), dark red (2.5YR 3/6; 10R 3/6), and pink (7.5YR 7/4). Rarely a lighter color or a combination of colors appears on the outside of the body. The effects of stacking in the kiln show in the darker slip color on the outside of the rim.

The inclusions are usually minute (occasionally small), white and/or black, often combined with mineral inclusions and varying in quantity.

Sometimes there are roughened bands on the body, though this is more characteristic of CRSW (see below). The slipped surfaces may have a metallic sheen.

Rouletted decoration on the outside of the rim, although characteristic, is not always present. Great variety is exhibited in these bands, which may be composed of one to three parts. The bowls usually have stamped decoration on the floor, with or without enclosing concentric grooves.

That such vessels were considered of value, worthy of repair, is illustrated by the mending of No. 153 with lead clamps. The importance of this type of bowl at Jalame is to illustrate the variety of detail for this shape in the second half of the 4th c.

145 (718–65). PH .026

Slip on outside of rim reddish brown (2.5YR 4/4) and very dark gray (5YR 3/1). **Fig. 7–9.**

146 (396–65). PH .034

Rounded ridge on inside below rim, another on outside wall. Lightly rouletted band on lower part of rim. **Fig. 7–9.**

147 (140–64). PH .04; D rim .28

Outside of rim dark reddish gray (5YR 4/2) and very dark gray (5YR 3/1). Top of rim beveled outward, rouletted band on lower two-thirds of rim. **Fig. 7–9.**

148 (146–64). PH .05; D rim .23, foot .12

Three concentric grooves at center floor, no stamped decoration preserved. **Fig. 7–9.**

149 (38bis–64). PH .03; D rim .218

Faint groove on top of rim; rouletted band on upper two-thirds of rim. **Fig. 7–9.**

150 (331–64). PH .041; D rim .195

Slight groove on top of rim; rouletted band around middle. **Fig. 7–9.**

151 (69–64). PH .044; D rim .299

Shallow groove on top of rim; rouletted band on lower two-thirds. **Fig. 7–9; Pl. 7–1.**

152 (92–64). PH .032; D rim .36

Broad shallow groove on top of rim; rouletted band on lower two-thirds. **Fig. 7–9.**

153 (42–65). H .064; D rim .28, foot .152

Parts of lead mends preserved. Broad shallow depression on inside of rim. Remains of rouletted band on lower two-thirds of rim, two concentric grooves on floor enclosing double-ribbed Greek cross. **Pl. 7–1 (top and bottom).**

154 (6–64). H .056; D rim .28, foot .134

Slip on outside of rim weak red (10R 4/2) and dark gray (2.5YR N3/). Double-ribbed Greek cross at center floor. **Fig. 7–9.**

155 (218–66). PH .047

Shallow groove on top of rim; rouletted band on lower two-thirds. **Fig. 7–9.**

156 (338–64). PH .031; D rim .233

Slip on outside of rim weak red (2.5YR 4/2) and dark gray (2.5YR N3/). **Fig. 7–9.**

157 (687–65). PH .032

Slip on outside of rim light reddish brown (5YR 6/3) and reddish brown (2.5YR 4/4). **Fig. 7–9.**

158 (327–64). PH .04; D rim .33

Shallow groove around top of rim, another below rim. **Fig. 7–9.**

159 (395–64). PH .026; D rim .23

Ridge below rim. **Fig. 7–9.**

160 (62–64). PH .041; D rim .267

Narrow groove with ridge below at bottom of rim on exterior. Two low ridges on upper exterior body, two roughened bands on interior. There may have been a rouletted band on rim. **Fig. 7–9.**

161 (443–64). PH .045; D rim .272

Traces of rouletted band on rim. **Fig. 7–9.**

162 (404–64). PH .035; D rim .256

Two roughened bands on interior. **Fig. 7–9.**

163 (522–65). PH .037; D rim .287

Ridge below rim on exterior. Two roughened bands inside. **Fig. 7–9.**

164 (340–64). PH (a) .041 (b) .037 (c) .035 (d) .033; D rim .272

Ridge around bottom of rim on exterior. Two-part rouletted band above. **Fig. 7–9.**

165 (403–64). PH .039; D rim .315

Two-part rouletted band on rim; two smeared grooves on top; deep groove on inside of rim. Roughened band on interior. **Fig. 7–9.**

166 (717–65). PH .03

Two to three roughened bands on interior and at least three on exterior. Rouletted band on lower half of rim. **Fig. 7–9.**

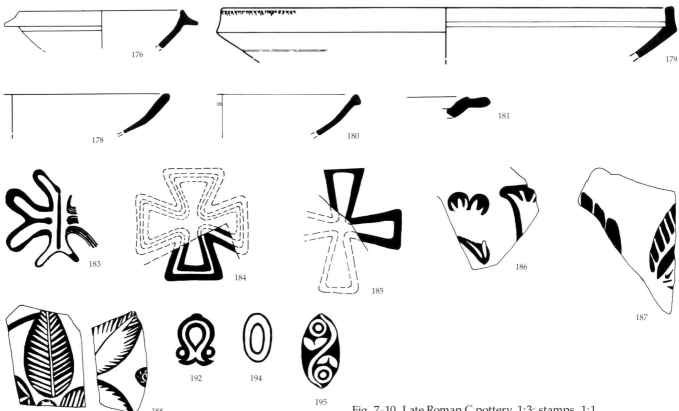

Fig. 7–10. Late Roman C pottery. 1:3; stamps, 1:1.

167   (394–64). PH .038; D rim .326

Rouletted band around middle of rim. **Fig. 7–9.**

168   (397–64). PH .025

Rouletted band on upper half of rim exterior; incomplete groove on top; narrow groove inside at middle of rim. **Fig. 7–9.**

Form 3, Small Varieties

169   (213–65). PH .024; D rim .192

Slip on outside of rim black (2.5YR N2.5/) and reddish brown (2.5YR 5/4). **Fig. 7–9.**

170   (336–64). PH .032

Slip on lower exterior rim dark gray (5YR 4/1) with a metallic sheen. **Fig. 7–9.**

171   (902–66). PH (a) .028 (b) .037; D rim .159

Exterior of rim red (2.5YR 4/6). **Fig. 7–9.**

172   (334–64). PH .029; D rim .19

Broad rough band on exterior below rim. **Fig. 7–9.**

Form 4 (Nos. 173–75). Three examples. They may be related to Form 3 (Hayes, *LRP,* 338, fig. 69).

173   (152–64). PH .024; D rim .172

Fine reddish brown clay (2.5YR 5/4), many white grits; slip reddish brown (2.5YR 4/4) on interior, dark red (2.5YR 3/6) on exterior body, outside of rim very dark gray (2.5YR N3/). **Fig. 7–9.**

174   (329–64). PH .026

Fine light red clay (2.5YR 6/8), many white and black grits and mineral inclusions; slip red (2.5YR 4/8) inside, dark red (2.5YR 3/6) outside. **Fig. 7–9.**

175   (524–65). PH .029

Fine light red clay (2.5YR 6/8), some white and black grits and mineral inclusions; red slip (2.5YR 5/8). Narrow ridge below rim on exterior. **Fig. 7–9.**

Form 8 (No. 176). Two fragments (Hayes, *LRP,* 342, fig. 70); the shape is not common in Palestine.[20]

176   (83–64). PH .031; D rim .155

Fine light red clay (2.5YR 6/8), a few white and black grits and mineral inclusions; slip red (2.5YR 4/8) on interior, red (2.5YR 5/8) and dark red (2.5YR 3/6) on exterior. Slight groove around middle of top of rim. Low rounded ridge on exterior below rim. **Fig. 7–10.**

Unclassified Late Roman C Forms

The clay, slip, and surface treatment of these pieces place them within the LRCW repertory.

Bowl with Plain Rim (No. 177). One example.

177   (454–64). PH .026; D rim .15

Fine light red clay (2.5YR 6/6), some white grits and

20. Bagatti-Milik, 136, fig. 32.10.

mineral inclusions; red slip (10R 4/6), outside of rim very dark gray (2.5YR N3/).

Thin-Walled Bowl (No. 178). Two examples. Pronounced transition from wide flaring rim to thin upper wall.

178   (505–66). PH .032; D rim .248

Fine light red clay (2.5YR 6/8), occasional white and black grits, some mineral inclusions; shiny light red slip (2.5YR 6/8) inside, red (2.5YR 4/8) outside. **Fig. 7–10.**

Bowl with Tall, Inward-Tilted Rim (No. 179). One fragment. The rouletted band around the interior wall is unusual.

179   (145–64). PH .041; D rim .353

Fine reddish brown clay (2.5YR 5/4), many white and yellow grits and mineral inclusions; dark red slip (2.5YR 3/6). Sharp, deep groove inside at junction of rim and body, another shallow one above it. Rouletted band on interior wall. **Fig. 7–10.**

Bowl with Knob Rim (No. 180). One piece. In profile somewhat similar to CRSW, Form 2.

180   (213–66). PH .034; D rim .219

Fine red clay (10R 5/6), some white and black grits and mineral inclusions, red slip (10R 4/6). **Fig. 7–10.**

Bowl with Horizontal Rim (No. 181). One fragment.

181   (70–65). Max dim .063; Est. D rim .28

Fine light red clay (2.5YR 6/8), a few white grits and mineral inclusions; red slip (2.5YR 5/8), outer edge of rim reddish brown (2.5YR 4/4) and weak red (10R 4/4). **Fig. 7–10.**

Fragments with Stamped Design (Nos. 182–95)

Crosses. Four kinds of cross occur: cross-monogram with pendants (No. 182),[21] double-ribbed Greek cross (Nos. 153–54, 183),[22] cross with double outline (No. 184),[23] plain cross (No. 185).[24]

182   (6–65). Max dim .07

Part of center floor, cross monogram with two pendants below arms. Fine weak red clay (2.5YR 4/2), a few white grits and mineral inclusions; reddish brown (2.5YR 4/4) and weak red slip. **Pl. 7–1.**

183   (18–64). Max dim .057

Part of center floor with double-ribbed Greek cross encircled by at least two concentric grooves. Fine light red clay (2.5YR 6/8), a few white grits and mineral inclusions; red slip. Similar is 321–65 (uncatalogued). **Fig. 7–10.**

184   (39–64). Max dim .04

Part of center floor, remains of Greek cross with double outline. Fine light red clay (2.5YR 6/8), a few white grits; slip same color as clay on interior, none on exterior. **Fig. 7–10.**

185   (40–64). Max dim .051

Part of center floor, remains of a plain cross. Fine light red clay (2.5YR 6/8), a few white grits and mineral inclusions; slip light red (2.5YR 6/8) on interior, red (10R 5/6) on exterior. **Fig. 7–10.**

Fleur-de-Lis. This pattern on No. 186 seems to be unique. The design is of interest for a similar one occurs on No. 334, a CRSW vessel.

186   (129–64). PH .017; D foot .14

Part of center floor, preserving design around it resembling a fleur-de-lis. Fine light red clay (2.5YR 6/6), a few white and black grits, many mineral inclusions; red slip (10R 5/6). **Fig. 7–10.**

Palm Branches. The palm branches on No. 187[25] appear alone, while those on No. 188 alternate with small rosettes with radiating spokes.[26]

187   (59–65). Max dim .049

Part of center floor, decoration of palm branches. Coarse reddish yellow clay (5YR 6/6), some white grits and mineral inclusions; red slip (2.5YR 4/6). **Fig. 7–10.**

188   (12–64). Max dim (a) .04 (b) .03

Part of center floor, at least two concentric grooves enclosing alternating palm branches and fringed circles around a central circle. Center of each branch smooth because of worn stamp. Fine light red clay (2.5YR 6/8), a few white grits and mineral inclusions; red slip (2.5YR 5/8). **Fig. 7–10.**

Lotus Bud. A rouletted band encloses the partially preserved lotus bud on No. 189. A somewhat similar lotus bud was found at Capernaum.[27]

189   (322–65). Max dim .038

Part of floor, beginning of ring foot. Rouletted band on floor enclosing lotus bud. Fine red clay (2.5YR 5/6), a few white grits and mineral inclusions; red slip (10R 4/6). **Pl. 7–1.**

Fish. Fish like that on No. 190 are unknown on LRCW but do occur on ARSW (Hayes, *LRP*, 256, fig. 47). None of the latter is exactly like ours.

190   (250–66). Max dim .037

Part of center floor, part of head of a fish preserved. Fine red clay (2.5YR 5/6), some white grits and mineral inclusions; red slip (2.5YR 4/6). **Pl. 7–1.**

21. Hayes, *LRP*, Motif 67, 363, fig. 78. For parallels in Palestine see Bagatti, *Nazareth*, 294, fig. 230.9; Loffreda, *Cafarnao 2*, 183, fig. 24.1, photo 21.1; Loffreda, *Sinagoga*, 77–79, fig. 3.14.
22. Hayes, *LRP*, Motif 69, 365, fig. 78. For parallels in Palestine see Loffreda, *Cafarnao 2*, 184, fig. 23.14, photo 22.8; Meyers, *Khirbet Shema*, 249, pl. 8.11.10, photo 8.4.
23. Hayes, *LRP*, Motif 71, 365–67, fig. 79. For parallels in Palestine see Bagatti, *Nazareth*, 307, fig. 236, 27; Baly, *Nessana 1*, pl. 59, C I; Loffreda, *Cafarnao 2*, 184–85, fig. 24.7, 9, fig. 26.2, 9, photo 22.9, 11, 12, 13.
24. Hayes, *LRP*, Motif 73, 367, fig. 79.

25. The Jalame example is closest to Hayes, *LRP*, Motif 1, j, 350, fig. 72.j. In contrast to what Hayes notes as the method of arrangement, our branches point outward.
26. Hayes, *LRP*, Motifs 1.d and 3, 350–51, fig. 72.
27. Ibid., Motif 12.m, 353, fig. 72. See Loffreda, *Cafarnao 2*, 178, fig. 27.5, photo 20.11.

Stylized Fish or Lotus Buds. The decoration on Nos. 191–92 is unclear. For possible comparisons with a lotus bud see Hayes, *LRP*, Motif 12, 353, fig. 73.l-p.

191   (94–64). PH .015; D foot .15

Part of side, floor, and ring foot, stylized fish or lotus buds at center floor within three concentric grooves. Fine red clay (2.5YR 5/6), a few white grits and mineral inclusions; red slip (10R 5/8). **Pl. 7–1.**

192   (51–65). PH .019; D foot .14

Part of side, floor, and ring foot. Shallow grooves on floor and lower side, stylized fish or lotus buds at center. Fine light red clay (2.5YR 5/6), a few white grits and mineral inclusions; red slip (10R 5/8). **Fig. 7–10.**

Hare. The lower body and one leg of a running hare (Hayes, *LRP*, Motif 35, 357, fig. 74.y) appears on No. 193.

193   (247–66). Max dim .0435

Part of center floor, lower part of hare enclosed by at least three concentric grooves. Fine red clay (10R 5/6), a few white grits and mineral inclusions; red slip (10R 4/6). **Pl. 7–1.**

Plain Oval. No parallel is known for No. 194. A plain oval, probably meant to be a leaf, was made with a worn stamp, resulting in what looks like the letter "C."

194   (345–64). PH .018; D foot .13

Part of side, floor, and ring foot. Four concentric grooves around floor, at least three more nearer center; between them a large plain oval. Stamp worn on one side and so resembles a C. Fine light red clay (2.5YR 5/8), a few white and black grits and mineral inclusions; red slip (2.5YR 5/8). **Fig. 7–10.**

S-Scroll. This design (Hayes, *LRP*, Motif 19, 353, 355, fig. 73) appears once (No. 195) on a badly worn sherd.

195   (55–64). PH .021; D foot .14

Part of side, floor, and ring foot, S-scrolls at center floor. Fine light red clay (2.5YR 6/6), a few white grits and mineral inclusions; light red slip (2.5YR 6/8). **Fig. 7–10.**

Fragments with Rouletting. Nos. 196–98 have a rouletted band on the floor, either alone or in combination with concentric grooves. It is unknown whether they had stamps. LRCW vessels with a rouletted band enclosing stamped decoration have been found at Capernaum.[28]

196   (117–64). PH .13; D foot .13

Part of side, floor, and ring foot. Three concentric grooves on floor, narrow rouletted band inside innermost, nearer the center four concentric grooves. Fine clay banded light red (2.5YR 6/6) and red (2.5YR 5/6), some white grits and mineral inclusions; slip red (2.5YR 4/6) inside very dark gray (2.5YR N3/) outside.

197   (56–65). PH .016; D foot .16

Part of side, floor, and ring foot. Two concentric roulett-

ed bands at center floor. Coarse light red clay (2.5YR 6/6), some white grits and mineral inclusions; red slip (2.5YR 5/6).

198   (122–64). PH .03; D foot .15

Part of side, floor, and ring foot. Two concentric rouletted bands around floor. Coarse light red clay (2.5YR 6/6), some white grits and mineral inclusions; dark red slip (2.5YR 3/6). **Pl. 7–1.**

Cypriote Red Slip Ware (CRSW)

Cypriote Red Slip Ware is the most popular of the Late Roman Fine wares at the site. According to present typology, 12 forms are known; of these, in descending order of frequency, Forms 2, 9, 1, 7, and 8 occur at Jalame. There are also several shapes not previously published as CRSW; these are described but have not been assigned form numbers.

The characteristics of clay, slip, surface treatment, and decoration are treated in Hayes, *LRP* (371–86, figs. 80–84). However, more variety in details of shape appear among the Jalame CRSW than is indicated in Hayes's study.

Useful as indicators of the ware are the metallic sheen of the slip (especially on Forms 1 and 9), roughened bands over which the slip is dull, dark streaks of dribbled slip or lighter patches resulting from an uneven distribution of the liquid over the surfaces.[29] All these factors contribute to the range of slip color. The outer surface of the rim is often a different color from the rest of the vessel because of stacking in the kiln.

Contexts suggest a date in the 3rd quarter of the 4th c. for the CRSW from Jalame.

Form 1 (Nos. 199–222).[30] 155 sherds. The basic features are a low ring foot and a rounded-off rim usually thickened and slightly incurved at the top. The lower body may be gently carinated.

Fine clay, most often light red (2.5YR 6/6, 6/8); other colors are reddish yellow (5YR 6/6), light reddish brown (5YR 5/3, 6/4; 2.5YR 6/4), and red (2.5YR 5/6). Occasionally the clay has a different colored core or is banded in combinations of the colors mentioned.

The slip varies greatly; generally more than one color appears on a sherd. The range is light red (2.5YR 6/6, 6/8), red (2.5YR 4/6, 4/8, 5/8; 10R 4/6), reddish brown (2.5YR 4/4, 5/4; 5YR 4/3), dark reddish brown (2.5YR 3/4), dark red (2.5YR 3/6), dusky red (2.5YR 3/2; 10R 3/4), and yel-

---

28. LRCW vessels with a rouletted band enclosing stamped decoration have been found at Capernaum. See Loffreda, *Cafarnao* 2, photo 20.

29. It seems that the vessels were usually dipped a single time with the rim downward and then turned upright. The excess slip then dribbled over the exterior leaving darker and lighter areas.

30. Adan, "Horvat Ammudim," 24, fig. 3.9; Bagatti, *Nazareth*, 289–90, fig. 227.6, 7; Ben-Tor, "Horvat Usa," 2, fig. 11.7 (called typical of 5th and 6th c.). Ben-Tor, "Tel Yoqneam," 73, fig. 8.6; Loffreda, *Cafarnao* 2, 168, 68, fig. 18.1–14; Loffreda, *et-Tabgha*, 80, fig. 3.3; Meyers, "Meiron 1976," 14, fig. 14.18. The body and foot in photo 71.11 in Corbo, *Kh. Siyar el-Ghanam* probably are Form 1. Possible examples of this bowl are to be found in Meyers, *Khirbet Shema*, 237, pl. 7.23.6–11, 24, 25. About these Meyers comments: "The bowls are not found as such in Hayes' corpus of Late Roman sigillata forms." However, the description and profiles indicate they are similar and may be variants of Form 1. The descriptions and profiles given in Delougaz-Haines, pl. 52.5, 6 may also be of Form 1 vessels. Though largely unpublished, Form 1 bowls regularly appear at Late Roman sites in North Sinai and the Gaza Strip.

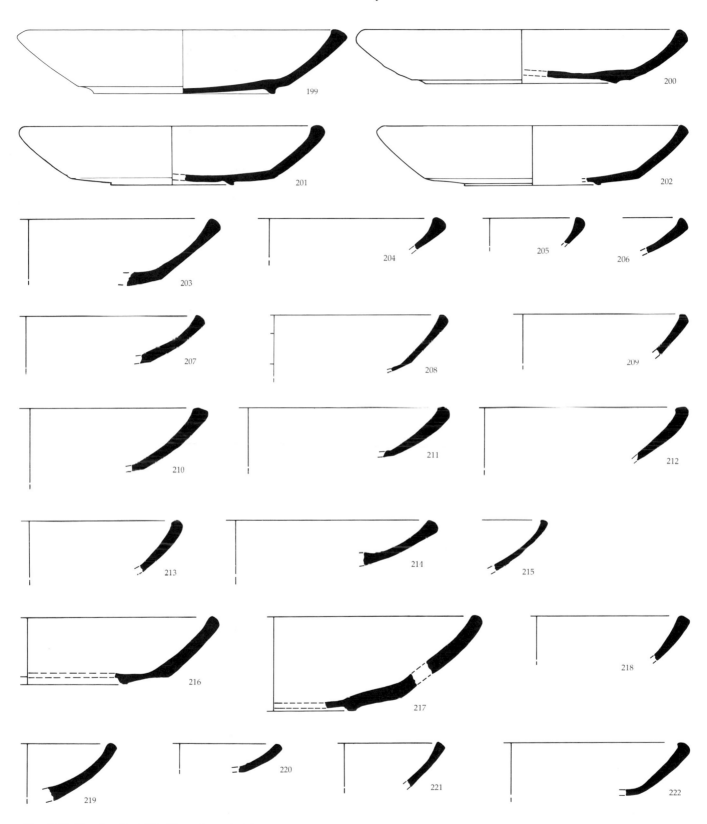

Fig. 7–11. Cypriote Red Slip Ware. Form 1. 1:3.

lowish red (5YR 5/8). When the outer surface of the rim has fired differently from the rest of the vessel the color is weak red (2.5YR 4/2), dark reddish gray (5YR 4/2), or very dark gray (2.5YR N3/).

199 (21–66). H .053; D rim .262, foot .145

A few white and black grits and mineral inclusions. **Fig. 7–11.**

200 (271–66). H .044; D rim .247, foot .15

Occasional white grits. **Fig. 7–11.**

201 (42–66). H .048; D rim .238, foot .096

Some white and black grits and mineral inclusions. Slip has a metallic sheen. Groove around underside inside foot. **Fig. 7–11.**

202 (39–66). H .049; D rim .247, foot .11

Some white and black grits. Slip has a metallic sheen, roughened band on interior. **Fig. 7–11.**

203 (1002–65). PH .053; D rim .29

A few white grits and mineral inclusions. **Fig. 7–11.**

204 (545–64). PH .025; D rim .262

Inclusions as No. 203. Slip reddish brown (2.5YR 4/4) on rim. **Fig. 7–11.**

205 (207–65). PH .022; D rim .15

Occasional white grits. Slip has a metallic sheen. **Fig. 7–11.**

206 (60–65). PH .029

Inclusions as No. 203. Slip dark reddish gray (5YR 4/2) on rim. **Fig. 7–11.**

207 (1179–66). PH .038; D rim .27

Inclusions as No. 203. Upper and outer surface of rim very dark gray (2.5YR N3/). Two roughened bands on interior. **Fig. 7–11.**

208 (61–64). PH .047; D rim .28

Occasional white grits. **Fig. 7–11.**

209 (548–64). PH .033; D rim .255

Many white, black, and yellow grits. **Fig. 7–11.**

210 (999–65). PH .05; D rim .278

Occasional white grits and mineral inclusions. **Fig. 7–11.**

211 (1000–65). PH .04; D rim .31

Occasional white and black grits. **Fig. 7–11.**

212 (1170–66). PH .043; D rim .313

A few white and black grits and mineral inclusions. **Fig. 7–11.**

213 (1169–66). PH .041; D rim .235

A few white grits and mineral inclusions. **Fig. 7–11.**

214 (997–65). PH .036; D rim .305

Occasional white grits. Exterior slip has a metallic sheen. **Fig. 7–11.**

215 (994–65). PH .041

Inclusions as No. 214. **Fig. 7–11.**

216 (111–64). H .053; D rim .287, foot .156

Many white and yellow grits. Three roughened bands on interior, another on exterior at point of carination. **Fig. 7–11.**

217 (996–65). Est H .075; D rim .32, foot .13

Occasional white and black grits. **Fig. 7–11.**

218 (1176–66). PH .035; D rim .23

A few mineral inclusions. **Fig. 7–11.**

219 (203–65). PH .046; D rim .14

Some white and black grits. Slip has metallic sheen on exterior. Four roughened bands inside, one outside. **Fig. 7–11.**

220 (1005–65). PH .024; D rim .16

Occasional white and black grits and mineral inclusions. Slip has a metallic sheen. **Fig. 7–11.**

221 (1171–66). PH .036; D rim .16

Inclusions as No. 214. Metallic sheen on exterior only from top of rim to just below. **Fig. 7–11.**

222 (541–64). PH .043; D rim .268

Occasional white and black grits. **Fig. 7–11.**

Form 2 (Nos. 223–51).[31] 266 fragments. Typical is a knob rim with one to three grooves around the top; there are exceptions such as No. 253, which has a plain rounded-off rim and one groove. The body may show a smooth curve or a gentle carination near the foot.

The rouletting, which almost always appears on the outside of the body (exceptions are Nos. 225, 227), varies greatly. On No. 228 the rouletting covers half of the preserved body. This indicates an unusual degree of carelessness in the process of decorating the vessels. The slip generally does not have a metallic sheen.

The clay is fine and occasionally variegated in color. The most common of the clay colors is light red (2.5YR 6/6, 6/8). To a lesser degree the following colors appear: red (2.5YR 5/6; 10R 5/6), light reddish brown (5YR 6/4), reddish brown (2.5YR 5/4; 5YR 5/3, 5/4), reddish yellow (5YR 6/6), yellowish red (5YR 5/6), reddish gray (5YR 5/2).

The most common slip colors are light red (2.5YR 6/6, 6/8) and red (2.5YR 4/6, 4/8, 5/6), often in combination with light reddish brown (2.5YR 6/4), reddish brown (2.5YR 4/4, 5/4; 5YR 5/4), dusky red (10R 3/3), weak red (2.5YR 4/2), dark red (2.5YR 3/6), very dark gray (2.5YR N3/), dark grayish brown (10YR 4/2), reddish gray (5YR 5/2), very pale brown (10YR 8/3), black (2.5YR N2.5/), and pink (7.5YR 7/4, 8/4).

31. Adan, "Horvat Ammudim," 24, fig. 3.11; Bagatti, *Nazareth*, 290–91, fig. 228.9, fig. 229.7, 14, 15; Corbo, *Kh. Siyar el Ghanam*, 71, fig. 22.22, photo 68.7; Crowfoot, *Samaria* 3, 360, fig. 84.9, 10; Delougaz-Haines, 31–32, pl. 32.5, 9; pl. 52.25, 27; Landgraf, *Tell Keisan*, 55, fig. 15.1, 2; Loffreda, *Cafarnao* 2, 169, 70, fig. 19.1–5; Loffreda, *Sinagoga*, 77–80, fig. 3.10, 12; Riley, "Caesarea Hippodrome," 37–38, no. 46; Saller, *Bethany*, 259–60, fig. 49.3385, fig. 50.2341 (?); Sellers-Baramki 12, 26, fig. 17.310, fig. 30.8.

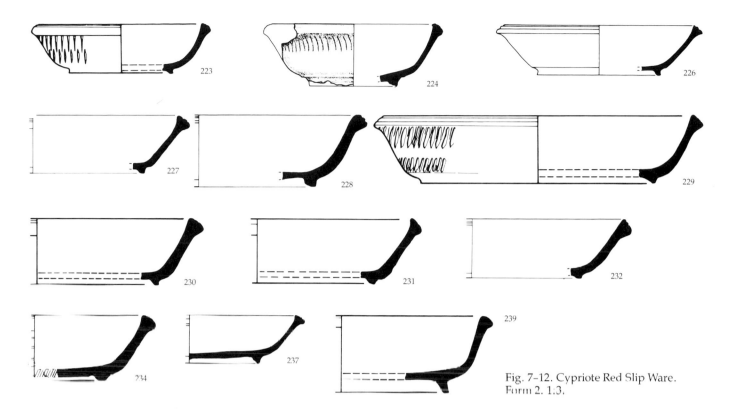

Fig. 7-12. Cypriote Red Slip Ware. Form 2. 1:3.

223 (163–65). H .034; D rim .14, foot .082

Occasional mineral inclusions. Two grooves on top of rim. Two-part rouletted band on upper two-thirds of body. **Fig. 7–12.**

224 (165–65). H .052; D rim .145, foot .072

Few white grits, some mineral inclusions. Two faint grooves on top of rim. Narrow two-part rouletted band below rim. **Fig. 7–12.**

225 (248–64). H .033; D rim .19, foot .125

Occasional white grits and mineral inclusions. Two grooves on top of rim. No rouletting. **Pl. 7–2.**

226 (5–64). H .042; D rim .164, foot .10

Occasional white grits, many mineral inclusions. Two grooves on top of rim. No rouletting. **Fig. 7–12.**

227 (67–65). H .048; D rim .25, foot .18

A few white grits and mineral inclusions. Two grooves on top of rim. Three-part rouletted band covering most of body. **Fig. 7–12.**

228 (1050–66). H .058; D rim .268, foot .185

A few white grits, many mineral inclusions. Two deep grooves on top of rim. Two- to three-part rouletted band on body covering half of the preserved area. **Fig. 7–12.**

229 (142–64). H .054; D rim .259, foot .185

A few white and black grits and mineral inclusions. Incomplete groove on top of rim. Smeared two-part rouletted band on most of body. **Fig. 7–12.**

230 (29–64). H .052; D rim .26, foot .191

Occasional white grits, some mineral inclusions. Two grooves on top of rim. Rouletted band on upper two-thirds of body, lower part faint. **Fig. 7–12.**

231 (325–65). H .052; D rim .26, foot .187

Occasional white grits, some mineral inclusions. One to three grooves on top of rim. Three-part rouletted band on upper two-thirds of body. **Fig. 7–12.**

232 (8–64). H .048; D rim .253, foot .173

A few white and black grits and mineral inclusions. Two grooves on top of rim. Two-part rouletted band on upper two-thirds of body. **Fig. 7–12.**

233 (164–65). H .051; D rim .235, foot .16

Occasional white grits, some mineral inclusions. Two grooves on top of rim. Two-part rouletted band on upper half of body; roughened areas and tool marks above and below.

234 (91–64). H .053; D rim .192, foot .13

Occasional white grits, many mineral inclusions. Two grooves on top of rim. Two-part rouletted band on upper two-thirds of body. **Fig. 7–12.**

235 (19–64). H .041; D rim .18, foot .10

A few white grits, many mineral inclusions. Two grooves on top of rim. Rouletted band on upper two-thirds of body.

236 (48–64). H .042–.052; D rim .176, foot .077

Some white grits and mineral inclusions. Groove on top of rim. Rouletted band of widely spaced strokes around upper third of body. **Pl. 7–2.**

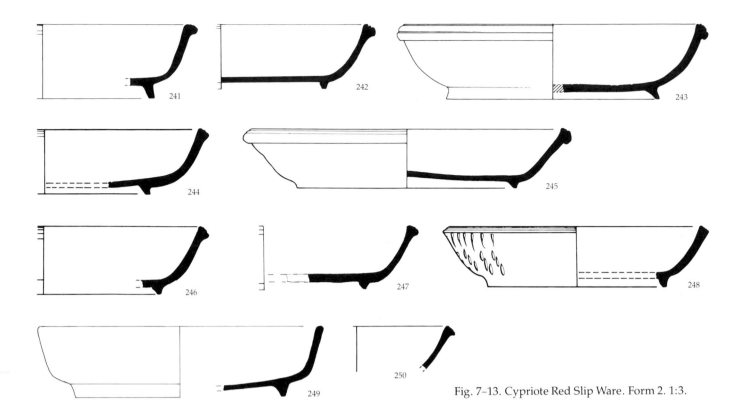

Fig. 7–13. Cypriote Red Slip Ware. Form 2. 1:3.

237   (3–64). H .039; D rim .183, foot .113

Occasional white grits and mineral inclusions. Two grooves on top of rim. Two-part rouletted band on upper two-thirds of body. **Fig. 7–12.**

238   (141–64). H .052; D rim .21, foot .17

Some white and black grits and mineral inclusions. Two grooves on top of rim, two grooves around center floor. Two- to three-part rouletted band on upper half of body.

239   (130–64). H .061; D rim .24, foot .172

Some white grits and mineral inclusions. Two grooves on top of rim, groove around outer edge of floor. Rouletted band on upper two-thirds of body. **Fig. 7–12.**

240   (66–65). H .064; D rim .24, foot .17

Occasional white and black grits and mineral inclusions. Two grooves on top of rim, another at bottom of rim on exterior, two concentric grooves around outer edge of floor. Rouletted band on upper half of body.

241   (46–65). H .06; D rim .25, foot .18

Some white and black grits and mineral inclusions. Two grooves on top of rim, another around outer edge of floor. One- to two-part rouletted band on body. **Fig. 7–13.**

242   (116–64). H .053; D rim .243, foot .166

Occasional white grits and mineral inclusions. Rough areas on interior wall. Surfaces shiny in places. Two grooves on top of rim. Two-part rouletted band on upper two-thirds of body, stamped decoration of palm branches on floor enclosed by two concentric grooves. **Fig. 7–13.**

243   (1–64). H .061; D rim .25, foot .17

Occasional white and black grits and mineral inclusions. Three grooves on top of rim, another below it on exterior. Two-part rouletted band on upper two-thirds of body. Two sets of two concentric grooves around floor; between are stamped fish. **Fig. 7–13; Pl. 7–2.**

244   (65–65). H .052; D rim .26, foot .167

A few white and black grits and mineral inclusions. Two grooves on top of rim. Rouletted band on upper half of body, at least one groove around center floor. Four roughened bands around interior wall. **Fig. 7–13.**

245   (72–65). H (a) .048; PH (b) .041 (c) .027 (d) .025; D rim .26, foot .175

Occasional white and black grits and mineral inclusions. Two grooves on top of rim. **Fig. 7–13.**

246   (7–64). H .051; D rim .252, foot .18

A few white grits and mineral inclusions. Three grooves on top of rim. Two-part rouletted band on upper three-fourths of body.

247   (89–64). H .052; D rim .245, foot .163

Occasional white grits, some mineral inclusions. Groove on top of rim. Two-part rouletted band on upper two-thirds of body. **Fig. 7–13.**

248   (31–64). H .048; D rim .21, foot .141

Occasional white grits, some mineral inclusions. Three grooves on top of rim. Two-part rouletted band on body. **Fig. 7–13.**

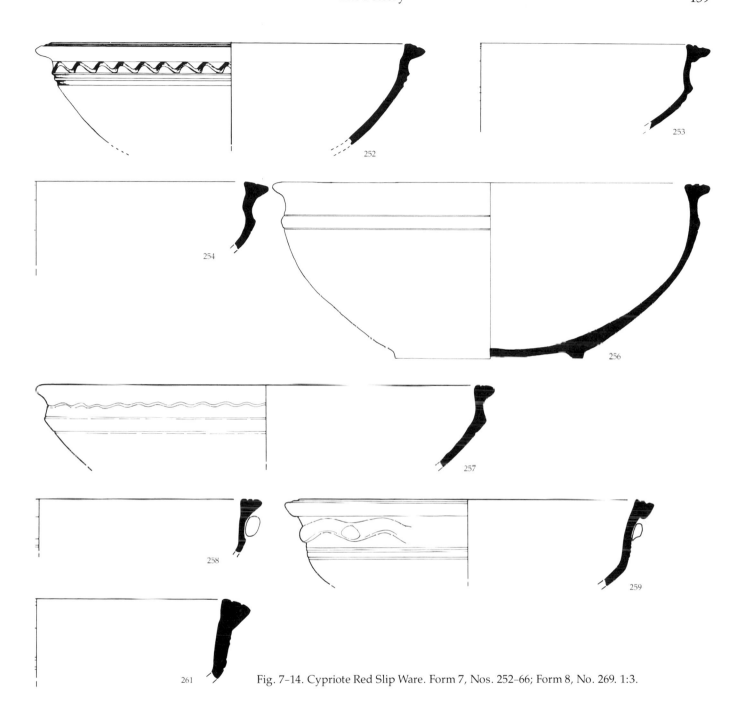

Fig. 7–14. Cypriote Red Slip Ware. Form 7, Nos. 252–66; Form 8, No. 269. 1:3.

249 (149–64). H (a) .057; PH (b) .043; D rim .23, foot .17

Occasional white and black grits and mineral inclusions. Groove on top of rim. Traces of rouletted band on body. **Fig. 7–13.**

250 (53–65). PH .035; D rim .15

Occasional white and black grits and mineral inclusions. Two grooves on top of rim. Rouletted band on upper two-thirds of body. **Fig. 7–13.**

251 (16–65). H .063; D rim .29, foot .20

Occasional white grits and mineral inclusions. Three

grooves around top of rim, rouletted band on body. On floor palm branches around a central fringed circle.

Form 7 (Nos. 252–63).[32] 135 examples. This deep bowl is carinated below the rim. Few bases were preserved, but the standard seems to have been a low ring foot, at times almost a false ring foot. The heavy knob rim has one to

32. Hayes, *LRP*, 377–79, fig. 81, and *LRP Suppl.* 1980, 529. In *LRP* only one example is illustrated; therefore differences in detail are not seen. It appears that Form 7 is a shape given to a good deal of variety which may have chronological significance. A thorough study of the form based on all known examples remains to be done.

three grooves around the upper surface. The concave area above the carination contains short incised zigzag lines. The vestigial coil handle is usually somewhat flattened, horizontally attached and often bears thumb impressions from pressing it on to the body. These impressions may also serve a decorative purpose. Sometimes a strip of clay was stretched across the middle of the handle to help secure it to the surface (See Nos. 260, 264–65). Rouletted decoration rarely appears on the exterior of the body (see No. 263).

The clay is fine, occasionally with a different colored core. The range is light red (2.5YR 6/6), red (2.5YR 5/6), weak red (2.5YR 5/2), reddish yellow (5YR 6/6, 6/8), light reddish brown (2.5YR 6/4), reddish brown (5YR 5/4). Cores are pinkish gray (5YR 6/2) or grayish brown (10YR 5/2).

The slip, which shows a variety of colors within the group and sometimes on the same vessel, rarely has a metallic sheen. The colors are red (10R 4/6, 5/6, 2.5YR 4/6, 4/8, 5/6, 5/8), light reddish brown (2.5YR 6/4), reddish brown (2.5YR 4/4, 5/4; 5YR 5/3, 5/4), reddish yellow (5YR 6/6), yellowish red (5YR 5/6), weak red (2.5YR 4/3), dusky red (10R 3/2), dark reddish gray (10R 4/1), very pale brown (10YR 8/3), light brown (7.5YR 6/4), pink (7.5YR 7/4), white (10YR 8/2).

The Jalame examples may be an early variety of Form 7.[33]

252 (64–64). PH .082; D rim .31

Occasional white grits and mineral inclusions. Two grooves on top of rim, another two on outside of body at carination. Incised zigzag below rim. **Fig. 7–14.**

253 (2–64). PH .069; D rim .365

A few white grits and mineral inclusions. Two grooves on top of rim, another two on outside of body below carination. Incised zigzag below rim, shallow groove above. **Fig. 7–14.**

254 (198–65). PH .055; Est D rim .37

Occasional white grits and mineral inclusions. Groove on top of rim, shallow one on exterior at carination, another just below. Incised zigzag and remains of applied coil handle below rim. **Fig. 7–14.**

255 (3–66). PH .071; D rim .365

A few white and black grits and mineral inclusions. Slip shiny on exterior. Two grooves on top of rim, thumb-impressed coil handle with strip of clay over middle. **Pl. 7–2.**

256 (346–64). PH .141; D rim .349, foot .156

A few white grits. Two grooves on top of rim, another two on exterior below carination, and another above. **Fig. 7–14.**

257 (467–64). PH .065; D rim .36

Occasional white grits and mineral inclusions. Two

grooves, one deep, one shallow, on top of rim, groove around exterior at carination, another just below. Incised zigzag below rim. **Fig. 7–14.**

258 (35–64). PH .043; D rim .35

Occasional white and black grits. Two grooves on top of rim, shallow groove on exterior at carination, another just below. Thumb-impressed coil handle with incised zigzag line next to it. **Fig. 7–14.**

259 (53–64). PH .068; D rim .291

Occasional white grits, some mineral inclusions. Two grooves on top of rim. Wavy, thumb-impressed coil handle below rim. One to two grooves at carination on exterior. **Fig. 7–14.**

260 (468–64). PH .055; D rim .36

A few white and black grits and mineral inclusions. Two grooves on top of rim, one to two smeared ones on exterior below carination. Flattened, thumb-impressed coil handle with incised zigzag to left. **Pl. 7–2.**

261 (1057–66). PH .064; D rim .34

Occasional white grits and mineral inclusions. Two grooves on top of rim, two on exterior below carination. Incised zigzag below rim. **Fig. 7–14.**

262 (147–64). PH .06; D rim .36

Occasional white and black grits. Two grooves on top of rim, groove on carination on exterior. Incised zigzag below rim. **Pl. 7–2.**

263 (27–64). PH .061; D rim .295

Fine light red clay (2.5YR 6/6), occasional white grits; red slip (2.5YR 4/6). Two grooves around top of rim, two below carination. Incised zigzag above carination. Lightly impressed rouletted band around body.

Form 8 (No. 264).[34] The decoration on the four fragments consists of an incised zigzag on the upper surface of the rim and a rouletted band on the outside of the body. No metallic sheen.

264 (50–64). PH .047; Est D rim .32

Fine light red clay (2.5YR 6/6), a few white and black grits and mineral inclusions; red slip (2.5YR 4/8, 5/6) inside and out (2.5YR 4/6, 5/6), parts of top of rim pink (7.5YR 7/4). Groove around outer edge of top of rim with incised zigzags inside. Rouletted band on outside of body. Two smeared roughened bands on inside of body. **Pl. 7–3.**

Form 9 (Nos. 265–99).[35] This is one of the most popular shapes at Jalame (137 fragments). The body may be gently

---

33. Bagatti, *Nazareth*, 290–92, fig. 228.6, 8; Crowfoot, *Samaria* 3, 361, fig. 84.21; Landgraf, *Tell Keisan*, 58–59, fig. 15.4–12; Loffreda, *Cafarnao* 2, 170, 70, fig. 19.7–8; Meyers, "Gush Halav," fig. 15.9, an example of Form 7 (?).

34. Hayes, *LRP*, 379, fig. 81.

35. Bagatti, *Nazareth*, 290, fig. 227.11, 12, fig. 228.13, 16, 17; Delougaz-Haines, 31–32, pl. 52.32–38, pl. 52.2, pl. 54.4, pl. 32.3; FitzGerald, *Beth Shan* 3, 38, pl. 30.19, pl. 34.46; Landgraf, *Tell Keisan*, 55, 58, 59, fig. 15.13–15; Loffreda, *Cafarnao* 2, 169, 68–70, fig. 19.10–14, fig. 20.1–3; Loffreda, *et-Tabgha*, 149, fig. 56.250; Loffreda, *Sinagoga*, 80, fig. 3.7; Prausnitz, *Shavei Zion*, 42–43, fig. 14.4, 6, 8–13; Riley, "Caesarea Hippodrome," 37–38, no. 45; Saller, *Bethany*, 259, fig. 49.5355 (Form 9?). Also Dothan, *Hammath Tiberias*, 62, 66–67, fig. 4.M, P where they are mistakenly called ARSW; however, this shape does not occur in the North African repertory. Rather it appears that they are bowls of CRSW, Form 9.

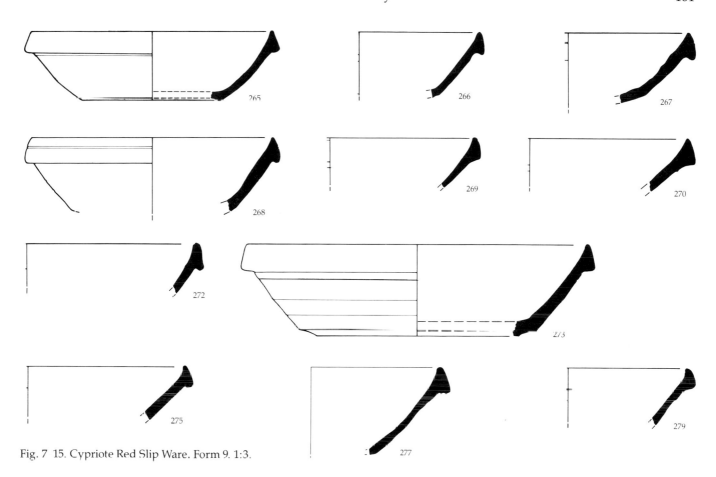

Fig. 7-15. Cypriote Red Slip Ware. Form 9. 1:3.

carinated near the foot. Great variety is seen in the profile of the knob rim. Rarely there is a rouletted band on the upper exterior body (see No. 283). The fine clay is occasionally banded or has a different colored core. Among the most common of the clay colors are light reddish brown (5YR 6/4; 2.5YR 4/4), reddish brown (5YR 5/3, 5/4; 2.5YR 5/4), light red (2.5YR 6/6, 6/8; 10R 6/6), and reddish yellow (5YR 6/6, 7/6). Others are red (2.5YR 5/6; 10R 5/6), weak red (2.5YR 5/2), reddish gray (5YR 5/2), gray (2.5YR N5/), very pale brown (10YR 7/4), pale brown (10YR 6/3), light brown (7.5YR 6/4), grayish brown (10YR 5/2), and strong brown (7.5YR 5/6).

The slip may have a metallic sheen, though it is not so common as on Form 1. Frequently variations in color occur on a single sherd; no one color predominates. Often the outer surface of the rim is fired darker than the rest of the vessel because of stacking in the kiln. Color range: red (2.5YR 4/6, 4/8, 5/6, 5/8; 10R 4/6, 5/6), weak red (2.5YR 4/2), dusky red (2.5YR 3/2), dark red (2.5YR 3/6; 10R 3/6), reddish yellow (7.5YR 7/6), yellowish red (5YR 4/8, 5/6, 5/8), light reddish brown (2.5YR 6/4; 5YR 6/4), reddish brown (5YR 4/3, 5/3, 5/4; 2.5YR 4/4, 5/4), dark reddish brown (5YR 3/2), dark grayish brown (10YR 4/2), very pale brown (10YR 7/4, 8/3, 8/4), pinkish gray (7.5YR 7/2), very dark gray (2.5YR N3/), brown/dark brown (7.5YR 4/2), black (2.5YR N2.5/), pink (7.5YR 7/4), and white (10YR 8/2; 5YR 8/2).

265 (148–64). H .056; D rim .19, foot .11

A few white and black grits. Four roughened bands on interior wall. **Fig. 7–15.**

266 (529–64). PH .053; D rim .192

A few white grits. Three roughened bands on interior wall, broad depression below rim on outside. **Fig. 7–15.**

267 (78–65). PH .057; D rim .191

A few white and black grits and mineral inclusions. Groove on top of rim through which runs a narrow ridge. **Fig. 7–15.**

268 (989–65). PH .059; D rim .19

Occasional white grits. Groove around middle of top of rim through which runs a ridge. **Fig. 7–15.**

269 (536–64). PH .04; D rim .234

A few white grits and mineral inclusions. Slip shiny on outside and upper half of inside. One to two roughened bands on exterior, one on interior. **Fig. 7–15.**

270 (530–64). PH .042; D rim .249

Occasional white and black grits and mineral inclusions. Ridge below rim on exterior. **Fig. 7–15.**

271 (1156–66). PH .037; D rim .25

Occasional white grits and mineral inclusions.

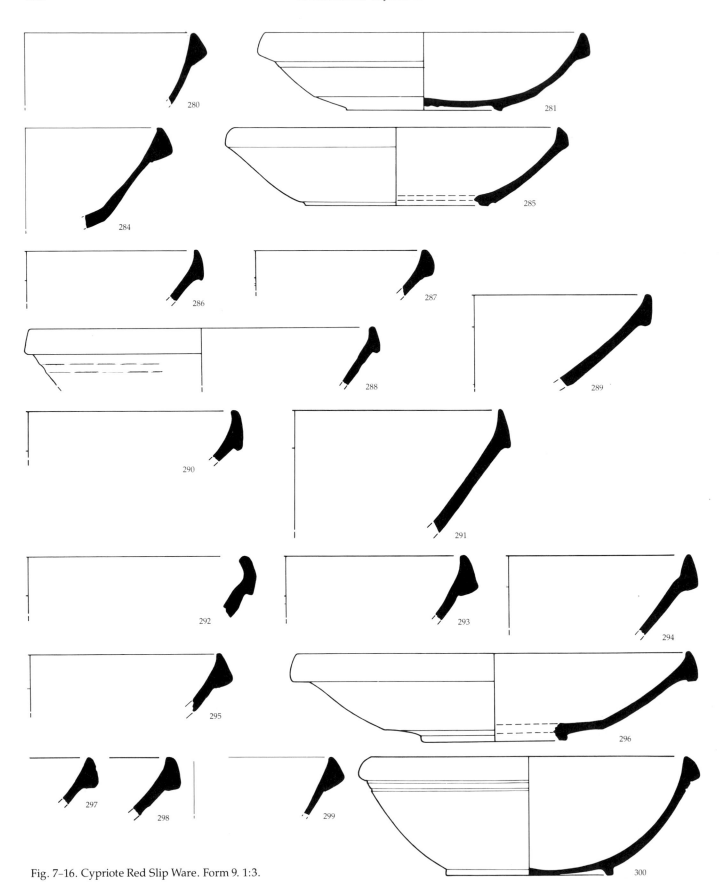

Fig. 7–16. Cypriote Red Slip Ware. Form 9. 1:3.

272 (881–65). PH .04; D rim .275

Occasional white grits. Slip shiny. **Fig. 7–15.**

273 (167–65). H .073; D rim .27, foot .16

Some white grits, a few mineral inclusions. **Fig. 7–15.**

274 (527–64). PH .049; D rim .18

Occasional white grits and mineral inclusions. Two roughened bands on interior.

275 (1163–66). PH .043; D rim .25

Some white grits and mineral inclusions. Slip slightly shiny on interior, unslipped areas on exterior. **Fig. 7–15.**

276 (1152–66). PH .047; D rim .24

Many white and black grits.

277 (1162–66) PH .07; D rim .214

Occasional white and black grits. Slip shiny over most of both surfaces. Three roughened bands on interior. **Fig. 7–15.**

278 (74–65). PH .053; D rim .30

A few white and black grits. Surfaces shiny. Two roughened bands on interior.

279 (533–64). PH .045; D rim .19

Inclusions as No. 277. Three to four roughened bands on interior. **Fig. 7–15.**

280 (524–64). PH (a) .058 (b) .056; D rim .28

Inclusions as No. 277. Slip shiny. **Fig. 7–16.**

281 (173–66). H .063; D rim .252, foot .123

Occasional white grits, some mineral inclusions. Thickened center floor with spiral groove on underside. **Fig. 7–16.**

282 (174–66). H .063–.073; D rim .27, foot .123

Occasional white grits. Thickened center floor with spiral groove on underside.

283 (535–64). PH (a) .037; Max dim (b) .107 (c) .069; D rim .28

Occasional white grits, many mineral inclusions. Three roughened bands on interior wall and floor. Rouletted band on exterior from below rim to just above carination.

284 (27–66). PH .081; D rim .224

Inclusions as No. 282. Slip shiny. **Fig. 7–16.**

285 (991–65). H (a) .063; PH (b) .051 (c) .04; D rim .257, foot .145

Inclusions as No. 282. Four roughened bands on interior wall and floor. **Fig. 7–16.**

286 (159–64). PH .04; D rim .27

Occasional white and black grits and mineral inclusions. Roughened band below top of rim on interior. **Fig. 7–16.**

287 (1153–66). PH .036; D rim .269

Inclusions as No. 278. Roughened band on exterior. **Fig. 7–16.**

288 (525–64). PH .046; D rim .273

Inclusions as No. 282. **Fig. 7–16.**

289 (86–64). PH .072; D rim .278

Occasional black grits and mineral inclusions. Incomplete slip, dribbled on exterior. Two roughened bands on interior wall. **Fig. 7–16.**

290 (975–65). PH .04; D rim .332

Some white and black grits. Slip shiny on interior. **Fig. 7–16.**

291 (43–65). PH .096; D rim .327

Occasional white grits. Roughened bands on interior and exterior. **Fig. 7–16.**

292 (884–65). PH .049; D rim .345

A few white and black grits. **Fig. 7–16.**

293 (79–65). PH .051; D rim .281

A few white and black grits; occasional large white ones have erupted though surfaces. **Fig. 7–16.**

294 (138–64). PH .064; D rim .288

Some white grits; occasional large ones have erupted through surfaces. Rough smeared areas on interior. **Fig. 7–16.**

295 (1159–66). PH .046; D rim .304

Inclusions as No. 277. **Fig. 7–16.**

296 (196–65). H .069; D rim .31, foot .114

Occasional white and black grits and mineral inclusions. **Fig. 7–16.**

297 (522–64). PH .038

Occasional white grits. Groove around exterior rim. **Fig. 7–16.**

298 (462–64). PH .047

Occasional white grits and mineral inclusions. Roughened band on interior. **Fig. 7–16.**

299 (1157–66). PH .048; D rim .226

Occasional white grits. Slip shiny on exterior. **Fig. 7–16.**

Unclassified CRSW Forms

Bowl with Grooves on Exterior (Nos. 300–302). Only one of the seven examples (No. 300) has decoration. No parallels are known for these bowls or for the other unclassified forms.

300 (23–64). H .096; D rim .252, foot .133

Fine reddish brown clay (2.5YR 5/4), occasional white grits and mineral inclusions; reddish brown (2.5YR 4/4, 5/4) and red slip (2.5YR 5/6). Two grooves below rim on exterior; two sets of concentric circles stamped on top of rim. **Fig. 7–16.**

301 (113–64). PH .066; D rim .25

Fine red clay (2.5YR 5/6), occasional white grits, a few mineral inclusions; slip red (2.5YR 5/6) on interior, light red (2.5YR 6/6) and red (2.5YR 5/6) on exterior, much of

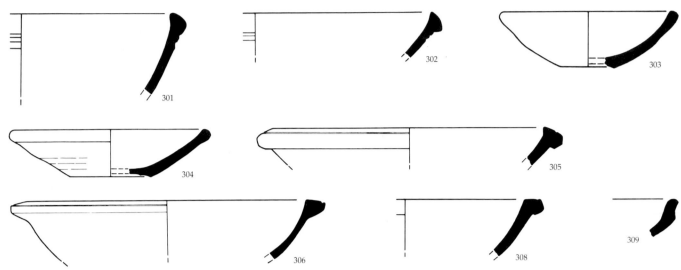

Fig. 7–17. Cypriote Red Slip Ware. 1:3.

rim reddish yellow (7.5YR 7/6). Two grooves below rim on exterior. **Fig. 7–17.**

302   (214–66). PH .037; D rim .28

Fine light reddish brown clay (5YR 6/4), some white, yellow, and black grits and mineral inclusions; slip reddish brown (2.5YR 5/4) on interior, red (2.5YR 5/8) and reddish brown (5YR 5/4) on exterior. Burnishing on body. Three grooves below rim on exterior. **Fig. 7–17.**

Small Bowl with False Ring Foot (Nos. 303–4). Three examples.

303   (253–66). H .046; D rim .14, foot .045

Fine reddish brown clay (2.5YR 5/4), a few white grits and mineral inclusions; slip reddish brown (2.5YR 4/4) on interior, weak red (10R 4/4) on exterior, outside of rim dusky red (10R 3/3). **Fig. 7–17.**

304   (323–65). H .039; D rim .159, foot .067

Fine brown clay (7.5YR 5/4), some white and black grits and mineral inclusions; slip yellowish red (5YR 5/6) and dark red (2.5YR 3/6) on interior, reddish brown (2.5YR 4/4, 5YR 5/4) on exterior. **Fig. 7–17.**

Bowl with Heavy Knob Rim (Nos. 305–8). Six sherds. No. 307 has rouletting on outside of body below rim.

305   (49–65). PH .031; D rim .24

Fine light red clay (2.5YR 6/6), occasional white and black grits and mineral inclusions; red slip (10R 4/6). Groove on underside of rim on exterior, another below top of rim on interior. **Fig. 7–17.**

306   (217–66). PH .047; D rim .25

Fine red clay (2.5YR 5/6), occasional white grits; red slip (2.5YR 5/6), outside of rim pink (7.5YR 7/4) and dark red (2.5YR 3/6). Groove around top of rim. **Fig. 7–17.**

307   (211–65). PH .025; D rim .201

Fine reddish brown clay (2.5YR 5/4), some white,

yellow, and black grits; reddish brown slip (5YR 4/4), outside of rim pinkish white (7.5YR 8/2). Groove around top of rim. Traces of rouletted band around body below rim.

308   (212–66). PH .046; D rim .215

Fine reddish brown clay (5YR 5/3), many white grits and mineral inclusions; slip reddish brown (5YR 5/4) on interior, exterior reddish brown (5YR 5/3) with areas of very dark gray (2.5YR N3/), rim dark red (2.5YR 3/6). Groove around top of rim. **Fig. 7–17.**

Bowl with Concave Rim (No. 309). One fragment.

309   (205–65). PH .031; D rim .16

Fine light red clay (2.5YR 6/6), occasional white grits and mineral inclusions; red slip (2.5YR 4/8). Two roughened bands on interior. **Fig. 7–17.**

CRSW Fragments with Stamps (Nos. 310–37). Many of the stamps have no parallels; some are similar to those on other Late Roman Fine Wares. A few examples have parallels among CRSW stamps (Hayes, *LRP*, fig. 84).

Cross. The plain cross on No. 310 has a parallel in Egypt (Hayes, *LRP*, fig. 84.h,j).

310   (1049–66). Max dim .036

Fine reddish brown clay (5YR 5/4), occasional white and black grits and mineral inclusions; reddish brown slip (5YR 5/4). One arm of a plain cross at center floor.

Trefoil and Standard. No. 311 is unique. Standards (?) in imitation of metal originals (note the two dots representing studs at the broad end) alternate with trefoils on which are concentric circles in relief (cf. Hayes, *LRP*, Type 83, fig. 44.a).

311   (13–64). PH .016; D rim .15

Part of floor and ring foot. Alternating crosses and standards. Fine reddish brown clay (5YR 5/3), occasional white and black grits and mineral inclusions; reddish brown slip

Fig. 7–18. Stamps on Cypriote Red Slip Ware. 1:1.

(2.5YR 5/4) on interior and exterior (2.5 YR 4/4, 5/4). **Fig. 7–18; Pl. 7–3.**

Concentric Circles

312 (9–64). Max dim .082

Part of center floor with band of concentric circles between two concentric grooves. Fine light red clay (2.5YR 6/6), occasional white grits; red slip (2.5YR 5/6). **Fig. 7–18.**

313 (54–65). PH .02; D foot .18

Part of side, floor, and high ring foot. Fine light red clay (2.5YR 6/6), occasional white grits; slip red (2.5YR 5/6) on interior, reddish yellow (7.5YR 7/6) and red (2.5YR 5/6) on exterior. Traces of rouletted band on outside wall, two concentric grooves on floor; between them is design of concentric circles, two concentric grooves around outer edge of floor. **Fig. 7–18.**

Rosette. The rosettes on No. 314 are unusual.

314 (268–66). Max dim .056

Wall with rosettes on exterior. Fine light brown clay (7.5YR 6/4), occasional white grits; red slip (10R 5/6) inside and out (2.5YR 5/8).

Circles with Cruciform Interior. Nos. 315–16 are unique. The former has a dotted circle, the latter a fringed one.

315 (451–64). Max dim .055

Floor with stamp of dotted circle with cross shape

inside. Dot in each quadrant formed by the cross. Fine reddish yellow clay (5YR 6/6), occasional white grits; slip light red (2.5YR 6/6) on interior, red (2.5YR 5/8) on exterior. **Fig. 7–18.**

316 (447–64). Max dim .066

Center floor, stamp of fringed circle with cruciform interior and arrow stem. Design worn. Fine brown clay (7.5YR 7/4), occasional white grits and mineral inclusions; yellowish red slip (5YR 5/8). **Fig. 7–18.**

Zigzags around Fringed Circle. The decoration of No. 317 is otherwise unknown. In style, though not in form, the design is similar to the chevrons on ARSW (Hayes, *LRP,* Types 75–77, 243, fig. 42). Fringed circles are also known on ARSW but not reported on CRSW (Hayes, *LRP,* Type 35, 236–37, fig. 40.r, s, t).

317 (504–66). Max dim .051

Center floor, zigzag lines around a fringed circle. Fine reddish brown clay (5YR 5/4) on interior, light reddish brown (5YR 6/4) on exterior. **Fig. 7–18.**

Star. The stars around concentric circles on No. 318 are otherwise unknown. The design is larger and cruder than usual. Only general comparisons can be made with designs on ARSW (Hayes, *LRP,* Types 24–29, 235–36, fig. 40) and LRCW (Hayes, *LRP,* Motif 2, 351, fig. 72).

318 (76–64). Max dim .075

Part of center floor, two sets of two concentric grooves with a band of six-pointed stars between them. Stamp

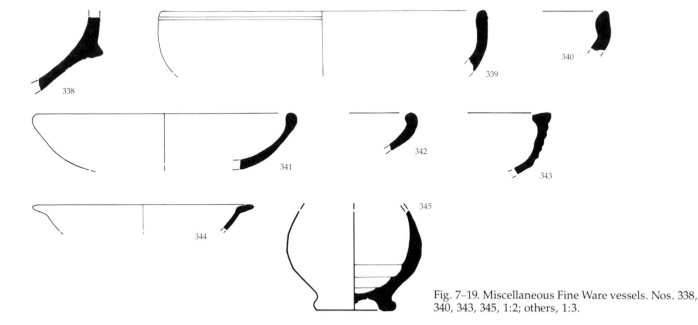

Fig. 7–19. Miscellaneous Fine Ware vessels. Nos. 338, 340, 343, 345, 1:2; others, 1:3.

worn. Fine brown clay (7.5YR 5/4), occasional white grits and mineral inclusions; slip light red (2.5YR 6/6) and light reddish brown (2.5YR 6/4) on interior, red (2.5YR 5/6) and light reddish brown (2.5YR 6/4) on exterior. **Pl. 7–3.**

Leaves. Nos. 319–25 include varieties of leaves without exact parallels. Nos. 319–21, with oval leaves, have a general resemblance to a leaf recorded for CRSW (Hayes, *LRP,* fig. 84.b). The leaf of No. 323 is not found on CRSW pottery (but see Hayes, *LRP,* fig. 44, 83–ARSW).

319   (248–66). Max dim .062

Part of center floor, oval leaves between two sets of two concentric grooves. Fine light brown clay (7.5YR 6/4), occasional white grits and mineral inclusions; slip yellowish red (5YR 5/6) on interior, red (2.5YR 5/6) on exterior. **Pl. 7–3.**

320   (118–64). Max dim .083

Part of center floor. Band of oval leaves with a triple outline enclosing raised dots. Fine light red clay (2.5YR 6/6), occasional white grits and mineral inclusions; slip red (2.5YR 5/8) on interior, reddish yellow (5YR 6/6) on exterior. A similar stamp is found on 269–66.

321   (75–64). Max dim .055

Part of center floor, band of abutting oval leaves that have two ridges with an irregular raised center. Dots outside and between the ridges. Fine light red clay (2.5YR 6/6), a few white grits and mineral inclusions; red slip (2.5YR 5/6). **Pl. 7–3.**

322   (871–65). Max dim .07

Part of center floor, triangular leaves formed of two ridges with depressed dots between. The leaves abut at the broad ends. Fine light reddish brown clay (5YR 6/4), occasional white grits; slip red (2.5YR 5/6), weak red (2.5YR

5/2), and reddish brown (2.5YR 5/4) on interior, weak red (2.5YR 4/2) on exterior. **Fig. 7–18.**

323   (874–65). Max dim .051

Part of center floor, band of leaves (the outline enclosing dotted circles) between two sets of concentric grooves. Left side of stamp worn. Fine reddish yellow clay (5YR 6/6), a few white grits and mineral inclusions; red slip (2.5YR 5/8). **Fig. 7–18.**

324   (125–64). Max dim .107

Part of floor, two concentric grooves enclosing the outward pointing heads of leaves with central stems. Fine reddish yellow clay (5YR 6/6), a few white grits; yellowish red slip (5YR 5/6). **Pl. 7–3.**

325   (61–65). Max dim .049

Part of center floor, two concentric grooves enclosing grape leaves. Fine light red clay (2.5YR 6/6), a few white and black grits and mineral inclusions; red slip (2.5YR 5/6). **Fig. 7–18.**

Palm Branch. Nos. 326–30 have palm branches with concentric grooves; No. 330 is of special interest since it has a cross at center floor composed of the same kind of leaves that appear around it. Nos. 332–33 have palm leaves set around a circle. The central fringed circle is not recorded for CRSW but is known in ARSW (Hayes, *LRP,* Type 30–40, 236–37, fig. 40). No. 334, with palm branches encircling a rosette, has no exact parallel. Somewhat similar rosettes occur on ARSW (Hayes, *LRP,* Types 44–66, 239–41, fig. 41).

326   (15–64). Max dim .061

Part of center floor, palm branches inside three concentric grooves. Fine reddish yellow clay (5YR 6/6), occasional white grits; red slip (2.5YR 5/8).

327 (74–64). Max dim .063

Part of center floor, palm branches outside two concentric grooves. Fine reddish yellow clay (5YR 6/6), occasional white grits and mineral inclusions; slip red (2.5YR 5/6) and reddish brown (2.5YR 4/4) on interior, red (2.5YR 5/6), reddish brown (2.5YR 4/4), and weak red (2.5YR 4/2) on exterior. **Pl. 7–3.**

328 (249–66). Max dim .058

Part of center floor, palm branches enclosed by a single groove at center and two concentric grooves, beyond branches. Fine reddish yellow clay (5YR 6/6), occasional white and black grits and mineral inclusions; slip light red (2.5YR 6/8) and red (2.5YR 5/8) on interior, red (2.5YR 5/8) on exterior.

329 (47–65). Max dim .093

Part of center floor, two sets of one to two concentric grooves enclosing palm branches. Fine light reddish brown clay (5YR 6/4), occasional white grits; red slip (2.5YR 5/6). **Pl. 7–3.**

330 (17–65). PH .022; D foot .19

Part of floor and ring foot. Two sets of two concentric grooves, between them radiating palm branches. Within inner set of grooves is a cross composed of palm branches. Fine light red clay (2.5YR 6/6), a few white grits and mineral inclusions; red slip (2.5YR 5/6) on interior and exterior (2.5YR 5/8). **Pl. 7–3.**

331 (251–66). Max dim .048

Part of center floor, concentric circles surrounded by palm branches (center of branch smooth). Fine light red clay (2.5YR 6/6), occasional white and black grits; slip red (2.5YR 5/6) on interior, on exterior light red (2.5YR 6/6) with areas of red (10R 4/6). **Pl. 7–3.**

332 (58–65). Max dim .045

Part of center floor, concentric circles surrounded by palm branches (bottom ending in raised dot). Fine reddish yellow clay (5YR 6/6), a few white and black grits and mineral inclusions; slip red (2.5YR 5/8) on interior, light red (2.5YR 6/6) on exterior.

333 (726–66). Max dim .03

Part of center floor, palm branches around a central rosette. Fine light red clay (2.5YR 6/6), some white grits; red slip (2.5YR 5/8).

Of the remaining stamps on CRSW, No. 334, with a design resembling a fleur-de-lis, has no parallel. The pomegranate (No. 335) is a decoration on CRSW, but none is quite like ours. The fish (Nos. 336–37), while unknown on CRSW, appears on ARSW (Hayes, *LRP*, Types 173–77, 256–57, fig. 47) in slightly different forms.

334 (16–64). Max dim .125

Part of center floor, two sets of two concentric grooves enclosing a band of fleur-de-lis. Fine reddish brown clay (5YR 5/4), occasional white and black grits and mineral inclusions; reddish brown slip (2.5YR 5/4). **Fig. 7–18.**

For a similar stamp on an LRCW piece see No. 186.

335 (73–64). Max dim .101; D foot .16

Part of floor and ring foot with randomly placed pomegranates. Fine light red clay (2.5YR 6/8), occasional white grits and mineral inclusions; slip red (2.5YR 5/8) on interior and exterior (2.5YR 4/8, 5/8). **Fig. 7–18.**

336 (11–64). PH .018; D foot .15

Part of floor and ring foot, two to three concentric grooves on floor; inside them is a band of fish with heads pointed to the center. Fine reddish yellow clay (5YR 6/6), occasional white and black grits; red slip (2.5YR 4/8). **Fig. 7–18; Pl. 7–3.**

337 (62–65). Max dim .054

Part of center floor, two concentric grooves enclose a fish design. Fine reddish yellow clay (5YR 6/6), occasional white and black grits and mineral inclusions; red slip (10R 4/6). **Fig. 7–18.**

Imitation Local Athenian Late Roman D Ware[36] (No. 338)

Imitation of a popular shape in the repertory of local Athenian vessels of the Late Roman period. These are characterized by a tall rim with a heavy keel at its lower end. Painted designs run along the outside of the rim and/or around the interior body. The date range is from 3rd–5th c., perhaps later. It is unusual to find the ware beyond Athens and extremely rare that an imitation is found.

338 (727–66). PH .062; Max dim .103

Part of body and keeled rim. Fine reddish brown clay (5YR 5/3), a few white and black grits. Incomplete dull slip. Interior slip weak red (10R 4/2), exterior reddish brown (2.5YR 5/2) and weak red (2.5YR 4/2). **Fig. 7–19.**

Unclassified Bowls (Nos. 339–44) and Closed Vessel (No. 345)

These examples are of unidentified types. Contexts suggest that Nos. 339–40 and 344–45 date before 351. For the others only a general Late Roman date can be offered.

339 (223–66). PH .05; Est D rim .33

Fine light reddish brown clay (2.5YR 6/4), some white, black, and yellow grits; slip weak red (10R 4/4) on interior and exterior (10R 5/4). **Fig. 7–19.**

340 (448–64). PH .021; D rim .31

Fine light red clay (2.5YR 6/8), occasional black inclusions; red slip (2.5YR 4/8). **Fig. 7–19.**

341 (82–64). PH (a) .045 (b) .027; D rim .208

Fine light red clay (2.5YR 6/6); red slip (2.5YR 5/6). **Fig. 7–19.**

36. The ware has been defined in Robinson, *Agora Pottery*, 60, n. 9, especially pl. 69.K19, K32. Evidence from Athens indicates a date range of 3rd–5th c., possibly later.

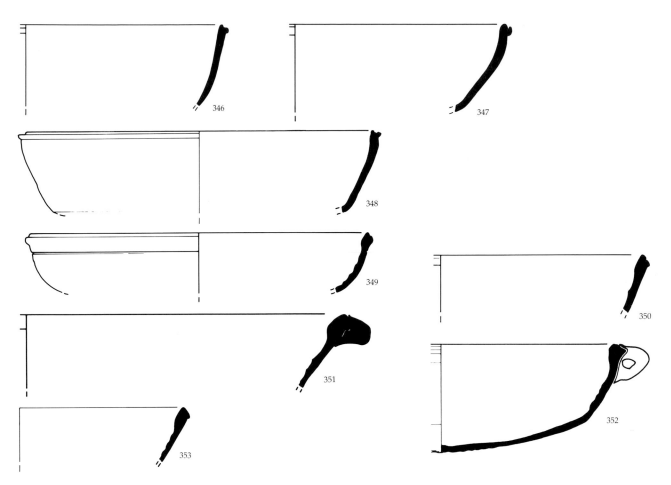

Fig. 7–20. Galilean Bowls. Variant 1, Nos. 346–48; Variant 2, Nos. 349–53. 1:2.

342   (528–65). PH .031

Fine light red clay (2.5YR 6/8), occasional white and black grits; red slip (10R 5/6), outer surface of rim and below pink (7.5YR 7/4). **Fig. 7–19.**

343   (434–66). PH .032; D rim .24

Fine light red clay (2.5YR 6/8), some white and black grits; red slip (2.5YR 5/6) on upper part of exterior. **Fig. 7–19.**

344   (165–66). PH .021; D rim .18

Wide everted rim with two grooves around outer edge of upper surface. Fine light red clay (2.5YR 6/8), a few white and black grits and mineral inclusions; variegated red (10R 5/8) and weak red (10R 5/6) slip. **Fig. 7–19.**

345   (209–66). PH .053; D foot .044

Fine light red clay (2.5YR 6/6), occasional white and black grits; red slip (2.5YR 4/8) on exterior except for bottom and underside of vessel. **Fig. 7–19.**

Bowls

Few of the bowls appeared in any quantity; exceptions

are the "Galilean" bowls and Forms 1 and 2 of the carinated bowls.

"Galilean" Bowls

These are ubiquitous on sites in Galilee; they are also found on the Golan, to which they are presumed to have been imported.[37] Although no kiln sites have been found, the excavators of Khirbet Shema gave the name "*Galilean*" bowls; this practice will be adopted here.

Sometimes the vessels have been published as cooking ware;[38] however, their size, shallowness, and lack of functional handles argue against actual use in cooking. The dark areas on the exterior body come from firing and not necessarily from immediate contact with fire.

The hard fabric is banded or has a core; rarely the color varies on a piece (No. 381). The clay is fine; most often red (2.5YR 4/6, 5/6, 5/8; 10R 4/6), occasionally light red (2.5YR 6/8), yellowish red (5YR 4/6, 5/8), or reddish brown (2.5YR 4/4). The surfaces, except for patches of weak red (10R 4/2,

---

37. The name is that given by the excavators of Khirbet Shema, who also report its occurrence on the Golan (Meyers, *Khirbet Shema*, 170).
38. Zevulun-Olenik, *Talmudic Period*, 73, nos. 193–94.

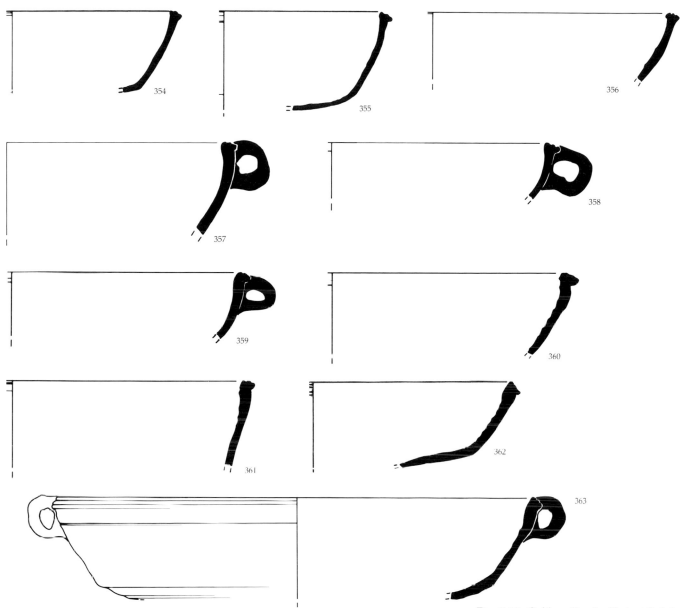

Fig. 7–21. Galilean Bowls. Variant 3. 1:2.

4/3, 4/4), dusky red (5YR 3/1), gray (2.5YR N5/), or dark gray (2.5YR N4/), show the same range of color as the clay.

Most examples come from a pre–351 (Period 2) context; an occasional piece was found in a 351–383 (Period 3) or post–383 (Period 4) context.

Here the five variants are based on a combination of information from Capernaum and Khirbet Shema.[39]

Variant 1 (Nos. 346–48).[40] 16 examples. Characteristics:

39. For distribution and division and relationship of types see Loffreda, "Evoluzione," and Meyers, *Khirbet Shema*, 170.

40. Variant 1 is equivalent to Loffreda Type 1 and Khirbet Shema, Type 1.1 (Loffreda, "Evoluzione," 240–43, figs. 1, 2; Meyers, *Khirbet Shema*, 172–73, fig. 7.1). See also Bagatti, *Nazareth*, fig. 226.4 (note that a ring handle is preserved on this fragment); Loffreda, *Cafarnao* 2, 36, 155, fig. 5.1–9; Loffreda, *et-Tabgha*, 80, fig. 31.11; Loffreda, *Sinagoga*, 66, fig. 1.1, 2. Exam-

groove around top of rim, no clear distinction between rim and body, no internal ribbing. No handles preserved.

346   (581–65). PH .044; D rim .218

Fine red clay (2.5YR 4/6), a few white grits and mineral inclusions. **Fig. 7–20.**

347   (679–65). PH .047; D rim .23

Fine red clay (2.5YR 5/6), a few white and black grits and mineral inclusions. **Fig. 7–20.**

348   (680–65). PH .044; D rim .192

Clay and color as No. 347. **Fig. 7–20.**

ple 2 in fig. 1 shows internal ribbing; this is not found on Variant 1 pieces at Jalame, nor is it recorded on Type 1.1 from Khirbet Shema.

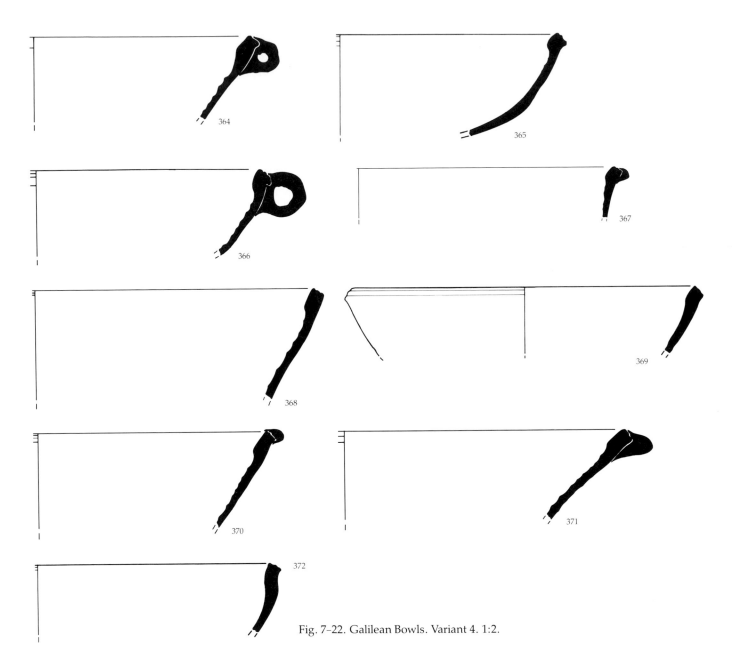

Fig. 7–22. Galilean Bowls. Variant 4. 1:2.

Variant 2 (Nos. 349–53).[41] 97 pieces. Characteristics: groove around top of rim, clear distinction between rim and body. Handles on 18 examples. On 5 the handle is an open ring (see No. 352); on 3 the pushed-together ring no longer has an opening; on 10 the handle is a lug.

349   (746–66). PH .031; D rim .184
    Clay and color as No. 346. **Fig. 7–20.**

350   (815–66). PH .03; D rim .22
    Clay and color as No. 347. **Fig. 7–20.**

351   (552–65). PH .039; D rim .34
    Clay and color as No. 347. **Fig. 7–20.**

352   (239–66). PH .058; D rim .195, bottom .08
    Clay and color as No. 347. **Fig. 7–20.**

353   (757–66). PH .029; D rim .18
    Clay and color as No. 346. **Fig. 7–20.**

Variant 3 (Nos. 354–63).[42] 40 examples. Characteristics: two grooves around top of rim, no clear distinction between

41. Variant 2 is equivalent to Loffreda Type 2 and Khirbet Shema Type 1.2 (Loffreda, "Evoluzione," 243, fig. 3, and Meyers, *Khirbet Shema*, 172–74, fig. 7, pl. 7.14–30). See also Loffreda, *Cafarnao* 2, 39, 156, fig. 5.10–15; Loffreda, *et-Tabgha*, 77, 80, fig. 30.1, 4, fig. 31.11; Loffreda, *Sinagoga*, 68, fig. 1.3–4.

42. Variant 3 is equivalent to Loffreda Type 3 (Loffreda, "Evoluzione," 243–46, fig. 4) and to Khirbet Shema Type 2.1 (Meyers, *Khirbet Shema*, 174, fig. 7.1, pl. 7.2:1–23). See for parallels Loffreda, *Cafarnao* 2, 38, 155–56, fig. 5.16–19, photo 6; Loffreda, *et-Tabgha*, 77–80, figs. 30.5, 31.10; Loffreda, *Sinagoga*, 68, fig. 1.5; Dothan, *Hammath Tiberias*, fig. 4.B, E, H, J, K, N for which a date of 4th–6th c. is proposed.

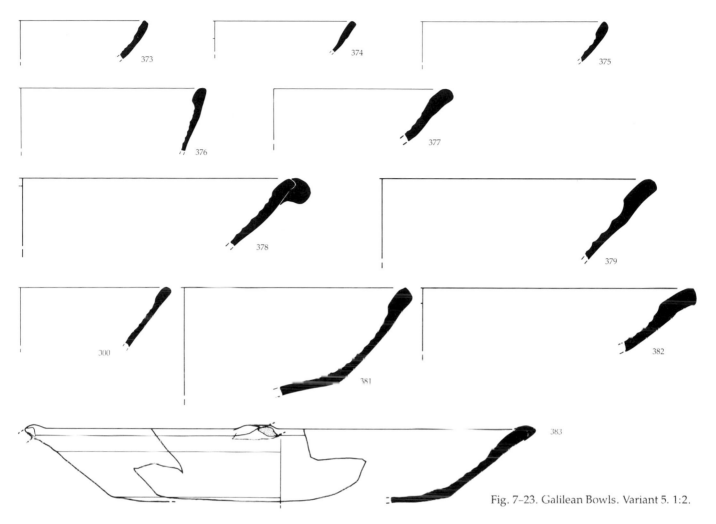

Fig. 7–23. Galilean Bowls. Variant 5. 1:2.

rim and body. Internal ribbing may or may not be present. All handles are open rings (see Nos. 357–59, 363).

354 (72–66). PH (a) .045 (b) .019; D rim .179
Clay and color as No. 347. **Fig. 7–21.**

355 (174–65). H .054; D rim .179, bottom .09
Clay and color as No. 346. **Fig. 7–21.**

356 (755–66). PH .036; D rim .26
Clay and color as No. 347. **Fig. 7–21.**

357 (759–66). PH .049; D rim .242
Fine red clay (2.5YR 4/8). **Fig. 7–21.**

358 (769–66). PH .03; D rim .24
Clay and color as No. 347. **Fig. 7–21.**

359 (668–65). PH .034; D rim .252
Clay and color as 347. **Fig. 7–21.**

360 (673–65). PH .043; D rim .262
Fine yellowish red clay (5YR 4/6). **Fig. 7–21.**

361 (768–66). PH .045; D rim .258
Clay and color as No. 347. **Fig. 7–21.**

362 (42 64). PH .046; D rim .22
Clay and color as No. 347. **Fig. 7–21.**

363 (268–65). H .054; D rim .262, bottom .17
Clay and color as No. 347. **Fig. 7–21.**

Variant 4 (Nos. 364–72).[43] 52 pieces. Characteristics: one or two grooves on top of rim, clear distinction between rim and body. Internal ribbing may or may not be present. Handles are open rings or lugs (see Nos. 364, 366, 368, 370–71).

364 (669–65). PH .045; D rim .24
Clay and color as No. 353. **Fig. 7–22.**

43. Variant 4 is equivalent to Loffreda Types 4 and 5 (Loffreda, "Evoluzione," 246, figs. 5, 6), Loffreda Type A14 (Loffreda, *Cafarnao* 2, 40, 156), and Khirbet Shema, Type 2.1 or 2.2 and 3.1 or 3.2 (Meyers, *Khirbet Shema*, 172, fig. 7.1).
For parallels see Loffreda, "Evoluzione," 246, figs. 5, 6, and Meyers, *Khirbet Shema*, 174, fig. 7.1; pls. 7.2:1–23, 7.2:23–24, 7.3:1–16, 23–27; Adan, "Horvat Ammudim," 20, fig. 2.2, 3, 4; Bagatti, *Nazareth*, fig. 226.1, 2, 14, 15; Loffreda, *Cafarnao* 2, 38, 40, 155–56, fig. 5.16, 20; Loffreda, *et-Tabgha*, 77, 80–82, fig. 30.5, 6, fig. 31.10, 13–14, 18; Loffreda, *Sinagoga*, 68, fig. 1.6–9; Ritterspach, "Meiron Cistern," 19–20, pl. 3.14–18; Dothan, *Hammath Tiberias*, 62, 67, fig. 4.A, D, G dated to the latest of Stratum II, that is, late 4th c.

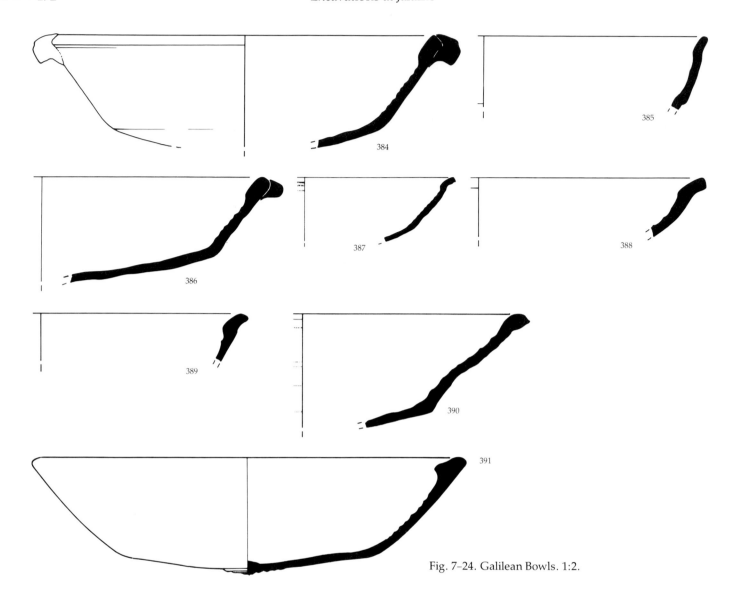

Fig. 7–24. Galilean Bowls. 1:2.

365   (158–66). PH (a) .049 (b) .055; D rim .238
Clay and color as No. 353. **Fig. 7–22.**

366   (670–65). PH .045; D rim .25
Clay and color as No. 346. **Fig. 7–22.**

367   (766–66). PH .04; D rim .42
Clay and color as No. 346. **Fig. 7–22.**

368   (589–65). PH .057; D rim .31
Clay and color as No. 353. **Fig. 7–22.**

369   (170–66). PH .036; D rim .188
Fine reddish brown clay (2.5YR 4/4). **Fig. 7–22.**

370   (429–66). PH .05; D rim .252
Fine yellowish red clay (5YR 5/8). **Fig. 7–22.**

371   (771–66). PH .048; D rim .306
Clay and color as No. 347. **Fig. 7–22.**

372   (161–65). PH .037; D rim .258
Clay and color as No. 353. **Fig. 7–22.**

Variant 5 (Nos. 373–91).[44] 131 fragments. Characteristics: rounded or flat rim without grooves, internal ribbing. Handles remain on 25 pieces. Of these 11 are pushed-together rings without an opening; 13 are lugs; 1 (not catalogued) is only a strip of clay carelessly smeared onto the body at the rim and below.

373   (622–65). PH .031; D rim .204
Clay and color as No. 353. **Fig. 7–23.**

44. Variant 5 is equivalent to Loffreda Type 6 (Loffreda, "Evoluzione," 248, figs. 7, 8) and Khirbet Shema, Type 4.1 or 4.2 (Meyers, *Khirbet Shema*, 172, fig. 7.1). For parallels see Meyers, *Khirbet Shema*, 174–75, fig. 7.1, pls. 7.8:24–30, 7.9:15–28, 7.10:1–19; Adan, "Horvat Ammudim," fig. 2.1, 5–7; Bagatti, *Nazareth*, fig. 226.3, 13; Loffreda, *Cafarnao* 2, 40, 156–57, fig. 5.21–23; Loffreda, *et-Tabgha*, 77, fig. 30.2; Loffreda, *Sinagoga*, 69, fig. 1.10, 11; Ritterspach, "Meiron Cistern," 19–20, pl. 3.18–20.

374 (782–66). PH .025; D rim .228
Clay and color as No. 347. **Fig. 7–23.**

375 (813–66). PH .032; D rim .30
Clay and color as No. 353. **Fig. 7–23.**

376 (580–65). PH .05; D rim .30
Clay and color as No. 353. **Fig. 7–23.**

377 (817–66). PH .027; D rim .19
Clay and color as No. 346. **Fig. 7–23.**

378 (426–66). PH .036; D rim .288
Clay and color as No. 353. **Fig. 7–23.**

379 (585–65). PH .042; D rim .292
Clay and color as No. 353. **Fig. 7–23.**

380 (591–65). PH .047; D rim .242
Clay and color as No. 353. **Fig. 7–23.**

381 (583–65). PH .057; D rim .242
Fine red (2.5YR 4/8) and reddish brown (2.5YR 5/4) clay.
Fig. 7–23.

382 (582–65). PH .033, D rim .29
Clay and color as No. 346. **Fig. 7 23.**

383 (244–64). PH .04; D rim .26, bottom .13
Clay and color as No. 353. **Fig. 7–23.**

384 (752–66). PH .06; D rim .208, bottom .10
Clay and color as No. 346. **Fig. 7 24.**

385 (584–65). PH .038; D rim .238
Clay and color as No. 353. **Fig. 7–24.**

386 (21–65). PH (a) .056 (b) .041; D rim .25, Est bottom .12
Clay and color as No. 346. **Fig. 7–24.**

387 (490–66). PH .07; D rim .318
Clay and color as No. 346. **Fig. 7–24.**

388 (812–66). PH .03; D rim .242
Clay and color as No. 369. **Fig. 7–24.**

389 (370–64). PH .025; D rim .222
Clay and color as No. 347. **Fig. 7–24.**

390 (314–65). PH .061; D rim .239, bottom .10
Fine light red clay (2.5YR 6/8). **Fig. 7–24.**

391 (86–65). H .063; D rim .23, bottom .08
Fine red clay (10R 4/6). **Fig. 7–24.**

Carinated Bowls

Form 1 (Nos. 392–93).[45] 105 fragments. Most common of the carinated bowls. Of the two examples catalogued No.

393 is unusually large; however, both display the wide rim everted to the horizontal or nearly so and the two ring handles set at rim and carination. The rim is often slightly concave on top. The vessels are of a hard fired red fabric; a core or banding is rare. White and black grits appear in varying amounts. The greatest number of pieces come from a pre–351 context; however, a few are from 351–383 or post–383 contexts.

392 (234–66). H .069; D rim .218, Est bottom .065
Fine red clay (2.5YR 5/6). **Fig. 7–25.**

393 (51–66). H .13; D rim .393
Fine red clay (2.5YR 5/6). **Fig. 7–25.**

Form 2 (Nos. 394–97). Typical is a wide rim everted to the horizontal or below. As with Form 1 the rim is often concave on top. These bowls are hard fired and usually have a gray core; occasionally the clay may be of a single color, banded or variegated. The gently carinated side of No. 397 makes it unusual. Contexts indicate that many of these bowls are probably before 351, while none is clearly of later periods.

394 (10 66). PH .046; D rim .323
Fine clay, dark gray core (2.5YR N3/), outer bands dusky red (2.5YR 3/2). **Fig. 7–25.**

395 (237–66). PH .072; D rim .269
Fine clay, dark gray core (2.5YR N4/), outer bands weak red (2.5YR 4/2). **Fig. 7–25.**

396 (310–65). PH .042; D rim .24
Fine clay, dark gray core (2.5YR N4/), outer bands reddish brown (2.5YR 5/4). **Fig. 7–25.**

397 (156–65). PH .063; D rim .36
Fine clay, dark gray core (2.5YR N4/), outer bands red (2.5YR 5/6). **Pl. 7–4.**

Form 3 (No. 398). One fragment. No good context; a similar bowl at Capernaum indicates a 4th c. date.[46]

398 (94–65). PH .068; D rim .33
Fine clay, dark gray core (2.5YR N4/), outer bands red (2.5YR 5/6), a few white and black grits; occasional white ones have erupted through surfaces. **Fig. 7–25.**

Form 4 (Nos. 399–400). Four examples. Contexts indicate a date before 351.

399 (701–66). PH .03; D rim .21
Fine clay, weak red core (2.5YR 4/2), outer bands red (2.5YR 5/6), some white and black grits, a few small ones. **Fig. 7–25.**

400 (702–66). PH .03; D rim .24
Fine very dark gray (2.5YR N3/) and red (2.5YR 5/6) clay, some white and black grits. **Fig. 7–25.**

Form 5 (Nos. 401–2). Two pieces. Contexts indicate a date

45. For parallels see Bagatti, *Nazareth*, 282, figs. 224.4–6; Loffreda, *Cafarnao* 2, 40–42, 157, fig. 6.1–7; Loffreda, *et-Tabgha*, 82, fig. 31.22; Loffreda, *Sinagoga*, 71–73, fig. 2.1–3; Meyers, *Khirbet Shema*, 180–88, pls. 7.10:20–29, 7.11, and 7.12:1–27; Ritterspach, "Meiron Cistern," 21, pl. 3.11–13.

46. For a parallel to Carinated Bowl, Form 3, see Loffreda, *et-Tabgha*, 112, fig. 37.11.

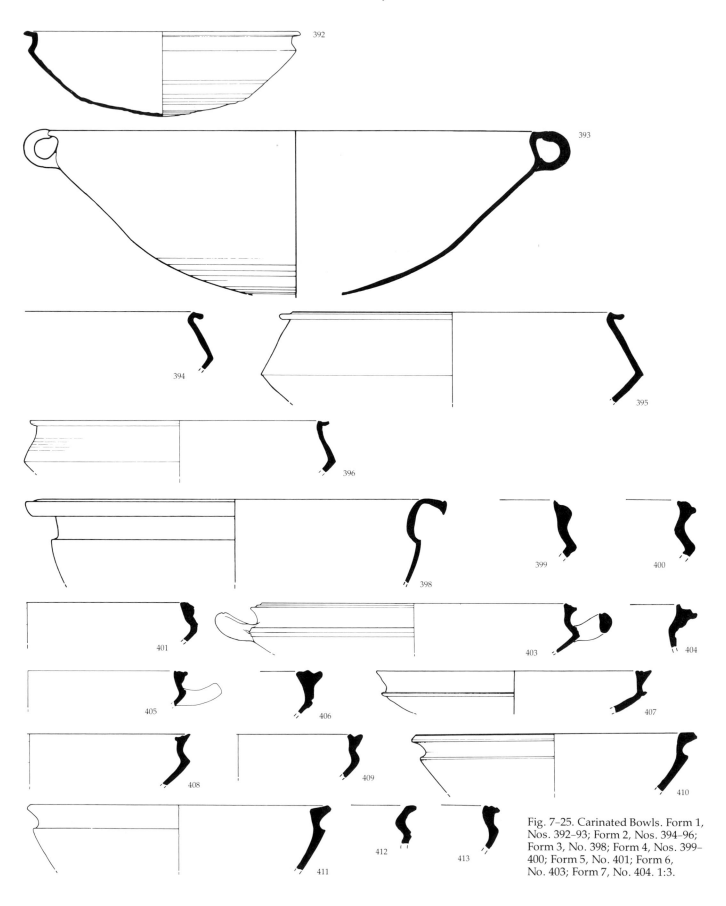

Fig. 7-25. Carinated Bowls. Form 1, Nos. 392–93; Form 2, Nos. 394–96; Form 3, No. 398; Form 4, Nos. 399–400; Form 5, No. 401; Form 6, No. 403; Form 7, No. 404. 1:3.

before 351. No. 402 has a twisted horizontal handle set at point of carination.

401 (620–66). PH (b) .032; Max dim (a) .083; D rim .269

Fine red clay (2.5YR 4/6), a few white and black grits; occasional ones have pitted the surfaces. **Fig. 7–25.**

402 (232–66). PH .034; D rim .23

Fine red clay (2.5YR 5/8), outer bands weak red (2.5YR 4/2), a few white and black grits.

Form 6 (No. 403). One example. Context suggests a date before 351.

403 (153–66). PH .04; D rim .26

Fine red clay (2.5YR 5/6), a few white and black grits, occasional ones have erupted through surfaces. **Fig. 7–25.**

Form 7 (No. 404). Two pieces. Contexts suggest that the form probably dates before 351.

404 (71–66). PH .023; D rim .19

Coarse clay, dark gray core (2.5YR N4/), outer bands red (2.5YR 5/6), a few white grits. **Fig. 7–25.**

Form 8 (No. 405). Three fragments. Contexts suggest a date of 351–383.

405 (197–64). PH .029; D rim .256

Coarse reddish yellow clay (5YR 6/6), some white and black grits; a few have erupted through surfaces. **Fig. 7–25.**

Form 9 (No. 406). One example.

406 (2–67). PH .023; D rim .24

Coarse reddish brown clay (2.5YR 4/4), a few white and black grits; outer surface fired gray (5YR 5/1) and very dark gray (5YR 3/1). **Fig. 7–25.**

Form 10 (Nos. 407–8). Two examples. No. 408 has a more inward tilted rim and body above the point of carination than No. 407. Contexts suggest a date before 351.

407 (34–65). PH .034; D rim .22

Fine clay, dark gray core (2.5YR N4/), outer bands red (2.5YR 5/6), a few white and black grits. **Fig. 7–25.**

408 (311–65). PH .043; D rim .26

Coarse clay, dark gray core (2.5YR N4/), outer bands reddish brown (2.5YR 5/4), a few white and black grits; occasional small white ones have erupted through surfaces. **Fig. 7–25.**

Form 11 (No. 409). One example.

409 (161–66). PH .036; D rim .198

Fine clay banded black (2.5YR N2.5/), dark reddish gray (10R 4/1) and reddish brown (2.5YR 4/4), a few white grits. **Fig. 7–25.**

Form 12 (Nos. 410–11). Two fragments. No. 410 has a blob of clay stuck on the top of the rim. This piece of clay may have been used for stacking in the kiln; it adhered to the rim and apparently could not be removed without damag-

ing the salability of the vessel. Contexts indicate a date in Period 3 (351–383).

410 (290–65). PH .047; D rim .22

Fine reddish brown (2.5YR 4/4) and dark gray clay (2.5YR N4/), some white and black grits, a few of which have erupted through surfaces. Flattened blob of clay on top of rim. **Fig. 7–25.**

411 (108–66). PH .053; D rim .241

Fine red clay (2.5YR 4/6), many minute to small white grits, a few of which have pitted surfaces, occasional black grits. **Fig. 7–25.**

Form 13 (No. 412). One example. Context suggests a date before 351.

412 (621–66). PH .021; D rim .20

Fine clay, reddish brown core (2.5YR 4/4), outer bands weak red (2.5YR 4/2), a few white and black grits. **Fig. 7–25.**

Form 14 (No. 413).

413 (479–65). PH .023; Est D rim .27

Fine clay, dark gray core (2.5YR N4/), outer bands reddish brown (2.5YR 4/4), some white and black grits, occasional mineral inclusions. **Fig. 7–25.**

Various Bowls with Everted Rim (Nos. 414–28)

These bowls are loosely bound together by the fact of an everted rim. Each is represented by one example except for No. 414 (2 pieces), No. 419 (3 examples), and No. 423 (1 other smaller fragment). From contexts, Nos. 418–21, 425, 428 all seem to date before 351; Nos. 417 and 423 appear to be dated near and after 383; Nos. 414–16, 422, 426, and 427 can be no more closely dated than Late Roman.

414 (404–65). PH .029; D rim .219

Coarse clay, gray core (5YR 5/1), outer bands yellowish red (5YR 4/8), some white and black grits and mineral inclusions. **Fig. 7–26.**

415 (659–65). PH .032; D rim .23

Coarse clay, light brown core (7.5YR 6/4), outer bands red (2.5YR 5/6), some white and black grits; a few have erupted through surfaces. **Fig. 7–26.**

416 (462–65). PH .046; Est D rim .20

Coarse clay banded yellowish red (5YR 4/8), reddish yellow (5YR 6/6), dark gray (5YR 4/1), and reddish brown (5YR 5/4), some white and black grits, a few of which have pitted surfaces. **Fig. 7–26.**

417 (441–66). PH .049; D rim .24

Fine clay, dark gray core (5YR 4/1), outer bands yellowish red (5YR 5/8), a few white and black grits, occasional ones have erupted through surfaces. **Fig. 7–26.**

418 (615–65). PH .035; D rim (warped) .196

Fine red clay (2.5YR 4/6), some white and black grits. **Fig. 7–26.**

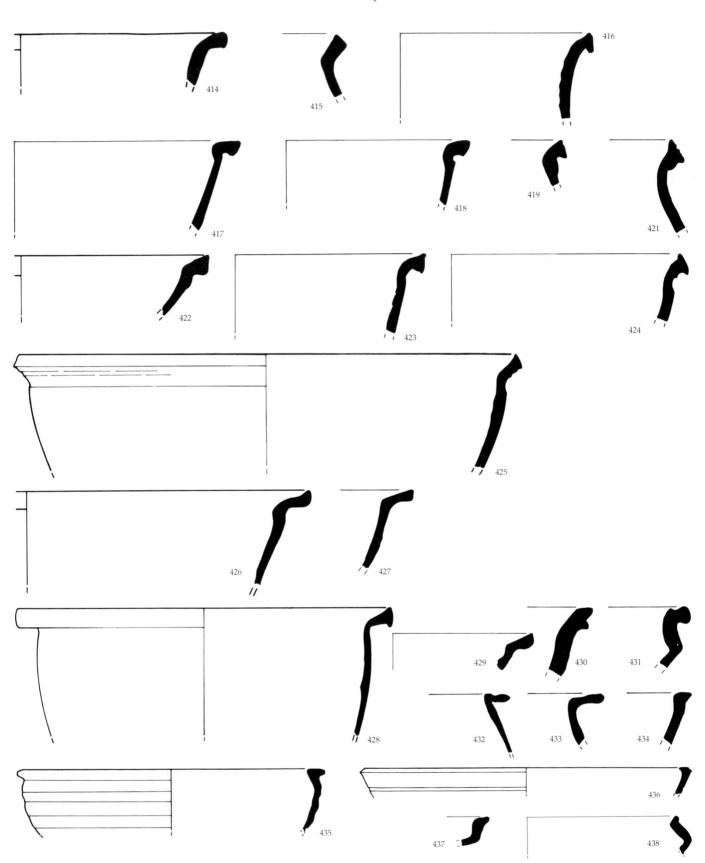

Fig. 7–26. Bowls (various kinds). Nos. 435–36, 438, 1:3; others, 1:2.

419 (644–65). PH .025

Coarse red clay (2.5YR 4/6), many white grits, some black ones, a few white ones have erupted through surfaces. **Fig. 7–26.**

420 (647–65). PH .02

Fine clay, dark gray core (2.5YR N4/), outer bands yellowish red (5YR 5/6), some white and black grits, a few of which have pitted the surfaces.

421 (480–65). PH .049; D rim .23

Coarse black (2.5YR N2.5/) and weak red (2.5YR 4/2) clay, some white and black grits, a number of which have pitted the surfaces. **Fig. 7–26.**

422 (164–66). PH .032; D rim .20

Coarse yellowish red clay (5YR 4/8), some white and black grits. **Fig. 7–26.**

423 (501–65). PH .043; D rim .202

Fine clay, dark gray core (2.5YR N4/), outer bands red (2.5YR 5/8), some white and black grits, a few white ones have erupted through the surfaces. **Fig. 7–26.**

424 (856–66). PH .03; D rim .20

Fine clay, very dark gray core (2.5YR N3/), outer bands reddish brown (2.5YR 5/4), a few white and black grits, occasional ones have pitted the surfaces. **Fig. 7–26.**

425 (499–65). PH .06; D rim .26

Coarse clay, dark gray core (2.5YR N4/), outer bands weak red (2.5YR 4/2), a few white and black grits, occasional ones have pitted the surfaces. **Fig. 7–26.**

426 (693–66). PH .051; D rim .30

Fine clay, gray core (5YR 5/1), outer bands yellowish red (5YR 5/8), some white and black grits, a few white ones have erupted through the surfaces. **Fig. 7–26.**

427 (668–66). PH .041; D rim .28

Coarse clay, gray core (5YR 5/1), outer bands yellowish red (5YR 5/6), a few white and black grits. **Fig. 7–26.**

428 (156–66). PH .068; D rim .199

Fine clay, dark gray core (2.5YR N4/), outer bands red (2.5YR 5/8), some white and black grits, a few white ones have erupted through the surfaces. **Fig. 7–26.**

Miscellaneous Bowls

Large Bowl with Wide Everted Rim (No. 429). One example. Context suggests that it may date before 351.

429 (284–65). PH .018

Coarse reddish yellow clay (5YR 6/6), some white, red, and black grits. **Fig. 7–26.**

Bowl with Heavy Everted Rim (No. 430). One piece. Context indicates a date after 383.

430 (307–64). PH .036; D rim .25

Coarse clay, light brown core (7.5YR 6/4), outer bands

brown/dark brown clay (7.5YR 4/2), many white and black grits. **Fig. 7–26.**

Carinated Bowl with Grooved Rim (No. 431). One fragment. Context offers no closer date than Late Roman.

431 (876–66). PH (a) .033 (b) .024; D rim .24

Fine light brown clay (7.5YR 6/4), some red and black grits, a few white ones. **Fig. 7–26.**

Bowl with Wide Horizontal Rim (Nos. 432–33). One example each of Forms 1 and 2. Contexts suggest a date before 351 for No. 432.

Form 1

432 (639–66). PH .032; D rim .16

Fine red clay (2.5YR 5/6), a few white and black grits. **Fig. 7–26.**

Form 2

433 (14–67). PH .027; D rim .27

Fine clay, light reddish brown core (5YR 6/4), outer bands yellowish red (5YR 4/8), a few white grits and some black ones. **Fig. 7–26.**

Bowl with Horizontal Rim (No. 434). One piece.

434 (782–65). PH .027; D rim .17

Fine clay, gray core (7.5YR N5/), outer bands brown (7.5YR 5/4), some white and black grits. **Fig. 7–26.**

Bowl with Heavy Horizontal Rim (No. 435). One fragment. Context suggests it may date after 383.

435 (25–65). PH .052; Est D rim .242

Fine clay, light brown core (7.5YR 6/4), outer bands reddish yellow (5YR 7/6), some white and black grits, occasional mineral inclusions. **Fig. 7–26.**

Bowl with Rim Undercut on Interior (No. 436). One example. Context indicates a date before 351.

436 (162–66). PH .022; D rim .258

Fine clay, red core (2.5YR 5/6), inner band reddish brown (5YR 5/3), outer band weak red (2.5YR 4/2), a few white and black grits. **Fig. 7–26.**

Bowl with Thickened Rim and Slightly Carinated Side (No. 437). One piece. Context suggests only a Late Roman date.

437 (495–65). PH .037; D rim .023–.028

Coarse clay banded reddish brown (2.5YR 4/4) and weak red (2.5YR 4/2), some white grits, a few mineral inclusions. **Fig. 7–26.**

Bowl with Slightly Inward-Beveled Rim (No. 438). One example. Context indicates only a Late Roman date.

438 (143–66). PH .026; D rim .24

Coarse clay, light brown core (7.5YR 6/4), outer bands yellowish red (5YR 5/6), some white, red, and black grits, occasional mineral inclusions. **Fig. 7–26.**

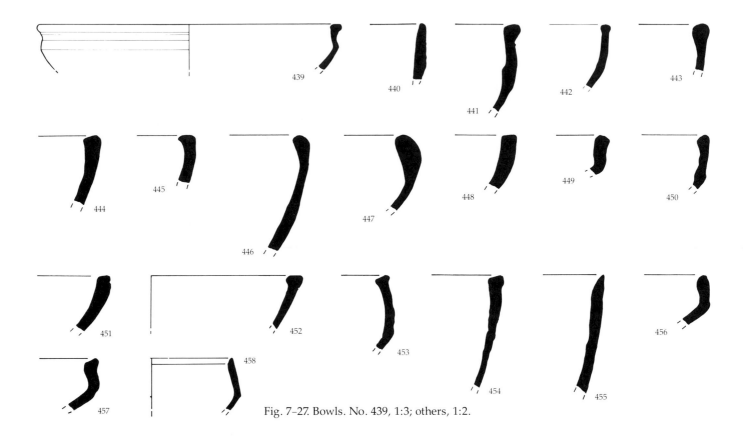

Fig. 7–27. Bowls. No. 439, 1:3; others, 1:2.

Bowl with Carinated Side and Knob Rim (No. 439). One piece. Contexts suggest only a Late Roman date.

439 (281–65). PH .038; D rim .239

Fine light red clay (2.5YR 6/6), some white and black grits. **Fig. 7–27.**

Bowl with Rounded-Off Rim (No. 440). One fragment.

440 (980–66). PH .029

Fine clay banded light brown (7.5YR 6/4) and strong brown (7.5YR 5/6), some white and black grits, occasional mineral inclusions. **Fig. 7–27.**

Bowls with Thickened Rim (Nos. 441–43). Three examples. These bowls are grouped together by virtue of their thickened rims. Contexts suggest a date of 351–383 for No. 441; a date before 351 for No. 442; and a date near and after 383 for No. 443.

441 (874–66). PH .046

Fine clay banded red (2.5YR 4/6) and light brown (7.5YR 6/4), a few white and black grits. **Fig. 7–27.**

442 (330–65). PH .05

Fine reddish brown clay (2.5YR 5/4), some black grits, a few white ones. **Fig. 7–27.**

443 (268bis–66). PH .025; D rim .13

Fine clay, very dark gray core (2.5YR N3/), outer bands reddish brown (2.5YR 4/4), a few white grits; occasional large ones have erupted through the surfaces. **Fig. 7–27.**

Bowl with Angular Thickened Rim (Nos. 444–45). Two pieces. Contexts offer only a Late Roman date.

444 (866–65). PH .036; D rim .18

Fine clay, light red core (2.5YR 6/6), outer bands reddish brown (2.5YR 4/4), some white grits, occasional mineral inclusions. **Fig. 7–27.**

445 (551–64). PH .025; D rim .19

Fine clay banded reddish brown (2.5YR 4/4), dusky red (2.5YR 3/2), and weak red (2.5YR 4/2), many white grits, a few black ones, and mineral inclusions. **Fig. 7–27.**

Bowl with Round Incurved Rim (No. 446). One example. Context indicates a date before 351.

446 (508–66). PH .061; D rim .26

Fine clay, very dark gray core (7.5YR N3/), outer bands brown (7.5YR 5/4), some white and black grits a few of which have erupted through surfaces, occasional mineral inclusions. **Fig. 7–27.**

Bowl with Heavy Incurved Rim (No. 447). One piece. Context suggests only a Late Roman date.

447 (328–65). PH .039; D rim .19

Coarse red clay (2.5YR 4/6), a few white and black grits, occasional mineral inclusions. **Fig. 7–27.**

Bowl with Flat Rim (No. 448). One example. The bowl comes from topsoil; the only date is Late Roman.

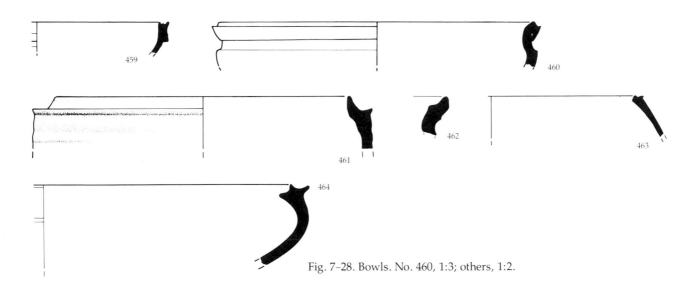

Fig. 7–28. Bowls. No. 460, 1:3; others, 1:2.

448 (384–64). PH .039; Est D rim .17

Coarse clay banded black (2.5YR N2.5/), dark reddish brown (5YR 3/2), and reddish brown (5YR 4/3), a few white and black grits. **Fig. 7–27.**

Bowl with Outward Beveled Rim (No. 449). One fragment. Context indicates a date in Period 3 (351–383).

449 (367–64). PH .021; D rim .19

Fine brown clay (7.5YR 5/4), some white grits, a few small and large ones have erupted through surfaces. **Fig. 7–27.**

Various Bowls with Inward-Beveled Rim (Nos. 450–55). This group is loosely held together by the fact that they all have an inward-beveled rim. One example of each. Contexts indicate a date probably before 351 for Nos. 450 and 452–54, while the only dates for Nos. 451 and 455 are Late Roman.

450 (976–66). PH .029

Coarse yellowish red clay (5YR 4/6), many white and black grits, a few white ones have pitted the surfaces. **Fig. 7–27.**

451 (879–66). PH .03; D rim .21

Fine red clay (2.5YR 5/6), a few white and black grits, occasional mineral inclusions, occasional small white grits at surface. **Fig. 7–27.**

452 (978–66). PH .029; D rim .162

Fine clay, dark gray core (5YR 4/1), outer bands yellowish red (5YR 4/6), a few white grits. **Fig. 7–27.**

453 (984–66). PH .04; D rim .21

Coarse clay banded reddish brown (5YR 5/4) and dark gray (5YR 4/1), many white grits, some erupted through surfaces, a few black grits and mineral inclusions. **Fig. 7–27.**

454 (507–66). PH .059; D rim .19

Coarse clay banded brown (7.5YR 5/2) and light olive gray (5Y 6/2), some white and black grits; a few white ones have pitted surfaces. **Fig. 7–27.**

455 (329–65). PH .062; D rim .18

Fine clay, reddish gray core (5YR 5/2), outer bands light reddish brown (7.5YR 6/4), many white and black grits; a few white ones have erupted through surfaces. **Fig. 7–27.**

Various Bowls with Carinated Side (Nos. 456–58). One example of each. Contexts for Nos. 456–57 are Late Roman; No. 458 comes from a pre–351 context.

456 (645–65). PH .026

Fine clay, reddish brown core (5YR 4/3), first outer bands dark gray (5YR 4/1), second outer bands reddish brown (5YR 5/4), some white and black grits; a few white ones have erupted through surfaces. **Fig. 7–27.**

457 (869–66). PH .027

Coarse light red clay (2.5YR 6/6), many white and black grits; a few white ones have erupted through surfaces. **Fig. 7–27.**

458 (1193–66). PH (a) .043 (b) .033; D rim .132

Fine clay, gray core (10YR 5/1), outer bands yellowish red (5YR 4/6), many white and black grits, some white ones erupted through surfaces, occasional mineral inclusions. **Fig. 7–27.**

Bowl with Rectangular Rim (No. 459). One piece. Context offers a date before 351.

459 (159–66). PH .027; D rim .207

Coarse red clay (2.5YR 4/6), a few white grits. **Fig. 7–28.**

Carinated Bowl with Outward-Folded Rim (No. 460). One fragment. Context indicates Late Roman date.

460 (95–65). PH .037; Est D rim .28

Fine very dark gray (5YR 3/1) and dark reddish gray (5YR 4/2) clay, a few white and black grits. **Fig. 7–28.**

Bowl with Inwardly Offset Rim (No. 461). One example. Context suggests no closer date than Late Roman.

461   (677–66). PH .029; D rim .156

Fine clay banded gray (5YR 5/1) and light reddish brown (5YR 6/4), a few white and black grits. Traces of very pale brown slip (10YR 8/4) on exterior. **Fig. 7–28.**

Bowl with Outwardly Offset Rim (No. 462). One fragment. The bowl comes from topsoil; the suggested date is Late Roman.

462   (129–66). PH .033; Est D rim .336

Fine clay, light brownish gray core (10YR 6/2), outer bands yellowish red (5YR 5/6), some white and black grits. **Fig. 7–28.**

Bowl with Two-Part Rim (No. 463). One piece. Context indicates Late Roman date.

463   (308–65). PH .035; D rim .237

Fine clay, reddish brown core (5YR 4/3), outer bands dark gray (5YR 4/1), some white and black grits. White (10YR 8/2) painted decoration of strokes on upper surface of rim and horizontal and vertical lines on outside of body. Too little remains for further description. **Fig. 7–28.**

Bowl with Three-Prong Rim (No. 464). One example. Context suggests a date before 351.

464   (66–66). PH .043; D rim .278

Fine clay, very dark gray core (2.5YR N3/), outer bands reddish brown (2.4YR 5/4), some white and black grits, a few erupted through surfaces. **Fig. 7–28.**

Basins

North Syrian Mortaria

The 85 fragments are divided into three variants; Variant 1 is the most common. Characteristic are the minute to large pieces of glass in the clay,[47] accompanied by combinations of white, black, red, or yellow grits in varying sizes. Sometimes the inclusions have erupted through or caused bulges in the surface. A few floor fragments (uninventoried) bear burnishing marks, apparently from use. Contexts date the vessels to the 3rd quarter of the 4th c., although some examples come from a post–383 context (Period 4).

Variant 1 (Nos. 465–74).[48] 81 pieces. The heavy rim, rectangular or square in section, serves as a continuous handle, as do the rims of the other variants. Three fragments show that the rim was added after the vessel had been formed. A distinct line appears on Nos. 465 and 472.

No. 473 shows that the upper wall was pulled outward and the rim pressed on under the extended part and upper body. The line of joining of the bottom of the rim can be seen on the interior of No. 472. That the mortarium was made in sections and pieced together is clear on No. 471, where the outside of the body is slightly offset in two places. A small thumb-impressed open spout is preserved on the rim of this piece. Another sherd (uninventoried) has a similar spout.

465   (260–64). PH .05; D rim .34

Coarse reddish brown clay (5YR 4/4). **Fig. 7–29.**

466   (315–65). PH .042; D rim .42

Coarse reddish brown clay (2.5YR 4/4). Rim undercut on interior. **Fig. 7–29.**

467   (257–64). PH .06; D rim .36

Clay and color as No. 465. **Fig. 7–29.**

468   (265–64). PH .048; D rim .40

Coarse yellowish red clay (5YR 4/6). **Fig. 7–29.**

469   (44–64). PH .074; D rim .36

Coarse clay, weak red core (2.5YR 4/2), outer bands reddish brown (2.5YR 4/4). Rim slightly undercut on interior. **Fig. 7–29.**

470   (457–66). PH .068; D rim .38

Coarse dark reddish brown clay (5YR 3/4). Rim slightly undercut on interior. **Fig. 7–29.**

471   (60–64). H .08; D rim .306, bottom .15

Coarse reddish brown clay (5YR 4/3). **Fig. 7–29; Pl. 7–4.**

472   (318–65). PH .034; D rim .34

Coarse red clay (2.5YR 4/6). **Fig. 7–29.**

473   (280–64). PH .042; D rim .42

Coarse weak red (2.5YR 4/2) and reddish brown (2.5YR 4/4) clay. Applied outer section of rim broken away. **Fig. 7–29.**

474   (319–66). PH .042; D rim .396

Clay and color as No. 465. **Fig. 7–29.**

Variant 2 (No. 475). This piece provides a link between the previous group and Variant 3. The wide rectangular rim is rounded off along the outer edge. In proportion to the width and weight of the rim the body below is quite thin.

475   (886–66). PH .033; Est D rim .39

Coarse clay banded dark reddish brown (5YR 3/3) and very dark gray (5YR 3/1). All or part of three oblique incised lines on underside of rim. **Fig. 7–29.**

Variant 3 (Nos. 476–77).[49] Three fragments found, each

---

47. The name is taken from the area of manufacture—the coastal region of Syria in and around Ras el-Basit. Hayes states that the clay contains lime and generally no mica. Common inclusions are white and black grits and "particles of what appears to be crushed glass" (J. W. Hayes, "North Syrian Mortaria," *Hesperia* 36 [1967] 337–47).

48. For general parallels see ibid., 342–46. For parallels in Palestine to Variant 1 see Loffreda, *Sinagoga*, 95, fig. 5, no. 10.1823; Loffreda, *Cafarnao 2*, 160, 53, fig. 12.1–6; Riley, "Caesarea Hippodrome," 36–37, nos. 41–42. Apparently of this variant is a piece from Kh. Siyar el-Ghanam (Corbo, *Kh. Siyar el-Ghanam*, 66–67, fig. 19.6, not described in text).

49. See Riley, "Caesarea Hippodrome," 41–42, nos. 65–68; no. 65 (p. 41) shows the same stamp as our No. 477. The North Syrian mortaria from the Caesarea Hippodrome were republished by D. E. Groh, "North Syrian Mortaria Excavated at Caesarea Maritima (Israel)," *Levant* 10 (1978) 165–69; no. 5 (p. 169) is Riley's no. 65. For other examples from Palestine see Groh. For pieces preserving a spout similar to No. 476 see Groh, 167, no. 1; Y. Israeli, "A Roman Pottery Mortarium," *Atiqot* 6 (1970) 79.

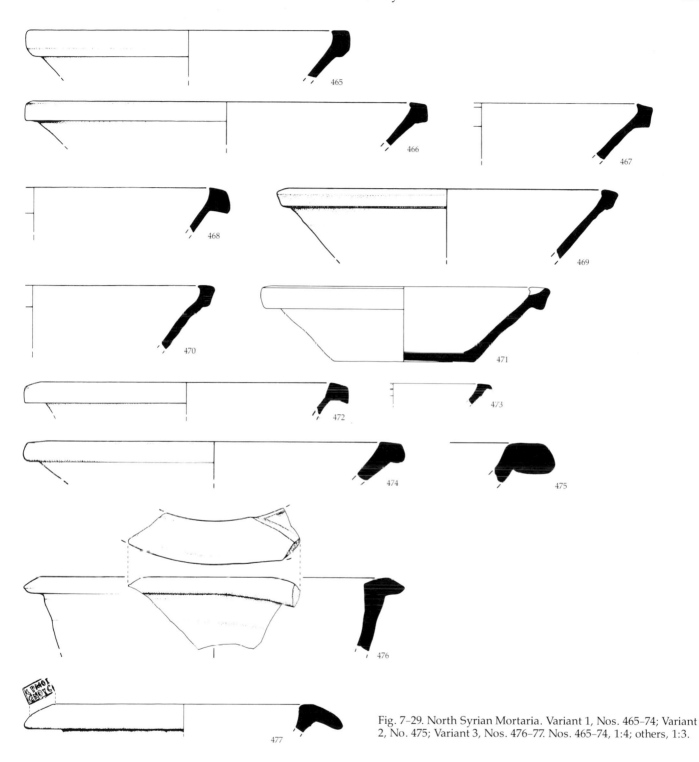

Fig. 7–29. North Syrian Mortaria. Variant 1, Nos. 465–74; Variant 2, No. 475; Variant 3, Nos. 476–77. Nos. 465–74, 1:4; others, 1:3.

with a wide horizontal rim convex on the upper surface and narrow at the outer edge; that of No. 477 is larger and heavier. No. 476 preserves part of an open triangular spout on the rim. Each of the two fabrics identified by Hayes ("Mortaria," 338, see n. 47) were recovered; No. 476 and a similar piece (uncatalogued) are of the "orange or orange-brown" variety, while No. 477 belongs to the larger group in a darker clay. Distinctive are the multiple stamps impressed around the rim. No. 477 preserves such a

stamp. The two-line inscription gives the maker's name, Hermogenes, in the genitive case. The short vertical stroke at the end of the second line is not part of the name; it is a simple termination mark.[50]

50. A termination mark is often a branch or floral element; however, the short vertical stroke, as on this piece, is well known. See Hayes, "Mortaria," 342, nos. 1–3; 343, nos. 7–32, 33, 40–46, 48–54, 54–64; 344, nos. 75–80, nos. 84–86; 344–45, nos. 97–113; 346, nos. 151, 152, 154, 156.

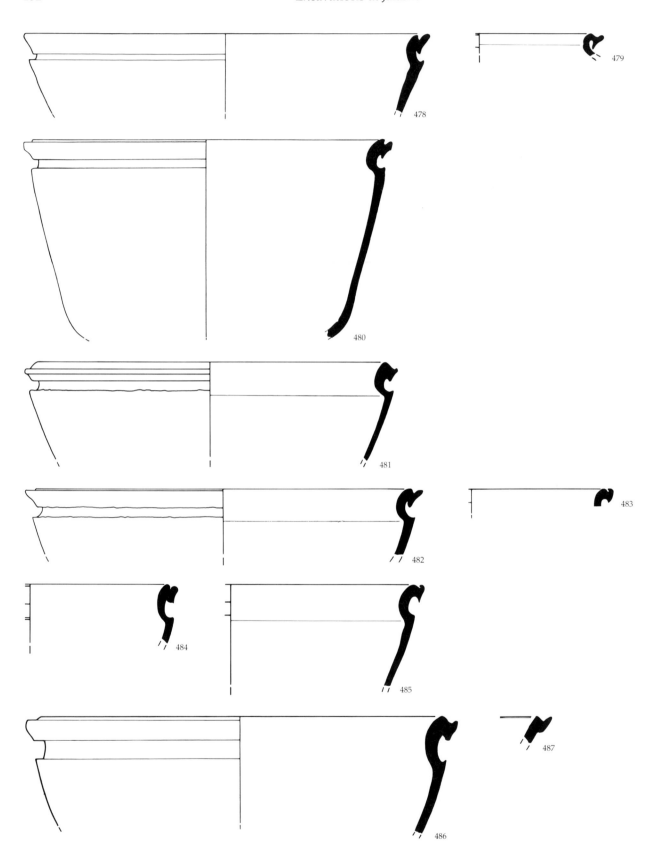

Fig. 7–30. Basins with carinated sides. 1:3.

476 (491–66). PH .078; Est D rim .40

Fine yellowish red clay (5YR 4/6). **Fig. 7–29.**

477 (29–65). PH .046; Est D rim .496

Fine clay, yellowish red core (5YR 4/6), outer bands dark gray (5YR 4/1). Shallow groove below rim on interior. Stamp on upper surface of rim: see discussion above. **Fig. 7–29; Pl. 7–4.**

Basin with Carinated Side (Nos. 478–87)

30 fragments. Fine clay, white and/or black grits and mineral inclusions in varying amounts; occasional small white grits have erupted through the surface. Clay color may be solid, banded, or have a core.

Common is a deep groove separating the rim into two parts. On No. 478 it is clear that the outer part of the rim was added. The other examples do not show this; tooling accounts for the crisp form. The deep vessel is carinated high on the body; below the side curves inward. No complete profile was recovered, but parallels indicate the bottom was convex, either with or without attached loop feet.[51]

The sharpness and size of the carination suggest that a cord may have been wound around the vessel in order to suspend it. The use of these basins is unknown. A public or commercial use has been proposed.[52] At Jalame they are scattered over the site with no concentration in one place. Contexts show they were in use by the mid–4th c.

478 (28–65). PH .064; D rim .32

Brown core (7.5YR 7/2), outer bands reddish brown (2.5YR 5/4). **Fig. 7–30.**

479 (619–66). PH .019; D rim .198

Red clay (2.5YR 5/6). **Fig. 7–30.**

480 (43–66). PH (a) .155 (b) .109; D rim .29

Light red clay (2.5YR 6/6). **Fig. 7–30.**

481 (487–64). PH .08; D rim .298

Clay banded red (2.5YR 5/8) and pinkish gray (7.5YR 6/2). **Fig. 7–30; Pl. 7–4.**

482 (285–65). PH .054; D rim .318

Reddish brown clay (2.5YR 5/4), occasional large grits erupted through surfaces. **Fig. 7–30.**

483 (157–66). PH .03; D rim .225

Pinkish gray core (5YR 6/2), outer bands red (2.5YR 5/6). **Fig. 7–30.**

484 (33–65). PH .047; D rim .238

Clay and color as No. 479. **Fig. 7–30.**

485 (1085–66). PH .081; D rim .309

Pinkish gray core (7.5YR 6/2), outer bands yellowish red (5YR 4/3). **Fig. 7–30.**

486 (287–66). PH .094; D rim .335

Core as No. 485, outer bands light red (2.5YR 6/6). **Fig. 7–30.**

487 (286–66). PH .023; Est D rim .325

Clay and color as No. 480. **Fig. 7–30.**

Basin with Everted Rim (Nos. 488–93)[53]

276 fragments make this the most common basin at the site. Characteristic are a wide heavy rim, gritty surfaces, and worn and pitted bottoms. The everted rim sometimes approaches the horizontal. A broad smeared area on the outside at the junction of side and bottom results from joining the two; a layer of clay was applied, roughly smoothed, and trimmed. The clay is fine or coarse; standard are many minute to small white, red, and black grits, a few of which have erupted through or pitted the surfaces. The clay color is evenly divided among reddish yellow (5YR 6/6), very pale brown (10YR 8/4), and pink (7.5YR 7/4). Traces of slip the same color as the clay are preserved on a few fragments. Contexts offer a date of 2nd half of 4th c.

488 (88–65). H .088; D rim .347, Est D bottom .216

Fine pink clay (7.5YR 7/4). **Fig. 7–31.**

489 (229–65). PH .049; Est D rim .32

Coarse very pale brown clay (10YR 8/4). **Fig. 7–31.**

490 (244–66). PH .092; D rim .397

Coarse pink clay (7.5YR 7/4). **Fig. 7–31.**

491 (151–66). H .10; D rim .38, bottom .25

Fine reddish yellow clay (5YR 6/6). **Fig. 7–31.**

492 (85–65). Est H .10; D rim .368, bottom .227

Clay and color as No. 491. Traces of pink slip (7.5YR 8/4) on rim. **Fig. 7–31.**

493 (228–65). PH .075; D rim .358

Clay and color as No. 491. **Fig. 7–31.**

Handmade Basin with Partial Slip (Nos. 494–512)

168 pieces. Basins with different rims are included, but all share the same clay and surface treatment as well as a similarity of shape below the rim. Typical are the flaring side and flat bottom. The soft clay varies in color. A common inclusion is straw, present in negative impressions. There are also many minute to small white grits as well as gray ones that in some cases are stones. A slip on interior may extend onto the outside of rim or upper body. Con-

---

51. For parallels see Avigad, "Beth Shearim, 1954," 209, fig. 3.4, Bagatti, *Nazareth*, 296, fig. 231.7–10; Meyers, *Khirbet Shema*, 205–6, pl. 7.17:15–20 and comparanda cited there; Meyers, "Meiron 1976," fig. 18.7, 8. Other examples are recorded by Adan, "Horvat Ammudim," 18, fig. 1.7; Loffreda, *Cafarnao* 2, 42, fig. 7, and Ben-Tor, "Tel Yoqneam," 73, fig. 8.12.

52. This suggestion was made by Meyers in *Khirbet Shema*, 205–6, based on the find spots of the vessels within the site.

53. For parallels see Avigad, "Beth Shearim 1954," fig. 3.8; Bagatti, *Nazareth*, 298, fig. 231.12–20.

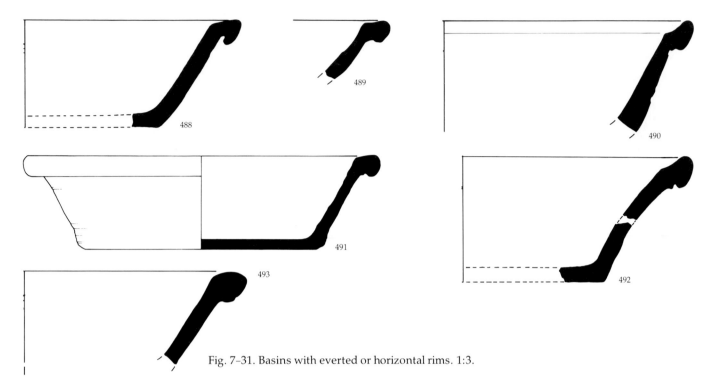

Fig. 7–31. Basins with everted or horizontal rims. 1:3.

texts give a date of 3rd quarter of 4th c. Twelve variants, some represented by only one example.

Variant 1 (Nos. 494–98).[54] The vertical rim is convex, concave, or flat on top. It may be the same thickness as the body or thicker. The body wall may be concave at midpoint on the exterior.

494   (85–64). H .131; D rim .23, bottom .188

Coarse reddish yellow clay (7.5YR 7/6); traces of red slip. **Fig. 7–32.**

495   (513–66). PH .088; D rim .27

Coarse reddish brown clay (5YR 4/4); traces of red slip. **Fig. 7–32.**

496   (331–65). PH .064; D rim .28

Coarse clay, incomplete gray core (5YR 5/1), outer bands pink (5YR 7/4); traces of red slip (2.5YR 5/6) on upper and outer surface of rim. **Fig. 7–32.**

497   (336–65). PH .072; D rim .32

Coarse clay, pink core (7.5YR 8/4), outer bands pink (5YR 7/4); red slip (2.5YR 5/6). **Fig. 7–32.**

498   (276–64). PH .098

Coarse clay banded light gray (10YR 7/2) and pink (5YR 7/4); traces of light reddish brown slip (2.5YR 6/4). **Fig. 7–32.**

Variant 2 (No. 499). Differs from Variant 1 in the broad rounded ridge on the exterior below the rim.

499   (510–66). PH .038; D rim .30

Fine clay, grayish brown core (10YR 5/2), outer bands reddish brown (5YR 5/4). **Fig. 7–32.**

Variant 3 (No. 500). Tall everted rim slightly undercut below top on interior. Decoration of a band of tool-made nicks around the inner and outer edge of the rim, enclosing two grooves.

500   (558–64). PH .062; D rim .36

Coarse clay, very pale brown core (10YR 7/4), outer bands pink (5YR 8/4); red slip (10R 5/6). **Fig. 7–32.**

Variant 4 (Nos. 501–2).[55] Characteristic is a vertical thickened rim either plain on the top or decorated with one or two grooves. The walls are thicker than usual for basins of this group.

501   (209–64). PH .06; D rim .44

Fine clay, very pale brown core (10YR 7/3), outer bands pink (7.5YR 7/4); light red (2.5YR 6/6) and red (2.5YR 5/6) slip.

502   (335–65). PH .056

Coarse pink clay (7.5YR 7/3); red slip (2.5YR 5/6). **Fig. 7–32.**

Variant 5 (No. 503). Similar to Variant 4 but thicker rim; two widely spaced grooves around top.

503   (514–66). PH .048; D rim .362

Coarse clay, gray core (5YR 5/1), first outer bands pinkish gray (7.5YR 6/2), second outer bands dark reddish

54. For parallels see Bagatti, *Nazareth*, 296, 298, fig. 232.5; Loffreda, *Cafarnao* 2, 59, 161–62, fig. 14.9; Loffreda, *Sinagoga*, 95, fig. 5.3.

55. See Loffreda, *Sinagoga*, 95, fig. 5.2.

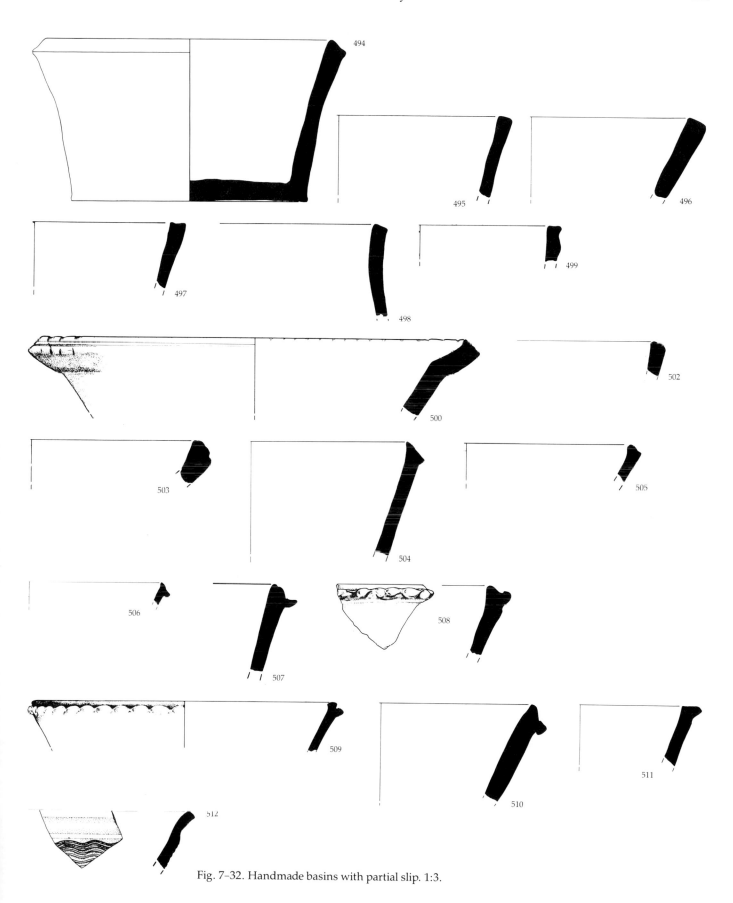

Fig. 7–32. Handmade basins with partial slip. 1:3.

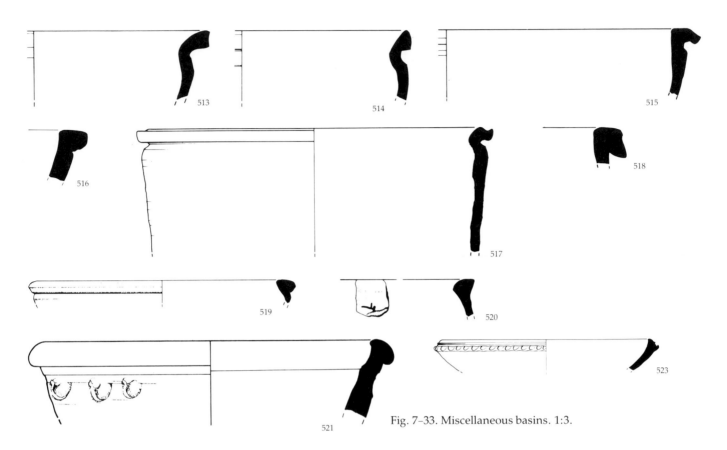

Fig. 7-33. Miscellaneous basins. 1:3.

gray (10R 4/1), third outer bands light red (2.5YR 6/6). **Fig. 7–32.**

Variant 6 (Nos. 504–5).[56] Rim triangular in section. It may be vertical or everted.

504 (188–66). PH (a) .092; Max dim (b) .071; Est D rim .255

Fine reddish yellow clay (5YR 7/6); red slip (2.5YR 5/6). **Fig. 7–32.**

505 (334–65). PH .042; D rim .354

Deep groove on top of rim. Coarse clay, dark gray core (7.5YR N4/), outer bands pink (5YR 7/4). **Fig. 7–32.**

Variant 7 (No. 506). Triangular rim concave on top, distinctly set off from body on exterior.

506 (511–66). PH .04; D rim .212

Coarse clay banded pink (5YR 7/4) and very pale brown (10YR 7/4); light red slip (10R 6/6). **Fig. 7–32.**

Variant 8 (Nos. 507–8).[57] Outer edge of triangular rim formed by a tool-notched band.

507 (182–65). PH .07; Est D rim .40

Coarse clay banded light reddish brown (10YR 6/4), gray (10R 5/1), and pink (5YR 7/4); light red slip (2.5YR 6/6). **Fig. 7–32.**

508 (34–64). PH .056; D rim .26

Shallow groove below rim on exterior. Fine pink (5YR 7/4) and very pale brown (10YR 7/3) clay; traces of red slip (2.5YR 5/6). **Fig. 7–32.**

Variant 9 (No. 509).[58] Vertical rim undercut on the interior; applied thumb-impressed band below.

509 (24–66). PH .06; D rim .363

Coarse clay, pinkish gray core (7.5YR 6/2), outer bands light red (2.5YR 6/6); red slip (2.5YR 5/6). **Fig. 7–32.**

Variant 10 (No. 510). Below the narrow rounded-off rim is an applied band decorated with thumb-impressions.

510 (78–66). PH .079; Est D rim .25

Coarse light gray clay (10YR 7/2). **Fig. 7–32.**

Variant 11 (No. 511). Wall thicker than normal. Vertical rim flat on top and slightly incurved. It is made into a wide horizontal rim by the addition of a triangular coil. On the outside below the rim is a broad shallow groove.

511 (502–66). PH .098; D rim .382

Shallow groove below rim on exterior. Coarse clay, light gray core (10YR 7/2), outer bands pink (5YR 7/4); light red slip (2.5YR 6/6). **Fig. 7–32.**

56. Ibid., fig. 5.9.
57. See Loffreda, *Cafarnao* 2, 59, 161–62, fig. 14.6, 7.
58. See Bagatti, *Nazareth*, 298, fig. 232.1.1a.

Variant 12 (No. 512). Seven-part combed wavy band on the body.

512 (44–66). PH .064; D rim .26

Fine clay, light gray/gray core (10YR 6/1), outer bands pinkish gray (7.5YR 6/2); traces of red slip (2.5YR 5/6). **Fig. 7–32.**

Miscellaneous Basins

Basin with Angular Everted Rim (No. 513). One example. Soft fabric.

513 (196–66). PH .056; D rim .278

Edge of handle attachment preserved (?). Broad shallow groove below rim on exterior. Fine clay incompletely banded red (10R 5/6) and light brown (7.5YR 6/4), some minute to small white, red, and black grits. **Fig. 7–33.**

Basin with Everted Rim and Slightly Carinated Side (No. 514). One example. Fabric soft as that of No. 513.

514 (186–64). PH .057, D rim .26

Fine clay, gray core (10YR 5/1), first outer bands yellowish red (5YR 5/6), second outer bands light red (2.5YR 6/6), many minute to small white, red, and black grits; some white ones have erupted and pitted the surfaces. **Fig. 7–33.**

Basin with Angular Horizontal Rim (No. 515). One example. Fabric soft as that of No. 513. Rim convex on top. Suggested date is 4th c.[59]

515 (52–66). PH .053; D rim .40

Broad shallow groove below rim on outside. Fine light red clay (2.5YR 6/6), some minute to small white, red, and black grits, a few white ones have erupted and pitted the surfaces. **Fig. 7–33.**

Basin with Heavy Horizontal Rim (No. 516). One example.

516 (59–66). PH .041; D rim .35

Rim distinctly set off from body on outside. Fine clay, light gray core (10YR 7/2), outer bands light red (2.5YR 6/6), many white and black grits, occasional small white ones erupted through surfaces. **Fig. 7–33.**

Basin with Offset Rim (No. 517). One example. Suggested date from context is before 351.

517 (176–65). PH .98; Est D rim .278

Rim sharply set off from body on outside. Broad, widely spaced ribbing on inside. Fine reddish brown clay (5YR 5/3), some white and black grits and mineral inclusions; a few black grits have caused bulges in the surfaces. **Fig. 7–33.**

Basin with Outward-Folded Rim (No. 518). One example.

518 (48–65). PH .032; D rim .30

Heavy rim roughly square in section. Very fine yellow-

ish red clay (5YR 5/6), occasional white grits and mineral inclusions; red slip (2.5YR 5/6) on interior extending to inner part of top of rim. **Fig. 7–33.**

Basin with Heavy Knob Rim (No. 519). Two examples. Outer part of rim added to vessel wall. This can be seen in section and also by a shallow depression or groove around inner edge of top of rim.

519 (539–66). PH .038; D rim .42

Coarse red clay, some white and black grits; traces of slip (?) of same color as clay. Similar is 746–65 (uncatalogued). **Fig. 7–33.**

Basin with Wide Heavy Rim (No. 520). One example. Outer part of rim formed by outward folding of clay from inner part. Graffito on outside of body. Without context.

520 (310–64). PH .06

Rim convex on top. Coarse dark gray clay (5YR 4/1), a few white grits and mineral inclusions. Graffito on outside of body. **Fig. 7–33.**

Basin with Thumb-Impressed Decoration (No. 521). One example. Surfaces gritty. Decoration made by pushing thumb from top to bottom in right to left direction. Since the fragment is from a disturbed context, no specific date can be given; however, nothing intrinsic to the piece prohibits a Late Roman date.

521 (20–64). PH .062; D rim .265

Knob rim, broad rounded ridge below on exterior. Below ridge a band of thumb-impressed decoration. Coarse reddish brown clay (5YR 5/3), outer bands light red (2.5YR 6/6), some white grits, a few mineral inclusions and straw temper; white slip (10YR 8/2) on both surfaces. **Fig. 7–33.**

Basin with Two-Part Rim (Nos. 522–23). Two examples the same except for the technique employed to make the decoration on the lower part of the rim. On No. 522 the broad notches were made by pressing the thumb inward toward the upper part of the rim. On No. 523 the notches are smaller and tool-made and do not bend inward toward the upper part of the rim. The context of No. 522 suggests a date in Period 3 (351–383); No. 523 came from the surface near the olive press.

522 (82–65). PH .034; D rim .32

Lower outer part of rim is an applied band with thumb-impressed decoration. Fine dark gray clay (2.5YR N4/), many white and black grits and mineral inclusions, occasional small white grits erupted through surfaces; remains of very pale brown slip (10YR 8/3) on exterior.

523 (119–66). PH (a) .052 (b) .05; Est D rim .34

Lower outer part of rim is an applied band decorated with small tool-made notches. Fine dark gray clay (5YR 4/1), some white and black grits and mineral inclusions; a few small and large grits have erupted through the surfaces. **Fig. 7–33.**

Body Sherds of Basins with Combed Decoration (Nos. 524–25). Two of the three body sherds of basins bearing combed

---

59. The basin was found in association with a Carinated Bowl, Form 2, dated by context probably before 351. See Carinated Bowl, Form 2, above.

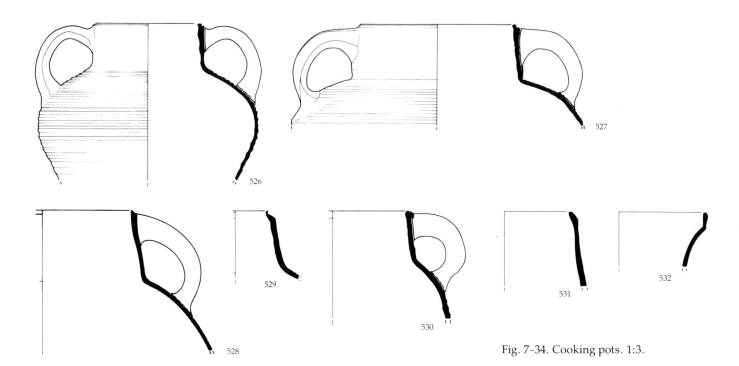

Fig. 7–34. Cooking pots. 1:3.

decoration are presented here; the design is similar to known examples of the Late Roman/Byzantine period.[60] No. 525 has a graffito on the exterior that may be a number.

524 (28–64). Max dim .099

Part of body, combed decoration of linked scallops. Fine clay, light brown core (7.5YR 6/4), first outer bands very dark gray (7.5YR N3/), second outer bands pink (5YR 7/4), a few white and black grits. **Pl. 7–4.**

525 (110–66). Max dim .085

Body sherd with handle attachment. Two horizontal bands of combed decoration with a wavy band between. Coarse clay banded brown (7.5YR 5/4) and dark gray (5YR 4/1), some white and black grits and mineral inclusions. Graffito on exterior body may be a number: IV. **Pl. 7–4.**

Cooking Wares

This category includes cooking pots, casseroles, pans, and lids. The greatest number of sherds comes from deep vessels, only a few of which, distinguished mainly by rim profile, appear in quantity; exceptions are Forms 1, 4, and 12. Unless otherwise stated, the following features may be assumed: (1) More or less globular body with convex bottom, wide mouth, and two vertical handles. (2) The handles are coils flattened or unflattened and with or without groove(s) or ridge(s) along the sides or outer surface. (3) Ribbing occurs on at least part of the body,

including the bottom. (4) Surfaces are gritty. (5) There are frequent minute to large grits, of which especially the white ones have erupted through the surfaces. Ancient sources (the Mishnah and Talmud) indicate that these vessels were used for cooking various foods.[61]

A much smaller number of casseroles and frying pans was recovered; the most common shape was shallow and open, with beveled rim, carinated side, and two horizontal handles twisted upward.[62] A few related, but deeper, containers have a curved or angular side with a beveled rim and two horizontal handles. These casseroles continued to be made without much change in shape until well into the Arab period.[63] The many lid fragments, some with combed designs, are remnants of casserole covers.[64]

Cooking Pots

Form 1: Cooking Pot with Grooved Rim (Nos. 526–30). 200 examples, one of the most popular of the pots. The fine or coarse clay has white and black grits in varying amounts and sizes; rarely are there mineral inclusions. Groove on top of rim sometimes deep enough to offset it into two parts. Contexts indicate a date of 351–383 and after; one piece may date before 351.[65]

60. For some basins with combed decoration see Aharoni, *Ramat Rahel 1959–1960*, 4, fig. 3.10, 11, 13, dated 6th–7th c.; Aharoni, *Ramat Rahel 1961–1962*, fig. 7.13, 16; 22.22 also dated 6th–7th c.; Delougaz-Haines, 37, pl. 33.17, 18.

61. For a discussion of these sources, see Zevulun-Olenik, *Talmudic Period*, 32–33.
62. For ancient written sources see ibid., 33–35.
63. To cite a single example, one may mention Baramki, "Kh. El-Mefjer," 71, fig. 13.1–9, 11–13.
64. For specific references and comments on these lids see notes 77 and 79 below.
65. For parallels in Palestine see Loffreda, *Cafarnao* 2, Type C2, 43, 152–53, fig. 10.1–4; Loffreda, *et-Tabgha*, 131–32, fig. 49.200, fig. 50.1 The cooking pot at Gush Halav in which a coin hoard was found is of the same type (Meyers, "Gush Halav," 37, 53–54, fig. 18.

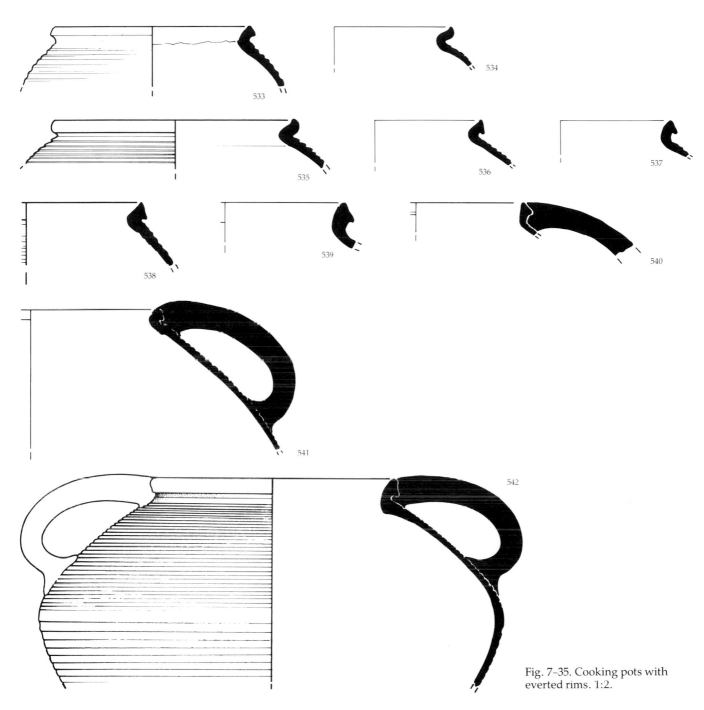

Fig. 7–35. Cooking pots with everted rims. 1:2.

526   (229–64). PH .127; D rim .087
Clay banded dark reddish gray (5YR 4/2) and red (2.5YR 4/8). **Fig. 7–34.**

527   (220–65). PH .083; D rim .125
Very dark gray (5YR 3/1) and red (2.5YR 4/8) clay. **Fig. 7–34.**

528   (9–66). PH (a) .116 (b) .058; D rim .142; Max dim (c) .093 (d) .099 (e) .074 (f) .049 (g) .071
Clay with incomplete dark gray core (2.5YR N4/), outer bands red (2.5YR 4/6). **Fig. 7–34.**

529   (387–66). PH .054; D rim .054
Red clay (2.5YR 4/6). **Fig. 7–34.**

530   (353–65). PH .086; D rim .125
Red clay (2.5YR 5/8). **Fig. 7–34.**

Form 2: Cooking Pot with Inward-Sloping Neck (No. 531). One fragment. Low rounded-off rim sharply tilted inward. Context is 351–383.

531   (902–65). PH .059; D rim .18
Two slight grooves on outside of rim, upper one narrow,

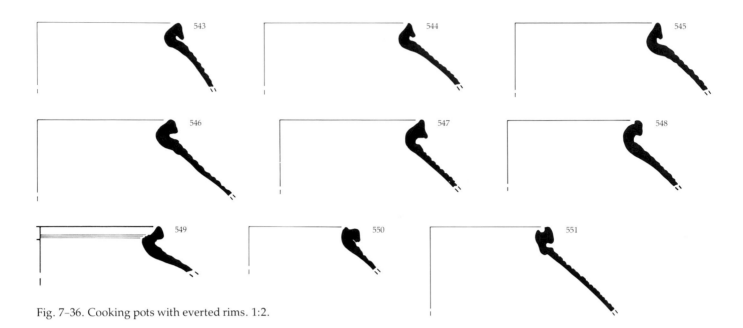

Fig. 7–36. Cooking pots with everted rims. 1:2.

lower one wide. Coarse dusky red (2.5YR 3/2) and red (2.5YR 5/6) clay, white and black grits and mineral inclusions; a few small white grits erupted through surfaces. **Fig. 7–34.**

Form 3: Cooking Pot with Vertical Rim (No. 532). One piece. The low rim sits atop a slightly flaring neck.

532   (970–65). PH .043; D rim .142
   Coarse weak red clay (2.5YR 4/2), some white grits and mineral inclusions. **Fig. 7–34.**

Form 4: Cooking Pot with Everted Rim (Nos. 533–58). 360 fragments make this pot even more common than Form 1 and illustrate the variety in the treatment of the everted rim. The group is divided into two variants on the basis of the rim: (1) upper surface plain or somewhat concave; (2) groove around upper surface. Ribbing on body sometimes smeared. The clay is usually coarse, rarely fine. White grits are common; infrequently there are black ones; both occur in varying amounts. Clay color is either banded or solid; only one has a core. Contexts indicate that such cooking pots were in use 351–383 (Period 3); they were also probably used both earlier and later.[66]

Variant 1

533   (1132–66). PH .032; D rim .108
   Clay banded dark gray (5YR 4/1) and reddish brown (5YR 4/4). **Fig. 7–35.**

534   (514–64). PH .021; D rim .126
   Clay banded very dark gray (7.5YR N3/) and dark reddish brown (5YR 3/2). **Fig. 7–35.**

535   (947–65). PH .025; D rim .132

66. For an example that seems to be of this type see Kelso, *Bethel*, 81, 109, pl. 75.6.

Clay banded dark gray (5YR 4/1), light reddish brown (5YR 6/3) and yellowish red (5YR 5/6). **Fig. 7–35.**

536   (1126–66). PH .023; D rim .116
   Clay banded dark gray (5YR 4/1) and yellowish red (5YR 5/6). **Fig. 7–35.**

537   (1117–66). PH .019; D rim .124
   Clay banded very dark gray (5YR 3/1) and dark reddish brown (5YR 3/3). **Fig. 7–35.**

538   (1124–66). PH .034; D rim .122
   Reddish brown clay (2.5YR 4/4). **Fig. 7–35.**

539   (1120–66). PH .024; D rim .136
   Clay and color as No. 538. **Fig. 7–35.**

540   (944–65). PH (including handle) .027; D rim .122
   Dark reddish gray core (5YR 4/2), outer bands yellowish red (5YR 4/8). **Fig. 7–35.**

541   (484–66). PH .079; D rim .148
   Coarse red clay (2.5YR 5/6). **Fig. 7–35.**

542   (47–66). PH .107; D rim .132
   Coarse red clay (2.5YR 4/6). **Fig. 7–35.**

543   (950–65). PH .034; D rim .154
   Clay banded weak red (2.5YR 4/2) and reddish brown (2.5YR 4/4). **Fig. 7–36.**

544   (1139–66). PH .033; D rim .16
   Clay banded reddish gray (5YR 5/2) and yellowish red (5YR 5/6). **Fig. 7–36.**

545   (1115–66). PH .035; D rim .154
   Clay banded dark gray (5YR 4/1) and red (2.5YR 4/6). **Fig. 7–36.**

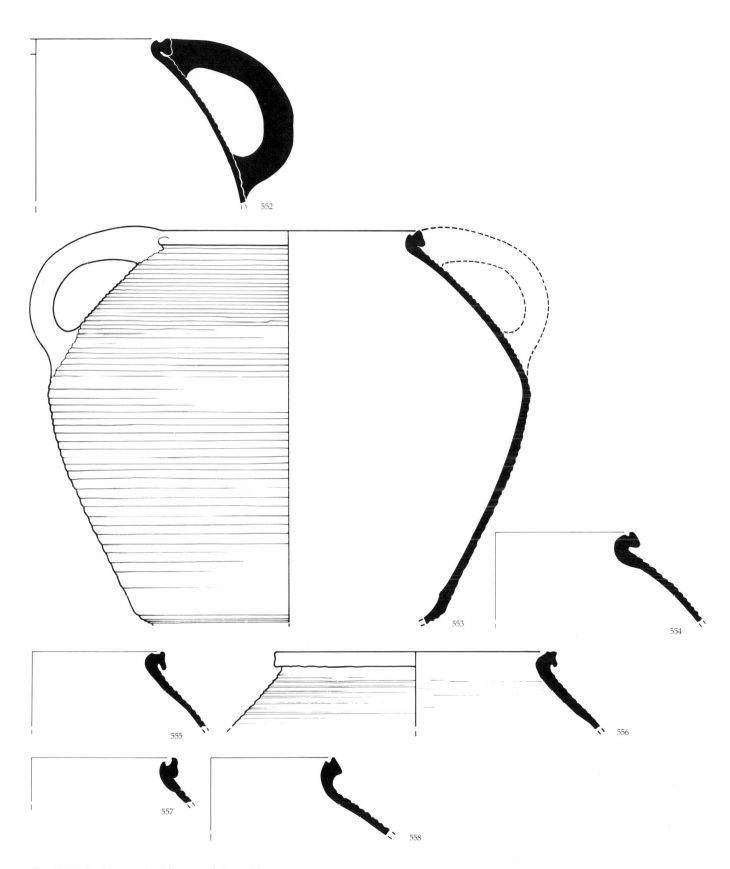

Fig. 7–37. Cooking pots with everted rims. 1:2.

546   (1134–66). PH .039; D rim .15

    Clay banded brown (7.5YR 5/4) and strong brown (7.5YR 5/6). **Fig. 7–36.**

547   (504–64). PH .035; D rim .156

    Clay and color as No. 542. **Fig. 7–36.**

Variant 2

548   (1141–66). PH .035; D rim .14

    Clay banded weak red (2.5YR 4/2) and red (2.5YR 5/6). **Fig. 7–36.**

549   (958–65). PH .024; D rim .13

    Clay banded brown (7.5YR 5/2) and weak red (2.5YR 5/2). **Fig. 7–36.**

550   (1123–66). PH .022; D rim .118

    Reddish brown clay (5YR 5/3). **Fig. 7–36.**

551   (1164–66). PH .044; D rim .13

    Clay banded dark reddish gray (10R 4/1) and red (2.5YR 4/6). **Fig. 7–36.**

552   (11–66). PH .087; D rim .174

    Clay banded very dark gray (5YR 3/1) and dark reddish brown (5YR 3/3). **Fig. 7–37.**

553   (8–66). PH .202; D rim .14

    Clay banded reddish gray (5YR 5/2) and reddish brown (2.5YR 5/4). **Fig. 7–37.**

554   (962–65). PH .047; D rim .152

    Clay and color as No. 542. **Fig. 7–37.**

555   (1121–66). PH .04; D rim .142

    Clay banded weak red (2.5YR 4/2) and red (2.5YR 4/6). **Fig. 7–37.**

556   (1133–66). PH .041; D rim .15

    Clay banded yellowish red (5YR 5/6) and red (2.5YR 4/6). **Fig. 7–37.**

557   (966–65). PH .024; D rim .154

    Clay banded weak red (2.5YR 4/2) and red (2.5YR 4/6). **Fig. 7–37.**

558   (515–64). PH .041; D rim .14

    Yellowish red clay (5YR 5/6). **Fig. 7–37.**

Form 5: Cooking Pot with Square or Rectangular Rim (Nos. 559–64). Six fragments. The rim, which may be flat, concave, or offset on the upper surface, is distinctly set off from the shoulder. Coarse clay, with white and black grits in varying amounts. Solid or banded clay. Contexts indicate a post–383 date.

559   (1137–66). PH .035; D rim .132

    Clay banded dark reddish gray (5YR 4/2) and red (2.5YR 4/6). **Fig. 7–38.**

560   (506–64). PH .054; D rim .145

    Reddish brown clay (2.5YR 4/4). **Fig. 7–38.**

561   (964–65). PH .027; D rim .134

    Clay banded reddish brown (2.5YR 5/4) and red (2.5YR 4/6). **Fig. 7–38.**

562   (1116–66). PH .037; D rim .122

    Red clay (2.5YR 4/6). **Fig. 7–38.**

563   (510–64). PH .044; D rim .118

    Reddish brown clay (5YR 5/3, 5/4). **Fig. 7–38.**

564   (503–64). PH .027; D rim .142

    Clay banded reddish brown (5YR 4/3) and yellowish red (5YR 4/6). **Fig. 7–38.**

Form 6: Cooking Pot with Outward-Folded Rim (No. 565). Three examples. Rounded, knob rim distinctly set off from ribbed shoulder. Contexts indicate a date of 351–383.

565   (954–65). PH .038; D rim .14

    Fine red clay (2.5YR 5/8), some minute to small white grits, a few black ones. **Fig. 7–38.**

Form 7: Cooking Pot with Two-Pronged Rim (No. 566). Three fragments. More or less square rim sharply divided on the exterior into two prongs. Another fragment (uninventoried) bears remains of a white slip. Contexts suggest a date after 383.[67]

566   (505–64). PH .039

    Coarse reddish brown clay (2.5YR 5/4), some white grits. **Fig. 7–38.**

Form 8: Cooking Pot with Heavy Outward-Folded Rim (Nos. 567–68). Two examples. Rim distinctly set off from ribbed shoulder.

567   (517–64). PH .037; D rim .15

    Fine clay, reddish yellow core (5YR 7/6), outer bands light red (2.5YR 6/8), many minute to large white grits. **Fig. 7–38.**

568   (922–65). PH .035; D rim .15

    Fine light red clay (2.5YR 6/8), some white and red grits; traces of pink slip. **Fig. 7–38.**

Form 9: Cooking Pot with Outward-Folded Grooved Rim (Nos. 569–73). 21 fragments somewhat similar in rim treatment to Variant 2 of Form 4. Most are fired harder and the surfaces are less gritty. Contexts suggest they were probably in use in Period 3 (351–383), and possibly later.

569   (1105–66). PH .02; D rim .15

    Coarse red clay (2.5YR 5/6), some white grits. **Fig. 7–38.**

570   (495–64). PH .035; D rim .132

    Fine clay banded reddish yellow (5YR 6/6) and yellowish red (5YR 5/6), some white and black grits. **Fig. 7–38.**

571   (366–64). PH .083; D rim .145

---

67. A pot with similar rim, but differing in resting point of rim and angle of shoulder, was found at Khirbat al-Karak (Delougaz-Haines, 32–33, pl. 53.37).

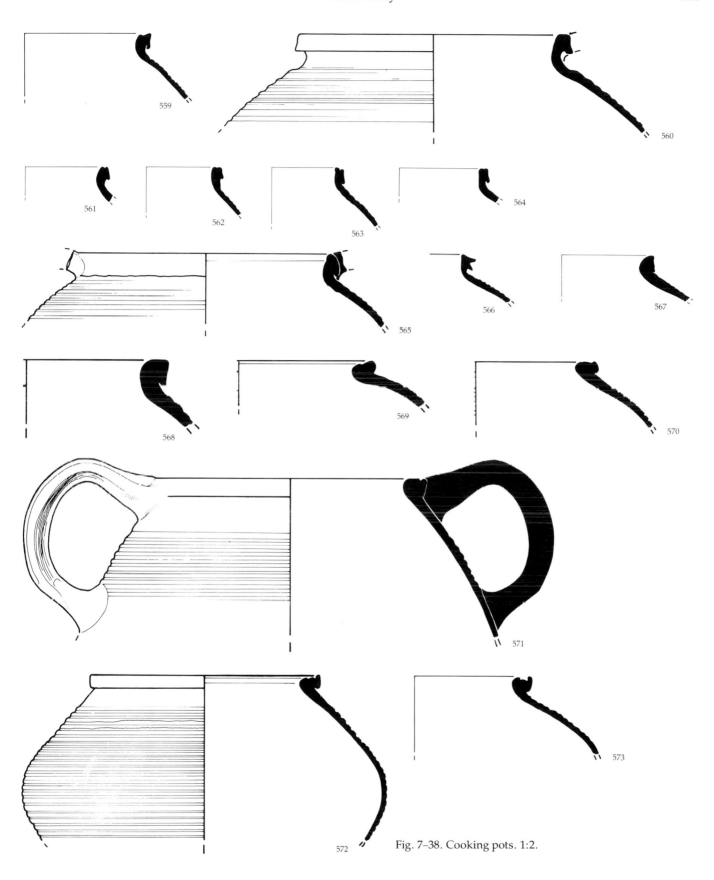

Fig. 7–38. Cooking pots. 1:2.

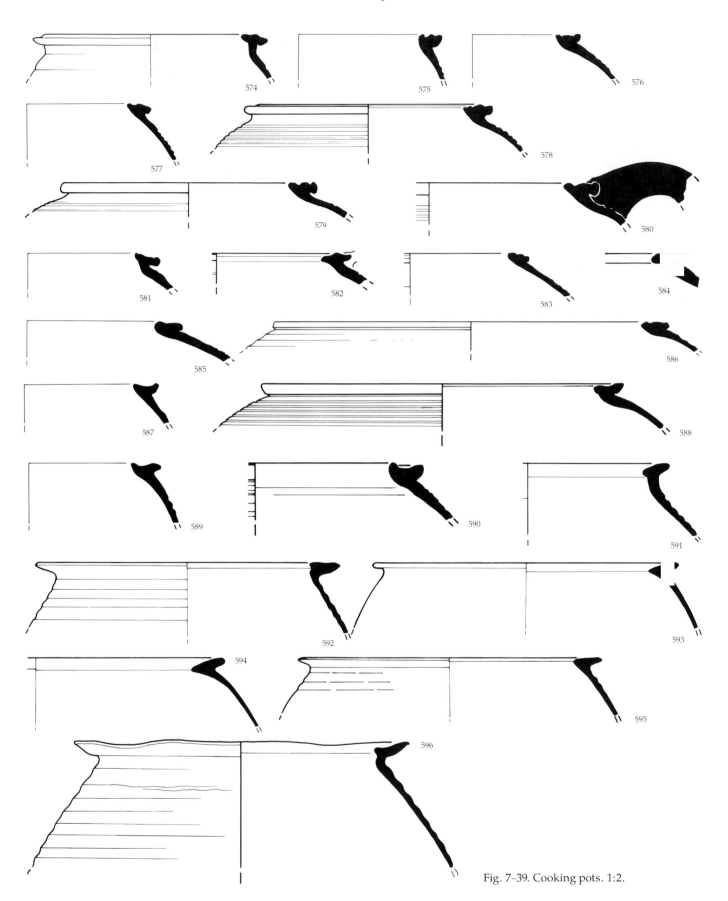

Fig. 7–39. Cooking pots. 1:2.

Fine clay banded dark gray (5YR 4/1) and reddish brown (5YR 4/4), a few white and black grits. **Fig. 7–38.**

572 (228–64). PH .088; D rim .122

Fine reddish gray clay (5YR 5/2), some white and black grits. **Fig. 7–38.**

573 (952–65). PH .04; D rim .124

Fine reddish brown clay (2.5YR 5/4), some minute to small white and black grits. **Fig. 7–38.**

Form 10: Cooking Pot with Wide Rim (Nos. 574–90). 29 examples. Divided into two variants on the basis of the rim: (1) one to three grooves on top; (2) concave on top. Variant 1 is more common. The clay is about evenly divided between fine and coarse; the white and black grits range from minute to large and occur in varying amounts.

Variant 1

574 (943–65). PH .023; D rim .124

Reddish brown clay (2.5YR 4/4). **Fig. 7–39.**

575 (500–65). PH .024; D rim .152

Reddish brown core (2.5YR 4/4), outer bands dark reddish brown (5YR 3/2). **Fig. 7–39.**

576 (940–65). PH .024; D rim .114

Reddish brown clay (5YR 5/4). **Fig. 7–39.**

577 (931–65). PH .03; Est D rim .132

Clay banded very dark gray (2.5YR N3/) and reddish brown (5YR 4/3). **Fig. 7–39.**

578 (938–65). PH .025; D rim .13

Brown clay (7.5YR 5/4). **Fig. 7–39.**

579 (1110–66). PH .018; D rim .136

Clay banded very dark gray (5YR 3/1) and reddish brown (5YR 4/3). **Fig. 7–39.**

580 (808–66). PH .022; D rim .18

Clay banded reddish brown (5YR 4/4) and dark gray (5YR 4/1). **Fig. 7–39.**

581 (930–65). PH .018; D rim .14

Dark red clay (2.5YR 3/6). **Fig. 7–39.**

582 (936–65). PH .016; D rim .142

Red clay (2.5YR 4/6). **Fig. 7–39.**

583 (1111–66). PH .023; D rim .126

Reddish yellow clay (5YR 6/8). **Fig. 7–39.**

584 (1100–66). PH .025

Brown core (7.5YR 5/2), outer bands dark gray (5YR 4/1). **Fig. 7–39.**

585 (942–65). PH .021; D rim .166

Clay banded reddish brown (2.5YR 4/4; 5YR 5/4). **Fig. 7–39.**

586 (934–65). PH .165; D rim .21

Clay banded red (2.5YR 5/8) and very dark gray (5YR 3/1). **Fig. 7–39.**

Variant 2

587 (1107–66). PH .021; D rim .142

Clay and color as No. 581. **Fig. 7–39.**

588 (935–65). PH .026; D rim .19

Reddish brown clay (5YR 5/4). **Fig. 7–39.**

589 (1108–66). PH .031; D rim .14

Clay and color as No. 588. **Fig. 7–39.**

590 (1112–66). PH .031; D rim .175

Reddish brown clay (2.5YR 4/4). **Fig. 7–39.**

Form 11: Cooking Pot with Wide Everted Rim (Nos. 591–98). 15 pieces. Rim is occasionally everted to horizontal; in one case it rests on the shoulder. There may be ribbing on the shoulder. These vessels resemble Form 10, but the rim is generally flat on top. Coarse clay, minute to small white and black grits in varying amounts. Contexts suggest a date in Period 3 and possibly earlier.[68]

591 (923–65). PH .038; D rim .15

Red clay (5YR 5/8). **Fig. 7–39.**

592 (1097–66). PH .039; D rim .16

Red clay (2.5YR 5/6). **Fig. 7–39.**

593 (924–65). PH .035; D rim .16

Clay and color as No. 592. **Fig. 7–39.**

594 (969–65). PH .037; D rim .20

Clay and color as No. 592. **Fig. 7–39.**

595 (1095–66). PH .032; D rim .16

Clay banded dark gray (5YR 4/1) and dark reddish gray (5YR 4/2). **Fig. 7–39.**

596 (619–65). PH (a) .068 (b) .03; D rim .177

Clay and color as No. 592. **Fig. 7–39.**

597 (1098–66). PH with handle .045; D rim .21

Clay and color as No. 592. **Fig. 7–40.**

598 (933–65). PH .022; D rim .15

Clay and color as No. 592. **Fig. 7–40.**

Form 12: Cooking Pot with Spherical Body (Nos. 599–604). 84 fragments with rim. Though two variants have been proposed,[69] on the pieces sufficiently well preserved from our site the grooves are not necessarily continuous around the rim; thus, the catalogued examples are presented as a single group. The angle of the low neck is vertical, occasionally tilting outward slightly. In contrast to most of the Jalame cooking pots, the fabric is hard, the surfaces

68. For parallels see Delougaz-Haines, 32–33, pl. 53.39; Loffreda, *Cafarnao* 2, Type C4, 46, 154, fig. 10.7–9; Meyers, *Khirbet Shema*, 217–18, pl. 7.18.26–29; Ben-Tor, "Horvat Usa," 2, fig. 11.4, 6 (noted as characteristic of 5th and 6th c.).

69. For the division into two groups see Meyers, *Khirbet Shema*, 193–96.

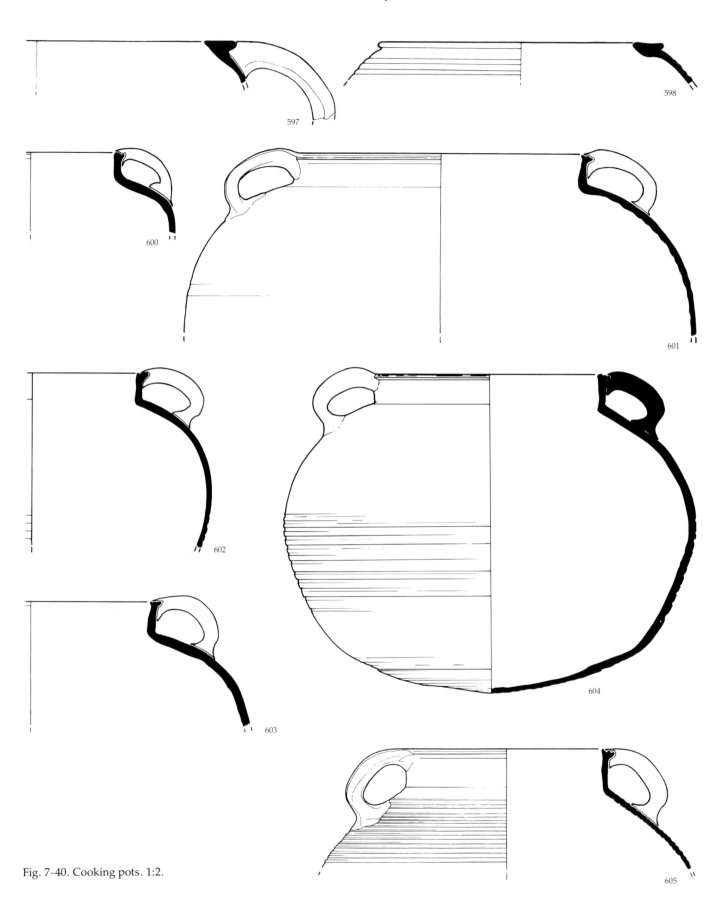

Fig. 7–40. Cooking pots. 1:2.

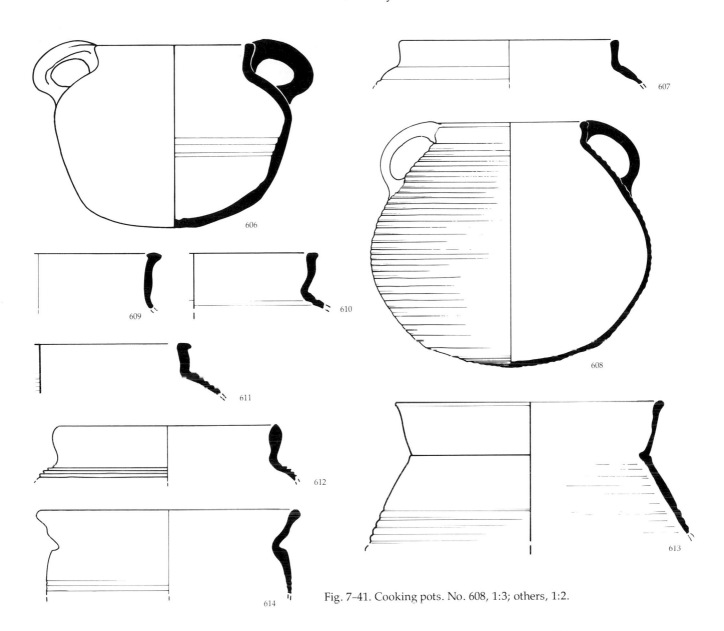

Fig. 7–41. Cooking pots. No. 608, 1:3; others, 1:2.

smooth, and grits infrequently pit the surfaces. Body lightly ribbed except for shoulder. No. 603 is unusual because the exterior was fired very dark gray. These pots come from contexts dating before 351.[70]

599 (242–64). PH .125; D rim .105

Fine red clay (2.5YR 5/6), some minute to large white and black grits.

600 (180–66). PH .043; D rim .10

Fine red clay (2.5YR 5/8), some minute to small white and black grits. **Fig. 7–40.**

601 (230–66). PH .095; D rim .155

Fine red clay (2.5YR 5/8), some minute to large white and black grits, occasional mineral inclusions. **Fig. 7–40.**

70. For parallels see Meyers, *Khirbet Shema*, 193–94, pl. 7.13.11–18, 7.13.19–26, 7.14.1–21, 7.15.7, 7.16.15, and bibliography cited.

602 (152–66). PH .091; D rim .124

Fine red clay (2.5YR 5/8), a few minute to small white and black grits. **Fig. 7–40.**

603 (191–66). PH .066; D rim .135; Max dim (b) .039

Fine red clay (2.5YR 5/6), some minute to small white and black grits; exterior very dark gray (2.5YR N3/). **Fig. 7–40.**

604 (30–66). H .169; D rim .125–.132, bottom .08

Fine red clay (2.5YR 5/6), occasional black and white grits. Ribbing on mid-body and bottom. From Cistern IV (See Chap. 2, Outlying Structures). **Fig. 7 40; Pl. 7 4.**

Form 13: Cooking Pot with Grooved Rim (No. 605). Five pieces. Two grooves on top of rim. Shape similar to Form 12, but the fabric is softer and the shoulder has a lower, gentler slope covered with ribbing. Grooves on inside of shoulder. An uninventoried fragment has banded weak red and dark reddish gray clay with surfaces fired dark reddish gray. No good context exists for this form; it is, however, associated with pottery dated 351–383 (Period 3) and after.[71]

605   (179–66). PH .065; D rim .11

Fine red clay (2.5YR 5/6), some minute to small white and black grits. **Fig. 7–40.**

Form 14: Cooking Pot with Angular Spherical Body (No. 606). One example. Small hard-fired pot, no ribbing. Context is Period 3 or later.

606   (92–65). H .097; D rim .085, bottom .06

Fine red clay (2.5YR 5/8), some minute to small white and black grits. **Fig. 7–41.**

Form 15: Cooking Pot with Vertical Rim (No. 607). One sherd. The low neck ends in a slightly thickened, rounded-off rim. It is associated with pottery of Period 3 and later.

607   (167–66). PH .024; D rim .117

Coarse clay banded dark reddish gray (10R 4/1) and red (2.5YR 5/6), some minute to small white and black grits. **Fig. 7–41.**

Form 16: Cooking Pot with Angular Everted Rim (No. 608). Three fragments. Globular pot, angular rim, ribbing on upper two-thirds of body. Associated with pottery of Period 3 and later.

608   (113–65). H .194; D rim .12, bottom .14

Coarse reddish brown clay (2.5YR 4/4), some minute to small white and black grits. **Fig. 7–41.**

Form 17: Cooking Pot with Rim Undercut on Interior (No. 609). One example. Low neck ends in knob-like rim convex on the top. Context indicates date before 351.

609   (160–66). PH .023; D rim .13

Fine red clay (2.5YR 5/8), a few white grits. **Fig. 7–41.**

Form 18: Cooking Pot with Rim Concave on Interior (No. 610). One fragment. Low neck bows outward sharply to a convex exterior and concave interior. Context suggests a date before 351.

610   (408–66). PH .03; D rim .132

Coarse light red clay (2.5YR 6/6), some minute to small white and black grits. **Fig. 7–41.**

Form 19: Cooking Pot with Low Rectangular Rim (No. 611). One piece. Low neck convex on exterior; shoulder ribbed on exterior.

611   (820–66). PH .029; D rim .16

Coarse clay banded red (2.5YR 5/8) and gray (2.5YR N5/), a few minute to small white and black grits. **Fig. 7–41.**

Form 20: Cooking Pot with Heavy Rim (No. 612). One fragment. Rim oval in vertical section. Sharp hatched ribbing covers shoulder.

612   (162–65). PH .03; D rim .12

Coarse dark reddish brown clay (2.5YR 3/4), some minute to small white and black grits. **Fig. 7–41.**

Form 21: Cooking Pot with Tall Flaring Rim (Nos. 613–15). Three fragments. All are similar in form; No. 613 is particularly hard-fired, with a sharp projection at the inside bottom of the rim, probably to hold a lid. No closer date than Late Roman can be given; No. 614 comes from a pre–351 context; No. 615 is from a 351–383 context. Vessels of the same general shape are known.[72]

613   (189–66). PH .071; D rim .145

Fine clay, light red core (2.5YR 6/6), outer bands light reddish brown (5YR 6/6), some minute to small white and black grits. **Fig. 7–41.**

614   (168–66). PH .045; Est D rim (warped) .14

Fine clay banded light red (2.5YR 6/6) and black (2.5YR N2.5/), some minute to large white and black grits. **Fig. 7–41.**

615   (607–65). PH .066; D rim .115

Fine red clay (2.5YR 5/6), some minute to small white and black grits. **Fig. 7–42.**

Form 22: Cooking Pot with Broad Rim (Nos. 616–18). Four fragments. Fine hard-fired clay. No ribbing on shoulder. Contexts indicate a date of before 351.

616   (231–66). PH (a) .038 (b) .026; D rim .155

Clay banded dark gray (5YR 4/1) and red (2.5YR 5/8), some minute to small white grits. **Fig. 7–42.**

617   (154–66). PH .053; D rim .155

Red clay (2.5YR 5/8), a few minute to small white grits. **Fig. 7–42.**

618   (60–66). PH .062; D rim .19

Reddish brown clay (2.5YR 5/4), some minute to small white and black grits. **Fig. 7–42.**

Form 23: Cooking Pot with Ribbed Neck (No. 619). One piece. Pronounced ribbing on inside and outside of neck and shoulder. A possible parallel is reported from Khirbet Shema.[73]

619   (789–66). PH .057; D rim .083

Fine clay banded yellowish brown (10YR 5/4) and yellowish red (5YR 4/6), a few white and black grits. **Fig. 7–42.**

---

71. Similar in profile but not described is a piece from Horvat Usa (Ben-Tor, "Horvat Usa," 2, fig. 11.2, noted as "characteristic of the 5th and 6th c. C. E.").

72. See Type 2.3 from Khirbet Shema, with a date range of 3rd–5th c. Meyers, *Khirbet Shema*, 198–200, pl. 7.15, nos. 6, 8, esp. 9, and perhaps 18; Riley, "Caesarea Hippodrome," 38, 41, no. 56; R. J. Bull and E. F. Campbell, Jr., "The Sixth Campaign at Balatâh (Shechem)," *BASOR* 190 (1968) fig. 11.1–7 dated 2nd half of 3rd and 1st half of 4th c.

73. Meyers, *Khirbet Shema*, 219, pl. 7.19:12.

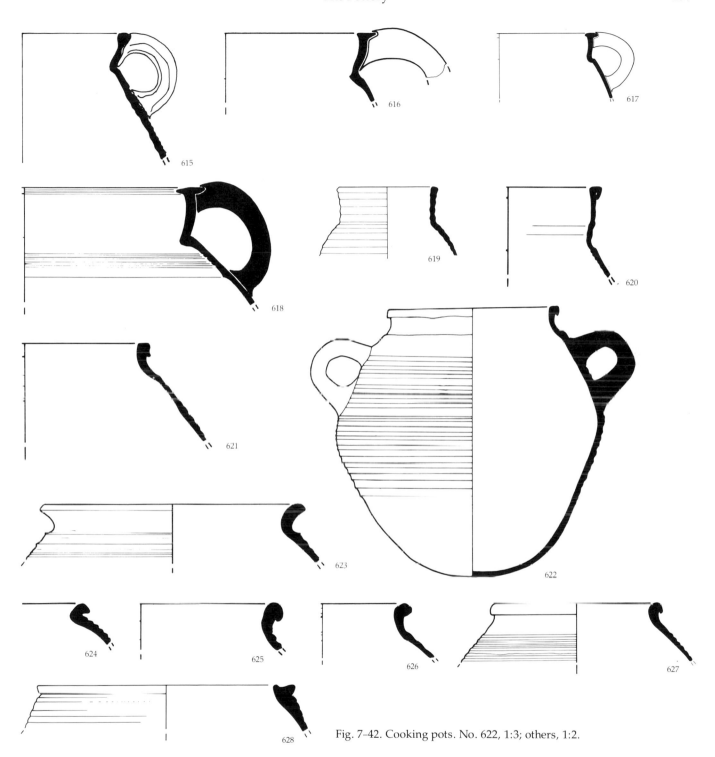

Fig. 7–42. Cooking pots. No. 622, 1:3; others, 1:2.

Form 24: Cooking Pot with Downward-Folded Rim (No. 620). One fragment of fine hard-fired clay. Sharp transition from low neck to shoulder. Context suggests a date before 351.

620 (1025–66). PH .049; D rim .095

Yellowish red clay (5YR 4/8), some minute to small white and black grits. **Fig. 7–42.**

Form 25: Cooking Pot with Slightly Carinated Shoulder (No. 621). One piece. Hard fabric, exterior fired gray. Rim square in section and concave along outer surface. Ribbing covers shoulder on exterior.

621 (243–64). PH .054; D rim .132

Fine light red clay (2.5YR 6/8), some minute to small

white and black grits; exterior dark gray (2.5YR N4/).
Fig. 7–42.

Form 26: Cooking Pot with Outward-Folded Rim (No. 622).
The one example of this globular cooking pot shows a
sharp transition from low neck to shoulder. Ribbing on
lower half of body only.

622   (104–64). H .21; D rim .133, bottom .06

Red to reddish brown clay, many white and black grits.
Fig. 7–42; Pl. 7–4.

Form 27: Cooking Pot with Outward-Rolled Rim (Nos. 623–27).
Five sherds held together loosely by the outward-rolled
rim. Exterior shoulder ribbed. Coarse clay, black and white
grits in varying amounts and sizes. No. 625 bears traces of
slip.

623   (217–64). PH .031; D rim .14

Clay banded light red (2.5YR 6/6) and dark gray (2.5YR
N4/). **Fig. 7–42.**

624   (955–65). PH .021

Red clay (2.5YR 5/8). **Fig. 7–42.**

625   (1119–66). PH .025; D rim .15

Light red clay (2.5YR 6/8); traces of pink slip (5YR 8/3).
Fig. 7–42.

626   (216–64). PH .03; D rim .095

Red clay (2.5YR 5/6). **Fig. 7–42.**

627   (957–65). PH .048; D rim .14

Yellowish red clay (5YR 4/6). **Fig. 7–42.**

Form 28: Cooking Pot with Wide Outward-Folded Rim (No.
628). One example. The wide heavy rim, concave on its
top, was folded outward until it came to rest on the shoulder without any separation between the two.

628   (929–65). PH .027; D rim .138

Coarse red clay (2.5YR 5/6), some minute to small white
grits. **Fig. 7–42.**

Form 29: Cooking Pot with Rounded Square Rim (No. 629).
One fragment. Rim has a groove around its top and is
heavy in proportion to the thin ribbed shoulder. Context
suggests a date before 351.

629   (1125–66). PH .03; D rim .13

Coarse brown clay (7.5YR 5/2); a few white grits; exterior
fired very dark gray (2.5YR N3/).

Casseroles and Pans

*Form 1: Casserole with Carinated Side and Twisted Horizontal
Handles* (Nos. 630–634). 610 fragments found, making
this the most popular casserole at the site. The characteristic carination of the side may be sharp or smooth and
set high or low on the body wall; a high point of carination is more common. The two handles set at the level of
the rim usually rise above it. Typically they have been
twisted and pulled upward. The method of attachment
that produced the twisted effect is as follows: One end of

a coil was attached to the body, then twisted and pulled
upward before the second end was attached. The groove
along the upper surface was made afterward. The clay is
coarse and may be solid, banded, or have a core. Black
and white grits occur in varying amounts and sizes. It is
on the beveled rim of these vessels and those of Form 2
that the decorated and undecorated lids discussed below
fitted. Contexts indicate these vessels were in use during
the period of the glass factory (Period 3) and probably
both before and after. Parallels are numerous.[74]

630   (37–66). PH (a) .077 (b) .051; D rim .271

Clay has a red core (2.5YR 4/6), outer bands reddish
brown (2.5YR 4/4). **Fig. 7–43.**

631   (235–64). PH .052; D rim .282

Clay banded reddish brown (2.5YR 5/4), weak red
(2.5YR 4/2), and red (2.5YR 4/6). **Fig. 7–43.**

632   (232–64). PH (a) .076 (b) .055; Est D rim .18–.22

Clay banded dark reddish gray (5YR 4/2) and dark reddish brown (5YR 3/2). **Fig. 7–43.**

633   (46–64). H .094; D rim .283, bottom .13

Red clay (2.5YR 5/6). **Fig. 7–43.**

634   (205–64). PH (a) .042 (b) .036 (c) .034 (d) .042; D rim
.254

Reddish brown clay. **Fig. 7–43.**

Form 2: Deep Casserole with Curving Side (No. 635). Two
examples. Inward-beveled rim. Two twisted horizontal
handles on body just below rim. Ribbing on lowest part of
body. Contexts do not allow close dating; parallels from
other sites indicate Late Roman period.[75]

635   (18–65). PH .146; D rim .20

Coarse clay banded reddish brown (5YR 5/4) and very
dark gray (5YR 3/1), many white grits, a few mineral inclusions. **Fig. 7–43.**

Form 3: Deep Casserole with Angular Side (No. 636). One
example. The shape, though more angular, is similar to
Form 2. Probably there were two horizontal handles. Rim
beveled for a lid. From the kitchen area, for which a date
after 383 is suggested (see Chap. 2). Parallels are known.[76]

74. Delougaz-Haines, 33, pl. 33.3, pl. 53.25, 28, pl. 54.10, 11; Bagatti,
Nazareth, 287, fig. 226.7, 10; Baly, *Nessana* 1, Shape 75, pl. 52.A2, A2a, A3,
A6; Loffreda, *Cafarnao* 2, Type C6, 48, fig. 11.7–10; Kelso, *Bethel*, 81, 109,
pl. 75.5, 7, 8; Avigad, "Beth Shearim, 1954," 209, fig. 3.14 dated 3rd c. and
1st half of 4th; V. Tzaferis, "A Tower and Fortress near Jerusalem," *IEJ* 24,
no. 2 (1974) 93, fig. 4.13 noted as characteristic of the 5th–6th c. See also
Zevulun-Olenik, *Talmudic Period*, 33–35, 64, nos. 159, 160. For their continuation into the Arab period see S. Ben-Arieh, "Survey between Raphia
and the Brook of Egypt, B. The Finds," *Atiqot* 7 (1974) 84, fig. 1.19.
75. See Bagatti, *Nazareth*, 287, fig. 226.8, 8a, 11, 11a; Baly, *Nessana* 1, pl.
52, Shape 74.B1; Delougaz-Haines, 33, pl. 33.4, 7; Aharoni, *Ramat Rahel
1961–1962*, fig. 8.3, 4, 5, 7, dated 6th–7th c.
76. FitzGerald, *Beth Shan* 3, 37, pl. 31.12; Aharoni, *Ramat Rahel
1959–1960*, 2–4, fig. 3.19, fig. 17.14; Baly, *Nessana* 1, pl. 52, Shape 74.B16;
Loffreda, *Cafarnao* 2, 48, Type C7, fig. 11.11–12; Prausnitz, *Shavei Zion*,
43–44, fig. 15.9; Saller, *Bethany*, 246, no. 3338, fig. 48, pl. 119.11, no. 4003,
fig. 48, pl. 119.14, and Zevulun-Olenik, *Talmudic Period*, 33–35, 64–65, nos.
161, 162. For their continuation into the Arab period see Kelso-Baramki,
Jericho and en-Nitla, 35, 36, pl. 28.N169, for which a date of 8th to early 9th
c. is given.

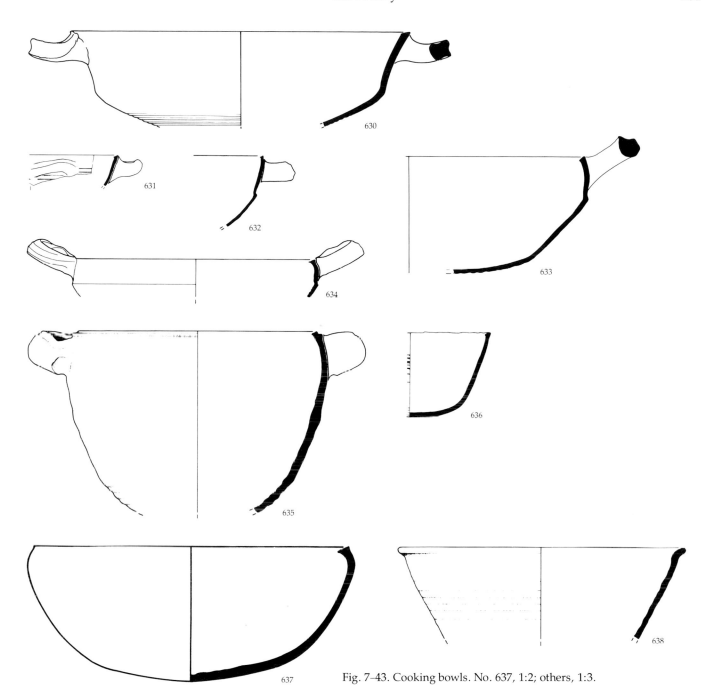

Fig. 7–43. Cooking bowls. No. 637, 1:2; others, 1:3.

636   (81–64). H .135; D rim .26, bottom .19

Coarse clay banded reddish brown (5YR 4/4) and very dark gray (5YR 3/1), many white and black grits and mineral inclusions. Low, widely spaced and interrupted ribbing on exterior. **Fig. 7–43; Pl. 7–4.**

Form 4: Small Pan with Inward-Beveled Rim (No. 637). One piece (no handles). Top of body curves inward to beveled rim. Faint random ribbing on the body.

637   (117–65). H .07; D rim .165

Coarse reddish brown clay, some white grits and mineral inclusions. **Fig. 7–43.**

Form 5: Cooking Pan with Outward-Rolled Rim (No. 638). Two fragments. Tall outward-rolled rim. Ribbing on interior and exterior. No handles preserved. Context gives a date after 383.

638   (313–65). PH .073; D rim .228

Coarse clay, very dark gray core (7.5YR N3/), outer bands reddish brown (5YR 4/3), some white grits and mineral inclusions. **Fig. 7–43.**

Lids (Nos. 639–57)

520 sherds. Typical is the low convex shape with beveled rim and knob handle. The knob may be solid, pierced with

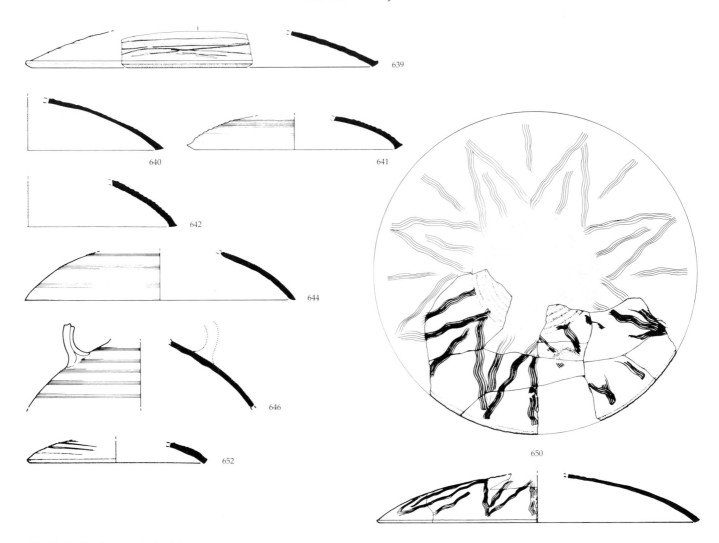

Fig. 7–44. Cooking pot lids. 1:3.

a small hole (for the escape of steam), or be a knob-shaped cylinder largely open at the top. When the knob itself has no hole it may be supposed that a hole was punched into the body. Unusual is No. 646, whose high-arching form is equipped with an open strap handle.

The fragmentary Jalame examples show that the outer surface may be plain (No. 639), ribbed completely or partially (Nos. 640–43), or have combed decoration (Nos. 644–51) made by dragging a comb-like tool across the surface. That the patterns could be quite elaborate is demonstrated by No. 650, on which is a large star composed of wavy lines with similar wavy ones between the points. A small sherd (No. 652) shows a number of deeply incised lines; too little remains for speculation on the overall decoration. None of the sherds has painted decoration, although such is known on covers for deep casseroles such as Forms 2 and 3.[77] Only No. 646 bears traces of a slip.

The clay itself is either fine or coarse. White and black grits and mineral inclusions appear in varying amounts and sizes. Frequently white grits have erupted through the surfaces.

The lids were a common item of household equipment and contexts indicate that they were in use before, during, and after the time of the glass factory, that is, from before 351 to after 383.[78] Parallels are numerous in Palestine.[79]

639   (225–64). PH .031; D rim .283

Fine brown clay (7.5YR 5/4). No decoration or ribbing.
Fig. 7–44.

77. Zevulun-Olenik, *Talmudic Period*, 33–35, 66, 67, nos. 166, 167.

78. See Chap. 1, Chronology and Stratigraphy.
79. Corbo, *Kh. Siyar el-Ghanam*, 74, fig. 24.1, 2; Delougaz-Haines, 32–33, pl. 43.33–36, pl. 54.16–17; FitzGerald, *Beth Shan 3*, pl. 30.13, 31.12; Loffreda, *Cafarnao* 2, 51, 159, fig. 11.13, fig. 33.13, photo 10.1–6; Loffreda, *et-Tabgha*, 133, fig. 49.202, fig. 50.2; Loffreda, *Sinagoga*, 112, fig. 12.4; Meyers, *Khirbet Shema*, 204–5, pl. 7.17:1–14; Saller, *Bethany*, 277, fig. 48.3996; Sellers-Baramki, 26–29, fig. 9, fig. 30.16; Aharoni, *Ramat Rahel 1961–1962*, fig. 8.2, dated 6th–7th c.; Tzaferis, "Tower and Fortress" (see n. 74 above), 91, fig. 3.10, called typical of the early Roman period; and L. Y. Rahmani, "Mirror Plaques," 54, fig. 2.8.

That lids accompanied the casseroles into the Arab period may be seen in J. A. Sauer, *Hesbon Pottery 1971*, Andrews University Monographs 7 (Berrien Springs, Mich., 1973) fig. 2.51, 52 (Late Roman), fig. 2.91, 92 (Byzantine), and fig. 3.109 (Umayyad); and Kelso-Baramki, *Khirbet en-Nitla*, 35, 36, no. 138, Type 25, pl. 28, N8, N169.

For general comments and a special technique of manufacturing such lids together with the deep casseroles see Zevulun-Olenik, *Talmudic Period*, 33–35, 64–65, nos. 161, 162.

640 (33–66). PH .043; D rim .22

Clay banded weak red (2.5YR 4/2) and red (2.5YR 4/6). Low ribbing over most of body. **Fig. 7–44.**

641 (103–65). PH .028; D rim .172

Red clay (2.5YR 4/6). Ribbing on outer half of body. **Fig. 7–44.**

642 (12–66). PH .038; D rim .24

Clay banded brown (7.5YR 5/4) and red (2.5YR 5/6). Ribbing on all of body as preserved. **Fig. 7–44.**

643 (267–66). PH .034; D rim .18

Black clay (2.5YR N2.5/). Low, widely spaced ribbing on all of body as preserved.

644 (236–66). PH .039; D rim .218

Clay has a reddish brown core (5YR 5/4), outer bands reddish gray (5YR 5/2). Three sets of concentric grooves on body. **Fig. 7–44.**

645 (269–65). Max dim .093

Reddish brown clay (2.5YR 5/4). Two sets of concentric grooves on body; low, widely spaced ribbing near center. **Pl. 7–5.**

646 (154–65). PH with handle .068; Max dim .18

Part of body and open strap handle. Red clay (2.5YR 4/6); pink slip (7.5YR 8/4) on exterior. Five sets of concentric grooves on body. **Fig. 7–44.**

647 (25–64). PH .041; D rim .25

Yellowish red clay (5YR 4/8). Wavy lines enclosed by and interrupting innermost two of three concentric grooves. **Pl. 7–5.**

648 (104–65). PH .036; D rim .12

Clay banded dark grayish brown (10YR 4/2) and reddish brown (2.5YR 4/4). Alternating concentric grooves and wavy lines on body.

649 (63–66). PH .03; D rim .27

Reddish brown clay (5YR 5/3). Combed decoration of two sets of concentric grooves enclosing and interrupted by zigzag lines. **Pl. 7–5.**

650 (29–66). PH .034; D rim .256

Yellowish red clay (5YR 4/6). Wavy lines forming a star with wavy lines between the points. Low, widely spaced ribbing at center of body. **Fig. 7–44.**

651 (22–66). PH .038; D rim .25

Reddish yellow clay (5YR 6/6). Combed decoration of two kinds of wavy lines. **l. 7–5.**

652 (301–65). PH .018; D rim .145

Clay banded light brown (7.5YR 6/4) and red (2.5YR 5/6). Four deeply incised lines on body. **Fig. 7–44.**

653 (238–66). PH .022; D handle .022

Part of body and knob handle. Dark gray core (2.5YR N4/), outer bands red (2.5YR 4/8). Hatched ribbing on body. **Pl. 7–5.**

654 (261–66). PH .02; D handle .013

Part of body and pierced knob handle. Clay banded reddish brown (2.5YR 5/4) and red (2.5YR 5/6). Wide rounded ribbing on body.

655 (198–64). PH .02; D handle .0135

Part of open knob handle and body. Yellowish red clay (5YR 5/6). Handle set off from body by shallow depression. **Pl. 7–5.**

656 (114–65). PH .011; D handle .022

Part of open knob handle and beginning of body. Clay banded dark reddish brown (5YR 3/2) and very dark gray (5YR 3/1). **Pl. 7–5.**

657 (266–66). Max dim .09

Part of body and open knob handle. Clay banded red (2.5YR 4/6), light reddish brown (5YR 6/4), and dark gray (5YR 4/1). Rounded, widely spaced ribbing around outer body, body offset at midpoint; shallow depression separates handle from body.

Late Roman Jugs

Although a large number of fragments were found, no types appeared in quantity.

Jug with Rounded-Off Rim (Nos. 658–63). One example of each. Contexts suggest a date before 351 for Form 1, Form 2 is possibly pre-351, while Form 5 may be placed in Period 3 (351–383). The only date for Forms 3 and 4 is Late Roman.

Form 1

658 (388–66). PH .063; D rim .044

Fine clay banded dusky red (2.5YR 3/2) and red (2.5YR 4/6), many minute to large white grits some of which have erupted through surfaces. Hard fabric. **Fig. 7–45.**

659 (233–64). PH .065; D rim .032

Fine clay banded weak red (2.5YR 4/2) and reddish brown (2.5YR 5/4), some white and black grits. Hard fabric. **Fig. 7–45.**

Form 2

660 (257–65). PH .076; D rim .085

Coarse clay, dark gray core (2.5YR N4/), outer bands reddish brown (2.5YR 5/4), some white and black grits and mineral inclusions.

Form 3

661 (284–64). PH .048; D rim .05

Fine light red clay (2.5YR 6/6), some white and black grits. **Fig. 7–45.**

Form 4

662 (268–64). PH .055; D rim .036

Fine reddish yellow clay (5YR 6/6), some black grits, a few white ones. **Fig. 7–45.**

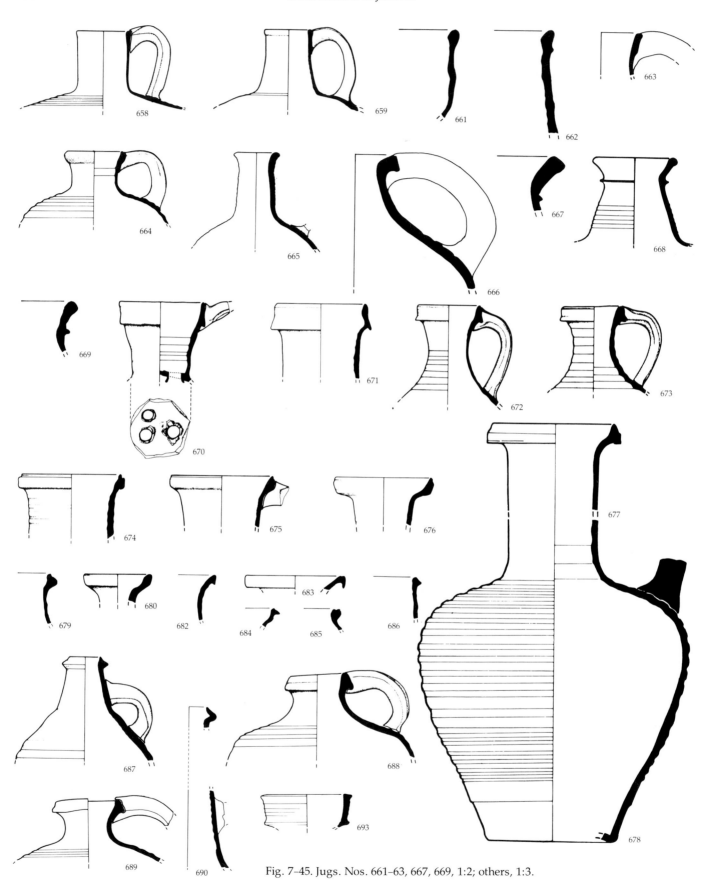

Fig. 7–45. Jugs. Nos. 661–63, 667, 669, 1:2; others, 1:3.

Form 5

663   (1022–66). PH .024; D rim .048

Fine light reddish brown clay (5YR 6/4), a few white and black grits. **Fig. 7–45.**

Jug with Outward-Flaring Rim (Nos. 664–69). One fragment each of Forms 1–3. Contexts suggest a date of probably pre–351 for Form 1 and possibly pre–351 into Period 3 (351–383) for Form 4, post–383 for Form 2, and only Late Roman for Form 3. Parallels are known for Form 4.[80]

Form 1

664   (155–66). PH .059; D rim .045

Fine clay banded dark gray (2.5YR N4/) and red (2.5YR 5/6), some white grits, a few erupted through surfaces. Surfaces gritty. **Fig. 7–45.**

Form 2

665   (150–66). PH .076; D rim .037

Fine yellowish red clay (5YR 4/8), many white grits, a few black ones. Surfaces gritty. **Fig. 7–45.**

Form 3

666   (747–65). PH .071; D rim .06

Coarse light red clay (2.5YR 6/6), many white grits, some erupted through surfaces, few black grits and mineral inclusions. **Fig. 7–45.**

Form 4

667   (142–66). PH .03; D rim .06

Fine red clay (2.5YR 5/6), some white and black grits, a few white ones erupted through surfaces. **Fig. 7–45.**

668   (31–66). PH .07; D rim .067

Fine clay variegated reddish brown (5YR 5/3) and red (2.5YR 5/6), some white and black grits, a few erupted through surfaces. **Fig. 7–45.**

669   (597–66). PH .027; D rim .06

Fine clay, dark gray core (2.5YR N4/), outer bands light red (2.5YR 6/6), a few white and black grits.

Jug with Tall Rim (Nos. 670–73). Forms 1, 2, and 4 represented by one example each; two fragments of Form 3. Contexts indicate a pre–351 date for Forms 3 and 4; Form 1 is post–383. The only date suggested for Form 2 is Late Roman.

Form 1

670   (54–64). PH .064; D rim .067

Fine red clay (2.5YR 4/6), some white grits. Three-holed sieve in neck. Hard fabric. **Fig. 7–45.**

Form 2

671   (193–64). PH .06; D rim .07

Fine clay, gray core (5YR 5/1), outer bands yellowish red (5YR 5/6), many minute to small white grits, a few pitting surfaces. Hard fabric. **Fig. 7–45.**

Form 3

672   (91–65). PH .078; D rim .051

Fine yellowish red clay (5YR 4/6), many white and black grits, a few erupted through surfaces. Hard fabric. **Fig. 7–45.**

Form 4

673   (214–65). PH .06; D rim .049

Fine clay banded dark gray (2.5YR N4/) and red (2.5YR 5/6), a few white and black grits. Hard fabric. **Fig. 7–45.**

Jug with Grooved Rim (Nos. 674–75). Two examples of Form 1 and one example of Form 2. Contexts suggest a Late Roman date.

Form 1

674   (219–64). PH .052; D rim .08

Fine clay banded dark gray (7.5YR N4/) and brown (7.5YR 5/2), some white grits, a few black, occasional white ones erupted through surfaces. Hard fabric. **Fig. 7–45.**

Form 2

675   (358–65). PH .041; D rim .081

Fine reddish brown clay (2.5YR 5/4), some white and black grits, occasional mineral inclusions. Surfaces gritty. **Fig. 7–45.**

Jug with Outwardly Offset Rim (Nos. 676–81). Three examples of Form 1 and two of Form 2. Forms 3–5 represented by one fragment each. No closer date than Late Roman may be offered for Forms 1, 2, and 5; contexts indicate a date in Period 3 (351–383) for Forms 3 and 4.

Form 1

676   (556–66). PH .039; D rim .08

Fine brown clay (7.5YR 7/2), many white and black grits, occasionally erupted through surfaces. Surfaces gritty. **Fig. 7–45.**

Form 2

677   (115–65). PH (a) .047 (b) .126; D rim .064

Coarse clay, pink core (7.5YR 7/4), outer bands reddish brown (5YR 5/4), many white and black grits, some erupted through surfaces. **Fig. 7–45.**

678   (116–65). PH .17; D bottom .068

Fine reddish brown clay (2.5YR 5/4), some white and black grits, a few white ones have pitted surfaces. **Fig. 7–45.**

Form 3

679   (855–66). PH .041; D rim .07

Coarse red clay (2.5YR 5/6), many white grits, a few erupted through surfaces, a few black grits. Surfaces gritty. **Fig. 7–45.**

---

80. Jugs similar to Jalame Form 4 dated Early Roman Period (63–135) into the Middle Roman Period (135–300) have been found at Capernaum (Loffreda, *Cafarnao* 2, Type 10b, 166, 36, fig. 4.6–10, photo 5; Loffreda, *Sinagoga*, 110, fig. 11.1).

Form 4

680   (83–66). PH .023; D rim .055

Fine red clay (2.5YR 4/6), some white and black grits. **Fig. 7-45.**

Form 5

681   (739–66). PH .071; D rim .068

Coarse reddish brown clay (2.5YR 5/4), some white grits, a few black ones.

Jug with Out-turned Rim (Nos. 682–84). This small group is loosely held together by the out-turned rim. One example of each form. Contexts suggest a date before 351 for Form 1 and before 351 or early in Period 3 (358–383) for Form 3. Form 2 may be dated only to the Late Roman period.

Form 1

682   (216–65). PH .036; D rim .08

Fine red clay (2.5YR 5/6), a few white and black grits. **Fig. 7-45.**

Form 2

683   (365–65). PH .012; D rim .08

Fine red clay (2.5YR 5/6), some white and black grits. **Fig. 7-45.**

Form 3

684   (141–66). PH .016; D rim .05

Fine light red clay (2.5YR 6/6), a few white and black grits. **Fig. 7-45.**

Jug with Thickened Rim (Nos. 685–86). One example of two forms loosely related by the thickened rim with a groove around the top. Contexts indicate a date after 383 for Form 2.

Form 1

685   (290–64). PH .017

Fine red clay (2.5YR 5/6), a few white and black grits. **Fig. 7-45.**

Form 2

686   (486–66). PH .033; D rim .09

Fine clay, very dark gray core (2.5YR N3/), outer bands reddish brown (2.5YR 4/4), some minute and small white grits. **Fig. 7-45.**

Jug with Triangular Rim (Nos. 687–90). Forms 1 and 3 represented by one example each; Form 3 by two. Contexts indicate a date before 351 for Forms 1 and 3. The only date for Form 2 is Late Roman.

Form 1

687   (81–65). PH .08; D rim .038

Fine clay banded reddish gray (5YR 5/2) and reddish yellow (5YR 7/6), some white and black grits. **Fig. 7-45.**

Form 2

688   (59–64). PH .065; D rim .046

Fine clay banded brown (7.5YR 5/4) and yellowish red (5YR 4/6), some white and black grits. Surfaces gritty. **Fig. 7-45.**

689   (194–64). PH .052; D rim .055

Fine clay incompletely banded red (2.5YR 5/6) and weak red (2.5YR 4/2), some white, red, and black grits, occasional mineral inclusions. Surfaces gritty. **Fig. 7-45.**

Form 3

690   (145–65). PH (a) .018 (b) .064; D rim (a) .034

Coarse grayish brown clay (10YR 5/2), many white grits, a few black ones. Surfaces gritty. **Fig. 7-45.**

Jug with Vertical Rim (No. 691). One example. Late Roman. Tall heavy rim has broad shallow depression on interior at junction with shoulder.

691   (1006–65). PH .04; D rim .075

Coarse yellowish red clay (5YR 5/6), many white and black grits; a few have pitted surfaces.

Jug with Inward-Beveled Rim (No. 692). One example with sharply beveled rim. Upper end of vertical coil handle attached on neck. The proposed date is Late Roman.

692   (413–64). PH .034; D rim .05

Fine reddish yellow clay (5YR 6/6), a few white and black grits, air holes.

Jug with Flanged Rim (No. 693). One fragment characterized by sharp flange at bottom of rim, separating it from the neck. Low ribbing on outside of rim. The proposed date is Late Roman.

693   (853–65). PH .028; D rim .075

Fine reddish gray clay (5YR 5/2), some black grits. **Fig. 7-45.**

Jug with Heavy Vertical Rim (No. 694). One sherd. Heavy rim below which the neck slopes sharply inward. Context suggests a date before 351.

694   (158–65). PH .038; D rim .093

Fine very pale brown clay (10YR 7/4), many black grits, a few red and white ones. **Fig. 7-46.**

Jug with Wide Everted Rim (No. 695). One piece. Hard fired. Upper end of a downward slanting coil handle attached just below rim.

695   (69–66). PH .052; D rim .075

Fine red clay (2.5YR 4/4), some white and black grits; a few have pitted the surfaces. **Fig. 7-46.**

Globular One-Handled Jug (No. 696). One example. Slightly out-turned rim. Lower end of small coil handle set on shoulder. Entire body ribbed except for two panels at mid- and lower-body.

696   (146–66). Est H .248; D rim .054, bottom .153

Coarse clay, dark gray core (5YR 4/1), outer bands light

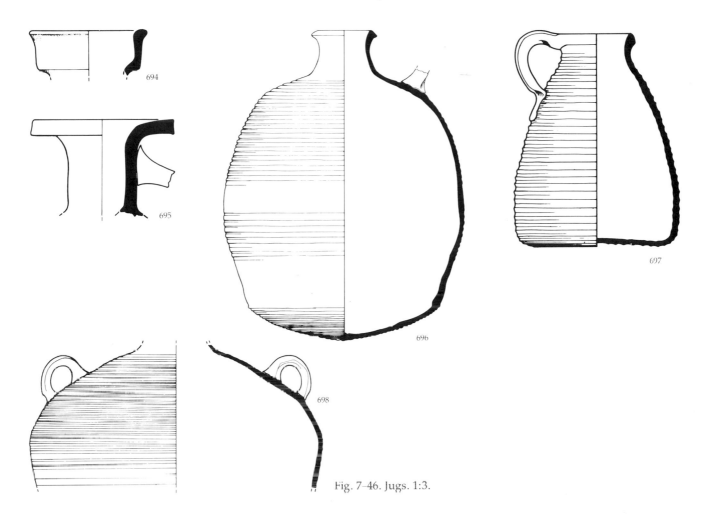

Fig. 7–46. Jugs. 1:3.

red (2.5YR 6/6), some white grits. **Fig. 7–46; Pl. 7–5.**

Jug with Pyramidal Body (No. 697). One example. Body and slightly concave bottom ribbed. Coil handle attached at rim and upper body. Suggested date is Late Roman.

697 (19–66). H .17; D rim .06, bottom .12

Coarse reddish yellow clay (5YR 6/6); yellow slip (10YR 7/6). **Fig. 7–46.**

Jug with Two Loop Handles (No. 698). One example. This vessel may have been used for boiling water.[81] Context offers a date before 351.

698 (217–65). PH .11

Fine red clay (2.5YR 5/8), some white and black grits. Hard fabric. **Fig. 7–46.**

Various Jugs (Nos. 699–709).

699 (1–65). PH .103

Fine clay, brown core (7.5YR 5/4), outer bands yellowish

81. For comments on their use, see Zevulun-Olenik, *Talmudic Period.* For parallels see Loffreda, *Cafarnao* 2, Bottle, Type A7, 32, 152, fig. 3.10, photo 4, dated Middle Roman Period (135–300); Bagatti, *Nazareth,* 284, fig. 220.5 and fig. 224.10; and D. Bahat, "A Roof Tile of the Legio VI Ferrata and Pottery Vessels from Ḥorvat Ḥazon," *IEJ* 24 (1974) 165, fig. 4.11.

red (5YR 4/6), some white and black grits and mineral inclusions. **Fig. 7–47.**

700 (359–65). PH .043

Fine red clay (2.5YR 5/6), many white and black grits; some white ones have pitted surfaces. **Fig. 7–47.**

701 (543–66). PH .054

Fine red clay (2.5YR 5/6), many white and black grits, a few white ones have pitted surfaces. Very pale brown slip (10R 8/3) on exterior. Surfaces gritty. **Fig. 7–47.**

702 (541–66). PH .045

Fine light red clay (2.5YR 6/6), many minute to small white grits, a few erupted through surfaces; some black grits. Surfaces gritty. **Fig. 7–47.**

703 (112–66). PH .076

Coarse reddish brown clay (2.5YR 5/4), some white and black grits and mineral inclusions. **Fig. 7–47.**

704 (436–64). Max dim .084; PH .038

Fine reddish brown clay (5YR 5/4), some white and black grits. Reddish yellow (7.5YR 7/6) painted decoration on exterior consisting of band at base of neck and shoulder, in field between unidentifiable decoration. **Fig. 7–47.**

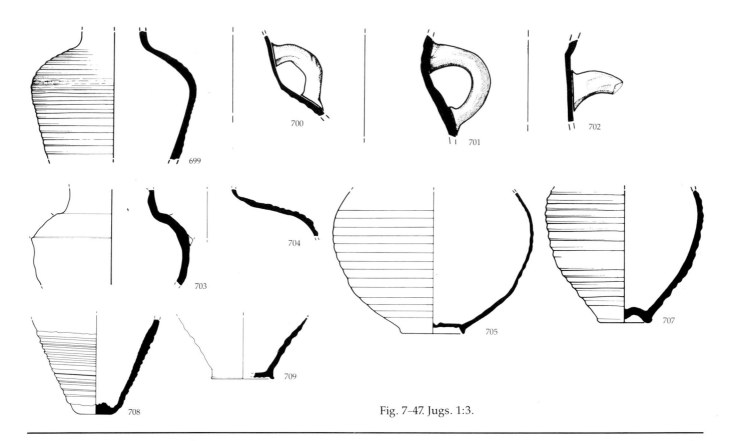

Fig. 7–47. Jugs. 1:3.

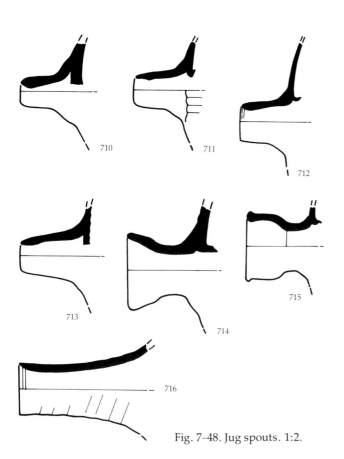

Fig. 7–48. Jug spouts. 1:2.

705 (233–66). PH .111; D foot .051

Fine red clay (2.5YR 5/6), some white and black grits, a few small white ones have pitted surfaces. Hard fabric. **Fig. 7–47.**

706 (7–66). PH .142; D bottom .075

Rim and handle missing. Fine reddish yellow clay (5YR 7/6), micaceous inclusions; a few small white stones have erupted through surfaces. **Pl. 7–5.**

707 (34–66). PH .105; D bottom .045

Fine clay, many white and black grits, some white ones have pitted surfaces. White slip (10YR 8/2) on exterior. **Fig. 7–47 .**

708 (501–66). PH (a) .104; Max dim (b) .066; D bottom .038

Fine clay, reddish gray core (10R 5/1), outer bands reddish brown (2.5YR 5/4), many white and black grits. **Fig. 7–47.**

709 (264–66). PH (a) .051; D foot .05

Coarse light red clay (2.5YR 6/6), many white and black grits. Surfaces gritty. **Fig. 7–47.**

Spouts (Nos. 710–16). A representative selection is presented. Contexts suggest that No. 711 is probably pre–351, No. 712 dates to Period 3 (351–383), while No. 713 is probably of Period 4. The others are Late Roman, not closely datable.

710 (236–64). L of spout .027; Max dim .049

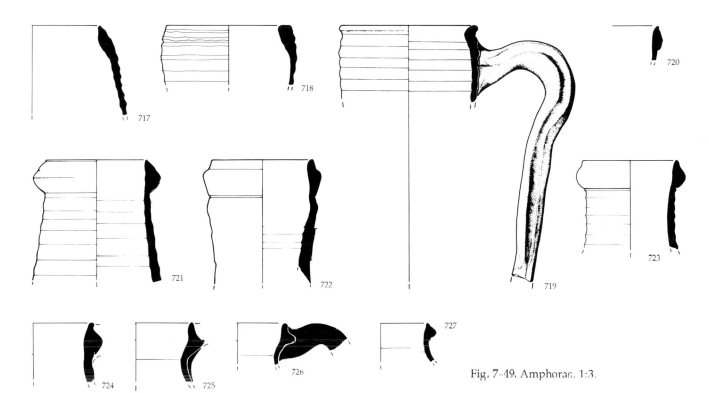

Fig. 7-49, Amphoras. 1:3.

Fine clay banded light red (2.5YR 6/6) and reddish gray (5YR 5/2), many white and black grits. **Fig. 7-48.**

711 (302-65). L of spout .027, Max dim .06

Fine red clay (10R 4/6), a few white and black grits. Hard fabric. **Fig. 7-48.**

712 (77-66). L of spout .027; Max dim .07

Fine reddish brown clay (5YR 5/4), a few white and black grits. Hard fabric. **Fig. 7-48.**

713 (149-65). L of spout .033; Max dim .046

Fine reddish brown clay (2.5YR 4/4), some white grits. Hard fabric. **Fig. 7-48.**

714 (304-65). L of spout .037; Max dim .072

Coarse clay banded reddish brown (5YR 5/4) and light reddish brown (2.4YR 6/4), many white and black grits; a few have pitted surfaces. Surfaces gritty. **Fig. 7-48.**

715 (144-65). L of spout .035; Max dim .052

Fine red clay (2.5YR 5/6), many white and black grits; a few have pitted surfaces. Hard fabric. **Fig. 7-48.**

716 (540-66). PL of spout .068

Fine yellowish red clay (5YR 5/6), some white and black grits and mineral inclusions. **Fig. 7-48.**

Amphoras

This section deals with two kinds of large jars: those whose primary use was as a shipping container (Amphoras Forms 1-4 and at least some of the rim fragments listed under Miscellaneous Amphoras); and those storage or water jars used locally in the Syro-Palestinian region. Of the transport amphoras only Forms 1 and 2 occur in quantity, although both Forms 3 and 4 are well known from the Late Roman period.

Amphora Form 1 (Nos. 717-28). 211 fragments. Coarse clay usually reddish yellow (5YR 6/6; 7.5YR 7/6), occasionally red, light reddish brown, reddish brown, or grayish brown. The color is usually solid through the section. Surfaces are gritty. The most common rim profile is triangular. No. 723 is probably a lower body and toe of this amphora type. Characteristic is the broad groove down one side of each heavy handle. Though no parallels are known, visual examination of the fabric suggests Palestinian origin. Contexts do not indicate a closer date than Late Roman (4th c.).

717 (448-66). PH .074; D rim .11

Coarse grayish brown clay (10YR 5/2); interior surface light gray (10YR 7/2), exterior gray (5YR 5/1). **Fig. 7-49.**

718 (685-65). PH .049; D rim .10

Coarse yellowish red clay (5YR 5/8). **Fig. 7-49.**

719 (485-65). PH .205 with handle; D rim .11

Coarse reddish yellow (5YR 6/6) and reddish brown (5YR 5/4) clay. **Fig. 7-49.**

720 (700-65). PH .028

Coarse reddish yellow clay (7.5YR 7/6). **Fig. 7-49.**

721 (170-65). PH .099; D rim .081

Coarse reddish yellow clay (5YR 6/6). **Fig. 7-49.**

722 (533-66). PH .099; D rim .081

Coarse red clay (2.5YR 5/6). **Fig. 7-49.**

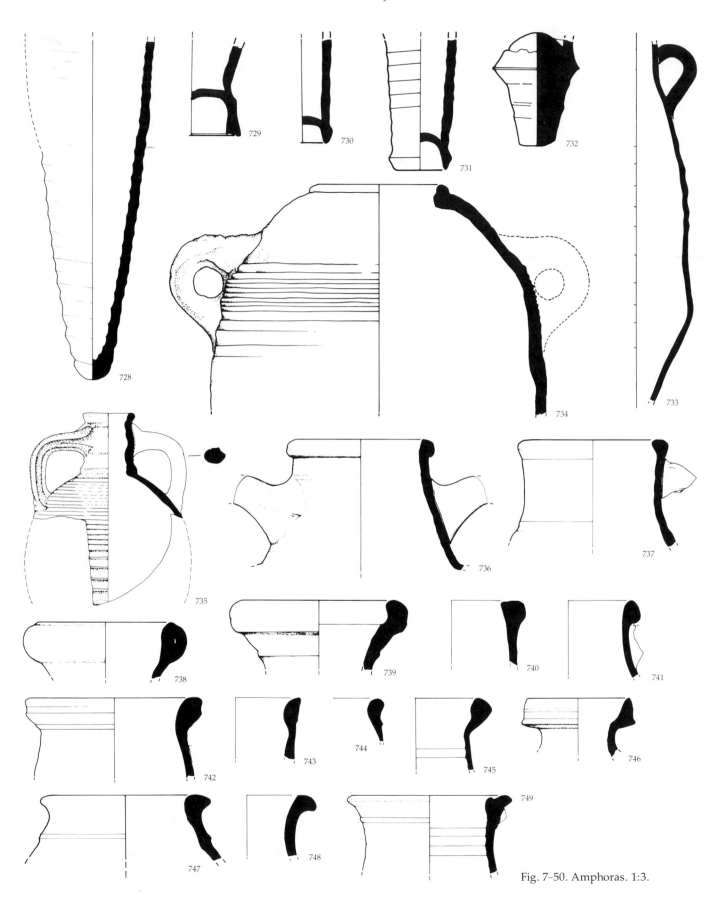

Fig. 7-50. Amphoras. 1:3.

723 (168–65). PH .07; D rim .08

Coarse light reddish brown clay (5YR 6/4). **Fig. 7–49.**

724 (475–65). PH .047; D rim .098

Clay and color as No. 721. **Fig. 7–49.**

725 (662–65). PH .049; D rim .094

Clay and color as No. 721. **Fig. 7–49.**

726 (872–66). PH .033; D rim .08

Clay and color as No. 721. **Fig. 7–49.**

727 (763–65). PH .031; D rim .08

Clay and color as No. 721. **Fig. 7–49.**

728 (41–66). PH .27

Clay and color as No. 721. **Fig. 7–50.**

Amphora Form 2 (Micaceous Water Jar) (Nos. 729–33). 382 pieces.[82] This long-lived shape has been found around the Mediterranean and beyond.[83] It appears in large and small sizes, each of which may have one or two handles depending on its place in the typological development. The largest published group comes from the Athenian Agora. It has been assumed these vessels were used for the shipment of wine since many have a mastic resin lining.[84] A recent study indicates that some contained an oily substance, perhaps an unguent.[85] The proposed place of manufacture is Asia Minor, probably the Maeander valley.[86]

Fragments of both the large and small size in the "highly micaceous reddish brown" fabric[87] were found at Jalame. The preserved neck/handle combinations indicate only two-handled jars, but the toes show the presence of the one-handled variety as well. No. 729, a tubular foot with thickened collar, is, according to current typology,[88] associated with a one-handled jar of the late 2nd-early 3rd c. Nos. 730–31 are characteristic of one-handled containers of the late 4th c.[89] No. 732, in the same fabric but with a tapering solid toe, resembles two-handled vessels from the late 4th c. and later.[90] The most completely preserved

example, No. 733, probably belongs late in the development of the small variety. Since the remains from Jalame are fragmentary, we can only note that such vessels whether large or small, one- or two-handled, but always in micaceous reddish brown clay, were in use from before 351 until after 383.

Amphoras of this sort are known from the Syro-Palestinian area.[91]

729 (279–66). PH .048; D toe .054

Fine reddish brown clay (5YR 4/3); interior surface reddish gray (5YR 5/2), exterior brown (7.5YR 5/4). **Fig. 7–50.**

730 (11–65). PH .055; D toe .028

Fine reddish yellow clay (5YR 6/6). **Fig. 7–50.**

731 (354–65). PH .069; D toe .028

Fine red clay (2.5YR 4/8). **Fig. 7–50.**

732 (559–64). PH .061

Fine reddish brown (2.5YR 4/4) and brown (7.5YR 5/4) clay. **Fig. 7–50.**

733 (102–64). PH .283

Fine reddish brown clay (2.5YR 4/4). **Fig. 7 50; Pl. 7 5.**

Amphora Form 3 (Gaza Amphora) (No. 734). Though well known and of wide distribution, only seven examples were found at Jalame.[92] Characteristic is the clay smeared on the rim and shoulder. Both short and tall varieties exist, with chronological differences based mostly on the form of the rim.[93] At our site only rim fragments were found with the exception of a piece (501a,b 66, uncatalogued) of the bottom of the taller variety.

That these containers are from the Gaza region is now generally accepted, but the question of their contents remains.[94] Gaza was famous for its wine in late antiquity, and it has been suggested that this vessel is the type in which wine was shipped.[95] Several factors confuse the

82. The sherd count is misleading since most of the fragments are small and recognizable only because of their distinctive micaceous clay.
83. For discussion of development, fabrics, sizes, and dates see Robinson, *Agora Pottery*, 17, under F65; M. Lang, "Dated Jars of Early Imperial Times," *Hesperia* 24 (1955) 227–85; Riley, "Coarse Pottery," Mid Roman Amphora 3, 183–85, 219–23. For the small variety only see C. Panella, *Ostia 3*, Part 2. *Studi Miscellanei* 21 (Rome, 1973) 460–62.
84. Robinson, *Agora Pottery*, 17, under F65; Riley believes the contents are unknown ("Coarse Pottery," 183–85, 219–23).
85. M. C. Rothschild-Boros, "The Determination of Amphora Contents," in G. Barker and R. Hodges, eds., *Archaeology and Italian Society. Prehistoric, Roman and Medieval Studies* (Papers in Italian Archaeology 2. BAR International Series 102), 79–89, 1981, esp. 79, 83, 86.
86. That these amphoras stem from the Maeander Valley in Asia Minor and not from formerly proposed points of origin is discussed in Riley, "Coarse Pottery," 184.
87. For fabrics and sizes see n. 83 above.
88. Robinson, *Agora Pottery*, 55, J46, pls. 11, 41; and Riley, "Coarse Pottery," fig. 83, no. 235.
89. Robinson, *Agora Pottery*, M277, 110, pl. 29; and Riley, "Coarse Pottery," fig. 83, nos. 230, 233, 234.

90. Robinson, *Agora Pottery*, M373, 119, pls. 34, 41. Jars with this pyramidal toe filled with a spherical or hemispherical plug of clay closing the top are common in the late 4th to early 5th c. Generally, there is a small opening at the lower end, or even if the lower end is closed it can be ascertained that the area below the plug is hollow. In contrast the Jalame toe, though provided with the plug, is solid below.
91. For parallels in Palestine to Nos. 730–31 see Saller, *Bethany*, 311, fig. 62, no. 412, pl. 129, a, 10, and Bagatti, *Nazareth*, fig. 220.4. A tapering toe like No. 732 but hollow on the inside and not closed at the bottom was found at Khirbat al-Karak (Delougaz-Haines, pl. 54, no. 18, pl. 38.10). For small containers like No. 733 see Avigad, *Beth Shearim* 3, 194–95, 197, fig. 94 12A, 12B; FitzGerald, *Beth Shan* 3, no. 13; and Meyers, *Khirbet Shema*, 237–38, pl. 7.23, nos. 26, 27, called amphoriskoi and dated 4th to early 5th c. A large one-handled example was recovered from the sea (Barag, "Survey of Pottery," 5B.10).
92. Riley, "Coarse Pottery," 219–23, and Zemer, *Storage Jars*, 61–66, pls. 18–19, nos. 49–53. For examples in Palestine see Riley, "Caesarea Hippodrome," Amphora Type 2, 27–31; Bagatti, *Nazareth*, 273, fig. 217.1, fig. 218, left, not specifically dated; Prausnitz, *Shavei Zion*, 41, fig. 11.14, pl. 25.3, dated Late Roman on basis of similar jar from a 4th c. tomb at Ashkelon; and Landgraf, *Tell Keisan*, 67, 69, 82; Barag, "Survey of Pottery," pl. 5B.9.
93. See Zemer in n. 92 above.
94. See Riley and Zemer in n. 92 above.
95. Riley, "Coarse Pottery," 219–23, and Riley, "Caesarea Hippodrome," 30, notes 19 and 20.

issue. At a northern Sinai site (unpublished)[96] these vessels contain fish bones. Recent scientific analysis indicates either olive or sesame oil as a commodity transported.[97]

734   (98–65). PH .178; D rim .11

Fine reddish brown clay (5YR 4/4). **Fig. 7–50.**

Amphora Form 4 ("Panel" Amphora) (No. 735). Five fragments. The name is derived from the broad area at midbody on which the ribbing is widely spaced or absent. Two fabrics have been noted, of which only the "normal" one occurred at Jalame. Characteristics are a sandy ware gritty to the touch and of a yellowish red color (5YR 5/6). Sometimes a very pale brown slip remains. [98] The question of its origin remains open.[99] It has been reported from few sites in Palestine; but it has a wide distribution.[100] The commodity shipped is not known; it may have been wine or oil or both.[101] No information from Jalame contradicts or modifies the established date range of 4th–6th c.

735   (109–64). PH .166; D rim .042

Coarse yellowish red clay (5YR 5/6), many white and black grits and mineral inclusions. **Fig. 7–50; Pl. 7–5.**

Miscellaneous Amphoras (Nos. 736–61). Little study has been given to amphoras of the Roman East. The fragmentary jars included here are rarely represented by more than one example. They serve mainly to illustrate the wide variety of amphoras at the site. Contexts offer a date before 351 for Nos. 746, 748; Period 3 (351–383) for No. 752; late in Period 3 for No. 759; Period 4 for No. 743.

736   (195–66). PH .105; D rim .115

Coarse reddish yellow clay (5YR 6/6), many white and black grits and mineral inclusions. Surfaces gritty. **Fig. 7–50.**

737   (283–65). PH .084; D rim .118

Fine reddish yellow clay (7.5YR 7/6), some white and black grits. **Fig. 7–50.**

738   (535–66). PH .045; D rim .13

Coarse reddish yellow clay (5YR 6/6), some white and red grits; white slip (10YR 8/2). **Fig. 7–50.**

739   (351–65). PH .055; D rim .14

Coarse clay, red core (2.5YR 5/6), outer bands pale yellow (2.5Y 8/4), a few minute to small white and black grits; pink slip (7.5YR 7/4). **Fig. 7–50.**

740   (538–66). PH .052; D rim .12

Fine clay banded light red (2.5YR 6/6) and reddish yellow (7.5YR 7/6), some minute to small white grits. **Fig. 7–50.**

741   (910–66). PH .062; D rim .11

Coarse light gray clay (2.5Y 7/2), many small black inclusions. **Fig. 7–50.**

742   (227–64). PH .065; D rim .14

Coarse light reddish brown clay (5YR 6/4), a few minute to small white, black, and red grits; white slip (2.5Y 8/2). **Fig. 7–50.**

743   (221–64). PH .051; D rim .11

Coarse yellowish brown clay (10YR 5/6), some white and black grits and mica; reddish yellow slip (7.5YR 7/6). Surfaces gritty. **Fig. 7–50.**

744   (364–65). PH .035; D rim .11

Fine reddish yellow clay (5YR 6/6), some white and black grits. **Fig. 7–50.**

745   (1025–65). PH .058; D rim .12

Coarse clay variegated light red (2.5YR 6/6) and reddish yellow (5YR 6/6), a few minute to small white and black grits; very pale brown slip (10YR 8/4). **Fig. 7–50.**

746   (282–65). PH .048; D rim .08

Fine reddish brown clay (5YR 5/4), occasional white and black grits, many mineral inclusions. **Fig. 7–50.**

747   (1033–66). PH (a) .054 (b) .047; D rim .138

Fine red clay (2.5YR 5/6), a few white and red grits, occasional small red ones; pale yellow slip (2.5Y 8/4). **Fig. 7–50.**

748   (673–66). PH .045; D rim .11

Fine clay, light red core (2.5YR 6/6), outer bands pale red (2.5YR 6/2), some minute to small white, red, and black grits; white slip (2.5Y 8/2). **Fig. 7–50.**

749   (537–66). PH .063; D rim .13

Fine red clay, light red core (2.5YR 6/6), outer bands gray (2.5YR N5/), some minute to small white and black grits, a few mineral inclusions; traces of white slip. **Fig. 7–50.**

750   (105–65). PH .125; D rim .116

Faint band of ribbing on neck at lower end of handle. Coarse light red clay (2.5YR 6/8), many minute to large white, black, and red grits, occasional sparkling inclusions; worn reddish yellow slip (7.5YR 7/6). **Fig. 7–51.**

751   (316–64). PH .052; D rim .095

Coarse light brown clay (7.5YR 6/4), many minute to small black grits, occasional white and red ones; white slip (2.5YR 8/2). **Fig. 7–51.**

752   (463–65). PH .045; D rim .10

Fine light red clay (2.5YR 6/8), a few minute to small black grits, occasional white ones. **Fig. 7–51.**

96. Zemer, *Storage Jars*, 61.
97. M. C. Rothschild-Boros, as in n. 85 above, 78–89, esp. 79, 86.
98. Riley, "Coarse Pottery," 212.
99. Ibid.
100. See Riley, "Coarse Pottery," 212–15; Zemer, *Storage Jars*, 76–79. For other examples from Palestine see Riley, "Caesarea Hippodrome," Amphora Type 5, 31, 33; Landgraf, *Tell Keisan*, 82; Dothan-Freedman, *Ashdod* 1, 34, 68–69, fig. 14.2, dated 6th c. on basis of parallels in the Athenian Agora; Saller, *Bethany*, 210, nos. 243, 245, fig. 41, pl. 114.1, 2, dated to Byzantine period.
101. Riley, "Coarse Pottery," 215.

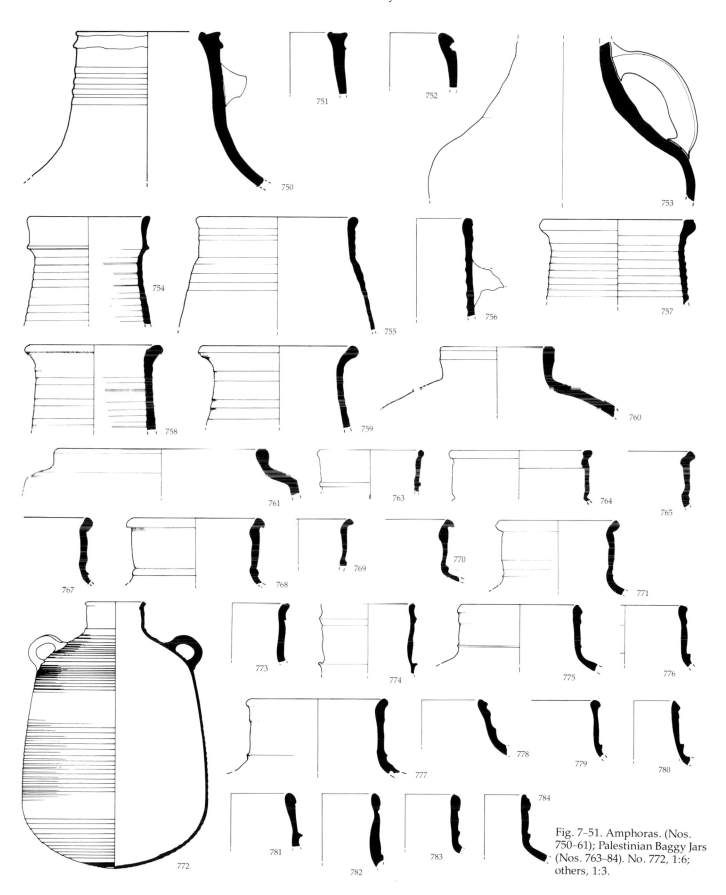

Fig. 7–51. Amphoras. (Nos. 750–61); Palestinian Baggy Jars (Nos. 763–84). No. 772, 1:6; others, 1:3.

753 (243–66). PH .135

Coarse yellowish red clay (5YR 5/8), many minute to small white and black grits. **Fig. 7–51.**

754 (152–65). PH .084; D rim .096

Coarse very pale brown clay (10YR 7/4), a few white and black grits. Surfaces gritty. **Fig. 7–51.**

755 (206–64). PH .088; D rim .127 (mouth oval)

Coarse red clay (2.5YR 5/6), some white grits, occasional small ones. Surfaces gritty. **Fig. 7–51.**

756 (710–66). PH .078; D rim .092

Coarse light reddish brown clay (5YR 6/4), a few white and black grits. Surfaces gritty. **Fig. 7–51.**

757 (286–65). PH .066; D rim .12

Fine yellowish red clay (5YR 5/6), a few white and black grits. **Fig. 7–51.**

758 (178–66). PH .07; D rim .11

Coarse brown clay (7.5YR 5/4), a few white grits, occasional small ones. **Fig. 7–51.**

759 (230–64). PH .066; D rim .12

Coarse reddish yellow clay (5YR 6/6), many white grits, a few black ones and mineral inclusions. Surfaces gritty. **Fig. 7–51.**

760 (239–64). PH .052; D rim .09

Coarse clay banded red (2.5YR 5/8) and weak red (2.5YR 5/2), some white and black grits, occasional small ones. **Fig. 7–51.**

761 (226–65). PH (a) .038 (b) .036; D rim .167

Coarse reddish yellow clay (5YR 6/6), some white and black grits, some small ones also. **Fig. 7–51.**

Palestinian Baggy Jars (Nos. 762–827). These jars, known variously as store jars, storage jars, bag jars, baggy jars, or water jars, are common at Late Roman sites in Palestine. The shape has a long history extending from the Hellenistic to the Arab period.[102] Although the height and girth may vary over time, certain features are always present: a baggy body, low neck, two small ear handles, convex bottom. Some of the body is ribbed; this ribbing may differ in prominence from one part of the body to another. A study of the typological development of this shape, particularly within the Late Roman period, remains to be done.

The jars occur in a number of fabrics; the most easily recognizable are red and black. The variety of fabric supports the assumption that many factories were producing for a local market. Increasingly these containers are found beyond the Syro-Palestinian area.[103]

102. P. W. Lapp, *Palestinian Ceramic Chronology 200 B.C.–A.D. 70* (New Haven, Conn., 1961); Baramki,"Kh. El-Mefjer," fig. 3.1–3, pl. 19:1–2.

103. See Robinson, *Agora Pottery*, 115, N329, N330, pls. 32, 35, 58, dated early 6th c. The painted decoration, although not the fabric, resembles some of the black jars from Jalame. A few of these storage jar sherds, especially the black ones, have been found at Corinth (information from personal examination).

What commodity they carried is unknown. It has long been assumed that a main use was as a water jar.[104] Then a lining was not necessary, because absorption into the body wall would have helped keep the water cool. Neither would a lining have been needed if the material contained was dry. Since there is no water supply on the low rocky hill of Jalame, many of the jars must have served to transport water for the domestic and commercial use of the inhabitants. Nothing chronologically, typologically, or stratigraphically suggests that these vessels were used in connection with the wine or olive press, especially as the amounts produced at these installations were probably mainly for home consumption. Dipinti or graffiti are uncommon;[105] none was found at Jalame.

Thousands of pieces were recovered from the site. Of these No. 762 is the earliest; a 2nd-c. date has been suggested.[106] Nos. 763–72, preserved mainly in small neck and rim fragments (an exception is No. 772), are characterized by a hard fabric and an everted rim. Parallels are known.[107] Nos. 773–77 are related to the previous group by virtue of the hardness of fabric; however, the rim is folded outward and concave on the outer surface. It sometimes flares slightly at the upper end, as on No. 777. Parallels are known for these as well.[108]

Three types (based mainly on the exterior surface color) predominate: the red jar (Nos. 798–809), the black jar (Nos. 810–23), and a third in a soft light red fabric (Nos. 788–89). The total sherd count of the red jars, not including those restored from a single deposit, is 900; the black jar total count is 1,663, of which 64 are handles and 957 rim fragments. The count for soft light red fabric jars was 2,882, mostly small body sherds. Among the fragments 20 were from the rim and 107 were handles. An unascertainable number of body sherds may belong to a large pot such as No. 858. The red and black surface colors vary from example to example as well as on a single vessel. The red jars range from red to reddish brown or light brown, while the black ones are a variety of gray.

The large deposit of red jars from Trench Q[109] illustrates

104. Although this assumption is reasonable because the container is common on Syro-Palestinian sites and similar vessels are used to this day, the increasing amount found beyond the region suggests they might have contained exportable commodities, the nature of which is not clear.

105. See Robinson, *Agora Pottery*, N330, 115, which has a graffito giving a capacity. For dipinti see Delougaz-Haines, p. 34, pl. 35.5; Zevulun-Olenik, *Talmudic Period*, p. 44, no. 97.

106. Personal communication from the late Prof. Paul Lapp.

107. Bagatti, *Nazareth*, 273, fig. 217.3, 4, dated 3rd to 5th c.; Loffreda, *Sinagoga*, 88–89, fig. 4.1, 6, dated to Roman period; Loffreda, *Cafarnao* 2, Type A2, 27, 143–44, fig. 1.2, 4, dated Middle (135–300) to Late (300–450) Roman; Loffreda, *et-Tabgha*, 90, fig. 35.38, dated 4th–5th c.; Meyers, *Khirbet Shema*, Type 1, 220–22, pls. 7.20, nos. 5–16, 33–51, and 7.21, nos. 1–4, dated ca. 200 into 5th c.

108. Delougaz-Haines, 34, pl. 55.4; Loffreda, *Sinagoga*, 89, 93, fig. 4.4; Loffreda, *Cafarnao* 2, Type A3, 27, 144, fig. 1.3, dated Middle and Late Roman; Loffreda, *et-Tabgha*, 81, 82, 150, figs. 31.17, 32.17, 56.257, 57.14; Meyers, *Khirbet Shema*, 222–25, pl. 7.20, nos. 17–31, dated early 3rd to early 5th c.

109. The jars of the deposit are from the north side of Trench Q, just to the southeast of the wine press. There were about 25 in all, some fragmentary. They include Nos. 798–808 and uncatalogued pieces 130–65, 132–40–65. They were found broken in place and begin ca. .40 below the surface, continuing to ca. 1.60–1.70 below. See Chap. 2, wine press.

the typical shape at Jalame. The baggy body is slightly constricted below the shoulder, which is marked by a sharp ridge. Two small ear handles are set on the shoulder at or just above the ridge. Another ridge is located around the bottom of the neck. The rim is thickened and may flare slightly. Ribbing covers the body except for a panel at the middle that is usually filled with painted decoration. The ribbing is sharper and narrower on the shoulder. Surface color is variegated, ranging through light reddish brown, reddish brown, light brown, brown, pinkish gray, and reddish gray. Rarely does a gray core show in section.

The evidence for painted decoration is greatest on the red jars for the simple reason that they are the best preserved. The most common design is a "guilloche" band around mid-body, enclosed and bisected by horizontal lines.[110] On other jars is a zigzag decoration or one composed of slanting lines enclosed and bisected by horizontal bands.

The black jars, though represented by a larger sherd count, are more fragmentary, a fact that affects a discussion of their shape. They are hard fired and clink when one sherd is struck against another. The clay color in section may be solid, banded, or have a core. Colors range through light red, red, weak red, reddish brown, brown, or very dark gray. Surface color is gray, dark gray, or very dark gray. Ribbing seems to cover more of the vessel than on the red jars. The painted decoration is put on over the ribbing if no clear panel has been left. Because of the fragmentary nature the painted decoration is less easily identified.[111] The patterns are more elaborate and cover a larger portion of the body. No. 824 has the guilloche and bands as on the red jars but combined with a vertical menorah-like element that rises at one point above the design of guilloche and lines. Vertical wavy lines that intersect and cover most of the body appear on Nos. 823, 822–27.

The amount of baggy jars from Jalame serves to show the importance of such vessels on a Late Roman site as well as the variety of detail within this common shape.

762 (1018–65). PH .029; D rim .107–.114

Coarse clay variegated red (2.5YR 5/6) and dark gray (2.5YR N4/), some white and black grits; pale yellow slip (2.5Y 8/4). **Pl. 7–5.**

763 (455–66). PH .033; D rim .08

Fine clay, dark gray core (2.5YR N4/), outer bands reddish brown (2.5YR 5/4), occasional white and black grits. **Fig. 7–51.**

764 (604–66). PH .04; D rim .09

Fine clay, dark gray core (2.5YR N4/); surface light reddish brown. **Fig. 7–51.**

765 (347–66). PH .045; D rim .09

Fine clay, dark gray core (5YR 4/1), outer bands yellow-

ish red (5YR 4/8), a few white grits, occasional large ones. **Fig. 7–51.**

766 (356–66). PH .041; D rim .10

Fine yellowish red clay (5YR 5/6), a few white grits.

767 (403–66). PH .053

Fine yellowish red clay (5YR 4/8), many white grits; very pale brown slip (10YR 8/3). **Fig. 7–51.**

768 (400–66). PH .053; D rim .11

Fine yellowish red clay (5YR 4/8), some white grits, occasional small ones; white slip (10YR 8/2). **Fig. 7–51.**

769 (353–66). PH .038; D rim .09

Fine clay, reddish gray core (5YR 5/2), outer bands yellowish red (5YR 4/8), many white grits, a few small ones, also a few black inclusions. **Fig. 7–51.**

770 (348–66). PH .05

Fine dark gray clay (2.5YR N4/), a few white and black grits, occasional small ones; surface reddish brown (2.5YR 5/4). **Fig. 7–51.**

771 (392–66). PH .06; D rim .10

Fine clay banded dark gray (5YR 4/1) and reddish brown (5YR 4/4), some white grits, a few small ones. **Fig. 7–51.**

772 (50–66). H .39; D rim .092, bottom .152

Coarse light red clay (2.5YR 6/6), some minute to small white grits. **Fig. 7–51.**

773 (471–66). PH .047

Fine reddish yellow clay (5YR 6/6), some white grits; light brown slip (7.5YR 6/4). **Fig. 7–51.**

774 (391–66). PH .056; D rim .076

Fine yellowish red clay (5YR 4/8), some minute to small white grits; very pale brown slip (10YR 7/3). **Fig. 7–51.**

775 (349–66). PH .053; D rim .095

Coarse clay, brown core (7.5YR 5/4), outer bands reddish brown (5YR 5/3), some minute to small white grits. Surfaces gritty. **Fig. 7–51.**

776 (345–66). PH .049; D rim .10

Coarse brown clay (7.5YR 5/4), some minute to large white grits. Surfaces gritty. **Fig. 7–51.**

777 (485–66). PH .06; D rim .112

Fine light reddish brown clay (5YR 6/4), some white and black grits. **Fig. 7–51.**

778 (475–66). PH .044; D rim .11

Fine clay banded dark gray (5YR 4/1), reddish brown (5YR 5/3), and yellowish red (5YR 5/8), a few white and black grits. **Fig. 7–51.**

779 (343–66). PH .046

Coarse clay banded gray (5YR 5/1), reddish gray (5YR 5/2), and yellowish red (5YR 5/6), a few white and black grits. **Fig. 7–51.**

110. Painted decoration like that on the Jalame red jars is found at Tell Keisan (Landgraf, *Tell Keisan*, fig. 24b.2, 7–9).
111. Decoration similar to that on the Jalame jars was found at Khirbat al-Karak on a jar with dark gray exterior (Delougaz-Haines, 34, pls. 35.1, 55.1).

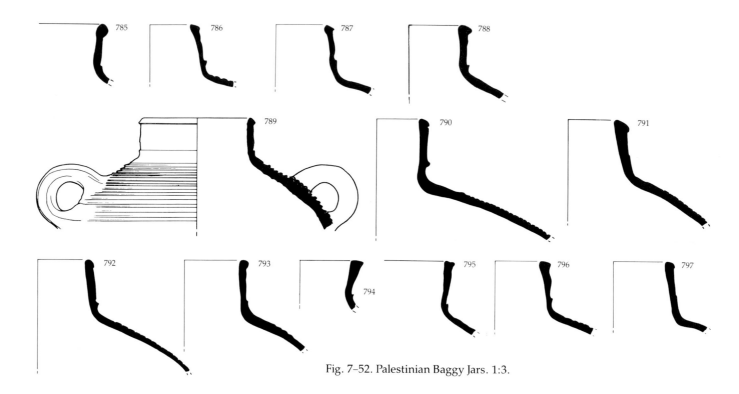

Fig. 7–52. Palestinian Baggy Jars. 1:3.

780 (337–66). PH .053; D rim .11

Coarse clay, dark gray core (5YR 4/1), outer bands reddish yellow (5YR 6/6), a few white and black grits. Traces of pinkish white slip (7.5YR 8/2). Surfaces gritty. **Fig. 7–51.**

781 (336–66). PH .038; D rim .10

Coarse brown clay (7.5YR 5/4), a few white and black grits; very pale brown slip (10YR 7/4). **Fig. 7–51.**

782 (404–66). PH .06; D rim .09

Coarse clay, very pale brown core (10YR 7/4), outer bands reddish yellow (5YR 6/6), a few black grits. **Fig. 7–51.**

783 (325–66). PH .049; D rim .08

Fine reddish yellow clay (5YR 6/6), some white and red grits, a few small white ones. **Fig. 7–51.**

784 (326–66). PH .055; D rim .07

Fine reddish yellow clay (5YR 6/6), some red and white grits. **Fig. 7–51.**

785 (1207–66). PH .05; Est D rim .08

Fine yellowish red clay (5YR 5/6), a few white and black grits and mineral inclusions. **Fig. 7–52.**

786 (328–66). PH .052; D rim .084

Coarse yellowish red clay (5YR 4/6), a few minute to small white and black grits; pink slip (7.5YR 7/4). **Fig. 7–52.**

787 (332–66). PH .054; D rim .094

Fine clay banded reddish gray (5YR 5/2), dark reddish gray (5YR 4/2), and yellowish red (5YR 5/6), some white grits; very pale brown slip (10YR 7/4). **Fig. 7–52.**

788 (351–66). PH .058; D rim .10

Coarse light red clay (10R 6/6), a few white grits. Soft fabric. **Fig. 7–52.**

789 (290–66). PH (a) .113 (b) .12; D rim .12

Same as preceding. White red, and black grits. **Fig. 7–52.**

790 (654–66). PH .097; D rim .082

Coarse light red clay (2.5YR 6/6), minute to large white and black grits. **Fig. 7–52.**

791 (176–66). PH (a) .085; Max dim (b) .083; D rim .084

Coarse yellowish red clay (5YR 5/6), minute to large white and black grits. **Fig. 7–52 .**

792 (219–65). PH .087; D rim .09

Coarse clay, gray core (5YR 5/1), outer bands yellowish red (5YR 5/8), minute to small white and black grits. Traces of pink slip (5YR 7/3). **Fig. 7–52.**

793 (329–66). PH .073; D rim .11

Fine clay, gray core (5YR 5/1), outer bands red (2.5YR 5/8), a few minute to small white and black grits; pink slip (7.5YR 7/4). **Fig. 7–52.**

794 (357–66). PH .04; D rim .10

Fine clay banded red (2.5YR 5/6) and dark gray (5YR 4/1), a few white and black grits. **Fig. 7–52.**

795 (394–66). PH .059; Est D rim .10

Fine clay banded reddish brown (2.5YR 5/4) and light red (2.5YR 6/6), some minute to small white and black grits; very pale brown slip (10YR 7/3). **Fig. 7–52.**

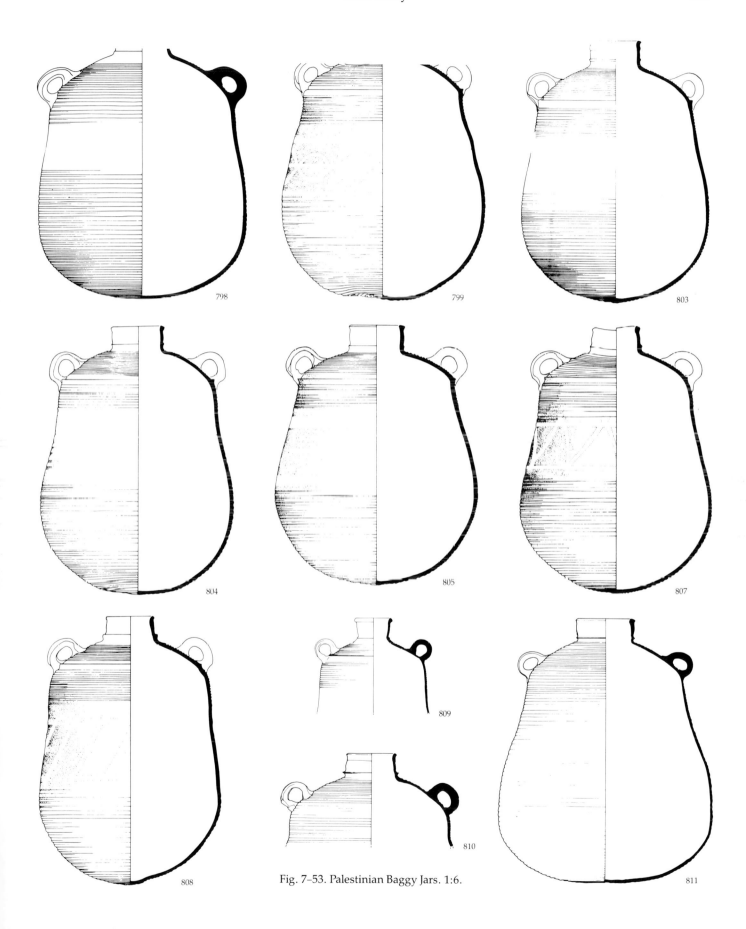

Fig. 7–53. Palestinian Baggy Jars. 1:6.

796   (331–66). PH .059; D rim .08

Fine dark gray clay (7.5YR N4/), some minute to small white and black grits; exterior surface reddish brown (2.5YR 5/4). **Fig. 7–52.**

797   (222–64). PH (a) .056 (b) .089 (c) .093; D rim (a) .10

Coarse clay, light red core (2.5YR 6/6), outer bands reddish yellow (5YR 6/6), minute to small white and black grits. Surfaces gritty. **Fig. 7–52.**

798   (120–65). H .44; D rim .092

Light brown clay. **Fig. 7–53; Pl. 7–6.**

799   (121–65). H .45; D rim .09, bottom .21

Surface variegated reddish brown (5YR 5/3), reddish gray (5YR 5/2), and pinkish gray (7.5YR 6/2). Three very pale brown bands (10YR 8/3) painted around mid-body. The middle one runs through a guilloche pattern enclosed by upper and lower bands. **Fig. 7–53.**

800   (122–65). H .44–.453; D rim .08, bottom .19

Coarse clay, gray core (7.5YR N5/), outer bands pinkish gray (7.5YR 6/2); white (10YR 8/1) decoration as on No. 799. **Pl. 7–6.**

801   (123–65). H .46; D rim .09

Surface color red (10R 5/6); white painted decoration (10YR 5/6) as on No. 799. **Pl. 7–6.**

802   (124–65). H .404–.414; D rim .09, bottom .17

Surface color weak red (2.5YR 5/2). White painted decoration (10YR 8/1, 8/2) around body—at least two horizontal bands enclosing a "running loop" pattern. **Pl. 7–6.**

803   (125–65). H .476; D rim .098, bottom .18

Surface variegated brown (10YR 5/4, 5/3), light reddish brown (2.5YR 4/4), reddish brown (2.5YR 5/4), and weak red (10YR 5/4). Very pale brown (10YR 8/3) painted decoration, pattern unclear, around mid-body. **Fig. 7–53.**

804   (126–65). H .454; D rim .092, bottom .17

Surface light yellowish brown (10YR 6/4). Traces of white painted decoration. **Fig. 7–53.**

805   (127–65). H .424; D rim .096, bottom .20

Surface light brown (7.5YR 6/4) and pinkish gray (7.5YR 6/2). Traces of white painted decoration. **Fig. 7–53.**

806   (128–65). H .37; D rim .094, bottom .28

Surface light brown (7.5YR 6/4). White decoration as on No. 799.

807   (129–65). H .438; D rim .082, bottom .17

Surface reddish brown (5YR 5/3). Two horizontal white bands painted around mid-body; zigzag pattern between and interrupting them. **Fig. 7–53.**

808   (131–65). Est H .446; D rim .084

Surface reddish brown (5YR 5/4). Very pale brown painted decoration around body: horizontal lattice pattern. **Fig. 7–53; Pl. 7–6.**

809   (112–65). PH (a) .25 (b) .17; D rim .102

Fine clay banded weak red (2.5YR 4/2) and reddish brown (2.5YR 4/4), many white grits. **Fig. 7–53.**

810   (411–64). PH .19; D rim .096

Fine reddish brown clay (5YR 5/3), partial gray core (5YR 5/1), many white, black, red, and yellow grits; exterior surface dark gray (5YR N4/). **Fig. 7–53.**

811   (106–65). H .445; D rim .102, bottom .17

Fine clay, reddish brown core (5YR 4/4), outer bands dark gray (2.5YR N4/), a few white grits; surfaces gray (5YR 5/1). White painted decoration (10YR 8/2), unclear pattern, on body. **Fig. 7–53; Pl. 7–6.**

812   (99–64). PH .28; D rim .10

Fine light red clay (2.5YR 6/6), occasional gray core (2.5YR N5/), white and black grits; interior surface light olive gray (5Y 6/2), exterior dark gray (2.5YR N4/). White painted decoration (5Y 8/2): vertically set, overlapping wavy lines. Horizontal band crosses wavy lines at upper body. **Fig. 7–54.**

813   (32–66). PH .305; D rim .11

Coarse light red clay (2.5YR 6/6), white and black grits and mineral inclusions; surfaces same as clay on interior, very pale brown (10YR 8/4) on exterior. **Fig. 7–54.**

814   (341–66). PH .043; D rim .10

Fine reddish brown clay (2.5YR 5/4), a few white and black grits; surfaces dark gray (2.5 YR N4/). **Fig. 7–54.**

815   (397–66). PH .051; D rim .09

Fine clay banded brown (7.5YR 5/4) and red (2.5YR 5/6), a few white and black grits; interior surface red (10R 5/6), exterior very dark gray (2.5YR N3/). **Fig. 7–54.**

816   (312–64). PH .045; D rim .11

Fine reddish brown clay (2.5YR 5/4), a few white grits; interior surface weak red (2.5YR 5/2), exterior dark gray (2.5YR N4/). **Fig. 7–54.**

817   (342–66). PH .038; D rim .12

Fine clay, reddish brown core (5YR 5/3), outer bands dark gray (5YR N4/), some white grits; surface very dark gray (2.5YR N3/). **Fig. 7–54.**

818   (491–65). PH .057; D rim .095

Fine reddish brown clay (2.5YR 5/4), some white grits, occasional small ones; surfaces dark gray (2.5YR N4/). **Fig. 7–54.**

819   (662–66). PH .064; D rim .10

Fine clay, weak red core (2.5YR 4/2), outer bands dark gray (2.5YR N4/); surfaces same as outer bands of clay. **Fig. 7–54.**

820   (442–66). PH .055; D rim .11

Fine dark gray clay (2.5YR N4/), a few white grits; surfaces variegated weak red (2.5YR 5/2) and dark gray (2.5YR N4/). **Fig. 7–54.**

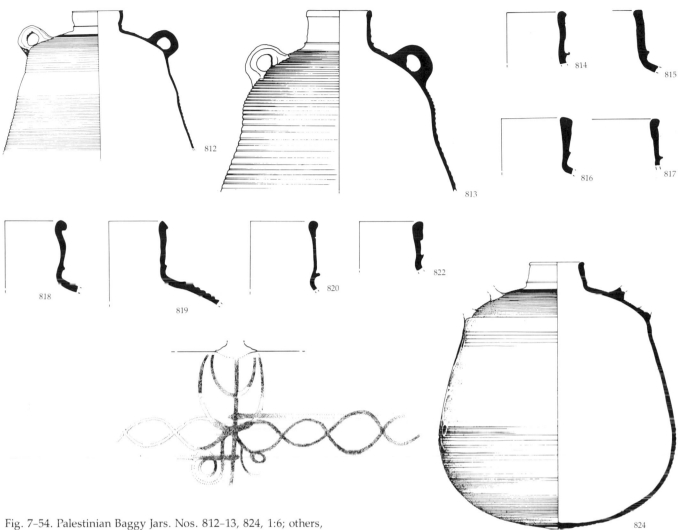

Fig. 7–54. Palestinian Baggy Jars. Nos. 812–13, 824, 1:6; others, 1:3.

821   (465 65). PH .049; D rim .09

Fine clay banded reddish brown (2.5YR 5/4) and dark gray (2.5YR N4/), some white and black grits; surface gray (5YR 5/1).

822   (354–66). PH .04; D rim .11

Fine clay, reddish brown core (5YR 5/4), outer bands very dark gray (2.5YR N3/), a few white grits; surfaces dark gray (5YR 4/1). **Fig. 7–54.**

823   (1213–66). PH .51; D rim .095

Coarse light red clay (2.5YR 6/6), a few white grits; surfaces variegated reddish brown (2.5YR 5/4), dark gray (5YR 4/1), and gray (5YR 5/1). Remains of white painted decoration (10YR 8/2). **Pl. 7–6.**

824   (75–66). H .44; D rim .094, bottom .208

Coarse red clay (2.5YR 4/6), minute to small white grits. White (10YR 8/2) painted guilloche pattern between horizontal bands with a vertical element resembling a menorah rising above. **Fig. 7–54.**

825   (98–64). PH .37

Fine reddish brown clay (2.5YR 5/4), some white and black grits, a few small white ones; interior surface light olive gray (5Y 6/2), exterior dark gray (2.5YR N4/). White (10YR 8/2) decoration as No. 812. **Pl. 7–7.**

826   (105–64). Max dim .30

Fine red clay (2.5YR 5/6), some white and black grits, occasional small white ones; interior surface reddish brown (2.5YR 5/4), exterior dark gray (2.5YR N4/). White painted decoration (5Y 8/1) as No. 812. **Pl. 7–7.**

827   (103–64). PH .266

Fine red clay (2.5YR 5/6), incomplete core/inner band of gray (2.5YR N5/), white and black grits, a few small to large white ones; interior surface weak red (2.5YR 5/2), exterior dark gray (2.5YR N4/). White (10YR 8/1) decoration as No. 812. **Pl. 7–7.**

Bell Lids

1,062 fragments; 398 belong to Variant 1 and 167 to Variant 2. Pieces preserving part of the body and/or body

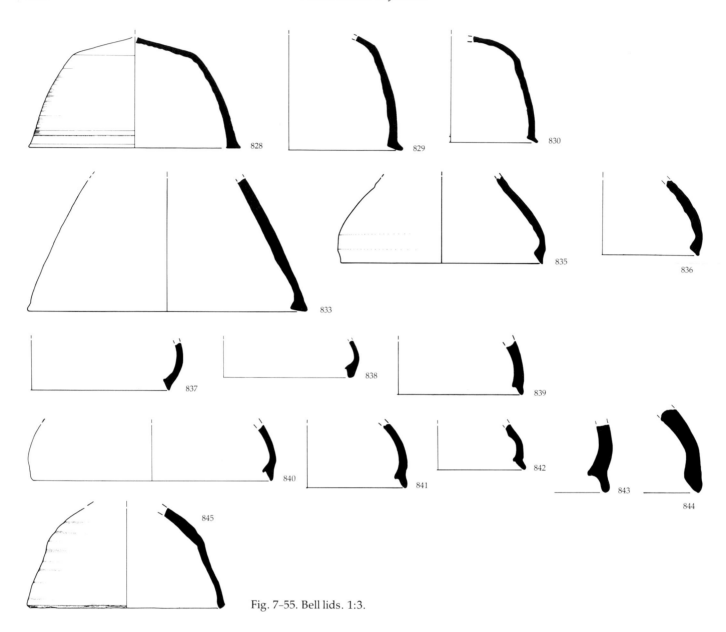

Fig. 7–55. Bell lids. 1:3.

and handle (497 in all) cannot be directly associated with either variant, although in fabric most are like Variant 1. For what kind of amphora or large jar these were intended is not indicated by the evidence from Jalame. They have not been found in such large numbers at any other site, as far as is known. However, similar lids have been recovered from nearby tomb caves (Ein Hashofet and Nahariya) and a jar with a bell-shaped lid in place is in the Museum Haaretz (MHR 278). It is logical to assume that such lids were used to seal amphoras and wine jars of the 3rd and 4th centuries. Such lids are discussed in Zevulun-Olenik, *Talmudic Period*, 26 (English section), 49 (Hebrew section), and figs. 110–12.

Variant 1 (Nos. 828–44). Typical is the inward-beveled rim. The bevel may be slight (No. 833) or quite pronounced (No. 834). It may lie in a straight line from the body or hook inward sharply. Much variety can be observed in the

treatment of the rim. The bevel may be flat, flat with a ridge around the inner edge, or concave with an inner ridge. The body wall usually presents a gentle curve accompanied by a definite transition to the shoulder. The fabric is soft, at times almost powdery. Frequently small white grits have pitted or erupted through the surfaces. Occasionally remains of slip can be seen (No. 833).

828   (893–65). PH .09; D rim .17

Shallow groove above rim on exterior, low random ribbing on interior. Fine clay, pinkish gray core (7.5YR 6/2), outer bands light red (2.5YR 6/6), many white and black grits. **Fig. 7–55.**

829   (160–65). PH (a) .093 (c) .052; Max dim .082; D rim .18

Low ribbing on interior shoulder. Fine reddish yellow clay (5YR 6/6), many white and black grits. **Fig. 7–55.**

830 (381–65). PH .087; D rim .14

Fine clay, dark gray core (2.5YR N4/), outer bands light red (2.5YR 6/6), many white, black, and yellow grits. **Fig. 7–55.**

831 (423–66). PH .041; D rim .19

Irregular incised line on body above rim. Fine clay banded reddish gray (5YR 5/2) and red (2.5YR 4/6), many white and black grits, occasional large white ones.

832 (438–66). PH .039; D rim .17

Fine red clay (2.5YR 5/6), some white grits, a few small ones.

833 (93–64). PH .106; D rim .224

Shallow groove above rim on exterior. Fine clay banded light brown (7.5YR 6/4) and light red (2.5YR 6/6), many white and black grits, a few small reddish ones. **Fig. 7–55.**

834 (433–66). PH .043; D rim .21

Fine light brown clay (7.5YR 6/4), a few white and black grits; remains of very pale brown slip (10YR 8/3) on interior.

835 (99–65). PH .071; D rim .161

Fine red clay (2.5YR 5/6), some minute to small white grits. **Fig. 7–55.**

836 (489–66). PH .06; D rim .155

Faint ribbing on interior body. Fine clay banded brown (10YR 5/3), light red (2.5YR 6/6), and reddish brown (2.5YR 5/4), many white and black grits, a few small white ones. **Fig. 7–55.**

837 (436–66). PH .039; D rim .22

Fine light red clay (2.5YR 6/6), some white and black grits. **Fig. 7–55.**

838 (437–66). PH .03; D rim .21

Fine red clay (2.5YR 5/6), some white grits. **Fig. 7–55.**

839 (790–66). PH .044; D rim .20

Shallow groove above rim on exterior. Fine clay, incomplete pink core (7.5YR 8/4), outer bands reddish brown (5YR 5/4), some white and black grits. **Fig. 7–55.**

840 (1008–66). PH .046; D rim .195

Fine clay banded red (2.5YR 5/6) and gray (5YR 5/1), some white and black grits, occasional small white ones. **Fig. 7–55.**

841 (421–66). PH .052; D rim .16

Coarse clay banded brown (7.5YR 5/2) and red (10R 5/6), many white and black grits, occasional small white ones. **Fig. 7–55.**

842 (449–66). PH .038; D rim .142

Two shallow grooves around exterior: one on rim, another at junction of rim and body. Fine clay, dark reddish gray core (10R 4/1), outer bands reddish brown (5YR 5/3), many white and black grits. **Fig. 7–55.**

843 (58–66). PH .036; Est D rim .14

Rim slightly misshapen. Fine clay, pale brown core (10YR 6/3), outer bands light brown (7.5YR 6/4), some white and black grits. **Fig. 7–55.**

844 (424–66). PH .044; Est D rim .16

Fine clay, pale brown core (10YR 6/3), outer bands yellowish red (5YR 5/6), some white and black grits. **Fig. 7–55.**

Variant 2 (Nos. 845–47). This group is distinguished from the former by its rounded-off rim, which may or may not be thickened. No. 847 is larger than usual, and its angular knob handle, concave on the top, presents the only instance in which a rim is associated with a handle (though the two parts do not actually join). Harder fabric than that of Variant 1, less inclined to be powdery.

845 (483–66). PH .08; D rim .16

Low ribbing on exterior. Fine reddish brown clay (5YR 5/4), some white and black grits, occasional small white grits. **Fig. 7–55.**

846 (430–66). PH .053; D rim .14

Faint random ribbing on inside and outside of body. Fine reddish yellow clay (5YR 6/6), some white and black grits. **Fig. 7–56.**

847 (118–65). Est H .18; D knob .035, rim .18

Low, widely spaced ribbing on interior and exterior shoulder. Coarse pink clay (7.5YR 7/4), some white and black grits, airholes. **Fig. 7–56.**

Body and Handle Fragments (Nos. 848–51). The greatest number of pieces closely resemble Variant 1 in fabric. Generally, the small knob handle is solid and pyramidal in shape. An exception is No. 850 on which the knob is smaller than usual and slightly convex on the upper surface. It also has another uncommon feature: around the shoulder on the exterior is an excess smeared area of clay that stuck there at some point during the manufacturing process. The lid may have been placed upside down on a clay chock, perhaps to finish the rim, with the result that some clay adhered to the shoulder and through lack of attention to detail was not removed. The small lid, No. 851, is unique in shape, handle, and fabric. There is no transition from body to shoulder, the handle is more a bulb than a knob, and the surfaces are gritty. As no rim is preserved it is not possible to determine whether the piece belongs to Variant 1 or 2 or neither. The contexts for bell lids at Jalame place them before 351. Many were found in the area of the olive press.[112] General parallels may be noted for the shape.[113]

848 (488–66). PH .084; D handle .029

Fine light red clay (2.5YR 6/6), some white and black grits, air holes. **Fig. 7–56; Pl. 7–7.**

112. See Chapter 2.
113. No parallels for Variant 1 are known. For a lid similar to Variant 2, No. 847, in handle and rim but with a lower, more rounded profile, see Bagatti-Milik, 138, fig. 32.24, and Ben-Tor, "Horvat Usa," fig. 12.2. A general parallel to Variant 2 lids may be seen at Shavei Zion (Prausnitz, *Shavei Zion*, fig. 11.9, 12, 13).

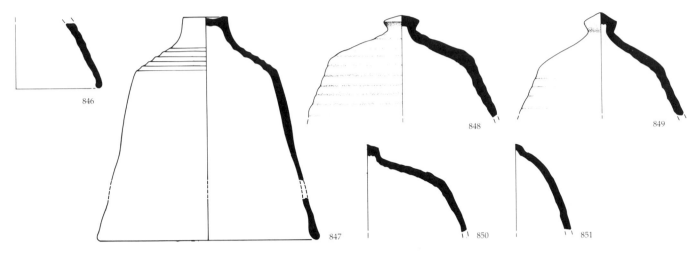

Fig. 7–56. Bell lids. 1:3.

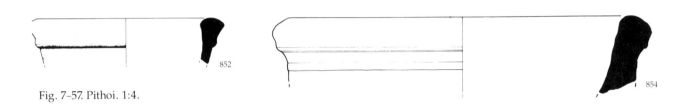

Fig. 7–57. Pithoi. 1:4.

849　(70–66). PH .087; D handle .027

Low, widely spaced ribbing on inside and outside of body. Fine reddish yellow clay (5YR 6/6), some white and black grits ranging from minute to large. **Fig. 7–56.**

850　(379–65). PH .07; D handle .019

Random ribbing on interior shoulder. Fine clay, very pale brown core (10YR 7/3), outer bands light red (2.5YR 6/6), some white and black grits, occasional small ones. **Fig. 7–56.**

851　(6–66). PH .07; D handle .015

Coarse reddish yellow clay (5YR 6/6), many white and black grits. **Fig. 7–56; Pl. 7–7.**

Pithoi

Three fragments. The fabric of Nos. 853–54 appears to be the same as that of the North Syrian Mortaria (see above). The context of No. 852 is Period 3, while Nos. 853–54 come from Period 4 contexts.

852　(534–66). PH .049; Est D rim .21

Fine clay, brown core (7.5YR 5/4), outer bands yellowish red (5YR 5/6), some minute to small white grits. **Fig. 7–57.**

853　(24–65). PH .133; Est D rim .38–.40

Coarse dark reddish brown clay (2.5YR 3/4), some minute to small white grits, many minute to small dark shiny bits.

854　(247–64). PH .084; Est D rim .40

Coarse clay variegated black (2.5YR N2.5/) and dusky red (2.5YR 3/2), many white grits and shiny bits, a few yellowish grits. **Fig. 7–57.**

Miscellaneous Shapes (Nos. 857–61)

No. 855 is a single example; the suggested date is Late Roman. Twenty-nine fragments of pots like No. 856 were found; a similar date of pre–351 is suggested. One hundred and two sherds like No. 857 were recovered. On one body fragment part of the exterior has been purposely roughened. The potter pulled clay upward in short strokes, leaving a relief pattern. This may have been intended as decoration. Contexts offer a date before 351. Some of the sherds recorded with the soft light red fabric storage jars (see above) may belong to pots like No. 858. It will be remembered that such jars were common in contexts ranging from before 351 to after 383. The saucer (No. 859) is from topsoil. The small lid (No. 860) is concave on the upper surface, in order to make removal from the container easier. No. 861 has a flat bottom and vertical lower side through which a number of holes were punched from the exterior. Other fragments of the same piece show that higher up the wall curves inward and was separated from the lower part by a broad collar. It is probably a lantern: light from a lamp placed inside would have shone through the holes. Its context offers a date before 351.

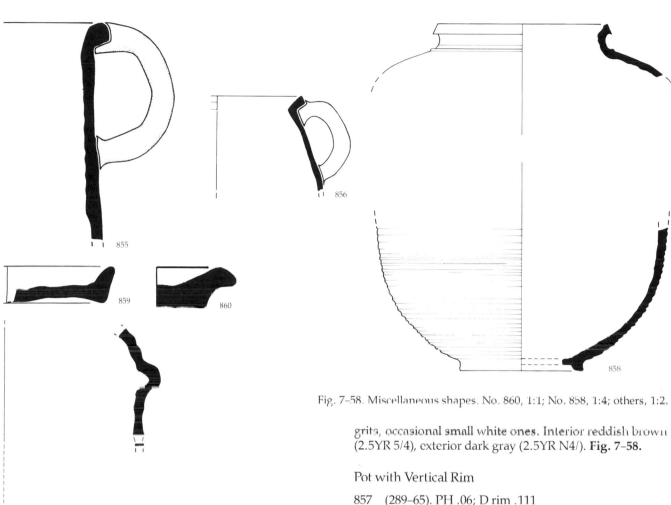

Fig. 7–58. Miscellaneous shapes. No. 860, 1:1; No. 858, 1:4; others, 1:2.

grits, occasional small white ones. Interior reddish brown (2.5YR 5/4), exterior dark gray (2.5YR N4/). **Fig. 7–58.**

Pot with Vertical Rim

857   (289–65). PH .06; D rim .111

Fine brown clay (7.5YR 5/4).

Pot in Soft Light Red Fabric

858   (121–66). PH (a) .058 (b) .15; H rest. .39; D rim .18

Fine clay banded light red (10R 6/6) and light brown (7.5YR 6/4), a few white and red grits. **Fig. 7–58.**

Saucer

859   (14–65). H .02; D rim .115, bottom .105

Fine light reddish brown clay (5YR 6/4), a few white grits; traces of reddish yellow slip (5YR 6/8). **Fig. 7–58.**

Lid

860   (2–66). H .02; D rim .044

Fine reddish yellow clay, a few white and red grits. **Fig. 7–58.**

Lantern

861   (277–65). PH (a) .05 (b) .069; D bottom .12

Coarse light red clay (2.5YR 6/6), some white and black grits. **Fig. 7–58.**

Deep Straight-Sided Pot

855   (208–64). PH .116; D rim .22

Coarse clay, incomplete yellowish red core (5YR 5/6), outer bands red (2.5YR 4/6), a few white and black grits, occasional small white ones. **Fig. 7–58.**

Pot with Wide Everted Rim

856   (207–64). PH .102; D rim .19

Coarse dark gray clay (5YR 4/1), some white and black

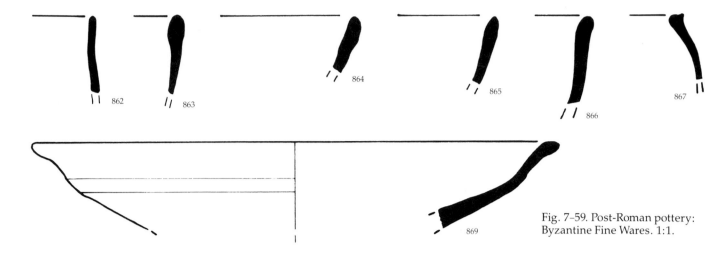

Fig. 7–59. Post-Roman pottery: Byzantine Fine Wares. 1:1.

Post-Roman Pottery

A small number of sherds dating as late as Crusader times represent the post-Roman period.

Byzantine Fine Wares

Gichon, in his basic study, identified three groups by ware.[114] Further distinctions were made according to surface treatment and decoration consisting of slipping, painting, burnishing, scraping, and rouletting. Both open and closed shapes occur, but bowls and cups are most common. Gichon notes that it is not yet possible to ascertain when these wares began to be made; however, they are in existence by the 5th c. and continue as late as the 10th. The distribution, "or their spread and frequency, was in the region west of the Jordan between Sinai and Samaria."[115] Eight fragments were found at Jalame, six of which are rims of hemispherical cups; the others are bowls. Although all three wares are represented, C appears most frequently. Only Nos. 863 and 866 have micro-rouletting.[116] Contexts at Jalame offer no closer date than 4th c.

Hemispherical Cups (Nos. 862–67)

862   (287-64). PH .02

Fine clay, dark gray core (2.5YR N4/), outer bands very dark gray (2.5YR N3/); remains of pink slip (5YR 8/4). **Fig. 7–59.**

863   (409-65). PH .021 D rim .07

Fine dark reddish gray clay (10R 4/1); light red slip (2.5YR 6.6) bands of dark reddish gray (10R 3/1). "Micro-rouletting" on both surfaces below rim. Scraped lines on interior. **Fig. 7–59.**

864   (546-65). PH .017; D rim .08

Fine clay, dark gray core (2.5YR N4/), outer bands light red (2.5YR 6/6); light red slip (2.5YR 6/6). **Fig. 7–59.**

865   (435-65). PH .024

Fine reddish yellow clay (5YR 6/6); pink slip (5YR 7/3) with bands of light red (2.5YR 6/6). Scraped lines on exterior. **Fig. 7–59.**

866   (423-65). PH .018

Fine clay incompletely banded reddish yellow (5YR 6/6) and gray (2.5YR N5/); pink slip (5YR 7/4) with bands of weak red (2.5YR N4/2). Reddish yellow (5YR 7/6) burnished band on exterior. "Micro-rouletting" on interior below rim. Scraped lines on both surfaces. **Fig. 7–59.**

867   (734-66). PH .019

Fine clay, dark reddish gray core (10R 4/1), thin outer bands weak red (10R 4/3); light gray slip (5YR 7/1). Scraped lines on both surfaces. **Fig. 7–59.**

Bowl with Out-Splayed Rim (Nos. 868–69)

868   (143-64). PH .012; D rim .14

Fine clay, dark gray core (2.5YR N4/), thin outer bands light red (2.5YR 6/6), slip light red (2.5YR 6/6) and pink (7/5YR 7/4), red (2.5YR 5/8) where burnished. Scraped lines present.

869   (144-64). PH .024; D rim .14

Fine clay, dark gray core (2.5YR N4/), outer bands light red (2.5YR 6/6); light red slip (2.5YR 6/6) with bands of weak red (2.5YR 5/2), red (2.5YR 5/6) where burnished. **Fig. 7–59.**

Umayyad Period (mid–7th to mid–8th c.)

Three categories of pottery date to this period. Nos. 870–79 illustrate the fragmentary nature of the 40 sherds of "White Wares" found.[117] No. 879 is mold-made and has a

114. M. Gichon, "Fine Byzantine Wares from the South of Israel," *PEQ* (1974) 119–39. For the several wares see 119–20.
115. Ibid., 136–39.
116. For a description of micro-rouletting see ibid., 121.

117. See Baramki, "Kh. el-Mefjer," 65–103.

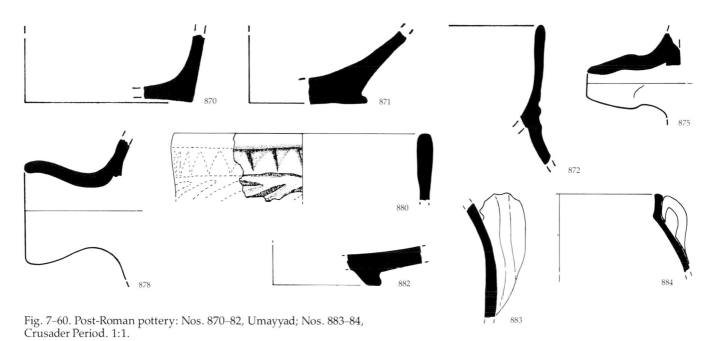

Fig. 7–60. Post-Roman pottery: Nos. 870–82, Umayyad; Nos. 883–84, Crusader Period. 1:1.

relief tongue pattern on the exterior. Three glazed sherds, of which No. 882 is the best preserved, also belong to this period.[118] Four sherds of bowls in the *Kerbschnittmuster* technique (of which Nos. 880–81 are catalogued) show the deeply cut geometric designs typical of this pottery.[119] No. 881 still preserves the painted decoration that often overlies the cut pattern.

"White Wares" (Nos. 870–79)

Bases

870 (94–66). PH .02; D bottom .09

Fine very pale brown clay (10YR 7/3), occasional black grits. **Fig. 7–60.**

871 (762–65). PH .019; D base .06

Fine light gray clay (2.5Y 7/2), a few black grits. **Fig. 7–60.**

Jugs

872 (43–64). PH .04

Fine light gray clay (10YR 7/2), a few black grits. Oblique incised lines around exterior below rim. **Fig. 7–60.**

873 (924–66). PH .028; D rim .11

Rounded-off rim. Coarse pink clay (7.5YR 7/4), some white, red, and black grits. Surfaces gritty.

118. See F. E. Day in Delougaz-Haines, 42–47, and Meyers, *Khirbet Shema*, 214–15.
119. For examples see Crowfoot, *Samaria* 3, 361–64, fig. 84a.4–8; FitzGerald, *Beth Shan* 3, 36, pl. 26.3; Ben-Tor, "Tel Yoqneam, 1977," 73, fig. 8.2–3.

874 (732–65). PH with handle .061; D rim .07

Triangular rim and handle. Coarse weak red clay (2.5YR 5/2), some minute to small white grits, a few black ones. Surfaces gritty.

Spouts

875 (1058–66). L of spout .042

Coarse clay, light yellowish brown core (10YR 6/4), outer bands reddish yellow (5YR 6/6), many white, red, and black grits, some erupted through surfaces. **Fig. 7–60.**

876 (266–65). L of spout .04; Max dim .058

Coarse light yellowish brown clay (2.5Y 6/4), many minute to small white and black grits and mineral inclusions.

877 (143–65). L of spout .054; Max dim .072

Coarse clay banded brown (7.5YR 5/2) and reddish yellow (5YR 6/6), many white and black grits and mineral inclusions. Surfaces gritty.

878 (267–64). L of spout .047; Max dim .082

Coarse reddish yellow clay (5YR 6/4), a few white and black grits; traces of pink slip (5YR 8/3). **Fig. 7–60.**

Mold-Made Vessel

879 (17–66). Max dim .05

Fine light gray clay (10YR 7/1), a few black grits. Relief tongue pattern on exterior, upper part smeared.

Kerbschnittmuster Technique Pieces (Nos. 880–81)

880 (1062–66). PH .034

Fine clay banded reddish brown (5YR 5/4), reddish gray (5YR 5/2), and gray (5YR 5/1), a few white and black grits.

Deeply cut triangular and oblique line decoration on exterior. **Fig. 7–60.**

881   (381–66). Max dim .042

Fine gray clay (5YR 5/1), occasional black grits. Deeply cut band of white painted triangles (10YR 8/2) around exterior, enclosed by two dusky red bands (10R 3/4).

Green-Glazed Vessel (No. 882)

882   (190–64). PH .02; D foot .12

Fine clay banded pinkish gray (7.5YR 6/2) and gray (5YR 5/1), a few black grits. Green to dark green glaze on interior and exterior except for underside of foot and bottom. **Fig. 7–60.**

Medieval Cooking Wares (Nos. 883–84)

Two examples, both in a fabric typical of the Crusader period. No. 883 with its distinctive arch handle horizontally set finds parallels among globular cooking pots with several different rim forms.[120] No. 884 is assigned to the Crusader period on the basis of its close similarity to No. 883.

883   (83–65). Max dim .076

Coarse light red clay (2.5YR 6/6), some black grits, a few small and large white ones. **Fig. 7–60.**

884   (306–65). PH .085

Coarse clay, dark reddish gray core (5YR 5/2), outer bands reddish brown (5YR 5/4), some minute to large white and black grits. **Fig. 7–60.**

120. See Meyers, *Khirbet Shema*, 192–93, fig. 7.6, dated 1150–1277; and A. Ben-Tor et al., "The Second Season of Excavations at Tel Yoqne'am, 1978," *IEJ* 29 (1979) 73–83, esp. 76–77, fig. 5.12.

8

WALTER BERRY

The Minor Objects

The small objects recovered in excavations on an ancient site usually reveal much of the conditions of daily life. At Jalame this portion of the archaeological record is somewhat obscured, for when the hilltop was finally deserted at some point in the 5th century, little of value was left behind. In addition, no significant pattern of distribution for the minor finds has appeared from study of the find spots. Thus they consist to a large extent simply of objects discarded or lost. Most can be dated to the later 3rd through early 5th century. A number of pieces are earlier, late 1st or 2nd century for the most part, while a few seem to belong to post-Roman times.

The finds have been divided by use under five headings: (1) Jewelry and Related Objects; (2) Instruments and Implements; (3) Vessels; (4) Structural Materials; (5) Miscellaneous. Find spots are given only when they are significant.

Jewelry and Related Objects

This category includes items of personal adornment. Over half of these are of glass, but in view of their rarity it is unlikely that most of them are products of the Jalame factory. Less than one-third come from the factory dump and nearly half from Trenches A–2 to A–6 (north portion of the excavated area).

Finger Rings (Nos. 1–4)

Three finger rings of glass were found and one of bronze. Glass rings ranging in color from transparent light green to opaque, apparently black, are found frequently in Roman and Byzantine contexts in Palestine.[1]

Despite their small size such objects are usually identified as finger rings, probably for children.[2] Possibly, they were worn as beads or pendants[3] or served as loops on glass vessels.[4] Nos. 1–2 show different methods of manufacture. The bronze signet ring is a variant of a common type.

1   (G238–65). Glass "finger ring"
Inner D .012. Opaque green. Small flattened bezel. **Fig. 8–1.**
Cf. Crowfoot, *Samaria* 3, 420; Bagatti-Milik, 159, fig. 37, no. 31 and pl. 41, photo 127, no. 41, 3rd or 4th c.; Erdmann, "Mezad Tamar," 111, pl. 8, no. 934, dated 3rd–5th c. This seems to have been made like the modern glass bracelets produced at Hebron: a lump of softened glass is pierced and held on one rod while the circuit of the ring is gradually widened with a second rod; see M. Korfmann, "Zur Herstellung nahtloser Glasringe," *BJ* 166 (1966) 48–61.

2   (G236–65). Glass "finger ring"
Inner D .011. Opaque light blue. Irregular oval ring with overlapping ends. **Fig. 8–1.**
Somewhat similar is Bagatti-Milik, 159, pl. 41, photo 127, no. 40, 3rd or 4th c. Produced from a drawn rod formed around a cylinder and joined by overlapping the ends, as seen in twisted glass bracelets, e.g., ibid., fig. 37, no. 34.

3   (G23–66). Glass ring, half (?) preserved, dark enamel-like weathering
Inner D .013; Th ca. .003. Colorless greenish. Five added yellow threads marvered into surface, twisted to produce spiral. Diameter varies, widening at one end. A finger ring, a looped handle of an instrument, or a vessel handle. **Fig. 8–1.**
Cf. Nos. 1–2, 28–29.

1. The variety of glass finger rings is reflected in F. Henkel, *Die römischen Fingerringe der Rheinlande* (Berlin, 1913) 154–58, 256–57, pls. 63–65, nos. 1697–1756; Petrie, *Daily Use* 15, pl. 11, nos. 15, 18; Harden, *Karanis*, 284, pl. 21, no. 855; and Davidson, *Corinth* 12, 233, 248, pl. 107, nos. 1992–93. For Palestine, see in addition to parallels for Nos. 1–2, Reisner, *Samaria* 1, 332, no. 2b. See also S. Loeschcke, "Frühchristliche Werkstätte für Glasschmuck in Trier," *Trier Heimatbuch* (Trier, 1925) 337f, 341f, 351f, 356f, pls. 2 and 5.

2. I believe the rings from Jalame and others with or without bezels cited below, which have an inner D of ca. .01 or more, are best termed "finger rings" in order to differentiate them from ring beads.
3. E.g., Charlesworth, "Glass," 245, fig. 132, two 3rd c. ring beads only slightly smaller than Nos. 1–2.
4. For glass rings used as loops on glass vessels, see Stern, *Custodia*, 142–45, pl. 4, no. 45, a Syrian beaker of 8th–9th c.

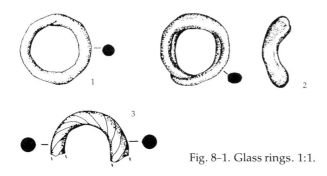

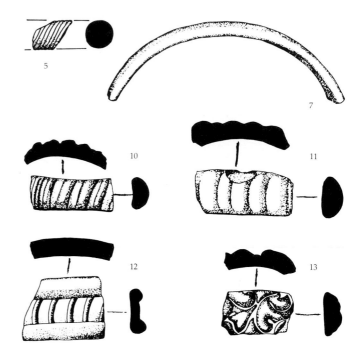

Fig. 8–1. Glass rings. 1:1.

4 (M8–64). Bronze finger ring, part of hoop missing

Inner D .02; L of bezel .023. Narrow oval hoop, circular in section, with angular joint to long narrow bezel. Intaglio, probably a head, obscured by corrosion. 2nd or 3rd c. **Pl. 8–1.**

Cf. Baramki, "Karm al-Shaikh," pl. 9, no. 1, from Grave 44, dated 2nd or 3rd c.

Glass Bracelets (Nos. 5–13)

Four types of glass bracelets were found: spiral (No. 5), semicircular plain (Nos. 6–9), semicircular with tooled decoration (Nos. 10–12), and semicircular with molded decoration (No. 13).[5] They were probably produced just as they are today[6] and were most likely worn on the wrist or upper arm.[7] Unless otherwise noted, all examples have white enamel-like weathering and iridescence.

5 (G104–65). Fragment broken at both ends

W .007. Purple. Twisted clockwise to produce close-set narrow spiral decoration. **Fig. 8–2; Pl. 8–1.**

Cf. Macalister, *Gezer* 1, 357, and 3, pl. 104, no. 19, blue, found in Tomb 147 with Late Roman "palm branch" lamps; Iliffe, "El Bassa," 89, pl. 24, no. 1a, dated 4th–8th c.; Makhouly, "el Jish," 47, pl. 32, nos. 2d and e, 4th or 5th c.; Sussman, "Rehovot," 69–71, pl. 13, no. 8, dated Late Roman; Bagatti-Milik, 156, fig. 37, no. 34, 3rd or 4th c. This type continues into the Byzantine period; see Davidson, *Corinth* 12, 262, pl. 112, nos. 2143–47, and A. von Saldern, "Glass from Sardis," *AJA* 66 (1962) 12, pl. 7, fig. 20, both with further references.

6 (G375, G392–64). Two non-joining fragments preserving half

Inner D .054; Max Th .004; Max W .005. Light blue. Irregular flat band. 4th–5th c. Found in Trench K, depth ca. 1.10, in Period 4 context.

---

5. The diversity of glass bracelets from Palestine is reflected in Reisner, *Samaria* 1, 332, nos. 3a–h; and in Bagatti-Milik, 159–60, pl. 40, photo 124, nos. 1–19; see also Loeschcke, as in n. 1, 353ff, pl. 5.

6. Korfmann, as in No. 1, above.

7. McCown, *Nasbeh* 1, 269, pl. 20, nos. 9, 12, illustrates a dark green glass bracelet (or armlet) on the upper arm of a female skeleton of Roman date. Diameters of bracelets at this site range from .041 to .077, those at Jalame from .054 to .075.

Fig. 8–2. Glass bracelets. 1:1.

For this and Nos. 7–9, cf. Macalister, *Gezer* 3, pl. 9, nos. 11–13, and pl. 104, no. 19, dated Late Roman or Early Byzantine; Baramki, "Karm al-Shaikh," pl. 6, no. 14, pl. 14, no. 5, and pl. 15, no. 3, undated; Iliffe, "El Bassa," 89, pl. 24, no. 2b, somewhat smaller, end of 4th c.; Bagatti-Milik, 160, pl. 40, photo 124, no. 4, 3rd or 4th c.; Avigad, *Beth Shearim* 3, 68–69 and 216, pl. 73, no. 22, several similar fragments from Catacomb 15 found with tooled bracelets like Nos. 10–11 and associated with glass vessels dated by Barag (in Avigad, *Beth Shearim* 3, 201–3) to first half of 4th c.

7 (G69–65). One-third preserved

Est. D .07. Light bluish green. Two similar fragments, one (G190–66) of same color, the other (G80–65) dark bluish green and thicker. 3rd–5th c. **Fig. 8–2.**

8 (G137–65). Small fragment

Est. D .07; PL .032. Opaque dark green. Surface find. Probably medieval.

9 (G193–64). Small fragment

Est. D .065; PL .065. Longitudinal red streaks on dark purple. Probably 3rd–5th c.

10 (G147–66). Small fragment

Est. D .06; PL .021. Opaque, apparently black. Interior smoothed; exterior deeply tooled diagonally to produce raised ribbing. Ribs ca. .003 wide. Mid–4th c. From early factory dump with coin of Constantine II (352–354). **Fig. 8–2.**

Cf. Macalister, *Gezer* 1, 339 and 3, pl. 94, no. 8, from "Byzantine" Tomb 99; and 1, 353 and 3, pl. 102, no. 12, of "black" glass, from disturbed Tomb 139; Baramki, "Karm al-Shaikh," pl. 6, nos. 8–9, undated Grave 24; Iliffe, "El Bassa," 89, pl. 24, no. 2a, late 4th c.; Bagatti-Milik, 160, pl. 40, photo 124, no. 15, 3rd or 4th c.; McCown, *Nasbeh* 1, 112, pl. 112, nos. 13, 15, "black . . . with corrugated outer surface," from Late Roman Tomb 6. Opaque "black" glass bracelets seem to appear in Palestine ca. mid-3rd c.; see Macalister, *Gezer* 2, 101; Rahmani, "Raqafot," 82, pl. 23, no. 3, not earlier than ca. 250; Erdmann, "Mezad Tamar," 111, nos. 932–33, plain semicircular examples similar to No. 5 in "black" glass dated mid-3rd to 5th c. Petrie, *Daily Use*, 8, pl. 7, nos. 100–101, shows that in Egypt this type continues into the Coptic period. Loeschcke, as in n. 1, 353f, no. 05.294e, pl. 5, 19 and pl. 6, 3, complete example also in "black" glass, dates (pp. 355f) the production of "schwarzem Glas" at Trier between 250 and 350.

11 (G134b–64). Small fragment

Est. D .07; PL .026. Opaque dark purple. Like No. 8, but less pronounced ribbing perpendicular to edge of bracelet. Ribs ca. .005 wide. Probably 4th–5th c. **Fig. 8–2.**

Cf. Macalister, *Gezer* 1, 333, and 3, pl. 109, no. 20, of "black resinous paste," from Tomb 76; and 1, 352, and 3, pl. 102, no. 13, of "black" glass, from Tomb 139, both from disturbed contexts; Baramki, "Karm al-Shaikh," pl. 6, no. 13, from undated Grave 24; Bagatti-Milik, 160, fig. 37, no. 35, and pl. 39, photo 122, no. 12, as well as pl. 40, photo 124, nos. 7–13, 3rd or 4th c.

12 (G143–66). Small fragment

Est. D .075; PL .022. Dark blue. Interior smoothed. Exterior edges thickened and rounded. Between edges a band of tooled diagonal ribs. Surface find. Probably 4th–5th c. **Fig. 8–2.**

Cf. Loeschcke, as in n. 1, 354, no. 16600, pl. 5, 21, fragment from Trier, dated Late Roman. T. E. Haevernick, *Die Glasarmringe und Ringperlen der Mittel- und Spätlatènezeit aus dem Europäischen Festland* (Bonn, 1960), mentions the Trier fragment, which she considers Celtic, not "Roman" (p. 65, Group 17a, pl. 14, 2).

13 (G68–65). Small fragment

Est. D .065; PL .019. Apparently black. Inner surface smoothed, outer decorated with molded relief design, perhaps floral. Surface find, without ancient parallel. **Fig. 8–2.**

Hairpins (Nos. 14–15)

It appears that the large number of bone and ivory pins found throughout the Roman Empire, classified here as hairpins, may also have served as cosmetic or toilet implements, or as clothing fasteners or dress ornaments.[8] The method of manufacturing them has been shown from debris of a workshop at Corinth.[9] The two examples from Jalame are typical of the Late Roman

8. See *DarSag*, s.v. Acus; Macalister, *Gezer* 2, 82–90; *Exploration archéologique de Délos faite par l'École Française d'Athènes*, vol. 18, *Le Mobilier Délien*, by W. Deonna (Paris, 1938) 277–81; Davidson, *Corinth* 12, 276–80; Chavane, *Salamine*, 166–72.

9. Davidson, *Corinth* 12, 278–79, pls. 147a, b, and 148b.

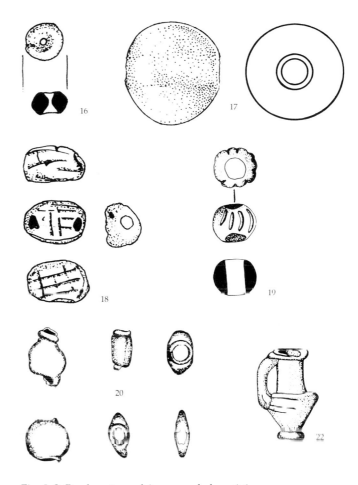

Fig. 8–3. Beads—stone, faience, and glass. 1:1.

period. Glass pins and rods are discussed in the section "Implements and Instruments."

14 (B2–65). End of shaft missing

L .055. Head and neck lathe-polished, remainder carved by hand. Four incised lines around shaft near neck. Conical depression at top. **Pl. 8–1.**

Cf. Bagatti-Milik, 159, fig. 37, no. 28 and pl. 42, photo 128, no. 17, 3rd–4th c.; Petrie, *Daily Use*, 24, pl. 19, no. 40, Roman; Davidson, *Corinth* 12, 284, pl. 118, no. 2324, from a 1st–2nd c. context; Chavane, *Salamine*, 170–71, pl. 47, no. 488, 3rd c., her type B1 (épingle à petite tête globulaire), extending from Roman into Early Byzantine times. Rahmani, "Shmuel ha-Navi," 144–45, pl. 20e, reports similar pins covered with gold foil, 3rd c.

15 (B7–66). Pinhead

H .016. Acorn shape, lathe-turned and polished. Shallow drilled depression on bottom partly overlapping an incised circle; possibly an indication of reworking. From factory dump. **Pl. 8–1.**

Cf. Baramki, "Beit Nattif," 7, pl. 9, no. 17, from Cistern 2, 3rd c. or later; Macalister, *Gezer* 1, 351f and 3, pl. 102, no. 9, from disturbed Tomb 139, found with "black" glass bracelets; Sellers-Baramki, fig. 19, no. 252; Crowfoot-FitzGerald, "Tyropoeon," pl. 21, no. 49 and fig. 21, no. 1,

Late Roman and Early Byzantine context; Davidson, *Corinth* 12, 283, pl. 118, nos. 2300–2302; Chavane, *Salamine*, 171, type B2.

Beads (Nos. 16–21)

Few beads were found and none could be dated with assurance.[10] Nos. 16–17 are probably Roman. The scaraboid No. 18 may be much earlier. More recent beads were also discovered, of which only a group of six (No. 20) is included.

16   (S28–65). Carnelian, chipped

D .01. Translucent reddish brown. Biconical, truncated; drilled from both ends. **Fig. 8–3; Pl. 8–1.**

Cf. Beck, "Beads," short bead type I.B.1.f.

17   (S29–65). Rock crystal, intact

D .026. Nearly spherical, large central hole drilled from both ends. From topsoil. Possibly medieval. **Fig. 8–3; Pl. 8–1.**

Cf. Beck, ibid., standard type I.C.1.a.

18   (S76–65). Serpentine

L .016 Scaraboid, roughly oval, pierced lengthwise, oval in section, flat bottom. Crude geometric pattern incised on all sides. Surface find. **Fig. 8–3.**

Cf. Beck, ibid., group 24, family B9.

19   (G235–65). Faience

H .009; D .011. Bluish green. "Melon bead," shallow grooves. **Fig. 8–3.**

Cf. Beck, ibid., gadrooned regular faceted type I.C.1.a. Very common type. Cf. Baramki, "Karm al-Shaikh," pl. 4, no. 10, from undated Grave 3; Crowfoot, *Samaria* 3, 396, fig. 92, no. 56, from 3rd–5th c. grave; Sussman, "Rehovot," 70, pl. 13, no. 8, end of Roman period, found with glass bracelet similar to No. 5; Meyers, *Khirbet Shema*, 137, pl. 8.11, no. 22, from Tomb 29 North (not "South," as in plate caption), late 2nd–early 5th c.

20   (G234–65). Six glass beads, no two identical, unweathered

Largest: L .016. Yellowish green to yellowish brown. Irregular blobs pierced lengthwise. Five preserve short spirals of excess glass at ends of holes. 5th c. or later. From r-s:9–10 (Trench A–6), depth 1.50. **Fig. 8–3; Pl. 8–1.**

21   (B1–67). Bone disk

D .01; Th .001. Flat thin disk, off-center suspension hole. Possibly medieval. **Pl. 8–1.**

Pendants (Nos. 22–23)

Two pendants are of special interest. The miniature glass pitcher (No. 22) belongs to a group of supposedly

Christian prophylactic objects called the "Two Vases of Joseph of Arimathea," while the bronze amulet (No. 23) contained a scroll.

22   (G237–65). Glass pitcher pendant

H .024; D at shoulder .012; D at lip .009. Opaque, apparently black. Small flattened circular base. Conical body, rounded, horizontal shoulder. Thick neck, approximately oval in section, vertical ridge at front. Trail forming handle attached below rim and to shoulder. Uneven coil rim. Possibly early 4th c. From I:25 (Trench M–1), depth .25, possibly Period 2 context. **Fig. 8–3; Pl. 8–1.**

Miniature handled vessels from Palestine are of two distinct types: a simple vase or pitcher form (e.g., G. A. Eisen and F. Kouchakji, *Glass*, 2 vols. (New York, 1927) 516, fig. 222, right) and a "guard" type in which the body of the vessel is enclosed within a network (Crowfoot, *Samaria* 3, 413, fig. 95, no. 19). Both types are usually made of dark blue or opaque "black" glass. Most examples of the simple variety have white or yellow trailed zigzag decoration around the body, perhaps imitating the openwork of the "guard" type; both types may imitate full-size openwork vessels. For an excellent summary of current knowledge of these objects see Stern, *Custodia*, 112–15, with numerous parallels. Cf. also V. Tzaferis, "Tombs in Western Galilee," *Atiqot* 5 (1969) 75, pl. 17, nos. 4–5, two pendants, one of each type, with workmanship of no. 5 and lack of decoration very similar to our No. 22, from a tomb at Yehiam in use late 3rd to first half of 4th c.; thus the two types were roughly contemporary. For the pitcher type, see also Macalister, *Gezer* 1, 377–78, and 3, pl. 119, no. 9, from Tomb 199, probably Late Roman; Lamon-Shipton, *Megiddo* 1, 157, pl. 102, no. 11 (pictured upside-down), a surface find. For the identification of these objects as amulets, see Eisen and Kouchakji, *Glass*, 515–16, 520–21, 694ff; and Stern, *Custodia*, 110–15. The connection between these objects and the so-called Vases of Joseph of Arimathea is dubious, but their use as amulets is plausible.

23   (M41–66). Bronze cylindrical amulet, one end damaged

L .059; D .008. Bronze sheet folded to form tube, suspension loop near one end, another probably at opposite end now missing. Tube contained tightly rolled thin metal sheet .047 wide, length undetermined. Analysis by Römisch-Germanisches Zentralmuseum, Mainz, determined sheet is 80% lead, 20% zinc. Probably mid–4th c. From early factory dump. **Pl. 8–1.**

For the cylinder, cf. F. Marshall, *Catalogue of the Jewellery, Greek, Etruscan, and Roman, in Department of Antiquities, British Museum* (London, 1911), 380–81, pl. 71, no. 3155, gold, with suspension chain, not earlier than 2nd or 3rd c., enclosing an earlier gold sheet inscribed in Greek, from South Italy; M. Siebourg, "Ein gnostisches Goldamulet aus Gellep," *BJ* 103 (1898) 125, pl. 7, nos. 9–11, gold, 3rd or 4th c. Bronze cylinders, e.g., Avigad, *Beth Shearim* 3, 109f and 214, fig. 101, no. 1 (no. 2 probably belonged to this), no doubt served some cosmetic function, while tubes like Macalister, *Gezer* 3, pl. 113, no. 23, from 4th c. Tomb 158 (ibid. 1, 365), may have contained scrolls now lost. Bronze

10. For Palestinian beads in general, see Macalister, *Gezer* 2, 104–15; McCown, *Nasbeh* 1, 267–68; Crowfoot, *Samaria* 3, 391–98. For bead production see M. Guido, *The Glass Beads of the Prehistoric and Roman Periods in Britain and Ireland*, Society of Antiquaries Reports 35 (London, 1978) 7–18.

or copper scrolls of a type similar to No. 23 were reported by Rahmani, "Maon Synagogue," 15–16, pl. 2, no. 1. These seem to have been enclosed in cloth and suspended from the neck; they are dated 4th–6th c. Two amulets, one of silver, one of bronze, were found in a Roman family vault in Amman: Harding, "Jebel Jofeh," 88, no. 244, pl. 27 (silver); 90, no. 310, pl. 28 (bronze). Most of the material seems to date to the 3rd c.

Instruments and Implements

A variety of objects ranging from cosmetic articles to a pickax is presented in this section. They have been arranged in the following order: toilet instruments; domestic, agricultural, and light industrial implements and equipment; balances and weights; hooks and rings; miscellaneous.

Toilet Instruments (Nos. 24–39)

A number of toilet articles were recovered, including glass pins, rods and spoons, a few fragmentary bronze instruments, and a bone spatula. The glass instruments fall into three general categories: pins,[11] rods,[12] and spatulas.[13] Though presumably no hard and fast separation in function existed among them, the rods (and certainly spatulas) probably would have been used in stirring or extracting cosmetics or unguents. Pins (and flat spatulas), while they could have been used for these purposes as well, seem better suited for applying makeup or perfumes.[14] Glass instruments appear in a variety of colors and often have spiral decoration. They were

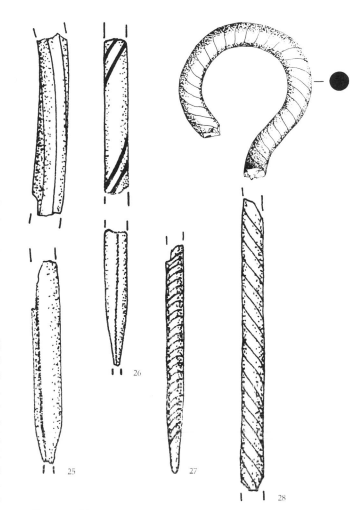

Fig. 8–4. Glass pins, rod. 1:1.

made from drawn rods, the spiral ones having been twisted with pincers.[15] A fragment of a twisted rod with pincer marks was found in the factory dump (No. 34).

Four glass pins were found (Nos. 24–27), one nearly intact (No. 24), along with numerous shaft fragments of other pins and rods (Nos. 33a–k, 34). Looped handles of three rods (Nos. 28–30) were also recovered, as well as two fragments of spoons (Nos. 31–32). A complete spoon of the sort that our fragments represent is illustrated on Pl. 8–1 (Israel Museum, No. 77.12.489). A large proportion of the glass instruments came from the factory dump, but it is uncertain if they were local products, nor can their date be established. Some white weathering and iridescence are present unless otherwise noted.

The bronze instruments (Nos. 35–38)—an ear spoon, two rod fragments, and a spatula—and the bone spatula (No. 39) are of well-known types and probably served purposes similar to the glass instruments.[16]

11. The most common form resembles the modern "ten-penny" nail, as in *Oppenländer Coll.* 215, no. 622 (identified as a hair pin) and Alarcão, *Conimbriga* 1965, 159, pl. 12, no. 312; both dated 1st or 2nd c. Avigad, "Jewish Quarter 1972," 200, pl. 46e, reports similar pins dated ca. 50 B.C. A less common variant of this type that tapers uniformly along the length of the shaft, e.g., *Oppenländer Coll.* 215, no. 621, and Auth, *Newark Glass* 157, no. 211, does not seem to appear among the Jalame fragments.

12. Rods appear in several forms and combinations. There are examples with flattened ends, but more common are applied disk ends, as in C. Simonett, *Tessiner Gräberfelder* (Basel, 1941) 83, fig. 16, no. 3, etc.; Isings, *Roman Glass*, 94–95, Form 79; all 1st or 2nd c. Also common are rods with one flat disk or globular end, and a looped handle; see Vessberg, "Cyprus Glass," 152–53, pl. 10, no. 15 and pl. 20, no. 6, with further references. Terminals of other types also occur, including birds, ducks, and claws, in combination with flat disks and looped handles; e.g., *Smith Coll.* 149, no. 298, "Syrian," 1st or 2nd c.; G. E. Wright, "Excavations at Tocra . . . ," *PEFQ* 95 (1963) 39, fig. 6a, from Tomb B, ca. 100 A.C.; *Bomford Coll.* 24, no. 83 a, c, 1st or 2nd c. (very close to No. 28).

13. Glass objects of this kind are clearly imitations of metal instruments. Harden, *Karanis*, 286–87, pl. 21, nos. 865–67, distinguishes two types, one with a flat bowl and very much like a spatula, the other concave. For spatulas see also *Bomford Coll.* 26, no. 94, 2nd or 3rd c., and McCown, *Nasbeh* 1, 265, pl. 105, no. 2, from Late Roman Tomb 33; and for spoons, Vessberg, "Cyprus Glass," 153, pl. 10, no. 19; and Auth, *Newark Glass*, 156 no. 210, "early Roman"; she conjectures that glass spoons served special uses where metal was avoided.

14. The use of some of these objects as cosmetic instruments is uncertain, and, though it may seem unlikely, their use in the arrangement of women's hair and clothing or in weaving cannot be ruled out. For cosmetics and perfumes in antiquity, see Forbes, *Studies* 3, 1–46, with bibliography; for the use of the kohl stick, see Stern, *Custodia*, 117–18.

15. Avigad, "Jewish Quarter 1972," 200, pl. 46d; G. D. Weinberg, "Glass Manufacture in Hellenistic Rhodes," *ArchDelt* 24 (1969) 146, pl. 81a; and Harden and Price, "Glass Vessels" in Cunliffe, *Fishbourne*, 366, fig. 144, nos. 106–7, 2nd or 3rd c. spiral rods.

16. Davidson, *Corinth* 12, 181–82; Macalister, *Gezer* 2, 116–17.

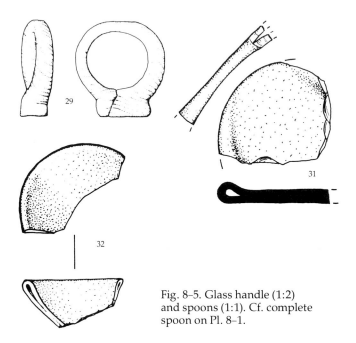

Fig. 8–5. Glass handle (1:2) and spoons (1:1). Cf. complete spoon on Pl. 8–1.

Glass Instruments

24   (G299–64). Pin, tip of point missing

PL .148; D shaft .006, head .014. Light bluish green. Flat circular head with rounded edges and indented circle in center of top. Shaft nearly circular in section, lateral ridge along entire length. Slight curve near point. Made from drawn rod; point pulled out and other end flattened to form head. From late wall built on top of east wall of furnace. **Pl. 8–1.**

For parallels for this and Nos. 25–26, see above, n. 11. Pins of this type have not been published from contexts later than 2nd c. (cf. Fremersdorf, *Denkmäler* 3, 55, pl. 124a,b).

25   (G149–66, G11–65). Pin. Two non-joining fragments, both broken at either end

PL (a) .055 (b) .046; D (a) .0065 (b) .007. Bluish green. Shafts circular in section with horizontal groove, (a) tapering to point. Probably similar to No. 24. Possibly 1st c. B.C.–2nd c. A.C. **Fig. 8–4.**

26   (G241–66). Pin (?). Two non-joining fragments, both broken at either end

PL (a) .036 (b) .041; D both .006. Yellowish green. Twisted shaft circular in section, with white spiral thread. Surface find. **Fig. 8–4 .**

27   (G83–66). Pin, top of shaft missing

PL .027; D .007. Light purple. Circular in section, spirally twisted, tapering point. From lowest part of factory dump, possibly from Period 2. **Fig. 8–4.**

Cf. McCown, *Nasbeh* 1, fig. 23, no. 12, a spatula with similar pointed end, from Tomb 33, Late Roman.

28   (G10–66, G14–66). Rod with looped handle. Two non-joining fragments, both broken

PL shaft .075; D .0058, handle .035; Th .005. Light bluish green. Spiral shaft circular in section. Handle bent to form loop. Factory dump. **Fig. 8–4.**

Cf. Macalister, *Gezer* 1, 344, and 3, pl. 98, no. 7, from Tomb 117, Roman; *Oppenländer Coll.*, 215, no. 619, with further references, "Eastern Mediterranean," 1st–2nd c. See also n. 12 above.

29   (G300–64). Looped handle, shaft broken off

H .051; Inner D .033. Transparent light green. Heavy twisted rod drawn out and narrowing toward one end, bent to form loop. Ends pushed together into roughly rectangular attachment for shaft. Loop oval in section, flattened on interior and at top. The large size of this handle is unusual, but rod fragments of similar thickness and color were found (No. 33e). **Fig. 8–5; Pl. 8–1.**

30   (G70–65). U-shaped instrument handle, broken at both ends

PL .068; D .007. Yellowish green. Spiral rod, circular in section, one end bent to form hooked handle. **Pl. 8–1.**

31   (G73–65). Spoon, portion of bowl preserved

L .028. Light green. Flattened bubble with air spaces, apparently oval. Bottom flattened, top slightly concave. From factory dump. **Fig. 8–5.**

Cf. Crowfoot, *Samaria* 3, 420; Harden, *Karanis*, 287, pl. 21, nos. 865–66.

32   (G148–64). Spoon, part of bowl preserved

L .034. Light bluish green. Flattened bubble pushed out to form concave, originally circular bowl. **Fig. 8–5.**

Cf. Harden, *Karanis*, 287, pl. 21, no. 867.

33   Instrument shaft fragments, broken at both ends; all but h, j, and k from factory dump. **Fig. 8–6.**

a (G161–66). D .006. Purple, unweathered. Slightly curved. Wide raised spiral bands.

b (G127–66). D .007. Light purple. Flattened spirals of slightly different shade. One similar fragment (G270–66).

c (G71–65). D .006. Light bluish green. Flattened spirals of varying width.

d (G68–66). D .0045. Bluish green. Rounded spiral bands, including two threads of darker blue.

e (G135–66). D .011. Partly devitrified. Light green. Spiral bands with narrow grooves between. Curved and thicker at one end. One similar fragment (G253–66).

f (G175–66). D .007. Light green. Spiral rod, slightly curved, thicker at one end. Similar fragment of bluish green (G318–66).

g (G12–67). D .0045. Light green. Flattened spiral bands, two white threads ending near center of fragment. Several similar fragments in poor condition found.

h (G200–64). D .006. Colorless greenish. Closely set rounded spirals, broader at one end.

i (G290–66). D .006. Colorless yellowish. Very closely set narrow spiral.

j (G233–65). D .005. Colorless with purple tinge. Spiral of five rounded ribs. One end tapers. Probably a pin.

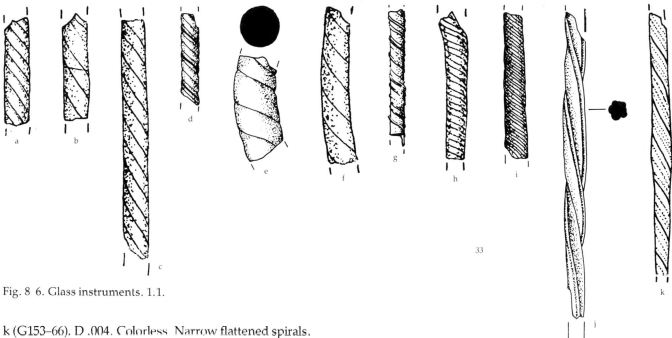

Fig. 8 6. Glass instruments. 1:1.

k (G153–66). D .004. Colorless. Narrow flattened spirals. Thicker at middle, tapering toward one end. Possibly a pin. From topsoil.

34 (G154–64). Instrument, broken at one end

PL .047; D shaft .006. Light green. Bulbous end of drawn rod, slightly twisted and circular in section. **Pl. 8–1.**

Cf. Vessberg, "Cyprus Glass," 153, pl. 10, no. 19, a glass spoon with similar terminal.

Bronze Instruments

35 (M48–65). Unguent or ear spoon, part of bowl and end of shaft missing

PL .058. Shaft circular in section, incised spiral near bowl. From M:4–5 (Trench A–5) depth 1.05, with coins dating 351 383. **Pl. 8 2.**

Such instruments are often found in association with Roman and Early Byzantine glass flasks, e.g., Barag, "Netiv," 81, fig. 2, no. 2, Byzantine. See also Milne, *Instruments*, 63–68, 77–78. The spiral decoration is a common feature, e.g., Davidson, *Corinth* 12, 184, pl. 82, no. 1323, Late Roman or Byzantine; Frere, *Verulamium*, 124, fig. 35, no. 70, dated 270–280.

36 (M62–65). Shaft, bent, broken at both ends

PL .06. Rectangular in section. Two horizontal grooves near one end. Pair of incised lines along wider sides, single lines on narrow sides. **Pl. 8–2.**

37 (M6–64). Rod, one end broken off

PL .052; Max D .005. Circular in section, thicker rounded bottom. Small bulbous collar at broken end. **Pl. 8–2.**

Similar terminals appear in a variety of instruments, e.g., Reisner, *Samaria* 1, 359, fig. 231, no. 1a, Hellenistic; Baramki, "Karm al-Shaikh," pl. 4, no. 9, from undated Grave 3, and pl. 9, no. 9, from Grave 44, probably 2nd–3rd

c.; Crowfoot, *Samaria* 3, 428, fig. 100, nos. 24–25, from Tomb E 220, 2nd–3rd c., and 446, fig. 104, no. 7, similar terminal identified as probe or kohl stick, Late Roman; McCown, *Nasbeh* 1, 265, pl. 105, no. 10, from Late Roman Tomb 33. See also Milne, *Instruments*, 53–56.

38 (M49–65). Spatula, point and part of shaft missing

PL .057; W .015. Flat narrow leaf-shaped blade. Shaft square in section. **Pl. 8–2.**

Cf. Baramki, "Karm al-Shaikh," pl. 11, no. 11, from Grave 3 of Chamber H, possibly first half of 4th c.; Husseini, "Beit Fajjar," 176, pl. 85, no. 3, similar spatula found in glass double kohl bottle, 4th c. See Milne, *Instruments*, 58–61; Davidson, *Corinth* 12, 181 82.

Bone Instrument

39 (B3–66). Spatula, two joining fragments, end missing

PL .074; W .024; Th .002. Flat blade widening toward blunt end. **Pl. 8–2.**

The purpose of bone spatulas is uncertain. In Palestine they have been identified as styli (Macalister, *Gezer* 2, 274); as "household implements" (Reisner, *Samaria* 1, 372); as "mesh gauges for making fishing nets" (Petrie, *Gerar*, 17); and most commonly as cosmetic instruments, though there is no direct evidence of such use (e.g., Crowfoot, *Samaria* 3, 461–62).

Domestic, Agricultural, and Industrial Implements and Equipment

This heterogeneous body of material has been arranged under four subheadings: iron tools and bind-

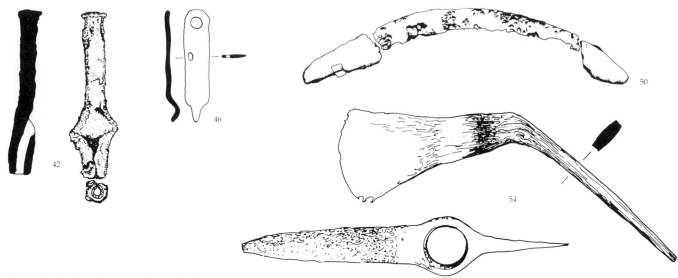

Fig. 8–7. Metal implements. Nos. 42, 46,
1:2; others, 1:3.

ings; bone implements and handles; tools and whorls of stone and clay; palettes, millstones, and presses. As many of these objects are very common types, some appearing as early as the Bronze Age on other sites, no definite dating is possible in most cases. With the exception of the flint tools, however, all the items are compatible with a late 3rd to early 5th c. date.

Iron Tools and Bindings (Nos. 40–58); *Bronze* (No. 59)

Almost all the iron tools are described. All were corroded when found, and most were cleaned at the laboratory of the Römisch-Germanisches Zentralmuseum, Mainz.

40   (M19-64). Needle, pointed end missing

PL .12; D .004. Thin rod, circular in section, one end flattened and pierced by oval eyelet. From topsoil.

41   (M36-65). Bodkin, one end broken off

PL .051; shaft .004 x .005. Shaft rectangular in section, pierced by elliptical opening near broken end, flattened beyond opening. From factory dump. **Pl. 8-2.**

42   (M34-65). Punch

L .087; Th of shaft .009; D of hole .005. Rectangular rod flattened and folded over at one end to form a circular nozzle. Other end flat with slightly projecting edges, probably from being struck with hammer. From factory dump. **Fig. 8-7.**

Cf. Brodribb, *Shakenoak* 1, 102, fig. 34, no. 26, "woodcarving chisel or punch for wood or leather," Roman. The Jalame example was probably used for leather, which might then have been stitched using a bodkin such as No. 41.

43   (M13-66). Tool, chisel, or gouge

L .049. Shaft rectangular in section, ending in short flat transverse blade. Found in factory dump. **Pl. 8-2.**

44   (M33-65). Tool, chisel, or stylus, parts of both ends missing

PL .092. Rod, probably square in section, one end flattened and triangular, other end curved, possibly pointed. **Pl. 8-2.**

Cf. Brodribb, *Shakenoak* 4, 120, fig. 58, nos. 402-3, two styli, 4th c.

45   (M15-65). Large awl or borer

L .252; Th .01. Shaft square in section, upper end hammered flat. Lower part bent 18° and tapering to point. Found at p–q:10–11, depth 1.50, with coin of Theodosius II (425–450). **Pl. 8-2.** L: as found; R: cleaned.

Similar, smaller object (M16-65) found in factory dump.

46   (M24-65). Latch

L .088; W .022; Th .04. Rectangular strip with circular hole at rounded end. Other end narrows to pointed flange bent into C-shape. Second hole along side near center of object. From factory dump. **Fig. 8-7; Pl. 8-2.**

47   (M25-65). Blade, one end damaged

L .082, W .007; Th .002. Small flat blade pointed at both ends. From factory dump. **Pl. 8-2.**

48   (M38-66). Blade, one end broken off

PL .098; W .023; Th .002. Flat blade with rounded hafted end. Single rivet preserved. From factory dump. **Pl. 8-2.**

49   (M4-64). Triple knife

L .186; W .03; Th of blades ca. .004. Three blades, the inner one slightly shorter, attached to each other by rivet at one end. Upper edges of blades straight, lower edges curved, being broader at point, narrower at riveted end. Final quarter of 4th c. From Y:14 (Trench A-2), at top of red fill. **Pl. 8-2.** L: as found; Cen: cleaned; R: profile.

This knife may have functioned like a clasp knife illustrated by Yadin, *Cave of Letters*, 88, fig. 31, no. 29, which may have been used in weaving "for cutting the weft, or the thread from a ball."

50 (M11–64, M26–65, M48–66). Sickle, three joining fragments

L .275; W at center ca. .023; Th .005. Curved flat blade, inner edge sharpened. Rounded point and flat blunt-ended shank with straight outer edge, remains of single rivet. **Fig. 8–7.**

Though this blade resembles a scythe, it lacks the characteristic handle at right angles to the cutting edge. Cf. Petrie, *Tools and Weapons*, 47, pl. 59, no. 34, described as a "pruning hook" of Roman date. See also White, *Implements*, 71–85, 98–103; S. E. Rees, *Agricultural Implements in Prehistoric and Roman Britain*, British Archaeological Reports, British Series 69, 2 vols. (London, 1979) 2:438–50; and Turkowski, "Agriculture," 101–3.

51 (M10–64). Pruning hook

L .195; D of haft .02; Th outer edge .004. Flat curved blade, inner edge sharpened. Haft hammered out to fit over wooden handle, fixed in place by two rivets, one preserved. Traces of wood in haft. Second half of 4th or first half of 5th c. From bottom of wine press tank. **Pl. 8–2.** L: as found; R: cleaned.

This is an example of the lightweight *falx arboraria* or *falx putatoria* used for removing small branches from trees and hedges, or for pruning vines. See Petrie, *Tools and Weapons*, 47–48, White, *Implements*, 85–88; and Turkowski, "Agriculture," 101–3. Most Palestinian pruning hooks reported are of the heavier type like Nos. 52–53. For similar light hooks, cf. Macalister, *Gezer* 1, 365f, and 3, pl. 116, no. 11, a socketed hook from Tomb 159, containing a coin of Constantine I; Delougaz-Haines, 28–29, 48, pl. 48, no. 7, mistaken for a sickle, from Tomb 3, Byzantine; Rees, as in No. 50, 2:450–52, 461–73.

52 (M19–65). Pruning hook

L .185; Th of outer edge .007. Flat curved blade, inner edge sharpened. Single rivet hole near end of haft. **Pl. 8–2.** L: as found; R: cleaned.

This and No. 53 are of the heavy *falx arboraria* type, used for clearing brush and for work in the orchard and vineyard. In Palestine it may have served the role of the classic *falx vinitoria*. See White, *Implements*, 93–96, and Petrie, *Tools and Weapons*, 48. Cf. FitzGerald, *Beth-Shan* 3, 41, pl. 37, no. 30, with socketed handle, from Cistern I, 6th c.; Delougaz-Haines, 29, 48, pl. 48, no. 8, "sickle" from Tomb 4, Byzantine; Bagatti, *Nazareth*, 120, fig. 75 and fig. 79, no. 31, similar, two rivets, 4th or 5th c.; and Meyers, *Khirbet Shema*, pl. 8.2, no. 13, 4th c. context.

53 (M21–65). Pruning hook, haft end of shank missing

PL .135; Th at outer edge .009. Hooked flat blade, inner edge sharpened. Made of two pieces hammered together. Late 4th or first half of 5th c. Found at s–t:9–10 (Trench A–6), depth 1.10. **Pl. 8–3.** L: as found; R: cleaned.

Fragments of three similar hooks (M2–66, M21–66, M37–66) found.

54 (M1–64). Pickax, tip of pointed blade broken off

L .285; W of flaring blade .065; D of hole .034. Wide

flaring blade with rounded edge. Circular hole for insertion of wooden shank. Thick flat pointed blade on opposite side. Metal "laminated" along sides of hole and underside of pointed blade. **Fig. 8–7; Pl. 8–3.**

Cf. Iliffe, "Tarshiha," 12, pl. 8, no. 14, late 4th c.; McCown, *Nasbeh* 1, 112, fig. 23, from Tomb 33, Late Roman. The flat pointed pick end is much less common than other forms; see Petrie, *Tools and Weapons*, 15–16, pl. 4. See also White, *Implements*, 61–64; Turkowski, "Agriculture," 25, fig. 1. According to White, the *dolabra* is referred to by ancient writers as having three main uses: in preparing land for cultivation, in breaking up clods after plowing, and in excavating or mining.

55 (M32–65). Blade fragment, broken at both ends

PL .099; W .035; Th .005. Flat blade, slightly curved. **Pl. 8–3.**

56 (M14–66). Knife or chisel, broken off at one end and along one side

PL .058; W .017; Th .003. Tang and portion of flat blade. From factory dump. **Pl. 8–3.**

57 (M47–66). Collar

D .025; W .015; Th .003. Flat strip wound to form ring. From early factory dump. **Pl. 8–3.**

Collars such as Nos. 57–59 are common on Roman sites but not often published. They could have served a number of uses but probably were bindings for hafted tools or reinforcements for wooden objects; see Yadin, *Cave of Letters*, figs. 30–31 and pl. 24.

58 (M26–66). Collar, half preserved

Est. D .03; W .042; Th .003. Wide band bent to form circular binding. From factory dump. **Pl. 8–3.**

59 (M16–66). Bronze binding fragment

PL .031. Wide flat curved strip. Binding from small tool. **Pl. 8–3.**

Bone Implements and Handles (Nos. 60–65)

The bone tools Nos. 60–62 are a representative selection. Made of readily available and easily worked material, some were probably improvised for a specific task and soon discarded. Others show a good deal of wear and seem to have been used for some time. These implements probably reflect the forms of a large number of wooden tools in use on the site but now lost. The three handles (Nos. 63–65) belonged to metal tools.

60 (B1–64). Scraper

L .065; W .042. Upper rib of large animal worked and rounded at both ends. Similar but fragmentary scraper (B2 66) found in factory dump. **Pl. 8–3** (two views).

61 (B4–66). Groover and scraper

L .059; W .013; Th .002. Fragment of long bone, pointed at one end and worked to form U-shaped scraper along one side near the other, blunted end. From factory dump. **Pl. 8–3.**

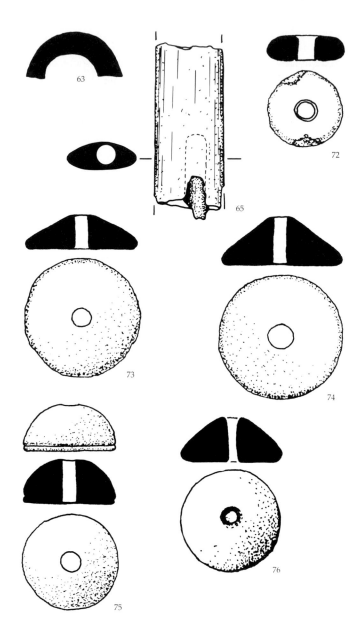

Fig. 8-8. Bone objects, stone and terracotta whorls. 1:1.

62   (B6–66). Awl or punch

L .038. Naturally shaped bone carved to form sharp point at one end. Five somewhat similar fragments (B2b–67, B3a-d–67) found. All from factory dump. **Pl. 8–3.**

63   (B3–65). Handle, three joining fragments preserving half

L .089; Outer D .026. Hollow cylinder with flat ends. Incised horizontal band and reserved ring at one end, raised horizontal band at other. From DD–EE:29–30 (Trench F–5), depth .50, in possibly Period 2 context. **Fig. 8–8** (section); **Pl. 8–3.**
Pl. 8–3.
   Cf. Macalister, *Gezer* 1, 355–58, and 3, pl. 104, no. 22, Tomb 147, Late Roman; Reisner, *Samaria* 1, 370, fig. 240, no. Fld, somewhat like, identified as kohl-pot or toilet box.

64   (B2–64). Tube, half preserved

L .03; outer D .022. Leg bone of animal carved into short cylinder; series of lightly cut grooves around exterior. Late 4th or first half of 5th c. From Y:24 (Trench F), depth 1.00, found with No. 101; Period 4 context. **Pl. 8–3.**
   Cf. Reisner, *Samaria* 1, 371, fig. 240, no. G8a, Roman; Cunliffe, *Portchester,* 222, fig. 119, nos. 118–19, with similar decoration, 1st half of 4th c.

65   (B1–65). Handle, broken at both ends

L .0465; W .007; D of hole .005. Buff (burned?) area on one side. Shaft a flat ellipse in section, hole drilled at one end. Carved and highly polished. **Fig. 8–8.**
   Cf. Yadin, *Cave of Letters,* 88, fig. 31, no. 28, first third of 2nd c.

Tools and Whorls of Stone and Clay (Nos. 66–92)

These objects have been subdivided into flint tools, whorls, and pounding, grinding, and rubbing stones.

Flint tools

66   Prismatic blades. Fragments, broken at both ends; both edges moderately utilized unless noted otherwise. Pl. 8 4.

a (S88–66). Intact. L .045. Half mottled gray flint, other half reddish brown limestone of core. Slight utilization of both edges.
b (S30–65). Intact. L .041. Light gray. One edge moderately worn, other cut with two C-shaped notches. One end worked as point.
c (S69–65). PL .028. Dark gray. Extensively utilized on both edges.
d (S32–66). PL .022. Mottled light gray.
e (S64–66). PL .019. Mottled pink.
f (S42–65). PL .043. Pink and light gray mottled. Heavily worn in use, chipped.
g (S94–66). PL .026. Mottled pink.
h (S12–66). Broken at one end. PL .032. Yellowish brown. Hafted blade, polished.
i (S21–65). One end broken off. PL .02. Light brown. End finished off, polished, and used as thumbnail scraper.
j (S46–66). PL .03. Gray. Utilized on straight side with wear from cutting plants or woodworking. Sickle blade?

67   (S9–66). Flaked blade, recent break at one end

PL .032. Mottled light gray. Backed, moderate wear on cutting edge. **Pl. 8–4.**

68   (S43–66). Cutting tool

L .034. Dark reddish brown. Backed, with utilized edge. Use uncertain. **Pl. 8–4.**

69   (S1–65). Punch

L .049. Brown. Utilized at point. One similar tool found. **Pl. 8–4.**

70   (S80–65). Scraper

L .06. Gray flint encased in white limestone. Utilized primary decortication flake. Wear on one edge. **Pl. 8–4.**

71 (S2–67). Tool

L .038. Yellow and gray mottled. Utilized shatter. Use uncertain. **Pl. 8–4.**

Whorls

Of "spindle whorls" Harden wrote half a century ago, "In archaeology such an identification of pierced objects often seems but a last despairing attempt at the concealment of ignorance."[17] The five whorls from Jalame (Nos. 72–76)[18] shed no light on this problem.[19]

72 (S8–64). Serpentine disk, chipped

D .019; H .007. Greenish, top and bottom flat, pierced by circular hole. Finely incised circle around bottom of hole; top of hole beveled and worn from use. From factory dump. **Fig. 8–8.**
Cf. Crowfoot, *Samaria* 3, 400, fig. 92a, no. 9, of limestone. Surface find.

73 (S31–65). Serpentine whorl, chipped

D .031; H .009. Green, conical, circular hole. Mid–4th c. From M:4–5 (Trench A–5), depth 1.05 in Period 3 context. **Fig. 8–8.**
Cf. Reisner, *Samaria* 1, 342, fig. 216, nos. 3, 9, of slate and "gray stone"; Baramki, "Karm al-Shaikh," pl. 4, no. 3 and pl. 6, no. 12, from Roman Graves 3 and 15, and pl. 14, no. 6, from possibly late 3rd c. context in Chamber J; McCown, *Nasbeh* 1, 271, fig. 74, nos. 6–7, of basalt; Crowfoot, *Samaria* 3, 399, fig. 92a, no. 7, three whorls of "black stone," one from Tomb E220, Late Roman; Meyers, *Khirbet Shema*, 250, pl. 8.8, no. 31, stone, Byzantine.

74 (S9–64). Serpentine, chipped

D .032; H .011. Like No. 73. **Fig. 8–8.**

75 (S27–65). Stone whorl

D .024; H .012. Dark brown with gold inclusions. Hemispherical, large central hole. Single incised line around outside of bottom edge. Surface find. **Fig. 8–8.**
Cf. Reisner, *Samaria* 1, 342, fig. 216, no. 10, gray stone, apparently Roman; Petrie, *Gerar*, 20, pl. 44, nos. 35–36, dated ca. 5th c. B.C.; McCown, *Nasbeh* 1, 271, fig. 74, no. 8,

basalt; Crowfoot, *Samaria* 3, 400, fig. 92a, no. 13, dark gray stone, dated not before 7th c. B.C., following Tufnell, *Lachish* 3, 398, pl. 54, no. 42, steatite whorl, from Tomb 106, dated ca. 600 B.C., but with 3rd or 4th c. A.C. reuse; Tufnell's conclusion is based in turn on Petrie, *Gerar*, p. 20.

76 (T4–65). Terracotta whorl

D .026; H .012. Dark gray gritty clay. Conical, small central hole. **Fig. 8–8.**

Pounding, grinding, and rubbing stones

Nos. 77–92 are representative of the many implements found on the site. They are common in Palestine from the Bronze Age onward.

77 (S8–65). Basalt hammer

L .075; W .064. Gray. Oval stone, two shallow worn depressions on top and bottom. **Fig. 8–9; Pl. 8–4.**
Chavane, *Salamine*, 22–23, identifies possible uses for such objects: grinder/pounder, small mortar, or pestle; her examples date from Geometric period through 4th c. A.C.; see also White, *Equipment*, 9. For Palestinian examples, see Reisner, *Samaria* 1, 340, fig. 215, no. 1c; McCown, *Nasbeh* 1, pl. 91, no. 3; both pre-Roman.

78 (S12–65). Chert pounder

D .056. Grayish brown. Roughly cubical, chipped all over except for one smooth face. One similar pounder (S6–66) found. **Pl. 8–4.**

79 (S61–66). Limestone grinder

D .054. White. Spherical, surface rough. **Pl. 8–4.**
Cf. S. Saller, *Discoveries at St. John's, 'Ein Karim, 1941–1942* (Jerusalem, 1946) 175, pl. 33, 2, nos. 6–7.

80 (S5–65). Limestone grinder

D .112. Like preceding but larger and heavier. Late 4th or first half of 5th c. From s–u:30–33 (Trench M) in Period 4 context. See Pl. 2–11B for the object in situ. **Pl. 8–4.**

81 (S32–65). Limestone grinder

D .054. White. Roughly cubical, surface rough. **Pl. 8–4.**

82 (S14–66). Limestone rubber

D .06; H ca. .04. White. Ovoid, flat bottom. Found built into northeast corner of furnace room wall. **Pl. 8–4.**

83 (S39–65). Marble grinder

D .058. Pink and yellow veined. Irregularly spherical, one face smoothed. **Pl. 8–4.**

84 (S18–65). Basalt grinder

L .14; W .06; H .055. Dark gray. Oval. Considerable wear. One similar fragmentary grinder (S13–66). **Pl. 8–4.**

85 (S3–65). Basalt rubbing stone, two edges broken off

L .088; Th .035. Dark gray. Flat bottom, rounded top, both worn smooth. Preserved edges flat. Two similar, fragmentary examples (S3–64, S4–64) found near bottom of wine press tank. **Pl. 8–4.**

86 Two rubbing stones. Both from factory dump. **Pl. 8–4.**
a (S47–66). Limestone encased flint nodule. L .093; D .03.

17. Harden, *Karanis*, 295.
18. Macalister, *Gezer* 2, 91, argues that these objects, whether of stone or bone, were too light and their perforations too small to have served as spindle whorls and should thus be considered buttons or ornamental pinheads. In Reisner, *Samaria* 1, 341, however, it is suggested that the small holes on some whorls (such as those at Jalame) may be due to their use on metal or ivory spindles, which were smaller in diameter than the more common wooden variety. G. M. Crowfoot (*Samaria* 3, 399) also points out, "even lighter whorls of wood, pottery discs or gourd rinds are known in modern primitive usage." For whorls preserved on their spindles, see Petrie, *Tools and Weapons* 53, pl. 66, nos. 141–47; and Aharoni, "Cave of Horror," 192, pl. 25 c, d, 1st half of 2nd c. Similar discs, apparently stoppers, are reported by Harden, *Karanis*, 295, and Vessberg, "Cyprus Glass," 152–53, pl. 10, no. 17. One argument against these being buttons is their absence from the grave goods on many sites, but there are enough exceptions, e.g., Baramki, "Karm al-Shaikh," pls. 4, 6, and 11, to preclude any firm conclusion.
19. Though appearing in the Bronze Age and continuing into the Byzantine period, they seem to have been in greatest use during the Hellenistic period; see Deonna, *Delos*, 267–71; Davidson, *Corinth* 12, 172, 296–98; Chavane, *Salamine*, 88–102. For Palestinian examples of all periods, see Petrie, *Gerar*, 19–20; Macalister, *Gezer* 2, 70–73, 90–93; Reisner, *Samaria* 1, 341–42; Crowfoot, *Samaria* 3, 398–402; McCown, *Nasbeh* 1, 271.

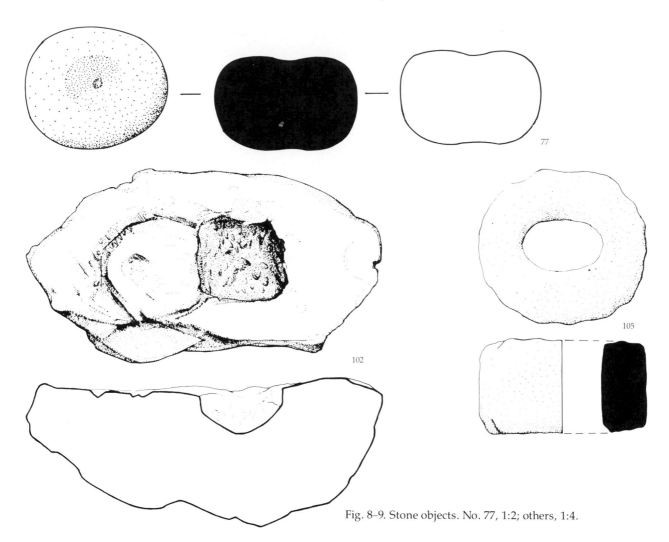

Fig. 8–9. Stone objects. No. 77, 1:2; others, 1:4.

White. Oval in section, pointed at both ends.
b (S75–65). Flint nodule. L .043; D .013. Gray, partly
enclosed in white limestone. Oval in section, tapering to
point at one end.

Cf. Macalister, *Gezer* 1, 342, and 3, pl. 97, no. 25, from
Hellenistic Tomb 103.

87   (S39–66). Sandstone rubbing stone, one end broken

L .098; W .035. Reddish. Rectangular in section,
rounded point. Topsoil. **Pl. 8–5.**

88   (S10–65). Basalt pestle, chipped

H .055; D at bottom .046. Pinkish exterior (burned?),
fine-grained gray interior. Roughly conical, flat smoothed
bottom. **Pl. 8–5.**

Common type, e.g., Crowfoot, *Samaria* 3, 464, fig. 117,
no. 1. See also Chavane, *Salamine*, 21, with further references; Forbes, *Studies* 3, 155–56.

89   (S23–65). Basalt pestle, top broken off

PH .058; D at bottom .048. Dark gray. Very much
like preceding. **Pl. 8–5.**

90   (T4–66). Terracotta rubbing stone or pestle

L .067; D .022. Gray. Sausage-shaped, roughly oval in
section; blunt rounded ends, both worn. One broad and
two narrow orange-colored terracotta bands on sides,
probably produced by rubbing on coarse ware. Possibly
connected with the production of objects such as No. 184.
Surface find. **Pl. 8–5.**

91   (T17–65). Terracotta pestle, one end broken off (?)

PL .053; D .02. Pinkish buff (7.5YR 8/4). Finger-like,
oval in section. Rounded point, other end chipped but flat, perhaps not broken. Made from amphora handle? From
Trench P, Period 4 context. **Pl. 8–5.**

92   (P1–66). Terracotta pestle

H .033; D at bottom .033. Reddish orange (2.5YR 6/8).
Coarse-ware vessel handle adapted for use as pestle. Con-
ical grip broadening to rounded bottom. Surface find.
Pl. 8–5.

Palettes, Millstones, Presses, Weights (Nos. 93–113)

These objects have been subdivided into palettes,
querns, millstones, small presses, and ring and pressure
beam weights. Mortars are described in Chap. 7.

Palettes

Palettes were used used in grinding pigments for cosmetics and paints.[20] The depression in the center of the upper surface of No. 94 probably indicates that grinding was done with a rotating motion using a pestle such as No. 89.

93 (S13–65). Slate palette, corners and one edge chipped

L .097; W .065; Th .007. Buff. Thin, flat rectangular shape, top smooth, worn at center. Wide beveled edges on bottom. For parallels, see n. 20. **Pl. 8–5** (2 sides).

94 (S33–65). Slate palette, corners and edges chipped

L .142; W .092; Th .011. Gray. Larger than preceding, beveled edges narrower. Deeply worn oval depression on top. From q–r:10–11 (Trench A–5), depth 1.50, in Period 4 context. Late 4th or first half of 5th c. **Pl. 8–5** (2 sides).

95 (S80–66). Slate palette, one corner preserved

PL .072; Th .006. Reddish brown. Like preceding. From factory dump. **Pl. 8–5.**

Querns

Fragments of the lower stones of small basalt and limestone "saddle querns," used for grinding grain, were found all over the site. They would have been used in conjunction with the pounding and grinding stones described above.[21]

96 (S52–65). Basalt quern, broken on three sides

PL .28; Th .049. Gray. Flat pitted top, rounded rough bottom. Edge rounded, original shape probably oval. Three similar fragments found. **Pl. 8–5.**

97 (S53–65). Basalt quern, broken on three sides

PL .30; Th .005. Gray. Top concave, some pitting, bottom rough. Finished edge straight and raised. Five similar fragments found. **Pl. 8–5.**

98 (S16–65). Limestone quern, two joining fragments

L .325; Th .04. White. Like No. 97, but raised ridge at edge curved. **Pl. 8–5.**

Millstones

No. 99 is of the "rubbing mill" type, and three grooved reused revetment fragments (Nos. 100a-c) probably belonged to a similar mill. No. 101 is the lower stone (*meta*) of an animal-powered *mola asinaria*. These mills, especially the latter, provided a means of grinding cereals much more efficiently and in much larger amounts than did the hand querns and grinders (Nos. 78–85, 96–98). These appear in the upper levels and may belong to the final period of occupation.

---

20. Macalister, *Gezer* 2, 272–73; Davidson, *Corinth* 12, 126, pl. 62 nos. 834–36.

21. See Macalister, *Gezer* 2, 35–36, figs. 227, 231; McCown, *Nasbeh* 1, pl. 91, no. 4, a quern in use. See also White, *Equipment*, 9–12; Robinson and Graham, *Olynthus* 8, 326–34, pl. 79, nos. 1–4, with numerous references.

(Nos. 78–85, 96–98). These appear in the upper levels and may belong to the final period of occupation.

99 (S26–65). Basalt millstone

L and W .36; H .11. Dark gray. Thick square slab, top and bottom flat, sides roughly finished, tapering inward toward top. Aperture .16 square at top, nearly circular at bottom (D .05), with four sloping triangular sides. Extending from opening at top, two rectangular slots .05 wide and .03 deep. Lower surface has parallel longitudinal grooves and irregular curved grooves radiating from central aperture. From o:35 (Trench F–3), depth 1.30. **Pl. 8–6.**

Similar millstones found at Ashdod, Gezer, Khirbat al-Karak, Samaria, Tel Mevorakh, Shiloh, and Oumm el-'Amed have been published; doubtless others have been found in the Palestinian area. Most of the published millstones of the form found in Palestine were not well understood until fairly recently. The type has a long history; it was used in Greece, South Italy, and Sicily as early as 5th c. B.C. (see Robinson-Graham, *Olynthus* 8, 327–34, and D. White, "A Survey of Millstones from Morgantina," *AJA* 67 [1963] 204–5) and possibly earlier in the Near East (see R. Amiran, "Millstones and the Potter's Wheel," *Eretz-Israel* 4 [1956] 46–49, and Forbes, *Studies* 3, 147–48). Found at many sites in the Greek mainland and islands as well as in Asia Minor, it also appears in the Fayum in early Roman times (unpublished: see Robinson-Graham, *Olynthus* 8, 330, n. 14). How late it continued in use is uncertain; the Jalame stone and others were found in Late Roman contexts but may have been reused for building material. The most comprehensive discussion remains that in *Olynthus* 8; there reference is made to a Hellenistic relief bowl on which is pictured a flour-mill clearly showing the method of using the millstone. The upper millstone was placed upon a flat grooved stone (like Nos. 100a-c) on a raised platform. One end of a long wooden shaft was placed in the two slots at the top of the mill and attached to them. Grain was poured into the central hopper and the mill moved back and forth over the lower stone. A diagram illustrating this operation (adapted from the relief bowl) is in *Olynthus* 8, 328, fig. 34; see also White, "Millstones," pl. 48, fig. 9. The entire flour-mill scene on the relief bowl was interpreted by Rostovtzeff as representing an early Hellenistic mime: *AJA* 41 (1937) 86–90, figs. 4–5 (a photograph of the bowl and an extended drawing of the scene). The closest parallel to the Jalame mill is E. Stern, *Excavations at Tel Mevorakh (1973–1976)* 1, *QEDEM* Monographs 9 (Jerusalem, 1978) 24, pl. 44, 5, dated Hellenistic.

100 Fragments of lower millstones. **Pl. 8–6.**

a (S6–64). Marble, broken all around. L .125; Th .019. White, fairly fine grained. One side flat, other picked with long narrow gouges, excepting .013 wide raised curved band. From Period 4 context in Trench K.

b (S59–65). Marble, broken all round. L .125; Th .02. Like preceding.

c (S49–66). Basalt, one side broken off. PL .50; W .42; Th ca. .095. Top cut with series of parallel grooves. Raised edge along one side. Sides and bottom roughly picked.

These slabs served as the lower millstones of rubbing mills such as No. 99. The first two seem to have been made from revetment fragments (see Nos. 161–62). Cf. Robinson-Graham, *Olynthus* 8, 329, pl. 79, nos. 5–7. Dothan-Freedman, *Ashdod* 1, 24, and Macalister, *Gezer* 2, 40–41, report these as common finds in Hellenistic contexts. B. Mazar et al., "Ein Gev, Excavations in 1961," *IEJ* 14 (1964) 18–19, pl. 7a-b, describe similar slabs as "basalt orthostats" with grooved ornamentation. It is likely these were reused millstones.

101   (S14–64). Limestone conical millstone; pitted

H .55; D .47 Conical with roughly cut irregular base. Apex cylindrical with central depression. Late 4th or first half of 5th c. From Y:24 (Trench F), depth .90. **Pl. 8–6.**

Cf. Delougaz-Haines, 26, pl. 22, no. 11, and pl. 49, no. 6, perhaps from 4th c. context. The *mola asinaria* is the hourglass-shaped grain mill well known from the bakeries of Pompeii. The mill consists of three parts: a stationary conical lower stone (the *meta*); a hollow biconical unit (the *catillus*), the bottom half of which fits over and rotates around the *meta* while the upper half acts as a hopper for the grain; and the harness attachment by which the *catillus* is turned. See L. Moritz, *Grain-Mills and Flour in Classical Antiquity* (Oxford, 1958) 98–101; Forbes, *Studies* 3, 94–98, 151–52; and White, *Equipment* 12–18, fig. 8.

Small presses

A press such as No. 102 was probably used in a household. The form and larger capacity of No. 103 suggest it was part of a pressing installation; it could have been used in the production of oil or wine, or in dyeing.[22]

102   (S1–64). Limestone press, chipped

L .38; H .146; W .19. White, soft. Irregular ovoid block, sides and bottom roughly carved. Top flat with oval groove (D .11, depth .01) next to and connected with a square depression (.10 sq., depth .058). When vegetable material was crushed within the oval space, liquid ran into the circular groove and drained into the receptacle. **Fig. 8–9.**

103   (S12–64). Limestone press, corners chipped

L .67; H .34; W .45. White. Block squared off at one end, irregular at other; perhaps a reused ashlar. Top flat with oval depression .20 x .25, depth .20. Circular opening (D .05) in one of the long sides. Late 3rd or first half of 4th c. From j:15 (Trench H), depth 1.00, possibly Period 2 context. **Pl. 8–6.**

Ring and pressure beam weights

In Palestinian oil and grape presses of the lever type, a wooden shaft or beam, one end of which was fixed in place, was laid over the material to be crushed, and weights were hung on its free end.[23] Nos. 104–5 seem to have belonged to small presses such as No. 103. The heavy pressure beam weight, No. 106, obviously belonged to a much larger press.

22. See Macalister, *Gezer* 2, 60–61, figs. 256, 257, and p. 65, fig. 259.
23. Ibid., 48–67, pls. 129–31; Z. Yeivin, "Two Ancient Oil Presses," *Atiqot* 3 (1966) 52–63; Forbes, *Studies* 3, 138–44.

104   (S2–64). Limestone ring weight

L .228; W .187; Th .10. White. Doughnut-shaped. One narrow end of oval perforation nearly flat, probably to aid movement of weight on pressure beam. Late 4th or first half of 5th c. From w–x:12–14 (Trench A–2), Period 4 context. **Pl. 8–6.**

105   (S55–65). Limestone ring weight (?)

D .175; Th .05. Like preceding but smaller and more roughly made. Oval hole, .09 x .06. Traces of red paint. Late 3rd or first half of 4th c. From z–AA:24 (Trench F–5), depth 1.45. **Fig. 8–9.**

106   (S13–64). Limestone pressure beam weight

H 1.25; L at top ca. .80, at bottom 1.15; W at top .50, at bottom ca. 1.00. Light gray. Roughly cut block, somewhat oval in section near bottom, tapering and becoming more rectangular in section toward top. Pierced near top by rectangular opening ca. .25 x .20 to receive press beam. Similar hole through flat top. On surface at extreme northwest corner of excavation. **Pl. 8–6.**

Balances and Weights

Balances of two types were found. No. 107 has simple transverse arms and two suspension pans and would have been used for weighing small items such as coins. No. 108 is a bronze steelyard. Both found in factory dump. A single, uninscribed lead weight (No. 109) was recovered.

107   Bronze suspension balance. **Fig. 8–10; Pl. 8–7.**

a (M53–65). Balance support. H .033. Two round-ended rectangular prongs attached to short conical stem. Each prong pierced by a rectangular opening and a circular hole at the bottom. Two incised horizontal lines at upper end. Stem constricted at join with prongs, tapers toward flattened circular suspension eyelet at top.
b (M47–65). Balance arm, end of shaft broken off. L .059. Thin shaft, circular in section, narrowing toward flattened circular end with suspension hole. Small ring of bronze wire attached.
c (M56–66, M57–66). Balance pan, two joining fragments. D .06. Thin circular sheet, three holes preserved near edge, 90° apart. Third quarter of 4th c.

Cf. Deonna, *Delos*, 139–40, pl. 53, nos. 399–400; Davidson, *Corinth* 12, 216, pl. 99, no. 1672, Byzantine or later; and Cunliffe, *Portchester*, 212, no. 62.

108   (M45–66). Bronze steelyard, one suspension hook and counterbalance missing

Overall L .169, of scale bar .112, of chain .225. Quadrilateral bar, thicker at one end. Loops for three fulcrum hooks and suspension chain attached at one end. Legend of weights inscribed on three sides of bar. Oval knob at end. Third quarter of 4th c. **Fig. 8–10; Pl. 8–7.**

This object is discussed in A. Mutz, *Römische Waagen und Gewichte aus Augst und Kaiseraugst*, Augster Museumshefte 6 (Augst, 1983) 21–22. Cf. also Deonna, *Delos*, 140f, fig. 164, pl. 53, no. 404; Davidson, *Corinth* 12, 207f, 214ff; D. Brown, "A Roman Pewter Hoard from

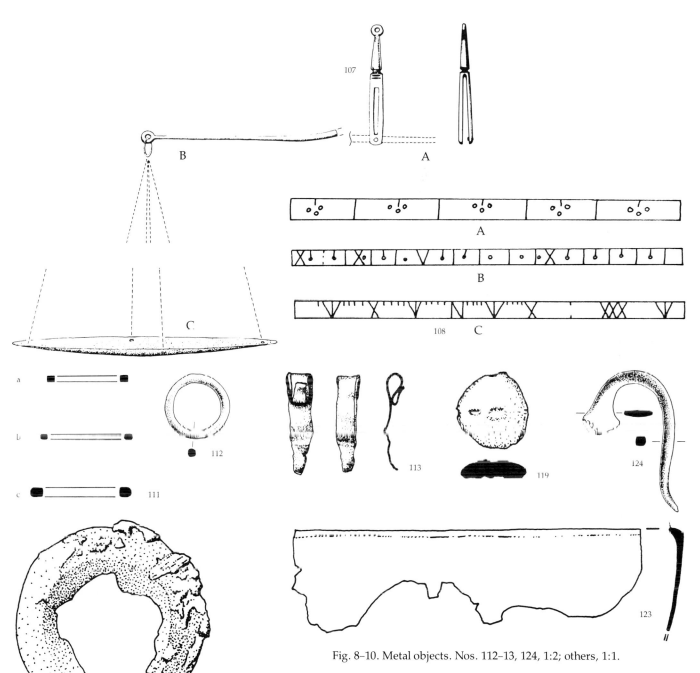

Fig. 8–10. Metal objects. Nos. 112–13, 124, 1:2; others, 1:1.

Appleford, Berks.," *Oxoniensia* 38 (1973) 195–97, fig. 6, no. 26, 4th c.; and Mutz, as above, 17–21, an example from Osterburken. The scales on the bar correspond to the position of the fulcrum hooks, and weights would have been read from the position of a sliding counterpoise (missing). Hung from the hook nearest the middle, scale A (see Fig. 8–10) is upright and reads right to left from 0 to 5 Roman pounds (*libra*, 0.721 lb. avoirdupois), with divisions at the

libra and *selibra* (half-pound). Suspended from the central hook, scale B reads from 5 to 20 *librae* in a similar fashion, with an "X" at 17.5. From the third hook, weights from 25 to 66 *librae* can be measured using scale C. The suspension chains may once have held a scale pan. See in addition *DarSag*, s.v. *Libra*, esp. 1227–31; D. K. Hill's discussion of a similar steelyard in the Walters Art Gallery, in "When Romans Went Shopping," *Archaeology* 5 (1952) 51–55; and A. Mutz, "Aus der römischen Metallbearbeitungstechnik," *Pro-Metal* 14 (1961) 523–29.

109   (M28–65). Lead weight, slightly pitted and scratched

L .09; W .089; Th .006. Nearly square, front flat with raised border (W .009). Back flat, slightly concave at center. Small rectangular flange near middle of one side. From n–o:35–36 (Trench F–3), depth 1.40, in Period 2 context, but probably earlier. **Pl. 8–7.**

Cf. Dothan, *Ashdod* 2–3, 67–68, pl. 25, nos. 1–2, without flange, Hellenistic; B. Lifshitz, "Bleigewichte aus Palästina und Syrien," *Zeitschrift des deutschen Palästina-Vereins* 92 (1976) 168–87, a catalogue of similar, inscribed weights. See also *DarSag*, s.v. *Pondus*; Davidson, *Corinth* 12, 203–7, with further references.

Hooks and Rings

Like many minor objects, hooks and rings are found frequently on ancient sites but seldom reported. They could have served a multitude of uses. They appear from the Bronze Age on.[24]

110 (M3–66). Iron hook

L .048. Flat strip, rectangular in section, folded over at one end to form small loop and bent into U-shaped hook at other end. From factory dump. One similar hook (M12–64) found. **Pl. 8–7.**

111 Bronze rings. **Fig. 8–10; Pl. 8–7.**

a (M54–65). Inside D .02. One similar ring found (M51–66).
b (M50–66). Inside D .02.
c (M55–65). Inside D .02. Polygonal in section.

112 (M22–65). Iron ring

Inside D .05. One similar ring (M27–65) found.
Fig. 8–10; Pl. 8–7.

113 (M50–65). Bronze loop

L .05; Th .001. Irregular narrow band tapering toward ends. One end folded to form closed S-shaped loop. Opposite end once folded in similar fashion but found unfolded. Single incised line along outer edge. From topsoil. **Fig. 8–10; Pl. 8–7.**

Miscellaneous (Nos. 114–21)

114 (M68–65). Bronze incense shovel handle, shovel broken off, corroded and pitted

PL .053; D of shaft .028. Hollow semicircular shaft, exterior plain, reinforced internally by diagonal rod. At unbroken end shaft broadens to form rounded band at join with perpendicular rectangular plate (H .025; W .038) closing off end of shaft. Remains of palmette ornament at top of plate. Interior of shaft contains bluish black residue, seems to be covellite (CuS). 1st or 2nd c. **Pl. 8–7.**

Cf. Yadin, *Cave of Letters*, 48–58, figs. 11–15, pls. 15–16, 1st or 2nd c., with further references.

115 (M59–65). Bronze bell, most of body broken off, clapper missing

PH .031. Thick solid oval loop (opening .013 x .009), broadening to form hollow flaring body of bell. Stub of iron loop that held clapper preserved. **Pl. 8–7.**

Cf. S. Saller, *The Memorial of Moses on Mount Nebo* 1

(Jerusalem, 1941) 312, pl. 137, fig. 2, no. 7, Byzantine.

116 (M18–66). Bronze arrowhead, end of tang missing

PL .089; Th .002; W .013. Flat narrow leaf-shaped blade. Tang square in section, tapering toward end. **Pl. 8–7.**

Cf. Lamon-Shipton, *Megiddo* 1, 144, pl. 80, no. 47, early 1st millennium B.C.

117 (M46–65). Iron arrowhead, one blade and part of tang missing, heavily corroded

PL .037; W ca. .016. Three-edged triangular shape, perhaps barbed. Late 3rd or first half of 4th c. Period 2 context in Trench F–5. **Pl. 8–7.**

Cf. Aharoni, "Expedition B," *IEJ* 11 (1961) pl. 9B, 2nd or 3rd c.; Yadin, *Cave of Letters*, 91, fig. 32, no. 38, 2nd c.; Yadin's no. 40 illustrates attachment of similar arrowhead to wooden shaft.

118 (M17–65). Lead fishnet weights, white incrustation

L .045. Flat strip folded over lengthwise to grasp edges of a net. Seven similar net weights found (M58–65 illustrated). **Pl. 8–7.**

Cf. Davidson, *Corinth* 12, 193, pl. 88, no. 1449.

119 Lead disks. **Fig. 8–10.**

a (M18–64). D .017; Th .005. Nearly circular, top slightly convex in section, scratched. Bottom flat. Small central depression on top, as in No. 171c. Weight or "gaming piece."
b (M57–65). D .014; Th .0015. Thin circular disk, flat on both sides. From factory dump.

120 (S45–65). Limestone object

H .057; D ca. .09. Light gray, many impurities. Roughly cut globular form, drilled hole off-center. Probably used as a weight. **Pl. 8–7.**

Cf. Dothan, *Ashdod* 2–3, 67, fig. 29, no. 9, a pierced stone used as a weight, 1st c. B.C.

121 (S34–66). Limestone object, edges chipped

D ca. .06; Th ca. .023. Light gray. Disk with rounded edges. Partially drilled hole in center, unfinished? Use uncertain. **Pl. 8–7.**

Cf. Macalister, *Gezer* 2, 37, fig. 229d, a "paint-grinder" quern; Dothan, *Ashdod* 2–3, 66, fig. 29, no. 6, a stone loomweight of similar size but with completed hole.

Metal and Stone Vessels

No complete vessels were found. Two fragments of bronze vessels, Nos. 122–23, have clipped edges that suggest they were used as scrap. No. 123 was found in the factory dump and may have been used in the glass manufacturing process.[25] To the pre-factory period can be assigned two iron vessel handles (Nos. 124–25), as well as a number of fragments of lathe-turned basins of porous limestone (Nos. 126–31). The latter are of a type

24. See Reisner, *Samaria* 1, 351, 357f, mostly of Hellenistic date; Robinson, *Olynthus* 10, 229, pls. 62, 63, nos. 833–946, who suggests they were used as fibulae, latch-attachments, handles, etc.; and Chavane, *Salamine*, 149–50, with further references.

25. The same may be true of other bronze fragments described below, Nos. 173–74.

well known from excavations in Jerusalem, where they appear chiefly in Herodian contexts, but they seem to have been produced as late as the 4th c.[26] At Jalame, all these were found in Period 2 contexts, except three small fragments from the factory dump.

Dowel holes in No. 129 suggest the object was either mended (and thus did not hold a liquid) or had some metal or wooden attachment (handle, latch hook, etc.). The latter seems more probable. Another fragment, No. 130, has a "palm branch" graffito, suggesting ceremonial use. The basins of marble and basalt (Nos. 132–39) are of types common throughout the Eastern Mediterranean.[27] No. 140, part of a rectangular limestone container, was possibly used in the factory (see Chap. 3). No. 141 is a lid cut from a fragment of revetment.

Metal Vessels (Nos. 122–25)

122 (M54–66). Bronze rim, broken off around neck, part of rim missing; heavily corroded, with traces of wood and straw

D .049. Slightly downturned rim, neck narrowing as in an oinochoe. First half of 4th c. or earlier. From below factory debris in Trench Y–3S. **Fig. 8–10.**

123 (M5–64). Bronze rim, clipped on three sides, flattened out

PL .093. Thickened and slightly inturned rim; upper portion of body preserved. From factory dump. **Fig. 8–10; Pl. 8–8.**

124 (M20–65). Iron handle, broken off at one end

PL .125. Curved, roughly oval in section, flattened at both ends for attachment to vessel. **Fig. 8–10; Pl. 8–8.**

125 (M18–65). Iron suspension handle

L .108. Curved bands, square in section, joined together and coming to point at each end. **Pl. 8–8.** L: as found; R: cleaned.

Limestone Vessels (Nos. 126–31)

These are of soft white local limestone. All body fragments have horizontal grooves and incised lines or raised bands. They average .47 in diameter and may have stood ca. .25–.30 high.

126 (S19–66, S65a,b–66). Three non-joining fragments preserving rim and part of body

PH .172; Est D of rim .49. S65a and b–66 from factory dump; S19–66 found in Trench S–1, depth 1.00. **Fig. 8–11.**

127 (S51a,b–65, S57a–65). Three non-joining fragments preserving part of base and wall

PH .21; Est D .46. Flat base, side almost vertical. From context of late 3rd or first half of 4th c. Both found at BB:24 (Trench F–5) among Period 2 earthquake debris, depth 1.25–1.50. Fragment (S57d–65) from wall of this or another basin found with these. Similar fragment (S63–65) found at x:34 (Trench F–4), depth 1.30. **Fig. 8–11.**

128 (S41–65). Fragment of rim and wall

PH .10; Est D .46. From Trench S, depth .80. **Fig. 8–11.**

129 (S40–65). Fragment of rim and wall

PH .117; Est D .46. Rounded rim, horizontal groove and three small holes drilled in upper portion of angular molding. Large dowel hole drilled below lip of this molding, perhaps for handle or latch pin. Incised line separating molding from two grooves at bottom of fragment. From bb:21–24 (Trench J–4), depth ca. 1.20. **Fig. 8–11.**

130 (S51c,d–65, S21–66). Three joining fragments preserving part of wall

PH .24; Est D .46. Rounded molding at top. Below this, vertical lines incised between and below two horizontal grooves producing a masonry-like pattern. Partly overlapping this, an incised "palm branch." Near bottom of fragment, a horizontal groove and incised line above a rounded molding set off by smaller grooves. From contexts of later 3rd or first half of 4th c., S51–65 found with No. 127; S21–66 found at BB:22 (Trench S–1), depth 1.10. Three other fragments may belong to this or a similar basin: S57b,c–65, found with No. 127; S31–66, from northeast corner of Trench OP–1, depth .45. **Fig. 8–11; Pl. 8–8.**

The stylized "palm branch" motif is often found in Jewish funerary art, either alone or in conjunction with the menorah and other cult objects; numerous examples are given in Goodenough, *Symbols* 3. Goodenough discusses the possible significance of this symbol (*Symbols* 4, 145–66) and connects it with both the *lulab* and the Classical "palm of victory" (*Symbols* 7, 121–24). In the proper context, this motif in both its Greco-Roman and Jewish forms may be interpreted as a symbol of immortality. Such an intent probably lies behind the palm branches scratched on Jewish limestone ossuaries and on the walls of burial chambers; e.g., Bagatti-Milik, 56–57, fig. 15, nos. 113 and 119, and B. Mazar, *Beth Shearim* 1 (Jerusalem, 1944) no. 2 on pl. 18. The possibility of such a meaning for the graffito on No. 130 is suggested by similar limestone vessels found in tombs at Jerusalem and Bethany; see Bagatti-Milik, 164, fig. 38, nos. 2–3; and Saller, *Bethany*, 335–39. Goodenough, *Symbols* 4, 150ff, cites a close relationship between the ceremonial use of the *lulab* and the ritual libations of water and wine during the annual Feast of Tabernacles.

26. R. Macalister and J. G. Duncan, "Excavations on the Hill of Ophel, Jerusalem, 1923–25," *PEFA* 4 (1926) 147–50, figs. 138–40, pl. 16, no. 6ff, dated Roman. Crowfoot-FitzGerald, "Tyropoeon," pl. 18, nos. 24–31, from disturbed context; Hamilton, "North Wall," 50, fig. 23, nos. 16–17, 3rd or 4th c.; Crowfoot, *Samaria* 3, 466, fig. 118, no. 6, unstratified; N. Avigad, "Jewish Quarter 1970," 6–7, pls. 3B, 4B, example of a complete high-footed vase, 70 A.C.; B. Mazar, "The Excavations in the Old City of Jerusalem near the Temple Mount. Second Preliminary Report, 1969–70 Seasons," *Eretz-Israel* 10 (1971) 18, nos. 1–2, Herodian; Dothan-Freedman, *Ashdod* 1, 35, fig. 15, no. 5 and pl. 11, no. 7, a mortarium (?), dated 4th c.; Eitan, "Rosh Ha-ayin," 67, fig. 15, no. 4, either ca. 90–150 or 250–350, from the Mausoleum. All the dates of lathed limestone basins cited above are open to question. The only securely dated finds are of the 1st c. B.C. or 1st A.C. from Jerusalem. For the method of manufacture, see A. Mutz, "Die Jüdische Steindreherei in herodianischer Zeit. Eine technologische Untersuchung," *Technik Geschichte* 45 (1978) 291–320.

27. See Macalister, *Gezer* 2, 38, fig. 233a–d; McCown, *Nasbeh* 1, pl. 91, nos. 1–2, a group of similar mortars.

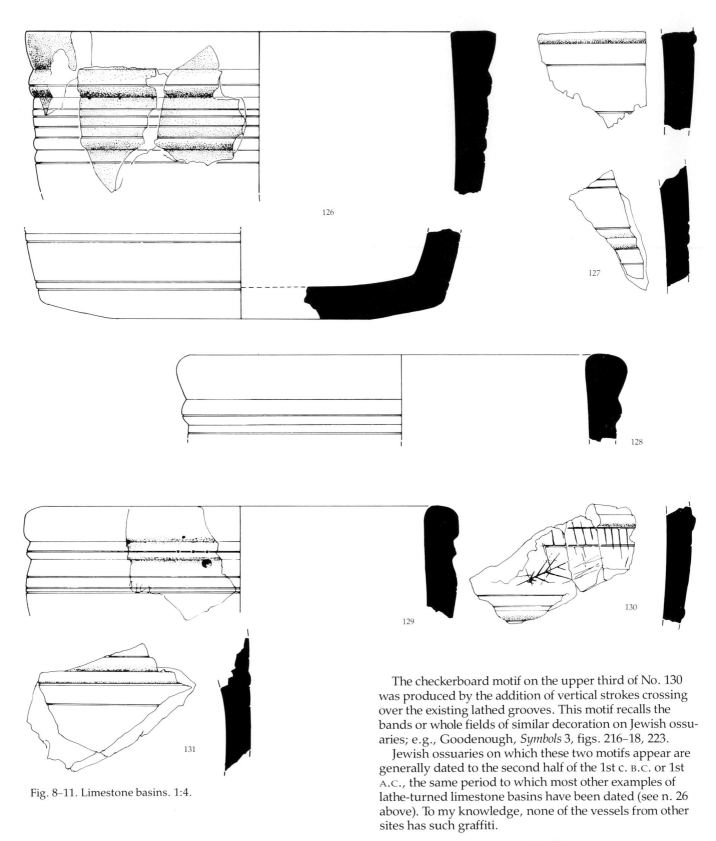

Fig. 8–11. Limestone basins. 1:4.

The checkerboard motif on the upper third of No. 130 was produced by the addition of vertical strokes crossing over the existing lathed grooves. This motif recalls the bands or whole fields of similar decoration on Jewish ossuaries; e.g., Goodenough, *Symbols* 3, figs. 216–18, 223.

Jewish ossuaries on which these two motifs appear are generally dated to the second half of the 1st c. B.C. or 1st A.C., the same period to which most other examples of lathe-turned limestone basins have been dated (see n. 26 above). To my knowledge, none of the vessels from other sites has such graffiti.

131   (S65c–66). Fragment of wall

PH .144. Found with No. 126. **Fig. 8–11.**

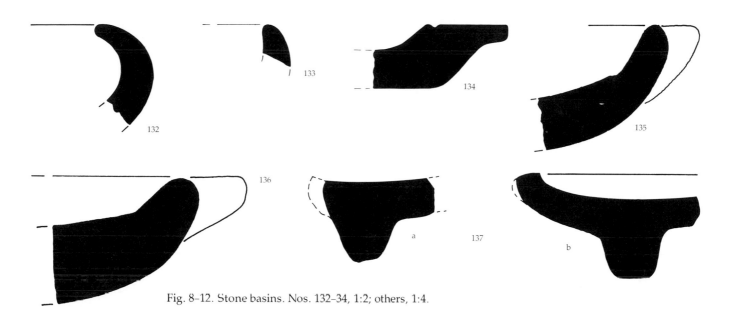

Fig. 8–12. Stone basins. Nos. 132–34, 1:2; others, 1:4.

Other Stone Vessels (Nos. 132–40)

132   (S70–65). Marble fragment, rim and wall of large shallow basin

PH .053. White, crystalline. Simple flat rim, inward curving side. **Fig. 8–12.**

Cf. Bagatti, "Nuovi apporti archeologici al 'Dominus Flevit' (Oliveto)," *LA* 19 (1969) fig. 7, no. 1, unclear context.

133   (S1–67). Marble fragment, rim

Max dim .046. Like No. 132, slightly smaller. From factory dump. **Fig. 8–12.**

134   (S67–65). Marble fragment, rim and wall of large shallow basin

H .034. Flat rim, short thick flat body. Single groove on upper surface of rim. Two similar fragments (S44–66, S51–66) found. **Fig. 8–12; Pl. 8–8.**

Cf. Deonna, *Delos*, 56–58, fig. 83, no. 8 (rim).

135   (S34–65). Basalt fragment preserving profile and handle

PH .06; Est D .16. Gray. Plain rim, flat lug handle starting at rim and tapering down wall. Body thickened and turning inward. **Fig. 8–12.**

136   (S19–65). Basalt fragment of rim and side preserving handle, burned on upper surface

PH .065; Est D .165. Purplish gray above (burned), gray along outer bottom edge. Like No. 135. From factory dump. One other fragment (S33–66) found. The burned interior supports the suggestion that basalt basins were sometimes used as "cooking trays" (Macalister, *Gezer* 2, 39–40). **Fig. 8–12; Pl. 8–8.**

137   Basalt tripod basins. **Fig. 8–12.**

a (S46–65). Fragment preserving entire profile and one

foot. H .098; Est D .24. Gray. Low rim, shallow interior, thick body. Lug handle at rim, conical foot (D ca .05). Surface find.

b (S48–65). Fragment preserving profile and one foot. H .112; Est D .34. Gray basalt. Thick rim, lug handle. Wall turned inward and broadening on exterior, base thinner, flat. Circular foot tapering toward bottom (D ca. .054). Interior surface smooth, exterior roughly cut. Surface find. Two similar fragments (S81–65, S10–66) found.

138   (S17–65). Limestone mortar; edges chipped

H .073; L .14. Light gray, soft stone. Irregular oval block, perhaps originally rectangular. Oval depression (D .09, depth .05) in center of flat top. Bottom flat but roughly cut. (See n. 27 above.) **Pl. 8–8.**

139   (S24–65). Limestone mortar, three corners broken off, bottom damaged

H .11; L .19. Light gray stone, many inclusions. Block was once cubical. Hemispherical depression (D .12; depth .05). Otherwise like preceding. Surface find. **Pl. 8–8.**

140   (S74–66). Limestone container, one upper corner preserved

PH .055; L of longest side .097; Th. wall .038. White stone. Top flat, edges beveled. Sides slope inward. Original form probably a rectangular or square box (see Chap. 3). Late 4th or first half of 5th c. context in Trench X–4. **Fig. 8–13; Pl. 8–8.**

Structural Material

These items used in construction or decoration of buildings on the site include iron and bronze nails (Nos. 141–42), water pipes (Nos. 143–48), and roof tiles (Nos.

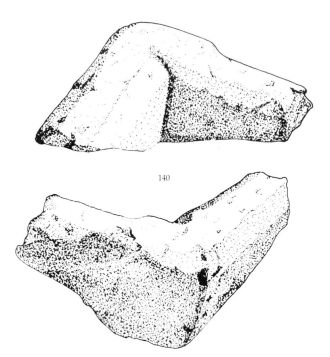

140

Fig. 8-13. Limestone container, two views. 1:2.

154–55). A few fragments of circular and rectangular bricks and wall flues (Nos. 149–53) indicate the presence of heated rooms and possibly a bath. A fragment of a Corinthian capital, pieces of pilasters and moldings, stone revetments and paving (Nos. 156–62), fragments of mosaic pavement and wall painting (Nos. 163–66) suggest some luxury, but at what period is uncertain.

Iron and Bronze Nails (Nos. 141–42)

Numerous fragmentary iron nails were found. Though their distribution shows no pattern, two concentrations are apparent: immediately north and west of the glass furnace and northwest of the wine press. The 65 intact examples inventoried all have square tapering shanks and flat or convex circular heads.[28] Nails that have been hammered into wood thicker than their length, and those that have been retracted, tend generally to retain their points. The fact that few points have been preserved among the Jalame nails indicates they were "clinched," i.e., pushed through pre-bored holes in the planks or beams to be joined, and the point then

bent and hammered flat.[29] The extant length of a "clinched" nail is thus roughly equivalent to the thickness of the wood it has been driven through. At Jalame this averages .04–.055. Most of the nails were originally about .07 in length; others varied from .035–ca. .10.[30]

The bronze nails accounted for only 6 percent of those found.[31] All but one came from the factory dump.

141   Iron nails, point and part of shank broken off unless otherwise mentioned. **Pl. 8-9.**

a (M44–66). PL .064; D of head .026. Long shank, thin convex round head. 11 inventoried.
b (M8–65). Intact. L .07, of head .014. Like No. 141a but with flat circular head, thinner shaft. 5 inventoried.
c (M13–65). PL .057, D of head .017. Like No. 141a but with smaller convex head. 11 inventoried.
d (M31–65). PL .062; D of head .021. Like No. 141b but with larger convex circular head. 2 inventoried.
e (M6–66). Intact (?), bluish green glass adhering. L .031; D of head .01. Head of undetermined form, short shank tapering to point. One similar nail, also covered with glass, found in factory dump.
f (M19–66). Intact. L .05; D of head .013. Flat head, square or circular thin shank. 3 inventoried.
g (M1–65). L .085; D of head .02. Thick rectangular shank tapering toward point. Convex circular head. 9 inventoried.
h (M41–65). Head missing. PL .102. Thick shank, circular in section. Probably a spike. 3 inventoried.
i (M4–66). L .057; D of head .024. Thick shank, large convex circular head. 4 inventoried.
j (M20–66). L .052; D of head .035. Broad convex circular head, tapering square shank. 3 inventoried.
k (M43–66). Burned? PL .033; D of head .025. Gray granular appearance. Large convex square head. Analysis by Dr. Henry E. Bent, Department of Chemistry, University of Missouri–Columbia: density of 6.85 ($\pm$1%), considerably lower than iron (7.86); porous appearance, but absorbs only about 1% of its volume in water; polishing on carborundum wheel produced metallic surface but not sparks characteristic of iron nails, or of soft or hard steel; only weakly magnetic. Dr. Bent concluded that No. 141k is of impure iron and may contain a considerable amount of slag. Found in factory dump.

142   Bronze nails, points broken off. All square in section. **Pl. 8-9.**

a (M9–64). PL .051; D of head .012. Convex circular head with flattened sides. Four examples found.
b (M60–65). PL .051; D of head .012. Like No. 142a but shank folded back on itself at junction with head.
c (M51–65). L .036; D of head .011. Convex circular head with beveled sides. Shank circular in section near head, square below. From factory dump.

28. Iron nails are often the most frequent metal finds on a Palestinian site of this period, but they are seldom published. For nails from Palestine see Macalister, *Gezer* 2, 246f; Reisner, *Samaria* 1, 349–50; Meyers, *Khirbet Shema*, pl. 8.3, nos. 9–12, 14–18; Mazar, *Beth Shearim* 1, 222–24; Avigad, *Beth Shearim* 3, 215; and P. D. Hammond, *The Excavation of the Main Theatre at Petra 1961–62, Final Report* (London, 1965) 66–67. A good deal of work has been done on Roman period nails in Britain; e.g., Frere, *Verulamium* 1, 186f; Brodribb, *Shakenoak* 3, 114f, and 4, 134, both with further references.

29. Examples of "clinched" nails illustrated in Meyers, *Khirbet Shema*, pl. 8.3, nos. 9–10, dated Early Byzantine.
30. The average lengths at Jalame are very close to those at Beth Shearim and Khirbet Shema.
31. See Macalister, *Gezer* 2, 246f; Reisner, *Samaria* 1, 353f; also Chavane, *Salamine*, 68f, with further references.

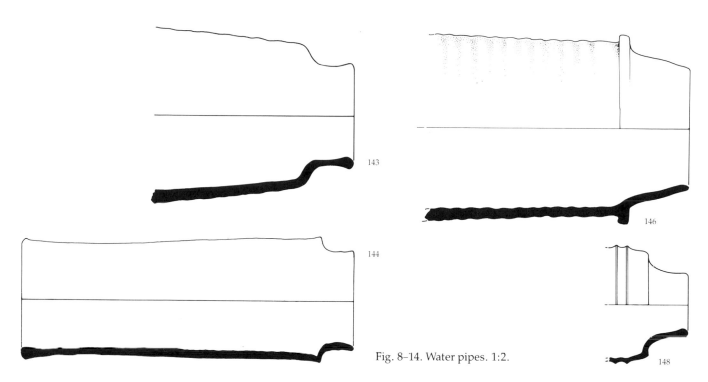

Fig. 8-14. Water pipes. 1:2.

Terracotta Water Pipes (Nos. 143–48)

Nos. 143–48 are representative of the pipes found.[32] Water must always have been scarce on the hilltop, and these pipes probably belonged to a system of conduits that carried rain water from the roofs and gutters of the buildings to a series of cisterns. The diversity of types probably stems from the succession of building phases to which they belong, as well as the differing functions they may have served. The separate tubes were linked by inserting the narrow end into the wide end of the next pipe and then sealing the join with plaster.[33]

143 (P90–65). Two joining fragments preserving profile of collar and part of body

PL .158; D of rim .085, of body ca. .14; L of collar .034; Th of body .01. Gritty red clay, exterior greenish buff (10YR 7/4), interior red (2.5YR 5/6). Thickened rounded rim. Collar slightly concave. Narrow flaring shoulder. Body lightly ribbed on exterior, circumference enlarging toward broken end. Four similar fragments inventoried. **Fig. 8-14; Pl. 8-9.**

Cf. Macalister, *Gezer* 3, pl. 50, no. 3, from the Roman bath; Fisher-McCown, "Jerash," 114, fig. 2a, 2nd or 3rd c.; Kelso-Baramki, *Jericho and en-Nitla,* 35, no. 128 and pl. 16, no. 5, of Byzantine date.

144 (T14–65). Many joining fragments preserving entire profile

32. See Vitruvius, *De architectura* 8, 6.5–6.10; *DarSag,* s.v. *Tubus*; Robinson-Graham, *Olynthus* 8, 309–11; Forbes, *Studies* 1, 152–55, 172–77.

33. For examples of drains in situ see Aharoni, *Ramat Rahel, 1959–60,* pls. 18–19, in bath of 2nd–4th c.; Hammond, *Petra,* 53f, pl. 43, nos. 2–3, dated 2nd c.

L .35, collar .03; D of body, .124, wide rim .128; Th of narrow rim, .006, wide rim .014, body ca. .01. Fine buff fabric (10YR 7/3). Plain narrow rim, collar somewhat concave on exterior, with raised band .016 from rim; interior convex. Narrow flared shoulder, slight ridge at junction with body. Thickened rounded rim. **Fig. 8-14; Pl. 8-9.**

Cf. Hamilton, "North Wall," fig. 23, no. 30, 3rd or 4th c., with ribbed body that No. 144 lacks.

145 (T1–65). Many joining fragments preserving all but wide end

PL .038; D narrow rim .052, of body .10; L of collar .039. Buff clay (10YR 7/3). Preserved rim plain (Th .006), collar widening toward body. Raised edge (D .123, Th .009) at join with body. From bb–cc:29 (Trench J-3), depth 1.55, Period 2 context. **Pl. 8-9.**

146 (P221–65). Eight fragments preserving profile of collar and part of body

PL .21; D of rim .095, of body .12; L of collar .047; Th of wall ca. .007. Red clay (2.5YR 6/8). Plain rim, collar convex and widening toward body. Raised edge (D .15, Th .009) at join with body. Body ribbed inside and out, thicker and wider toward broken end. Found in Trench F-6, Period 2 context. **Fig. 8-14; Pl. 8-9.**

147 (T24–65). Three joining fragments preserving portion of collar and body

PL .116; D of body ca. .138. Reddish-buff (5YR 6/4). Like No. 146, but somewhat thinner and lacking groove on body side of raised ridge (D .15, Th .006). From YY–dd:27 (Trench J-3), depth ca. 1.75, Period 2 context. **Pl. 8-9.**

148 (P84–66). Five joining fragments preserving part of collar and body

PL .062; D of rim .051, at shoulder, .08; L of collar .032; Th of collar .005, of body .003. Fine buff clay (10YR 7/3). Thickened, rounded rim, sloping collar broadening to flat shoulder. Body ribbed outside, smoothed flat inside. From just above bedrock in Trench OP. **Fig. 8–14; Pl. 8–9.**

Terracotta Flues (Nos. 149–51)

Flues (*tubuli*) were used during the Roman period not only in bath structures but also in heating parts of other types of buildings.[34] These flues resemble narrow rectangular boxes, open at both ends, with open slots along the sides. They were arranged vertically in rows within the walls of the building and conveyed hot air up from a space below the floor, which was heated by a furnace (cf. Masada installation, Pl. 8–10). The flue fragments found on the site were limited to the area northeast of the wine press. The presence of circular bricks (Nos. 152–53) in the same contexts suggests the villa contained heated rooms.

149   (T10–65). Eight joining fragments preserving entire profile; parts of one narrow side missing

H .235; L .13; W .076; av. Th .008. Light red fabric (2.5YR 6/6). Exterior smooth, interior rough and uneven, showing use of fingers and edged tool in manufacture. Narrow sides pierced by rectangular openings (L .13, W .03). From Trench J–3, Period 2 context. Two similar large fragments (T11–65, T31–66). **Fig. 8–15; Pl. 8–10.**

150   (T13–65). Two fragments preserving two corners and part of narrow side

PH .05; L .048; W .073; Th .01. Red fabric (2.5YR 5/6). Like No. 149. Break at one corner shows side panels were formed from a flat sheet folded and reinforced with rolls of clay pressed and smoothed along the inside corners by hand. Sharp tool used to finish edges and cut out vents before firing. From Trench J–4, Period 2 context. **Pl. 8–10.**

151   (T5–66). Four joining fragments preserving most of one broad face and part of both narrow sides

PH .292; L .187; W .074; Th .012. Like No. 149, but of buff fabric (10YR 8/3) and heavier. Five similar large fragments (T12–65, T16–65, T18–65, T19–65, T24–66) and many smaller ones found in lower levels in eastern part of site, from Trenches OP to J–5. **Pl. 8–10.**

Terracotta Bricks (Nos. 152–53)

Circular and rectangular baked bricks were commonly used to support the floors of heated rooms.[35] A nearly complete circular example is No. 152a. Six other similar

fragments were inventoried from among the relatively small number found. They range in diameter from .13 to .25, and in thickness from .30 to .33 (Pl. 8–10). Circular brick fragments were found in the eastern part of the site, in the same contexts as the flues (Nos. 149–51), and in the factory dump. Rectangular bricks were more numerous but had the same distribution. Though no complete example was found, these appear to have been roughly square, about .20 on a side and either about .033 or .04 in thickness. Both types were probably formed in wooden frames. The upper surfaces retain the marks of a wooden (?) tool drawn across the brick and forming a slightly raised ridge along the outer edges. The sides also have marks from a tool drawn horizontally along them. As these bricks were stacked one on another, they show evidence of heating and smoke only on the sides. The variations in thickness seem to indicate that there were two sizes of both varieties of bricks, perhaps employed in rooms of differing sizes or uses.

152   Circular bricks. **Pl. 8–10.**

a (T3–65). Partly burned. Th .045; D .20. Coarse red (2.5YR 5/6) clay, large white inclusions.
b Group of brick fragments, all ca. same diameter and approximately same clay.

153   Rectangular bricks. **Pl. 8–10.**

a (T10–66). One-half (?) preserved. Th .039; PL .11; W .193. Light grayish buff (5Y 8/2) gritty, brittle clay.
b (T53–66). Corner preserved. Th .04; PL .13; PW .18. Pinkish buff (5YR 7/4) exterior, clay red (2.5YR 6/4), gritty, white inclusions. Stained with soot on sides.
c (T54–66). Corner preserved. Th .033; PL .146; PW .093. Like No. 154b but thinner. Impressions of grass on bottom.

Terracotta Roof Tiles (Nos. 154–55)

Among the inventoried objects, only No. 154 can be positively identified as a *tegula* (flat roof tile) fragment, and three (represented by No. 155) as *imbrex* (curved roof tile) fragments.[36] The paucity of these finds suggests they did not come from the excavated structures on the site but were employed as lids for clay sarcophagi (see No. 182).

154   (T25–65). *Tegula* fragment, broken on three sides, worn

H .052; Th of plate .03. Light red to buff (2.5YR 6/6) gritty clay with many dark inclusions. Flat vertical flange (H .025, W .026). Bottom rough with adhering dark gravel. **Fig. 8–15.**

34. Vitruvius, *De architectura*, 5.10; F. Kretzschmer, "Hypokausten," *Saalburg Jahrbuch* 12 (1953) 7–41; A. Grenier, *Manuel d'archéologie gallo-romaine* (Paris, 1931–1960) 4, 238–41.
35. See D. Barag, "Brick Stamp-Impressions of the Legio X Fretensis," *BJ* 167 (1967) 250–51, with further references; and B. Maisler, M. Stekelis, and M. Avi-Yonah, "The Excavations at Beth Yerah (Khirbet al-Kerak) 1944–1946," *IEJ* 2 (1952) 218–22, a Late Roman bath with rectangular bricks in situ.

36. See Barag, as in n. 35, 251; and discussions in G. Spitzlberger, "Die römischen Ziegeltempel im . . . Raetien," *Saalburg Jahrbuch* 25 (1968) 104f, and A. C. C. Brodribb, "A Survey of Tile from the Roman Bath House at Beauport Park, Battle, E. Sussex," *Britannia* 10 (1979) 140–44. For an example of a clay sarcophagus covered with roof tiles see Zevulun-Olenik, *Talmudic Period*, 91, fig. 235, 2nd or 3rd c., from Nahariya.

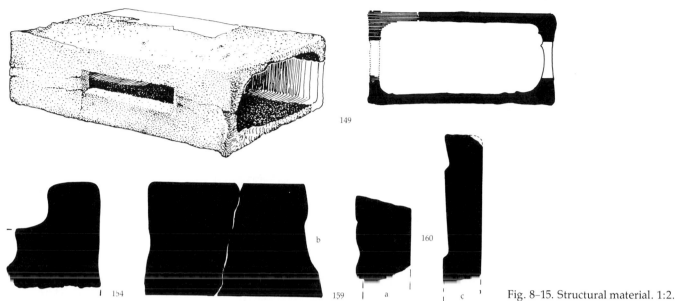

Fig. 8–15. Structural material. 1:2.

155 (T26–66). *Imbrex* fragment, broken on two sides, corner and part of center ridge preserved

PL .113; PW .091; Th ca. .007. Reddish buff (7.5YR 7/6) gritty clay. Rounded thickened edges. Shallow grooves on upper surface from fingers drawn lengthwise across the tile during manufacture. Interior rough. Tile turned inward 45° at center, original width probably ca. .14. Possibly too lightweight to have been an *imbrex*. Provenience not recorded. Another roughly similar fragment (T18–66) found on surface. **Pl. 8–11.**

Stone Structural and Decorative Material (Nos. 156–62)

The distribution of these fragments indicates the majority can be associated with the villa. Nearly 30 percent of the inventoried stone structural and decorative material was found east and northeast of the wine press. Sixty percent came from among the debris in the factory dump, and only 10 percent from the central two-thirds of the site. Another indication of an early date for most or all of this material is the reuse of the column drum (No. 157) as a mortar and of pieces of marble revetment as millstones (No. 100). These fragments, more than any others, give an idea of what must have been a somewhat sumptuous building. A Corinthian order seems to have been used in at least part of the villa, and carved moldings appear to have framed its windows and doorways. Panels of marble and other revetment covered some parts of its walls, and slabs of polished flooring were found. Of the revetment and flooring, 47 fragments were inventoried. Of these, 39 were of marble of different types, 6 of limestone, and 1 each of granite and porphyry. A representative selection is presented in Nos. 161–62.

156 (S5–64). Marble Corinthian capital fragment, one corner of abacus, angle-volute, and portions of upper and lower leaves of acanthus ring preserved

PH .27; W .21. White coarse-grained marble. Fragment triangular from top view. Summary carving. Stem of lower leaves suggested by two parallel vertical grooves. Flanking round-edged leaves indicated by crescent and tear-drop-shaped depressions. Similarly carved leaf extends below tightly coiled scroll of volute. Narrow groove between volute and simple abacus with broad horizontal groove. **Fig. 8–16.**

157 (S11–64). Limestone column drum, gouge in side, reused as mortar

H .48; D .385. Light gray. Roughly cut cylinder, both ends flat. Hollowed to form receptacle (D .275, depth .20) at one end. From Trench K, Period 4 context. **Pl. 8–11.**

158 (S4–66). Limestone base fragment, broken on three sides

H .085; W .051. Light gray. Two flat faces, rounded corner between. Hole drilled through one face; part of second hole preserved at opposite end. **Pl. 8–11.**

159 Marble pilaster fragments. **Fig. 8–15; Pl. 8–11.**

a (S41–66). Broken all around. L .06; Th .032. White. Three narrow parallel grooves on finished face. From factory dump.

b (S4–65, S14–65, S84–66). Three joining fragments. L .34; Th .06. Light gray, fine grained. Finished face highly polished, reverse picked in spots. Possibly from corner molding or pilaster.

160 Stone fragments with molded borders. **Fig. 8–15; Pl. 8–11.**

a (S66–66). Marble, possibly burned, broken all around. L .061; Th .028. Gray crystalline. One face flat and smooth,

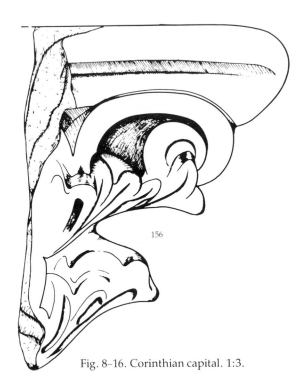

156

Fig. 8–16. Corinthian capital. 1:3.

other cut by two parallel grooves setting off two rounded moldings.

b (S3–66). Marble, broken all around. L .068, Th .028. Like preceding but with broader moldings.

c (S54–66). Marble, broken all around. L .10; Th .022. Gray. One side flat and smooth. Broad shallow indented band across center of opposite face.

d (S79–66). Marble, one edge preserved, burned. L .10; Th .033. White. Raised ridge on one face, other side smooth. Preserved edge rounded.

e (S7–64). Serpentine molding, two edges preserved. L .06; Th .037. Dark greenish. Wide groove along one side of polished face. One edge smoothed and rounded, other more roughly finished. All these found in factory dump.

161   Stone slab fragments finished on both sides. **Pl. 8–11.**

a (S86–66). Marble, one edge preserved. L .103; Th .017. White, fine crystalline. Preserved edge roughly cut.

b (S36–65). Marble, broken all around. L .18; Th .035. White, highly polished on both sides.

c (S45–66). Marble, three joining fragments, broken all around. L .18; Th .0185. White with gray streak. From topsoil.

d (S87–66). Limestone, part of one edge preserved. L .115; Th .037. Bluish gray streaked with white. Edge flat. From topsoil.

e (S81–66). Limestone, one edge intact. L .121; Th .025. Gray. One face cut with single slightly curved diagonal groove. Finished edge rounded. From topsoil.

162   Stone fragments finished on one face only; no edges preserved. **Pl. 8–11.**

a (S17–66). Marble. L .114; Th .024. White crystalline. Possibly flooring. From topsoil.

b (S20–65). Marble. L .24; Th .044. White veined with blue. Flooring.

c (S20–66). Marble. L .099; Th .018. Purple and pink. Possibly revetment.

d (S68–65). Marble. L .123; Th .026. Multicolored (purple, yellow, pink, and white). Finished side polished. Possibly flooring.

e (S72–65). Granite. L .055; Th .014. Pink. Finished face very smooth. Probably revetment.

f (S9–65). Porphyry. L .09; Th .015. Reddish brown. Probably revetment. From factory dump.

Mosaic Tesserae (Nos. 163–64)

163   Limestone tesserae from the wine press floor. **Pl. 8–12.**

a. Fragment of floor, heavy lime incrustation. L .07; Th ca. .03. Nine light gray limestone cubes (av. L .02). Roughly set in thick whitish mortar with many small inclusions of charcoal and crushed potsherds.

b (S83–65). Tessera. L .019; H .017. Light gray. Almost cubical. Typical of the tesserae from the wine press.

c (S84–65). Tessera. L .035; W .029; H .02. Light gray. Large coarse cube. This type not uncommon in wine press floor. Late 3rd or early 4th c.

164   Representative small limestone tesserae

L ranges from ca. .01 to .017. Colors range from almost white to dark gray among the common examples; reddish brown is infrequent, black (basalt) even more so. All roughly cubical. Late 3rd or early 4th c. **Pl. 8–12.**

Painted Wall Plaster (Nos. 165–66)

165   (T20–23–65, T37–66, T38–66). 21 non-joining fragments

W of largest fragment .05; av. Th .005. Irregular pieces, flat smoothed-out surfaces. Simple designs in red over yellow and white grounds. A possible reconstruction is suggested in Fig. 8–17: an imitation marble dado in red daubed over a yellow ground adjoining a geometric design (a lattice?) in red on a white field. Preliminary layer of plaster thick (.04) and mixed with coarse small gravel and sand. Final layer thin (.01) and finer. Yellow and white grounds applied first, then the division between the upper and lower levels drawn in red with a small brush. The remainder completed with larger brush and without further preliminary drawing. All but three fragments from the "dado." Late 3rd or early 4th c. From Trench F–4, Period 2, earthquake fall. **Fig. 8–17.**

166   (T11–64). 230 fragments

L of largest fragment .05; av Th .005. Like No. 165 but different design. Distribution of colors: 42 fragments with red on white (19 are parts of bands of W .012 and .006); 16 yellow on white (2 are parts of a band, W .01); 170 white only. Two further fragments have both red and yellow on white and are handled in a freer style than the linear

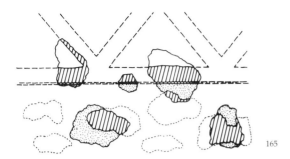

Fig. 8–17. Wall stucco. 1:2.

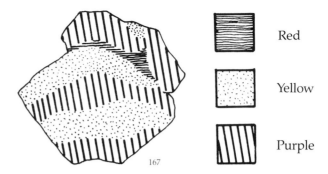

Fig. 8–18. Glass inlay. 2:1.

bands. The overall design cannot be reconstructed. From Trenches A and A–1.

Miscellaneous (Nos. 167–98)

This final section presents a heterogeneous group of objects organized by material: glass, bronze, iron, lead, terracotta, stone. One noteworthy object is a Canaanite bronze figurine, No. 169, from the Middle Bronze Age. It is a type fairly well known in northern Israel and southwest Syria. Few of these figurines have been found in their original context. The origin of this one probably is Tell Amar, just north of Jalame. Other objects include segments of glass inlay (No. 167), a fragment of a lead openwork ornament (No. 176), fragments of three figurines and a mask of terracotta (Nos. 179–80), and several fragments of clay sarcophagi from nearby graves.

167   Glass inlay fragments. **Fig. 8–18; Pl. 8–12.**
a (G506–64). Heavy white weathering, two edges preserved. L .025; Th .002. Light green. Flat sheet, intact edges have curvilinear contours. From factory dump.
b (G221b–65). Slight iridescence. L .019; Th .001. Transparent light bluish green with faint striations. Flat sheet cut to form pointed, hook-like shape.
c (G116–66). Weathered, some pitting, no edge preserved. L .02; Th .003. Red, purple, and yellow marbled bands. Fragment flat with rough surface. From factory dump.
d (G471–66). Heavy greenish weathering with blackish patina, three edges preserved. L .029; Th .003. Bright red layer visible in section now covered on both sides by black and green mottled weathering. Flat sheet, one preserved edge slightly curved. From factory dump.
Cf. Harden, *Karanis*, 298–302, pl. 22; Davidson, *Corinth* 12, 143f, pl. 73, no. 1060. Both illustrate fragments of various colors and shapes from glass plaques used as inlay. The Karanis material dates 3rd–5th c. and was used on "boxes, trays, or pieces of furniture" and for wall decoration. The Corinthian finds were used for the latter purpose and are dated 4th c.

168   (G24–66). Glass counter, heavy weathering
D .017; H .007. Opaque dark. Oval with convex top and

rough, flat bottom. From aa:3 (Trench J–4) on bedrock. **Fig. 8–19.**
Cf. Deonna, *Delos*, 308f, pl. 90, no. 794, identified as glass settings for jewelry; Davidson, *Corinth* 12, 217–19, 223, 226, separates these into "gaming pieces" and "gems" by shape; Harden, *Karanis*, 291, pl. 21, no. 897. At Samaria more than 100 were found; none was found in the glass factory waste or in Byzantine contexts. There they seem to date 1st or 2nd c.; see Crowfoot, *Samaria* 3, 392, with parallels from Pompeii. Charlesworth in Frere, *Verulamium* 1, 214, suggested the variety of colors found in these glass gaming pieces was "so that different players can distinguish their pieces." See also R. C. Bell, "Games Played at Corstopitum," *Archaeologia Aeliana*, ser. 5, 6 (1978) 174–76, pl. 8, an apparently complete set of 53 similar counters.

169   (M29–65). Bronze figurine, cast, some corrosion, pitting, and flaking; short flange (L ca. .004) at top of head broken off, as are lower portions of both arms
H .075; Th .004. Schematic human figure with heavy base. Bent slightly forward above waist, backward above shoulders. Back flat, front somewhat rounded but unmodeled. Oval head, now damaged, on long narrow neck. Arms pinched out from shoulders. Lower body thicker, legs separated by vertical groove. No indication of sex but probably male. Middle Bronze Age, ca. 1850–1700 B.C. Found at cc:19 (Trench J–4), depth 1.46. **Pl. 8–12.**
This figurine shares a number of characteristics with late pre-Hyksos figurines considered to be of Canaanite origin. The closest parallels for the Jalame example appear within the "'Syrian' Group" of O. Negbi's Type 1, Class A of flat-cast "male warriors in 'Anatolian' pose," in *Canaanite Gods in Metal. An Archaeological Study of Ancient Syro-Palestinian Figurines*, Tel-Aviv University Institute of Archaeology 5 (Tel-Aviv, 1976) 8–9; cf. pl. 7, no 31. Certain details of No. 169 are also quite similar to those encountered in several of the representations of "war gods" in joined multiple figurines, also published by Negbi and considered by her to be closely related (ibid., 4–5, 9). Field drawings of No. 169 show that prior to photographing and cleaning, there was a flange at the top of the head, as seen, for instance, in several examples in the Louvre; see A. Parrot, "Acquisitions et inédits du Musée du Louvre," *Syria* 41 (1964) 219–25, pl. 12.3 and fig. 9. Negbi ("Dating Some Groups of

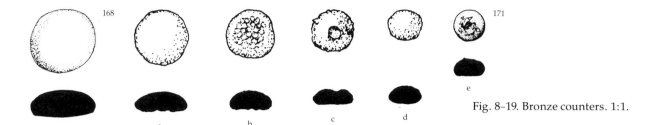

Fig. 8–19. Bronze counters. 1:1.

Fig. 8–20. Lead ornament. 1:1.

Canaanite Bronze Figurines," *PEQ* 100 [1968] 45–55) remarks that all figurines of this type may originally have had such flanges. Corrosion and flaking of the head of No. 169 have obliterated the facial features, but as can be seen in Pl. 8–12, there remains the trace of what may have been a "pinched" nose; cf. Negbi, *Canaanite Gods*, fig. 3. It is likely that the missing portions of the arms would have been bent forward to hold attributes. If, as seems quite probable, the figurine represents a "Syrian war god," these attributes might have included one or a pair of spears or daggers. It is also possible the figure was fitted with a short "kilt," which would explain the lack of genitalia and the pinched-in appearance of the lower torso; cf. ibid., p. 9, in ref. to no. 37. The base is similar to those of several published by Negbi, e.g., ibid., pl. 3, no. 5. A mold for a related type of figurine is illustrated by M. Dothan, "The excavations at Nahariyah, Preliminary Report (Seasons 1954/55)," *IEJ* 6 (1956) pl. 6.

170   (M49–66). Bronze rod, broken off at both ends

PL .084; Th .003. Thin rod, square in section, twisted to produce spiral. Ends not twisted. Bent into C-shape. A bracelet fragment, or possibly a vessel handle or the shaft of an instrument. From factory dump. **Pl. 8–12.**

Cf. Cunliffe, *Portchester*, 205, fig. 111, no. 27, bracelet, dated 1st half of 4th c.

171   Bronze disks, convex on top. **Fig. 8–19.**

a (M52–66). D .014; H .006; weight 5.998 g. Circular, top convex, bottom flat and rough.
b (M40–66). D .013; H .006; weight 4.565 g. Like preceding but with shallow indentations on top.
c (M31–66). D .012; H .005; weight 3.308 g. Like preceding but with single central depression on top.
d (M53–66). D .009; H .006; weight 2.108 g. Like No. 171a; more rounded in section.
e (M65–65). D .007; H .005; weight 1.209 g. Like preceding. Fragments of light green glass attached. All these found in factory dump.

Cf. Davidson, *Corinth* 12, 220, pls. 99–100, nos. 1712–14, from Late Roman and Byzantine contexts. Such objects may have been gaming pieces, small weights, or possibly pinheads. The four most regular of these from Jalame (a–d) range in weight from just over 2 to nearly 6 g. If accepted as weights, they might represent the following: (a) is the rough equivalent of 1/60 *libra* (halfway between a *sicilius* and a *sextula*; (b) is nearly 1/72 *libra* or one *sextula*; (c) is about 1/96 *libra*, or one *drachma*; and (d) is 1/144 *libra* (one *dimidia-sextula*); see A. Mutz, as in No. 108 above, 525–28.

They might represent part of a set of weights belonging to the bronze suspension balance, No. 107. However, it is possible they are pinheads. Cf. Baramki, "Karm al-Shaikh," pl. 4, no. 7, from Grave 3, Roman; and Brodribb, *Shakenoak* 2, 106, fig. 45, no. 69, a Roman glass pinhead attached to a bronze wire shaft. The bottom surfaces of all the Jalame examples have central depressions, and No. 171c also has a small blob of added bronze. Perhaps this is evidence of attachment of wire shafts.

172   (M3–64). Bronze disk, probably a boss

D .06; Th .002. Thin lathed disk with central hole (D .005). Around hole on outer face, concentric narrow raised ring, broad rounded band and wide concave indentation. Reverse slightly convex, broad flat band near outer edge. Raised lip along one-third of outer edge. Small square depression on outer face. **Pl. 8–12.**

173   (M58–66). Gilt bronze sheet fragment, broken off at either end

PL .05; W .018 (folded); Th .001. Very thin sheet, several fine incised parallel lines on one face. One edge folded back to middle of fragment; seems intentional. Possibly ornamental border attachment for item of cloth or leather. From factory dump. **Pl. 8–12.**

174   (M55–66). Bronze sheet fragment, edges clipped off, crumpled

PL .069; Th .002. Originally probably a flat rectangular sheet. Portions clearly clipped off. Small tool marks (?) on both sides: single and double L's, and single T and I forms. Scrap used in glass production? Original use unknown. From late factory dump. **Pl. 8–12.**

175   (M45–65). Iron rod, intact?

L .132; Th .003. Long thin rod, square in section. **Pl. 8–12.**

176   (M29–66). Lead ornament, bent and fragmentary;

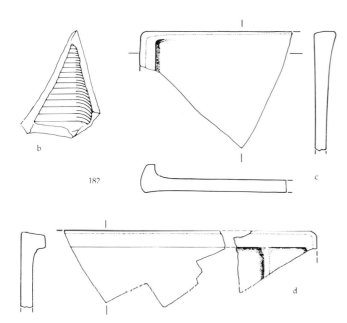

Fig. 8–21. Above: sarcophagus from Beth Shearim (restored). Drawing courtesy of author. Below: sarcophagus fragments. 1:4.

portions of interior decoration and part of one side broken off; coated with white corrosion

L .055; W .023; Th .001. Flat rectangular strip pierced with openwork decoration. Strip divided into eight unequal rectangular cells by one horizontal and three vertical bands inside border decorated with chevrons. Remains of openwork within each cell, originally probably central hexagons with radiating spokes. At damaged end, two protruding flanges. Cast; poor workmanship. An ornamental fitting or possibly a pendant (hung from a hypothetical C-shaped terminal at the damaged end). **Fig. 8–20; Pl. 8–12.**
Cf. Iliffe, "Tarshiha," 12, pl. 8, no. 15, a circular lead ornament, late 4th c.

177   (M56–65). Lead mend, ends of two rivets broken off, third preserved but bent flat; white corrosion

L .032; W .024; H .013. Irregular oval disk with three projecting rivets. **Pl. 8–12.**

178   (M7–64). Lead hook, white corrosion

L .042; Th .002. Flat strip, rectangular in section, bent to form hook. From topsoil. **Pl. 8–12.**

179   Terracotta figurine fragments, broken off all around. **Pl. 8–12.**

a (T7–66). L .025; Th .005. Fine buff clay (7.5YR 7/4). Three

rows of small spiral curls bordering neck or face of probably human figure. Interior rough, thickness uneven. Molded.
b (T8–66). L .042. Fine buff clay (7.5YR 7/4), exterior painted black. Irregular curved fragment. Raised band of tooled clay perhaps representing mane of a horse or lion.
Cf. L. Rahmani, "Notes on some Acquisitions," *Atiqot* 5 (1969) 81, fig. 1, a figurine of a human-headed animal with similar "mane," 9th or 8th c. B.C.
c (P103–66). L .045; Th .004. Reddish buff clay (2.5YR 6/6) with traces of red slip (2.5YR 5/8) or paint on exterior. Raised band with central incised groove running across fragment, curving inward at one end. Drapery from standing human figure or possibly fragment of small mask.

180   (P23–65). Terracotta mask fragment, broken all around

L .07; W .028. Very fine buff to light orange clay (10YR 8/4 to 5YR 7/6) with soft white inclusions (probably limestone). Irregular fragment preserving portion of undulating surface and heavy rounded ridge with incised groove along one edge. Part of suspension hole also preserved along edge of opposite side. Back rough. Apparently not mold-made. **Pl. 8–12.**
Cf. Davidson, *Corinth* 12, 21, pls. 40–41, nos. 440, 443, 444, 1st c.

181   Terracotta disks, chipped from vessels after firing. **Pl. 8–13.**

a (P274–65). D .049; Th ca. .008. Buff clay (7.5YR 7/4), flat thick-walled vessel (?), ribbed on both sides.
b (P374–66). D .03; Th .006. Light red clay (7.5YR 7/6), ribbed surface, probably from water jar.
c (P114–66). D .032; Th .006. Buff clay (7.5YR 8/2), probably from cooking pot.
d (P131b–66). D .037; Th .006. Very light orange clay (5YR 8/4).
e (P148–66). D .025; Th .008. Light orange clay (7.5YR 7/4). From heavy ribbed vessel.
f (P494–66). D .035; Th .007. Light red clay (5YR 7/3).
g (T12–64). D .03; Th .006. Red clay (10R 6/6). From fineware sherd.
h (P131a–66). D .04; Th .005. Reddish clay (10R 6/3), perhaps from cooking pot.
Many such objects were found at Jalame. Disks of terracotta and stone are plentiful on most ancient sites but not often published. They have been identified as stoppers for vessels or as gaming pieces. Cf. Macalister, *Gezer* 2, 301–3; Chavane, *Salamine*, 26, 30, nos. 84–85, with references; Meyers, *Khirbet Shema*, pl. 8.11, no. 7.

182   Terracotta sarcophagus fragments. **Fig. 8–21; Pl. 8–13.**

Several fragments of clay coffins were found in and around the burial caves north of the excavated area. They are of a type well represented in northwestern Israel and are commonly dated 2nd to 4th c.[37] Examples, such as one found at Beth Shearim (Fig. 8–21), are narrow and shallow, with rims splayed out to receive flat lid tiles.[38] The following are representative:

a (T9–66). Upper corner, broken off at bottom and along both sides. PH .23; PL of longest side .21. Gritty buff clay. Outer surfaces smoothed, rounded corner. Interior less well finished, corner thickened as in flue No. 150. Rim (W .08) flares out from body at 45° angle; top and outer edge flat. Surface find.

b (T44–66). Lower corner, broken off at top and along both sides. PH .165; PL of longest side .155. Buff, fairly fine clay. Bottom flat (Th .03). Straight sides, overlapping and smoothed at corner.

c (T47–66). Corner of a lid, six joining fragments. PL .36; PW .115; Th .018. Gritty buff clay. Flat tile with thickened upturned edges (H of rim .085). From Tomb 1 (see Fig. 2–10).

d (T48–66). Corner and portion of side of a lid, four joining fragments. PL ca. .22; PW .06; Th .02. Buff gritty clay. Like preceding but with a raised band on upper side near corner.

e (T10–64). Portion of side of lid. PL .12; PW .09; Th .018. Like preceding, excepting broad groove along inside of raised rim. From Trench J–4, depth 1.00.

f (T26–65). Portion of side of lid. PL .088; PW .077; Th .017. Grayish buff (7.5YR 7/3) clay. Raised rim (H. .021, W .037) flat on top with beveled sides. Incised lines from tool drawn along length of top and sides of rim. Upper surface smooth, underside marked with straw impressions. From factory dump.

g (T51–66). Portion of side of lid. PL .14; PW .097; Th .03. Light red (2.5YR 6/6) gritty clay. Upper surface smoothed, bottom rougher. Preserved rim flat with projecting rounded band along top.

183 (P4–65, P372–66, etc.). Coarseware sherds used as backing for wall facing or pavement, worn, with plaster adhering to one or both sides

Av. L .05. Primarily reddish orange (2.5YR 6/6) and triangular in shape. Greatest concentration of inventoried sherds associated with pithoi and press in north-central area of site. **Pl. 8–13.**

184 (S50–65). Marble disk

D .085; Th .018. Grayish white marble revetment fragment roughly cut into circular shape. Both faces smooth, one polished. Possibly stopper or lid for water jar. **Pl. 8–13.**

Cf. Chavane, *Salamine* 6, 26–29, pls. 8–9, with further references and an example of such a lid in place.

185 (S3–67). Limestone slab, two edges preserved

PL .14; Th ca. .03. Light gray soft limestone. Use uncertain, too soft for revetment? From topsoil. **Pl. 8–13.**

186 (S7–66). Basalt object, one side broken off and missing, some areas chipped off

H .056; PL .026; W .04; D of hole .01. Black fine-grained basalt with white inclusions. Irregular rectangular block. Broadest face flat, opposite face convex and beveled at one end. Preserved edge also flat. All finished surfaces smoothed, corners rounded. Pierced lengthwise by drilled hole now exposed along broken side of object. From factory dump. **Pl. 8–13.**

Window Glass

Evidence for the manufacture or use of window glass at Jalame is scarce, but some fragments may be from crown-glass panes. These circular panes, which became common everywhere in medieval times, are said to have been manufactured in the East as early as the 4th c.[39] They have been found at Samaria,[40] in Jerusalem,[41] and at Gerasa.[42] They are conspicuous by their absence at other sites, e.g., Shavei Zion[43] and Sardis,[44] where quantities of roller-molded sheet glass were found. The use of circular panes in the 4th c. cannot have been extensive; they are more common in the 5th and following centuries. The Jalame fragments would allow for a later dating, since all but one (No. 188) were found around the site, not in the factory dump. No fragments were found that could be identified as sheet glass.

It is also possible that most of the Jalame fragments are bottoms of large bowls. Against this supposition is the extreme thickness of some of the pieces (e.g. Nos. 189–91). And the two rim fragments (Nos. 187–88) cannot be from bowls—they are both too thin and too flat. One fragment (G301–65) without a finished edge (but not including the center) has abraded concentric lines, perhaps indicating some panes were finished in this way (see also No. 188).

Despite the uncertain nature of the Jalame fragments, they are published here tentatively as window glass.

Rim Fragments

187 (302–65). D rim ca. .195; Th rim .004, pane .0015

Pale greenish blue. Tiny bubbles. Concentric abraded lines on upper surface, possibly slight wheel-polishing along bottom of thickened rim. **Fig. 8–22.**

37. Avigad, *Beth Shearim* 3, 182–83 and 223, n. 166.

38. Ibid., 183, fig. 91. Illustrated by permission of the author. Standard roof tiles (see Nos. 154–55) could also be used as covers.

39. D. B. Harden, "Domestic Window Glass: Roman, Saxon and Medieval," in *Studies in Building History,* ed. E. M. Jope (London, 1961) 40. Earlier publications are mentioned here in n. 1.

40. Crowfoot, *Samaria* 3, 420–21. The earliest pieces come from 4th c. context; the others are assigned to 4th–5th c. or later.

41. Crowfoot-FitzGerald, "Tyropoeon," pl. 21, nos. 16, 19–21. These are dated by context to 5th–6th c.

42. Baur, "Gerasa Glass," 527, fig. 23, published as dishes, but circular panes are mentioned on p. 546.

43. Barag in Prausnitz, *Shavei Zion,* 69–70. The dates are 5th and 6th c. It is pointed out that roller-molded glass has been found at a number of other Palestinian sites well into the Byzantine period.

44. Saldern, *Sardis Glass,* 91–92. Quantities of roller-molded glass were found, dated 5th–7th c.

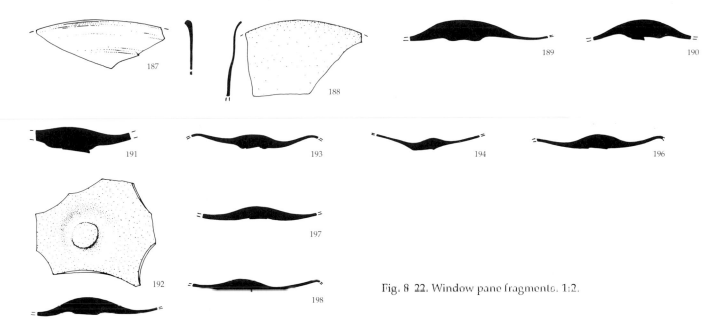

Fig. 8-22. Window pane fragments. 1:2.

188   (466–66). D rim ca. .16; Th rim .001, pane .002

Pale green. Rim cut and turned slightly downward. From factory dump. **Fig. 8–22.**

Center Fragments

189   (127–64). Max dim .08; Th center .007

Greenish blue. Tiny bubbles. Bottom slightly concave, large boss with rounded edge. **Fig. 8–22; Pl. 8–13.**

190   (61–64). Max dim .051

Greenish blue. Boss on bottom, like preceding. Pontil mark (D .011). Floor seems horizontal. **Fig. 8–22; Pl. 8–13.**

191   (186–65). Max dim .051

Olive green with yellow streaks. Boss on bottom, pontil mark (D .021). Floor begins to turn slightly upward. **Fig. 8–22; Pl. 8–13.**

192   (465–66). Max dim .062

Light greenish blue. Thickened center with boss and pontil mark (D .013). Floor extends slightly upward. **Fig. 8–22.**

193   (43–65). Max dim .07

Light green. Few tiny bubbles. Small boss on bottom, pushed in by pontil (D .01). Floor extends up and then downward. **Fig. 8–22.**

194   (343–66). Max dim .052

Light greenish blue. Boss on bottom, pontil mark (D .01). Floor extends irregularly upward. **Fig. 8–22.**

195   (288–64). Max dim .07

Light green. Bottom almost flat, with low boss, irregular pontil mark (D ca. .01). Floor flat as far as preserved.

196   (378–64). Max dim .065

Yellowish green. Tiny bubbles. Bottom flat, pontil mark

(D .01). Floor turns upward and then slightly downward. **Fig. 8–22.**

197   (503–64). Max dim .061

Light greenish blue. Bottom completely flat, pontil mark (D .01). Floor turns slightly upward. **Fig. 8–22.**

198   (86–64). Max dim .065

Light greenish blue, striations from blowing. Bottom flat, pontil mark (D .01). Floor extends upward and then begins to turn down. **Fig. 8–22.**

Appendix: Inscriptions
by Joseph Naveh and G. D. Weinberg

Only two inscribed objects were found at Jalame, but both are of considerable interest. The first (No. 199) consists of eight letters inscribed on a jar handle before it was fired; despite its brevity and the ordinary quality of the jar, it throws new light on legal practice in Palestine. The second (No. 200) is a sealing that must have been affixed to an object. Its origin and meaning are obscure and subject to discussion.

199   (P384–66). Inscribed jar handle

Max dim .067. Fine clay with dusky red core (2.5YR 3/2), outer bands reddish brown (2.5YR 4/4), many white and black grits. **Pl. 8–13.**

On the jar handle is an Aramaic inscription consisting of eight Jewish (square Hebrew) letters incised before firing. Its reading and translation are: *ḥnny' śd,* "Hanania, witness."

Palaeographically, the two *nun*s and the *he* seem to indicate a date some hundred years earlier than that of the Palestinian Aramaic and Hebrew synagogue inscriptions

Fig. 8–23. Clay sealing (No. 200). 1:1.

of the Late Roman and Byzantine periods. The spelling *ḥnny'*, with a final *alef*, instead of writing the theophorous element as usual -*yh*, is unknown in those synagogue inscriptions. This spelling is, however, quite frequent in Elephantine texts of the 5th c. B.C. and occurs in some inscriptions on Jewish ossuaries of the Herodian period. It is, therefore, reasonable to date the inscription on the Jalame jar handle to 1st c. A.C. or somewhat later.

The Aramaic word *śhd* (or its Hebrew equivalent *'d*) meaning "witness" is frequent in the lists of witnesses at the ends of Aramaic legal documents. In these deeds *śhd* or *'d* attached to a person's name shows that the person testified to the specific contract. The inscription *ḥnny' śhd* on the jar handle from Jalame may indicate that Hanania had the function of guaranteeing the measure of the jar.

On a large soapstone stamp is a similar Aramaic inscription of the 4th c. B.C. reading *šlmy | h'd*, "Shelomi the witness."[45] According to Cross this large stamp might have been used for marking or sealing sacks. One may also suggest that by sealing the sacks Shelomi might have certified that he attested to the quality or the weight of the merchandise in the sacks.

There is, however, a third epigraphic text in which the word *śhdh* "the witness," occurring after a personal name, cannot be interpreted as in the two inscriptions mentioned, on the stamp and the jar handle. Among the dedicatory inscriptions of the 6th–7th c. synagogue at Kh. Susiya (south of Hebron) was found a fragmentary Aramaic dedication on a mosaic pavement: *dkyrn lṭb mnḥmh yšw' śhdh wmnḥmh š[*—"Remembered be for good the 'comforter' Yeshua' the witness and the 'comforter' Sh[".[46] That the donor is mentioned here as "Yeshua' the witness" seems to indicate that "the witness" was his per-

manent title and perhaps a professional designation of Yeshua'. Moreover, it seems likely that the other title of Yeshua'—*mnḥmh*, literally, "the comforter"—may speak in favor of the assumption that *śhdh* designates a profession in the court of justice; *mnḥmh* can be explained as a loan translation of the Greek παρακλητος, meaning advocate.[47]

The three texts mentioned above may indicate that from the Persian to the Byzantine period there were among the Jews publicly authorized witnesses,[48] although no other evidence of such a profession in Jewish law at that time is known. If this is correct, it may be that *śhd* ("witness") was Hanania's permanent title and that the writing of this name and the title only indicated Hanania's ownership of the jar.

J.N.

200   (T12–66). Clay sealing

H ca. .03, of stamp .016; PL of stamp .026. Lump of dark gray, fine, very hard clay (2.5YR N2.5/) broken all around. Part of a rectangular stamp on one face and remains of another on an adjacent surface. On the back, grooves apparently made by cords. **Fig. 8–23; Pl. 8–13.**

The left end of one rectangular stamp is preserved. It is framed by a ridge within which are letters in relief. While the letters seem clear, they have not been entirely deciphered. The first impression of several archaeologists who saw the stamp shortly after it was excavated was that the letters could not be Semitic. The clay is totally unlike that of any of the pottery found at Jalame. Various Oriental scholars who examined the photograph thought it might be Chinese, and one who saw the object itself thought the clay resembled that used during the Han Dynasty. None of the Oriental specialists, however, could read the inscription.

Finally, Prof. Moshe Sharon of the Hebrew University, Jerusalem, was able to read the name "Ali." He dated the sealing about 9th c. The find-spot, near the surface at the extreme southeast end of the excavated area, is compatible with a late date. This object was probably dropped at the same time as the few Islamic potsherds and glass fragments (see Chaps 4 and 7).

G.D.W.

45. F. M. Cross, "Judean Stamps," *Eretz-Israel* 9 (1969) 26–27, pl. 5, 3–4 (non-Hebrew section).

46. S. Gutman et al. "Excavations in the Synagogue at Khirbet Susiya," *Qadmoniot* 5 (1972) 51, pl. 1 opposite p. 44 (in Hebrew). J. Naveh, *On Stone and Mosaic: The Aramaic and Hebrew Inscriptions from Ancient Synagogues* (Jerusalem, 1978) 118–19 (in Hebrew).

47. J. Naveh, "The Titles ŚHD/'D and MNḤM in Jewish Epigraphic Texts," *Studies in Bible and the Ancient Near East in Honor of Prof. S. E. Loewenstamm* (Jerusalem, 1978) 303–7 (in Hebrew).

48. See above (n. 45) Cross's translation, "Shelomi the notary."

9

ROBERT H. BRILL

Scientific Investigations of the Jalame Glass and Related Finds

The excavation at Jalame is the most comprehensive investigation of an ancient glass factory site to date, undertaken *because* the site was that of a glass factory and not just as an ancillary part of another excavation. In keeping with the goals of the excavation, it was decided at the outset to take advantage of all scientific techniques that could be applied to work in the field and in the laboratory studies to follow.[1]

The Jalame excavation offered an unparalleled opportunity for chemical study of glasses made in a single factory during a limited time. Because thousands of fragments were found, we could carry out enough analyses for them to be statistically significant in assessing the variability of chemical composition within the production of a single factory. We also expected that informative relationships could be established between the glass itself and the other materials uncovered, such as waste and refractories. Ultimately, the Jalame studies are expected to yield a chemical and mathematical model for investigating the production of other ancient glass factories.

As this report is being written, a considerable body of data and observations is available. Nevertheless, some work remains to be done, particularly in completing a more comprehensive mathematical analysis of the chemical analytical data (which requires the aid of a computer) and in understanding the functional interrelationships between the waste glass and various types of "furnace debris" uncovered. A fuller account of our findings in these areas will be presented in the future.[2]

The overall objectives of the studies described here are to learn as much as possible about the Jalame factory and its glass through laboratory work and to interpret the findings, where possible, so as to expand our general understanding of glass manufacturing in ancient times. It now appears, as far as the laboratory work is concerned, that we have learned more about the glass itself than about either the furnaces in which it was made or the work processes used. As for the furnace structures, certain rudimentary chemical information has been obtained, but reconstruction of the structures depends primarily on archaeological interpretation of the remains. Views on what kind of containers the glass was melted in remain conjectural (see Chap. 3).

Studies of the Glass and Raw Materials

Chemical Analyses

Characterization of the Jalame Glass as a Material

Quantitative chemical analyses and semiquantitative emission spectrographic analyses of 53 samples have been completed. Among these, 40 were selected because they were believed to be representative of glass made at Jalame from cullet brought to the factory. This group includes 19 samples of cullet and 21 vessel fragments. The other 13 samples were designated "special objects," meaning that they differed somehow from the main body of finds.

Analyses of individual samples are reported in Tables 9–1 through 9–5. In the first four tables, the group of 40 is reported. In addition, mean compositions of the 40 glasses, separated as above, are reported in Tables 9–6 through 9–8. The most important of these is Table 9–8, which gives the composition of what we call "Jalame

---

1. For a survey of some such techniques see R. H. Brill, "The Scientific Investigation of Ancient Glasses," *Proceedings of the VIIIth International Congress on Glass* (London and Sheffield: The Society of Glass Technology, 1968) 47–68.

2. The author is preparing a monograph on scientific aspects of ancient glass, using the Jalame findings as a model for mathematical treatments of analytical data from other sites.

The author expresses his thanks to Paul Perrot, Sidney Goldstein, John Wosinski, and Frederick Matson for help in the field as well as for countless hours of discussion; also to the following people in Israel who provided scientific and other assistance: Moshe Ish-Shalom and R. Hammer of the Technion, Haifa, Uri Kafri of the Hydrological Division of the Geological Survey, the late Zeev Goldmann of the Municipal Museum, Akko, and, with special fondness, Hannah Katzenstein, formerly of the Department of Antiquities. Nina McPhilmy, Judy (Seal) Snyder, and Florence (White) Edwardson helped in the recording and calculation of data.

Table 9–1. Jalame Cullet (No Manganese)

		aqua 619	green 620	green 621	green 626	aqua 633	bl. aqua 636	aqua 638
SiO$_2$	Δ	~69.48	~68.74	~71.23	~69.55	~69.38	~68.47	~69.62
Na$_2$O	a	14.8	16.8	16.1	16.4	14.8	17.0	16.1
CaO	a	10.5	8.95	8.02	8.90	10.5	9.25	9.38
K$_2$O	a	0.64	0.79	0.81	0.42	0.87	0.64	0.69
MgO	a	0.80	0.92	0.45	0.90	0.66	0.87	0.48
Al$_2$O$_3$	a	2.87	2.97	2.63	2.91	2.96	2.76	2.65
Fe$_2$O$_3$	a	0.42	0.40	0.31	0.47	0.39	0.55	0.38
TiO$_2$		0.10	0.07	0.08	0.09	0.07	0.08	0.08
Sb$_2$O$_5$	a	–	–	–	–	–	–	–
MnO	a	0.086	0.086	0.079	0.049	0.058	0.094	0.31
CuO		0.001	0.001	0.001	0.001	0.001	0.001	0.001
CoO		–	–	–	–	–	–	–
SnO$_2$		–	–	–	–	–	0.001	–
Ag$_2$O		0.001	0.0005	0.001	0.001	–	–	0.0005
PbO		0.005	0.002	0.002	0.002	0.001	0.001	0.005
BaO		0.04	0.04	0.04	0.04	0.07	0.04	0.07
SrO		0.07	0.07	0.07	0.07	0.07	0.07	0.07
Li$_2$O		0.0005	0.0005	0.0005	0.0005	0.0005	0.0005	0.0005
Rb$_2$O		–	–	–	–	–	–	–
B$_2$O$_3$		0.02	0.01	0.01	0.02	0.02	0.02	0.01
V$_2$O$_5$		0.001	0.001	0.001	0.001	–	–	–
Cr$_2$O$_3$		0.001	0.0005	0.0005	0.0005	0.0005	0.0005	–
NiO		–	–	–	–	–	–	–
ZnO	a	0.013	0.011	0.011	0.012	0.0077	0.0077	0.010
ZrO$_2$		0.005	0.005	0.005	0.005	0.005	0.005	0.005
P$_2$O$_5$	c	0.15	(0.13)	0.15	(0.16)	(.14)	(.14)	(.14)

Notes (Tables 9–1 through 9–8)

All analyses by Robert H. Bell and Brant Rising of Lucius Pitkin, Inc., New York City.

a   atomic absorption.

c   colorimetry; ( ) estimated P$_2$O$_5$, not quantitative.

SiO$_2$ estimated by differences from 100%.

All other values by emission spectography, except where reported to more than one significant figure.

—   Sought, but not found.

Δ   All values are reported as weight percentages.

*   Not normalized to 100%, therefore direct comparison with compositions in Tables 9–6 and 9–8 is complicated slightly by presence of MnO. To compare data, multiply values in Table 9–7 by 1.03 (for cullet) and 1.01 (for vessels).

glass." These are the values that best summarize the basic composition of the glass. Glasses with deliberately added manganese or colorants are not included. The compositions in Tables 9–6 through 9–8 are expressed as mean values of the oxides plus or minus two standard deviations around the nominal values, corresponding to 95 percent confidence limits. (For trace elements, the ranges are reported instead of confidence limits.)

It can be seen that the five mean compositions do not differ markedly from one another, except for the distinction between those containing additive levels of manganese and those without manganese.[3] Statistically, there is no significant difference between the vessel glass and the cullet in their major and minor oxides.

The compositions are about what one would anticipate for glass of this period and region. The glass has a soda-lime-silica composition (Na$_2$O : CaO : SiO$_2$) and contains the usual impurities at the usual concentra-

3. The presence of manganese or other additives reduces the percentages of all other oxides, because the total must be 100%. In our more refined calculations the MnO and CuO are subtracted and the other oxides normalized to a 100% summation. This provides a better basis for deriving the formulation of the Jalame factory. The data from manganese-containing glasses used for calculating the mean composition of Jalame glass was normalized in this way beforehand.

aqua 639	olive-green 644	green 645	aqua 814	olive 622	olive 629	olive-amber 647
~69.37	~71.27	~71.75	~71.08	~70.48	~70.13	~71.76
17.2	15.3	15.0	15.2	15.7	16.6	14.2
8.77	8.47	8.68	8.83	8.90	8.48	8.77
0.64	0.91	0.75	0.77	0.66	0.81	0.77
0.66	0.48	0.50	0.59	0.75	0.56	0.60
2.64	2.54	2.56	2.78	2.64	2.55	2.82
0.34	0.36	0.32	0.36	0.43	0.37	0.40
0.08	0.08	0.07	0.09	0.09	0.10	0.09
–	–	–	–	–	–	–
0.039	0.28	0.094	0.056	0.052	0.11	0.30
0.003	0.001	0.003	0.003	0.001	0.003	0.001
–	–	–	–	–	–	–
–	–	–	0.001	–	–	–
0.001	0.0005	0.0005	0.0005	0.0005	–	0.0005
0.005	0.002	0.003	0.001	0.005	0.01	0.005
0.07	0.07	0.04	0.04	0.04	0.04	0.07
0.08	0.07	0.07	0.06	0.07	0.07	0.07
0.0005	0.0005	0.0005	0.0005	0.0005	0.0005	0.0005
–	–	–	–	–	–	–
0.02	0.01	0.01	0.03	0.03	0.01	0.02
0.001	0.001	–	–	0.001	–	0.001
–	–	0.0005	0.0005	0.0005	0.0005	–
–	–	–	–	–	–	0.001
0.012	0.0093	0.0074	0.0083	0.010	0.0079	0.012
0.005	0.005	0.005	0.005	0.005	0.005	0.005
0.067	(.14)	(.14)	(0.09)	(0.13)	(.14)	0.10

tions. The potassium oxide (K_2O) and magnesium oxide (MgO) levels place the composition squarely within the low K_2O-low MgO category.[4] This is evidence that natron was used as the alkali in the glassmaking batch (see below).

Manganese (MnO) was an intentional additive to only some of the 40 glasses. It is difficult to draw a sharp dividing line between an intentional additive and background impurities, but we have assumed that at a level of about 0.4% or greater, manganese was clearly an intentional additive. Twelve such glasses are recorded, with an average of about 1.9% MnO. We regard .02 to .10% as the expected background impurity level for manganese in ancient glasses. Therefore, the observed range of about .02 to .15% in most of the Jalame glasses indicates only manganese impurities, not deliberately added manganese. The intermediate values of approximately 0.1 to 0.3% (found in only 3 samples) probably indicate remelted mixtures of two or more lots of cullet, some containing more manganese than others.

Antimony (Sb_2O_5) was not found in any of the samples analyzed. The alumina (Al_2O_3) borders on the high side but is not without numerous precedents among ancient glasses. The iron (Fe_2O_3),[5] titanium (TiO_2), barium (BaO), strontium (SrO), and boron (B_2O_3) are all in line with other ancient glasses, as are other trace elements. Lithium oxide (Li_2O) was seen close to our spectrographic limit of detection and is estimated to be present in Jalame glass at a level of about .0005%.

4. See E. V. Sayre, *Advances in Glass Technology*, part 2 (New York, 1963) 263–82, and Brill, as in n. 1.

5. The iron is present as a mixture of FeO and Fe_2O_3, but, by the usual convention, it is reported here as if it were all Fe_2O_3.

Table 9–2. Jalame Vessels (No Manganese)

	green 815	green 816	aqua 818	green 827	green 828	green 829	green 831	aqua 837	aqua 841
SiO_2 △	~71.35	~70.27	~68.34	~71.63	~72.07	~71.22	~71.53	~69.68	~71.85
Na_2O a	16.2	16.4	15.9	15.3	14.7	16.0	14.9	16.2	14.8
CaO a	7.60	8.52	10.3	8.27	7.97	8.10	8.62	9.15	8.42
K_2O a	0.70	0.67	0.96	0.90	0.74	0.76	0.73	0.89	0.94
MgO a	0.70	0.51	0.67	0.53	0.68	0.46	0.52	0.54	0.46
Al_2O_3 a	2.60	2.74	2.83	2.60	2.60	2.64	2.86	2.65	2.72
Fe_2O_3 a	0.35	0.37	0.49	0.31	0.47	0.36	0.39	0.40	0.32
TiO_2	0.10	0.10 .	0.10	0.08	0.08	0.10	0.10	0.09	0.09
Sb_2O_5 a	–	–	–	–	,–	–	–	–	–
MnO a	0.043	0.014	0.067	0.102	0.37	0.12	0.061	0.059	0.066
CuO	0.003	0.003	0.005	0.003	0.001	0.003	0.001	0.002	0.002
CoO	–	–	–	–	–	–	–	–	–
SnO_2	–	–	–	–	–	–	–	0.001	0.001
Ag_2O	–	0.0005	–	0.0005	0.0005	0.0005	0.0005	0.0005	0.0005
PbO	0.005	0.005	0.05	0.002	0.05	0.003	0.001	0.04	0.11
BaO	0.04	0.06	0.04	0.04	0.04	0.04	0.04	0.04	0.04
SrO	0.06	0.06	0.06	0.07	0.05	0.06	0.07	0.07	0.07
Li_2O	0.0005	0.0005	0.0005	0.0005	0.0005	0.0005	0.0005	0.0005	0.0005
Rb_2O	–	–	–	–	–	–	–	–	–
B_2O_3	0.02	0.02	0.02	0.01	0.02	0.01	0.02	0.03	0.01
V_2O_5	0.001	–	–	0.001	0.001	–	–	–	–
Cr_2O_3	–	–	0.0005	0.0005	–	0.0005	0.0005	0.0005	0.0005
NiO	–	–	–	–	–	–	–	–	–
ZnO	0.015	0.012	0.011	0.0078	0.016	0.0084	0.0070	0.014	0.0073
ZrO_2	0.005	0.005	0.005	0.005	0.005	0.005	0.005	0.005	0.005
P_2O_5 c	0.21	0.24	(0.15)	(.14)	(.14)	(0.11)	(.14)	(.14)	(0.09)

Rubidium oxide (Rb_2O) was not detected and is presumed to be below our .001% limit of detection.

In addition, numerous histograms and both two-element and three-element graphs were plotted. Graphs of oxide ratios and various groupings of oxides were also plotted against one another. Separate calculations were made that eliminated the compositional effects of deliberately added manganese. (The manganese and colorants were subtracted and the compositions normalized to 100%.)[6]

The most significant analytical results are that the 40 selected glasses appear statistically homogeneous and that no clear subclassifications could be distinguished among them (except for those containing manganese). All vessel types appear to have approximately the same composition.[7] The cullet is virtually the same as the vessel glass except that the lime (CaO) may be a little lower in the vessels than in the cullet. If true, this is curious, because when cullet is remelted to be made into vessels, the vessels would be expected to become higher in lime, owing to corrosion of the refractory surfaces. Also, setting aside the purple cullet, there seem to be fewer examples of cullet with intentionally added or intermediate manganese (3 intermediate out of 14) than there are of vessel fragments (7 additive, 1 intermediate out of 21). This suggests that the vessel glasses containing manganese—if presumed to have been manufactured by resoftening cullet brought to the site—acquired their manganese by its addition when the cullet was resoftened to be worked.

Interesting information also comes from comparisons between the trace element analyses of the glasses with manganese and those without. The addition of manganese also introduced some iron, copper (CuO), vanadium (V_2O_5), nickel (NiO), and barium. We have seen examples from elsewhere (unpublished) of all these elements being associated with manganese. Presumably they were present as impurities in the original manganese-containing ingredient, although it is possible

6. The results of these plots and calculations are not included here because they are complicated and space-consuming, but the remarks below, including those regarding relationships between the glasses and raw materials, are based on consideration of all those different treatments of the data.

7. There may be some correlation between certain vessel types and composition, but the calculations required to either prove or disprove this rigorously have not been completed.

green 844	aqua 845	green 846	green 854	olive 853
~69.50	~70.39	~72.81	~70.73	~71.54
16.9	15.8	14.7	16.0	15.8
8.72	8.70	8.17	8.53	8.14
0.84	0.87	0.70	0.69	0.74
0.46	0.57	0.43	0.56	0.41
2.75	2.73	2.44	2.64	2.64
0.38	0.43	0.31	0.35	0.30
0.07	0.10	0.08	0.10	0.07
-	-	-	-	-
0.11	0.061	0.090	0.12	0.074
0.001	0.003	0.003	0.003	0.002
-	0.001	-	-	-
0.0005	0.0005	0.0005	0.0005	0.0005
0.005	0.05	0.002	0.005	0.001
0.04	0.04	0.04	0.04	0.04
0.06	0.06	0.06	0.06	0.08
0.0005	0.0005	0.0005	0.0005	0.0005
0.01	0.03	0.01	0.02	0.03
-	-	-	-	-
-	0.0005	0.0005	0.0005	0.0005
-	-	-	-	-
0.010	0.016	0.012	0.0074	0.014
0.005	0.005	0.005	0.005	0.005
(.14)	(.14)	(.14)	(.14)	(0.11)

that the iron and copper were introduced by some crushing tool, balance, or sieve used for preparing that ingredient. If they are impurities, these elements would have been present in the original manganese-containing ingredient to the following extents (expressed as percentages of MnO present): $Fe_2O_3 \sim 5\%$; $CuO \sim 0.1\%$; $V_2O_5 \sim 0.2\%$; $NiO \sim 0.07\%$; $BaO \sim 1\%$.

Among the other trace elements, there is some indication that the vessel glass contains slightly more copper and lead (PbO) than does the cullet. This may have resulted from use of a bronze tool in preparing the cullet for resoftening. The occasional traces of tin (SnO_2) in the glasses, even those without deliberately added manganese, may have come from some similar operation. The tin is sometimes associated with traces of lead.

Special Objects (Table 9-5)

Because these objects show features differing from Jalame glass as a whole, they were not included in the calculation of the composition of Jalame glass. Nine of these were chosen either on an *a priori* basis or because they contain deliberately added colorants. Four more were added after having been analyzed and found to

have minor compositional features that differ from the main group. The special objects include four light and medium blue glasses, a piece of dark blue waste glass, a conical lamp fragment with applied decoration (two samples), four overblows (moils), and two vessel fragments with borderline analyses.

The light and medium blue glasses are two samples of trail decoration from vessels (Nos. 820–21) and two of waste glass (Nos. 3612–13). All four were colored with copper oxide only. The analyses of the trails resemble one another. The two waste glasses also resemble each other but differ somewhat from the trail specimens. Statistically, none of these glasses differs significantly from the Jalame glass as a whole, although a few elements are near the 95% confidence limits. The blue color was apparently achieved by adding a colorant to the regular Jalame glass (see below).

No. 3611 is a piece of dark blue waste glass or cullet (possibly from a knock-off), colored with cobalt oxide (CoO). There is nothing in its analysis to indicate it was not made at the same place and time as the main body of Jalame glass. The iron, alumina, and zinc (ZnO) values are somewhat higher than in the uncolored glass and it also contains some nickel, vanadium, and lead. However, all these elements can be readily accounted for as having come in with the cobalt containing ingredient that was added to the regular Jalame glass.

Samples No. 3600, from the uncolored base glass of a conical lamp, and No. 3601, one of its applied blue blobs, are especially interesting. The lamp is a common type (see Chap. 4, Nos. 404ff.). Because dark blue decoration was relatively scarce at Jalame, there could be a question as to whether this lamp was produced at Jalame or found its way to the site from elsewhere. Except for the cobalt colorant in the blue glass, and other elements brought in with the cobalt, the analyses of the colorless base glass and that of the blue glass are quite close to each other. The blue glass was clearly made by adding a cobalt colorant to the colorless glass in use at the factory where this glass was made.[8] The two glasses do not differ significantly from Jalame glass in a statistical sense, but they do hover near the borderline on some elements. Lead isotope determinations on the same dark blue glass samples are discussed below.

The four samples Nos. 3196–99 are moils or overblows, cracked off from conical lamps. In their analyses,

8. This may seem obvious, but it is an important point. Because cobalt occurs in very few places in the world, that used by glassmakers was traded in some form over long distances. In this instance, at least, the cobalt must have been obtained not as a ready-to-use blue glass but either as a cobalt mineral or, more likely, as a concentrate such as *wad* or a highly concentrated glass cullet corresponding to the smalt of later times. We are inclined to believe that Persia was the source of most cobalt used in ancient glasses. For further information see R. H. Brill and I. L. Barnes, "The Flight into Egypt, from the Infancy of Christ Window (?): Some Chemical Notes," *The Royal Abbey of Saint-Denis in the Time of Abbot Suger (1122–1151)* by S. McK. Crosby et al. (New York, 1981) 81.

Table 9–3. Jalame Cullet (with Manganese)

	colorless 623	purple 624	purple 649	purple 811	purple 812
SiO_2 $\lrcorner$	~68.19	~67.12	~68.50	~67.20	~66.26
Na_2O a	16.0	16.0	15.6	15.2	15.3
CaO a	9.18	9.91	8.41	8.80	9.11
K_2O a	0.87	0.90	0.88	0.84	0.88
MgO a	0.55	0.52	0.45	0.56	0.61
Al_2O_3 a	2.75	2.71	2.56	2.61	2.76
Fe_2O_3 a	0.40	0.43	0.43	0.51	0.68
TiO_2	0.08	0.08	0.10	0.10	0.10
Sb_2O_5 a	–	–	–	–	–
MnO a	1.69	2.00	2.79	3.77	3.89
CuO	0.003	0.003	0.003	0.003	0.005
CoO	0.002	0.002	–	–	–
SnO_2	–	–	0.001	0.002	–
Ag_2O	0.0005	0.0005	0.0005	0.001	0.0005
PbO	0.005	0.005	0.005	0.09	0.005
BaO	0.04	0.04	0.07	0.08	0.12
SrO	0.07	0.07	0.07	0.06	0.10
Li_2O	0.0005	0.0005	0.0005	0.0005	0.0005
Rb_2O	–	–	–	–	–
B_2O_3	0.01	0.01	0.01	0.01	0.01
V_2O_5	0.001	0.001	0.005	0.005	0.008
Cr_2O_3	0.0005	0.0005	0.0005	0.0005	–
NiO	0.001	0.001	0.001	0.001	0.003
ZnO a	0.012	0.013	0.009	0.009	0.008
ZrO_2	0.005	0.005	0.005	0.005	0.005
P_2O_5 c	(.14)	(0.18)	(0.10)	(.14)	(.14)

several elements fall near the borderline of Jalame glass. Statistically, however, there is not sufficient difference to reject them as having a common origin with the rest of the Jalame finds. Minor compositional aberrations might be indicative of a short-lived variation in raw materials, composition, or formulation. Hence, the lamps from which they came might have been made only during a limited period of the factory's existence.

The remaining two objects in Table 9–5 are vessel fragments (Nos. 823, 835). Although their compositions are borderline in some elements and they contain higher traces of lead and tin than most of the glass, they probably are Jalame wares. Their compositional peculiarities might reflect a short-lived variation from routine practices.

Comparisons with Glasses from Other Sites

The analyses and the mean composition characterize

the Jalame glass very well and serve several useful functions in themselves. But they take on added importance in that the composition can be used to distinguish Jalame products from glasses made at other ancient factories.

No comprehensive library of compositions of glasses from known ancient factories exists and possibly none ever will. Therefore, the best we could do was to compare the Jalame analyses with those of glasses from the few factories we do know and from certain excavations that have yielded large numbers of glass finds. The latter were selected because they represent the outputs of individuals, although unknown, of factories, or of limited regions. After making comparisons, it was concluded that differences in the major and minor oxides (Na_2O, CaO, K_2O, MgO, Al_2O_3, and Fe_2O_3) are, surprisingly, sufficient in themselves to separate Jalame glass from all other sizable bodies of analyses completed (see sample No. 451 for one exception). Comparisons of the inten-

Table 9–4. Jalame Vessels (with Manganese)

	green 833	green 836	p. green 843	olive 852	colorless 855	p. purple 857	colorless 858
SiO_2 Δ	~68.52	~68.73	~69.98	~71.09	~69.76	~67.73	~67.76
Na_2O a	17.7	17.2	15.3	14.9	15.2	15.9	16.4
CaO a	8.29	8.43	8.53	8.48	8.51	8.96	8.67
K_2O a	0.69	0.74	0.66	0.80	0.75	0.83	1.01
MgO a	0.50	0.48	0.68	0.69	0.69	0.51	0.78
Al_2O_3 a	2.66	2.44	2.69	2.62	2.87	2.64	3.01
Fe_2O_3 a	0.39	0.47	0.44	0.47	0.49	0.38	0.56
TiO_2	0.05	0.07	0.09	0.10	0.08	0.07	0.09
Sb_2O_5 a	–	–	–	–	–	–	–
MnO a	0.80	1.06	1.29	0.55	1.32	2.62	1.38
CuO	0.003	0.003	0.003	0.003	0.003	0.005	0.007
CoO	–	–	–	–	–	–	–
SnO_2	–	0.001	0.001	–	–	–	–
Ag_2O	0.001	0.0005	0.0005	0.0005	0.0005	0.0005	0.0005
PbO	0.07	0.09	0.001	0.005	0.002	0.02	0.005
BaO	0.07	0.04	0.08	0.04	0.08	0.08	0.00
SrO	0.07	0.08	0.06	0.07	0.07	0.08	0.07
Li_2O	0.0005	0.0005	0.0005	0.0005	0.0005	0.0005	0.0005
Rb_2O	–	–	–	–	–	–	–
B_2O_3	0.01	0.01	0.03	0.02	0.02	0.01	0.02
V_2O_5	–	–	0.001	–	0.001	0.005	0.001
Cr_2O_3	0.0005	0.0005	0.0005	0.0005	0.0005	–	0.0005
NiO	0.005	–	0.001	–	0.001	0.001	0.001
ZnO a	0.018	0.0098	0.012	0.015	0.0077	0.010	0.0073
ZrO_2	0.005	0.005	0.005	0.005	0.005	0.005	0.005
P_2O_5 c	0.15	(.14)	(.14)	(.14)	(.14)	(.14)	(.14)

tional additives, manganese and antimony, and of trace impurities such as TiO_2, BaO, SrO, and B_2O_3 augment the separation. Even though the comparisons have in some instances been made with glasses distant in date and provenience from those of Jalame, they illustrate the important point that glasses made in different factories, or at different times, can be distinguished on the basis of their compositions. If this were not true, chemical analyses of ancient glasses would be much less useful.

Among the more distant sites tested,[9] some of which

9. Most of these data are unpublished. The samples were contributed (with permission of the proper authorities) by D. F. Grose (Cosa), G. M. A. Hanfmann and J. Scott (Sardis), R. L. Scranton (Kenchreai), G. Scanlon (Fustat), H. Salam (Qasr Al-Hayr), J. H. Pedley (Apollonia), G. F. Bass (Serçe Liman), D. Barag, N. Avigad, B. Mazar, Y. Aharoni, Y. Israeli, Y. Tsafrir, and E. Ben-Dor (various sites in Israel). The samples from Tel Anafa were submitted by D. F. Grose on behalf of S. Herbert, director of the University of Missouri-University of Michigan excavations.

are also separated by centuries from the Jalame factory, are the following: Cosa (Italy), 19 vessels, 2nd–3rd c.; Sardis (Turkey), 23 vessels, Hellenistic period–7th c. A.C.; Kenchreai (Greece), 20 vessels, 4th c.; Fustat (Egypt), 27 samples, 9th–13th c.; Qasr Al-Hayr (Syria), 18 samples, Islamic period; Apollonia (Libya), 8 samples, Late Roman period; the Serçe Liman wreck (Turkey), 82 vessels and cullet, 11th c.; and numerous samples of Sasanian and early Islamic glass. Jalame glass can also be distinguished from a group of twelve *diatreta*, a group of fifteen Roman cameo glasses, and a jug made by Ennion (1st c.) excavated in Jerusalem.

Of greater interest, because they presumably came from factories that would be expected to have utilized sources of raw materials similar to those used for Jalame glass, are comparisons with glasses from the following

Table 9–5. Jalame Special Objects

	lt. blue 821	blue and colorless 820	gr. aqua 823	aqua 835	colorless-gr. aqua 3196	colorless-gr. aqua 3197	colorless-gr. aqua 3198	colorless-gr. aqua 3199
SiO_2 Δ	~68.52	~69.44	~69.45	~71.13	~69.65	~72.36	~71.12	~70.04
Na_2O a	16.9	17.1	14.8	13.6	15.8	14.3	15.0	16.3
CaO a	8.07	8.06	9.81	9.56	8.50	7.81	8.36	7.97
K_2O a	1.10	0.94	0.94	1.05	0.68	0.58	0.58	0.58
MgO a	0.64	0.63	0.64	0.57	0.57	0.52	0.52	0.62
Al_2O_3 a	2.74	2.79	2.81	3.00	3.00	2.65	2.65	2.62
Fe_2O_3 a	0.45	0.42	0.51	0.43	0.36	0.36	0.28	0.40
TiO_2	0.10	0.10	0.10	0.10	0.08	0.08	0.08	0.08
Sb_2O_5 a	-	-	-	-	-	-	-	-
MnO a	0.054	0.072	0.12	0.061	1.03	1.07	1.13	1.13
CuO a	0.99	0.087	0.003	0.003	0.003	0.003	0.003	0.003
CoO	-	-	-	-	-	-	-	-
SnO_2	0.03	0.005	0.005	0.003	-	-	-	-
Ag_2O	0.001	0.0005	0.0005	0.001	0.001	0.001	0.001	0.001
PbO	0.07	0.02	0.53	0.20	0.001	0.001	0.001	0.001
BaO	0.08	0.08	0.04	0.04	0.04	0.04	0.04	0.04
SrO	0.07	0.07	0.07	0.08	0.08	0.05	0.05	0.05
Li_2O	0.0005	0.0005	0.0005	0.0005	0.0005	0.0005	0.0005	0.0005
Rb_2O	-	-	-	-	-	-	-	-
B_2O_3	0.03	0.03	0.02	0.02	0.02	0.02	0.02	0.02
V_2O_5	-	-	0.001	-	0.001	0.001	0.001	0.001
Cr_2O_3	0.0005	0.005	0.0005	0.0005	-	-	-	-
NiO	-	-	-	-	0.0005	0.001	0.001	0.001
ZnO a	0.0072	0.0068	0.0086	0.012	0.0078	0.0090	0.0078	0.0075
ZrO_2	0.005	0.005	0.005	0.005	0.005	0.005	0.005	0.005
P_2O_5 c	(.14)	(.14)	(.14)	(0.13)	0.17	0.14	0.15	0.13

sites: Karanis (Egypt), 22 vessels from the main periods of activity, 150–200 and ca. 250–450; Tel Anafa (Israel), 10 bowls ca. 125–75 B.C.; Kafr Yasif (Israel), 16 vessels and cullet, probably 5th c.; Beth Shearim (Israel), 8 vessels, 4th c.; the Cave of Horror (Dead Sea, Israel), 5 vessels, early 2nd c.; Rehovot (Israel), 3 painted glasses, 5th c.; Tiberias (Israel), 15 glasses of varying dates, some considerably later than Jalame glass; and Arsuf (Israel), a large piece of cullet, undated.

Kafr Yasif, about 25 km from Jalame, was the site of another glassmaking operation, where many pieces of cullet and vessel fragments were found. The Kafr Yasif compositions resemble Jalame glass but differ sufficiently (especially in their Na_2O:CaO relationships) to distinguish the two. This is noteworthy because it suggests that, although the two groups of glasses almost certainly were made from similar raw materials, something in the actual selection of the raw materials, the precise source of the raw materials, the glass formulation, or processing led to distinguishable compositional differences. Neither cullet nor vessel fragments found at Kafr Yasif contained intentionally added manganese.

Similar findings resulted from comparison of Jalame glass with bowls from Tel Anafa. Although much earlier than the Jalame glass, they were probably made from similar raw materials. Even so, technological differences of some sort made the two groups distinguishable, adding further strength to the arguments for specificity of compositions relative to time and/or place of manufacture.

Only one glass from any of the above sites has a composition that matches Jalame glass. That is our sample No. 451, which consists of a few fragments of a thin-walled blown vessel of aqua glass (shape unknown) from Beth Shearim. The sample, submitted for analysis by Dr. D. Barag, had been excavated in Catacomb XV.[10]

Raw Materials and the Jalame Batch

In order to prepare a soda:lime:silica glass—the basic formulation of all ancient glasses—it is obviously necessary to introduce these three major components into a

---

10. The glass vessels from this catacomb are dated first half of 4th c.: Avigad, *Beth Shearim* 3, 69.

	aqua 3600	dk. blue transp. 3601	dk. blue transp. 3611	lt. blue 3612	lt. blue 3613
	~68.87	~67.28	~68.11	~67.44	~66.63
	17.2	16.7	15.3	14.8	14.7
	8.10	8.27	8.92	8.07	8.42
	0.75	0.75	0.80	0.70	0.80
	0.48	0.49	0.66	0.35	0.38
	2.97	3.14	2.88	2.84	2.93
	0.55	1.58	0.96	0.58	0.99
	0.10	0.10	0.10	0.10	0.10
	–	–	–	–	–
	0.59	0.76	1.22	0.097	0.11
	0.005	0.18	0.13	3.75	3.69
	–	0.10	0.15	–	–
	–	0.005	–	0.25	0.35
	0.003	0.002	0.002	0.02	0.02
	0.10	0.30	0.35	0.65	0.65
	0.05	0.05	0.10	0.05	0.05
	0.05	0.05	0.05	0.05	0.05
	0.0005	0.0005	0.0005	0.0005	0.0005
	–	–	–	–	–
	0.02	0.02	0.02	0.01	0.01
	–	0.005	0.005	–	–
	–	–	–	–	–
	0.015	0.03	0.08	0.017	0.017
	0.005	0.042	0.043	0.005	0.005
		0.005	0.005		
	(0.14)	0.14	0.11	0.22	0.10

batch,[11] and to do so within a rather limited range of proportions. Otherwise, the resulting glass might not melt well or be stable when made into objects. Present-day glassmakers accomplish this by weighing out three separate pure ingredients, one for each component. But in ancient times, we believe, there were two different formulations, each of which made use of only *two* ingredients to introduce the *three* components.[12]

In more easterly regions the two ingredients were relatively pure quartzite pebbles (which introduced silica) and plant ash (which introduced both soda and lime). This was established by chemical analyses in connection with a study of cuneiform glassmaking texts.[13] This two-ingredient formulation accounts for the high K_2O–high MgO compositions typical of Mesopotamian, Sasanian, and Islamic glasses. The same ingredients were still being used as late as 1977 in a glass factory in Herat, Afghanistan.[14]

A different two-ingredient formulation accounts for the low K_2O-low MgO compositions of Jalame glass and probably also for those of many of the Hellenistic, Roman, and Byzantine glasses made farther west. In this formulation the two ingredients were natron, a relatively pure form of soda, and a beach sand containing both silica and lime. The major source of natron (possibly the only source used for glassmaking) was Wadi Natrun, in the desert between Cairo and Alexandria. Sands that fit the requirements perfectly, having just the right proportions of silica and lime for making a stable glass, are found on the beach at the mouth of the Na'aman River, the Belus River of antiquity. The silica

11. For descriptions of glass chemistry written for archaeologists see R. H. Brill, "A Note on the Scientist's Definition of Glass," *JGS* 4 (1962) 127–38, and "Ancient Glass," *Scientific American* 209, No. 5 (Nov. 1963) 120–31.

12. At present we believe three-ingredient batches may not have come into general use until the 12th or 13th c. and that even then two-ingredient batches continued to be used. The subject deserves further study.

13. See R. H. Brill, "The Chemical Interpretation of the Texts," in *Glass and Glassmaking in Ancient Mesopotamia* by D. Barag, R. H. Brill, A. L. Oppenheim, A. von Saldern (Corning, 1971).

14. Unpublished observations, related in "The Glassmakers of Herat," a 16–mm color sound film produced by Elliott Erwitt for The Corning Museum of Glass, 1979.

Table 9–6. Analyses of Jalame Glasses (without MnO)

	Cullet (n=14)			Vessels (n=14)		
	mean values			mean values		
SiO_2 Δ	68.0	70.17	72.4	68.6	70.92	73.3
Na_2O a	13.9	15.80	17.7	14.3	15.69	17.1
CaO a	7.62	9.03	10.4	7.24	8.52	9.79
K_2O a	0.48	0.726	0.97	0.59	0.795	1.00
MgO a	0.33	0.659	0.99	0.35	0.536	0.72
Al_2O_3 a	2.43	2.73	3.04	2.46	2.67	2.89
Fe_2O_3 a	0.27	0.393	0.52	0.26	0.374	0.49
TiO_2		0.084			0.090	
Sb_2O_5 a	—	nf	—	—	nf	—
MnO a	0.039	0.12	0.31	0.013	0.076	0.14
CuO	0.001	0.0016	0.003	0.001	0.0025	0.005
CoO	—	nf	—	—	nf	—
SnO_2	nf	0.0005	0.001	nf	0.0005	0.001
Ag_2O	nf	0.0005	0.001	nf	0.0004	0.0005
PbO	0.001	0.0035	0.01	0.001	0.024	0.11
BaO	0.04	0.05	0.07	0.04	0.04	0.06
SrO	0.06	0.07	0.08	0.05	0.06	0.08
Li_2O	0.0005	0.0005	0.0005	0.0005	0.0005	0.0005
Rb_2O	—	nf	—	—	nf	—
B_2O_3	0.01	0.02	0.03	0.01	0.02	0.03
V_2O_5	nf	0.0006	0.001	nf	0.0002	0.001
Cr_2O_3	nf	0.0004	0.001	nf	0.0004	0.0005
NiO	nf	0.0005	0.001	nf	0.0005	0.0005
ZnO a	0.0074	0.010	0.013	0.007	0.011	0.016
ZrO_2	0.005	0.005	0.005	0.005	0.005	0.005
Bi_2O_3	—	nf	—	—	nf	—
P_2O_5 c	0.06	0.122	0.19	0.03	0.152	0.27

comes from quartz sand grains, and the lime from mixed-in shell hash, that is, the skeletal remains of marine fauna. There may be other beaches along the same coast that have sands with similar compositions,[15] but this rather fortunate coincidence is, almost certainly, the reason for the ancient renown of the mouth of the Belus River as a source of glassmakers' sand.

During the excavations the author made several trips to the Belus River beach, about 20 km from Jalame. On one of these trips (10 July 1965) many samples of sand were collected from the small dunes covering the beach. The sand on the leeward side of the dunes, having been sorted by prevailing sea breezes, was fine-grained and clean—at least as clean as anything on that badly polluted beach could be. On a later occasion (11 July 1966) the author collected additional sand samples and made an extensive photographic survey of the area extending from the medieval city walls of Akko (the Crusaders' St.

Jean D'Acre) to Tel Akko, along the beach front and into the inland marshes near the Village of Napoleon.[16] At the north side of the river mouth was observed (over a period of three years) a roughly circular ridge of dunes, about a meter in height, surrounding a shallow depression about 40 m in diameter, filled with beach grass. Whether this depression is connected with the account of Josephus,[17] who states that there was at the mouth of the River Belus "a circular depression approximately 100 cubits across" (ca. 50 m) from which sand was taken for glassmaking, is a question that might be answered by excavation.[18]

We believe that Belus River sand was one of the ingredients of Jalame glass. Even though the basic glass material is thought not to have been made at Jalame (see

15. The beaches between Akko and Haifa are generally similar to that at the river mouth. North of Akko for some distance there are no sandy beaches, and what "sand" there is, is simply broken-up limestone from the beach shelf. There are said to be "white, sandy beaches" farther north toward Tyre.

16. To be published in the monograph cited in n. 2.

17. Josephus, *De Bello Iudaico* 2.10.2.

18. The depression was examined again with Paul Perrot in 1967. Nearby, at the railway bridge, a small extension of the river formed a pond of relatively still water. It could be imagined to resemble the location where "numerous small boats put in" to remove sand to be transported to glassmaking centers. One's enthusiasm is dampened, however, by recalling that landmoving must have accompanied the building of the modern bridge.

Table 9-7. Analyses of Jalame Glasses (with MnO)*

	Cullet (n=5)			Vessels (n=7)		
	mean values			mean values		
SiO$_2$ Δ	65.7	67.45	69.3	66.6	69.08	71.6
Na$_2$O a	14.9	15.62	16.4	14.0	16.09	18.2
CaO a	7.97	9.08	10.2	8.13	8.55	8.98
K$_2$O a	0.44	0.874	1.31	0.62	0.745	0.87
MgO a	0.42	0.538	0.66	0.38	0.619	0.86
Al$_2$O$_3$ a	2.50	2.68	2.86	2.38	2.65	2.93
Fe$_2$O$_3$ a	0.26	0.490	0.72	0.35	0.440	0.53
TiO$_2$		0.092			0.079	
Sb$_2$O$_5$ c	—	nf	—	—	nf	—
MnO a	1.69	2.83	3.89	0.55	1.29	2.62
CuO	0.003	0.0034	0.005	0.003	0.0038	0.007
CoO	—	nf	—	—	nf	—
SnO$_2$	nf	0.001	0.002	nf	0.001	0.001
Ag$_2$O	0.0005	0.0006	0.001	0.0005	0.0006	0.001
PbO	0.005	0.022	0.00	0.001	0.020	0.00
BaO	0.04	0.07	0.12	0.04	0.07	0.08
SrO	0.06	0.07	0.10	0.06	0.07	0.08
Li$_2$O	0.0005	0.0005	0.0005	0.0005	0.0005	0.0005
Rb$_2$O		nf	—	—	nf	—
B$_2$O$_3$	0.01	0.01	0.01	0.01	0.02	0.03
V$_2$O$_5$	0.001	0.004	0.000	nf	0.001	0.005
Cr$_2$O$_3$	nf	0.0004	0.0005	nf	0.0005	0.0005
NiO	0.001	0.0014	0.003	0.0005	0.0013	0.005
ZnO a	0.008	0.010	0.013	0.0073	0.011	0.018
ZrO$_2$	0.005	0.005	0.005	0.005	0.005	0.005
Bi$_2$O$_3$	—	nf	—	—	nf	—
P$_2$O$_5$ c	0.10	0.14	0.18	—	0.15	—

below), it must have been made in the vicinity. Ten sand samples were analyzed chemically and examined microscopically. A mean composition of the seven cleanest and finest-grained samples is given in Table 9-9. These came from four parts of the dunes. The "best" came from near the top of the leeward edge, which rose a little less than a meter above the apparent beach level. The sand that collected there had been "sorted" into a finer fraction (as it might have been in ancient times in "the circular depression"). Samples from nearer the bottom of the leeward surface proved to have a greater lime content than those higher up and closer to the active edge of the dune, as did samples from the crown. The fourth location was at a windswept flat on the windward side, from which the dune had most recently receded. Here the sand was coarser and much darker. A chemical analysis of the darkest of three dark-colored samples showed it to contain 25.1% CaO as compared to a mean value of only 8.93% for seven samples of clean sand. It also contained proportionately more magnesia and iron and less alumina. This dark-colored fraction was taken to be rep-

resentative of the black veins of sand common on that beach, as on beaches all over the world.

Microscopically, the dark-colored fractions are intriguing. The material consists primarily of tiny fragments of shell, from very small crustaceans. Mixed in also is an abundance of fragmentary or occasionally complete mollusk shells. None of these were more than 2 mm in greatest dimension, and the majority were less than 1 mm.[19] (Large shells were not common on the beach.) This shell hash gives the Belus River sand its high lime content and makes it suitable for a two-ingredient glass recipe.

We have also analyzed twelve samples of natron from Wadi Natrun. Eight of these were modern samples col-

19. About twenty distinct species were separated out, several of which resembled familiar Atlantic, Gulf Coast, and Caribbean species. Among these were a few *Tellinidae* and *Lucinidae* bivalves; possibly a scallop or pecten; numerous univalves resembling augers, turrids and volutes, a top and a wentletrap; several kinds of *Cypraeidae* (cowries); several kinds of *Caecidae* with ringed and grooved surfaces; several kinds of *Scaphopoda* (tusks and/or tooth shells); and three varieties of what looked like tiny chambered nautilus shells, some white, some with black spirals. These shells will be studied more carefully and the results reported in a future publication.

Table 9–8. Jalame Glass

	Base Composition without Additives (n=28,35,40)		
	mean values		
SiO_2	68.2	70.54	72.9
Na_2O	14.1	15.74	17.4
CaO	7.44	8.73	10.02
K_2O	0.54	0.758	0.97
MgO	0.32	0.601	0.88
Al_2O_3	2.43	2.70	2.96
Fe_2O_3	0.26	0.383	0.50
TiO_2	0.08	0.086	0.09
Sb_2O_5	—	nf	—
MnO	0.01	0.11	0.30
CuO	0.001	0.0020	0.003
CoO	—	nf	—
SnO_2	nf	0.0005	0.001
Ag_2O	nf	0.0005	0.001
PbO	0.001	0.014	0.10
BaO	0.04	0.046	0.07
SrO	0.05	0.067	0.08
Li_2O	0.0005	0.0005	0.0005
Rb_2O	—	nf	—
B_2O_3	0.01	0.017	0.03
V_2O_5	nf	0.0004	0.001
Cr_2O_3	nf	0.0004	0.001
NiO	nf	0.0005	0.001
ZnO	0.007	0.011	0.016
ZrO_2	nf	0.005	0.01
Bi_2O_3	—	nf	—
P_2O_5	0.05	0.135	0.23

glass to the known percentages of SiO_2 and Na_2O in Jalame glass. (Once these conditions were fixed, all the other oxide values also became fixed mathematically.) The fact that the results of that calculation (not shown here) were in remarkably close agreement with the analyzed composition of Jalame glass goes a long way toward verifying that Belus River sand and Wadi Natrun natron were the two basic ingredients used for making Jalame glass.

But the calculations can be refined even further. The proportions of the weights of the two ingredients mentioned are close to 5:2 or 2.5:1. While this is reasonable, one might feel more confidence in a recipe having an even simpler small-number ratio. Therefore, similar calculations were tried using volume instead of weight measurements. First, the bulk densities of Belus River sand and a crushed (but not pulverized) sample of natron were determined experimentally. Values of 1.44 g/ml (for the sand) and 1.24 g/ml (for the natron) were obtained. Using these densities, it was possible to calculate the composition of a glass that would result from a simple recipe of 2:1 parts by volume of sand to natron (see Table 9–9). The calculated composition of that glass is in excellent agreement with the Jalame glass, particularly in respect to the major and minor components (SiO_2 through Fe_2O_3). The agreement on some trace elements varies from good to fair. Because most of the analyses of the trace elements are only spectrographic estimates, one cannot expect quantitative agreement for them. The only disturbing discrepancies are those where an element appears in the Jalame glass but not in either of the raw materials. This is true for tin, chromium, and nickel, but in each case the element was not found in every Jalame sample and was seen only near our limits of detection. There is no obvious explanation for the presence of lead in trace quantities in the glass but not in either raw material, unless it had to do with the glass-making processes.

The fact that calcium does not seem to match the analyzed Jalame composition as closely as the other major and minor elements (being always a little on the low side) is troubling. There are two likely ways extra lime could have gotten into occasional pieces—refractory corrosion, or the accidental inclusion of higher-lime portions of sand in the batch. In fact, four specimens of Jalame glass had conspicuously greater lime contents than the rest, all in excess of 10%. Because the high CaO contents were correlated with increases in MgO and Fe_2O_3, and since these were lacking in the limestones we studied, it was concluded that the four high-lime samples had resulted from the use of sand of lower purity. In collecting the sand, the glassmakers may have included an occasional "shovelful" of the darker-colored, coarse sand, and this found its way into the glass. That inclusion (4% of contaminated sand or 1 of every 25 mea-

lected (in 1964) and studied by Zaki Khalil Hanna.[20] We repeated his chemical analyses and also analyzed four ancient samples of natron from the author's collection that had been excavated in Egypt. X-ray diffraction patterns were obtained by John Geiger of Corning Glass Works. A composite analysis is reported in Table 9–9. While we refer to these salts as natron, they are in reality trona, or the sesquicarbonate $Na_2CO_3.NaHCO_3.2H_2O$.

Calculations show that if Belus River sand and Wadi Natrun natron were mixed together in proportions of 4.92 to 2 parts by weight and melted, the resulting glass would have a composition closely resembling that of Jalame glass (see Tables 9–3 and 9–9). These particular weight proportions were selected to fit the resultant

20. Z. K. Hanna, "Study of Ancient Glass and Raw Materials in Wadi El-Natrun" (M.S. Thesis, Department of Physical Sciences, The American University, Cairo, 1966).

sures) would have led to the exact composition given in the last column of Table 9–9. Similar minor aberrations could account for other small discrepancies between the calculated compositions and the analyzed Jalame glass.

These calculations establish that Jalame glass was almost certainly made from Belus River sand and Wadi Natrun natron, following a recipe of two parts of sand to one part of natron, measured by volume. Although in ancient times most solid commodities, probably including glass cullet, were sold by weight, just as today throughout the Middle East and Central Asia, practical glassmakers would have discovered that they could make glass just as well by using the much more convenient method of measuring ingredients by volume.

Color Chemistry of the Jalame Glass
(Co-author, J. W. H. Schreurs)

Terminology and Explanations

The vast majority of Jalame glass, both cullet and vessel fragments, is either aqua or green. The cullet is more or less evenly divided between the two, but the vessel glass may favor the green color. Other colors include a range of olive to olive amber, which is quite well represented in the cullet; purple, which occurs mainly as a relatively small quantity of cullet; and dark and light blues. The blues occur only in small quantities, mostly as applied decoration. There are also many colorless (decolorized) vessel fragments. All the Jalame glass is transparent; none is opaque.

The discussion that follows has been divided into two parts. First descriptions of colors and the terminology are presented, along with chemical explanations of how the colors are formed. The second part, of a more technical nature, contains discussions of the transmission spectra of the glasses and redox effects related to variations in melting conditions. Details of a still more technical nature are included in the Appendix.

The terminology used here is subjective; nevertheless, the nine terms are intended to convey rather precise colors. These terms should be clear to anyone who has handled much glass. Transmission spectra, given in the second part, place the terminology on a more objective basis.

The terms selected for the colors (all transparent) are:

—Aqua: a somewhat greenish blue; sometimes modified to bluish aqua or greenish aqua
—Green: distinctly more yellowish than aqua
—Colorless: water-white, decolorized
—Amber: a warm, orangish brown
—Olive: sometimes confused with amber but cooler, with a pronounced greenish tinge
—Olive-amber: between olive and amber, distinguished only by comparison with the other two: a refinement, but an important one

—Purple: the familiar manganese "amethyst" color; differing from violet in that it contains a substantial red component
—Light Blue: the familiar "copper blue" (think of copper-sulfate solutions). We avoid *turquoise* because it implies opacity
—Dark Blue: the familiar "cobalt-blue"; the hue contains more red than do copper blues

The "natural" aqua color of Jalame glass is typical of much Roman glass. Visually, it is a pale greenish blue; chemically, it results from iron oxide at concentrations of about .3 to .6%. This level of iron can be accounted for by the known levels of iron impurities in the raw materials. All four of the most abundant Jalame colors—aqua, green, olive, and olive-amber—are a result of naturally occurring iron impurities, sometimes modified by manganese. The color of any particular piece of glass depends on its chemical composition and on whether it was melted under oxidizing or reducing conditions. The combinations of colorants and redox (oxidation-reduction) conditions responsible for the observed colors are:

Common Colors (manganese may or may not be present)
—Aqua: Iron; neutral or reducing conditions; Fe^{++} predominates
—Green: Iron and ferri-sulfide; somewhat more reducing conditions; Fe^{++} with relatively lower concentrations of ferri-sulfide (sometimes aqua streaked with amber also looks green)
  Olive: Iron and ferri-sulfide; strongly reducing conditions; Fe^{++} with relatively higher concentrations of ferri-sulfide
—Olive-amber: Same, with greater ferri-sulfide to Fe^{++} ratio

Less Common Colors
—Purple: Manganese; oxidizing conditions; Mn^{+++} predominates
—Colorless (decolorized): Manganese and iron; oxidizing conditions; balanced Fe^{++}, Fe^{+++} (?), and Mn^{+++}, Mn^{++} (?)

Rare Colors (or Migrants)
—Light Blue: Copper; neutral or oxidizing conditions; Cu^{++}
—Dark Blue: Cobalt; neutral or oxidizing conditions; Co^{++}

Iron exists in glass as two ionic species—the chemically reduced ferrous ion (Fe^{++}), which confers a bluish color to the glass, and the oxidized ferric ion (Fe^{+++}), which confers a much weaker yellowish color. Atom for atom, the ferrous is so much stronger a colorant that the effects of the ferric ion can be neglected in considering the color chemistry of the Jalame glasses.

In glass melts, redox reactions occur in which these ions can be converted from one to the other. When melted under reducing conditions, a glass colored only by iron will have a bluish color. The origin of the ferrous coloration is actually a strong absorption peak in the

Table 9–9. Raw Material Analyses and Glass Compositions

	Belus River Beach Sand* (n=7)	Wadi Natrun "Natron"† (Trona + salts) (n=6–11)		Oxides	Sand as oxide mixture (Normalized to 100%	"Natron" as oxide mixture (Normalized to 100%
SiO_2 g	79.90%	0.49%	SiO_2	SiO_2	84.68%	1.19%
Na_2O a	0.781	93.25	$Na_2CO_3 \cdot NaHCO_3 \cdot 2H_2O$	Na_2O	0.828	94.51
		1.32	NaCl			
CaO a	8.93	1.49	$CaSO_4$	CaO	9.47	1.48
K_2O a	0.798	0.404	KCl	K_2O	0.846	0.618
MgO a	0.503	0.550	$MgCO_3$	MgO	0.533	0.637
Al_2O_3 a	2.98	0.251	Al_2O_3	Al_2O_3	3.16	0.608
Fe_2O_3 a	0.325	0.274	Fe_2O_3	Fe_2O_3	0.344	0.661
TiO_2	0.04	0.05	TiO_2	TiO_2	0.042	0.12
MnO a	0.03	0.0017	MnO	MnO	0.032	0.0041
CuO	0.0005	0.0005	CuO	CuO	0.0005	0.0012
SnO_2	--	--		SnO_2	--	--
Ag_2O	0.0005	--		Ag_2O	0.0005	--
PbO	--	--		PbO	--	--
BaO	0.02	0.008	$BaSO_4$	BaO	0.03	0.012
SrO	0.02	0.09	$SrSO_4$	SrO	0.04	0.12
Li_2O	0.005	0.0005	Li_2O	Li_2O	0.005	0.0012
B_2O_3	0.01	0.01	B_2O_3	B_2O_3	0.01	0.02
V_2O_5	--	0.0002	V_2O_5	V_2O_5	--	0.0005
Cr_2O_3	--	--		Cr_2O_3	--	--
NiO	--	--		NiO	--	--
ZnO a	0.0063	--		ZnO	0.0067	--
ZrO_2	0.01	0.0052	ZrO_2	ZrO_2	0.01	0.012
P_2O_5	ns	ns	P_2O_5	P_2O_5	ns	ns
		1.20	H_2O in excess			
Σ	94.3593%	99.395%			100.038%	99.995%
CO_2 ε	5.73					
Other	0.03					
less O	0.015					
Σ	100.104%					

*   Mean composition of seven samples as described in text (p. 000). Oxide was subtracted to accommodate replacement by analyzed chloride.
†   Mean composition of 6–11 samples selected from seven modern specimens and four XVIIIth-dynasty specimens (see text p. 000). Not all specimens were used for all oxides because of organic contamination, presence of other salts, etc. The distribution of the anions and water among the metal oxides is arbitrary. Other salt and hydration mixtures would also match the analyses. However, as long as valence requirements are satisfied, the particular distribution chosen has no effect on the calculations of glass compositions, because those calculations depend only on the non-volatile metallic oxides.
** Calculations based on experimentally determined bulk densities of the analyzed specimens. The natron was crushed but not pulverized. Density of natron 1.24 g/ml. Average density of two sands 1.44 g/ml. (Individual values, 1.43 and 1.45.)

Jalame Glass	Glass Comp. 5:2 ratio by weight	Percent Relative Error (to nearest 1%)		Glass Comp.** 2:1 ratio by volume
70.54%	72.18%	+2%	+1%	71.43%
15.74	14.85	+6	0	15.69
8.73	8.27	−5	−6	8.20
0.758	0.812	+7	+7	0.810
0.601	0.548	−9	−8	0.550
2.70	2.78	+3	+2	2.75
0.383	0.392	+2	+3	0.395
0.086	0.054			0.055
0.121	0.028			0.027
0.002	0.0006			0.0006
0.0005	--			--
0.0005	0.0004			0.0004
0.014	--			--
0.046	0.027			0.024
0.067	0.052			0.044
0.0005	0.0044			0.0045
0.017	0.012			0.013
0.0004	0.00008			0.00008
0.0004	--			--
0.0005	--			--
0.011	0.0057			0.0055
0.005	0.011			0.011
0.135	--			--
95.959%	100.027%			100.010%

Analytical methods:
g   gravimetric (for SiO_2)
a   atomic absorption
e   acid evolution followed by absorption
ns   not sought

   All analyses by Brant Rising, Robert H. Bell, and co-workers at Lucius Pitkin, Inc., New York City.

Table 9-10. Colorant Species and Their Spectra

Colorants and Relative Strength	Wavelength Ranges and Colors Absorbed *	Wavelength Ranges and Colors Transmitted †
Reduced iron, Fe^{++} Strong	~600-700; red (Tail of 1100 peak in IR extending into visible. Extends further at higher conc.)	1. At higher conc.: ~400-580 2. At lower conc.: ~400-640
Oxidized iron, Fe^{+++} Very weak	~400-450; violet	1. At higher conc.: ~450-700 2. At moderate conc.: ~400-700
J Fe^{++} + Fe^{+++} Strong, Fe^{+++} predominates	~400-450; violet (weak) ~580-700; red (strong)	~400-580
Ferri-sulfide complex Very strong	~400-540; violet, blue	~540-700
J Ferri-sulfide + Fe^{++} Slightly reduced Both strong	~400-470; violet, blue ~640-700; red	~470-640
J Ferri-sulfide + Fe^{++} Strongly reduced Both very strong	~400-500; violet, blue 680-700; red	~500-680
J Oxidized Manganese, Mn^{+++} Strong	~440-580; green	~400-440 ~580-700
J Fe^{+++}, Mn^{++}, some Fe^{++} & Mn^{+++} (Balanced for decolorization)	All to more-or-less equal extent	All to more-or-less equal extent

J   Occurs at Jalame.
*   Wavelengths expressed in millimicrons or nanometers.
†   Because the maximum spectral sensitivity of the human eye is to green light (about 555 nm), the transmission in that region is especially important in relating wavelengths to color perceptions.

infrared-red region. When sufficient ferrous iron is present, that peak tails out into the red region of the visible spectrum. The absorption of the red light leaves the ferrous-containing glass with the greenish blue color we have called aqua. The higher the concentration of ferrous ion, the further the tail extends into the visible and the bluer the glass appears, because the extended tail removes more green than blue. The result is that more reducing melting conditions lead to a bluer tinge, while more oxidizing conditions (which decrease the amount of iron in the ferrous state) lead to a greener tinge. However, if a glass also contains sulfur (as the Jalame glasses do), the picture may change, because under certain conditions sulfur can form the amber-colored ferri-sulfide colorant. When that color is superimposed on the color of the ferrous iron, a range from green to olive can result.

There is some question as to whether amber colors in ancient glass are produced by an iron-sulfur complex (the ferri-sulfide colorant) or result simply from interac-

Approx. Transmission Peak in Visible	Color Sensation Perceived and Example
490	1. Bluish aqua (DZO)
520	2. Greenish aqua (DZP)
480	1. Slight yellowish
480	2. Colorless (3395)
510	Aqua (blue + green); bluish and greenish variants according to conc. of Fe^{++}. (633)
670	Amber (yellow + red) (3212)
555	Green (blue + green + yellow) (620)
585	Olive (green + yellow + red) (629, compare with 3212)
400, 700	Purple (violet + red) (624)
--	Colorless (neutral gray, or weak yellowish green) (Many vessels)

tion between iron and manganese. (We incline to the first explanation.)[21] None of the Jalame glass can be classified as true amber, but it has been proved that olive and olive-amber glasses from Jalame contain the ferri-sulfide complex, which modifies the basic aqua of the ferrous ion to olive and olive-amber. A similar effect produces the common green color. Furthermore, true amber glasses from other ancient sources have been found to be colored with the same ferri-sulfide complex.

21. Unpublished findings by the authors.

The Basic Aqua, Green, and Olives

As explained above, the "natural" aqua color results primarily from iron in the ferrous state. When, by accident or by design, the melting conditions became slightly more oxidizing or reducing, the aqua color would shift slightly, creating a range of greenish or bluish variants of aqua. However, most of the green glass, perhaps half of all the glass excavated, owes its color to a different effect, a mixture of ferrous blue with traces of the ferri-sulfide amber colorant. In very low concentrations, the amber of the ferri-sulfide is diluted to a yellow that modifies the aqua, producing green.

Olive and amber are common among ancient glasses, and olive is well represented in Jalame cullet. There is a distinction between these two colors (see above), although chemically they may differ more in degree than in kind. In their transmission spectra (Fig. 9–1) amber glasses show a relatively higher transmission in the red region (600–700 nm) than in the green. In contrast, the transmission curves of olive glasses fall off noticeably in the red, relative to their green transmission. It is the relative amounts of red versus blue and green transmitted that differentiate amber from olive.

Amber colors are produced by a combination of iron and sulfur in a strongly reduced melt, forming a complex that is an extremely intense colorant,[22] stronger probably even than cobalt. Three conditions are essential for the formation of the amber color: the presence of sulfur (very little is required), strong reducing conditions to reduce some of the sulfur to sulfide, and the presence of ferric iron. All these conditions would have been met frequently in ancient glass factories.

Plant ashes are often rich in sulfate;[23] therefore any glass that contained plant ash as its source of alkali (either soda or potash) would probably become amber if melted under strongly reducing conditions. Since the Jalame glasses were made not with plant ash but with natron, the sulfur was probably introduced from the natron itself. Natron from the Wadi Natrun is often found in association with sodium sulfate. All twelve natron samples analyzed contained some sulfate, ranging from .18 to 2.54%.

22. The chemical nature of the colorant has been argued for many years. One picture currently in favor is that of Douglas and others (R. W. Douglas and M. S. Zaman, "The Chromophore in Iron-Sulphur Amber Glasses," *Physics and Chemistry of Glasses* 10 [August 1969] 125–32.) They see the colorant as consisting, in simplified terms, of a ferric ion and a sulfide ion. In that case, the glasses are most accurately described as ferri-sulfide glasses. Previously, they were known as iron polysulfide glasses, a term some still prefer. Historically they have been called "carbon ambers," a misleading term. The name arose because carbon-containing batch materials, such as coke or coal, were added to produce a reducing melt. These often contained sulfur impurities, and the resultant color was mistakenly attributed to the carbon. The present author's views appear in R. H. Brill and J. W. H. Schreurs, "Iron and Sulfur Related Colors in Ancient Glasses," *Archaeometry* 26 (1984) 199–209.

23. See reference cited in n. 13.

Table 9–11. Ferrous/Ferric Ratios and Sulfur Contents of Some Ancient and Medieval Glasses

Sample No.	Source	Color	Total Sulfur* (as S, wt.%)	Total Iron† (as Fe$_2$O$_3$, wt. %)	Fe^{++} Conc.** (as "Fe$_2$O$_3$", wt. %)
619	Jalame	aqua	0.030%	0.42%	0.281%
633	"	"	0.047	0.37	0.249
636	"	"	0.082	0.51	0.324
814	"	"	---	0.36	---
620	"	green	0.041	0.35	0.246
621	"	"	---	0.31	0.231
644	"	olive-green	---	0.36	---
645	"	"	---	0.32	---
629	"	olive	0.027	0.40	0.349
622	"	"	---	0.43	0.374
647	"	olive-amber	0.014	0.40	0.314
649	"	purple	0.035	0.43	---
28359§	"	amber	0.022	0.40***	---
28360§	"	green	0.030	0.42***	---
623	"	"colorless"	---	0.40	<0.043
624	"	purple	---	0.43	<0.013
3210	Helln-Roman	amber	0.074	0.34	0.246
3212	"	amber	0.113	0.31	0.261
3214	"	colorless	0.179	0.86	0.056
3508	Rhodes, Helln.	amber	0.062	0.36	---
3395	Greece, 4th c. B.C.	colorless	0.136	0.425***	0.018
5301	Nishapur, Islm.	aqua	0.089	0.78	---
5322	" "	colorless	0.115	0.27	---
2525	St. Maur, Med.	amber	0.124	0.92	---
54985§§	Synthetic Meso.	amber	0.102	0.19***	0.186
5499	" "	blue	0.096	0.22***	0.128
DZO	Exptl melt	bl. aqua	0.005	0.58	0.432
DZP	" "	green	0.015	0.58	0.158

Compositionally, nothing sets the olive and olive-amber specimens apart from other Jalame glasses. Some have intentionally added manganese and some do not. The few samples analyzed (by Bruce Swinehart) seem to have about the same sulfur level (see Table 9–11). Although the sulfur levels are low, the percentage of sulfide required to form an amber color is even lower, perhaps only about .005% or less. Hence, even without any separate addition of a sulfur-containing ingredient, the Jalame glass contains enough sulfur as an impurity to allow an amber color to develop, if it is strongly enough reduced.[24]

Parallel color and chemical sequences can be followed in the aqua-green-olive Jalame glasses. The aqua glasses are not strongly enough reduced for any ferri-sulfide colorant to have formed. When they are a bit further reduced, a moderate amount of ferri-sulfide begins to form, and the color becomes green. Upon further reduction, still more ferri-sulfide forms and the strong amber component turns the glass olive.

The redox states of iron and sulfur in a glass are affected by two factors: variations in furnace atmosphere and the presence of other oxidizing or reducing agents in the melt. Whenever there was a strong draft through the melting zone of a furnace, a greater proportion of the iron and sulfur present would be in an oxidized state. A poor draft or a smoky atmosphere would reduce these elements. Recalling that many vessel fragments tend to be paler and more yellowish than the cullet (even when examined in equal thicknesses) it might be surmised that the resoftening of the cullet was carried out under more oxidizing conditions than those under which the cullet was manufactured. The melting containers were necessarily smaller than the original melting "tanks," and since they must have been adjacent to working ports, they would have been better ventilated.

24. It should be remembered that the sulfur retained in the glass is limited by its solubility in the glass melt, and that is rather low. No matter how much sulfate is added to the original batch, it will escape during melting until the saturation concentration is reached. That level is probably about 0.1% for glasses with Jalame-like compositions.

Fe^{+++} Conc.[††] (as Fe$_2$O$_3$, wt.%)	Redox Balance (% total iron present as Fe^{++})[**]
~0.13%	67%
0.13	67
~0.18	64
---	--
---	70
~0.10	75
---	--
---	--
---	87
---	87
---	79
---	--
0.09	~80 (EPR)
0.13	~69 (EPR)
---	<11
---	< 3
0.05	72
0.05	84
---	7
---	--
---	4
---	--
---	--

0.04	91
0.15	62
---	74.5
---	27.2

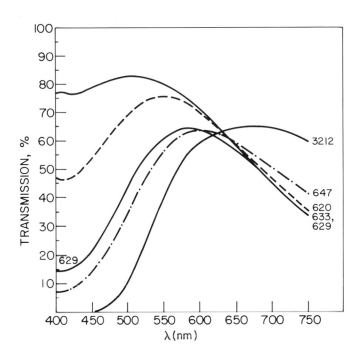

Fig. 9–1. Transmission spectra in the visible region for four glasses from Jalame and an amber Hellenistic bowl, which is thinner than the other glasses. If it were thicker, its transmission throughout would be markedly decreased.

*   Infrared sulfur determinator values by Bruce Swinehart and Yao-Sin Su of Corning Glass Works.
†   Analyses from Tables 9–1 through 9–5, by Brant Rising and co-workers at Lucius Pitkin, Inc., averaged with repeat analyses by Gerald D. Schuckers of Corning Glass Works, where available.
**   Determined optically, using DZO as a reference sample.
††   From EPR.
§   Adjacent parts of single piece of cullet.
§§   See p. 113 of reference cited in n. 12.
*** Analyses by Gerald D. Schuckers of Corning Glass Works.

Among the metallic oxides in the Jalame glasses, only manganese is present in sufficient quantities to have had a noticeable effect on the redox state of the iron. Generally, but not always, the cullet and vessel fragments that contain deliberately added manganese are more yellowish and paler than those without manganese. This is because the manganese oxidized part of the ferrous iron to its nearly colorless ferric state.

In some of the green cullet, particularly that containing manganese, the glass is not at all homogeneous. The green color is produced by streamers of a yellowish or amber color passing through the more bluish aqua matrix. Electron paramagnetic resonance studies have proved that these streaks correspond to zones that contain the amber ferri-sulfide colorant, which is absent (at least, undetected) in the aqua matrix (see Appendix). Obviously the dry glass batch or the glass melts (most likely both) were not well mixed because they contain zones reflecting widely varying redox conditions.

It is difficult to say whether the furnace atmosphere or the presence of redox reactants in the batch was the controlling factor in determining the redox state of the iron in Jalame glass. Given time, the furnace atmosphere will predominate if it is in a redox tug-of-war with internal reactants, and eventually it can control every redox species in the melt. However, unless a melt is vigorously stirred, gases in the atmosphere can react only with the surface of the glass. Reaction with the body of molten glass is limited by the diffusion of the furnace gases into the melt—a sluggish process. For shorter melting and "soaking" times, internal redox reactants have the advantage of intimacy with the iron and sulfur in the melt. Therefore, it is not surprising that Jalame glasses are sometimes quite heterogeneous in color.

We conclude that color differences between green and aqua glasses on the one hand, and olive and olive-amber on the other, could have been brought about (accidentally or intentionally) solely by variations in the furnace atmosphere. In actual practice, if the glassmaker set out to make an olive-amber, that could have been facilitated by adding something like powdered charcoal to the batch or by placing moist plant matter in the furnace chamber. Unfortunately, we have no way of checking analytically for a batch additive, because these organic materials burn away without leaving easily detected chemical traces.[25]

This subject was investigated further by reheating small portions of Jalame cullet of various colors in strongly reducing and strongly oxidizing atmospheres.[26] The five glasses have different total contents of manganese, but the total iron contents are about the same. These glasses are:

> 633 Aqua cullet, MnO = 0.058%, Fe$_2$O$_3$ = 0.39%
> 647 Olive cullet, MnO = 0.30%, Fe$_2$O$_3$ = 0.40%
> 649 Purple cullet, MnO = 2.79%, Fe$_2$O$_3$ = 0.43%
> J65Z Aqua cullet (not analyzed)
> J65Z Green cullet (not analyzed)

Pieces were placed in platinum foil, softened, and heated at 1220°C for two hours. They were purged continuously while over 500°C with either oxygen or forming gas (92% N$_2$ and 8% H$_2$). In the oxygen atmosphere the aqua, green, and olive glasses all became colorless (with a pale pink tinge if manganese was present). The purple glass became a still stronger purple. In the reducing atmosphere, all five glasses developed streaks and large patches of amber coloration within an aqua matrix. (The purple glass turned colorless but retained a spot of purple, showing how sluggish reactions between the interior of a glass melt and furnace gases can be.)

These results demonstrate that Jalame cullet, regardless of composition or color, can be converted by strong oxidation or reduction to either of the color extremes observed. They also serve to summarize the color chemistry of Jalame glass. In the most oxidized state the cullet is colorless, because its iron is almost exclusively in the weakly coloring ferric state. When strongly reduced, the glass acquires an olive or olive-amber color owing to the presence of ferrous iron and the amber ferri-sulfide colorant. If manganese is present in minor quantities, it will, in the most oxidized state, give a slight pinkish tinge to otherwise colorless glass; if present in higher concentrations, it produces a strong purple color. Almost all the cullet and vessel glass falls somewhere between these extremely oxidized and extremely reduced colors. The ranges of bluish-aqua to aqua to greenish-aqua, then to green to olive to olive-amber, which account for a large part of Jalame glass, represent a palette produced primarily by variations in furnace atmosphere. The role played by traces of sulfur

in the formation of the ferri-sulfide colorant, which accounts for the green color of so much of the glass, may be a general phenomenon among ancient glasses. That question is being pursued further.

Unfortunately, the most interesting question remains unanswered. Did the glassmakers manipulate these furnace variations to control color or were they simply, as the old saying goes, at the mercy of the furnace gods? Conceivably, they might not have even cared what colors resulted.

Purple, Blues, and Colorless

"Colored glasses," relatively scarce at Jalame, are limited to purple, light blue, and dark blue. If decolorized glass is considered a "colored glass," the number may be expanded substantially, but defining which pieces are deliberately decolorized and which are accidentally "less-colored" is difficult.

Several large and many small pieces of purple cullet—or colorless and purple-streaked—were found, but relatively little purple was found in vessel fragments or as applied decoration. The color of the cullet results from the presence of manganese, which ranges from 1.69 to 3.89% (as MnO) in the five samples analyzed. The cullet probably served as a manganese concentrate to be remelted with uncolored cullet. The manganese would either act as a decolorizer or modify the aqua to a paler yellowish green, depending on melting conditions. The original source of manganese was probably the mineral pyrolusite (MnO$_2$). This, when powdered, will dissolve in glass, but laboratory experiments have shown that adding pyrolusite directly to a glass melt (or even a glass batch) will not result in as uniform distribution as will adding crushed purple cullet. The intermediate level of about .12% MnO found in the green vessel glass could have been attained by adding about 4 parts of purple cullet to 100 parts of aqua cullet.

Precise values of the manganese content in Jalame cullet are not meaningful because the glass is quite heterogeneous in MnO. For example, the purple-streaked region of one piece of cullet (No. 624) contained 2% MnO, while an adjacent colorless zone of the same piece (No. 623) contained 1.69% MnO. The difference in color resulted from the fact that the redox reaction between manganese and iron had gone further toward completion in the colorless zone.

The decolorizing property of manganese results from its reaction with iron in a glass melt. The two elements are said to form a redox couple. As was mentioned earlier, this equilibrium is displaced strongly to the right.

$$Fe^{++} + Mn^{+++} \text{———} Fe^{+++} + Mn^{++}$$

blue   pink   weak   weak

yellowish   yellowish (?)

---

25. If something like powdered charcoal had been added, it probably would have left the amber glass noticeably seedier than the aquas and greens, and this was not found to be the case.

26. The experiments were carried out by E. E. Harris of Corning Glass Works, using an electric muffle furnace.

Two color effects are involved. First the manganese oxidizes the iron, lowering the concentration of the strongly coloring ferrous ion and substituting for it the weaker ferric colorant. If the reaction proceeds to just the right extent, it can yield a balanced mixture of the four colors, which offset one another and give a relatively flat transmission curve corresponding to a neutral gray color. Some Jalame vessel fragments can be described as "colorless." Many are thin-walled, heightening their water-white appearance. Those analyzed (Nos. 855 and 858) contain some additive manganese.

The presence of manganese raises a puzzling point that is usually overlooked. A great many ancient glasses from about the 2nd century B.C. through the Middle Ages contain intentionally added manganese.[27] It is usually assumed that manganese was intended as a decolorizer, because that is how it has been used in more recent times. In many instances among ancient glasses, including the two colorless glasses from Jalame just mentioned, the manganese did, indeed, act effectively as a decolorizer. But in many other instances the manganese-containing glasses have a pronounced greenish color. Among Jalame vessels, those with deliberately added manganese are *not*, for the most part, effectively decolorized. Evidently, the "correct" decolorizing balance was not achieved. Our experience with laboratory melts shows that approximately equal weight percentages of MnO and Fe_2O_3, when added to a batch, constitute a good proportion for decolorization.[28] Several of the green Jalame glasses fulfill this condition. Our experiments also show, however, that if laboratory melts are made in a strongly reducing atmosphere, the effects of the furnace atmosphere overwhelm the effectiveness of the manganese as an oxidant, thereby inhibiting its decolorizing action. The manganese seems to oxidize enough iron to give the glass a greenish-aqua color, but not enough to really decolorize it. The fact that so many ancient glasses containing manganese are green instead of colorless (in addition to those from Jalame) suggests there might have been some other reason for adding manganese. Perhaps it was sometimes used intentionally to make green instead of aqua glass.

Blue glass occurs at Jalame only in small quantities, mainly as trailing or applied blobs of decoration (see Chap. 4). Two specimens, Nos. 820–21 (Table 9–5) are trails on aqua and colorless body glasses. Their color is the light transparent blue typical of copper-colored glasses. In each case a little tin and lead are also present, indicating that the copper colorant was probably derived from bronze. Possibly it was an oxide scale formed by heating some scrap bronze or bronze coins.[29] In No. 820 the copper colorant is quite dilute. In No. 821, however, the levels are a little higher, and although the tin and lead are only spectrographic estimates, one may guess at a copper:tin:lead composition of about 90:3:7.

In addition to the trails, two specimens of light blue waste glass were analyzed (see Special Objects and Table 9–5). No. 3612 came from a small group of blue drippings and trailings. Because its copper, tin, and lead are at higher levels, a more reliable parent alloy composition can be estimated: approximately 79:5:16, which fits well with the heavily leaded bronzes used for Late Roman coinage, small artifacts, and sculpture. An almost identical alloy composition, 77:7:16, was estimated for the copper colorant in No. 3613, another piece of light blue waste glass.

Very little dark blue glass was found at the site; two specimens were analyzed (Table 9–5). No. 3611 is waste glass or cullet. No. 3601 is from a decorative blob on a conical lamp. Both are colored with cobalt. The complete analyses of the six blue glasses are discussed in the section on Special Objects.

Transmission Spectra

Percent transmission curves in the near-ultraviolet, visible, and infrared regions were measured for polished plates prepared from 13 specimens of Jalame cullet.[30] The curves for 4 of the glasses are plotted in Fig. 9–1, as references for understanding the four basic colors of Jalame glass. Table 9–10 may also be helpful for interpreting the curves. The wavelength ranges used to describe the colors, in nanometers (nm), are only approximate and somewhat arbitrary. Because the maximum spectral sensitivity of the human eye is in the green region, at about 555 nm, the transmission in that region is especially important in determining the colors perceived. Nos. 633 and 620 are the "natural" aqua and green. In the spectrum of No. 633 the ferrous iron absorbs much of the light in the red region, toward the right side of the graph. Consequently, the transmitted

27. Antimony was used as a decolorizer in many ancient glasses, but only by acting as an oxidant. It does not have the offsetting absorptions effect. Antimony would also have acted as a fining agent.

28. In fact, quite a wide latitude in the total iron and total manganese concentrations will produce a "colorless" glass. We have analyzed water-white ancient glasses from other sources, in which the MnO contents were about half, equal, or double the Fe_2O_3 weight percentages. Our experimental glasses show a stoichiometric balance to be very effective.

29. At the factory in Herat, Afghanistan, copper-scale was used.

30. These curves are part of an unpublished "color library" of transmission spectra of ancient glasses compiled by The Corning Museum of Glass. Most of the curves were run by R. C. French of Corning Glass Works. These curves show the percentages of different wavelengths (different colors) of visible light transmitted through the sample measured. A water-white piece of glass yields a nearly flat curve that crosses the spectrum as a horizontal line at about 92% (approximately 8% of the light is lost by reflection). A completely opaque sample would give a horizontal line at 0%, since no light of any color is transmitted. Colored glasses, or any other transparent colored matter, transmit different percentages of different incident wavelengths. Thus the light that finally emerges is richer in some wavelengths than others. The eye sees such light as being colored.

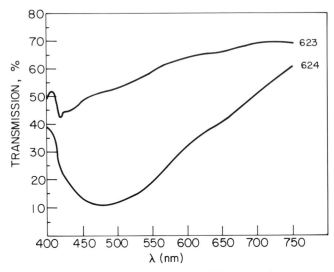

Fig. 9–2. Transmission spectra in the visible region of two samples cut from a streaked nugget of cullet.

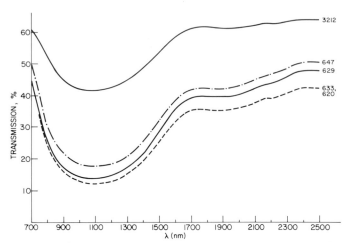

Fig. 9–3. Transmission spectra in the infrared region for the same samples shown in Fig. 9–1. Sample thicknesses are: No. 620, 4.8 mm; No. 629, 4.72 mm; No. 633, 4.91 mm; No. 647, 3.2 mm; No. 3212, 1.85 mm. Because No. 3212 is thinner than the other four glasses, its curve lies well above the others. Absorption near 1100 nm is caused by the ferrous ion. For discussion see Appendix.

light is deficient in red and relatively rich in blue and green. Hence, No. 633 has a bluish color. No. 620 also absorbs much of the red light, but in addition quite a lot of the violet and blue, owing to the presence of a small amount of ferri-sulfide (absent in No. 633). The remaining light transmitted has a peak at about 550 nm, which we perceive as green.

The curve for No. 3212 (a Hellenistic ribbed bowl) shows the transmission of a good ferri-sulfide amber. The ferri-sulfide complex absorbs very strongly in the near ultraviolet and allows virtually no transmission up to almost 500 nm. The light it does transmit is deficient in violet and blue wavelengths and quite low in green. Its main transmission is of yellow, orange, and some red wavelengths, which we perceive as a warm amber color.

No. 629 shows some absorption due to the ferri-sulfide colorant, but its spectrum falls off rapidly in the red region. Its peak is at about 580 nm. If the transmissions at any wavelengths in the green and red regions are compared to one another (for example, 540, 620, and 700 nm), it will be seen that the amber glass (No. 3212) contains about twice as much red as green, whereas No. 629 contains about twice as much green as red. Thus, No. 629 has a distinctly greener transmission than No. 3212, and this is seen as olive. The curve for No. 647 is intermediate between olive (No. 629) and amber (No. 3212). Visually, its color is different from both, and even before running the curve we had labeled it "olive-amber."

Fig. 9–2 shows the spectra for a piece of Jalame cullet with intermingled streaks of colorless and purple. The colorless region (with a pinkish tinge) is No. 623. The curve for No. 624, a purple region of the same piece, shows the strong absorption characteristic of the oxidized manganic ion, Mn^{+++}. It transmits only some violet and red, accounting for its strong purple color.

Physical Properties

The Viscosity-Temperature Curve

One of the most important physical properties characterizing a glass is its viscosity-temperature curve.[31] This curve, giving the viscosity at different temperatures, defines the temperatures required to carry out specific glassmaking operations with a particular glass.

Fig. 9–5 shows viscosity-temperature curves for two Jalame glasses (run by Eugene Fontana of Corning Glass Works). Each sample consisted of a few dozen pieces of cullet from various parts of the site. One sample was made up of green cullet and one of aqua. The chemical differences causing the color differences were not expected to have any observable effect on the viscosities, and the two curves do, in fact, track one another closely and may safely be assumed to represent the working properties of Jalame glass.

The general shape of viscosity-temperature curves is similar for most glasses. The curves drop rapidly, indicating that as glass is heated, viscosity decreases owing to the rupture of chemical bonds. Toward higher temperatures the decrease in viscosity is more gradual, and the curves flatten out. The differences among glasses with different compositions is reflected in the shapes of

31. The viscosity of a liquid is its resistance to flow; thus, viscosity is the opposite of fluidity. For a discussion of viscosity curves see R. H. Brill, "A Note on the Scientist's Definition of Glass," *JGS* 4 (1962) 127–38.

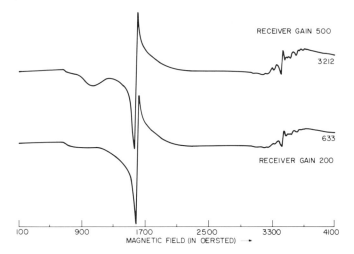

Fig. 9–4. Derivative of electron paramagnetic resonance absorption spectrum for an aqua and an amber glass. For discussion see Appendix.

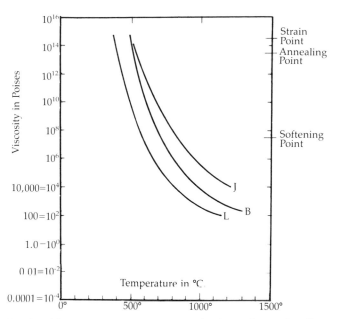

Fig. 9–5. Viscosity temperature curves for three glasses. J, cullet from Jalame; B, typical borosilicate; L, high lead art or optical glass. Jalame curve is very similar to modern soda lime glasses. For comparison, the viscosities near room temperature for the following substances (in poises) are: water ~ .01; motor oil ~ 1.; molasses ~ 10; cheddar cheese ~ 10^8; pitch ~ 10^9; lead metal ~ 10^{11}; aluminum metal ~ 10^{15}.

the curves and their relative placements along the temperature scale. For comparison with the Jalame samples, we have plotted data for other glasses. That labeled "B" is "harder" (requiring a higher temperature to achieve any given viscosity); that labeled "L" is "softer." The viscosity-temperature curve of Jalame glass is much like that of a modern window glass.

Table 9–12 lists some viscosity values for Jalame glass. From these we can infer the temperatures required in order to carry out various operations.[32] It is estimated that the glass had to be raised to 1000–1100°C in order to be gathered onto a blowpipe and blown. The softening, annealing, and strain points were also estimated. These points help to fix the viscosity values at lower temperatures. They also indicate that it would have been necessary to cool Jalame vessels slowly through the range of about 500–575°C in order to anneal them.

Viscosity curves for some forty other ancient glasses have also been determined. Some are softer and some harder, but most of the soda-lime glasses are not very different from Jalame glass, because their compositions are similar. Hence, the temperatures listed here for various operations with Jalame glass can be used as a guideline for ancient glasses in general, providing only soda-lime glasses are involved. Because the table may be of general use, some operations are included that were not practiced at Jalame. Some additional characteristics derived from a liquidus study have been added.

A viscosity-temperature curve was also determined

for a sample from the Beth Shearim slab.[33] This glass has a much higher lime content than Jalame glass and, consequently, was subject to devitrification during cooling, a fact consistent with the relatively steep slope of its viscosity curve.[34] It would have set up quickly upon cooling, probably with devitrification, and would have been extremely difficult to work.

Annealing State

Annealing is an integral part of the glassmaking process. If a hot glass object is allowed to cool too quickly, it will be highly strained by the time it reaches room temperature; it may even break during the initial cooling. Highly strained glasses break easily if exposed to thermal shock (rapid temperature change), or if they receive some mechanical shock. In order to prevent excessive strain, a glass object must be cooled slowly through a

32. This table was compiled from "common knowledge" and from information in H. H. Holscher, "The Relationship of Viscosity to Processing of Glass," Owens-Illinois Technical Center, April 1968; J. R. Hutchins III and R. V. Harrington, "Glass," *Encyclopedia of Chemical Technology*, 2nd ed. 10 (1966) 533–604; R. H. Brill, "An Inlaid Glass Plate in Athens, Part II. Laboratory Examination," *JGS* 4 (1962) 37–47.

33. For description and scientific studies see R. H. Brill and J. Wosinski, "A Huge Slab of Glass in the Ancient Necropolis of Beth Shearim," *Proceedings of the VIIth International Congress on Glass, Preliminary Papers*, sec. B, paper 219 (Brussels: International Congress on Glass, 1965), and R. H. Brill, "A Great Glass Slab from Ancient Galilee," *Archaeology* 20 (1967) 88–95. A large part of the excavation work on the slab was done by Paul Perrot, whose name does not appear in these publications.

34. A comprehensive crystallization study of the Beth Shearim slab glass yielded a higher liquidus (1130°C) and a crystallizing range of about 795–1130°C. Its maximum rate of crystallization occurred at about 980–1000°C. The major devitrification phase was beta-wollastonite ($CaO.SiO_2$).

Table 9–12. Temperatures required for Various Operations*

Operation or Property	Approximate [†] Viscosity Range log η	Approximate Temperature Range (°C.)
Strain point	14.5	490°, 491°C.
Annealing point	13	529°, 528°
Softening point	7.65	699°, 702°
Working point	4	~1000°
Critical annealing temperature	12.7	~525° C.
Annealing range (modern practice)	11–14	~500–575°
Sagging under own weight	10	~600°
Sharp edges will round	10	~600°
Indented by a firm tool	10	~600°
Hot pieces join on contact	~10 (?)	~600° (?)
Fusing of powder grains	6	~800°
Fusing into millefiori pattern (1 hour)	6	~800°
Sphericalization of bubbles (1 hour)	6	~800°
Mold sagging	5.3	~850°
Folding rims	5	~900°
Shearing	5	~900°
Drawing canes	4.3	~950°
Mold pressing	4	~1000°
Drawing threads	4	~1000°
Blowing	≤ 4	≥1000°
Marvering	3.2 – 4	~1000–1100°
Gathering	3.2 – 4	~1000–1100°
"Melting" (modern practice)	2–3	~1150–1300°
"Melting" (ancient practice)	≤3.5	≥1050°

* Some of these values are based on information in the references cited in n. 32.
† The viscosity is measured in poise units. The numbers are so high that they are commonly expressed as powers of 10. For convenience, the table gives the logarithm of the viscosity. For example, = 10^5 poise, log = 5.

certain critical temperature range—usually an interval of about 100°C beginning just below its annealing point. The annealing range differs for glasses of different compositions, and the time required for annealing depends on the size and shape of the object. The larger and thicker a piece of glass, the more likely it is to develop strain and, therefore, the more slowly it must be cooled through its critical range.

Today, careful glassmakers draw up annealing schedules, specifying times and temperatures of cooling. But in ancient times and even into this century annealing was a haphazard process. Ancient glassmakers probably annealed their wares in much the same way as do present-day glassmakers in Cairo and in Hebron (and in Herat until recently). The finished hot glass objects would have been placed either in a separate annealing furnace or in a chamber adjacent to the main furnace and allowed to cool slowly, perhaps overnight. The annealing chamber might have been filled with ashes to support the glasses and to prevent them from becoming misshapen or welded together by heat. Because the annealing was not well controlled, some of the wares were unstable and broke easily. What the glassmakers did not know is that the overall cooling process is not so important as the slow cooling of the glass through the critical range mentioned above. If the glass is placed in the annealing chamber after it has cooled below that range, it is too late, and the glass will turn out strained.

It is possible to detect whether a piece of glass is strained by examining it with a polariscope or, more simply, between two crossed polarizing plates. Light and dark patterns trace out zones of strain in the glass. We have examined cullet, vessel fragments, drippings, trailings, and knock-offs from Jalame. As expected, the

Table 9-13. Some Physical Properties of Jalame Glass*

Property	Jalame **	Modern Window	Typical Borosilicate	Optical (30% PbO)
Density in g/cc (d)	2.480--2.502--2.531	2.47	2.23	3.030
Refractive index (n_d)	1.516--1.519--1.524	1.512	1.474	1.572
Coefficient of thermal expansion (α) (0-300°); x 10^7/°C.	94.7--97.4--103.4	92.0	32.5	87.0
Liquidus temperature	924-935°C.	~800-900°	~1070°	~700°
Major devitrification phase	devitrite	devitrite	cristobalite	tridymite

*   Measurements by Loren Morse, Joseph Giardiana, and John Fisk, all of Corning Glass Works.
**   Averages and ranges of eight samples of cullet.

knock-offs are highly strained, for they were chilled rapidly in contact with the rigid iron blowpipe, which accentuated the strain. Similarly, the thicker bits of waste glass were also found to be highly strained. The cullet examined was strained, but not nearly as much as the knock-offs because it was composed of large pieces. As strain developed, internal shattering occurred, which released the strain. The nugget-sized pieces of cullet that resulted contain the less strained parts of the glass. Of the vessel fragments, only about 10% of those examined showed strain. This is the result of three factors: first, the vessels generally were thin-walled; second, the glass makers understood the necessity of annealing and made an attempt that, though only partially effective, improved the quality of their wares; third, since all the pieces examined were fragments, the objects from which they came had already broken, and that breakage would have released the strain, leaving the least-strained parts intact.

Strain also tends to be concentrated where a piece of hot glass has been applied to an already partially cooled vessel. Therefore, one looks for strain where a pontil, a handle, decorative trailing, or blobs have been attached. Only a few examples of such features were examined. On samples No. 3600–3601 (wall of a conical lamp with applied blue blob) there was not much strain where these glasses joined. However, the reheating that had to follow the application of a blob, in order to give it a smooth contour, would have reduced any incipient strain. The pieces with trailing did not show much strain either. They, too, must have been lightly reheated; in any event, the walls and trailing were both so thin that not much strain would develop.

Ancient objects from other sources examined in polarized light do show some strain, usually at junctions such as those mentioned. In general, however, glassmakers of ancient times seem to have been relatively successful in annealing their wares.

Liquidus and Devitrification (Table 9–13)

The necessity of cooling a glass object slowly through a certain critical temperature range has been pointed out. However, if a glass is cooled too slowly through another range of temperature, a different and sometimes harmful effect can result. When a glass is held for a long time at a certain temperature, it can be rigid enough not to sag but fluid enough that atoms and ions in the glass can rearrange themselves into crystals. Thus the glass becomes devitrified, that is, partially crystallized. The maximum temperature at which crystals can exist in a glass without being dissolved is called the liquidus temperature. The maximum rate of crystal formation and growth is usually about 50–150°C below the liquidus.

The liquidus for a mixture of several pieces of Jalame cullet against contact with air was found to be 935°C, and the internal liquidus 924°C. The devitrification product was identified petrographically as devitrite, $Na_2O.3CaO.6SiO_2$. These experiments indicated that Jalame glass becomes heavily devitrified when held in a range of about 790–880°C. The crystals were clusters of needles radiating spherically from central nuclei. After 24 hours of heating, the longest surface needles were about 0.5 mm.

Thermoluminescence

Thermoluminescence has proved useful for dating early pottery and certain other materials. In 1968, with the collaboration of Mark Han at the University of Pennsylvania, we undertook experiments to see if the method could be applied to dating ancient glasses. Attempts to run glow curves on several specimens proved unsuccessful; the only glasses that gave detectable glow curves were those containing crystalline inclusions such as devitrification stones. A sample of the Beth Shearim slab proved to be highly luminescent, because it was heavily devitrified (some parts are more than 50% crystallized).

At the time, it was thought that the failure of glasses to give glow curves might be related to their transparency—that the centers that cause the glow are bleached out optically by ambient light. In order to test this hypothesis, several cullet and vessel fragments were excavated in subdued light one night in Trenches M and L at Jalame.[35] Since that time these specimens, in their original soil contexts, have been stored in total darkness; glow curves have not yet been run.

Other Physical Properties

Other physical properties of Jalame glass are listed in Table 9–13. The values reported are the mean values determined for 8 samples of cullet. These values, all functions of composition, may be useful as estimates for ancient glasses in general. Values for a few types of modern glasses are included in order to give some idea of the ranges of these properties.

Weathering

The nature and extent of weathering suffered by ancient glass were controlled primarily by five factors: chemical composition, time of exposure to weathering elements, environmental factors (including moisture), the prevailing pH (a measure of acidity or alkalinity), and temperature. Of these, the chemical composition and amount of moisture in the macroclimate are most likely to vary widely. Other factors affecting corrosion, usually to a lesser extent, are the thermal history of the glass (strain or partial devitrification), the accumulation of weathering products, abrasion of the surface before burial, and the presence of unusually corrosive chemicals or atmospheric pollutants. Salinity is a factor with glasses from underwater sites.

Standards for describing extent of weathering are still quite subjective. We use the terminology *heavily, moderately,* or *lightly weathered,* or *unweathered,* coupled with terms describing the nature of the weathering. In general, Jalame glass is either moderately or lightly weathered, with occasional pieces being "unweathered." The weathering occurs mostly in the form of iridescence and pitting. Some pieces have a surface scum of weathering products, and many have a calcareous surface accretion from the soil. Since the Jalame composition is relatively stable—not too high in soda, just about right in lime, and with a little more alumina than many other ancient glasses—and since the climate of the area is only moderately wet, the observed extent of weathering is what one would expect. Scanning the chemical analyses while examining the objects, one finds no striking correlation between composition and weathering.

It may be noted that ancient manganese-containing

35. R. H. Brill, *Field Notes,* 5 July 1964.

glasses can often be spotted immediately if they are weathered. As the glass structure deteriorates, the manganese leaches out and tends to redeposit as a thin skin of black manganese dioxide on the surface of the weathering crust. Microscopically, these skins show the dendritic form characteristic of that compound. Although most Jalame glass is not heavily weathered, occasional vessel fragments do show this effect.

Imperfections

Four types of imperfections are ordinarily found in glass: stones, cords, bubbles or "seed," and inclusions. All are common in ancient glasses. These affect the aesthetic quality of a glass in terms of transparency and optical purity. Judged by present-day standards, the Jalame glass would not be considered high quality, but in comparison with other ancient glasses its quality is good.

Stones are inclusions of unmelted batch materials and refractory detached during melting, or crystals from devitrification. Batch and refractory stones are rare in Jalame vessel glass, and even in the cullet they are by no means numerous. The only notable exceptions are certain large chunks of cullet filled with unmelted batch, but these are clearly a special case. Refractory stones tend to occur in parts of the cullet that were close to interfaces with refractory surfaces. Devitrification stones are rare, except when they emanate from the occasional batch or refractory stones, or exist in waste glass that was obviously spilled and accidentally heated for a long time.

Cords are striations or streamers that give glass a wavy appearance. They result from poor mixing of a glass batch or melt. The streamers are caused by differences in refractive index, which, in turn, result from compositional differences. The Jalame cullet is quite cordy, as is to be expected. Cordiness becomes most obvious where compositional differences involve coloring species such as the yellowish and amber streamers mentioned above. Often, too, cords stretch out from stones in the glass. When worked into vessels cordiness becomes diminished, and in this respect Jalame vessels are about the same as, or possibly a little better than, most ancient glasses. Cordiness becomes accentuated by weathering. The zones having compositions less resistant to moisture weather preferentially, leaving a sculptured surface that follows the original cord patterns.

Bubbles become trapped in glass because of the evolution of gases during melting, because of stirring or gathering that accidentally envelops air, or because of moisture and other volatile substances evolved from contact with refractories. Very small bubbles are called "seed." These are difficult to eliminate because they are not very buoyant and rise only slowly through a viscous melt.[36] Nowadays, fining agents are used to remove seed. Although some ancient glasses may have been fined by adding antimony oxide, the Jalame glasses were not. The vessel glass is certainly seedy and bubbly but, on the whole, no more so than other ancient glass.

Some pieces of Jalame cullet are seedy, but many are not; some seem to contain only a few bubbles. When glass is gathered, bubbles are sometimes elongated and often break up into chains of smaller bubbles. As working continues, these chains can lose their identity, and the final glass object may appear seedy.

All in all, we regard Jalame glass as a very respectable example of the glassmaking accomplishments of the ancient world. The care taken in preparing high-quality glass for non-luxury uses testifies to the pride the glassmakers took in their work.

The fourth type of imperfection, inclusions of foreign matter, varies widely in occurrence among ancient glasses. Some individual objects and groups of related objects contain a multitude of microscopic debris of mineral, ceramic, or metallic nature. This is usually evidence of extensive reworking or careless manipulation of the glass. Flakes of iron, rust, and copper scale are often found in ancient glasses. These are not evidence so much of poor quality glass as of poor quality metal tools. Flakes of rust are rarely found in Jalame cullet and vessels but are abundant in knock-offs and moils. Half or more of the knock-offs contain sizable flakes of rust dislodged from tips of blowirons. Many large flakes (some nearly a centimeter in greatest dimension) remain at the surface of contact with the tool. Considering how abundant such flakes are in the knock-offs, it is surprising that more rust did not find its way into finished vessels. Clearly the glassmakers took care not to include contaminated knock-offs in cullet to be remelted.

Knock-offs

We have examined about 200 roughly semicircular knock-offs, in an effort to learn more about the blowirons. Some are aqua or olive, but the vast majority are green—a little paler and more yellowish than pieces of green cullet of the same thickness (they probably contain some manganese). The outside diameters of most of the knock-offs are about .035, and the inside diameters about .017. A few seem to have come from larger irons (ca .04 and .021) and a few from smaller irons (ca .029 and .011). Thus the ends of the blowirons most commonly used probably were somewhat larger than .035 in diameter and had a bore diameter of about .017. In profile, the outer curvatures of the knock-offs are sometimes convex

36. If a bubble is one-fifth the diameter of an adjacent bubble, it will take 25 times as long to rise through a glass melt.

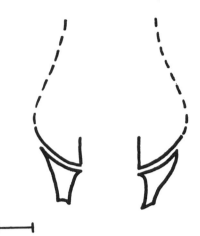

Fig. 9–6. Schematic composite profile of a Jalame knock-off and a possible reconstruction of the end of a blowiron. Scale marker is 1 cm.

and sometimes concave, stretching directly downward. Either form or a combination of both would be expected at the neck of a parison.

Most interesting is that the profiles of the knock-offs, where they were in contact with the ends of the irons, are distinctly curved. These are the surfaces where rust flakes are frequently found. Hence, the ends of the blowirons must also have been curved. These may have just been thickened at the ends and rounded off, or perhaps they were more or less "knob-like" (see Fig. 9–6.) The ends of the medium-sized irons must have had a curvature radius of about .027. This wide end would have afforded a structurally stronger and longer-lived tip, necessitated by the poor quality of the iron. A thin-walled, tube-like blowiron would not have lasted very long. A small fragment of metallic iron, set up from a puddle of molten metal, was found at the site; it could have been related to the manufacture of a blowiron.

Glass Manufacture (Co-authored by John F. Wosinski)

Glassmaking can be divided into two operations: an engineering stage, producing the material from its ingredients,[37] and a handcrafting stage, fashioning the mate-

37. The manufacture of glass material is described as an engineering process because the ingredients must be assembled, prepared, perhaps purified, pulverized, measured, mixed, and then heated to high temperatures for long periods in order to produce the chemical reactions that cause these ingredients to form a glass melt. The initial chemical reactions evolve considerable gaseous products (and water vapor) that cause the batch to froth vigorously. We know from Mesopotamian texts that in the 7th c. B.C.—or perhaps as early as the 12th c. B.C.—glassmaking materials were first heated to form a frit, that is, they were partially reacted in large open trays, allowing the gaseous products to escape and leaving the solid materials in the form of a friable, granular frit. The frit was then crushed and remelted without the complications of the evolution of gases and frothing (see reference in n. 13).

rial into objects. After the glass has been made, it can be worked immediately, as it is in the continuous tanks of modern industrial plants, and as it was in the Herat factory, where only 150 objects were made on a typical day. On the other hand, the glass can be cooled and transported as cullet to another factory, to be resoftened and fashioned into objects. The second factory might be nearby or many miles away, closer to a profitable market. Thus, when cullet is remelted for small-scale operations, it can be done at the glassmakers' convenience and under circumstances that enable them to concentrate on craftsmanship.

There is ample evidence that in ancient times the two stages were sometimes separate, for sizable chunks of cullet occasionally turn up in unexpected places, where they were either in transit or being held to be made into objects. Examples are the cullet aboard the Serçe Liman wreck and that found at Aphrodisias.[38] This division of stages may also be inferred from a passage in the Talmud.[39] Here it is implied that two kinds of glass were transported: one consisting of vessels which, if dropped to the ground and broken, would be ruined; the other, lumps of glass, if dropped and broken, would still be usable.

We surmise that Beth Shearim was a place where glass was made as a material, and Jalame a place where cullet was made into objects. The types of waste materials expected to have accompanied the engineering stage of glassmaking (partially reacted batch, raked-off froth, spilled glass filled with foreign matter, etc.) were conspicuously absent at Jalame.[40]

Refractory Materials

On the western slope of the site, in the factory dump, were found many large pieces of what seemed to be refractory materials, furnace debris, and nondescript waste. These were apparently dumped there when the glass furnace was repaired from time to time. Most of these finds must have been associated with glassmaking, because they had been heated to high temperatures and consisted generally of glass intermixed with limey material. In some cases this appears to be heavily calcined limestone; in others it looks more like a plastery conglomerate (see Chap. 2). In many instances molten glass had run down surfaces of the host material, while

in others numerous fingers of molten glass had penetrated the matrix itself.

Embedded in some of the plastery conglomerates (in the area identified as sorting floors, see Chap. 2) are thousands of glass splinters, fragments of blown vessels and cullet. Most of the pieces of glass preserved sharp edges and showed no evidence of sagging. Hence, that conglomerate had never been brought to red heat. An X-ray diffraction pattern of a sample of one of them showed the plastery matrix to be calcite, not gypsum. Hence the floor from which this piece came was made of lime plaster or local soil, not gypsum plaster.

When some large pieces were sawed open, the results were surprising. Pieces that looked like a stony substance on the surface were often found to have interiors consisting of once-molten glass intermingled with disintegrating limestone. The glass in such pieces is heavily devitrified because it is rich in dissolved calcium. The predominating crystal phase is wollastonite, $CaO.SiO_2$. The devitrification, along with the disintegrated state of the host substance, indicates that hot glass had been in contact with the limestone for several hours or even perhaps a few days. The maximum temperature must have been at least 900–950°C. The shapes of some large chunks suggest they were architectural elements in the furnace structure. Some had squared-off corners and others had adhering glass in shapes which suggest that the glass had run down into crevices between loosely joined blocks.

Among the hundreds of large pieces of cullet excavated, quite a number have a distinctive opaque, oatmeal-colored appearance and a pebbled surface texture. Almost all preserve one flat surface—the top of the original glass melt. The opacity is caused by unreacted batch materials, principally silica, which accumulated on the surface of the melt and formed a hard, dense, frothy layer of "scum" upon cooling. The layer often extends .05 or more into the glass, gradually thinning. There is no sharp demarcation between scum and clear glass. Petrographic examinations and X-ray diffraction patterns established that the scum consists of unreacted sand grains that had been largely transformed into cristobalite, a high-temperature crystalline modification of silica. In some regions the glass had also partially devitrified, forming crystals of wollastonite and a little $Na_2O.2CaO.3SiO_2$, a devitrification phase resembling devitrite ($Na_2O.3CaO.6SiO_2$). Near the surfaces some of the crystalline phases had weathered to calcite ($CaCO_3$). Under the microscope individual grains show a core of alpha-quartz (the original crystalline phase of the sand) which is internally shattered, having passed through the alpha-quartz to beta-quartz inversion. The cristobalite envelops the remains of the reacting quartz grains.

It is tempting to regard this scum as reacting batch

38. G. F. Bass, "The Shipwreck at Serçe Liman, Turkey," *Archaeology* 32 (1979) 36–43; and Brill, as in n. 1, pp. 51–52.

39. *Babylonian Talmud, Shabbath*, 154. See Chap. 3, n. 2, for details.

40. Examples of such material are the partially reacted batch at the bottom of the Beth Shearim slab (see n. 33), some unpublished materials from Arsuf, a few bits from the Viking settlement excavations at York (unpublished examination of samples provided by Dr. Addyman), and finds from the 18th c. Amelung factory (for a general description see I. N. Hume, "Archaeological Excavations on the Site of John Frederick Amelung's New Bremen Glass Manufactory, 1962–1963," *JGS* 18 [1976] 137–214).

materials brought to the surface during melting. However, because the material is so well melted beneath, and because the melt was probably heated from above, we believe the scum to be a residue of a dry batch loaded onto an already existing glass melt that, for some reason, was never heated sufficiently to take the new batch completely into solution. It would have been much more difficult for the Jalame glassmakers to make objects from this scum-containing cullet than from the regular cullet. The latter could have simply been softened at about 1050°C and worked directly. That contaminated with the scum would have had to be heated perhaps 50–100°C hotter and soaked for several hours in order to fully dissolve the cristobalite and yield a glass suitable for use.

The Furnace

The remains of a structure thought to have been the glass furnace are described in detail in Chap. 3. The remains comprise a foundation enclosing a rectangular area filled from wall to wall with material quite different in appearance and properties from the soil on the rest of the site. Its gritty nature and generally reddish color suggested the nickname *Red Room*. The fill had clearly been fired to a high temperature, and the inner surfaces of the foundation stones had been partially calcined. This, then, is presumed to have been the location of the glass furnace, albeit by default. Nowhere else on the site was there evidence of the heavy burning that must be associated with a furnace. Surrounding the foundation walls were floors with splinters of glass and vessel fragments embedded in them.

The fill of the room (measuring 2.40 x 3.60, average depth about .60) extended from below topsoil down to the thin layer of brown soil immediately on bedrock. As mentioned in Chap. 3, that thin layer seemed to have been tamped down to make an even floor. The gritty material that made up the bulk of the fill was stratified in horizontal bands clearly visible when freshly exposed. The chemical composition and microscopic appearance of the materials in each of these bands, however, were so similar as to make them indistinguishable. A typical profile in one central location showed that five distinct bands were colored as follows:

Topsoil	whitish, limey	0–.08
Band I	strong orange	.08–.15
	orangey transition	
Band II	brick red	.24–.37
	orange transition	
Band III	brick-red/purplish	.45–.55
	whitish	.55–.60
	brown soil	varying to bedrock

The color variation evidently resulted from variations in the oxidation state of the iron in each band. Presumably, a long time was required to generate this large volume of fill, so the five bands appear to represent long-term variations in the prevailing redox conditions.

Chemical analyses (Table 9–14) indicate that despite the color differences, the material consisted almost entirely of calcium carbonate. The table also shows analyses of the local limestone, foundation stones, and the powdery white soil accumulated in pockets throughout the site. Hand specimens of the Red Room fill could be crumbled into nut-sized irregular lumps with uneven surfaces. When further worked between the fingers, they could be reduced to still smaller lumps and a powdery material. Dissection under the microscope showed that all the material consisted of three components and that the difference between lumps and powder was purely one of state of aggregation.

The calcite (calcium carbonate) was stained a reddish color by iron oxide. From its color and texture, one could mistake this material for disintegrated clay brick, were it not that chemical analysis showed it to contain a much greater proportion of calcium carbonate than of any clay-like or siliceous substances. When treated with acid, the material was found to contain approximately six times as much carbonate as siliceous material. Occasional lumps resembled remains of bricks or plastered surfaces because they had a somewhat laminar appearance and sometimes contained fine impressions of vegetable fiber such as are usually associated with temper. However, these pieces also were much richer in carbonate than in siliceous components.

In addition to the limey phase with red staining, pockets of a very fine-grained, pure white material were dispersed throughout the grit bed. Chemical analysis, X-ray diffraction, and petrographic examination all confirmed that this material was also calcite, but this phase is a secondary deposit that must have originated from the calcining of natural limestone. This would have yielded finely powdered calcium oxide, which would later have hydrated and reacted with carbon dioxide either from the air or from dissolved carbonate in percolating ground water. In either event, finely divided calcium carbonate would have been reprecipitated. Possibly the material was redissolved by ground water and redeposited several times within the grit bed during its sixteen centuries in the earth.

The third component is a mixture of several minor mineralogical phases which together account for about 10–15% of the fill material as an acid-insoluble residue. Only small quantities of silica and moderate quantities of clay-like residues are present. Silica in the form of sand grains was rarely found in the fill.

Table 9-14. Analyses of Red-Room Fill, Limestones, and Soils

	"Red Room" (Band II) 694	"Red Room" (Band I) 4326		Limestone (Bedrock) 4320	Limestone (Block) 4321	Limestone (Calcined) 4322
Acid-Soluble Portion*						
$CaCO_3$	76.2	68.2	$CaCO_3$	99.07	97.82	101.39
$Ca(OH)_2$	3.14	13.7	$MgCO_3$	0.36	0.42	0.38
Al_2O_3	3.76	4.76	Na_2CO_3	< 0.01	< 0.01	0.05
Fe_2O_3	1.46	2.19	K_2CO_3	< 0.01	0.03	0.07
MgO	0.66	0.78	Al_2O_3	0.03	0.07	0.07
Na_2CO_3	0.67	1.16	Fe_2O_3	0.012	0.034	0.028
K_2CO_3	0.43	0.39	SiO_2	0.0X	0.X	0.X
MnO_2	0.03	0.03	TiO_2	nf	0.00X	0.00X
CuO	0.008	0.010	BaO	nf	nf	0.00X
ZnO	0.010	0.011	SrO	0.0X	0.0X	0.0X
			MnO_2	0.000X	0.000X	0.000X
			CuO	0.000X	0.000X	0.000X
Σ	(86.37%)	(91.23%)	Σ	~99.6%	~98.9%	~102.5%
Acid-Insoluble Portion						
SiO_2	10.17	13.01				
R_2O_3 †	0.42	0.87				
Σ	(10.59%)	(13.88%)				
Σ	96.96%	105.11%**				

If the stones enclosing the Red Room represent the foundation of the furnace, the remains of the interior must represent the firing chamber. The fill would have been generated by the ashes of the fuel and by calcium oxide sifted down from the calcining of the furnace structure. Chemical analyses did not show the presence of much alkali (particularly potassium), magnesium, or phosphorus, all of which would be expected to have made up a good part of the ash. No charred remains of organic matter were found. The lack of alkali and magnesia in the fill can be rationalized by assuming that they were leached out over many years of exposure to ground water. Some of the calcium now present as carbonate would have come in with the fuel, but most of it can be accounted for only by the calcining of parts of the furnace structure or refractories. The lack of charred remains can be explained only by assuming that the fuel was in small pieces and that the firing was strongly oxidizing.

Eight samples of the red, orange, and purplish bands in the fill were removed for thermoremnant magnetism measurements. These measurements were carried out by Dr. Martin Aitken of the Research Laboratory for Art and Archaeology at Oxford.[41] He reported mean values

41. M. J. Aitken and H. N. Hawley, "Archaeomagnetic Measurements in Britain-IV, Appendix," *Archaeometry* 10 (1967) 135. Also Brill, *Field Notes*, 20 July 1965.

for the samples of I = 46.6° and D = 2.3°E and also noted that the values for individual samples agreed with one another. Because no reference data for that part of the world were available, the measurements were not useful for dating the material. However, that the samples had measurable magnetic fields whose orientations agreed with one another proved the gritty fill had been fired in situ and was not simply a mixture of fired materials from other locations that had been dumped into the space enclosed by the walls. This proves the Red Room was the firing chamber of a pyrotechnological installation.

The only contents of the fill recorded by this author, other than the gritty material, were four small potsherds. The largest of these (from Band III) was ca .07 in greatest dimension. By comparison with samples of pottery heated in a gradient furnace, it is estimated that the fill where these potsherds were found never reached a temperature in excess of 875–900°C. A small potsherd found nearby showed the beginning effects of prolonged accidental heating; it had probably reached a temperature approaching 900°C. Another potsherd (lost in the Corning flood) from the white ashy layer at the bottom of the fill was recorded as having been heavily burned; it had probably reached 900–950°C.

The components found in the fill are consistent with its being the ashy remains of the firing chamber of a fur-

	Drifted Soil 691	Drifted Soil 692
$CaCO_3$	49.4	49.7
$Ca(OH)_2$	18.7	14.1
MgO	1.05	1.08
Na_2CO_3	0.31	0.14
K_2CO_3	0.81	0.84
Al_2O_3	3.25	3.16
Fe_2O_3	2.16	2.16
SiO_2+ insol. R_2O_3 (Ave. of 2 detn.)	~24.6	~ 32.6
Σ	~100.3%**	~103.8**

* Quantitative atomic absorption analyses for all metals, and evolution for CO_2. Anions were not analyzed, and those reported for the salts are arbitrarily chosen. Taken up in ~ 10% HCl.
† R_2O_3 consists of oxides of Na, K, Ca, Mg, Al, and Fe.
** Acid-soluble analysis run on different sample, accounting for part of the error in summation. Arbitrary selection of anions also contributes.
†† This calcined block may have contained some $Ca(OH)_2$ instead of being all $CaCO_3$. This would account for the high summation.
nf Not found.
Data reported as X instead of numerical digits are spectrographic estimates. Elements sought spectrographically but not found: Zr, V, Ni, Cr, B, Li, Mo, Zn, Bi, Sn, Cd, In, Be, Ga, Ge, P, Co, W, Sb, Pb.

nace. What was missing, however, was glass in any form. A few bits of broken vessel glass and some cullet were found in crevices between the fill and the foundation. Only four or five small pieces were found inside the foundation walls; these had not been misshapen by accidental firing and thus had not been heated in situ to a temperature of 650–700°C or greater for more than a few minutes. No foreign matter, such as the grit that made up the fill, was adhering to their surfaces. Thus it is likely that these pieces of glass were intrusions.

It is difficult to reconcile this lack of glass finds of any sort—drippings, waste, rundown, misshapen blobs, etc.—with the structure's presumed role as a glass furnace. It seems almost inconceivable that glass in some form would not have found its way into the firing chamber, unless there was a physical barrier isolating the firing chamber from the part of the furnace containing softened glass. Of this no evidence remains.

The dilemma is this: In order to accept the Red Room as the location of the glassmaking furnace, one must either (1) hypothesize the existence and removal of an isolating barrier, or (2) place the entire glass-working part of the furnace outside the walls (for which there is no evidence), or (3) abandon certain preconceived notions about what kind of evidence constitutes a condition for assigning a glassmaking function to a structure.

There is an interesting similarity—but a more signifi-

cant dissimilarity—between the Red Room and the Beth Shearim slab.[42] This huge piece of glass (8.8 tons) was excavated in a silted-up cistern adjacent to the ancient necropolis, about 5 km southeast of Jalame. The slab was melted (probably between the 4th and 7th centuries), in a rectangular tank made of limestone blocks, and left there to cool. After the glass set up, most of the superstructure and the tank walls were removed. Excavation revealed that the slab still rested on the bottom of the tank in which it had been melted. The outer dimensions of the slab, 1.95 x 3.40 (.45 in thickness) are quite close to the inner dimensions of the Red Room, 2.40 x 3.60. One might imagine that these measurements represent traditional dimensions for glassmaking structures in ancient times in that part of the world. Alternatively, the similarity might be fortuitous and represent a size that pyrotechnologists of the time could manage conveniently.

The tank in which the Beth Shearim slab was melted was not heated from below, since it would have been impossible for heat to penetrate blocks .15–.20 thick and melt the glass above without completely disintegrating the limestone. Excavation verified this obvious fact; the blocks on the tank bottom rested directly on some 1.50 of fine silt that showed no evidence of thermal damage where the two came in contact. Five firing chambers were found to have surrounded the tank on three sides. The bases of these chambers were at about the level of the bottom of the tank. The hot gases from the firing chambers were carried by a draft into the main part of the tank and reverberated downward, melting the glass batch.

The dissimilarity between the Red Room and the slab is that at Beth Shearim five ancillary firing chambers located at the level of the tank heated one large working volume. In contrast, in whatever furnace structure one hypothesizes for the Red Room at Jalame (see Chap. 3), a single large firing chamber must have been located beneath smaller glassworking areas. The two installations undoubtedly performed entirely different functions, and the structural remains appear more unlike than like each other.

With sparse evidence and with most of the structural elements scattered and broken, reconstruction of the superstructure of the Red Room must be conjectural. The partial reconstruction illustrated in Fig. 3–8 is believed by the field director possibly to fit the evidence. The only disappointing aspect of the excavation was the impossibility of achieving a completely convincing picture of the appearance of the glass furnace.

42. See n. 33.

Glass-Melting Containers

Considerable doubt remains about the nature of the containers in which the glass was melted. No remains of ceramic crucibles were found. Crucibles made of clay used for the household wares found on the site would not have withstood the temperatures required to make or work Jalame glass. Gradient furnace experiments were made on two samples of this pottery sawed into strips. Their appearance was altered noticeably by heating the strips to about 890–910°C for 24 hours. Thus the original firing must have been below that temperature. If the pottery was raised to about 1000°C, it swelled, frothed, and eventually began to vitrify. At a temperature of 1040–1100°C, it collapsed to a fluid liquid that set up as a clear, dark brown glass upon cooling.

Judging from the physical remains, it appears that the melting containers were made of local limestone, improbable as that may seem. Apparently, they were rectangular in shape, probably cut from a single block, leaving walls and a base of generous thickness. They would have had to be heated from above. Limestone can hardly be regarded as a satisfactory refractory material. When heated to about 900°C, its main component, calcium carbonate, gives off carbon dioxide, leaving calcium oxide. If heated long enough, even a large piece of limestone becomes calcined, disintegrating into a fine powdery material. Experiments with native bedrock and unheated foundation stones from Jalame proved that both disintegrate to a floury powder at or below 900°C. Also, we know from the viscosity curve of Jalame glass that in order to be resoftened sufficiently to be blown into vessels, the glass has to be heated to at least 1000°C. Gradient furnace experiments were done in which both natural limestone and preheated samples of limestone were heated in contact with softened Jalame glass. The natural limestone retained its shape at 900°C but became soft and chalky. The preheated limestone (really calcium oxide) dissolved completely and quickly in the softened glass. On this small scale, then, the limestone has no refractory properties. Nevertheless, its use for a glass-melting tank is not impossible. This is demonstrated on a huge scale at Beth Shearim: that tank was made of limestone. As we have described, a reverberatory arrangement was used whereby the glass batch was melted from above. As a result, the batch was raised to a temperature considerably higher than that of the tank, and the bottom of the batch was not completely reacted. While the upper surface of the tank floor was somewhat chalky, the lower part retained its physical integrity, remaining about as hard as shell.

A similar arrangement on a smaller scale at Jalame would have allowed cullet to be remelted in limestone containers. In fact, this system is consistent with the evidence, although the hot glass must eventually have corroded the limestone severely. As the corrosion advanced, accelerated by the thermal disintegration of the calcium carbonate, it produced the composite intermediate zone observed in many of the large pieces of conglomerate found in the dump. Although the limestone in contact with the glass would have failed rapidly, that near the bottom of the container would have survived longer. If the melt was "topped off" continuously by the addition of cullet—and the whole was not stirred vigorously—the glass at the top would probably have remained clear and satisfactory for use, only occasionally dissolving enough lime to make it unusable.

Because limestone is relatively soft[43] and it would have been easy to make new containers when the old ones failed, there is no serious objection to this picture if the process was of short duration. Such a system would be extremely wasteful of glass, and this is corroborated by the massive quantities of discarded glass and conglomerate found at Jalame. The author is uneasy in concluding that the Jalame glass was melted in limestone containers, but that is the picture that seems to fit the archaeological evidence best, while still maintaining plausibility.

Isotope Studies

Lead Isotope Ratios (Tables 9–15 and 9–16)

The determination of lead isotope ratios has become routine in studying ancient objects containing lead.[44] The method allows one to identify ancient mining regions that could have been the source of any particular lead sample, and those that could not have been. Isotope ratios for five specimens of metallic lead from Jalame were analyzed.[45] The samples came from a lead votive or mirror, from an object of unidentified use, from a lead weight, from a piece of lead sheeting, and from a lead dripping. The data are reported in Table 9–15 and summarized in Table 9–16. Three samples of lead extracted from glasses were also run.

The metallic samples are similar but not identical to one another isotopically. Three (Nos. Pb–220, 222, and 223) fall in the Group X type of lead, a type frequently

43. We refer here to the natural, relatively unweathered local limestone, not the exposed weathered stone that is almost chalky in appearance and texture. The latter would be an even worse refractory, because the weathered stone reacts much more rapidly with hot glass.

44. For general information see R. H. Brill and J. M. Wampler, "Isotope Studies of Ancient Lead," *AJA* 71 (1967) 63–77; R. H. Brill, "Lead Isotopes in Ancient Glass," *Annales, JIV* (1967) 255–61; R. H. Brill, "Lead Isotopes in Ancient Coins," *Special Publication No. 8*, Royal Numismatic Society (Oxford, 1972) 279–303; R. H. Brill, "Scientific Studies of the Panel Materials," *Kenchreai, Eastern Port of Corinth* (Leiden, 1976) 225–55. See also reference in n. 49.

45. By I. L. Barnes, E. C. Deal, and J. M. Wampler (then a guest worker) of the National Bureau of Standards.

Table 9–15. Lead Isotope Ratios*

Sample No.	Pb^{207}/Pb^{206}	Pb^{208}/Pb^{206}	Pb^{204}/Pb^{206}	Isotopic Type
Jalame				
Pb–219	0.8429	2.0822	0.05382	E/X
Pb–220	0.8393	2.0750	0.05355	X
Pb–221	0.8417	2.0815	0.05378	E/X
Pb–222	0.8382	2.0759	0.05351	X
Pb–223	0.8403	2.0785	0.05367	X
Pb–1189	0.8408	2.0808	0.05365	X
Pb–1190	0.8417	2.0821	0.05374	X
Beth She'arim				
Pb–657	0.8433	2.0881	0.05389	E
Pb–191**	0.846	2.088	0.0535	E (?)

*   All samples were analyzed by Emile Deal and J. Marion Wampler (then a guest worker) at The National Bureau of Standards, collaborating with I. Lynus Barnes and William R. Shields.
**   Early data, may not be as reliable.

encountered in leads associated with a region extending from Alexandria along the Palestinian and Syrian coast and around the southern shore of Turkey, also including parts of Mesopotamia. The actual mining regions that supplied this lead remain unidentified, although some leads of this type may occur in central Turkey, Syria, and possibly in the Zagros mountains. The two other samples (Nos. Pb–219 and 221) fall on the borderline of the E and X Groups. They are close to a group of leads in bronzes associated with Constantinople. It is not uncommon for leads from a single Near Eastern site to have this much isotopic spread. Because the region does not produce lead,[46] the metal was often salvaged and reused, resulting in mixtures of leads from different mines.

Of greater interest are isotopic analyses of lead extracted from three Jalame glasses. Sample Pb–1190 came from the light blue glass No. 3612. This contained about .65% PbO. It was colored by copper, believed to have been derived from leaded bronze coins or an artifact. Isotopically, the lead in this glass is like that in Pb–221, the lead votive, falling within the isotopic range containing both metallic leads and leads from bronzes associated with Constantinople. That same kind of lead was in use there for centuries. Soon it should be possible to identify the actual mining region from which it came.

Two other glasses (Nos. 3611, 3601) are colored with

cobalt and contain only traces of copper. They are interesting because findings from our laboratory and the National Bureau of Standards (unpublished) show that the cobalt in ancient dark blue glasses is often accompanied by small quantities of lead. There are many ramifications of this research, but especially interesting is the fact that isotope analyses of the lead in dark blue glasses reveal patterns that should eventually allow us to identify the mining regions that supplied the cobalt. The leads in many of these glasses are of the Group E type. They resemble the lead associated with Constantinople, while others differ somewhat. At least some of the leads and, therefore, some of the cobalt appear to have come from Iran.[47] Other possible sources are being investigated.

It is significant that two cobalt-colored glasses from Jalame contain leads of different isotopic composition. Pb–1189, from No. 3611, contained .35% PbO. Its lead is on the borderline of Groups E and X. This waste material, possibly a knock-off, was directly related to glassmaking. The lead in Pb–1188, the dark blue blob from No. 3601, has considerably lower ratios. That lead came from a different region, and presumably its cobalt colorant did as well.

Table 9–16 lists the eight Jalame samples in order of their descending Pb^{207}/Pb^{206} ratios, along with other analyzed leads with similar isotope ratios. Proximity in the table indicates similarity in isotopic composition

46. We have heard of galena deposits in "Syria" but have not been able to obtain samples of them or information on their locations.

47. See reference to Brill and Barnes cited in n. 8.

Table 9–16. Some Leads Similar to the Jalame Leads +

Sample Numbers	Brief Descriptions
Pb-657	Beth Shearim, Late Roman Imperial bronze coin (beneath slab.)
Pb-600 series	Five somewhat similar bronze coins from Alexandria, Heraclia, Antioch, and Phoenicia. They date from 2nd c BC through 4th c AC
*	
260 series	Zerek Camii, leads and stained glass, ca 1125
460 series	Kenchreai panels, six red opaque glasses, ca 365 AD
418	Denderah, red opaque glass, 1-2nd c AC
433	Beth Shan, yellow opaque tessera, 5th c AC
Pb-219	Jalame, lead drippings
662	Syria (?), bronze head of Julia Domna, ca 200
Pb-221	Jalame, lead weight
Pb-1190	Jalame, light blue glass drippings (no. 3612)
431	Ravenna, green opaque tessera, 4-6th c
Pb-1189	Jalame, dark blue waste glass (no. 3611)
204	Shavei Zion, green opaque tessera, 4-5th c
205	Shavei Zion, red opaque tessera, 4-5th c
1030	Islamic cameo cut glass, emerald green, 10-11th c
415	Egypt, yellow opaque glass, 4-2nd c BC
1015	(?), yellow opaque, ribbon glass, 1st c AC
434	Beth Shan, green opaque tessera, 5th c AC
438	Hagia Sophia, red opaque tessera, 9-10th c
Pb-223	Jalame, lead weight
224	Soli, Cilicia, lead medallion with heads of Aratos and Chrysippos, ca 250-240 BC
* (?)	
229	Ganei-Hamat, Tiberias, lead, 8-10th c
432	Beth Shan, red opaque tessera, 5th c AC
Pb-220	Jalame, lead sheet
228	Ganei-Hamat Tiberias, lead, 8-10th c
Pb-222	Jalame, lead mend
430	Ravenna, red opaque tessera, 4-6th c
*	
1182	Hagia Sophia, dark blue tessera, 9-10th c
Pb-1188	Jalame, dark blue blob on lamp (no. 3601)
1183	Hagia Sophia, dark blue tessera, 9-10th c

* Indicates a significant difference between the samples it separates. Samples that are single-spaced are virtually identical. Samples that are double-spaced are similar but not identical.

† Most of these samples are unpublished. Pb–622 was published in R. H. Brill, "New Directions in Lead Isotope Research," in W. Young, ed., *Application of Science in Examination of Works of Art* (Museum of Fine Arts, Boston, 1970) 73–83. For Kenchreai glass see R. Brill, "Scientific Studies of the Panel Materials," in L. Ibrahim, R. Scranton, and R. Brill, *Kenchreai, Eastern Port of Corinth* (Leiden, 1976) 225–55. For bronze coins see R. H. Brill, "Lead Isotopes in Ancient Coins," in E. T. Hall and D. M. Metcalf, *Methods of Chemical and Metallurgical Investigation of Ancient Coinage*, Special Publication No. 8, Royal Numismatic Society (London, 1972) 279–303. Sample Pb–224 was submitted by H. Ingholt.

Table 9–17. Calculated and Experimental O^{18} Contents of Some Jalame Glasses

Sample	$\delta_{calc.}$†	$\delta_{calc.}$**	$\delta_{exptl.}$
0–163	14.7$_9$	14.3$_4$	14.17
0–165	14.5$_5$	14.1$_3$	14.64
0–168	14.6$_7$	14.2$_4$	14.07
0–167	–	–	14.40
0–170	–	–	15.17

* δ_{calc} values were calculated by treating δ as an additive property.

+ The following values were assummed:
δ_{SiO_2} = 10.93 (Belus River beach sand, quartz fraction)
δ_{CaO} = 29.02 (Belus River beach sand, shell-hash fraction)
δ_{Na_2O} = 39.77 (modern natron from Wadi Natrun)
$\delta_{K_2O} = \delta_{Na_2O}$
$\delta_{MgO} = \delta_{CaO}$
$\delta_{R_2O_3}$ = 15.00

** The following fractionation effects were assumed:
in melts: $\delta_{CO_2} - \delta_{melt}$ = 3.0
in dolomite: $\delta_{CO_2} - \delta_{dol}$ = 4.0

and, hence, likelihood of a common lead-mining source.[48]

Oxygen Isotopes (Table 9–17)

The determination of O^{18} contents is extremely valuable in investigating ancient glasses.[49] The study of five fragments of cullet from Jalame played an important role in developing the theory behind this research and produced evidence concerning the raw materials used for making the glass.

The large majority of oxygen atoms in nature have a mass of 16 atomic units, designated O^{16}. But approximately one out of every 500 atoms is a heavier isotope O^{18}. Because oxygen atoms freely interchange with one another in nature, the element fractionates (separates partially into its isotopes) relatively easily. Consequently, different atmospheric, liquid, and mineral occurrences of oxygen and its compounds contain slightly different percentages of O^{18}. The O^{18} contents of many such materials have been determined by geochemists and geologists. The O^{18} content of any particular sample is expressed by Δ.[50]

48. We have extensive data on many other ancient glasses containing lead, reported at the 79th General Meeting of the Archaeological Institute of America in Atlanta, Ga., Dec. 1977.

49. See R. H. Brill, "Lead and Oxygen Isotopes in Ancient Objects," *The Impact of the Natural Sciences on Archaeology* (The British Academy, London, 1970) 143–64.

50. Δ is the deviation in parts per thousand of the O^{18} content of the sample from that of an accepted standard designated as standard mean ocean water (s.m.o.w.). Thus, the O^{18} content of standard mean ocean water has by definition a value of zero on the scale of Δ values. Substances having a positive Δ value have an excess of O^{18} over the standard; those with negative values are deficient in O^{18}.

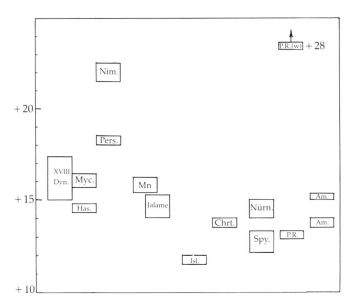

Fig. 9-7. Summary of oxygen-isotope data for approximately 75 samples of early glasses. Boxes contain varying numbers of samples from different periods and sites or regions. Boxes proceed in chronological order from left to right. Five Jalame glasses are labeled. Other abbreviations are for XVIIIth Dynasty Egypt, Mycenae, Hasanlu, Nimrud, Persepolis, manganese-containing glass of the Roman period, Islamic glasses, stained glasses from Chartres, Nürnberg, and Speyer, Port Royal in Jamaica, and the Amelung factory site. P.R.(w) is a weathered glass from Port Royal. All determinations were made by Robert N. Clayton and Toshiko Mayeda.

Since many of the raw materials of which glasses are made differ in their O^{18} contents, and oxygen is the most abundant element in glass, some 45–50% by mass, it was postulated that the O^{18} contents of the glasses might reflect the O^{18} contents of the ingredients from which they were made. The O^{18} contents of 75 man-made glasses spanning some 34 centuries and coming from widely separate origins were determined in order to see what range of values of Δ they would show.[51] As Fig. 9–7 shows, the range of Δ values for these glasses is considerable. Thus the prospects are promising for developing a scheme for classifying ancient glasses on the basis of O^{18} contents in a manner like that based on chemical analyses. Most important, oxygen isotope studies provide an essentially independent means of classification. For example, glasses with similar chemical compositions may have entirely different O^{18} contents if they were made from raw materials from different sources.

The O^{18} contents determined for the five samples of cullet from Jalame are reported in Table 9–17 and plotted in Fig. 9–4. Four of the Δ values agree very well with one

51. These determinations were made by Prof. Robert N. Clayton and Mrs. Toshiko Mayeda of the Fermi Institute, using techniques they devised for their studies of silicate and carbonate rocks and minerals.

another (Nos. 163, 165, 167, and 168) while the fifth, No. 170, is a little higher.

Assuming that Belus River sand was used for making the glasses, Δ is fixed for the silica at 10.93 and Δ for the lime at 29.02. These are the experimentally determined mean values for the quartz and calcium carbonate-bearing fractions of three samples of sand collected from dunes at the mouth of the river. We selected a value of 39.77, the mean of experimentally determined values for two samples of modern natron from Wadi Natrun, as the most likely for the alkali of Jalame glasses. By assuming an additive relationship and corrections for fractionation processes occurring during melting, values were calculated for glasses having the analyzed chemical compositions of the Jalame specimens. The results are in close agreement with the experimentally determined values for the actual Jalame glasses (see Table 9–17). These results strongly support the hypothesis that Jalame glasses were made from ingredients resembling modern Belus River sand, with its shell hash, and an alkali source having an O^{18} content like that of the two natron specimens. Thus, the O^{18} results are an independent verification of conclusions drawn from chemical analyses.

Catalogue

Glass, Vessels

Fragments with Trail Decoration

*815   Bottle, neck fragment with trail decoration. Green, lightly weathered. Probably like G260 J64. D .045. J64 29. Trench A, no. 29.

*816   Bottle, rim fragment with trail decoration. Green, moderately weathered. Like G155 J64. D .06. J64–43.

*818   Bottle or flask, rim fragment with trail decoration. Aqua, moderately weathered. Type like No. 816. D .01. Trench M–3, topsoil.

s820   Vessel, wall fragment with trail decoration. Colorless with blue trailing, moderately weathered. J65–AZ, Trench M–1, no. 7 (mixture of blue and colorless).

s821   Jug, rim fragment with trail decoration. Pale green with blue trailing, moderately weathered. Probably like G403 J64. Sample is of pale green glass mixed with blue glass. Trench A–5, no. 42.

Base Fragments of Small Vessels and Lamps

s823   Cup or bowl, base fragment. Greenish aqua, lightly weathered. Pushed-in and flattened, air space at fold. D .045. Trench A–5, no. 42.

*827   Lamp, base fragment with part of body. Green, moderately weathered. Solid base, tooled, wall spreading out and up. Pontil mark. Like G220 J65. D .035. Trench L, no. 21.

*828 Beaker or lamp, base fragment with part of body. Green, moderately weathered. Solid base, tooled, wall spreading out and up. Pontil mark. D .04. Trench J–6.

*829 Beaker or lamp, base fragment with part of body. Green, lightly weathered. Solid base, tooled, wall spreading out and up. Pontil mark. D .04. Trench A–5, no. 42.

*831 Beaker or lamp, base fragment with part of body. Green, lightly weathered. Solid base, tooled, wall spreading out and up. Pontil mark. D .035. J64–8

Rim Fragments of Large Vessels

*833 Bowl, rim and wall fragment. Green, moderately weathered. Rounded rim with thickened horizontal rib below wall, bending in gently as far as preserved. Probably from large, shallow footed bowl.

s835 Bowl, rim and wall fragment. Aqua, lightly weathered. Thickened, rounded rim, outfolded with air space. Probably from large bowl. D .28. Trench A–5, no. 42.

*836 Trailed decoration from large globular vessel. Green, moderately weathered. Trench M–1, no. 7.

Rim Fragments of Small Vessels

*837 Bottle, rim fragment with single trail. Aqua, moderately weathered. Rounded rim tapers into conical neck with thick single trail applied horizontally. Like G78 J 65. D .07. Trench A–5, no. 42.

*841 Bowl, rim and wall fragment. Aqua, lightly weathered. Rounded rim with thickened horizontal rib below rim. Wall bends in gently as far as preserved. From large deep bowl. Like No. 833. D .026. Trench J, no. 17.

*843 Bowl, rim and body fragment with wheel-abraded decoration below rim. Pale green, slightly weathered. Unworked rim, possibly lightly ground, spreading out and up from constriction above globular body. Trench L, no. 46.

Base Fragments

*844 Plate or bowl, base fragment. Green, slightly weathered. Trench L, no. 43.

*845 Dish or plate, foot and wall fragment. Aqua, moderately weathered. Trench A–5, no. 39.

*846 Bowl, base and wall fragment. Green, moderately weathered. Flat vessel with tubular base-ring. D .07. Trench L, no. 21.

*852 Bowl or plate, tubular base ring and wall fragment. Olive, moderately weathered. Small tubular base-ring bending in and down as far as preserved, wall spreading up and out. Trench L, no. 12.

*c853 Vessel, tubular base-ring fragment. Olive, lightly weathered. Trench L, no. 12.

Miscellaneous

*854 Bottle, wall fragment with thick vertical rib. Green, moderately weathered. Trench L, no. 21.

*855 Vessel, thick-walled fragment. Colorless, moderately weathered. J67–N.

856 Vessel, thin-walled vessel fragment. Purple, heavily weathered, black weathering crust. J65–AJ. Trench M–1, no. 25.

*857 Vessel, thin-walled vessel fragment. Pale purple, heavily weathered, black weathering crust. Trench M–3, topsoil.

*858 Vessel, thin-walled fragment. Colorless, heavily weathered. J64–105. Trench A–3, no. 105.

Glass, Special Objects

s3600 Lamp, fragment of wall with applied blobs and scratched horizontal decoration. G150 J66. Colorless body with dark blue transparent blobs, moderately weathered. Sample of colorless glass only.

s3601 Same object as No. 3600. Sample of blue glass only.

3610 Reference glass JL. Consists of powdered mixture of numerous pieces of Jalame glasses.

s3611 Waste glass, possibly knock-off. Dark blue transparent, moderately weathered.

s3612 Drippings and trailings. Light blue transparent, heavily weathered with surface devitrification. Could be drippings from tool or gather or furnace run-down. Trench X–1, no. 136.

s3613 Fragment of waste glass (G250 J66). Light blue transparent, filled with winding bubbles, heavily weathered. Contains few patches of accidental red opaque (cuprite) color. Trench X–1, no. 169.

s3196 Cracked-off overblow or moil. Colorless-pale greenish aqua, very slight iridescence, possibly strained. Apparent complete o.d. .012. Trench L, no. 25.

s3197 Cracked-off overblow or moil. Colorless-pale greenish aqua, black weathering crust, possibly strained. Apparent complete o.d. .012. Trench L, no. 8.

s3198 Cracked-off overblow or moil. Colorless-pale greenish aqua, black weathering crust, strained. Apparent complete o.d. .014. Trench M–1, no. 30.

s3199 Cracked-off overblow or moil. Colorless-pale greenish aqua, black weathering crust, possibly strained. Apparent complete o.d. .013. Trench L, no. 25.

Lead Samples

Pb–219 Lead drippings (not inventoried). Trench Y–3S, no. 86.

Pb–220 Fragment of thin lead sheet (not inventoried). Trench A–3, no. 198A.

Pb–221 Lead weight (M28–65). J65 BN; Trench F–3, no. 76.

Pb–222 Lead mend (M56–65). J65BO; Trench A–6, no. 81.

Pb–223   Lead fishnet weight (M58–65). Trench A–2.

Pb–1188   Blob of dark blue transparent glass decorating lamp fragment. Chem. anal. no. 3601. (PbO ~ .3%).

Pb–1189   Fragment of dark blue transparent waste glass. Chem. anal. no. 3611. (PbO ~ .35%).

Pb–1190   Drippings of light blue transparent glass. Chem. anal. no. 3612. (PbO ~ .65).

Other Materials

Red-Room Fill

694   Hardened nuggets and gritty material with "brick-red" color; from Band II. J64–e.

4326   Hardened nuggets and gritty material with "strong-orange" color; from Band I. J65–BJ.

Limestones

4320   Limestone bedrock from near olive press. Represents local rock. J66–DD.

4321   Architectural limestone block of irregular shape from south wall of Red Room. Represents architectural stonework. J66–DE.

4322   Calcined, white architectural block from near center of north wall of Red Room. Represents friable, chalky stone partially calcined by exposure to heat. J66–DF.

Soils

691   Fine, white, powdery silt accumulated over few days by wind action. From west wall of Red-Room. Represents natural soil found in similar pockets all over site. J65–BA.

692   Fine, white powdery silt accumulated over few days by wind action. Represents natural soil of site (somewhat coarser texture than No. 691). J65–BB.

Appendix: Ferrous to Ferric Ratios
J. W. H. Schreurs

Optical transmission spectra in the ultraviolet, visible, and near infrared (IR) regions and electron paramagnetic resonance spectra (EPR) were obtained for Jalame glasses, as well as for some other ancient glasses, in order to learn what color centers are present. These studies were augmented by chemical analyses.

Fig 9–3 shows the IR spectra of four Jalame samples and of the Hellenistic ribbed bowl fragment, No. 3212. The sample thicknesses, which affect the transmission logarithmically, are given in the caption. The absorption band near 1100 nm is characteristic of Fe^{++}. Although the total iron contents are not very different, there are large differences in the Fe^{++} concentrations, indicating considerable variation in the oxidation states of these glasses. Generally, the purple and colorless glasses have a low Fe^{++} concentration, that is, they are oxidized, while the aqua, green, olive, or amber glasses have higher Fe^{++} concentrations, or are reduced.

Fig. 9–4 gives the derivative of the EPR absorption spectrum of samples 633 and 3212. In these two glasses, the spectrum is mainly due to Fe^{+++} with a small admixture of Mn^{++} (and a trace amount of V^{++++}), both showing up primarily in the region around 3400 Oersted. The presence of V^{++++} also points to the reduced character of these samples. In most of the other ancient glasses there is so much Mn^{++} that it seriously interferes with determining the Fe^{+++} concentration from the EPR spectrum. To determine the absolute Fe^{++} and Fe^{+++} concentrations in the ancient glasses, two experimental glasses, DZO and DZP, were melted for use as standards. DZO was melted under strongly reducing conditions, while DZP was melted under somewhat oxidizing conditions.

From the ratio of the Fe^{+++} intensities in the EPR spectra and the Fe^{++} concentration ratio as determined from the IR spectra, it was determined that in DZO 25.5% of the iron is present as Fe^{+++} and 74.5% as Fe^{++}, while in DZP the percentages are 72.8 and 27.2, respectively.

Assuming the optical extinction coefficient of Fe^{++} in the two experimental glasses is the same as in the ancient glasses, it is possible to calculate the Fe^{++} concentration from the IR transmission spectra. The results are presented in Table 9–11. This assumption is reasonable, because the base glass composition of the ancient glasses is quite close to that of the experimental glasses. However it leads to an underestimate for the Fe^{++} concentration in some of the glasses, as shown by EPR.

In glasses that contain little Mn^{++} (for example, Nos. 633, 3210, 3212, 28359, and 28360) it is possible to calculate the Fe^{+++} concentrations from a comparison with an EPR standard of known Fe^{+++} concentration. These numbers are also given in the table (see Fig. 9–4). The numbers for the three Jalame samples are consistent with the optically determined values for Fe^{++}, but the Fe^{+++} concentrations in the two Hellenistic samples are considerably less than the optical data suggest.

From the table it is clear that the aqua, green, olive, and amber samples are quite reduced, with about 65% or more of the iron in the Fe^{++} state. Also the glasses become more reduced in going from the aqua to the amber glasses. On the other hand, the colorless (No. 3395) and purple (No. 624) glasses are strongly oxidized. No. 3395 was decolorized by oxidation with antimony oxide, while a higher valence manganese oxide (MnO_2) was used to oxidize No. 624.

The EPR spectrum of No. 3212 in Fig. 9–4 (as well as of Nos. 3210, 28359, 5498, 629, and some other Jalame glasses) shows an absorption near 1050 Oersted not seen in the spectrum of No. 633. This absorption is due to a ferri-sulfide complex. It is invariably observed in the amber glasses and, although weaker, in the olive-amber and olive glasses. This center is formed under strongly reducing conditions, when a minute amount of the sulfate present in the glass batch is reduced to the sulfide ion. The sulfide ion forms a complex with some of the remaining Fe^{+++}. This ferri-sulfide chromophore has a very high extinction coefficient[52] and is responsible for

the absorption band near 420 nm observed in the visible spectra of these glasses (Fig. 9–1.) The concentration of this center, virtually absent in the aqua glasses, increases in going from the green to the amber glasses. In the green glasses the concentration is too low for the center to be observed by EPR. From Table 9–11 it is also evident that the ancient glasses contain ample sulfur to form the ferri-sulfide chromophore.

52. D. Loveridge and S. Parke, "Electron spin resonance of Fe^{+++}, Mn^{++}, and Cr^{+++} in glasses," *Physics and Chemistry of Glasses* 12 (1971) 19–27. See also reference in n. 22 above.

Black-and-White Plates

A

B

C

Pl. 1–1. A. Appearance of the site in 1963, before excavation.
B. Jalame from the north. Slope of Mount Carmel at the right.
(Also in color.) C. Jalame from the north, closer view.

Pl. 2–1. A. Ashlar block of Period 1 in situ (bottom foreground). B. Retaining walls running west from unit II (from west, above). C. Unit XVI—courtyard from south. D. Units XVIII and XVI, from west. E. Fallen blocks in unit VIII. F. Southeast corner of unit XVI (at lower left).

A

B

C

D

E

F

Pl. 2–2. A. Unit XVIII from east. B. Doorway in south wall of unit XVIII. C. South part of unit VII with doorway to VIII (from north). D. Unit IX from south. E. Doorway in north wall of unit V (from north). F. Stone weight for early olive press (from west).

Pl. 2–3. A. Ovens or bins in Unit XVI (from south). B. Westernmost oven in unit XVI. C. Detail showing oven construction. D. Lowest floor southwest of unit XIX. E. Pavement in south part of villa. F. Plaster-lined tank in villa basement.

Pl. 2–4. A. Northernmost oven or bin at north end of villa.
B. Three architectural phases represented by early wall at center, later wall at left, wine press wall across top. C. The wine
press (general view from west). D. Wall dividing upper vats
(from north). E. Wine press vats as found (left), and central
room (from northeast). F. North side of central room and tank,
showing plastered surface. G. Central room of wine press
(from north, above).

A

B

C

D

E

F

Pl. 2–5. A. Rock cutting for south wine press wall, east end.
B. Rock cutting for south wine press wall, west end. C. Bedding for mosaic floor of central room. D. Two niches and dividing wall on east side of central room. E. Southern niche, showing mosaic floor. F. Northern niche, showing rock-cut channel.

Pl. 2–6. A. Northern niche, plastered back. B. Stones reinforc-
ing back of northern niche. C. Cut blocks in middle of central
room (from northwest). D. Channel in mosaic floor—central
portion (from south). E. Channel in mosaic floor—west end
(from east). F. The large lower tank (from the west, above).
G. Detail view of tank.

Pl. 2–7. A. General view of olive presses (from west). B. The olive crushing mill (from northwest). C. Crushing mill, rock-cut channel at bottom. D. Southern olive press (from south). E. Northern olive press (from west). F. Upper sorting floors cut by Period 4 wall (from south).

Pl. 2–8. A. Bedrock with fill removed (from north). B. Floor 3 (foreground), Floor 3a (right center). C. Floor 4 (from southeast). D. Floor 5 (from south). E. Glass factory dump, section from south.

A

C

B

D

Pl. 2–9. A. Broad areas of conglomerate, Trench Y–3 (from south). B. Brick fragments and other debris dumped in Trench Y–3. C. Intact glass jar (Chap. 4, No. 357) found in factory dump. D. Long west wall (Period 4), from south in unit XIX.

A

D

B

E

C

Pl. 2–10. A. Storage jar deposit in southeast corner of Period 4 compound. B. View from east of units VII and V. C. Wall laid east-west across unit V in Period 4. D. Typical masonry of Period 4 (unit V, east wall); glass fragments in packing between stones. E. Section of villa west wall rebuilt in Period 4.

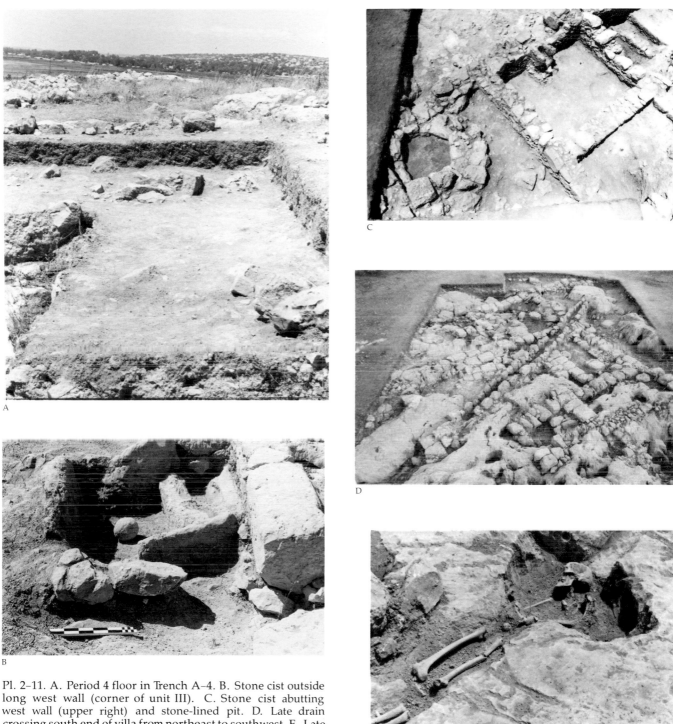

Pl. 2–11. A. Period 4 floor in Trench A–4. B. Stone cist outside long west wall (corner of unit III). C. Stone cist abutting west wall (upper right) and stone-lined pit. D. Late drain crossing south end of villa from northeast to southwest. E. Late burial in Trench A (Grave B).

A

D

B

Pl. 3–1. A. Trench A–2, just uncovered,
from southeast. B. Calcined stones found
in Trench A–2 (north wall). C. Foundation
of furnace room, north side.
D. Northwest corner of furnace room.
E. North side of furnace room.

C

E

Pl. 3–2. A. Northeast corner of furnace room. B. East side of
furnace room. C. View of furnace from east.

Pl. 3–3. A, B. The largest siege fragment recovered. C, D. Rectangular parallelepipeds of glass from containers.

Pl. 3–4. A. Stone blocks with curved surfaces. B. Bricks from the furnace walls and crown.

A

B

Pl. 3–5.

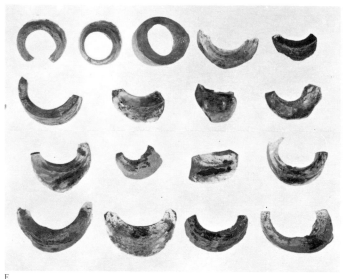

A. Pontil with remains of glass.
B, C. Pontil knock-offs.
D. Discoid pontil knock-offs.
E. Blowpipe crack-offs (moils).
F. Mass of discards from
blowpipes and pontils.

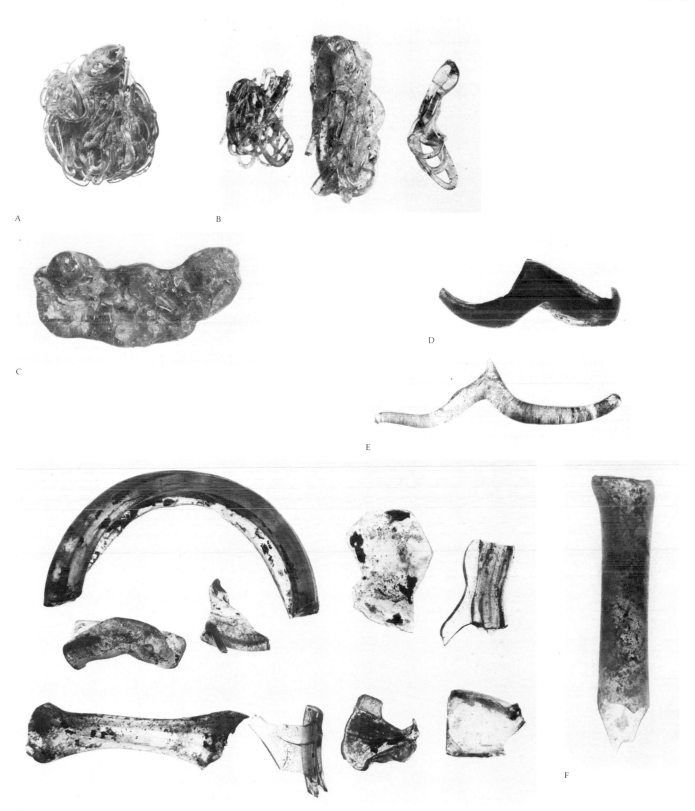

A, B. Threads drawn out from hot blobs. C. Shapeless
lump showing tooling. D, E. Trails for decoration.
F. Vessels distorted during blowing. 1:2.

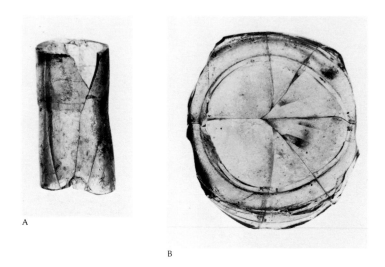

A

B

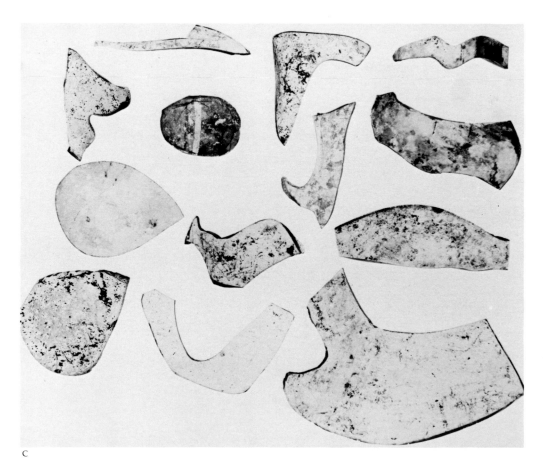

C

Pl. 3–7. Vessels damaged during annealing.

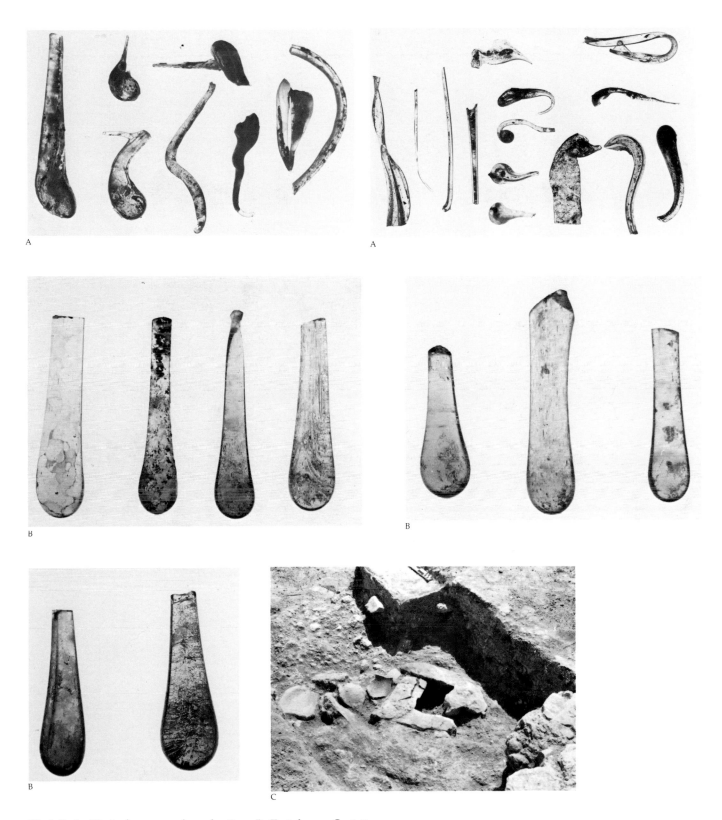

Pl. 3–8. A. Waste from vessel production. B. Test drops. Ca. 1:2.
C. Remains of stone box and pot fragments.

Pl. 4–1.

Bowls with flaring rim: yellowish green and greenish blue.

6   Bowl with thickened rim.

Bowl with outfolded rim, Missouri (see Chap. 4, n. 10).

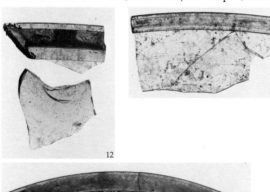

Bowls with outfolded rim.

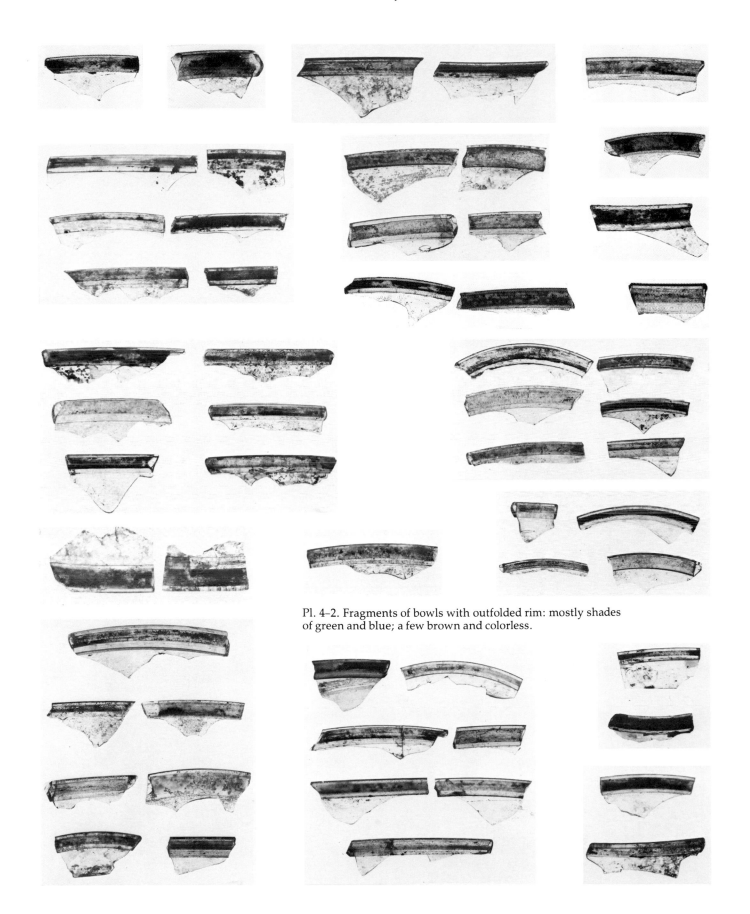

Pl. 4–2. Fragments of bowls with outfolded rim: mostly shades of green and blue; a few brown and colorless.

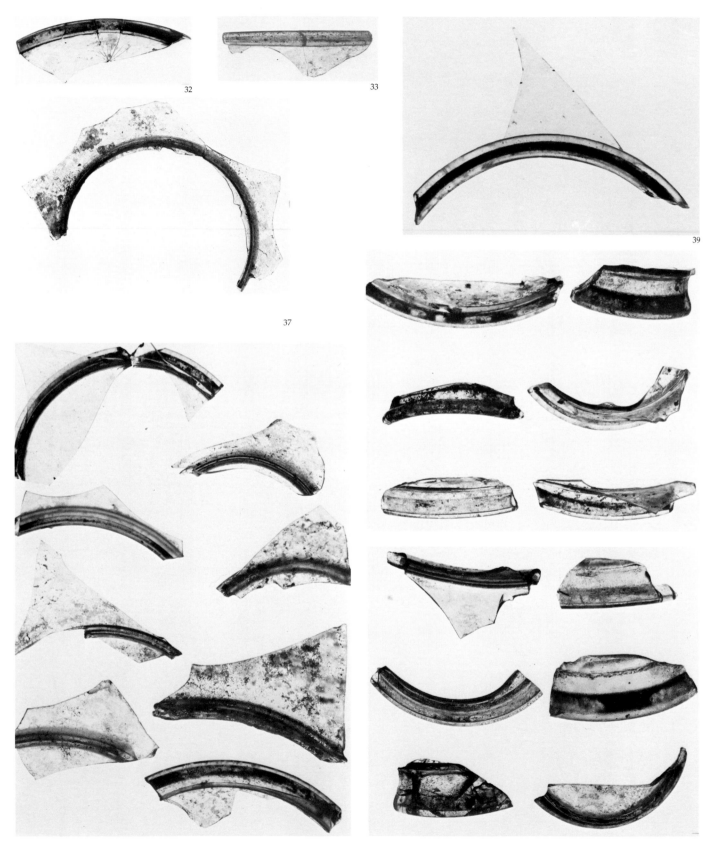

Pl. 4–3. Bowls with outfolded rim: nos. 32–33 rim fragments; others base fragments, bluish green, green, and brown.

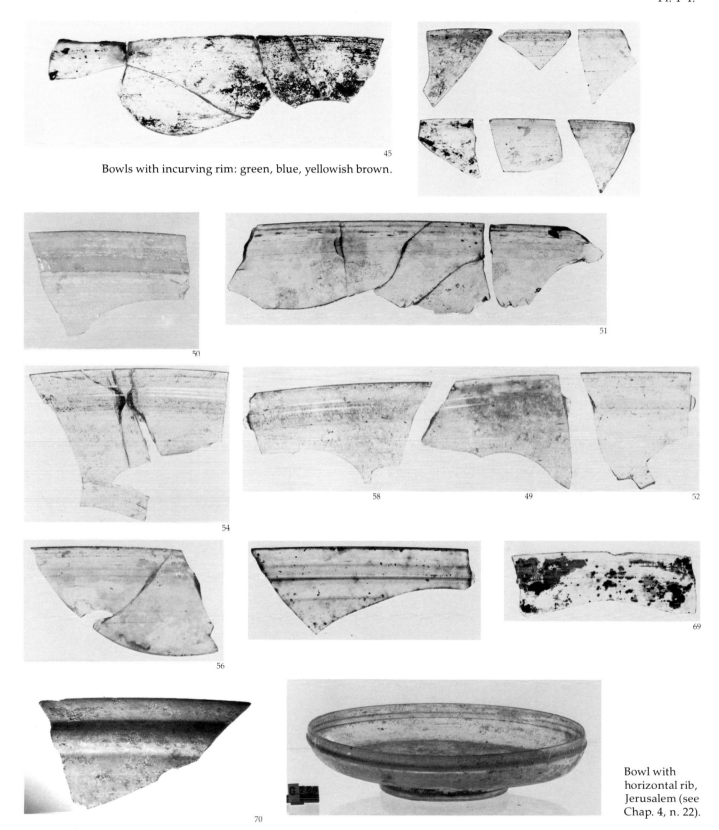

Bowls with incurving rim: green, blue, yellowish brown.

45

50

51

54

58   49   52

56

69

70

Bowls with horizontal rib.

Bowl with
horizontal rib,
Jerusalem (see
Chap. 4, n. 22).

Pl. 4–5.

Fragments of bowls with horizontal rib: bluish green, green, olive green.

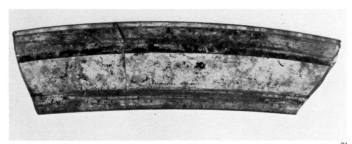

71

73

74

75

76

Bowls with folded
collar: shades of
blue and green,
one colorless.

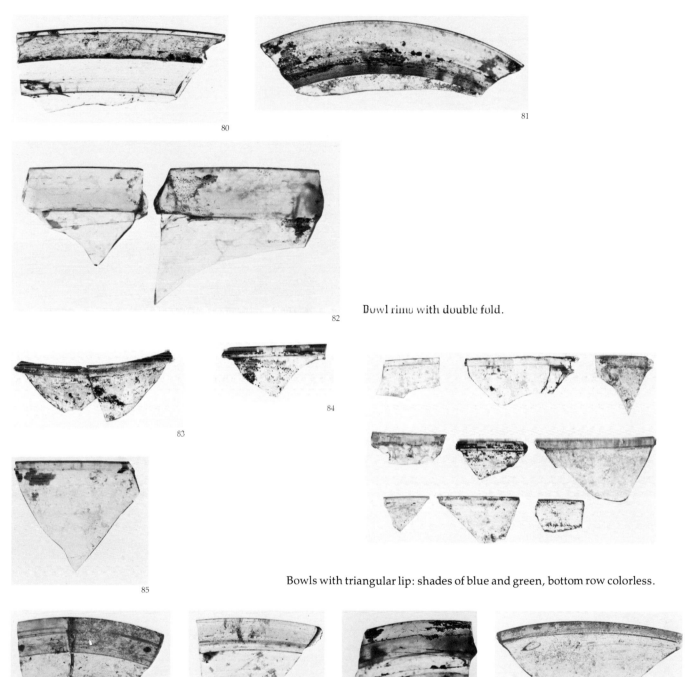

80

81

82

Bowl rims with double fold.

83

84

85

Bowls with triangular lip: shades of blue and green, bottom row colorless.

88

89

90

91

Bowls with infolded rim.

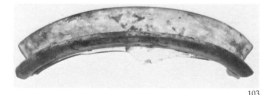

103

105

Bowl rims with tooled-out fold.

Pl. 4–7.

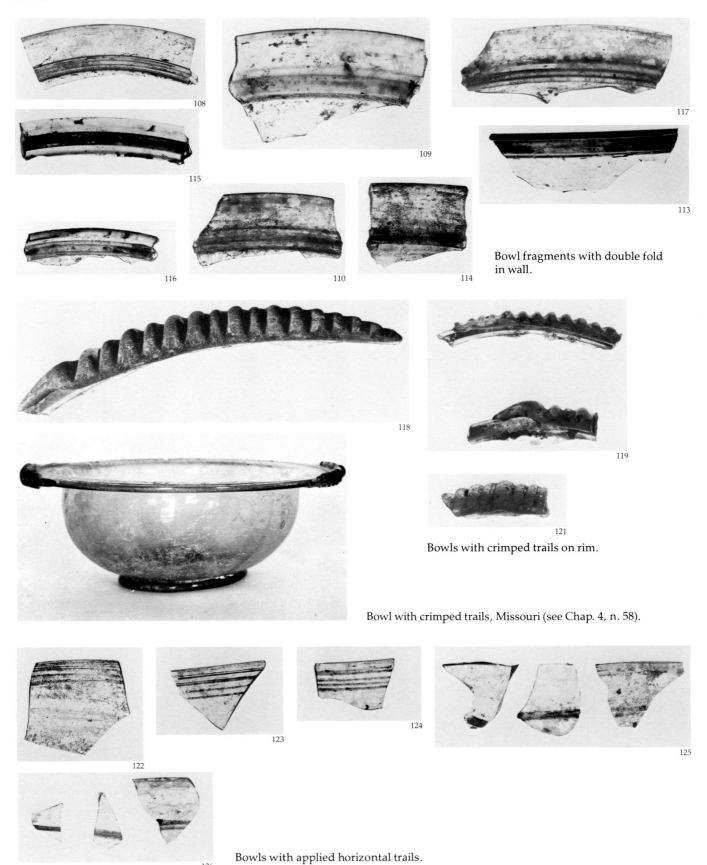

Bowl fragments with double fold in wall.

Bowls with crimped trails on rim.

Bowl with crimped trails, Missouri (see Chap. 4, n. 58).

Bowls with applied horizontal trails.

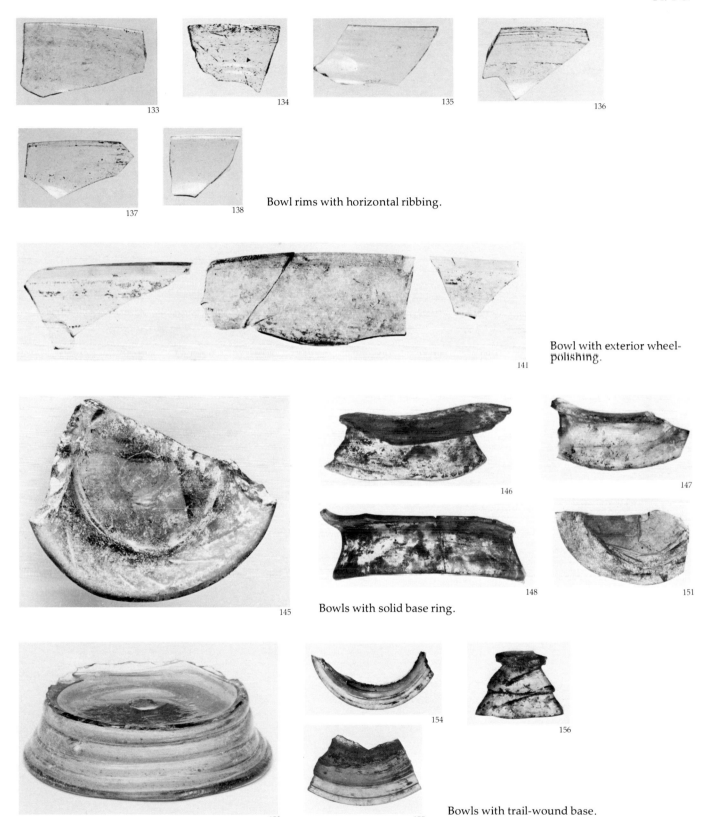

Bowl rims with horizontal ribbing.

Bowl with exterior wheel-polishing.

Bowls with solid base ring.

Bowls with trail-wound base.

Pl. 4–9.

Cup with solid base, Missouri (see Chap. 4, n. 88).

Cups with solid base.

Cups with pushed-in base.

198

Cups with concave bottom
(rim fragments).

Conical vessel, Missouri (see
Chap. 4, n. 100).

207

208

209

216

Jugs with spiral trail.

Jug with single trail, Corning (see Chap. 4, n. 107).

217

221

222

226

228

Jugs with single trail.

Pl. 4–11.

230

233

234

235

240

Jug bases.

242

243

244

250

251

252

253

254

255

256

Fragments of strap handles from jugs, many purple, others yellow, green, blue.

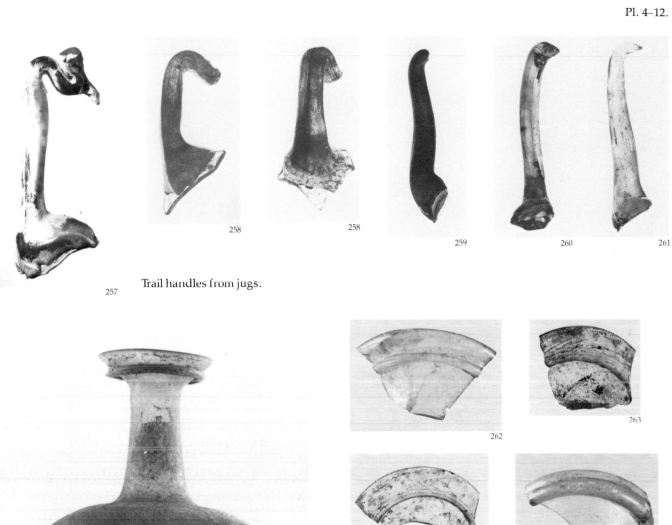

Trail handles from jugs.

Bottle with single trail, Jerusalem (see Chap. 4, n. 110).

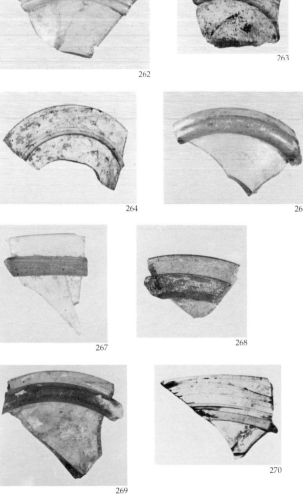

Globular bottles with single trail on rim.

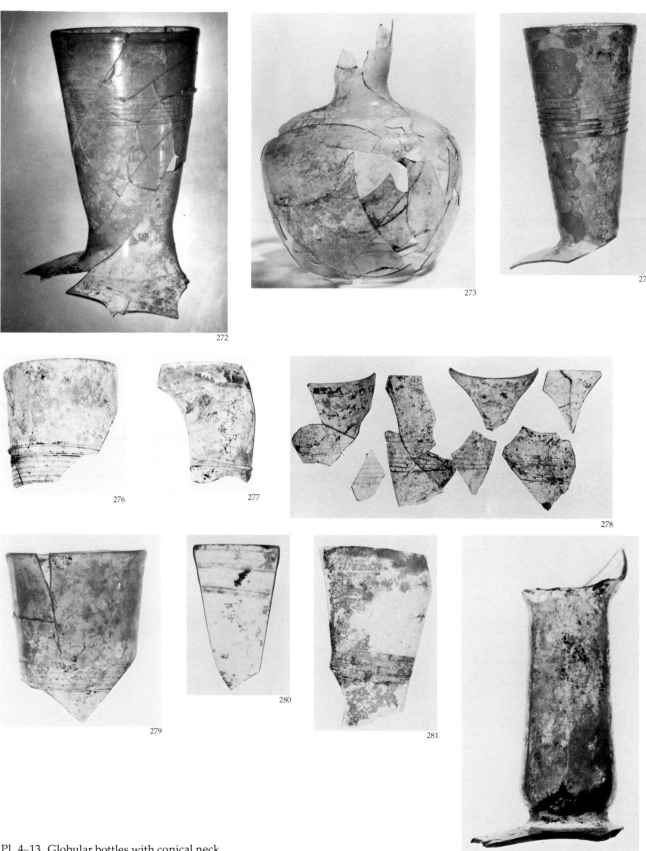

Pl. 4–13. Globular bottles with conical neck.

Bottle with ribbed rim.
289

297

298

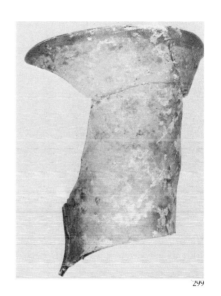

299

Various large bottles.

301

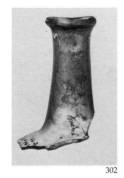

Small bottles.

302

306

321

Various flasks.

322

325

327

Pl. 4–15.

Spouted vessel, Missouri (see Chap. 4, n. 147).

Ribbed flask, Missouri (see Chap. 4, n. 151).

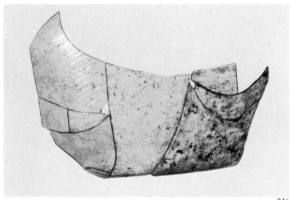

346

344

345

347

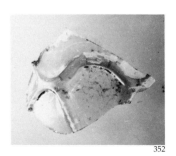

349

350

Mold-blown vessels.

351

352

356

Vessels with pinched ribs.

Fragment with applied trails.

Pl. 4–16.

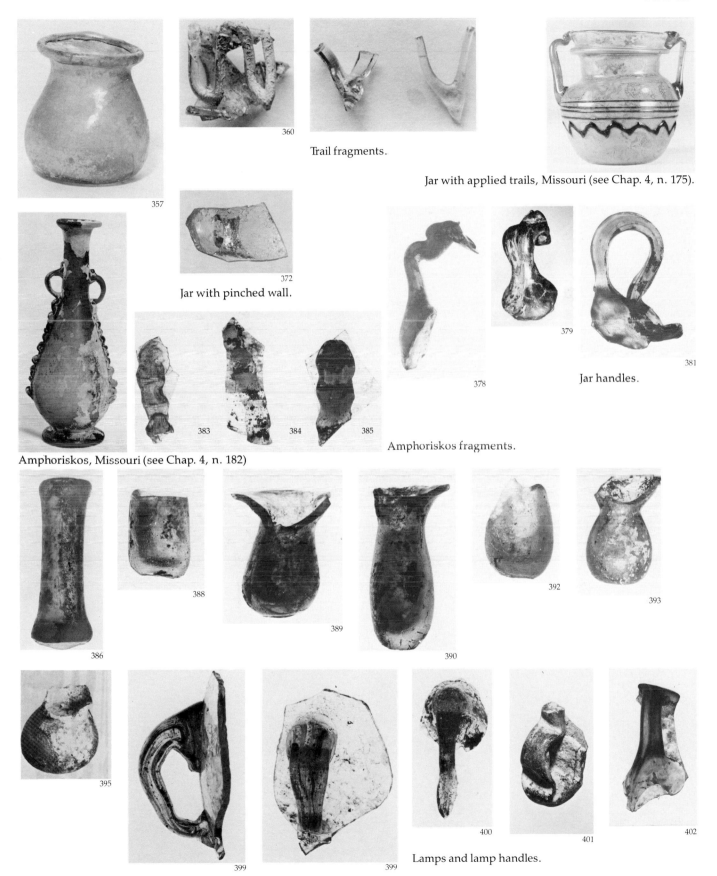

357

360

Trail fragments.

Jar with applied trails, Missouri (see Chap. 4, n. 175).

372

Jar with pinched wall.

378

379

381

Jar handles.

383   384   385

Amphoriskos fragments.

Amphoriskos, Missouri (see Chap. 4, n. 182)

386   388   389   390   392   393

395   399   399   400   401   402

Lamps and lamp handles.

Pl. 4–17.

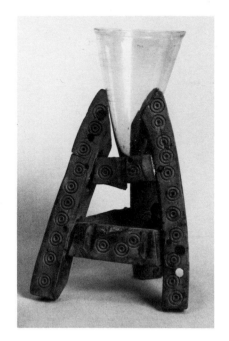

Wooden tripod holding lamp.
Photo courtesy of Kelsey
Museum, University of Michigan.

Conical lamp, Missouri (see Chap. 4, n. 191).

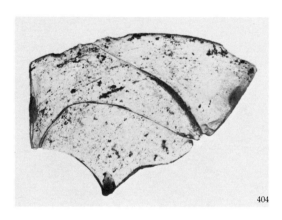

404

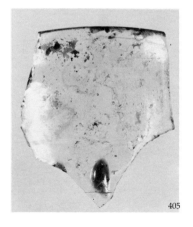

405

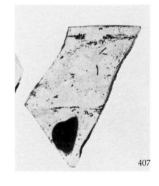

407

411

412   Fragments of conical vessels with blue blobs.

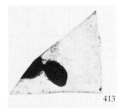

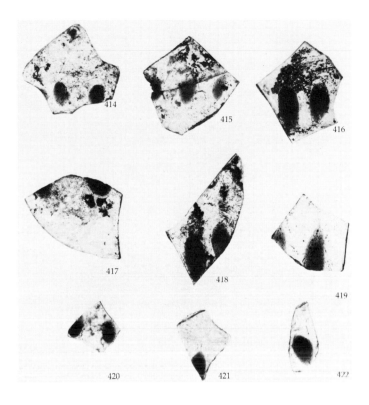

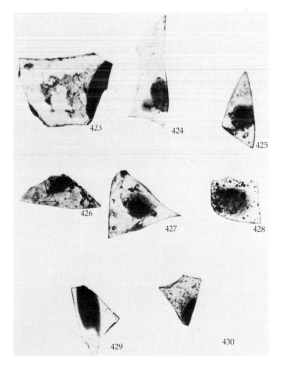

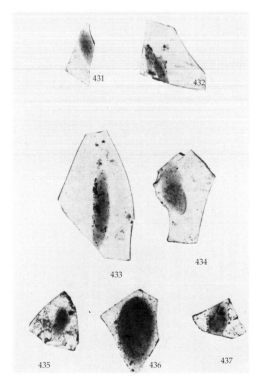

Pl. 4–18. Wall fragments of conical vessels with blue blobs. No. 438 has greenish blue blob.

Pl. 4–19.

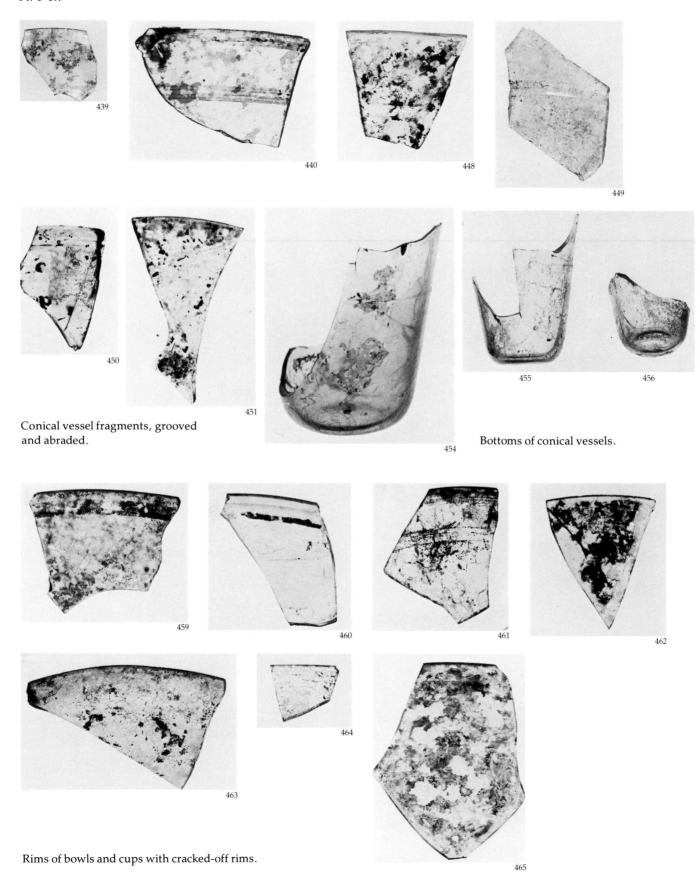

439

440

448

449

450

451

Conical vessel fragments, grooved
and abraded.

454

455   456

Bottoms of conical vessels.

459

460

461

462

463

464

465

Rims of bowls and cups with cracked-off rims.

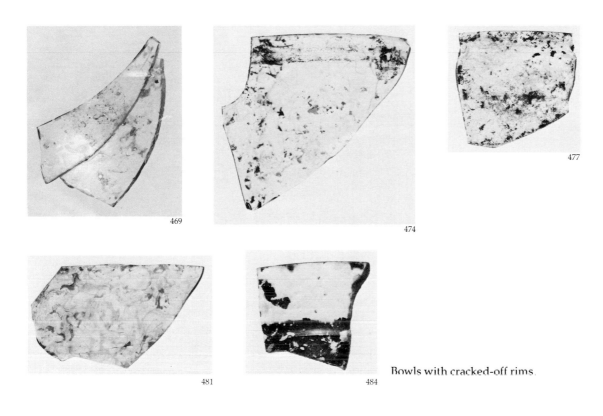

469

474

477

481

484

Bowls with cracked-off rims.

Bowls with ground and polished rims:
mostly shades of green.

Bowls with ground and polished rims,
thin-walled: mostly colorless.

Pl. 4–21.

Trial matching of moil and vessel fragments.

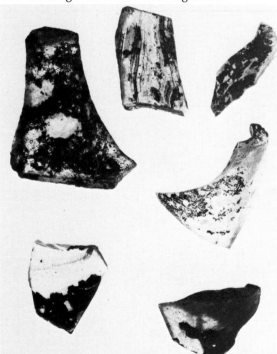

Fragments of upper parts of moils: yellowish green.

Fragments of upper parts of moils: shades of green, colorless at lower right

Moil fragments .0015 thick.

Moil fragments .001 thick.

Pl. 4–22. A. Moil fragments .002 thick.
B. Moil fragments .0025 thick. C. Moil
fragments .003 thick. D. Moil fragments
.004 thick.

Pl. 4–23.

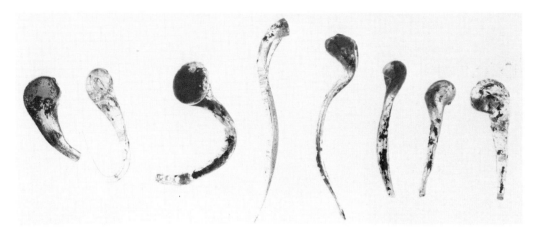

Glass trails possibly used to wrap around conical vessels, to remove moils.

Mass of discarded trails, from decorating vessels.

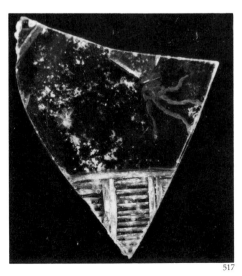

517

518

519

Vessel fragments with engraved designs. No. 517, 2:1; Nos.518–19, 1:1.

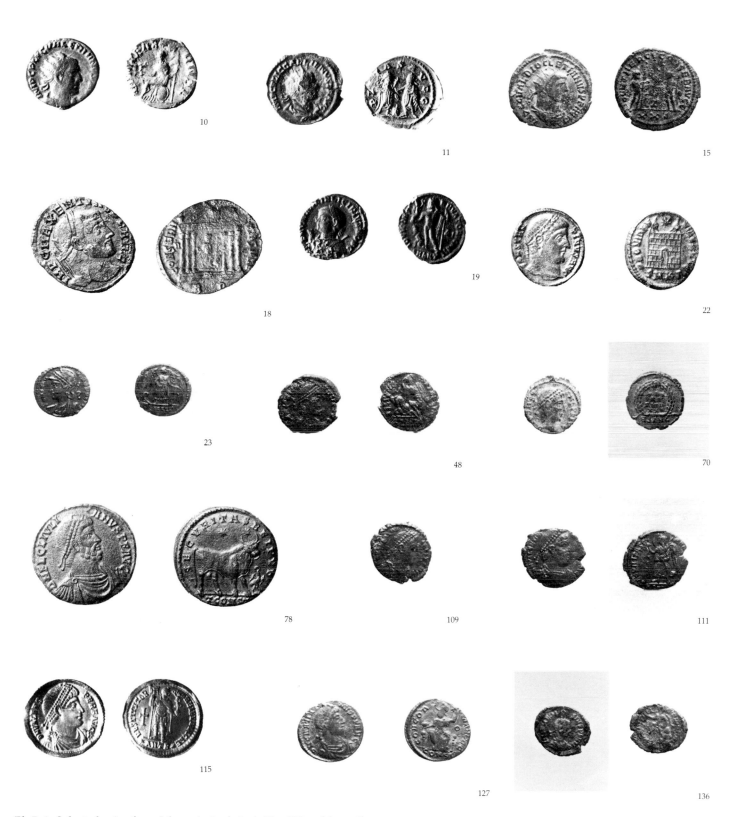

Pl. 5–1. Selected coins from Jalame (actual size). No. 115, gold; rest bronze.

Pl. 6–1.

1

2

3

3

4

4

5

8

6

7

7

Hellenistic and Early Roman Terracotta Lamps.

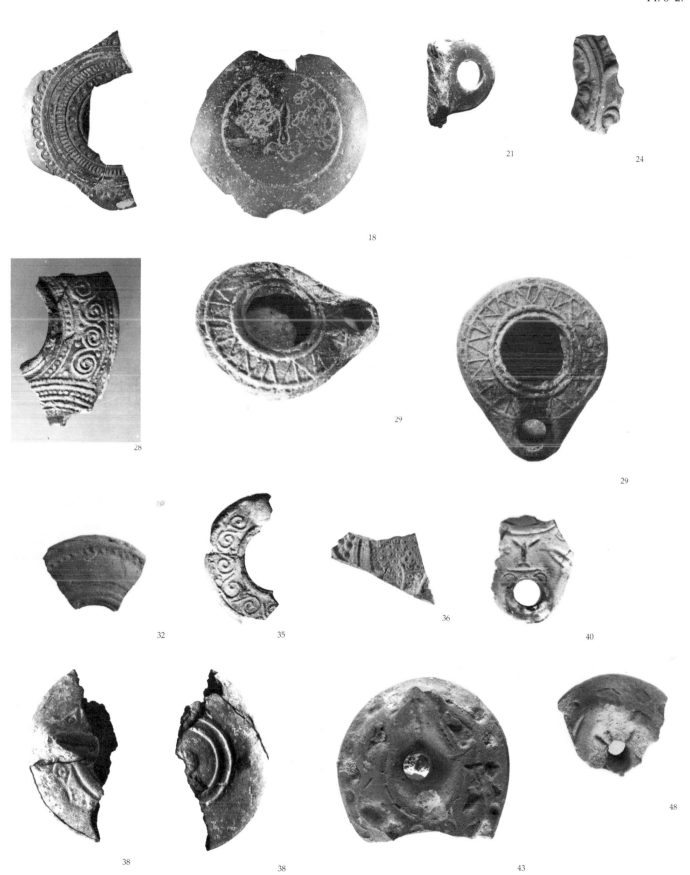

21

24

18

28

29

29

32 35 36 40

38

38 43 48

Terracotta Lamps, 2nd–4th century.

Pl. 6–3.

Terracotta Lamps, 4th century.

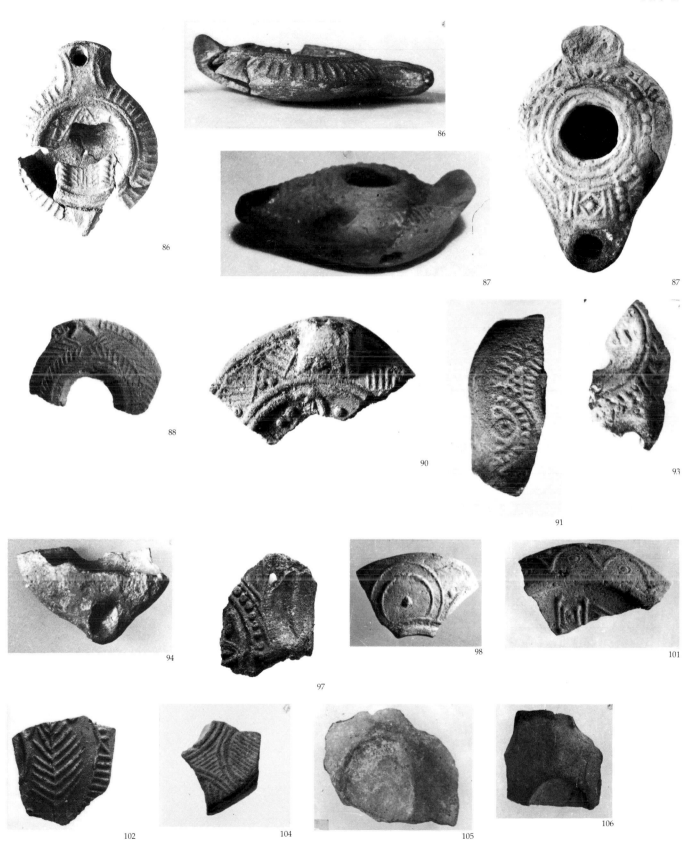

Terracotta Lamps, 4th century and later.

Pl. 6–5.

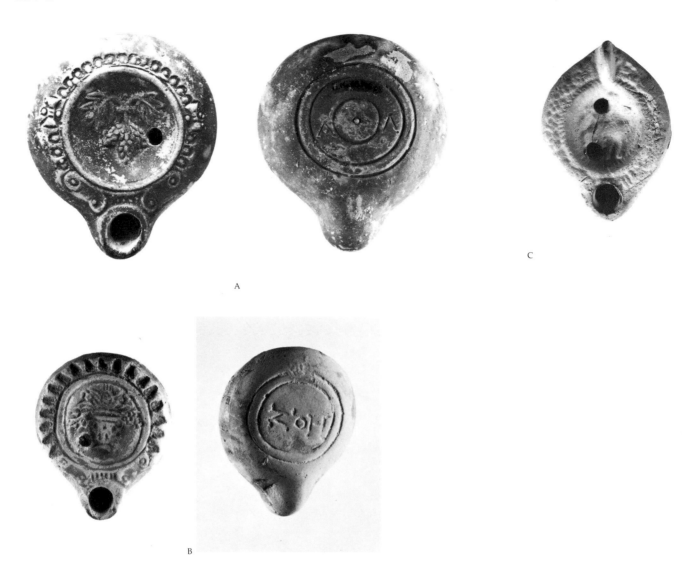

A

B

C

Pl . 6-5. Lamps in the Museum of Art and Archaeology, University of
Missouri-Columbia. A. No. 68.146c (see Chap. 6, No. 10 and n. 25). B.
No. 68.301 (see Chap. 6, n. 26). C. No. 59.72.21 (see Chap. 6, No.37).

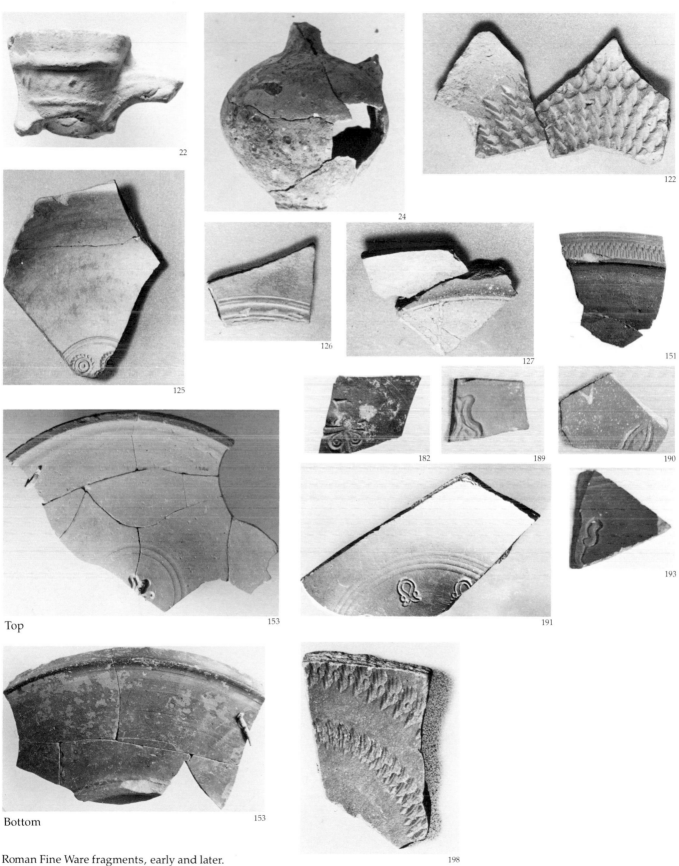

Top

Bottom

Roman Fine Ware fragments, early and later.

Pl. 7–2.

Late Roman Fine Ware Vessels.

264

319

318

321

311

327

329

324

336

331

330

Late Roman Fine Ware fragments.

Pl. 7–4.

Late Roman Basins and Cooking Pots.

Pl. 7–5.

Late Roman Cooking Pot Lids and Coarse Ware vessels.

Pl. 7–6.

Palestinian Baggy Jars.

825

826

827

848

851   Palestinian Baggy Jars, Bell Lids.

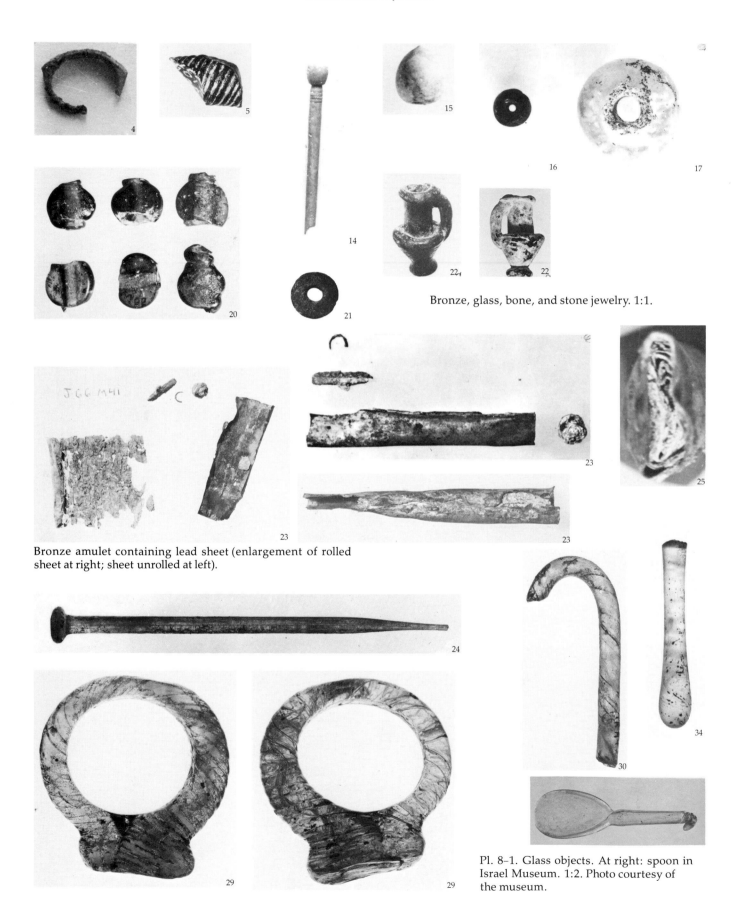

Bronze, glass, bone, and stone jewelry. 1:1.

Bronze amulet containing lead sheet (enlargement of rolled
sheet at right; sheet unrolled at left).

Pl. 8–1. Glass objects. At right: spoon in
Israel Museum. 1:2. Photo courtesy of
the museum.

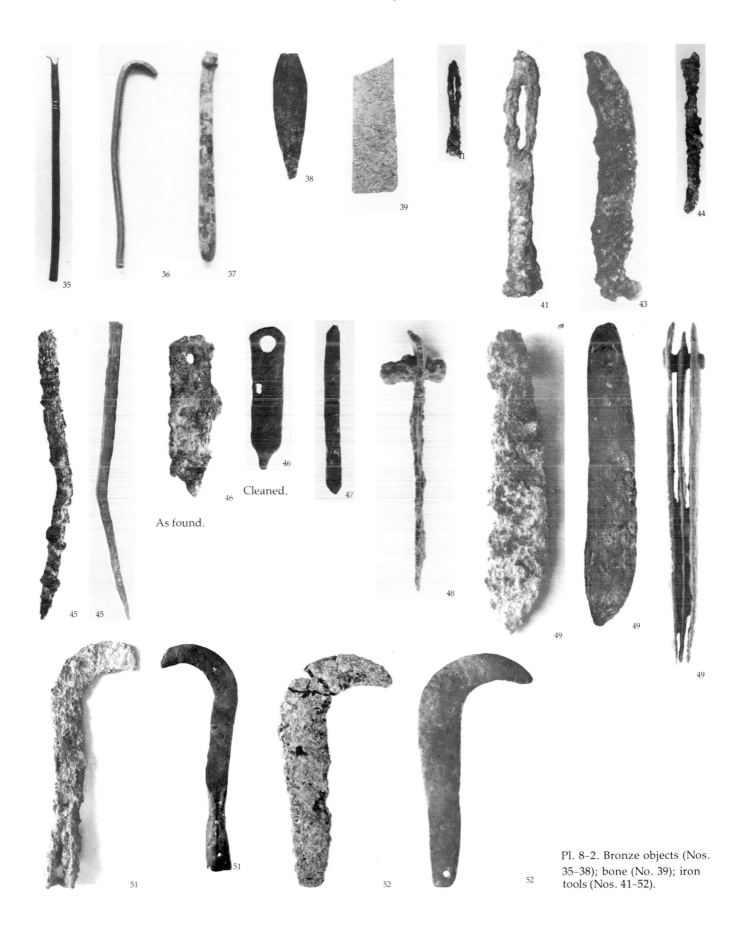

Pl. 8–2. Bronze objects (Nos. 35–38); bone (No. 39); iron tools (Nos. 41–52).

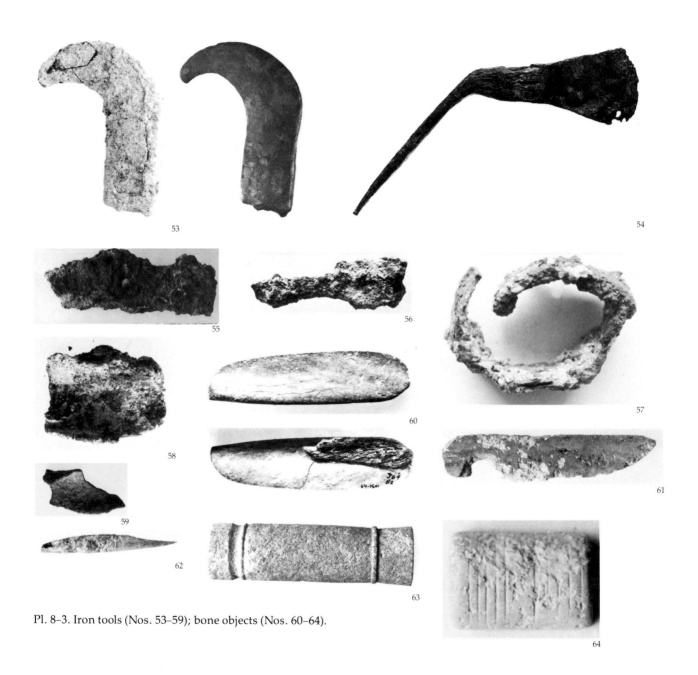

Pl. 8–3. Iron tools (Nos. 53–59); bone objects (Nos. 60–64).

Pl. 8–4. Stone tools.

Pl. 8-5. Stone and terracotta tools (Nos. 87–92); stone palettes
(Nos. 93–95); stone querns (nos. 96–98).

99   99

100a   100b   100c

101   103

104   106

Pl. 8–6. Millstones (Nos. 99–
100); stone press and weights
(Nos. 101–6).

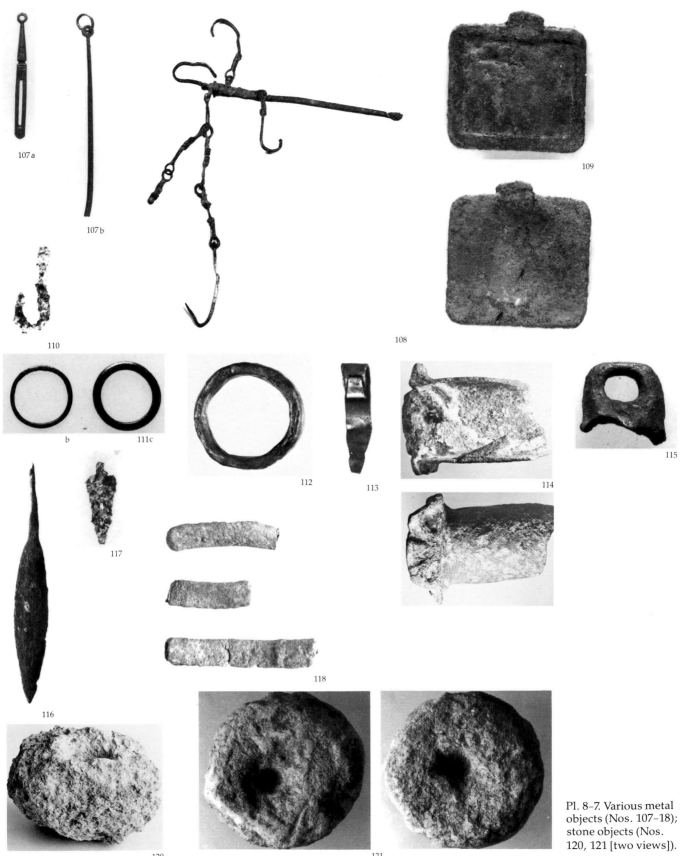

107 a

107 b

110

108

109

b 111c

112 113 114 115

116 117 118

120 121

Pl. 8–7. Various metal objects (Nos. 107–18); stone objects (Nos. 120, 121 [two views]).

Pl. 8–8. Metal objects (Nos. 123–25); stone objects (Nos. 130–40).

Pl. 8–9.

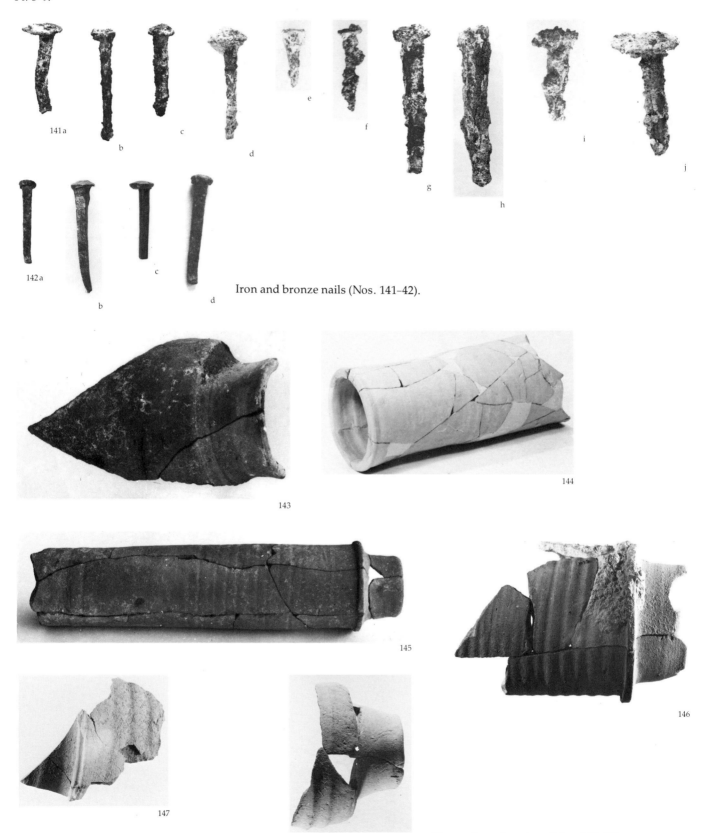

Iron and bronze nails (Nos. 141–42).

Terracotta water pipes (Nos. 143–48).

Flues found in situ at Masada. Photo courtesy of Y. Yadin.

149

150

151

152 a

152 b

153 a

153 b

153 c

Terracotta flues,
tiles, and bricks.

Pl. 8–11.

155

157

158

159b

160a

160d

160e

161a

161d

161e

162b

162d

162e

162f

Stone structural and decorative material.

Pl. 8–12. Mosaic tesserae (No. 164);
glass inlay (No. 167); bronze figurine,
front, side, and back (No. 169); metal
objects (Nos. 170–78); terracotta
figurines (Nos. 179–80).

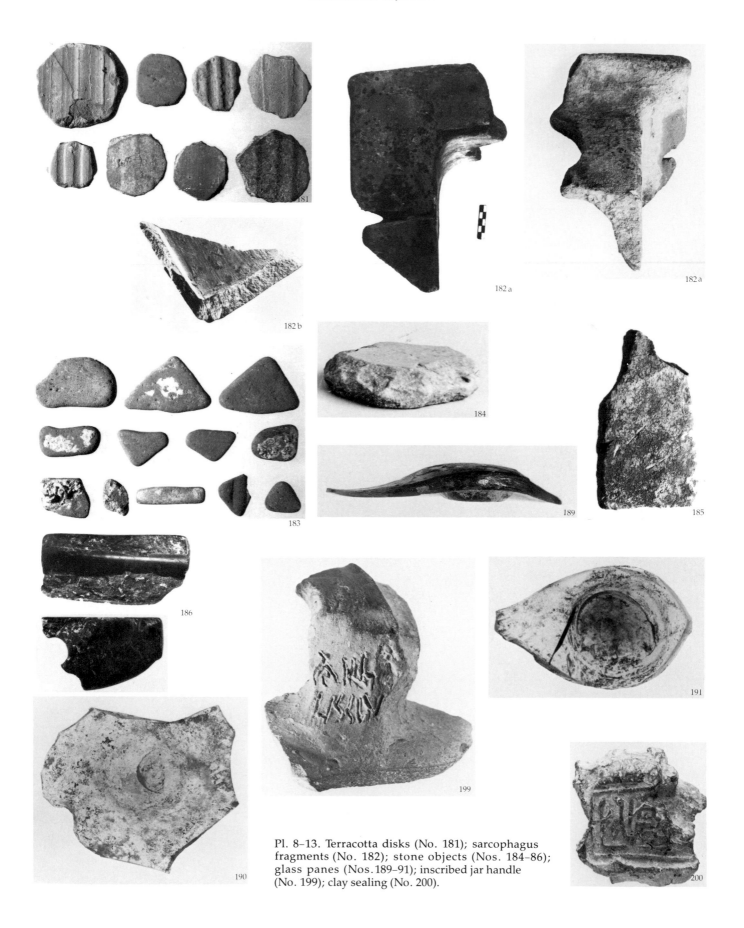

Pl. 8–13. Terracotta disks (No. 181); sarcophagus fragments (No. 182); stone objects (Nos. 184–86); glass panes (Nos. 189–91); inscribed jar handle (No. 199); clay sealing (No. 200).

Concordances

Inv. No.	Cat. No.	Inv. No.	Cat. No.	Inv. No.	Cat. No.	Inv. No.	Cat. No.	Inv. No.	Cat. No.
79	216	166	159	283	66	66	373	186	443
81	369	167	27	284	295	69	154	189	
82	220	168	366	285	410	70	144	191	464
83	242	169	376	286	111	71	344	193	480
84	163	170	51	287	6	72	247	195	430
85	461	171	155	300	39	75	303	198	348
86	329	172	105	303	196	77	506	203	67
92	321	173	45	304	142	78	139	207	349
94	347	179	400	305	294	82	372	212	417
95	325	180	385	306	206	84	367	214	126
96	140	182	94	475	468	86	458	237	100
98	281	183	384	476	492	88	477	243	184
100	258	189	62	502	267	89	494	251	141
102	285	191	292	507	55	91	448	256	434
103	244	193	131	508	60	92	455	258	498
105	438	196	181	509	516	94	374	262	512
107	454	197	117	510	66	97	44	269	157
109	289	199	128	**1966**		105	260	271	92
110	371	201	473	3	424	106	505	275	221
111	401	203	377	4	432	107	407	278	404
112	156	204	106	5	182	108	429	281	227
114	323	205	125	6	457	110	435	283	439
115	283	206	1	8	469	111	422	287	166
118	427	208	143	9	254	113	423	288	408
120	293	209		11	17	114	240	289	215
122	386	210	152	17	118	117	416	291	31
123	396	211	173	19	169	118	517	292	322
124	85	212	397	20	252	124	21	294	467
128	5	213	18	21	20	126	419	295	200
130	108	215	160	22	217	128	332	296	359
136	120	216	360	25	205	129	428	298	119
138	197	217	38	26	380	130	368	301	394
140	132	218	309	27	484	131	483	302	93
141	402	219	176	28	389	132	405	304	352
143	114	222	13	30	482	133	357	305	350
144	241	223	476	31	78	134	449	306	148
145	259	224	475	32	56	135	388	307	500
146	466	225	361	34	109	137	406	309	121
149	113	226	245	35	81	138	414	311	353
149a	115	227	282	37	496	139	370	313	186
150	465	228	341	39	129	140	433	315	268
151	474	229	63	40	362	144	460	316	223
152	195	240	421	41	101	145	445	322	149
153	342	241	425	53	399	151	413	323	305
154	253	265	147	54	183	160	88	329	251
156	514	266	86	56	381	163	383	334	447
157	507	270	286	59	304	170	478	337	64
159	493	275	441	61	40	171	133	338	502
160	178	276	468	62	68	174	89	342	3
164	174	278	451	64	246	183	442	349	334
165	411	282	52	65	249	184	471	350	288

Inv. No.	Cat. No.	Inv. No.	Cat. No.	Inv. No.	Cat. No.	Inv. No.	Cat. No.	Inv. No.	Cat. No.
355	243	468	446	41	206	46	185	50	194
356	28	469	489	42	199	51	98	51	34
368	450	470	486	43	2	52	45	52	69
370	8	472	509	46	151	53a	112	53	161
371	284	474	513	47	152	53b	167	56	169
373	162	477	510	51	72	59	10	59	81
374	99	478	290	52	105	60	122	60	131
375	324	481	265	56	32	67	118	61	117
376	456	482	499	57	106	68	178	62	187
376a	312	484	74	58	174	69	146	63	87
378	310	486	462	59	80	70	62	67	113
379	314	487	50	61	175	73	128	69	163
380	248	488	61	63	191	74	168	73	179
382	315	489	53	65	6	75	203	74	88
387	22	490	47	66	35	76	85	75	54
388	15	492	508	67	26	77	21	76	99
389	4	493	504	68	9	80	193	78	134
390	158	494a	135	**1965**		81	11	79	188
391	391	494b	136	1	18	82	36	84	44
392	7	494c	137	2	149	83	84	85	55
394	511	494d	138	3	153	84	7	86	17
395	503	**1967**		4	176	86	150	87	33
396	497	1	420	5	78	87	23	88	186
398	409	2	365	6	22	88	29	89	158
400	403	3	382	8	183	89	5	90	123
405	440	5	12	9	1	90	70	91	180
414	198	10	415	10	82	94	144	92	181
415	54	13	340	11	91	94a	141	93	124
416	269	19	339	12	177	95	109	94	97
421	167	20	459	13	94	96	24	96	156
426	452			15	143	97	3	97	170
428	165	Chapter 5,		16	25	99	132	98	110
433	316	Coins		17	154	104	53	99	66
434	168	**1964**		18	67	105	50	100	171
435	110	1	115	20	155	106	107	102	46
436	232	1a	86	22	127	107	8	103	42
437	77	2	120	23	189	**1966**		105	51
439	25	6	159	25	90	8	4	106	195
445	453	8	65	26	184	10	126	107	77
446	398	10	83	27	121	14	71	110	157
447	333	11	166	29	76	16	142	111	57
448	479	12	139	30	56	21	20	112	111
451	301	14	103	31	200	26	79	115	68
455	470	15	64	32	95	29	201	117	162
456	35	19	207	35	182	32	198	119	125
460	291	25	104	36	192	35	133	121	108
461	185	26	190	38	75	37	40	122	77
462	472	27	39	38a	61	39	164	123	73
463	87	38	31	40	140	40	12	124	30
464	199	39	148	41	19	42	43	125	13
467	444	40	52	44	49	47	89	126	16

Inv. No.	Cat. No.	Inv. No.	Cat. No.	Inv. No.	Cat. No.	Inv. No.	Cat. No.	Inv. No.	Cat. No.
127	48	12	65	112	96	**1967**		64	252
128	196	13	32	113	9	3	84	69	151
129	202	15	60	117	30	**1968**		73	335
130	96	16	103	118	83	1	6	74	327
131	100	20	55	127	79			75	321
133	165	23	56	131	68	Chapter 7,		76	318
134	129	26	82	140	5	Pottery		79	120
136	60	30	90	145	70	**1964**		81	636
137	93	31	61	146	31	1	243	82	341
139	38	32	76			2	253	83	176
140	74	33	86	**1966**		3	237	84	118
141	145	35	39	7	54	5	226	85	494
145	160	40	16	8	100	6	154	86	289
148	135	**1965**		10	59	7	246	89	247
151	205	1	87	13	45	8	232	91	234
156	27	2	97	16	8	9	312	92	152
158	58	5	63	17	38	10	125	93	833
161	101	6	52	23	11	11	336	94	191
162	137	7	46	24	58	12	188	98	825
164	130	8	81	26	74	13	311	99	812
165	204	12	48	33	62	15	326	102	733
172	59	15	64	34	41	16	334	103	827
173	119	17	94	35	75	18	183	104	622
178	41	18	89	36	93	19	235	105	826
179	172	19	102	37	95	20	521	108	22
180	197	20	4	43	40	23	300	109	735
181	114	21	3	46	42	25	647	111	216
182	28	22	43	49	51	27	263	112	139
184	37	25	35	50	49	28	524	113	301
185	92	28	18	54	10	29	230	116	242
186	136	29	25	58	72	30	119	117	196
191	147	30	101	65	37	31	248	118	320
1967		32	2	66	80	34	508	122	198
1	63	34	85	67	44	35	258	123	121
2	102	39	47	68	67	38bis	149	125	324
3	116	40	50	72	78	39	184	127	133
4	47	41	27	73	7	40	185	129	186
5	173	45	28	76	1	42	362	130	239
8	138	48	31A	77	21	43	872	138	294
9	15	50	12	86	17	44	469	140	147
		67	73	90	71	46	633	141	238
Chapter 6,		68	106	91	15	48	236	142	229
Lamps		69	92	92	20	50	264	143	868
1964		75	58	93	36	52	114	144	869
1	19	79	33	95	26	53	259	145	179
2	99	83	13	99	91	54	670	146	148
4	105	85	105	101	57	55	195	147	262
8	29	91	34	105	14	59	688	148	265
9	53	107	23	106	69	60	471	149	249
10	88	108	98	107	77	61	208	152	173
11	22	111	66	133	24	62	160	155	128

Inv. No.	Cat. No.	Inv. No.	Cat. No.	Inv. No.	Cat. No.	Inv. No.	Cat. No.	Inv. No.	Cat. No.
186	514	315	50	536	269	78	267	165	224
188	26	316	751	541	222	79	293	167	273
190	882	327	158	545	204	81	687	168	723
192	140	329	174	548	209	82	522	170	721
193	671	331	150	551	445	83	883	174	355
194	689	334	172	558	500	85	492	176	517
195	141	336	170	559	732	86	391	182	507
197	405	338	156	560	25	88	488	183	4
198	655	340	164	561	32	91	672	192	144
200	59	345	194	562	38	92	606	195	115
205	634	346	256	**1965**		93	74	196	296
206	755	366	571	1	699	94	398	198	254
207	856	367	449	6	182	95	460	203	219
208	855	370	389	11	730	97	83	204	91
209	501	384	448	14	859	98	734	205	309
213	78	394	167	16	251	99	835	207	205
216	626	395	159	17	330	103	641	209	117
217	623	397	168	18	635	104	648	211	307
219	674	403	165	20	12	105	750	213	169
221	743	404	162	21	386	106	811	214	673
222	797	411	810	24	853	112	809	216	682
225	639	413	692	25	435	113	608	217	698
227	742	436	704	28	478	114	656	219	792
228	572	443	161	29	477	115	677	220	527
229	526	447	316	33	484	116	678	226	761
230	759	448	340	34	407	117	637	227	20
232	632	451	315	39	14	118	847	228	493
233	659	454	177	42	153	120	798	229	489
235	631	459	286	43	291	121	799	234	131
236	710	460	137	46	241	122	800	236	101
239	760	462	298	47	329	123	801	238	98
242	599	467	257	48	518	124	802	239	92
243	621	468	260	49	305	125	803	240	93
244	383	487	481	50	123	126	804	243	116
247	854	495	570	51	192	127	805	244	108
248	225	503	564	52	132	128	806	246	106
257	467	504	547	53	250	129	807	248	109
260	465	505	566	54	313	131	808	249	103
265	468	506	560	55	112	143	877	257	660
267	878	510	563	56	197	144	715	266	876
268	662	514	534	58	332	145	690	268	363
271	60	515	558	59	187	149	713	269	645
276	498	517	567	60	206	152	754	277	861
280	473	522	297	61	325	154	646	281	439
284	661	524	280	62	337	156	397	282	746
287	862	525	288	65	244	158	694	283	737
290	685	527	274	66	240	160	829	284	429
307	430	529	266	67	227	161	372	285	482
310	520	530	270	70	181	162	612	286	757
312	816	533	279	72	245	163	223	289	857
314	46	535	283	74	278	164	233	290	410

Inv. No.	Cat. No.	Inv. No.	Cat. No.	Inv. No.	Cat. No.	Inv. No.	Cat. No.	Inv. No.	Cat. No.
301	652	440	52	732	874	1000	211	59	516
302	711	462	416	747	666	1002	203	60	618
304	714	463	752	762	871	1005	220	63	649
306	884	465	821	763	727	1006	691	66	464
308	463	467	76	782	434	1007	71	69	695
310	396	475	724	847	65	1018	762	70	849
311	408	479	413	853	693	1019	27	71	404
313	638	480	421	866	444	1020	37	72	354
314	390	483	53	871	322	1021	35	75	824
315	466	485	719	873	142	1022	28	77	712
318	472	491	818	874	323	1025	745	78	510
322	189	495	437	877	135	1026	36	83	680
323	304	499	425	878	136	1027	39	94	870
324	104	500	575	881	272	1028	43	103	87
325	231	501	423	884	292	1029	42	108	411
326	55	502	19	893	828	**1966**		110	525
327	21	522	163	902	531	2	860	112	703
328	447	524	175	922	568	3	255	119	523
329	455	528	342	923	591	4	24	121	858
330	442	539	75	924	593	6	851	125	11
331	496	543	72	929	628	7	706	129	462
334	505	546	864	930	581	8	553	132	6
335	502	552	351	931	577	9	528	134	10
336	497	580	376	933	598	10	394	141	684
340	100	581	346	934	586	11	552	142	667
348	107	582	382	935	588	12	642	143	438
349	124	583	381	936	582	17	879	145	44
351	739	584	385	938	578	19	697	146	696
352	9	585	379	940	576	21	199	150	665
353	530	589	368	942	585	22	651	151	491
354	731	591	380	943	574	24	509	152	602
358	675	607	615	944	540	26	138	153	403
359	700	615	418	947	535	27	284	154	617
360	82	619	596	950	543	29	650	155	664
363	47	622	373	952	573	30	604	156	428
364	744	644	419	954	565	31	668	157	483
365	683	645	456	955	624	32	813	158	365
366	85	647	420	957	627	33	640	159	459
371	84	659	415	958	549	34	707	160	609
376	1	662	725	962	554	37	630	161	409
379	850	668	359	964	561	39	202	162	436
381	830	669	364	966	557	41	728	164	422
396	146	670	366	969	594	42	201	165	344
404	414	673	360	970	532	43	480	167	607
407	56	679	347	975	290	44	512	168	614
409	863	680	348	989	268	47	542	170	369
414	77	685	718	991	285	49	17	173	281
417	64	687	157	994	215	50	772	174	282
423	866	700	720	996	217	51	393	176	791
425	67	717	166	997	214	52	515	177	45
435	865	718	145	999	210	58	843	178	758

Inv. No.	Cat. No.	Inv. No.	Cat. No.	Inv. No.	Cat. No.	Inv. No.	Cat. No.	Inv. No.	Cat. No.
179	605	283	80	441	417	603	66	898	13
180	600	286	487	442	820	604	764	902	171
188	504	287	486	448	717	611	69	909	8
189	613	290	789	449	842	619	479	910	741
191	603	319	474	455	763	620	401	911	5
195	736	325	783	457	470	621	412	924	873
196	513	326	784	471	773	639	432	976	450
200	81	328	786	475	778	654	790	978	452
207	143	329	793	483	845	662	819	980	440
208	111	331	796	484	541	668	427	984	453
209	345	332	787	485	777	673	748	1008	840
212	308	336	781	486	686	677	461	1022	663
213	180	337	780	488	848	679	2	1023	86
214	302	341	814	489	836	680	48	1025	620
215	130	342	817	490	387	693	426	1033	747
216	122	343	779	491	476	701	399	1046	15
217	306	345	776	501	708	702	400	1049	310
218	155	347	765	502	511	704	49	1050	228
223	339	348	770	504	317	710	756	1051	134
224	113	349	775	505	178	726	333	1057	261
225	102	351	788	507	454	727	338	1058	875
230	601	353	769	508	446	733	62	1062	880
231	616	354	822	509	7	734	867	1085	485
232	402	356	766	510	499	739	681	1095	595
233	705	357	794	511	506	746	349	1097	592
234	392	373	88	513	495	752	384	1098	597
236	644	381	881	514	503	755	356	1100	584
237	395	382	89	516	99	757	353	1105	569
238	653	385	14	517	95	759	357	1107	587
239	352	387	529	518	96	766	367	1108	589
240	23	388	658	522	94	768	361	1110	579
243	753	391	774	524	97	769	358	1111	583
244	490	392	771	528	110	771	371	1112	590
247	193	394	795	533	722	782	374	1115	545
248	319	397	815	534	852	789	619	1116	562
249	328	400	768	535	738	790	839	1117	537
250	190	403	767	536	63	808	580	1119	625
251	331	404	782	537	749	812	388	1120	539
253	303	408	610	538	740	813	375	1121	555
254	126	416	18	539	519	815	350	1123	550
255	105	421	841	540	716	817	377	1124	538
256	90	423	831	541	702	820	611	1125	629
261	654	424	844	543	701	855	679	1126	536
264	709	426	378	556	676	856	424	1132	533
266	657	429	370	558	79	869	457	1133	556
267	643	430	846	592	61	872	726	1134	546
268	314	433	834	593	73	874	441	1137	559
268bis	443	434	343	594	58	876	431	1139	544
270	127	436	837	597	669	879	451	1141	548
271	200	437	838	598	54	886	475	1152	276
279	729	438	832	601	68	890	16	1153	287

Inv. No.	Cat. No.	Inv. No.	Cat. No.	Inv. No.	Cat. No.	Inv. No.	Cat. No.	Inv. No.	Cat. No.
1156	271	90	143	302	187	25	47	53	171d
1157	299	221	146	**1966**		26	50	54	122
1159	295	274	181a	10	28	28	109	55	174
1162	277	**1966**		14	28	29	169	56	107c
1163	275	1	92	23	3	31	141d	57	107c
1164	551	84	148	24	168	32	55	58	173
1169	213	103	179c	68	33d	33	44	Stone	
1170	212	114	181c	83	27	34	42	**1964**	
1171	221	131a	181h	116	167c	36	41	1	102
1176	218	131b	181d	127	33b	41	141h	2	104
1179	207	148	181e	135	33e	45	175	5	156
1193	458	372	183	143	12	46	117	6	100a
1207	785	374	181b	147	10	47	107b	7	160e
1209	34	384	199	149	25	48	35	8	72
1210	29	494	181f	153	33k	49	38	9	74
1211	30	Glass		161	33a	50	113	11	157
1213	823	**1964**		175	33f	51	142c	12	103
1214	31	61	190	241	26	53	107a	13	106
1215	33	86	198	290	33i	54	111a	14	101
1216	40	127	189	343	194	55	111c	**1965**	
1217	41	134b	11	465	192	56	177	1	69
1967		148	32	466	188	57	119b	3	85
2	406	154	34	471	167d	59	115	4	159b
3	3	193	9	**1967**		60	142b	5	80
4	129	200	33h	12	33g	62	36	8	77
10	57	288	195	Metal		65	171e	9	162f
11	70	299	24	**1964**		68	114	10	88
14	433	300	29	1	54	**1966**		12	78
18	51	375	6	3	172	3	110	13	93
		378	196	4	49	4	141i	14	159b
Chapter 8,		392	6	5	123	6	141e	16	98
Minor Finds		503	197	6	37	13	43	17	138
Bone		506	167a	7	178	14	56	18	84
1964		**1965**		8	4	16	59	19	136
1	60	11	25	9	142a	18	116	20	162b
2	64	43	193	10	51	19	141f	21	66i
1965		68	13	11	50	20	141j	23	89
1	65	69	7	18	119a	26	58	24	139
2	14	70	30	19	40	29	176	26	99
3	63	71	33c	**1965**		31	171c	27	75
1966		73	31	1	141g	38	48	28	16
3	39	104	5	8	141b	40	171b	29	17
4	61	137	8	13	141c	41	23	30	66b
6	62	186	191	15	45	43	141k	31	73
7	15	221b	167b	17	118	44	141a	32	81
1967		233	33j	18	125	45	108	33	94
1	21	234	20	19	52	47	57	34	135
Pottery		235	19	20	124	48	50	36	161b
1965		236	2	21	53	49	170	39	83
4	183	237	22	22	112	50	111b	40	129
23	180	238	1	24	46	52	171a	41	128

Inv. No.	Cat. No.	Inv. No.	Cat. No.	Inv. No.	Cat. No.	Inv. No.	Cat. No.	Inv. No.	Cat. No.
42	66f	76	18	45	161c	**1967**		23	165
45	120	80	70	46	66j	1	133	24	147
46	137a	83	163b	47	86a	2	71	25	154
48	137b	84	163c	49	100c	3	185	26	182f
50	184	**1966**		54	160c	Terracotta		**1966**	
51a	127	3	160b	61	79	**1964**		4	90
51b	127	4	158	64	66e	10	182e	5	151
51c	130	7	186	65a	126	11	166	7	179a
51d	130	9	67	65b	126	12	181g	8	179b
52	96	12	66h	65c	131	**1965**		9	182a
53	97	14	82	66	160a	1	145	10	153a
55	105	17	162a	74	140	3	152	12	200
57a	127	19	126	79	160d	4	76	26	155
59	100b	20	162c	80	95	10	149	37	165
67	134	21	130	81	161e	13	150	38	165
68	162d	32	66d	84	159b	14	144	44	182b
69	66c	34	121	86	161a	17	91	47	182c
70	132	39	87	87	161d	20	165	48	182d
72	162e	41	159a	88	66a	21	165	51	182g
75	86b	43	68	94	66g	22	165	53	153b
								54	153c

About the Contributors

A 1979 graduate of the University of Missouri–Columbia, **Walter Berry** has been engaged since 1975 in several interdisciplinary projects in southern Burgundy. First, in collaboration with a joint UMC–University of North Carolina at Chapel Hill team, and then with the research group *Association Burgundie*, he has been involved in the archaeological investigation of Roman and medieval sites at Le Mont Dardon, Autun, and Nevers; in addition, he has made a study of the development of medieval rural settlement in the Autunois. At present he is completing a regional study of the Romanesque parish churches in this area. A Ph.D. candidate in the Department of Art History and Archaeology at UMC, he is also a member of the *Unité' de Recherche Archéologique* 26 of the CNRS, based at the University of Lyon II.

Robert H. Brill received a B.S. in Chemistry from Upsala College in 1951, and in 1954 a Ph.D. in Physical Chemistry from Rutgers University. After teaching for six years at Upsala College, he joined the staff of The Corning Museum of Glass and has remained there as Research Scientist. After the disastrous Corning flood of 1972 he served as Director until 1975, supervising the recovery effort. He then returned to research. Brill has traveled and lectured widely and has published extensively in scientific and archaeological journals.

Sidney M. Goldstein received a B.A. from the University of Missouri–Columbia and M.A. and Ph.D. (1970) degrees in Classical Archaeology from Harvard University. He has excavated in Israel and Turkey and has studied glass from sites in Egypt, Jordan, and Italy. Goldstein taught Art History and Archaeology at the University of Wisconsin–Milwaukee before joining the staff of The Corning Museum of Glass in 1973, first as Curator of Ancient Glass and then as Chief Curator. He has been Associate Director at The Saint Louis Art Museum since 1983.

Barbara L. Johnson received a B.A. from Southeast Missouri State College and then studied at the University of Missouri–Columbia, from which she obtained an M.A. in 1971 and a Ph.D. in 1973. Her work in Roman and Late Roman pottery, especially that of the Syro-Palestinian area, began at the University of Missouri and has been supplemented with work at numerous excavations in Israel and Greece. She taught for seven years at Ben-Gurion University of the Negev in Beer-Sheva, Israel. At present she is affiliated with the Albright Institute of Archaeological Research, in Jerusalem.

Anna Manzoni Macdonnell studied at Connecticut College (B.A.), University of Missouri (M.A.) and University of Southern California (Ph.D. 1985). She has been Instructor at the Art Center College of Design in Pasadena since 1985. She has participated in excavations in Israel, Greece and Turkey. Her current project is a study of Roman trade patterns in Southeast Asia.

Gloria S. Merker received an M.A. from the University of Missouri–Columbia (1963) and a Ph.D. from Bryn Mawr College (1970). She was Lecturer at the Hebrew University, Jerusalem during the years 1971-1976. In 1977 she joined the faculty of Rutgers University in Newark and is now Director of the Classics Program. Besides her work in numismatics, her professional interests include Greek sculpture, pottery, metalwork, and terracotta figurines.

Joseph Naveh is Professor of Ancient Semitic Languages and Archaeology at the Hebrew University of Jerusalem.

Paul N. Perrot studied at the Institute of Fine Arts, New York University from 1946 to 1952 and then joined the staff of the Corning Museum of Glass (1952–1972), becoming Director in 1970. From 1972 to 1984 he was Assistant Secretary for Museum Programs at the Smithsonian Institution. Since 1984 he has been Director of the Virginia Museum of Fine Arts in Richmond, Virginia. He is also currently President of the International Center for Conservation in Rome. Formerly editor of the *Journal of Glass Studies,* Perrot is the author of numerous articles on various aspects of glass history, museum management, and preservation.

Gladys D. Weinberg studied at New York University (B.A., 1930) and Johns Hopkins University (Ph.D., 1935). She worked chiefly at the American School of Classical Studies at Athens from 1932 to 1939, when she became Assistant Curator of Ancient Art at the Art Museum of Princeton University. In 1943–1945 she served in the Foreign Service Auxiliary of the U.S. Department of State, in Istanbul and Athens. After two years as Assistant and Acting Librarian at the American School, she edited *Archaeology* Magazine (until 1967) and from 1962 to 1977 was on the staff of the Museum of Art and Archaeology of the University of Missouri–Columbia. She has excavated at a number of sites in Greece and at others in Israel following the Jalame dig, publishing the results in several books and numerous articles.

Saul S. Weinberg, Professor Emeritus of Classical Archaeology at the University of Missouri–Columbia, studied at the University of Illinois (B.A., 1932, M.A. 1933) and at Johns Hopkins University (Ph.D., 1936). Thereafter he was a Fellow of the American School of Classical Studies at Athens and then a member of the Institute for Advanced Study. He served in the U.S. armed forces during World War II, subsequently was assistant to the Director of the American School, and joined the faculty of the University of Missouri–Columbia in 1948, retiring in 1977. He also was Archaeological Director of Hebrew Union College, Jerusalem (1966–1967) and headed the archaeological museums in Jerusalem (1969–1971), while teaching at the Hebrew University of Jerusalem (1969–1972). His excavation experience has been extensive, including sites in Greece, Cyprus, and Israel, and has resulted in numerous publications.

Index